D0225507

◀ MAY 7 - 1992
NOV 2 2 1993

DEC 1 7 1993

Topics in Information Systems

Editors:

Michael L. Brodie
John Mylopoulos
Joachim W. Schmidt

This book is based upon work supported in part by the National Science Foundation under Grant No. ECS-841383F; the Defense Advanced Research Projects Agency under SAI Subcontract No. 15-850009-82, Subproject No. 1-491-37-607-02; the United States Geographic Survey under Order No. 000749, and Computer Corporation of America; also the National Science and Engineering Research Council of Canada, the Canadian Institute for Advanced Research and the Department of Computer Science of the University of Toronto.

Any opinions, findings, conclusions, or recommendations expressed in this publication are those of the authors and do not necessarily reflect the views of the National Science Foundation, the Defense Advanced Research Projects Agency, United States Geographic Survey, the National Science and Engineering Research Council of Canada, the Canadian Institute for Advanced Research, the University of Toronto and Computer Corporation of America.

Series Editors

Michael L. Brodie
Computer Corporation of America
4 Cambridge Center
Cambridge, MA 02142
U.S.A.

Joachim W. Schmidt
Fachbereich Informatik
Johann Wolfgang Goethe-Universität
Dantestr. 9
6000 Frankfurt
Federal Republic of Germany

John Mylopoulos
Department of Computer Science
University of Toronto
Toronto, Ontario M5S 1A4
Canada

ERINDALE
COLLEGE
LIBRARY

CR Classification (1984) : H.1, H.2, H.3, I.2.4

Library of Congress Cataloging in Publication Data
On knowledge base management systems.
  (Topics in information systems)
  Bibliography: p.
  Includes index.
  1. Expert systems (Computer science)   2. Artificial
intelligence.   3. Data base management.   I. Brodie,
Michael L.   II. Mylopoulos, John.   III. Series.
QA76.76.E9505   1986   006.3'3   86-11889

© 1986 by Springer-Verlag New York Inc.
All rights reserved. No part of this book may be translated or reproduced in any form without
written permission from Springer-Verlag, 175 Fifth Avenue, New York, New York 10010,
U.S.A.

The use of general descriptive names, trade names, trademarks, etc. in this publication, even if
the former are not especially identified, is not to be taken as a sign that such names, as
understood by the Trade Marks and Merchandise Marks Act, may accordingly be used freely by
anyone.

Printed and bound by R.R. Donnelley & Sons, Harrisonburg, Virginia.
Printed in the United States of America.

9 8 7 6 5 4 3 2 1

ISBN 0-387-96382-0 Springer-Verlag New York Berlin Heidelberg
ISBN 3-540-96382-0 Springer-Verlag Berlin Heidelberg New York

On Knowledge Base Management Systems

Integrating Artificial Intelligence and Database Technologies

Edited by
Michael L. Brodie
John Mylopoulos

Springer-Verlag New York Berlin Heidelberg
London Paris Tokyo

Topics in Information Systems is a series intended to report significant contributions on the integration of concepts, techniques, and tools that advance new technologies for information system construction. The series logo symbolizes the scope of topics to be covered and the basic theme of integration.

The logo will appear on each book to indicate the topics addressed.

	Artificial Intelligence	Databases	Programming Languages
concepts			
techniques			
tools			

The first book of the series, "On Conceptual Modelling: Perspectives from Artificial Intelligence, Databases and Programming Languages", Michael L. Brodie, John Mylopoulos, and Joachim W. Schmidt (Eds.), February 1984, which deals with concepts in the three areas, has the logo:

	Artificial Intelligence	Databases	Programming Languages
concepts	●	●	●
techniques			
tools			

The second book, "Query Processing in Database Systems", Won Kim, David S. Reiner, and Donald S. Batory (Eds.), March 1985, which deals with Database and Programming Language Concepts, AI and Database techniques, and Database system tools, has the logo:

	Artificial Intelligence	Databases	Programming Languages
concepts		●	●
techniques	●	●	
tools		●	

The third book, "Office Automation", Dionysios C. Tsichritzis (Ed.), March 1985, which deals with the design and implementation of Office Systems, has the logo:

	Artificial Intelligence	Databases	Programming Languages
concepts		●	
techniques	●	●	
tools	●	●	●

Future books in the series will provide timely accounts of ongoing research efforts to reshape technologies intended for information system development.

March, 1985

Michael L. Brodie
John Mylopoulos
Joachim W. Schmidt

Topics in Information Systems

Series Description

Dramatic advances in hardware technology have opened the door to a new generation of computer sytems. At the same time, the growing demand for information systems of ever-increasing complexity and precision has stimulated the need in every area of Computer Science for more powerful higher-level concepts, techniques, and tools.

Future information systems will be expected to acquire, maintain, retrieve, manipulate, and present many different kinds of information. These systems will require user-friendly interfaces; powerful reasoning capabilities, and shared access to large information bases. Whereas the needed hardware technology appears to be within reach, the corresponding software technology for building these systems is not. The required dramatic improvements in software productivity will come from advanced application development environments based on powerful new techniques and languages.

The **concepts, techniques,** and **tools** necessary for the design, implementation, and use in future information systems are expected to result from the integration of those being developed and used in currently disjoint areas of Computer Science. Several areas bring their unique viewpoints and technologies to existing information processing practice. One key area is **Artificial Intelligence** (AI) which provides knowledge bases grounded on semantic theories of information for correct interpretation. An equally important area is **Databases** which provides means for building and maintaining large, shared databases based on computational theories of information for efficient processing. A third important area is **Programming Languages** which provides a powerful tool kit for the construction of large programs based on linguistic and methodological theories to ensure program correctness. To meet evolving information systems requirements, additional research viewpoints and technologies are or will be required from such areas as **Software Engineering, Computer Networks, Machine Architectures,** and **Office Automation.**

Although some integration of research results has already been achieved, a quantum leap in technological integration is needed to meet the demand for future information systems. This integration is one of the major challenges to Computer Science in the 1980s.

Foreword

Current experimental systems in industry, government, and the military take advantage of knowledge-based processing. For example, the Defense Advanced Research Projects Agency (DARPA), and the United States Geological Survey (USGS) are supporting the development of information systems that contain diverse, vast, and growing repositories of data (e.g., vast databases storing geographic information). These systems require powerful reasoning capabilities and processing such as data processing, communications, and multidisciplinary scientific analysis. The number and importance of such systems will grow significantly in the near future.

Many of these systems are severely limited by current knowledge base and database systems technology. Currently, knowledge-based system technology lacks the means to provide efficient and robust knowledge bases, while database system technology lacks knowledge representation and reasoning capabilities.

The time has come to face the complex research problems that must be solved before we can design and implement real, large scale software systems that depend on knowledge-based processing. To date there has been little research directed at integrating knowledge base and database technologies. It is now imperative that such coordinated research be initiated and that it respond to the urgent need for a technology that will enable operational large-scale knowledge-based system applications.

In the long term, research is needed to find ways for knowledge-based system technology to support database systems and *vice versa*. In the near term, research is needed to develop tools that support the design and development of systems that require an integrated set of knowledge base and database system tools. Both long and short term goals are closely related to what have been called Knowledge Base Management Systems (KBMSs). Hence, KBMSs will emerge as an important focus of research.

The Islamorada Workshop on Large Scale Knowledge-based Systems was funded jointly by the National Science Foundation, DARPA, USGS, and the Computer Corporation of America. It was organized to address the integration of AI and Database Technologies. The long-term goal is to produce a new generation of intelligent knowledge/database systems capable of providing multiple access to large, shared knowledge/databases.

The workshop brought together members of both the AI and Database research communities to focus on the problems and opportunities offered by such an integration of technologies. This book captures, to some degree, the interactions between the researchers both at the workshop and in the months preceding and following the workshop. We hope that the book will help to inspire the needed research.

The workshop initiated a new dialogue that helped to define and to make more concrete the essence of potential interaction between AI and Database technologies. However, there is still a long way to go. AI and Database researchers must work together more closely to share ideas and approaches to problems, and to construct a new generation of design and development software tools for the new generation of large- and small-scale knowledge-based systems.

We hope that the immediate future will see a rapid growth in research in this area and progress towards a technology for building large-scale knowledge base system applications.

Mr. Ted M. Albert, USGS
Dr. Bernard Chern, NSF
Commander J. Allen Sears, DARPA

Washington, D.C.,
December 1985

Preface

A major reason for the interest in interactions between Artificial Intelligence (AI) and Databases is the realization that, on the one hand, significant improvements in productivity and functionality of information systems requires treating information as **knowledge** and providing AI techniques for reasoning, problem solving, and question-answering such as those offered by knowledge based systems in AI. On the other hand, practical applications of this technology, especially ones that involve large amounts of information, require progress in implementation techniques such as those addressed in Database research.

Such realizations are leading to a new class of information systems capable of powerful and at the same time efficient knowledge-based processing over large shared knowledge/databases. A technology for building such systems must provide methods for the storage, retrieval, manipulation, and reasoning with respect to knowledge bases. At the same time, it must ensure the robustness of information systems by making allowances for concurrency control, error recovery, distributed processing, and security.

Current AI technologies do not provide access to or efficient management of large, shared, or distributed knowledge bases. Current Database technology does not accommodate knowledge bases and lacks the inference capabilities required for even the simplest forms of reasoning with respect to a knowledge base. The lack of effective integration of AI and Database technologies leaves a significant technological gap that needs to be amended. The research reported in this book addresses precisely this gap. The contributions of leading AI and Database researchers attests to the importance of the topic.

The book itself attempts to address the gap by providing related surveys, position statements, and research results in terms understandable to both AI and Database communities. Before we outline AI-Database interactions and describe the contents of this book and the workshop used to develop it, we briefly examine a potential focal point for the integration of the two technologies, the emerging concept of a **Knowledge Base Management System** (KBMS). At this early stage, the KBMS concept suggests a class of potential and actual systems that integrate selected features from both AI and Database systems and are intended to provide a complete environment for the construction and access of a knowledge base. KBMS requirements, functionality, knowledge representation capabilities, and architecture are open issues, as is the nature of the required technology integration. The situation is reminiscent of the early days of Database Management when there was an open discussion of desirable features and capabilities for database management systems (DBMSs) and a total lack of a theoretical framework addressing issues of data modelling, concurrency control, security and the like.

The particular features of a KBMS might be chosen from a menu of AI and DBMS features to meet specific requirements (i.e., to offer specific services to software components and human users). DBMS features on the menu include traditional database management functions for large shared databases such as: (semantic) data models, languages (i.e., for definition, query/browsing, manipulation, transaction specification), semantic integrity definition and maintenance, storage/search structures, search and update optimization, concurrency, security, error recovery, and distribution of data and processes. The AI menu of features might contribute co-existing knowledge representation schemes, effective control structures for deductive, plausible, and inductive reasoning; means for knowledge acquisition, refinement and validation; explanation facilities and dynamic human intervention.

Interactions Between AI and Database Research

The idea that AI and Databases have something to offer each other is not new. It began during the adolescence of AI and during the infancy of Databases with early natural language front ends for file management systems, limited "deductive" databases, and primitive "semantic" data models. Since 1975, the interaction between the two areas has broadened and has become more systematic. On the topic of natural language front ends to databases, prototypes such as Bill Woods' LUNAR and Larry Harris' ROBOT have led to the acceptance of natural language as a useful communication medium between databases and casual users (see the Natural Language survey in this volume). Such prototypes also have been responsible for the first commercial applications of AI. Following Jean-Pierre Abrial's seminal work, a host of semantic data models were proposed (see the Database Management survey), many of which borrowed elements of semantic network representations. The relevance of Mathematical Logic to data modelling also was established during the same period (see the Logic and Databases survey). Ray Reiter's closed world assumption has been recognized by Database and AI researchers alike as an important contribution to data/knowledge base theory. The arrival of expert systems in the '80s (see the Knowledge-Based System survey) opened yet another avenue of interaction leading to systems that couple a database with an expert system.

The history as well as the nature of the interaction between the two research areas has been well-documented in workshops, symposia, panel discussions, and survey papers. The **Logic and Databases** workshops organized by Herve Gallaire, Jean-Marie Nicolas and Jack Minker between 1977 and 1982 addressed key issues on the applications of Logic to Databases. The Pingree Park workshop in 1980 gathered AI, Database, and Programming Languages researchers and included interesting presentations of position statements and heated discussions. The 1983 NYU symposium on "AI Applications in Business" focused on the general topic of AI and Databases. A 1983 survey by Jonathan King published in the SIGART newsletter lists over 30 research projects that focus on the interaction of AI and Databases. Panels at the 1983 International Joint Conference on AI in Karlsruhe and recent Very Large Databases Conferences present additional evidence for the need for interaction. The Intervale workshop in 1983 included surveys, research papers, and discussions on AI, Databases, and Programming Languages. Finally, the Kiawah Workshop on Expert Database Systems held in 1984 in Kiawah, South Carolina addressed AI-Database issues and has established the need for an international conference on that topic.

In the past, the interaction between AI and Databases has been by and large a one-way street with AI serving as source of ideas and research results and Databases serving as the recipient. As discussed throughout this book, it now appears that the interaction can work in the other direction as well, with the application of Database concepts, techniques and methodological tools in the development of AI systems.

This Book and the Islamorada Workshop

In 1985, the Islamorada workshop was held as a forum for detailed technical presentations and discussions of research into the integration of AI and Database technologies. This book is the result of the workshop. The goals of the workshop and of this book are to:

- Identify actual and potential areas of integration of the two technologies using the concept of a KBMS as focal point for the discussion,

- Stimulate and improve communications between the AI and Database research communities,

- Identify future directions for KBMS technology, as well as potential research frameworks and related research methodologies.

In early 1984, Michael Brodie initiated the workshop by assembling and chairing an advisory committee that included Danny Bobrow, Ronald Brachman, John McDermott, John Mylopoulos, John M.

Smith, and Michael Stonebraker. The committee selected the topics to be discussed at the workshop and solicited participants based on current research interests and contributions, striving to achieve a balance of AI and Database views and expertise in each relevant research area. Before the workshop, surveys were distributed to each participant on several topics relevant to the workshop so that everyone would have the opportunity to participate fully in the proceedings. At the workshop there were 31 researchers of whom 15 were primarily in AI, 14 in Database, and 2 in AI-Database research. Throughout the workshop, emphasis was placed on discussions rather than on formal presentations of research and position papers.

During the year after the workshop, three activities developed. First, the surveys, position papers, and research papers were revised to reflect what was discussed at the workshop. They were interrelated and written so that they can be read by both AI and Database audiences. These revised papers constitute the chapters of this book. The survey chapters present the basic AI and Database concepts relevant to the other chapters. The briefer chapters present position statements that are highly speculative, forward looking, and, at times, opinionated. The remaining chapters provide technical details of recent research results and challenges. Chapters are grouped into sections that differ slightly from their grouping at the workshop.

In the second activity, the discussions, the heart of the workshop, were transcribed, editted and revised by all participants. The synopses are included in the book at the end of each section. In the third activity, four AI and four Database researchers worked together to identify the key technical challenges that face the integration of AI and Database technologies. This unique research project is presented in the Epilogue and is accompanied by equally unique AI and Database perspectives on the central topics of the workshop.

The Islamorada workshop was the third in a series devoted to the integration of AI and Database technologies. The first, Pingree Park in 1980, focused on data abstraction and emphasized identifying areas of interaction and defining terms. The second, Intervale in 1982, focused on conceptual modelling and emphasized comparing concepts, tools, and techniques from the AI, Database, and Programming Language areas. The Islamorada workshop, in February 1985, was a forum for North American researchers and focused on the notion of KBMSs. A companion workshop was held in Hania, Crete, in June 1985 on the same topic and format as the Islamorada workshop, but for European researchers. Its results, the European viewpoint on KBMSs, will appear as another volume in the *Topics in Information Systems* series, and will be edited by Joachim Schmidt and Costantino Thanos.

Acknowledgements

This book is the result of a two year effort. It is a pleasure for us to acknowledge the contributors. We are particularly thankful for financial support from the National Science Foundation, the Defense Advanced Research Projects Agency, the United States Geographic Survey, and Computer Corporation of America. Allen Sears of DARPA was instrumental in developing support for the workshop. Allen Sears, Bernard Chern, and Caroline Eastman, both of NSF, Ted Albert of USGS, and John M. Smith of CCA each enthusiastically supported the workshop and contributed directly to its success.

The value of this book is in the ideas it presents. They were ferreted out by the advisory committee, who worked together for a year, and were developed by the authors with stimulus from the workshop itself. We thank them for their enormous efforts, for sharing their ideas, and for enthusiastically venturing out of their traditional areas.

The heart of the workshop, the discussions, are brought to you by the synoptic brigade who faced immense challenges and innumerable what-I-meant-to-say's. We are grateful for this effort to Brian Nixon and Martin Stanley, and to Ellis Chang, Goetz Graefe, and Kieth Williamson. We are also very thankful to Joanne Mager, John Hogg, and David Darcy for their extraordinary devotion and ability to make real chapters out of a rather long string of bits. Finally, we would like to thank the folks at Cheeca Lodge on Islamorada in the Florida Keys for their warm sun, beautiful ocean vistas, and southern hospitality extended to our group of rather preoccupied adults who bore striking resemblance to a group of clerics visiting from Minnesota.

Michael L. Brodie
John Mylopoulos

January, 1986

Contents

Part I

Knowledge Base Management Systems

1
On Knowledge Base Management Systems

John Mylopoulos[1]

ABSTRACT *This position statement examines briefly the purpose, nature and impact of Knowledge Base Management Systems and outlines a comparison with Database Management Systems.*

This position statement briefly examines the purpose, nature, and impact of Knowledge-Base Management Systems (hereafter KBMSs), and outlines a comparison with Database Management Systems (DBMSs). The background for this statement can be found in [MYLO80], which sketches research on Knowledge Representation and its applications to databases carried out at the University of Toronto since 1975; also in [BM85] and [BROD85a] which discuss some of the underlying premises of this research. Our-long term objective has been to establish a new technology for software development. We assume that this software will include programs as well as databases ("persistent data") and that it might or might not provide sophisticated interpretation capabilities (see the chapter by Szolovits) of the kind associated with so-called expert systems. Our basic premise has been that software development can be usefully viewed as a knowledge-base construction task. KBMSs are intended to provide the representational framework and the computational environment for carrying out this task.

By analogy to DBMSs, we see the main purpose of KBMSs as being to facilitate the management of large, shared knowledge bases. At the same time, we see a number of major differences between DBMSs and KBMSs:

---

[1] University of Toronto, and Senior Fellow, Canadian Institute for Advanced Research

- The former make a clear distinction between "generic" knowledge, incorporated in the schema, and "ground" knowledge that is included in the database. Moreover, the schema is constructed by designers during the database design phase, while the database is constructed and accessed by end users during the production phase. For KBMSs, the distinction between "generic" and "ground" knowledge disappears (or becomes a concern only during "physical design," i.e., when an efficient version of the knowledge base is generated for a production environment).

- The functions offered by DBMSs (query languages, report generators, etc.) concentrate on the end users and their needs. On the other hand, KBMSs focus on the needs of the knowledge-base designer. In fact, it makes more sense to think of a KBMS as a prototyping facility for a particular kind of software (a knowledge base) than as a facility that offers efficient and robust management of large databases.[2]

- As a consequence of the previous point, a KBMS, unlike a DBMS, should provide facilities for physical design through which efficient code can be generated once one is satisfied that the knowledge base is epistemologically adequate.

A second area of comparison between DBMSs and KBMSs concerns their features. Both types of system need to address the issues of sharing by concurrent users, error recovery, and efficient access to information stored on primary and possibly secondary memory on one or several machines. For KBMSs, however, **reasoning facilities** need to be provided, which subsume aspects of deductive and abductive reasoning.[3] In addition, **explanation facilities** are needed, to allow a user of the knowledge base to find out the state of the reasoning process, to offer advice, and to get justification for a particular conclusion reached by the system. Considering that an important goal of the KBMS user is to generate a piece of software for a production environment, implementation facilities need to be provided as well. These should support the interactive generation of conventional software (e.g., COBOL code)

---

[2] If the KBMS is not intended to provide interfaces for the end user, it is fair to ask what does. An interesting possibility is to include in the KBMS framework facilities for representing lexical, grammatical, and pragmatic knowledge as well, so that one can generate a piece of software *and* its user interfaces. [PILO83] provides an initial exploration of such an alternative.

[3] The latter involves inferences of the type

"If A implies B and B has been observed, hypothesize A"

which are particularly useful for expert systems dealing with a diagnostic or other interpretation task.

from a given knowledge base, taking into account issues of efficiency and robustness all-important in a production environment. The chapter by Jarke briefly sketches a well-thought-out framework for carrying out this "compilation" of a knowledge base. An interesting aspect of this proposal is that it takes a strong stand on the linguistic levels relevant to this transformation from knowledge bases to "code", and on the features these levels should support.

The starting point in designing a DBMS is to choose the data model that will be supported (i.e., the data structures and operations to be used to store and operate on a database). A similar claim can be made for the design of a KBMS where the starting point is the *knowledge-representation framework* to be offered to the designer of a knowledge base; in other words, the nature of the units constituting a knowledge base. There are two sets of issues that need to be addressed by any such framework. Firstly, the framework should be *descriptively adequate*, allowing, among other things, for representing and reasoning with respect to negation, disjunction, and quantification. Secondly, since the knowledge bases to be developed may be large, a knowledge representation framework must support *organizational principles*, in the same sense that programming languages support program structuring principles intended to help the programmer in structuring a program. Candidates for such principles include generalization, aggregation, and classification, already used extensively in knowledge-representation languages and semantic data models. New principles are also included, such as:

1. **Projection**: This is intended to capture the semantic relationship between a physical object and its projection on some plane, or between a physiological event (e.g., a heart beat) and its projection on some medium (e.g., an ECG signal), or even a data structure with associated operations (e.g., a linked list along with push and pop operations) and its projection into an abstract plane (e.g., where the linked list may be viewed as a pushdown stack). Versions of this abstraction mechanism are used in [SHIB85] and [RICH82]. The mechanism also bears some resemblance to data abstraction as used in programming languages [LZ74b].

2. **Exceptions**: Knowledge is viewed with respect to this dimension as a multilayered structure of rules, exceptions to the rules, exceptions to the exceptions, etc. It is important to note that exception handling constitutes an essential feature of any software development technology intended for **flexible** software systems. The proposals outlined in [BORG85b] can serve as a basis for the introduction of such an organizational dimension.

3. **Reflection**: "Control" knowledge (i.e., knowledge about the reasoning process itself rather than domain knowledge), has been a

topic of interest and importance in expert-system research. This dimension of knowledge organization would allow one to organize a knowledge base depending on whether it represents domain knowledge, knowledge about reasoning with respect to domain knowledge, knowledge about reasoning about reasoning with respect to domain knowledge, etc. [SMIT82] and [KRAM86] are just two examples of proposals for reflection mechanisms that would allow a system to "reflect" about its own state, goals, achievements, etc.

4.   **Relativity**: By and large, present-day knowledge bases assume that there exists an objective view of the domain, and that differences in viewpoints (e.g., different accounts about how a hospital operates), can be resolved before knowledge is added to the knowledge base. Unfortunately, this is a naive view which is violated by many applications where large amounts of knowledge from many different sources are relevant. Well-accepted mechanisms for knowledge-base structuring, such as contexts/partitions, [HEND75], are too simple-minded to deal with the complications that arise from the co-existence of multiple viewpoints within one knowledge base. Recent work within the OMEGA project [HEWI85b] includes a powerful notion of "viewpoint" which seems a more appropriate starting point towards a structuring mechanism that provides an adequate treatment of subjectivity in knowledge bases.

This is necessarily a partial list of candidate mechanisms for knowledge organization. In closing this topic, it is important to stress that the organizational mechanisms supported by a particular knowledge- representation framework must assume that the units being organized are, in fact, representations of knowledge, rather than text, rules, program segments, or data structures. Also, to emphasize that *the knowledge engineer needs structuring facilities permitting the structuring of a (large) knowledge base as much as software engineers, for their part, are concerned with the construction of (large) programs.*

DBMSs already exist, and are widely, and successfully, used. An important methodological question is whether we should treat them as starting points and move in an evolutionary fashion towards KBMSs[4]. Likewise, one can begin with existing environments for building expert systems like KEE and LOOPS[5], and add to them features such as efficient use of secondary storage, concurrency control, error recovery, and query optimization. This is clearly a correct strategy for research

---

[4] Semantic Data Models, including Prolog-related ones, seem to have been doing just that.

[5] A more complete list of such environments can be found in [BM85].

and development work with a relatively short-term outlook. An alternative, *revolutionary*, approach begins with a knowledge- representation framework to be supported by a KBMS, and develops a theory of KBMSs based on the features of this representational framework, much as was done with the Relational Data Model. In the long run, the second approach is the correct one. Extensions of existing technologies for building DBMSs and expert systems are bounded by their point of origin, and can only be stretched so far towards yielding more "intelligent" DBMSs or more efficient and robust expert-system shells. A variation of this point is also made by David Israel in the chapter on knowledge bases and databases.

A serious and powerful argument against the KBMS framework presented here derives from the computational intractability of basic operations in a KBMS that uses a knowledge-representation framework with the expressiveness outlined earlier. (See the chapters by Brachman and Levesque, also Vassiliou.) How useful can a KBMS be, if the answers to simple questions are provably "hard"[6] from a computational viewpoint? A possible response to this argument is that computational intractability is an issue only as long as one is unwilling to focus on a particular knowledge base or, rather, specific questions asked of a specific knowledge base. Acceptance of a design/production environment dichotomy allows the provision of powerful representation tools in the design phase of a knowledge base, ignoring tractability issues. Once the design is complete (i.e., the designer is satisfied with the contents of the knowledge base), generation of efficient code can be achieved by restricting the range of operations over the knowledge base, taking its contents into account. The result of such a process is a limited knowledge base which nevertheless operates effectively in its intended production environment. This scenario for dealing with efficiency issues stresses the availability of implementation/compilation facilities that help the knowledge engineer and/or software designer to generate code.

Finally, it is worth emphasizing the importance of research that will hopefully be generated with KBMSs as its focal point. For a very long time, computer scientists have viewed software development as a task involving the construction of programs and/or databases. This paradigm has led to much research and great progress in areas such as Programming Languages, Databases, Software Engineering, and Office Automation. Software development, however, has remained a bottleneck in the use of computers. If anything, software is today a bigger bottleneck in terms of cost, availability, and quality than it was a decade ago, partly at least because of tremendous strides in research

---

[6] Here, "hard" can range from NP-completeness to undecidability.

into hardware and computer architecture. I believe that it is time to reconsider the software development paradigm in favour of one that views software- development primarily as *knowledge-base construction.* This shift of viewpoint is bound to have a tremendous impact on large and established research areas within Computer Science concerned with software development. Moreover, the shift can only come about when KBMSs become widely available.

1. References

[BM85]   [BORG85b]   [BROD85]   [HEND75]   [HEWI85b] [KRAM86]   [LZ74b]   [MYLO80]   [PILO83]   [RICH82]   [SHIB85] [SMIT82]

2
The Knowledge Level of a KMBS

Ron Brachman[1]
Hector Levesque[2]

There are a number of more or less orthogonal ways of looking at the kind of knowledge-base management system (KBMS) envisaged in this book. Nonetheless, two very distinct viewpoints seem to dominate. The first deals with what has been called the symbol level, and focuses on the data structures and algorithms needed to process and make available to a wide variety of users the large amounts of information present in (potentially distributed) KBs. Proposals here might involve using locking, parallelism, inheritance hierarchies, backward-chaining inference, database-style management of secondary storage and other mechanisms.[3] This level deals with how a *machine* views and processes the information in a KB.

For lack of a better name, the second viewpoint might be called the system engineering level, and focuses on a KBMS from the point of view of a KB designer, especially on what a designer needs for coping with the structural complexity of large information systems. In other words, this level deals with the organizational aspects of a KB; and techniques here include successive refinement by specialization, part whole decomposition, version management, exception handling, and various other information-abstraction mechanisms that help a KB designer manage his or her design.[4] In other words, this level deals with how *people* view and process the information in a KB.

What we recommend is yet a third viewpoint for looking at these information systems, the knowledge level. The idea, roughly, is to consider exactly what knowledge is represented or is representable in a scheme, treating knowledge as an abstract commodity, quite independent of the symbol level concerns of efficiency and integrity on the one hand, and the system engineering level concerns of understandability and maintainability on the other.[5] In other words, the Knowledge Level

---

[1] AT&T Bell Labs

[2] University of Toronto

[3] See, for example, the chapter by Stonebraker.

[4] See, for example, the chapter by Borgida et al.

[5] See the survey by Levesque for more motivation regarding this level, and the next chapter for some technical issues.

looks at the *information content* of a KB without considering how that content might be dealt with either by machines or people (the symbol and system engineering levels respectively).

To summarize, whenever we discuss a KB in terms of the data structures actually manipulated by a program, we are talking at the symbol level. If our discussion of a KB is in terms of how it can be defined, accessed, and changed by a KB designer, we are dealing with system engineering level concerns.[6] Finally, if we ask what the KB tells us about the world, we are asking about its Knowledge Level properties.

Our claim is that the knowledge level view is central to understanding what service a knowledge base is providing to the rest of the system using it. Since the *raison d'etre* of a knowledge base is, after all, the storage and maintenance of the beliefs (a more accurate term here than "knowledge", which implies the *truth* of what is represented) of the system in which it is embedded, what those beliefs (and their inferential consequences) are is the first and foremost thing to consider. Thus a knowledge level account of a KB is *primary*, the symbol and system engineering level accounts must play a supporting role.[7] A knowledge level analysis is especially important when considering combining representation schemes.[8] Indeed, one can imagine wanting to combine schemes with wildly different and incomparable implementation structures on the one hand and organizational facilities on the other. In this case, the only common ground between the schemes might be that they represent related kinds of knowledge about the world. This might be true even for the integration of two databases, arguably the simplest kinds of knowledge bases.[9] At the symbol level, for example, the integration of an IMS database and a System R database might seem like an arbitrary and misguided undertaking. However, the two databases could be *about* related domains and, thus, at the knowledge level, their integration would be rational and even desirable.

---

[6] In a programming language setting, for example, the system engineering level might deal with the features of a high-level programming environment, while the symbol level might involve the object code that is executed after compilation.

[7] This is not to say that a knowledge level account of a KB would not benefit from organizational facilities of some sort to make it more understandable to people (at the system engineering level), or could not be captured by suitable data structures to make it machine accessible (at the symbol level). But this is a separate issue that amounts to treating a knowledge level *account* itself as information to be used by people or by computers, over and above the information contained in the KB.

[8] See, for example, the chapter by Fox and McDermott.

[9] See the survey by Levesque for more on this.

In addition to combining multiple representations, there are a number of other KBMS issues that seem best dealt with at the knowledge level. A major one involves discovering why or what kind of (deductive) reasoning is necessary in a KBMS. It is at the knowledge level that it becomes clear what information about the world is explicit and implicit in a KB. For example, databases typically have an implicit Closed World Assumption; rule-based systems imply the chaining of rules. Either way, it is up to a KBMS to make available both the implicit and explicit information contained in a KB and therefore, for different schemes, more or less deductive activity will be necessary. Elsewhere we have argued that the amount of reasoning required provides a useful metric for comparing schemes at the knowledge level.[10] Indeed, there appears to be a tradeoff between how expressive a scheme is and how computationally tractable the necessary reasoning is. This is certainly something to keep in mind when contemplating the combination of multiple schemes. For one thing, the reasoning demands of one scheme may undermine the computational advantanges of another. To take an extreme example, retrieval of clauses is not a bottleneck for Resolution Theorem Provers, so all the careful DBMS retrieval techniques in the world will not prevent one from thrashing in the worst case. At the very least, one does not want to combine inference *mechanisms* ("inheritance", etc.) without considering the knowledge level consequences.

Another issue at the knowledge level involves the different *kinds* of knowledge that we might want to represent. The question then becomes how these affect one another. For example, a simple fact such as "Alcatraz is an island" obviously interacts with a definition such as "An island is a body of land completely surrounded by water." Moreover, there are propositions that on the surface look similar, but have quite different force. For example, we have facts like "Every bank on Bay Street has rich customers," implied laws like "Every bank on Bay Street is closed on Sundays," and definitional properties like "Every bank on Bay Street is a financial institution." In all three cases, we are dealing with a simple universal implication, but that alone obviously does not tell us the whole story. In the next chapter, we illustrate a knowledge level account of a system that integrates terminological (definitional) and assertional (sentential) representations. It is our position that, in general, we will need to consider *hybrid* approaches to the structure of knowledge bases, since, in addition to definitions and simple belief sentences, there are pieces of knowledge like rules, methods, and heuristics to be taken into account. It is at the knowledge level that the import and interrelation of these kinds of

---

[10] See again the survey by Levesque.

knowledge have to be sorted out.

In sum, it is easy to forget that a representational scheme is first and foremost *representational*, and that consideration of how to tailor a scheme either to machines (at the symbol level) or to people (at the system engineering level) must be preceded by a good understanding at the knowledge level of what knowledge a scheme can or cannot represent.

3
Knowledge Level Interfaces to Information Systems

Hector J. Levesque[1]
Ronald J. Brachman[2]

ABSTRACT *The knowledge level view advocates treating knowledge bases (KB) roughly as abstract data types: what is required of a KB is to be completely specified functionally, without regard to how it is implemented. We elaborate on this view, here, by providing detailed knowledge level accounts of several different types of languages for specifying KB. These accounts are expressed mainly in terms of two operations applicable to KB:* TELL, *which allows a system to tell a KB something about its application domain; and* ASK, *which allows the system to ask the KB questions about the domain. We also consider some of the important things that can be shown about an information system (a DBMS or a knowledge-base system) once the Knowledge Level description is in hand.*

1. Introduction

Traditionally, the goal of knowledge-representation systems in Artificial Intelligence has been to provide flexible ways of creating, examining, and modifying collections of symbolic structures forming what have been called "knowledge bases." In fact, virtually the only way to learn about what an AI representation system can do is to look at how the implementation code manipulates the data structures. The representational "power" of the system is usually assumed to have

[1] Department of Computer Science, University of Toronto Toronto, Ontario, Canada M5S 1A4; Fellow of the Canadian Institute for Advanced Research

[2] AT&T Bell Laboratories, 600 Mountain Ave., Murray Hill, New Jersey 07974

something to do with the complexity of the frame structures in it or the variety of links in its semantic network. How fancy the property inheritance mechanism is seems to be the determinant of the inferential power of the system.

Up to this point, the field has been able to sell its representation systems by appealing to the complexity of the mechanisms and the number of features a system offers. Somehow, the intuitive appeal of frames (or whatever) has been enough to make systems usable. However, with extremely large and complex information systems on the horizon, a mechanistic understanding of knowledge representation promises to be increasingly problematic. In fact, even with the currently popular frame systems, we can see evidence of serious inconsistencies in the interpretation of data structures (see [BFL83a] for some details on this), allowing users of the systems to draw inferences that in any reasonable sense do not logically follow from what is represented. Users simply do not know what they are getting, when all they get are data structure-manipulation packages.

Here we investigate a different approach to representation systems in AI, where knowledge bases are characterized, not in terms of the structures they use to represent knowledge, but *functionally*, in terms of what they can be asked or told about the domain. Essentially, a knowledge base (KB) is treated as an *abstract data type* that interacts with a user or system only through a small set of operations. We concentrate, not on what we call the symbol level of data structures and property inheritance, but rather on a knowledge level of what the system knows about the world in which it is embedded, (see the chapter by Levesque for more on this distinction). In our case, we consider only two basic interaction operations with a KB at this level, roughly analogous to database query and update operations: one of them allows a system to ASK the KB questions about some application domain and the other allows the system to TELL the KB about that domain. The complete functionality of a KB is measured in terms of these operations; the actual mechanisms it uses to maintain an evolving model of the domain are its own concern and not accessible to the rest of the knowledge-base system.

In the end, the details of what data structures are being manipulated is going to be of little use to the user of a knowledge-representation system. What he really wants to know is what the system knows at any given time, what follows from what it knows, and what questions about that knowledge the system is capable of answering. Once an account of this sort is given, the user will be able to correctly predict the behavior of the system; (he will, in fact, be able to prove certain consequences of what the system knows, as we illustrate later), and he will be able to verify the correctness of the implementation in hand, since he will have an independent specification of the appropriate behavior.

In this chapter, we illustrate some details of this functional view of knowledge representation. First, we present a general sketch of the knowledge level, and say a few words about the role of logic in representation, given this view. We then illustrate in some technical detail what an actual knowledge level account might look like. We do this by giving formal TELL and ASK specifications of three representation languages— a simple, first-order one, to illustrate the fundamentals of the approach; a "hybrid" language that allows the formation of complex predicates; and, finally, an "autoepistemic" language that allows a modal knowledge operator.

2. The Knowledge Level

In a recent paper [NEWE80], Newell introduces the idea of a knowledge level, an abstraction in terms of which intelligent agents can be described. For the rest of this section,[3] we will show how this idea applies equally well to KB and, indeed, motivates our functional approach to knowledge representation.

2.1. Competence

A major characteristic of the knowledge level is that knowledge is considered to be a *competence* notion, "being a potential for generating action".[4] There are actually two ways of looking at this. First, we might want to say that, to a first approximation, if an agent believes p, and if p logically implies q, then he is likely to believe q. In this case, competence might be thought of as a plausible abstraction (or heuristic) for reasoning about the beliefs of an agent. But there is another way of looking at this: we can say that if an agent imagines the world to be one where p is true, and if p entails q, then (whether or not he realizes it) he imagines the world to be one where q also happens to be true. In other words, if the world the agent believes in satisfies p, then it must also satisfy q. The point is that the notion of competence need not be one where an agent is taken to have appreciated the consequences of what he knows, but merely one where *we* examine those consequences.

So the analysis of knowledge at the knowledge level is really the study of what is *implicit* in what an agent holds as true, precisely the domain of *logic*. As Newell points out: "Just as talking of

---

[3] Much of this section is borrowed from [LEVE84a].

[4] All quotations in this section are from [NEWE80].

programmerless programming violates truth in packaging, so does talking of a *non-logical analysis* of knowledge". This is not to imply that agents do, can, or should use some form of logical calculus as a representation scheme, but only that the analysis of what is being represented is best carried out in this framework.

But what does this analysis amount to? Are there any purely logical problems to be solved? Indeed, once what Newell calls the symbol level—the level of symbol-manipulating programs—has been factored out, is there *anything* concrete left to say? Newell admits the following:

> However, in terms of structure, a body of knowledge is extremely simple compared to a memory defined at lower computer system levels. There are no structural constraints to the knowledge in a body, either in capacity (i.e., the amount of knowledge) or in how the knowledge is held in the body. Indeed, there is no notion of how knowledge is held; (*encoding* is a notion at the symbol level, not knowledge level). Also, there are not well-defined structural properties associated with access and augmentation. Thus, it seems preferable to avoid calling the body of knowledge a memory.

So it appears that, at the knowledge level, there is nothing to say about the *structure* of these abstract bodies of knowledge called knowledge bases. This does not mean that there is nothing at all to say. Although Newell does not go into any details, he insists that "knowledge is to be characterized *functionally*, in terms of what it does, not *structurally* in terms of physical objects with particular properties and relations."

2.2. Functionality

Newell's view of knowledge at the knowledge level is very similar to the standard notion of an abstract data type [LZ74a]: to specify what is required of a desired entity (or collection of related entities), and to specify the desired behavior under a set of operations, not the structures that might be used to realize that behavior. The canonical example is that of a *stack* that might be specified in terms of the following operation:

Create:	→ STACK
Push:	STACK × INTEGER → STACK
Pop:	STACK → STACK
Top:	STACK → INTEGER
Empty:	STACK → BOOLEAN

By defining these functions (over abstract stacks), we specify *what* the behavior should be, without saying *how* it should be implemented. Of course, we have not said how stacks can be used in general to do other things (like implement recursion, for instance), but we have provided the primitives of this usage. In this sense, the specification is functional.

How might similar considerations apply to knowledge? To answer this, we have to discover the primitive operations that will be composed to form complex applications of knowledge (such as problem solving, learning, decision making, and the like). At least two orthogonal operations suggest themselves immediately.

First, if the behavior of an intelligent agent is to depend on what is known, a primitive operation must be to *access* this knowledge. Very roughly speaking, we have the following:

ASK: KNOWLEDGE × QUERY → ANSWER.

In other words, we can discover answers to questions using knowledge. This is the analogue of the *Top*, *Pop*, and *Empty* operations which were also retrieval-oriented. Secondly, if we consider learning to be an intelligent activity, then we need the analogue to the *Push* operation: we have to be able to *augment* what is known:

TELL: KNOWLEDGE × ASSERTION → KNOWLEDGE.

Again, roughly, knowledge can be acquired by assimilating new information. There are, presumably, a large number of TELL and ASK operations corresponding to the many ways knowledge can be accessed and acquired (including non-linguistic ways). There are also other kinds of operations worth considering, including an analogue of *CREATE* as well as a *FORGET*, an *ASSUME*, and others. However, for our purposes, we can restrict our attention to these two operations.

2.3. Some Simplifications

To be able to say anything concrete about the operations of TELL and ASK and to simplify a lot of the machinery to come, a few assumptions are necessary. First of all, if we assume that "the knowledge attributed by the observer to the agent is knowledge about the external world," then we can assume that what a knowledge base is told or asked is also about the external world. In addition, if we now restrict ourselves to *yes-no questions*, we can assume (without loss of generality) that both the *queries* and the *assertions* are drawn from the same language. The only difference between a (yes-no) *query* and an *assertion* is that a knowledge base will be *asked* if the former is true and *told* that the latter is true.

So, for some language L that can be used to talk about an external world, we have the following functional specification of a KB:

$$\text{TELL:} \quad \text{KB} \times L \rightarrow \text{KB};$$

$$\text{ASK:} \quad \text{KB} \times L \rightarrow \{yes, no\}.$$

What remains to be done is to settle on a suitable language L that can be used as a basis for any knowledge level specification, and to come up with an appropriate abstract notion of a KB in terms of which these two operations can be defined.

2.4. Misdirection, Using Logic

Given the need for a language that might universally support knowledge level analyses, it is tempting to jump immediately to the obvious choice: we could take L to be a dialect of the first-order predicate calculus, and use a theorem-proving program to provide the answers to ASK's. One concrete possibility is to represent a KB as a "connection graph" of first-order logical sentences (where only potentially resolvable sentences are linked together—see [KOWA75]), and compute theoremhood for additional sentences by running a resolution theorem prover over that graph (as in [STIC82]). In this case, TELL and ASK would be defined in the following manner (where κ is a connection graph and α is a first-order sentence):

$$\text{TELL}(\kappa,\alpha) = \quad \begin{array}{l} \kappa', \text{ where } \kappa' \text{ is the connection graph} \\ \text{that results from adding and} \\ \text{appropriately linking } \alpha \text{ to } \kappa \text{ (as in [STIC82]).} \end{array}$$

$$\text{ASK}(\kappa,\alpha) = \begin{cases} yes, & \text{if the graph resulting from linking} \\ & \neg\alpha \text{ to } \kappa \text{ can be shown by resolution} \\ & \text{to be inconsistent;} \\ no, & \text{otherwise.} \end{cases}$$

In other words, we TELL something to a KB by conjoining to it a new sentence, and we determine the answer to ASK by negating the sentence α and running the theorem prover to detect any contradiction.

On the face of it, this seems quite reasonable. It is just a standard first- order system—albeit disguised in terms of two operations—like the kind discussed in [GM78] (where talk of a single-query operation is much more common). But we have been misled by the formality of first-order logic. As precise as such a specification might be, it simply does not address the issue of a knowledge level account any more than defining the stack operations in terms of operations on linked lists (or arrays) would. These definitions in terms of sentences, linking, and theorem proving are at a different level—the symbol level—where the symbolic structure of the KB has been decided. In this attempt at specifying TELL and ASK, we have already committed ourselves to particular *programs*, rather than having specified abstractly what such programs should compute.

This is not to say that there are no further design decisions to be made. In the stack case, for example, we would have to decide how to implement linked lists (maybe using arrays). Here, we have to decide how to realize a suitable theorem-proving behavior over connection graphs (i.e., there are many ways to actually run the resolution theorem prover). But the crucial choice was to *represent the knowledge symbolically*, using a connection graph, and reduce the operations on a KB to theorem-proving operations over it. As Newell argues,

> Logic is fundamentally a tool for analysis at the knowledge level. Logical formalisms with theorem proving can certainly be used as a representation in an intelligent agent, but [that] is an entirely separate issue (though one we already know much about, thanks to the investigations in AI and mechanical mathematics over the last fifteen years).

Regardless of whether or not we decide to use sentences of a first-order logical language to represent what is known, a separate decision must be made about L, the language for the TELL and ASK operations. It is the expressive power of this interface language that will determine what a KB can be said to know.[5] Since we are primarily interested in KB whose world knowledge can be represented in first-order terms, we will start with a first-order language—but without commitment to symbolic structures or particular programs for reasoning.

---

[5] The situation is complicated here by the fact that the TELL and ASK operations may not allow precisely the same subset of the interface language to be used. As an extreme case, TELL may be restricted to atomic sentences (as in relational style databases) while ASK may allow a full, first-order query language. For example, you might be able to find out if $(p \vee q)$ is true, but only be able to inform the KB that p is true or that q is true.

3. A First-Order Representation Language

In this section, we consider a knowledge level account of a first-order representation language. In subsequent sections, we show how this account can be generalized along two separate dimensions, one allowing complex predicates as in KRYPTON [BFL83a, BFL83b], the other allowing a modal knowledge operator (i.e., one that might allow us to ask explicitly: "Do you know where all the blocks are"?)

The language we will use for the moment is that of a pure (that is, function-free) predicate calculus. The grammar, then, is the following:

$\langle wff \rangle$ ::= $(\langle k-predicate-symbol\rangle\langle var\rangle_1 \cdots \langle var\rangle_k)$ $k \geqslant 0$
| **(NOT** $\langle wff \rangle$)
| **(OR** $\langle wff \rangle$ $\langle wff \rangle$)
| **(EXISTS** $\langle var \rangle$ $\langle wff \rangle$).

It is assumed that the other usual logical connectives (such as conjunction, material implication (simple "if/then"), material equivalence, universal quantification) can be defined syntactically in terms of the ones provided here; (we will use standard, logical, typography for these when convenient).

The semantics of this language is defined in terms of functions from predicate symbols to relations of the same arity over some domain. Given a domain of individuals and such a mapping, it will be possible to specify the truth value of every sentence.[6] For formulas in general, we also need the notion of an *environment*, which is a function from variables to elements of some domain. Given an environment V, a variable x, and an object o, we also define $V[x/o]$ to be the environment that is exactly like V except that x is mapped to o. The truth of a formula is defined in terms of a mapping E and an environment V as follows:

Let D be any set.

Let E be any function from predicate symbols to relations over D such that $E(s)$ has the same arity as s.

Let V be any environment over D.

Then for any wff α, we define the *truth* of α wrt to E and V by

1. $(P\ x_1 \cdots x_k)$ is true iff $\langle V(x_1),...,V(x_k)\rangle$ is in the relation $E(P)$,

---

[6] By a *sentence*, we will always mean a closed wff of the language.

2.   (NOT α) is true iff α is not true,

3.   (OR α β) is true iff either α or β is true,

4.   (EXISTS $x\alpha$) is true iff for some d in D, α is true wrt to E and $V[x/d]$.

One thing to notice about this definition is that the truth of *sentences* is indeed just a function of the set D and the mapping E.

3.1. Outcomes and Knowledge Bases

Using the notion of truth just defined, we can define an *outcome* as a complete specification of what the world could be like. In subsequent sections we will need a more complex notion of outcome, but, for the present, an outcome is simply a *truth valuation*, defined as follows:

Let w be a mapping from sentences to {true,false}.

w is a *truth valuation* iff

there is a set D and a function E as above over D such that for any sentence α, $w(\alpha)$ = true iff α is true wrt E.

So a truth valuation is any mapping from sentences to truth values that follows the definition of truth given earlier. Note that an outcome does not tell us what the domain is or what the extensions of the various predicates are, but only which sentences are true and which are false.

While an outcome is a complete specification of what the world is like, a *knowledge base* is considered a partial specification of the same. Formally, we define a knowledge base to be any *set* of outcomes. (This is the usual convention of treating a partial world model as the set of all complete world models that are 'consistent' with it.) So the outcomes that are members of a KB are those that are consistent with the information available to the KB; the outcomes that are not members of the KB are those that can be ruled out based on the information available to the KB. So, for example, if a KB knows only that α is true, the outcomes it will contain are all those where α is true. This is not to say that the KB does not know about other truths. For example, in all of the outcomes in this KB, (OR α β) is also true. Moreover, for any KB at all, all of its outcomes have the property that every valid sentence of logic comes out true.

3.2. The Operations on First-Order Knowledge Bases

We are now in a position to define what operations are available on these abstract-knowledge bases. These are the operations that define the system at the knowledge level, and the only ones that an implementation has to provide to a user.

As we discussed, there are two operations provided by a first-order system of the kind we are envisaging. The first, called ASK, is used to determine what the world is like according to what is known. Informally, ASK takes a sentence and a KB and returns 'yes' or 'no'. The second, called TELL, is used to inform the KB of what the world is like. It takes a sentence and a KB and returns a new KB that knows that the sentence is true. More formally, we have:

$$\text{TELL}[\alpha, \text{KB}] = \text{KB} \cap \{w \mid w(\alpha) = true\}.$$

$$\text{ASK}[\alpha, \text{KB}] = \begin{cases} yes, \text{ if for each } w \text{ in KB, } w(\alpha) = \text{true}, \\ no, \text{ otherwise}. \end{cases}$$

So TELL rules out the possibility that its argument is false by retaining only those outcomes where it comes out true. Similarly, ASK answers 'yes' precisely when the possibility that α is false has been ruled out.

It is important to note that this specification of the 'input/output' behavior of TELL and ASK is just that—a specification. It is not a description of anything like a program, but rather a declarative measure of how *any* program that implements this knowledge level description must behave. KB here are defined abstractly, not by mechanisms or particular implementation structures. Note the contrast between this abstract account and our earlier attempt that resorted to theorem-proving and a particular first-order logic representation for KB. Here the idea of "adding" something like a sentence of first-order logic is inappropriate, whereas in the earlier, symbol level account, conjoining a new sentence to a KB was an appropriate mechanism for implementing TELL.

Given the details of this Knowledge Level account, there are a number of important properties that we can prove.[7] For example, it is easy to show that ASK and TELL have the right relationship, (i.e., that

$$\text{ASK}[\alpha, \text{TELL}(\alpha, \text{KB})] = \text{yes},$$

[7] Again, note that the fact that we are doing this at the Knowledge Level means that we can prove properties of *any* system that satisfies the account, regardless of implementation (symbol level) details.

for any KB, as well as any subsequent KB (TELL works *monotonically*—anything that is believed continues to be believed as new facts or new definitions are told). Another thing we can show is that the symbol level specification given earlier, of TELL and ASK in terms of theorem-proving is correct: TELL need only conjoin its argument to a sentence representing the KB, and ASK need only determine if its argument is a logical consequence of that sentence (i.e., prove that it is a theorem). In general, because we can *prove* such things of arbitrary symbol level implementations (as long as they are correct with respect to the Knowledge Level specification), this kind of knowledge level account plays a vital part in providing a predictable, reliable, interface for consumers of the knowledge-representation service.

4. KRYPTON: A Hybrid Representation Language

We now consider how the knowledge level approach we have been discussing can be generalized to deal with the kind of terminological structure found in KRYPTON. In a nutshell, KRYPTON is a hybrid system with two main components, one that specializes in terminological reasoning (the *TBox*), the other in assertional reasoning (the *ABox*). This split mirrors the distinction between definitions of terms and the use of such terms to state contingent facts about the world.[8] Each component has its own language, and its own inference mechanism: the ABox language is that of a first-order predicate calculus, while the TBox language is a special-purpose, frame-based language of descriptions, detailed below. The heart of KRYPTON is the connection between the two components: predicates used in the ABox are actually defined in the TBox. Thus, all of the analytic inferences computed by the frame-based TBox must be available for consumption in the logic-based ABox.[9]

---

[8] As intimated in our earlier paper in this volume, one of the basic motivations for the hybrid nature of KRYPTON is that there are propositions that on the surface look similar, but which have different force. See the examples about banks on Bay street.

[9] The mapping between symbols and their definitions is maintained by a *symbol table*, shared by the TBox and ABox. Please consult [BFL83a] and [BFL83b] for more on the structure of the system.

4.1. Knowledge Level Operations

Although our basic ABox is a standard first-order predicate logic, its proper integration in KRYPTON demands that complex terms defined in the TBox be available for use as predicates in assertions. Thus, if the resulting assertional capability is considered as a predicate logic, then it is a non-standard one, in that it has both the normal sentential operators and special operators used for constructing complex predicates. In this section we will demonstrate the hybrid semantics necessary to explain the integration. Having presented the syntax of KRYPTON's languages and their semantics, we will then rigorously specify the interface that a KRYPTON system presents to an outside user. In particular, we will precisely define operations that allow questions to be answered about the world or about the conceptual vocabulary being used, as well as operations that allow new information about the world to be accepted and new terms to be defined.

4.2. Syntax and Semantics

The language currently implemented in the TBox has two main categories: *concepts* and *roles,* corresponding to one-place predicates and two-place predicates (relations), respectively. These are defined in terms of each other by the following simple BNF grammar:[10]

$$\langle concept \rangle \quad ::= \quad \langle 1-predicate-symbol \rangle$$
$$| \quad (\textbf{ConGeneric} \ \langle concept \rangle_1 \cdots \langle concept \rangle_n) \quad n \geqslant 0$$
$$| \quad (\textbf{VRGeneric} \ \langle concept \rangle \ \langle role \rangle \langle concept \rangle)$$
$$\langle role \rangle \quad ::= \quad \langle 2-predicate-symbol \rangle$$
$$| \quad (\textbf{RoleChain} \ \langle role \rangle_1 \cdots \langle role \rangle_n) \quad n \geqslant 1.$$

The ABox language is the first-order language discussed in the previous section. But note that one-place (concept) and two-place (role) predicate symbols are both terms of the TBox language and components of the ABox language. To make this intersection explicit, we also define the following categories:

---

[10] While the formal semantics given here is sufficient to explain the meaning of these operators, the reader might wish for a more intuitive account; for such, see [BFL83a] and [BL84a]. Some simple examples appear below. Also, please note that this language is only a subset of the kind of TBox language we have talked about in those earlier papers. While the implementation described here is complete and fully integrated, it is still only a small experimental prototype, intended as a testbed for our ideas on hybrid reasoning architectures.

$\langle TBox - symbol \rangle$ $::= \langle 1 - predicate - symbol \rangle \mid \langle 2 - predicate - symbol \rangle$

$\langle gsymbol \rangle$ $::= \langle k - predicate - symbol \rangle \quad k \geqslant 0$

$\langle gterm \rangle$ $::= \langle gsymbol \rangle \mid \langle concept \rangle \mid \langle role \rangle$

So gterms, as they will be understood here, are either predicate symbols or composite TBox expressions, and each gterm has an associated arity (1 for concepts, 2 for roles, and k for each k-place predicate symbol).

The semantics of the TBox and ABox languages is defined in terms of mappings from gsymbols to relations of the same arity over some domain. Given a domain of individuals and such a mapping, it will be possible to specify the extension of every gterm and the truth value of every sentence. For the ABox language, this is exactly as it was before; for the TBox language, the semantics is defined as follows:

Let D be any set,

Let E be any function from gsymbols to relations over D such that $E(s)$ has the same arity as s,

Then for any gterm e, we define the *extension* of e wrt E by

1. The extension of any gsymbol s is $E(s)$.
2. The extension of (**ConGeneric** $e_1 \cdots e_k$) is the intersection of the extensions of the e_i, and D if k is 0.
3. The extension of (**VRGeneric** e_1 r e_2) are those elements x of the extension of e_1 such that $\langle x,y \rangle$ is in the extension of r only when y is in the extension of e_2.
4. The extension of (**RoleChain** $r_1 \cdots r_k$) is the relational composition of the extensions of $r_1 \cdots r_k$.

For example, the extension of:

(**VRGeneric** *Person Child Doctor*)

would be the elements x of the extension of *Person* such that any y for which $\langle x,y \rangle$ is in the extension of *Child* is also in the extension of *Doctor*, that is, the complex term stands for those people whose children are all doctors.[11] Similarly, the extension of

(**RoleChain** *Child Child*)

is the set of all pairs $\langle x,z \rangle$ such that for some y, $\langle x,y \rangle$ is in the

---

[11] As a matter of terminology, we will say that the fillers of the *Child* role are constrained to be in the extension of *Doctor*.

extension of *Child* and $\langle y,z \rangle$ is also in the extension of *Child*, that is, the expression stands for the *Grandchild* relation.

So far, the only relation between the semantics of the TBox and the ABox languages is that both depend on the assignment E of relations to gsymbols. However, the coupling is closer than this, since TBox symbols can be *defined*, that is, associated with other gterms that become their definitions. The net effect is to constrain the mapping E so that the extension of the defined symbol is the same as the extension of the gterm. To make this precise, we introduce the notion of a *symbol table* as follows: a symbol table S is a function from 1-place predicates to concepts and 2-place predicates to roles; for any TBox symbol g, $S(g)$ is the gterm which is the definition of g under S. Strictly speaking, we should be careful to avoid circular definitions[12] in a symbol table, but will not do so here. In fact, we will use the convention that a gsymbol is undefined whenever $S(p)$ equals p itself. In other words, for any gsymbol g, we say that g is *primitive* wrt S when g equals $S(g)$.[13]

A key notion, given a symbol table S, is that of a mapping E being an *extension function*:

Let D be any set,

Let S be a symbol table,

Let E be any function from gsymbols to relations over D such that $E(s)$ has the same arity as s,

E is an *extension function* wrt S iff for every gsymbol g, $E(g)$ is the same as the extension of $S(g)$ wrt E.

In other words, an extension function is a mapping that obeys the definitions specified by S. For example, if p is defined by S to be the gterm (**ConGeneric** q r), then $E(p)$ would have to be the intersection of $E(q)$ and $E(r)$.

4.3. Outcomes and KRYPTON Knowledge Bases

Using the notion of an extension function defined above, we can define what it means to be a *truth valuation* and a *subsumption relationship* with respect to a symbol table, which together will tell us what the world is like and how the gterms relate to each other. We define the

---

[12] An example of a circular definition might be one where $S(p)$ is (**ConGeneric** q r) and $S(q)$ is (**ConGeneric** p s).

[13] In particular, we assume that all k-place predicates for k greater than 2 are primitive.

first as follows:

> Let S be a symbol table,
>
> Let w be a mapping from sentences to {true,false},
>
> w is a *truth valuation* wrt to S iff
>
>> there is a set D and an extension function E wrt S over D such that $w(\alpha) =$ true iff α is true wrt E.

The only difference here from the previous definition is that a truth valuation must find a mapping, from predicate symbols to relations which is an extension function *for the given symbol table.* In other words, it must follow the definition of truth given earlier *and* respect the definitions given by S. For example, if p is defined by S to be q, then any truth valuation that says that (**EXISTS** x $(p\ x)$) is true, must also say that (**EXISTS** x $(q\ x)$) is also true.

For terms, we define the subsumption relationship as follows:

> Let S be a symbol table,
>
> Let e_1 and e_2 be gterms,
>
> e_1 *subsumes* e_2 wrt S iff
>
>> for any set D and any E that is an extension function wrt S, the extension of e_1 is a superset of that of e_2.

So, for example, the gterm p always subsumes (**ConGeneric** $p\ r$), and if q is defined by S to be (**ConGeneric** $p\ r$), then p subsumes q with respect to S (for any p, q, and r).

The notion of an *outcome* now is that of a complete specification of what the world is like and how the gterms are interrelated. It is defined by the following:

> An *outcome* is a pair $(\Rightarrow, w)$ where, for some symbol table S,
>
> 1. $\Rightarrow$ is the subsumption relationship wrt S (so, $\Rightarrow \subseteq$ *gterm* $\times$ *gterm*).[14]
>
> 2. w is a truth valuation wrt S (so, w is a function from sentences to truth values).

Note that an outcome does not determine a unique symbol table. As a

---

[14] Note that $q \Rightarrow p$ means that p subsumes q.

very simple example, if the relation $\Rightarrow$ says that the gterms p and (**ConGeneric** q r) subsume each other, it could have been the case that p was defined as (**ConGeneric** q r) or as (**ConGeneric** r q) or even as some other expression that subsumes and is subsumed by (**ConGeneric** r q). The actual syntactic form of the definition of p is not considered to be relevant; what counts is the relationship between p and all other gterms.

While an outcome is a complete specification of what the world and vocabulary are like, as before, a *knowledge base* is considered a partial specification of the same, that is, any set of outcomes. So, for example, if p is defined to be (**ConGeneric** q r), the outcomes it will contain are all those where p subsumes (**ConGeneric** q r) and vice-versa. Again, this is not to say that the KB does not know about other truths or subsumption relationships. For example, in all the outcomes in the KB, p also subsumes (**ConGeneric** r s q), and for any KB at all, all of its outcomes have the property that p subsumes (**ConGeneric** p q).

4.4. The Operations on KRYPTON Knowledge Bases

We are able once again to define what operations are available on these abstract-knowledge bases. These are the operations that define KRYPTON, and the only ones that an implementation has to provide to a user.

The ABox operations provided by KRYPTON are the ASK and TELL operations defined earlier but generalized to deal with the new outcomes.

$$\text{TELL}[\alpha,\text{KB}] \ = \ \text{KB} \ \cap \ \{(\Rightarrow,w) \mid w(\alpha)=\text{true}\}.$$

$$\text{ASK}[\alpha,\text{KB}] \ = \ \begin{cases} yes, \text{ if for each } (\Rightarrow,w) \text{ in KB}, \ w(\alpha)=\text{true}, \\ no, \text{ otherwise}. \end{cases}$$

The TBox equivalent to TELL is DEFINE. It takes a TBox symbol, a TBox expression, and a KB and tells the KB that the symbol is defined by the expression. The equivalent to ASK is called SUBSUMES. It takes two TBox terms and returns 'yes' or 'no' according to whether the first subsumes the second, based on what is known about the terms. These are defined as follows:

$$\text{DEFINE}[g,e,\text{KB}] \ = \ \text{KB} \ \cap \ \{(\Rightarrow,w) \mid g\Rightarrow e \text{ and } e\Rightarrow g\}.$$

SUBSUMES$[e_1, e_2, \text{KB}]$ =
>   *yes*, if for each $(\Rightarrow, w)$ in KB, $e_2 \Rightarrow e_1$,
>   *no*, otherwise.

It is worth emphasizing here that DEFINE involves nothing like the "addition" of a particular definition to a system. Rather, it constrains the outcomes to be only those where the symbol (g) and the expression (e) are mutually subsuming.

The TBox also has operations that have no (current) analogue in the ABox. These operations are questions that return sets of gsymbols, instead of 'yes' or 'no'.[15] The intent is that we should be able to find out what symbols have been defined and to reconstruct, for each such symbol, a definition for it. It may not be the actual definition that was used, but its effect overall would be the same. The three operations are VOCAB, which returns the gsymbols that have been defined; PRIMS, which, given a TBox term, returns the ultimate primitives[16] that make up the expression; and ROLEPAIRS, which, given a concept, returns a list of pairs $\langle c, p \rangle$ where p is a primitive concept and c is a list of primitive roles, and where the gterm constrains the fillers of the chain of c to be in the extension of p. These operations are defined in the following way:

VOCAB$[\text{KB}]$ = $\{p$, a gsymbol |
>   there is a different gsymbol q such that SUBSUMES$[q, p, \text{KB}]$ = yes$\}$.

PRIMS$[e, \text{KB}]$ =
>   if e is a concept then
> $\{p$ in 1-predicate-symbol | p is not in VOCAB$[\text{KB}]$ and
>   SUBSUMES$[p, e, \text{KB}]$ = yes$\}$
>   if e is a role then $(q_1 \cdots q_k)$ where
>   no q_i is in VOCAB$[\text{KB}]$ and
>   SUBSUMES$[(\textbf{RoleChain } q_1 \cdots q_k), e, \text{KB}]$ = yes.

ROLEPAIRS$[e, \text{KB}]$ = $\{\langle (q_1, \cdots, q_k), p \rangle$ |
>   neither p nor any q_i is in VOCAB$[\text{KB}]$ and
>   SUBSUMES$[(\textbf{VRGeneric } e \ (\textbf{RoleChain } q_1 \cdots q_k)p), e, \text{KB}]$ = yes$\}$.

Note that a gsymbol is a primitive exactly when it is not defined, that is, when it is not in VOCAB.

---

[15] Stickel's theorem prover provides answers to some assertional "wh-questions", but the question of an appropriate set for knowledge-representation purposes is still an open one.

[16] Recall that a primitive is a symbol that has no definition. Thus what constitutes a primitive may vary as definitions are acquired.

Given the details of this Knowledge Level account, there are a number of important properties of KRYPTON that we can prove. For example, it can be shown that DEFINE and SUBSUMES have the obvious proper relationship, for example:

and

$$\text{SUBSUMES}[s,e, \text{DEFINE}(s,e, \text{KB})] = \text{yes}$$

$$\text{SUBSUMES}[e,s, \text{DEFINE}(s,e, \text{KB})] = \text{yes} \quad \text{(for any KB)}.$$

We can show that all of the appropriate subsumption relationships [BL84a] hold in the TBox, as in, for example:

$$\text{SUBSUMES}[p_1, (\textbf{ConGeneric } p_1 \; p_2), \text{KB}] = \text{yes} \quad \text{(for any KB)}.$$

It can also be shown that the form of a definition expanded into only primitives (using the results of PRIMS and ROLEPAIRS) is equivalent to the original definition. Finally, and most cogent to the focus of this paper, it can be shown that the ABox and the TBox have the desired relationship. For example, universal assertions that should follow directly from definitions can be shown to do so:

$$\text{ASK}[\forall x \; man(x) \supset person(x),$$
$$\text{DEFINE}[man, (\textbf{VRGeneric } person \; sex \; male), \text{KB}]] = \text{yes} \quad \text{(for any KB)}.$$

In other words, the KB that results from defining "man" as those people whose sex is male thinks that all men are people. So the definition of "man" in the TBox has had the correct effect on the ABox.

5. *KL*: An Autoepistemic Representation Language

One of the properties of this knowledge level viewpoint of knowledge bases is that it does not specify what language a KB might actually use to represent the information it has, but only specifies the language whose sentences are arguments to TELL and ASK. This raises the possibility of having an interaction language that is more powerful than that of a first-order logic, without necessarily placing additional representational burdens on the resulting KB. In this section, we generalize the arguments to TELL and ASK to a language called *KL* that includes a modal operator **K**, where for any sentence α, **K**α is intended to be read as "the KB knows that α."

The motivation for having such an operator has been covered at length elsewhere ([LEVE81],[LEVE84a],[LEVE84b]). Suffice it to say that this operator allows us to examine what a KB knows in finer detail than is possible with a purely first-order language. For example, we can now distinguish between asking a KB if something satisfies a certain property and asking it if it *knows* something that satisfies the property. Similarly, we can ask the KB if it knows all instances of a certain predicate. Moreover, because a KB may not know whether or not it knows all the instances, by using sentences of *KL* as arguments to TELL, we can inform a KB that it satisfies this type of closed-world condition. The surprising fact proven in [LEVE84a] is that even when a KB can be told arbitrary sentences of *KL*, the resulting information is always representable (at the Symbol Level) in purely first-order terms. So while the interaction language *KL* is more expressive than first-order logic, the resulting KB are always first-order representable.

5.1. Syntax and Semantics

The syntax of *KL* is very much like that of the first-order language presented earlier but with a **K** operator (which we will sometimes write as **KNOWN**) and a few extra complications. Since we want to be able to talk about knowing what (or who) satisfies a certain property, we need a language of *singular terms* to refer to things over and above the variables used for quantification. First, we will include function symbols of every arity as in regular first-order languages.[17] The assumption is that terms formed from these need not refer to distinct elements of the domain nor name every element of the domain. In particular, there will be a special equality predicate to state when two of these terms are or are not identical. But, in addition, we include a denumerable set of *standard names* to refer unambiguously to objects in the domain. The assumption here is that, unlike terms made from function symbols, no two standard names corefer and every object in the domain is named by one of them. More formally, we have the following:

---

[17] Function symbols of arity 0 are called *constants*.

$$\langle term\rangle ::= (\langle k-function-symbol\rangle\langle term\rangle_1 \cdots \langle term\rangle_{k)} \quad k\geqslant 0$$
$$\quad | \quad \langle variable\rangle$$
$$\quad | \quad \langle standardname\rangle$$

$$\langle wff\rangle ::= (\langle k-predicate-symbol\rangle\langle term\rangle_1 \cdots \langle term\rangle_{k)} \quad k\geqslant 0$$
$$\quad | \quad (\textbf{EQUALS } \langle term\rangle \langle term\rangle)$$
$$\quad | \quad (\textbf{NOT } \langle wff\rangle)$$
$$\quad | \quad (\textbf{OR } \langle wff\rangle \langle wff\rangle)$$
$$\quad | \quad (\textbf{EXISTS } \langle var\rangle \langle wff\rangle)$$
$$\quad | \quad (\textbf{KNOWN } \langle wff\rangle).$$

We will let KL stand for the sentences of this language, L stand for sentences without a **K**, and T stand for the closed terms. If α is any formula, α_t^x is the result of replacing in α all free occurrences of x by t (and similarly, u_t^x, for any term u).

Since we have standard names to work with, the semantics of this language can be defined without talking about elements of any domain. To do so, we start with the notion of a coreference relation over closed terms.

A *coreference relation* over T is any equivalence relation such that

1. Every term has a coreferring standard name.

2. No two standard names corefer.

3. If u and v corefer, then for any term t, so do t_u^x and t_v^x.

Given this definition, we can define truth valuations for sentences without **K** operators as follows:

A *truth valuation* is any function from L to *true* or *false* such that

1. There is a coreference relation such that (**EQUALS** u v) is true iff u and v corefer.

2. If (**EQUALS** u v) is true, then α_u^x and α_v^x have the same truth value.

3. (**NOT** α) is true iff α is false.

4. (**OR** α β) is true iff α is true or β is true.

5. (**EXISTS** $x\alpha$) is true iff for some standard name n, α_n^x is true.

A truth valuation tells us what is true but does not deal with knowledge at all. To define the truth conditions for sentences with **K** operators, we have to specify what is known by a KB. To do so, we think of an *outcome* as before, as being a truth valuation, and a KB is then a set of truth valuations. As before, something is known when it comes out true in all outcomes. So to interpret arbitrary sentences of *KL*, we need a set of outcomes (*i.e.,* the KB that tells us what is known) and a single outcome (*i.e.,* the truth valuation that tells us what is true independent, of the KB). So the semantics of *KL* is defined as follows:

Let *w* be a truth valuation and KB be a set of truth valuations.

The *truth* of any sentence of *KL* wrt *w* and KB is defined by

1. If α is in *L*, then its truth value is $w(\alpha)$.
2. (**NOT** α) is true iff α is false.
3. (**OR** α β) is true iff α is true or β is true.
4. (**EXISTS** $x\alpha$) is true iff for some standard name *n*, α_n^x is true.
5. (**KNOWN** α) is true iff for every w' in KB, α is true wrt w' and KB.

The only new clause here is the one dealing with $\mathbf{K}\alpha$, which stipulates that something is known when it is true over all truth valuations in the KB, precisely the convention we had been using for ASK and TELL all along. Other properties of this semantics, as well as a sound and complete proof theory, can be found in [LEVE84a].

5.2. The Operations on *KL* Knowledge Bases

Given that the language *KL* already talks about what is known, there really is not much left to specifying how ASK and TELL should behave. Specifically, ASK will return **yes** for a given α and KB precisely if $\mathbf{K}$ α is true with respect to that KB.

$$\text{ASK}[\alpha, \text{KB}] = \begin{cases} yes, & \text{if for each } w \text{ in KB}, \alpha \text{ is true wrt } w \text{ and KB}, \\ no, & \text{otherwise.} \end{cases}$$

$$\text{TELL}[\alpha, \text{KB}] = \text{KB} \cap \{w \mid \alpha \text{ is true wrt } w \text{ and KB}\}.$$

The properties of this ASK and TELL are described in detail in [LEVE84b]. One worth discussing briefly here, however, is the fact that *KL* presents no additional representational burden to a KB at the Symbol Level. To see this, we need to specify what it means for a sentence (or set of sentences) of *L* to represent a KB:

A sentence κ of *L* *represents* a KB iff the KB is the set of all truth valuations where κ is true.

What this amounts to saying is that the KB knows *exactly* κ in that it knows κ and any KB with less information (i.e., with additional truth valuations) does not know κ. The theorem proven in [LEVE84a] is the following:

Theorem Suppose a KB is represented by a sentence κ. Then, for any sentence α of *KL*, there is a sentence β of *L* such that TELL$[\alpha,\text{KB}]$ is represented by (**AND** κ β).

This theorem guarantees that even if we TELL a KB sentences of *KL* (such as a closed-world assertion) we will always be able to represent what we just learned by conjoining a first-order sentence to what we had before. This is not to say that this operation is *decidable*, of course. We gave up decidability well before this. But it does guarantee that we can get by at the Symbol Level with strictly first-order theorem proving if we so desire.

6. Conclusion

We have presented several examples of how the Knowledge Level view can be applied to particular knowledge-representation systems. Under this view, it is possible to predict the behavior of a representation system with respect to the *knowledge* it can be considered to have. The user is not restricted to having to guess what an implementation "means" nor is he left to his own interpretation of the system's data structures. It should also be clear from our accounts that first-order logic is an important tool to be used in analyzing representation systems at the knowledge level, regardless of its connection with the actual implementation of a system. Further, the logical apparatus used in the account of a standard first-order language carries over to support the analysis of more sophisticated representation languages.

7. References

[BFL83a]   [BFL83b]   [BL84a]   [GM78]   [KOWA75]   [LEVE81] [LEVE84a]   [LEVE84b]   [LZ74a]   [NEWE80]   [STIC82]

4
On Knowledge-Based System Architectures[1]

Frank Manola
Michael L. Brodie[2]

ABSTRACT *This chapter investigates architectural issues of Knowledge-Base Management Systems (KBMSs) that might result from the integration of Knowledge-Base (KB) systems and Database Management Systems (DBMS) technology. A hypothetical KBMS architecture is presented that assumes the decomposition and current KB systems and DBMSs into components that may themselves be KB systems. The architecture is for a system of heterogeneous, distributed, cooperating KB components that actively participate in problem solving (e.g., Knowledge Management and KB application components cooperate, a DBMS query optimizer cooperates with other KB planning components.) The architecture is used to investigate the systems concept of a KBMS, its potential functionality, related systems issues, and types of integration.*

[1] This work was supported in part by the Defense Advanced Research Projects Agency and by the National Science Foundation, Grant ECS-841383F. The views and conclusions contained in this paper are those of the authors and do not necessarily represent the official policies of the Defense Advanced Research Projects Agency, the National Science Foundation, or the U. S. Government.

[2] Computer Corporation of America

1. Introduction

Many current information systems involve large centralized databases under the control of a Database Management System (DBMS). Although most programs using the DBMS access only small fractions of the database, there are significant advantages to using the database-centered approach, such as:

a. Controlled data sharing

b. Central control of data security and redundancy

c. Maintenance of common semantics and consistency among shared data

d. Potential for optimization of access

e. Flexibility of access and system development

Distributed database systems provide, in addition to central control, resource distribution facilities for:

f. Location of data near where it will be used

g. Increased system reliability

h. Increased system performance through use of parallelism

i. Ability to add additional processing power transparently, by adding additional nodes

The database community generally views such information systems as having an architecture consisting of "application programs" clustered around a central DBMS (see Figure 1).

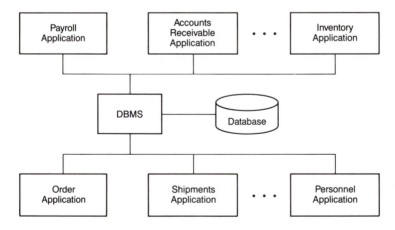

Figure 1: Conventional Database System Architecture

Recent investigations into applying (KB) system technology to components of this architecture raise important issues about the architecture itself. Examples of such investigations include:

a.   DBMS interfaces for existing KB systems (e.g., expert systems)

b.   Use of KB techniques in performing "database management" functions (e.g., "semantic query optimization" techniques, and use of "semantic data models")

c.   KB tools for database and DBMS development (e.g., database design)

This chapter identifies important system-design issues that arise when extending the database-centered architecture (by infusing its components, where appropriate, with KB capabilities) to an architecture for Knowledge-Base Management Systems (KBMSs). A hypothetical KBMS architecture is proposed, within which many previously-made observations are combined to develop a deeper understanding of the potential functionality and structure of KBMSs and the KB systems they will support. Further investigations will be required at the "organization" level (see the chapter by Fox and McDermott), the "knowledge" level (see [BLP84] and the two chapters by Brachman and Levesque), and the "symbol" level.

We conclude the introduction with a position statement. For the same reasons that motivated the database-centered architecture for information system applications, we propose a KBMS with a knowledge-base-centered architecture for KB system applications. Although a KBMS will be required by individual KB applications with large or complex knowledge bases, we propose a larger role for KBMSs. The KBMS will "manage" the "knowledge resources" of a collection of KB applications (e.g., all those of an organization). The knowledge resources will include complex data types and knowledge structures with associated processors and languages that are new to DBMS technology. Although incorporating these capabilities poses significant challenges, the greatest challenge is to provide *knowledge sharing*, the KBMS analog of the fundamental property of DBMSs, data sharing. Knowledge sharing will be new to both database and KB systems. It will require unified control schemes for consistency, semantics, and knowledge content (i.e., what knowledge resources the KBMS has) as well as for redundancy, reliability, and security.

The position statement is somewhat philosophical. Although we believe that DBMS technology is applicable, the knowledge-base-centered approach can include non-shared knowledge and knowledge not stored in the central knowledge bases. Further, we assume the need for different interpreters for different knowledge resources, and the need to store that same knowledge redundantly, in different ways, possibly inconsistently under some form of control.[4] The assumptions are based on current KB system technology in which single KB applications have several subcomponents, each with specialized knowledge. In fact, similar problems exist when a "single knowledge-base component" consists of multiple cooperating subcomponents, each with specialized knowledge in the knowledge base.

Finally, we assume that KBMS components will actively cooperate in problem solving. Hence, related control should be placed in the KBMS so as to achieve overall system objectives. To determine the role of DBMS components in the problem-solving process, components must be examined individually, rather than treating the DBMS as a monolithic unit. This allows DBMS components to be compared with KB system components that accomplish similar functions, so that they can cooperate or be integrated (e.g., KB system planning and DBMS query optimization components).

2. Motivating Example

This work was motivated by specific investigations of architectures for systems that extend the database-centered architecture with KB components, including systems for:

a.   Cartographic information (with a central, "earth model" database).

b.   CAD/CAM information (with a central design/manufacturing database.,

c.   Tactical Communications, Command, Control, and Intelligence (C3I) (with a central database of tactical situation and platform characteristics information).

Details of the C3I system are now presented to motivate further discussion.

Figure 2 shows processing components, knowledge, and data that might exist in a future C3I system.[5] The components are described below.

Components shown on the left side of Figure 2 handle input and output. They interpret data and translate it into required forms. For

---

[4] A federated, heterogeneous, distributed database system provides unified control over the common parts of the distributed database and mechanisms for resolving related inconsistencies. Not all data is under that control.

[5] The hardware configuration and "labeling" of groups of components as separate subsystems is not relevant here. The important issue is that the components must interact closely.

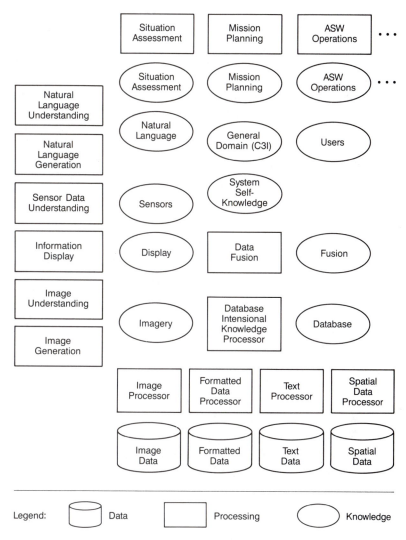

Figure 2: A Strawman C3I System

example, a Natural Language Understanding component might interpret English language text in incoming messages and create data in forms required for specific reports or for storage in the system's database. Components shown across the bottom form the "database management" facility. They store and retrieve various types of data in response to requests from other components. Components shown across the top represent applications using data from the I/O components and the database components. Still, other components perform system functions such as output display and routing of information between components.

The system continually accepts input from multiple data sources (e.g., message systems or human users) and attempts to maintain a description of the current (tactical or strategic) situation based on the new data and inferences it makes. System components may make recommendations (e.g., identifying threats, noting actions to take), or formulate plans (e.g., missions or various other operations) in response to specific requests, or in response to specific queries.

The structure and intended uses of this architecture illustrate important requirements that appear to be common to future KBMS applications. The remainder of this section outlines these requirements.

Large Knowledge Bases

Unlike current KB systems, some future KB systems will have large knowledge bases (e.g., rule sets and facts) for the following reasons:

a. Some KB systems will have to deal with large databases of facts (even when there is little higher-level knowledge) that will require DBMS support.

b. Knowledge bases for individual components cannot always be formulated concisely (e.g., as a small set of production rules). For example, the component's knowledge may be in the form of scenarios or previously-encountered situations [GBW83].

c. A knowledge-base-centered approach (like that in Figure 2) suggests that the KBMS will contain all the knowledge bases of all KB components. This would result in large "central" knowledge bases.

Heterogeneous Knowledge Bases

In typical database-centered environments, DBMSs provide interfaces for application programs written in multiple programming languages, as well as for other specialized languages such as query languages, report writers, and application development languages. Current KB system technology and knowledge bases are being developed using multiple-knowledge-representation languages and systems. Heterogeneous knowledge bases and databases will continue to be developed, and will have considerable value in future KB systems.

Knowledge Sharing

Data-and knowledge-sharing will be required. For example, messages concerning antisubmarine warfare (ASW) missions that contain English text will require interpretation by the Natural Language Understander, using general linguistic and domain knowledge and ASW Operations knowledge. This latter knowledge also is required by the ASW Operations expert. Knowledge of user intent also might be shared. For example, the goal of the person expressing a sentence is important in Natural Language Interpretation (see chapter by Webber). A similar type of knowledge might help a database access planner (e.g., a query optimizer) to plan access strategy or data movements (e.g., prestaging data the user is likely to ask for next).

Multiple Data Types

The system will process multiple types of data that include the usual formatted data types, spatial data, imagery, signals, etc. The architecture may have to support associated special storage devices and processors. The storage and retrieval of some data types may require KB processing. (This is discussed in the chapter by Dayal and Smith.)

Communication Between Components

At arbitrary times, any data source or system component may produce data of interest to one or more other components. There must be a flexible and efficient communication facility to allow the necessary flow of information.

Integrated Input/Output

Effective presentation is required, of information generated by the system *as a whole*. It may be necessary to present, on the same display, coordinated results from several KB components. For example, the Situation Assessment component might have to contribute to a display that also includes weather data on a map background, without obscuring other display information. A KB component is required to coordinate the separate contributions to the display. Similar comments can be made for input [BH80].

System Modularity

The system will probably grow continuously (e.g., by the addition of KB components, data types, and processors). Ideally, the integration of these new components into the overall system would not require each new component to possess excessive information about existing components.

Self-understanding

The system will be large and complex. Users should be able to interrogate the system about available data and processing resources, their capabilities, and how to use them. This requires a degree of system self-understanding. Ideally, the system also would be capable of explaining aspects of its own behavior.

Parallelism

Some system components must operate in parallel. For example, processing of sensor data must take place in parallel with situation assessment, requested mission planning, and support of ad hoc user queries and continuous display updates. This will require distributed processing by heterogeneous components tailored for specific types of data or processing (e.g., inference).

Component Adaptability

Some components will be specialized for particular applications (e.g., the Situation Assessment and ASW Operations components). They correspond to the application programs of conventional database-centered systems. However, it would be desirable if more general-purpose components could be used in multiple environments, just as generalized DBMSs are now.

3. Architectural Issues

This section identifies architectural issues that arise when addressing the above requirements, in order to:

- Decide on key system design decisions,

- Provide a common framework for examining the design decisions (and associated considerations),

- Make use of the framework and compare components used in KB systems and DBMS, particularly those with similar functionality.

Most of the issues have been investigated in the artificial intelligence literature (e.g., in connection with distributed problem solving). Special cases have been addressed in the database literature (although often under different names). In this section, we consider the issues together, since they are highly interrelated. In future KBMSs, the above issues cannot be considered in isolation.

3.1. Knowledge Integration and Access

Issues concerning the control of and access to knowledge can be divided into two sets, those that arise in:

- Treating knowledge *as data* (i.e., in dealing with the *representation*, at the "symbol level")

- Dealing with the knowledge per se, at the "knowledge level-" [BLP84] (See also the chapters by Brachman and Levesque.)

The first set of issues concerns traditional "database" problems applied to potentially large heterogeneous knowledge bases shared by multiple KB components. One example is the problem of "knowledge management considered as data management" [JV83] for which [BALZ80] suggested using a DBMS as an internal KB system component. Another issue is the control of concurrent access to shared knowledge that may be updated by multiple components. Depending on the knowledge representation involved, conventional database concurrency control mechanisms may not be ideal. Another such issue is the efficiency and storage structures and search techniques in various knowledge representation schemes. An example is the use of the RETE algorithm in finding relevant production rules in OPS [FORG79]. A study of such methods in a database context may be found in [DHMR84].

These issues apply not only to conventional knowledge representations (e.g., production rules, logic clauses, semantic nets) but also to unconventional *data* types. Current database research incorporates data types for spatial data, imagery, voice, etc. into DBMSs. (See the chapter by Dayal and Smith.)

The second class of issues concerns the knowledge level. For the architecture to result in a *system*, knowledge contained in system components must be coordinated. This does not necessarily require a central knowledge repository, nor a single knowledge representation scheme. It does, however, require the maintenance of semantics common to all (or even pairs of) system components, even if the knowledge is distributed for processing purposes. A business of the future might use numerous KB components in various aspects of its automated activities. Undoubtedly, common entities (employees, parts, etc.) and associated relationships will be referenced by more than one component. Semantics will need to be kept consistent throughout the components, even when some of the associated semantics are intentionally inconsistent.

Such knowledge-level concerns require the evaluation of the system at that level. Techniques are needed for identifying and validating the required consistency. Such techniques must refer to both the knowledge representations and too their interpretations provided by associated processors. Shared "metaknowledge" (e.g., knowledge about employee and part entities) should be available for use in designing and implementing components. A database analogy is the use of the DAPLEX model in the Multibase heterogeneous distributed database system [GKLS81, LR82]. In Multibase, DAPLEX is used as a "supermodel." Schema objects and relationships in the data models of individual database systems are mapped to DAPLEX objects and relationships so as to resolve data inconsistencies throughout the system. The problem in heterogeneous distributed databases is complicated enough. The problem in heterogeneous knowledge representations is far more complex. Investigations in this area also will be the key to allowing different views of the same knowledge.

A closely related issue (also connected to the communications issues discussed below) is knowledge communicated between components about tasks to be performed. A database example would be the communication of data requirements from an application to a DBMS. The set oriented queries processed by relational DBMSs provide more knowledge of the intention and the application (namely to process the specified data set) than a series of record-at-a-time accesses. Incorporating "knowledge of" recursion in DBMSs would represent a further step (pursued in detail in chapters by Dayal and Smith, Ullman, Naqvi, and Bancilhon). Another step could be the communication of application data requirements in the form of a series of IF <condition> THEN <request> statements. Probabilities could be supplied for conditions based on transaction input (or calculated for conditions based on previous retrievals). Such transaction statements are currently used in some database design methods. How far DBMSs should go in this direction is an interesting question. The problem is much more complex when KB components are involved.

3.2. System Organization

Issues of system organization concern the components that make up the system, their roles, and their interactions. Processing and communication constraints must be considered. Processing constraints limit the effectiveness of individual components and tend to suggest distribution for increased performance. Communication constraints limit the dissemination of information among distributed components. As a result, it is necessary to give processing components well-designed assignments based on task requirements, available components, and available communications. [CMS83] identifies key issues in this area. The discussion in this section relies heavily on their comments. The issues are well-known in the distributed-systems community, and special cases appear in the design of distributed database systems.

One group of issues involves the system's *organizational policy* [CMS83]. This specifies how a larger task is decomposed into smaller tasks that can be assigned to individual components. The set of required roles must be determined, and the policy must assign specific roles to each of the components. For example, roles determine which components have "authority" over others. This authority may include the right to assign roles to other components, the right to allocate scarce resources among competing components, etc. The criteria for specific assignments should also be specified. Ideally, this assignment will enable the components to work relatively independently, ensuring maximum parallelism and minimum communication. The policy also specifies communication paths among components. It defines which components must communicate with each other, as well as the nature of the communication required. The policy should keep irrelevant communication to a minimum, while facilitating relevant communication. The policy also must take cognizance of processing and communication resources available to given components, since, for example, assignment of authority requires sufficient resources for effectively coordinating subordinate components. The choice of system organization is usually between some type of hierarchy and a flat, "cooperating experts" approach. The choice depends on the problem to be solved, the degree of coordination required, the capabilities of the components, and the communications channels available, etc.

A method is required to determine the most appropriate policy. It should specify:

- When organizational structuring takes place, and whether a structure can be changed dynamically

- How roles are assigned to components

- Whether components are directed to assume roles or, instead, to determine their own roles based on information relayed about the problem to be solved

- Whether components negotiate with each other in assuming roles

A second group of organization issues concerns *information distribution policies* between components. The objective is to support necessary communication between cooperating components and to make efficient use of available communications channels. These policies are constrained by the organizational policy, since it determines component tasks (including communication), and decides what information the components must share and how frequently it must be shared. Information distribution policy must determine, for example:

- Broadcast or selective communication

- Unsolicited or on-demand communication, such as whether components communicate only when information is requested, or whether they infer the information needs of other components and communicate accordingly

- Acknowledged or unacknowledged communication

- Representation of communication by explicit message, some form of "subroutine call," or shared memory (such as a "blackboard"), etc.

- Such details as communication channel bandwidth channel reliability and load, timing constraints, and the relative cost and time of computation versus communication

The knowledge content of individual communications is also an important issue. Protocols and knowledge of other components can be used to reduce the amount of communication. Protocols are a type of knowledge-representation technique, since they encode knowledge; (e.g., "When you see the ship I've been telling you about, take over tracking and notify me.") Having knowledge of other components can be carried to the extreme of maintaining executable simulations of other components. Choices involve evaluating communications versus computation tradeoffs. As a result, relevant issues are: how much knowledge components have of other components' capabilities, what those other components are doing, the current situation or task at hand, etc.

A final system-organization issue is adaptability. For example, to what extent is a given component capable of adapting to different organizational policies (e.g., carrying out multiple roles) or different information- distribution policies (e.g., using messages in one instance and a blackboard in another). In a human "system," the "components" usually are quite adaptable, but limits can be reached. For example, in a typical business, people trained differently, and who use different terminology, are able to communicate with reasonable success. However, in an organization like the United Nations, the diversity is such that the special role of "translator" becomes necessary. Such roles may be considered in computer systems as well.

3.3. Relevant Technical Trends

We conclude this section by listing three trends which will require consideration of the above KBMS architecture issues. One trend is the potential use of KB techniques in performing DBMS-related activities. Developments illustrating this trend include:

- Semantic data models in DBMSs and associated implementation techniques [CFLR81, CDFG83, DAYA83] (See also the chapter by Dayal and Smith.)

- Semantic query optimization and other types of KB user interfaces (See the chapters by Webber, by Stonebraker, and by Jarke.)

- Flexible integrity control mechanisms [BBC80, HM75] (See also the chapters by Borgida and by Borgida, Mitchell, and Williamson.)

- Flexible concurrency control mechanisms [BG84, GARC83] (See also the chapter by Carey and DeWitt.)

- Network partition recovery in distributed databases [BCGK83]

The integration of KB and DBMS capabilities gives rise to two possibilities that might significantly affect the KBMS architecture. First, if DBMSs provide appropriate KB capabilities, KB "applications" could offload functions that are best performed centrally. For example, the DBMS could provide a general, production-rule-based alerting facility so that KB components could ask to be alerted by the DBMS when specific situations arose (e.g., information or events from outside the system or from other components). This would reduce the need (in a system such as that described in Section 2) for component/component communications, and for repeated polling of the DBMS. Second, KB components in the DBMS might be able to communicate, i.e., cooperate, with other KB components providing similar functions. For example, the query optimizer that plans DBMS queries could communicate with other planning components to determine system data access patterns.

A second trend is the potential use of DBMS technology in KB systems. One example is coupling database and expert systems. (See the chapter by Fox and McDermott.) Another example is the use of a DBMS containing a "demon" (alerting) capability as a component supporting the blackboard of HEARSAY-III [BALZ80]. [DF84] identifies DBMS capabilities necessary to support AI reasoning. Some of these capabilities are similar to those identified in the chapter by Dayal and Smith for supporting spatial data.

A final trend is DBMS developments not motivated by KB processing but relevant to it. The following examples are facilities that could be provided by the KBMS as a whole or by individual KB components:

- Recursive processing. This is an important issue in the interface between DBMSs and certain types of KB systems, such as those using Prolog. (See [CH82c] and the chapters by Bancilhon, by Naqvi, and by Ullman.) Important spatial data types (cartographic data, engineering data, and networks of various sorts) require recursive processing capability, whether KB components are involved or not. (See [AU79] and the chapter by Dayal and Smith.)

- Improved variable length data facilities (e.g., for new data types) such as text and spatial data. [LORI81] describes such needs for CAD/CAM data.

- Improved adaptability in adding new specialized data types (voice, imagery, spatial data) and associated generalized processors. (See the chapter by Dayal and Smith.)

- Real-time processing capabilities to support process control and sensor data applications, and possibly real-time KB system applications. (see the chapter by Fox and McDermott.)

4. A Knowlege-Base System Architecture

This section presents a hypothetical KBMS architecture to illustrate the concept and the issues. (The chapter by Carey and DeWitt also deals with DBMS architectures.) There are two basic ideas behind the architecture:

1. Increasing demand for KB capabilities in DBMSs and the consequent knowledge-processing requirements may lead to DBMS components that are KB systems themselves.

2. In this case, the entire architecture becomes that of a distributed, heterogeneous collection of KB systems in which "knowledge management" components actively cooperate with more application-oriented components.

Treating the DBMS as a distributed KB system permits us to compare, establish communication between, and possibly integrate components that perform similar functions. Such a breakdown will help to identify common problems and applicable technology from both DBMSs and KB systems. The objective of this chapter is to stimulate ideas for architectures of systems (e.g., KBMSs) that integrate KB and database components. Such architectures will include new interfaces and components that do not exist when DBMSs are considered merely as monolithic storage repositories for external KB systems. The design and implementation of such architectures will depend on many specific details and problems not addressed here.

The architecture illustrated in Figure 3 consists of a number of KB components.

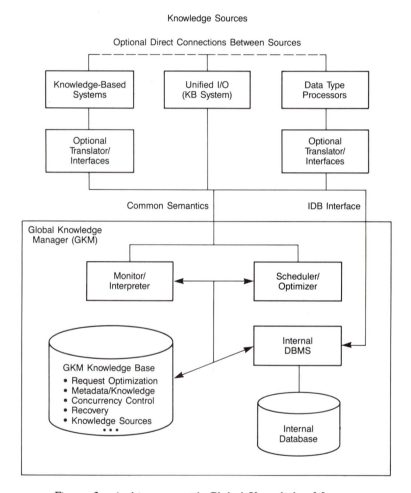

Figure 3: Architecture with Global Knowledge Manager

These components fall into the following classes:

a.   A *Global Knowledge Manager* (GKM) serves as a general coordinator and planner. It consists of two KB components, a Monitor/Interpreter, and a Scheduler/Optimizer, which use knowledge contained in the GKM Knowledge Base. The GKM contains an Internal DBMS that provides DBMS facilities for the GKM, and it also may be used by other components via the separate IDB interface.

b.   A *Unified I/O Interface* that enables system components to produce integrated displays and other I/O.

c.   *Knowledge Sources* (KSs) that fall into two categories:

•   "Knowledge-Based Systems" -- application-oriented KB systems or KB systems that provide dedicated services to the entire system

•   "Data Type Processors" -- specialized data repositories for different types of data (e.g., conventional DBMSs and text processors)

The connection between the GKM and the KSs is labeled "common semantics" to indicate that communication between these components requires a certain degree of shared understanding of the environment, tasks to be performed, etc.

d.   *Translator/Interfaces* that provide translation, when necessary, between the KSs and the GKM. Translator requirements depend on KS capabilities and the degree of integration with the GKM. For example, translators can be relatively "dumb" for KSs that act only as data repositories but must be more intelligent to translate between KS knowledge representations and the GKM. Translators also play a role in maintaining "common semantics."

The architecture permits (and Figure 3 conceals) many architectural variants. For example, various GKM subcomponents, including the Internal Database and GKM Knowledge Base, are logically but not necessarily physically part of the GKM. The Internal DBMS and its database could be a dedicated KS distributed and possibly coresident on processing nodes containing other KSs. Similarly, the GKM Knowledge Base might be stored in one or more dedicated KSs, including the Internal DBMS. One or more of the KSs may themselves be GKMs with additional attached KSs, and so on.

Potential GKM functions are best described in terms of interactions with other KB components. The simplest type of interaction occurs when components interact with the GKM much as conventional database applications interact with a DBMS. Requests enter via the Unified I/O interface from an external user, or are passed directly from a KS to the GKM. Such requests, which would be submitted to the GKM in a high-level form and result in data, would be processed as follows (assuming they were similar to conventional database queries):

1.   The optimizer/scheduler would convert the request to an optimized access plan. In doing this, the optimizer/scheduler would use knowledge about the data as well as, knowledge available on and

processing capabilities provided by the KSs, knowledge about request optimization itself, available communications paths, and semantics that might be used to improve the efficiency of the request, etc. The access plan would be stored in an internal database maintained by the Internal DBMS (in effect, a "blackboard").

2. The monitor/interpreter would carry out the plan by interpreting the steps stored in the internal database. Individual steps in the plan would be carried out by passing messages to (or leaving tokens in the blackboard for)[6] individual KSs requesting operations to be performed, accepting intermediate results from the KSs, and either moving these results to other KSs or retaining them in the internal database for further processing. During the interpretation, the monitor/interpreter would use knowledge about concurrency control, recovery techniques, etc., to control the overall course of the processing.

3. After any final processing, results would be returned to the requesting component by the monitor/interpreter.

Another simple type of interaction between a KS and the GKM occurs when the KS behaves toward the GKM as a stored data repository. In this case, the KS accepts requests for data and returns the requested data to the monitor/interpreter. Some such KSs may provide only data retrieval, whereas others may *derive* data by some form of reasoning. Thus, this type of interaction describes only the form of the interface, not necessarily the total functions of the component. The component might have functions other than those it reveals to the GKM (e.g., it might have a separate interface to human users).

The most interesting type of interaction between the GKM and a KS is "cooperative interaction," which is possible because the GKM is itself knowledge-based. The GKM can allow access to its own explicitly-represented plan(s) and knowledge. The GKM can accept knowledge (e.g., of requirements or plans) from KB components (e.g., accept requests to monitor situations and perform actions) and allow other components to modify its plans. The GKM's "plan" may merely be a goal for the KSs to work on or respond to. "Reactions" to the plan by the other components, changes in status, intermediate results, etc., may trigger reoptimization or other alterations in the plan by the GKM.[7] The GKM can send similar types of knowledge to other KB

---

[6] We show use of shared memory (blackboard/internal database) as the communications method in some places and messages in other places only because these approaches are used in the analogous places in the Multibase architecture. In fact, the particular method used for communication would be a matter of design based on factors discussed in the previous section.

[7] Such dynamic optimization also has been considered in the context of distributed database systems, but, generally, it has not been implemented.

components. This mode of operation also applies to cooperation between the scheduler/optimizer and the monitor/interpreter *within* the GKM. This allows the monitor/interpreter to notify the scheduler/optimizer of changes that affect the plan and might require rescheduling. In effect, the GKM's internal blackboard can be used to coordinate the activities of multiple KB systems. Other components may use the GKM as a blackboard server, since the internal DBMS can contain the necessary structures (and alerters to act as blackboard demons) to serve in this role. (This might require the use of special "real time DBMS" techniques to obtain sufficient performance.)

Central control over knowledge could be maintained by giving the GKM access to the components' knowledge bases. All knowledge bases would then form a heterogeneous distributed-knowledge base. The amount of central control would be "negotiated" between the components.

Not all access plans need be interpreted. Plans that correspond to database transactions might be precompiled and stored in the GKM Knowledge Base. In response to an external request, they would simply be extracted and run. This is an extension of SDD-1's transaction "preanalysis" that allows for especially simple concurrency control methods to be used for selected transactions [BSR80].

The architecture (in Figure 3) shows how KB components within the GKM would allow for interfaces at many levels. The actual interfaces would be the subject for design, and would depend on the nature of the various components involved, their processing capability, how tightly integrated the system was to be, etc.

The architecture raises many issues that were identified in Section 3. For example:

- What processing capacity would be required for the GKM to act as a central coordinator in a particular case? Would the GKM itself be a distributed KB system?

- There is an important tradeoff between general knowledge processing capability and computational efficiency [BLP84]. Is there a subset of KB processing tasks that can be performed efficiently, and that also could serve as a kernel for GKM facilities?

- What methods of communication are appropriate for interactions between the GKM and the KSs? What are the tradeoffs and design criteria?

- How can common semantics that must exist between specific components be specified and maintained?

- What knowledge about other components can be used to produce efficient interactions between components?

- Maintaining control within a set of KB components such as this will not be an easy task. What are the requirements for control in specific situations, and what mechanisms exist for implementing it?

5. Conclusions

We have identified important design issues and interesting system concepts that arise when extending a DBMS with increased knowledge-base processing capacity. This work is at a very early stage and has been performed in preparation for examining specific system architectures and component requirements for particular KBMSs. There is a great deal of work to be done to realize such KBMS architectures. Progress toward this goal, and toward supporting the system requirements identified in Section 2, will need to come from the knowledge-base and database technical communities, working together in applying their own specialized technologies and insights.

6. Epilog

Many chapters in this book deal with specific aspects of integrating KB and DBMS technology in situations that require the facilities of a KBMS — a system that extends DBMS functionality such as storage, management, and efficient search and access of data to KB functionality over large or complex knowledge bases. Several other chapters discuss specific KBMS features (see chapters by Brachman and Levesque, Mylopoulos, Bancilhon, Mitchell, Jarke, Woods); or the concept of a KBMS (see chapters by Dayal and Smith, Fox and McDermott). The present chapter brings together many of the potential concepts with proposed functionality, features, and issues, and places them in a systems framework (i.e., a KBMS architecture). The purpose of this chapter is to identify the requirements and issues that arise in creating such a system concept and to stimulate thinking about KBMSs.

Since this chapter hypothesizes a close integration of KB and DBMS technology in a general-purpose setting, some of the ideas presented may be unfamiliar to both the AI and database communities. The chapter does not present a specific system, but investigates the concept of a KBMS, a type of system. One goal is to consider the *systems* aspects peculiar to complex DBMSs. Such systems concerns may not be so evident in KB systems, which tend not to have the complex architecture of DBMSs. Also, KB systems are generally special-purpose systems, whereas DBMSs are designed for a broad class of applications.

The KBMS concept discussed here is intended to describe a general-purpose system that will serve a broad class of KB applications. However, like DBMSs, a particular KBMS will be designed for particular requirements (e.g., support particular knowledge-representation schemes and reasoning, or have particular functions).

In summary, this chapter investigates the KBMS concept by identifying potential functionality, features, and issues. The hypothetical KBMS architecture provides a framework within which to investigate how these things might interact (e.g., might relate to basic issues such as the role of a DBMS in future KBMSs). The architecture should not be construed as the blueprint for a real system.

The approach proposed here contains several insights. First, KBMSs should be designed to reflect a deep integration of the technologies involved, rather than merely to interface monolithic systems. This insures greater potential for applying the most advanced results from KB system and Database system technologies, for producing more flexible, integrated systems, for cooperative problem solving, and for avoiding system redundancy. Second, the architecture can be used to identify the more challenging problems facing KBMSs, including semantic consistency, cooperation, etc.

Acknowledgements

The authors would like to thank John Smith and Umesh Dayal for their contributions to the ideas described in this chapter, and Bill Modlin for his editorial comments.

7. References

[AU79] [BALZ80] [BBC80] [BCGK83] [BG84] [BH80] [BLP84] [BSR80] [CDFG83] [CFLR81] [CH82c] [CMS83] [DAYA83] [DF84] [DHMR84] [FORG79] [GARC83] [GBW83] [GKLS81] [HM75] [JV83] [LORI81] [LR82]

Discussion

John Mylopoulos discussed his research, aimed at developing a new technology for the production of software (consisting of programs, databases and, possibly, expert system-like interpretation modules). He views software development as involving (a) knowledge acquisition, (b) knowledge base construction and evaluation, and (c) generation of efficient code.

Comparing DBMSs with KBMSs he noted that DBMSs start with a data model while KBMSs start with a knowledge representation language which, in his view, should have (a) at least the power of first order logic, (b) facilities to specify and handle exceptions, (c) organisational principles to structure a large knowledge base. It was also noted that KBMSs do not distinguish generic and ground information, focus on the needs of knowledge base designers, rather than the needs of end users and require reasoning and explanation facilities.

He contrasted two methodological approaches to the development of KBMSs: (a) The "evolutionary approach" starts with an existing technology, such as DBMSs or expert system shells and moves toward a KBMS by extending the functionality of these systems; alternatively, (b) the "revolutionary approach" starts with a knowledge representation language and then builds around it appropriate KBMS facilities. He favours this second approach as a long term research strategy to yield a new technology.

Ron Brachman is not sure that a revolutionary approach is needed. He felt researchers should consider "the path", i.e. whether the revolution should be within one of the fields discussed at the workshop. He felt that knowledge representation research has proceeded beyond what it should.

Ron Brachman presented three orthogonal views of KBMSs: (a) The Symbol Level view, concerned with data structures, algorithms and efficiency, focuses on "machine-oriented" issues such as providing data integrity, concurrency and efficiency; (b) the System Engineering (or Manager) Level view, concerned with understandability and maintainability, addresses "people-oriented" issues, such as dealing with the complexity of large systems; approaches used here include abstraction principles and exception handling; (c) the Knowledge Level, concerned with information content and described by Newell [NEWE81], considers what knowledge can be represented. Brachman believes that the Knowledge Level is independent of, and more fundamental than, the Symbol and System Engineering Levels.

It is important to consider the Knowledge Level in a variety of situations such as (a) when combining multiple information sources, be they databases or knowledge bases, (b) when considering what kind of reasoning is needed in a KBMS, noting that there is a tradeoff between the tractability of reasoning and the expressiveness of a representation scheme, or (c) when considering the types of knowledge to be represented in a KBMS and whether HYBRID approaches (such as combining definitions and heuristics) need to be considered, and should be analysed at the knowledge level. Their research paper gives a knowledge-level account of combining terminological and assertional representations.

Ron Brachman felt that database people seem to be approaching AI-DB research as a means for improving DBMSs by dropping "particles of intelligence" (lots of little bright AI ideas) onto DBMSs. He is aiming at a better integration.

Hector Levesque presented a Knowledge Level view of knowledge bases as abstract data types. According to this view, a knowledge representation system is defined functionally, in terms of operations and their effects, not their implementation. In the proposal, two operations are provided for knowledge bases: (a) **Tell** adds to a knowledge base more information about a domain, (b) **Ask** extracts information about a domain from a knowledge base.

Knowledge Level accounts are then presented for several Knowledge Representation systems: (a) a first order representation language (without the notion of the Closed World Assumption), (b) an hybrid language (KRYPTON), (c) a language with a modal knowledge operator, where one can ask whether a property is satisfied, as well as whether the knowledge base knows that a property is satisfied. The language of interaction between the knowledge base and the the user is more expressive in the last case, but the resulting knowledge bases are first order.

Ron Brachman feels that the most important aspect of the Knowledge Level view is a measure of the correctness of a knowledge system. There are some kinds of initial specifications, some logical abstractions of what one likes to implement without worrying about the data structure. Bill Woods added a complementary view. He observed that discoveries are often made when a technology has interesting behaviour and one finds out years later that one does not understand what the behaviour is.

Mike Stonebraker asked if Hector Levesque and Ron Brachman were interested in engineering real expert systems, since most purchasers do not understand First Order Logic. "You are providing a technology the world cannot programme", he said.

Ron Brachman felt it is important to consider what the systems are about. For instance, in a banking systems, one should consider different types of accounts, without worrying about data structures, etc. Mark Fox said that it is important to understand what has been created in AI systems. Rusty Bobrow added that customers want to use a system with several features (e.g., concurrency, recovery), but that they do not have to understand the technology.

Ron Brachman felt that First Order Logic is not the most crucial aspect of the proposal. Rather, it is a convenient language which has certain desirable properties, including a formal semantics.

Jeff Ullman pointed out that only monotonic reasoning is allowed; no updates are permitted. Also, the handling of contradictions is not explicitly in the model, but has to be considered when designing a system. Levesque is not sure how to implement this. Gio Wiederhold added that the model lacks facilities for the representation of and reasoning with uncertainty. He noted that uncertainty permits generalisations, and is the basis of human understanding.

John McDermott asked whether the simplified model presented will be able to be extended to handle features like incompleteness, uncertainty, contradictions and non-monotonicity. Ron Brachman replied that good research is ongoing in those areas, and that a consideration of the knowledge level viewpoint may be of assistance in those areas.

John Mylopoulos and others, while agreeing with the Knowledge Level/System Engineering Level distinction, felt that engineering considerations should not be shoved off to a different level, but should be made part of every other level. Such considerations focusing on the Symbol Level have been addressed by software engineers and have led to abstraction mechanisms, programming methodologies and environments. Likewise, such considerations focusing on the Knowledge Level have led to knowledge organization and acquisition techniques, explanation facilities and the like.

Hector Levesque and Ron Brachman stressed that they are not suggesting that one should think of constructing a KBMS, by first of all, doing the analysis of knowledge to get that right, then doing the implementation of it, and getting that right with respect to knowledge level, and then doing some manager level, user interface, and keeping track of the knowledge base and getting that right, and then selling it. All three levels should be considered simultaneously, allowing them to affect each other. The reason why they focus on the knowledge level is because they are taking the knowledge in a KBMS very seriously. But they do not give implications for design methodology.

Frank Manola presented several architectural issues that arise when all components of a database system become more knowledge-based, assuming a **distributed** computing environment. As a result, he is concerned with the maintenance of consistency while at the same time allowing knowledge to be shared. He emphasized that many architectural issues and policy alternatives arise from the desire to provide large, heterogeneous knowledge bases (viewed as both knowledge and data) which support self-understanding, inter-component communication, continuous growth, and concurrency.

Frank Manola said that their work might be characterised as a "blender" approach. The key requirement for their system (which consists of several components) is going to be the maintenance and sharing of semantics which have to exist across different components. He also explained that their architecture does not assume a particular knowledge representation language. It can accommodate different kinds of representation languages.

Peter Szolovits noted that in large AI systems, people have been able to identify features which contributed to their success, such as having a small number of axes of representation, and having a particular architecture. He asked what particular features are in the proposed architecture. Frank Manola responded that he has adopted an evolutionary view of DBMSs. He sees his task as trying to understand the engineering issues while he is constructing a system. For example, an explanation facility requires a huge range of cooperating capabilities. Mike Brodie added that their purpose is not to propose a particular architecture. They don't have a particular solution, but they do have an idea of what the solutions might be.

Rusty Bobrow said that there is the possibility of doing a generalised DBMS with a specific architecture on the basis of example database systems. However, there isn't a sufficient number of knowledge based systems on which to base an architecture for a KBMS.

Mike Stonebraker felt that if one is going to replicate a system ten thousand times, to aid that many people, one has to figure out how to highly leverage one's software tools. That is a very important engineering problem.

Bruce Buchanan felt that the issue of communication among the components is an essential part of their design. It just can't be settled until one looks at the detail and the routine engineering. Moreover, he felt that the issue itself is neither routine nor engineering. Frank Manola responded that the different components of the system have to be considered, and one has to see what the best kind of communication between components is. There are many things to consider before one concludes that one of the best approaches is to build on top of a conventional database system.

Ron Brachman also expressed concern about the generalised architecture. He does not think that he will get much from the generalised architecture until he knows what they want the system to do. He observed that often expertise resides in particular knowledge about a particular task. He felt that there is a difference between large routine data operations and reasoning.

Peter Szolovits asked what would happen if tools are developed without an overall methodology. He drew a comparison with scientific programming where some people do things the same way as 20 years ago, because a general architecture has not been developed. Gio Wiederhold responded that one of the reasons for databases being forced together to cooperate is when the manager realizes that the very cost of data collection (which is often greater than the database management that actually processes the programme) makes it economically necessary to share the data and hence share the resources. There isn't an analogous management direction in scientific programming, because independent programmes are working in separate areas, with separate objectives, and there is no manager to see that it is economical to bring them together. He asked what the situation is with a KBMS. Are researchers aware that management is concerned with the cost of putting knowledge together? The high cost of knowledge acquisition might lead us towards the notion of a KBMS.

Part II

Knowledge Bases versus Databases

5
A View Of Knowledge Representation

Hector J. Levesque[1]

ABSTRACT *This is a thinly-disguised position paper that is more about logic and databases than anything else.*

There exist already at least two broad (and widely available) surveys of Knowledge-Representation work [BD81b and ML84], so my intent is not to repeat or even summarize that material here. I will instead assume familiarity with these surveys, and suggest a different way of looking at Knowledge-Representation, based on some of my recent work.

One feature shared by the two knowledge representation (KR) overviews mentioned above is that they focus almost exclusively on the *mechanisms* provided by the various schemes:[2] one offers inheritance hierarchies and cancellation; another provides active slot values and if then rules. The proliferation of potentially useful but completely dissimilar mechanisms found in KR schemes makes it very difficult to compare them even from an AI point of view, not to mention how they relate to the schemes found in Database Management. The question that immediately arises is what global perspective can be taken for comparing and evaluating a broad range of KR schemes. What I would like to do here is to investigate such a global perspective, instead of looking at the advantages and disadvantages of particular approaches. Essentially, the idea is that, instead of examining the representational structures and operations provided by a scheme at what has been called the symbol level [NEWE81, LEVE84, BRLE84], we focus instead on the knowledge level and ask what kinds of information about the world a KR scheme allows us to express.

---

[1] Department of Computer Science, University of Toronto, and The Canadian Institute for Advanced Research

[2] Following Hayes [HAYE85], a scheme is taken to any sufficiently precise notation that can be used in, or by, a computer.

Informally, and as further discussed in the Brachman and Levesque position paper, a knowledge-level analysis of a knowledge base (KB) is one that is concerned with its *information content*: what it tells us about the world it represents. At the symbol level, on the other hand, the issue is the way information is represented, that is, what symbolic structures are being used and what algorithms are used to manipulate and access these structures. Any mechanism or technique for dealing with represented information is therefore a symbol-level concern. To use first-order logic as an example of a scheme, at the knowledge level we care about the consistency and logical implications of a KB as defined by the semantics of the language; at the symbol level, we care about about topics like Skolemization, clausal normal forms, unification, connection graphs, resolution-refinement strategies, and the like.

For a more concrete example, consider the following case. Think of a KB that is a finite set of sentences in a language of a first-order logic with equality. We will choose some finite set of constant symbols (call it "C" and a finite set of predicate symbols (call it "P"; and call the set of first-order sentences that uses only these non-logical symbols "L". Now I want to consider a KB that can only contain certain sentences of L. First of all, the KB must contain the sentences

$$(x)[x = c_1 \lor x = c_2 \lor \cdots \lor x = c_n]$$

and

$$\text{not } (c_i \neq c_j) \quad i, j, \text{ distinct}$$

where the "c"s here range over all the elements of C. The rest of the KB must be a collection of sentences, one for each element of P, of the form

$$(x)[p(x) \longleftrightarrow x = c_1 \lor x = c_2 \lor \cdots \lor x = c_k]$$

where "p" is an n-place predicate symbol in P, "x" is an n-place vector of variables and the "c"s are n-place vectors of constants chosen only from C. We will say that a KB of this type is in "DB" form (for reasons that will soon be apparent). What is special about a first-order KB in DB form is that given *any* sentence of L, there is a way to determine whether or not it is a logical consequence of the KB. In other words, the problem of deciding whether or not

$$KB \vdash a$$

is (recursively) solvable, something that would not be true if the KB contained arbitrary sentences of L (since the so-called decision problem for full first-order logic is provably unsolvable). But, more importantly here, not only is the problem solvable, we can easily describe a mechanism to solve it, as follows. First translate the KB into a (more or less standard) relational database: consider the predicate symbols in P to be n-place relations over the domain C (think of C as strings or numbers). For each predicate "p", provide the tuples "c_1", "c_2" ... "c_k" as determined by the sentence above. Now treat the sentence "a" as a yes-no query to this database, where variables are understood as ranging over the domain C. It should be clear that "a" is a logical consequence of the KB exactly when the answer to the database query is "yes". What we have done is reduced logical implication for KBs in DB form to very simple database retrieval.

Let us call databases that can be viewed as the result of this type of translation "simple" and note that not every database is going to be simple. For instance, any database that use numbers in special ways (for example, to answer queries like "does any employee earn more than his/her manager") will not be simple since nothing in the KB language treats numbers or relations like "less than" as special.[3] Similarly, any database that uses strings in a special way (for example to answer the query "is there an employee whose last name starts with 'leve'") will not be simple. Ditto, for databases with null values, and for those that support views. However, for simple databases, we can always find a KB in DB form and vice-versa.

The point of this translation exercise is not that we can sometimes reduce first-order logic to relational databases, but rather that we can explain the information content of simple databases as a certain *restricted* type of first-order theory in such a way that the answers to queries are implicit in the theory (i.e., logical consequences of it). This is not to suggest that we might want to answer a query by doing theorem proving of some sort; that would be like cracking an egg with a hammer. Rather, it is precisely because the first-order theory is restricted in a certain way (namely, that it is in what I have called "DB form") that something like resolution is not necessary, and simple database retrieval is sufficient for sound and complete logical inference. What the first-order account gives us is *what* the answers to queries should be, not *how* to compute them (at least in this case). In other words, we are interested in using first-order logic at the knowledge level, not at the symbol level.

Why should this be translated into first-order logic when there is a perfectly good specification provided by the relational algebra? Indeed, there is nothing special about the language of first-order logic per se. What counts here is using a sufficiently general *knowledge representation language*, that is, a language that expresses the kinds of things that can be believed, namely sentences or, more strictly, propositions. Tuples in a relation, nodes in a semantic network, and wffs in a first-order theory

---

[3] We are, however, assuming that "equals" is special.

can be used to represent knowledge only to the extent that they can be understood as expressing propositions. Thus we ask questions like "Does this piece of data in the *employee* relation mean that John is Bill's manager?" or "Does this link between 'dog' and 'mammal' mean that every dog is a mammal?". What we get from first-order logic (and the only thing that concerns us here) is a reasonably general and precise *language of sentences* and a clear way of understanding the propositions expressed by complex sentences as a function of those expressed by the simple ones. Unfortunately, the propositions expressed by atomic sentences will be as undetermined as with a language of tuples or nodes and links. For example, in a particular application, "emp(a,b,c,d)" might express the proposition that there is an employee whose name is "a", whose age in years is "b", whose manager's name is "c", and whose yearly salary in kilodollars is "d", but Tarskian semantics will not tell you this.[4]

What I am suggesting is that we look at all KR schemes (including databases) as allowing us to express information about the world, information that can be understood as (declarative) sentences. Moreover, if we can express these sentences in a sufficiently general sentence language (like that of first-order logic), we can compare the schemes by asking what *range* of sentences in that language we are allowed (or forced) to express. So, for example, a simple database corresponds to (expresses the same information as) a first-order theory that is in DB form. At this knowledge level of analysis, the notions of data structure and algorithm are completely irrelevant. Similarly, notions of organization and abstraction are not at issue; all that counts here is what the sentences can or cannot say about the world. In fact, the set of sentences themselves need not even be finite (although they correspond to a finite structure in some KR scheme). So, for example, if we wanted to account for numeric operators in non-simple databases, we might want to include in the KB the infinite supply of arithmetic sentences that databases know implicitly about numbers.

The reason we are concerned with the logical implications of the sentences in the KB (rather than just the sentences themselves) is that, at the knowledge level, we want to know *what* the KB says about the world, not *how* it says it. In other words, it is not so much the actual content of the KB that counts, but *what the world it talks about has to be like.* So, for example, if the KB contains sentences of the form

    if A then B

and

---

[4] Axioms about "emp" (or database integrity constraints) might *constrain* its interpretation but, by themselves, they cannot tell us what the relation is about.

A,

then the world it describes must satisfy "B" even though the KB says so only implicitly. It is precisely to determine what is (logically) implicit in a collection of sentences that *inference* is required at all, although the key observation is that the amount and kind of reasoning that is needed will depend, in general, on the form of the KB.

The actual details of a knowledge level account of databases are not crucial here.[5] Elsewhere [LEVE84c], I have sketched how in simplified form, representation schemes such as production systems (or logic programs), semantic networks, and frames might be understood at the knowledge level as restrictions on collections of first-order sentences. What is important, I think, is the moral presented in [LEVE84c], namely, that there is a tradeoff between how expressive a KR scheme is (i.e., how unrestricted a logical theory it can express) and how difficult it is to reason correctly and completely within the scheme.[6] Again, to go back to the database case, as soon as we relax the form of the KB, for example, by allowing the knowledge-level equivalent of arbitrary disjunctions or existential quantifications, the implications of what the KB says about the world can no longer be calculated using standard database technology.[7] If a theory in DB form is an extreme position on this expressiveness/tractability spectrum, the other extreme might be to allow a completely unrestricted first-order theory, while requiring a full theorem-prover as a reasoner.

The interesting point about this knowledge-level analysis of KR schemes, however, is that there are, indeed, useful positions between full, first-order logic and what I have ca8lled "DB form". For example, the production system KR languages that form the basis of so-called expert systems appear to correspond to function-free Horn theories, a class that allows the problem of implication to be solved using a depth-first backtracking search strategy. Similarly, the logical restrictions imposed by (certain forms of) semantic networks allow reasoning based on tree traversal algorithms (inheritance of properties) that also have attractive computational features. The claim here is that much of the work in KR language design has to do with finding what amounts to an expressively useful, though limited, logical language, and providing reasoning algorithms that exploit these limitations to full advantage.

---

[5] See [REIT84] for an attempt along these lines for relational databases.

[6] It must be considered just how important it is to reason completely and correctly. See David Israel's survey for some ideas on this. For now, and to a first approximation, it is important.

[7] On the other hand, certain restricted forms of disjunctions and quantifications such as those allowed by "null values" may be quite tractable and amenable to extended database techniques. Similarly, view processing is a limited form of inference that meshes well with pure database retrieval.

So what does this expressiveness, that is the bane of efficient reasoners, really amount to? As hinted at above, one of the main things that a language like full first-order logic provides is the ability to represent knowledge that is *incomplete*: to be able to say that one of two sentences is true, without saying which (disjunction); to be able to say that something has a certain property, without saying what that is (existential quantification); to be able to say that everything with a certain property has another property, without saying what either property is (universal quantification); and so on. Indeed it might be said that the expressive power of first-order logic lies not so much in what it allows you to say but *in what it allows you to leave unsaid.* But this is certainly not the whole story, and much more work needs to be done to characterize how expressive power is used and why it presents difficulties to reasoners.[8]

One thing that seems clear is that the tradeoff between expressiveness and tractability is especially relevant for large-scale KB management systems that are required to do reasoning of some sort. First of all, we have to consider how systems that currently work acceptably will scale up. But, more significantly, we have to worry about combining representation schemes. By focussing only on the increase in expressive power, we may overlook relinquishing whatever computational advantage each scheme had. This is especially true when we try to apply database retrieval technology to KR problems. The efficiency of a reasoning component for a large-scale knowledge-based system is more than merely the careful management of secondary storage. Indeed, if the language is expressive enough, that aspect might be swamped completely by combinatorial explosions, unless somehow we restrict the kinds of reasoning we have to perform.[9] Unfortunately, again for sufficiently expressive languages, it is not at all clear that there are any semantically well-motivated kinds of inference lying anywhere between retrieval and full, logical implication. (Although see [LEVE84d] for a proposal in this direction and, again, David Israel's survey for more general discussion).

To summarize, I have suggested that a useful way of understanding and comparing KR and database schemes is to ask what restrictions they impose at the knowledge level on what can be expressed about the world. From this vantage point, it is often possible to demonstrate the possibility or impossibility of efficient reasoning mechanisms, a crucial

---

[8] For example, the power of first-order logic is also useful for stating laws (as in integrity constraints) and in forming definitions: a person x is an *uncle* of a person y iff ... . See [BL84b] for some concrete results regarding the tradeoff as applied to definitions of terms.

[9] View processing, for example, is crucially dependent on the limited expressive power available.

concern for large-scale KB management systems. Perhaps more to the point, the knowledge level account factors out the mechanisms used by the KR schemes to represent knowledge, and thus allows us to see clearly where they represent the same or different kinds of information. This is especially important when we try to combine multiple representation and reasoning systems (the so-called hybrid systems) and need to establish communication among the components while avoiding redundancies. I do not want to suggest that the knowledge level account is enough, however. Decisions made at the symbol level (in terms of the choice of operations and representational structures) and decisions regarding the use of a KR scheme (the facilities it provides for reliably designing and maintaining large KBs) are very critical concerns that the knowledge level does not address.

1. References

[BD81b] [BL84b] [HAYE85] [LEVE84a] [LEVE84c] [LEVE84d] [ML84] [NEWE80] [REIT84]

6
AI Knowledge Bases And Databases

David Israel[1]

ABSTRACT *In which the author expresses general* scepticism about proposals for a trouble free marriage of **AI Knowledge Bases** and **Databases** (narrowly and tendentiously construed.) The author argues, as well, against a shotgun wedding.

1. Introduction

The following idea is oft bruited about: **AI Knowledge Bases** are *small*(ish) in size; but oh so *complex* in the structure of their entries. **Databases** are (very) *large* in the number of their entries; but oh so *simple* with respect to the structure of these items. **AI Knowledge Bases** are, perforce, going to be getting much, much larger. (One can imagine here grave mumblings about "real world" problems and "real world" applications. See, for example, the chapter by Fox and McDermott.) And who knows but what **Databases** must succumb to the siren song of complexity? (See, for example, the chapter by Dayal and Smith.) Finally, then, mustn't the two "*technologies*" merge? (For an especially pointed statement of this perspective, look to Mylopoulos's chapter in Section I.)

Maybe.

In one direction, the above story sounds plausible enough. A central family of problems in the design and analysis of **Databases** has its origin precisely in considerations of sheer size; in particular, problems of storage and retrieval. Other important concerns are a function of the distributed character of projected **Databases** and of associated "information management" systems; these include data security — questions of

---

[1] SRI International

protection, access and integrity. Whatever problems of this sort arise in the case of large, distributed **Databases**, will arise as well in the case of large, distributed AI systems. Moreover, many of these problems are quite independent of the kind of information involved and independent, also, of the format(s) in which the information is embodied or encoded. Surely, then, AI researchers and AI system designers will have much to learn from their **Database** colleagues.

2. Caveats and Stipulations

That said, I would now like to enter a few **caveats**. One has to do with the very notion of **Databases**. How are we to understand this notion? We could, I suppose, take it to encompass precisely the kinds of systems that now exist and that are regularly called "**Databases**" and no more than these. In this vein, we could even refrain from entertaining hypotheses as to what these had in common — if anything — in virtue of which they all went by that name. This way boredom lies. We *could* try to make something out of the notion of **data**, in contrast to knowledge or information. There may be something to this; but to do justice to what there may be, would take me (us?) too far afield into the philosophy of science for this occasion. (It is this intuition about the contrast between data and knowledge that Prof. Wiederhold latches on to in the chapter immediately following this one. More power to him.)

In the absence of any general, theoretically well-motivated constraints, I shall **stipulate**. I hereby stipulate that the crucial feature of what I shall henceforth understand and mean by **Databases** has to do with their expressive power, measured in a certain way. In particular: From the perspective of their expressive resources, **Databases** are *finite collections of ground atomic sentences*, each such sentence consisting of an n-place predicate symbol and a sequence of n individual terms, the latter to contain no variables.

A few comments are in order. First, and despite appearances, it must not be thought that our stipulated defining characteristic has to do with representational format. Talk of collections of atomic sentences can be misleading. The characteristic I have in mind has nothing to do either with the nature of the format of the physical database, nor even — directly, anyway — with the nature of the abstract data types over which the database processes (conceived of as independent from physical implementation) are defined. The condition has rather to do with the kinds of content that **Database** entries can express. This brings us to our second point — the "unit of measurement." I am making the simplifying, and perhaps simple-minded, assumption that, in assessing expressive power, we can use interpreted quantificational languages as generating a universally applicable measuring scale. (See the chapter by Brachman & Levesque, "The Knowledge Level of KBMS," for more on this theme.) Intuitively, what the stipulation amounts to is that **Database** entries express only particular **"facts"**. (The quotes are required because I intend no implication of veridicality. Note, also, that there is an unhappy built-in relativity to an interpreted quantificational language in my notion of "fact".) To put the point negatively, such entries can neither express any element of generality nor manifest any degree of incompleteness in specificity. Finally, one absolutely crucial comment: as I suppose is evident, when I speak of **Databases**, I am abstracting from the expressive powers of their associated query languages and the algorithms implemented in their associated query processors. Query languages can be thought of as, e.g., full first order languages; query processors can implement sound and complete proof procedures over such languages. (Here, I'm fudging a little, especially with regard to negation; for, by stipulation, **Databases** are modelled by sets of **atomic** sentences. There is now a huge literature on this aspect of things; see Naqvi's "Negation in Knowledge Base Management Systems" in Section III.) Moreover, I am assuming that **data models** are in the minds of the designers and are, hence, extrinsic to the **Databases**.

3. Consequences

No doubt much could be said against this characterization. What can be said for it, on the other hand, is that it's simple, fairly precise — modulo one's settling, in a particular case, on a particular interpreted language — and that it is fairly faithful to Codd's original position. (Especially so, if one limits oneself to first order languages.) Moreover, it yields a framework for understanding the import of various **conventions of interpretation**, especially *the closed world assumption* and *the domain closure axiom*. It provides, then, a way of understanding how these conventions allow for interpretations of **Databases** to transcend the expressive resources of their entries. (For much, much more on this, see Reiter's [REIT84]. I should note, though, that Reiter and I end up on diametrically opposite sides of the question: are relational **Databases** best thought of model-theoretically or proof-theoretically? He argues and opts for the latter; I just opt for the former. Still, I owe a great debt to his essay.)

Among the consequences of my stipulation, one in particular deserves some mention. As Reiter noted, the various conventions alluded to above are not encoded as part of the data representation in **Databases**. (Of course, one could imagine them being expressed in the query language, which — as we noted above — can be thought of as a full first-order language, say with equality.) Such conventions are best thought of as constraints on interpretations of data representations. In this regard, think of the way in which integrity contraints are realized. The same would go for the importation into the **Database** world of taxonomic **IS-A** hierarchies, or the constraints they embody. Thus imagine we are concerned with a university's **Database** and we want to specify that every undergraduate is a student and that graduate students are students as well. This can be understood in various ways. If we adopt *the domain closure* and *closed world assumptions*, perhaps together with some form of *the unique names assumption*, the corresponding universally quantified conditionals:

$$(x) \ (\text{UnderGrad} \ (x) \ \text{-->} \ \text{Student} \ (x))$$

$$(x) \ (\text{GradStudent}) \ (x) \ \text{-->} \ \text{Student} \ (x))$$

can — without loss — be thought of as mere abbreviations for the (finite) conjunction of their instances. Remember: we are assuming that every entity in the domain of the interpretation has a (perhaps unique) name, and that, for each entity **e** that is a student (resp. undergrad, grad), there are the corresponding atomic sentences consisting of the predication of the associated monadic relation symbol to the name of **e**. In these circumstances, we must not suppose that the fact that the **Database** conforms to the *inheritance relations*, is to be understood solely in terms of the representational format or expressive powers of its entries. We must also take into account facts about the various processes which involve the **Database**, including processes of interpretation by users. In a certain sense, such conformance is in the minds of the designers and users of the **Database**. Again, this is really roughly Reiter's idea. (Or so I would urge.)

For instance, when Stonebraker talks of implementing *rules* in **Database** systems, or correlatively, of *inference* in such systems, he precisely confines himself to **Databases** in my sense: that is, to those components of systems which can be thought of finite collections of atomic sentences. (See his chapter in Section IV, "Inference in Database Systems by Lazy Triggers".) In these cases, the quantified sentences which express the relevant relationships ("rules") can be thought of as finite conjunctions or disjunctions of atomic sentences, under some scheme or convention of interpretation. Such a conception can't capture the import of such constraints when they are meant to apply "in all possible cases," or to an open ended range of cases. Imagine, that is , that we don't apply either the *domain closure* or the *closed world* assumption. It is then not the case that the universally quantified sentences are merely abbreviations for a finite conjunction of instances. Correlatively, in such cases, the import of the corresponding rules of inference is not exhausted — conformity to them, not insured — by the fact that for every instance in the database of an object's having the property of being (e.g.) an undergraduate attributed to it, there is an instance of that very same object's having the property of being a student attributed to it.

4. Conclusion

SO — you may well ask — **WHAT**? Here's what: the development of large, distributed AI systems, subject to access by many different people and systems, requires that system developers look to the Database community for help and guidance. It would be idiotic for people in AI to reinvent all those wheels. Moreover, as reinvented, they'd probably end up as irregular polyhedra. On the other hand, I think it's a mistake to think of **Databases** transmuting themselves — *growing up* — into something they're not. If one conceives of the *domain closure* and *closed world assumptions,* or of the subsumption relations embodied in **IS-A** hierarchies as being explicitly expressed, say by way of first order sentences, then one is no longer thinking about **Databases**.

Relational Databases — note: not the relational data model — seem to me precisely delimitable objects. They can be embedded in lots of different ways in lots of different systems; but — to close on a religious note — they cannot gain the world without thereby losing their soul.

Acknowledgments

This research was supported in part by a gift from the System Development Foundation.

5. References

[REIT84]

7
Knowledge versus Data

Gio Wiederhold[1]

ABSTRACT *This note defines the terms knowledge and data as complements of each other. Knowledge identifies information about general concepts, data is information about specific instances. The distinction is visible in most systems where general concepts are used to control or abstract object instances. The distinction is essential to select an architecture for large systems, and to deal with update issues. There remains some context dependence, so that knowledge in one model may become data for another model.*

1. Preamble

The terms *knowledge* and *data*, and *knowledge bases* and *databases* are frequently seen in papers discussing future information systems. They are rarely defined precisely and little aggreement exists about the domain and scope encompassed by these terms. This note presents one set of definitions how these terms may be used to make useful distinctions in the systems we are building.

By defining these two terms -- and not letting the two be synonymous -- we establish a classification scheme for objects seen in information systems. We are aware that classifications as proposed here are artificial. We have to consider what the objective is for the classification being proposed here since objects may be classified along more than one dimension. For instance, a classification used for flowers by a botanist is not necessarily useful for a florist who is concerned with costs and sales nor for a gardener who is concerned with planting seasons.

---

[1] Department of Computer Science, Stanford University

2. The Model

In our work we are concerned with describing systems which provide information, typically information to be used for decision-making in enterprises. These systems automate tasks which, in a traditional environment, are carried to a large extent by people, using computers only to store and communicate data. At the point of decision-making an expert, armed with knowledge, considers data which has been selected as relevant to the problem at hand and makes the decision. The selected data provides information. The knowledge provided by the expert has been obtained through education and experience. Figure 1 shows the flow leading to decision making.

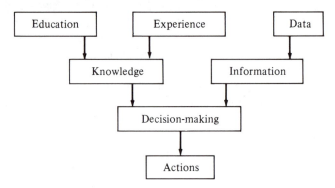

Figure 1: Function of Knowledge and Data In Enterprises

We have not sketched or named the processes which permit these transformations.   Neither have we indicated in this sketch the feedback loops through which the systems gain new data and new knowledge. Such feedback is essential to assure long-term stability of information systems. Feedback into the data box occurs through the collection of observations, modeling the *real world.* Feedback into the knowledge box occurs through the development of generalizations and abstractions, perhaps formalized through the scientific loop of hypothesis generation, hypothesis verfication, review, publication, and dissemination.

Our model of knowledge-based systems follows this description of use of information knowledge, and data.   The objective of the classification we propose in this note is to assist in the design and organization of information systems where these functions are being automated.   Organization in turn is necessary in order to make large systems manageable.

The automation of the decision-making processes means that both knowledge and information have to be accessed, so that for the inferencing process both categories must be accessible. We observe however that typically the source for the knowledge, namely the expert, and the source for the information, the collected data, is distinct. Only in academic exercises do we find that expert has time to also gather and validate the data. In industry the collected data is not provided by the expert. The expert may specify, using expert knowledge, the selection and processing steps to reduce data to information. We define *information*, following Shannon [SW48], as data that conveys material that was previously unknown to the receiver.

3. The Test to Distinguish Data and Knowledge

From these observations we derive a litmus test for distinguishing knowledge versus data:

> If we can trust an automatic process or clerk to collect the material then we are talking about *data*. The correctness of data with respect to the real world can be objectively verified by comparison with repeated observations of the real world. Eventually the state of the world changes, and we have to trust prior observations.
>
> If we look for an expert to provide the material then we are talking about *knowledge*. Knowledge includes abstractions and generalizations of voluminous material. These are typically less precise and cannot be easily objectively verified. Many definitions, necessary to organize systems, are knowledge as well; we look towards experts for the definitions which are important building stones for further abstractions, categorization, and generalization [SS77].

This definition permits us to now make processing distinctions between data and knowledge.

Since data reflects the current state of the world at the level of instances it will include much detail, will be voluminous, and will appear in reports which are used at lower levels of the enterprise for verification. Where instances change rapidly much data must be collected over time as well, if a complete historical picture is desired.

Knowledge will not to change as frequently. Knowledge may be complex but will deal with generalizations and hence refer to entity types rather than to entity instances.

The differences also mean that different data structures may be appropriate for the representation of data and the representation of knowledge, at least in the pre-processing stages before the decision-making process occurs. Structures for data are often simple, to accommodate frequent updates; knowledge, being updated by experts or learning systems, can benefit from more complex representations.

4. Consistency of Data and Knowledge

Data which are newly aquired may conflict with existing knowledge. Integrity constraints in databases may prevent some such data to be entered, to protect the database. Other data will enter, perhaps altering the generalizations made in the associated knowledge base. For instance, QUIST makes the assumption, acquired from human experts, that supertankers are not found in the Mediterranean [KING80b]. This generally valid assumption has only an economic, but not a legal or a physical basis. It may be violated by unusual instances, perhaps a supertanker enters the Mediterranean for repairs. For query optimization in the domain of transportation the QUIST generalization, attached to the abstraction of "supertanker", will remain valid.

Many artificial intelligence systems deal with expert provided estimates of uncertainty of knowledge. If the uncertainty is quantified, as in MYCIN and its successors, new instances of conflicting data will increase the degree of uncertainty [SABM73]. Learning techniques must be embedded to automate updating of certainty factors.

Systems which do not manage uncertainty, as those based on logic, have a problem dealing with conflicting data. Checking for conflicts is in itself costly. When a conflict is identified either the data must be considered to be in error or the knowledge must be false. Without an expert's presence the former alternative must be taken, even if now the state of the real world is not correctly represented.

An expert, before revising the knowledge, will verify the data, since in large databases we will always find some erroneous observations. Even in the case that the data is verified to be correct then the general base knowledge may not be wrong, it is more likely that it was incomplete. Now new knowledge must be added which will cover the case in question and similiar cases which can be foreseen.

Note that in this discussion the role of data versus knowledge seems obvious. We have found the distinction clear in all our experiments [WIED84].

5. Problems

We must, however, consider problems of our definition of data and knowledge. Items which appear as data at a higher level in the enterprise may appear to be knowledge to personnel involved in a lower level. In general, the assignment of data and knowledge is situation dependent. In large-scale systems which serve multiple objectives some further categorization may be necessary.

Unfortunately, we have no practical experience in dealing with this degree of complexity. Neither have we seen results of systems of such scope.

One candidate information system structure is to permit multiple layers, and let the knowledge component of one system layer become the supporting data for the next system layer. Such a structure appears to be nice and general but may be quite difficult to manage. A realistic current example of multiple level data is found when database systems manage aggregate or derived data. Aggregate data is a combination of knowledge, defined by an aggregation routine, and the source data on which the knowledge operates.

Another approach to deal with alternative knowledge definitions is to use a model based on views over knowledge, similar to views over data. This concept was proposed by us in [MW84] and is a current research topic here. It appears that the view concept in databases raises many problems which are best dealt with at a higher level of abstraction. Such an approach requires a conceptual extension of view definition and processing schemes that now support the notion of views in databases [KELL86]. Views over knowledge structures may, for instance, support distinct hierarchical categorizations of knowledge, each appropriate to some set of applications.

6. Conclusion

The question remains whether our classification is generally useful. It may not be useful if only concepts of querying of knowledge and associated data are being considered.

We are convinced of its power when we design systems to deal with large collections of data. The concerns in such systems include processing mechanisms and architecture. The ability to deal with the largest fraction of the system content, namely the data, in a regular and simple way is worth much to us. The distinction becomes a basis for modularity.

When we consider isues as update, errors in data, and uncertainty of knowledge the distinctions become essential. For instance, in large databases, the probalility of existence of errors approaches certainty, and we cannot afford to disable general inferencing because of spurious errors in the database.

In applications where the domain is sufficiently large or complex the knowledge must be incomplete. In such systems conflicts of data instances with the general knowledge will remain. We can see that applications aiding management in planning will depend on the knowledge being adequate for processing, and ignore outlying instances of data. Administrative functions may analyze the database for exceptions, that is conflicts of data and knowledge. The distinction of these application types is rooted in the distinction we make of data and knowledge.

Acknowledgement

This research was supported by the Defense Advanced Research Projects Agency, contract N39-84-C-211 for Management of Knowledge and Database. Experience leading to these conclusions came from work as described in [WBW85]. Michael Brodie provided detailed and helpful comments.

7. References

[KELL86] [KING80b] [MW84] [SABM73] [SS77] [SW48] [WBW85] [WIED84]

8
Knowledge Bases vs Databases

Michael L. Brodie[1]
John Mylopoulos[2]

ABSTRACT *This position statement argues that an important difference between knowledge bases and databases is that the former require a semantic theory for the interpretation of their contents, while the latter require a computational theory for their efficient implementation on physical machines.*[3]

Both AI and Database researchers have accepted the importance of developing systems with access to large information bases.[4] In AI such information bases are called "knowledge bases" on the grounds that they contain information *about something,* whereas in Databases these information bases are called "databases," and are viewed mostly as large complex data structures that allow efficient storage and retrieval. This brief chapter examines the terms "knowledge base" and "database" and argues that they are fundamentally distinct. Similar issues are discussed in the chapters by Brachman and Levesque.

The reason for arguing this point is that the two notions have been compared repeatedly in the literature, or have been used side by side without any consistency. For example, [RH83] explicitly treat "knowledge base" and "database" as synonymous:

Our approach is based on the idea that there is a far reaching intersection between both (knowledge representation languages and data models) and that they should be treated under a unifying approach. Therefore, throughout this paper we use the terms

---

[1] Computer Corporation of America

[2] University of Toronto

[3] Earlier versions of this statement appear in [REIT83b] and [BM86].

[4] For our purposes "information base" will mean a large collection of information; databases and knowledge bases will be treated as particular kinds of information bases.

"data model" and "knowledge representation language" as well as "database" and "knowledge base" as synonyms.

For other researchers, the distinction between the two terms hinges on the nature of the information handled by the data/knowledge base. Thus, in [WM77] the distinguishing characteristic between knowledge bases and databases is that knowledge bases will:

> include large amounts of abstract knowledge, e.g., knowledge about the relationship between the departments where an employee and his manager work, and a small amount of (less interesting) concrete knowledge, e.g., each employee's department...

while databases:

> were designed mostly for concrete knowledge..., e.g., each employee's department...

A different view of the distinction is found in [WIED84] where:

> a database is a collection of data representing facts.... A knowledge base, as opposed to a database, contains information at a higher level of abstraction.

Thus, according to [WIED84] (see also the chapter by Wiederhold entitled "Knowledge versus Data").

> Mr. Lee's age is 43 years.

is data, while

> Middle age is 35 to 50.

is knowledge.

Although we agree wholeheartedly with the basic message conveyed here, that databases and knowledge bases have something in common, we cannot help but note that the three accounts differ about what that commonality is.

Beyond these examples, one can find in the AI literature many other instances when the two terms appear to be used interchangeably. For instance, [HEWI72] describes an AI language called PLANNER, one of the early proposals for a (procedural) knowledge representation system, and uses the term "database" rather than "knowledge base" to refer to a collection of assertions, presumably about some world. Likewise, [DK75] describes a production system architecture as consisting of a collection of rules and a database which:

> is simply a collection of symbols intended to reflect the state of the world, but the interpretation of those symbols depends in

large part on the nature of the application.

Are then databases synonymous with "simple" knowledge bases? Are knowledge representation languages more powerful (and less efficient) versions of data models?

We argue that there is a fundamental difference between data models and knowledge representation languages that can help distinguish between databases and knowledge bases, and between AI and Databases. The distinction is that:

> **any knowledge representation language must be provided with a (rich) semantic theory for relating an information base to its subject matter, while a data model requires an (effective) computational theory for realizing information bases on physical machines.**

Thus **knowledge bases** have to have an associated theory for interpreting the information they contain, whereas **databases** are expected to meet performance standards for response time, robustness, reliability, security, etc. Note that our thesis distinguishes between *information* and the *meaning* of information. We can talk about the generation, transmission, and reception of information without assuming anything about its interpretation. We can study how it can be efficiently stored or retrieved, how to build a robust multi-user environment for an information base, or how to guarantee the security of the information base management system, and still assume nothing about the meaning of the information. Conversely, we can develop an elaborate semantic theory for temporal knowledge, beliefs, goals, etc., and yet say nothing about storing all this knowledge on a machine, using secondary storage, or making it accessible to multiple users.

To summarize then, a knowledge base contains knowledge **about something** represented in a suitable notation, whereas a database stores (large amounts of) shared data. In the case of databases, there is only an elementary and largely intuitive interpretation of the information stored in the database. Database semantics make little commitment, if any, to an interpretation. For knowledge bases there must be such a commitment. Thus a relational database, for example, stores tuples, and one can ask: "Is there a tuple x such that $Q(x)$?" Moreover, the answer to this question can only be "yes" or "no", *because the subject matter for the query is a data structure stored inside a machine*. With a knowledge base, however, we are storing information about people, accounts, etc., and a query takes the form: "Is there an employee x such that $P(x)$?". Now the answers can be "yes", "no", or "I don't know"; (there are other possibilities, too) and the subject matter is the external world. The distinction is clearly reflected by the terms used for the notations we have developed in order to construct, manipulate, and search databases and knowledge bases. A Data Model (such as the relational data model) offers a set of data structures and associated operations for the construction and manipulation of a database. Each data model commits its user to a particular way of visualizing whatever information is stored in a machine, and frees him from the details of the implementation (what Codd and others call **logical data independence**, [CODD70]). A knowledge representation language, on the other hand, offers tools for the representation and organization, of knowledge and commits its user to a particular way of viewing the world.

In closing, it is fair to add two points. First, the distinction we are making here between databases and knowledge bases is by no means absolute. For example, proposals for the treatment of "null values", extensions of the Relational Model (e.g., [CODD79]), or revisions (e.g., [REIT84]) do lead to versions of the Relational Model that make some semantic commitments. Second, whereas no AI system has a DBMS in the database sense, no Database system provides "intelligence" in the AI sense. In the AI community, "database" tends to mean a collection of data. "Intelligent" queries over a database are limited to model theoretic evaluation, whereas "intelligent" inference (or queries) in AI systems frequently are proof theoretic.

1. References

[BM86] [CODD70] [CODD79] [DK75] [HEWI72] [REIT83b] [REIT84] [RH83] [WIED84] [WM77]

9
Knowledge Based and Database Systems: Enhancements, Coupling or Integration?

Yannis Vassiliou[1]

ABSTRACT *Position: The technologies in the areas of Knowledge Based or Expert Systems (KBS) and of Database Management Systems (DBMS) will play a major role in future Information Systems. Research issues present in a combined use of the two technologies have attracted researchers, both from Artificial Intelligence and Databases.*

This short paper examines possible research strategies. They are basically three: (a) enhancements of existing systems, (b) coupling of independent systems, and (c) technology integration resulting in a new class of systems, which are not constrained by the objectives and design characteristics of Knowledge Based and Database Systems.

The position taken is: system enhancements present a short-term partial solution, coupling presents an easy and practical solution and although integration is elegant and promising, it may never lead to a practically acceptable solution.

1. Issues

Knowledge Based Systems research started several years ago with laboratory successes and recent attempts for commercialization. A KBS is based on two principles: the appropriate representation of the application domain knowledge or "slice of reality," and the control of this

---

[1] Graduate School of Business Administration New York University

knowledge. These two principles are embodied in the two top-level components of the KBS architecture: a knowledge base and an inference engine or reasoning capability.

Database Management Systems research has visible practical successes. At the core of DBMS research are implementation aspects and operational characteristics of database systems. Data models that have been developed for DBMSs share the same objectives with knowledge representation schemes for KBSs, namely, to represent an application domain or "slice of reality."[2]

Clearly, the combination of the two technologies would benefit to some extent both KBSs and DBMSs [JV84]. The main contribution of KBS technology to a DBMS will be on better semantic models - clear understanding of what knowledge is represented. In addition, there will be limited but useful reasoning ability at least for dealing with the operational issues in DBMSs (e.g., transaction management, optimization). The contribution of DBMS technology to a KBS will be on the ability to have "larger" knowledge bases and to apply features such as concurrency control, data security and protection, optimized access, and secondary storage management to at least some part of the knowledge base.

It is with respect to knowledge representation access and control that commonalities between KBS and DBMS research can be drawn. Abstracting, while ignoring application domain size, richness of the representation, and the degree of reasoning capabilities, it can be said that KBSs and DBMSs have similar architectural characteristics. Both types of systems are based on a subsystem that selects the appropriate structures to represent the knowledge and the appropriate mechanism to answer questions or deduce new knowledge. However, this subsystem for KBSs emphasizes reasoning and rich representation, while for DBMSs, it emphasizes the efficient access and manipulation of a more permanently structured, stored representation of reality. These differences are not coincidental, as explained in the sequel.

It is elegantly demonstrated in [BL84b] that the provision of full service of a knowledge representation subsystem for a complete knowledge base is intractable (computationally), independently of the knowledge representation formalism used. The obvious approach, as with other computationally intractable problems, is its avoidance in practical systems. This is done with different forms of minimization [BL84b]. For instance, KBSs may minimize it by employing automatic theorem proving techniques which avoid obvious redundancies (e.g.,

---

[2] We adopt here the view of [BL84b] that databases are interpreted as large knowledge bases of a certain limited form (i.e., the data level component of a knowledge base.)

Prolog) or by relaxing their notions of correctness (e.g. providing unknown answers after a certain time limit). Such partial solutions are made possible within a small knowledge base. Analogously, DBMSs minimize the intractability problem by employing incomplete representations and language constructs (e.g., avoiding disjunction, negation, and existential quantifiers), thus limiting the reasoning capabilities. The minimization techniques used in KBSs and DBMSs reflect their respective design objectives and explain their capabilities and differences.

2. Research Strategies

One major strategy in combining the two technologies is to develop a "better" Knowledge Based or Database system. This is done with **system enhancements**. This strategy can be subdivided based on which of the two systems (KBS or DBMS) is used as the pivot (major component). For instance, a KBS may be enhanced with a sophisticated data access component, one that is commonly found in DBMSs, to deal with very large knowledge bases. Furthermore, if needed, operational DBMS aspects (concurrency control, security) may be added to a KBS. Alternatively, the enhancements of a DBMS with reasoning capabilities may have a profound effect in "intelligent" database use, and "intelligent" database operation [JV84].

A second major research strategy for the combination of the two technologies is the **coupling of a KBS with a DBMS**. Such coupling implies the existence of a communication mechanism between the two systems. This strategy can be further divided depending on the degree of coupling, loose and tight, corresponding respectively to a "static" and a "dynamic" use of the communication mechanism.

If KBSs are to be applied in the commercial world they will need access to "external" data sources. Typically, "external" data are operational databases managed by a DBMS and shared by other applications. Issues like data volatility (frequency of database updates), data currency (how important is an up-to-date representation), and data security and protection influence the decision of whether to access the "external" data through the DBMS, or whether that data can be duplicated, restructured, and permanently stored as part of the KBS's own knowledge base.

Using tight coupling, interactions between a DBMS and a KBS can take place at any moment. On the one hand, the DBMS may employ the KBS functions for more "intelligent" processing, while on the other hand, the KBS may play the role of an "intelligent" user of a generalized DBMS that manages a very large database.

Among the above research strategies to combine KBS and DBMS technology proposed, the author considers tight coupling of a KBS with a DBMS as the most attractive short- and long-term solution. Employing tight coupling, minimal modifications to each system are to be made (if any). Therefore, the systems retain their identity and do what they are designed to do best, while still getting many benefits from the operation of their partner. On the other hand, evolving a KBS or a DBMS by adding facilities **not in spirit with the design objectives** of each system (see the minimization approaches for the intractability problem), results in yet another patch-up with very small improvements over the previous system state. More constructive improvements may require an expensive restructure and redesign of the system.

A more ambitious research strategy is to take a fresh look at the goals and objectives of future information systems and create a new class of systems which are not constrained by KBS and DBMS design characteristics. Thus, the Knowledge Based Management System (KBMS) enters into the picture.

As contrasted with the evolutionary nature of the previous research strategies, this strategy is revolutionary. Proposals as to how such systems should look like are around (see, for instance, the article by Manola and Brodie in this volume) and constitute the major topic in this volume - a new source of constructive controversy among AI and Database researchers.

Such proposals and the ensuing discussions demonstrate that we do not know what a KBMS is or, at a minimum, we can not agree on its characteristics. Consequently, we have an open research problem and there lies the challenge.

As researchers, we have to answer convincingly fundamental questions such as, "What is a KBMS?", "What are its architectural characteristics?", "How do we realize them?", and then proceed by building KBMSs. This brings us back to the tractability problem and appears to require brand new ways for its minimization. Considering that, there are serious doubts as to whether practical systems can be soon (or ever) realized.

As application-minded and goal-driven researchers we have to answer convincingly questions such as, "Is there a practical need for KBMSs?", or turning it around, "Can KBMSs meet the challenge of providing future Information Systems with multiple functionality?"

3. References
[BL84b] [JV84]

Discussion

David Israel presented a position paper on what he called a "moving target: knowledge bases and databases". According to him, databases are simple knowledge bases; simple in that they only contain assertions in a canonical normal form and their expressive power is limited. Moreover, there is an implicit closed world assumption being made in the minds of their users. By contrast, knowledge bases are databases, where one can express more kinds of things in a direct way. At the moment most knowledge bases are small. AI people should either learn the Databases techniques for dealing with large amounts of data, or get people from that database side to transfer some of their techniques to the AI realm. The "revolutionary" approach suggested by John Mylopoulos involves the toughest job.

In discussing the database vs. knowledge base issue, and in particular when comparing knowledge representation languages, Ron Brachman expressed the view that since there are so many versions of IS-A hierarchies, it is hard to know what it really means. He would prefer to see a first-order logic with a standard interpretation to pin down the semantics.

Shamim Naqvi asked whether adding the ability to do recursive queries to a database somehow makes it a knowledge base.

Michael Brodie offered the explanation that in "... AI there is more dedication to interpretation (i.e., in the Tarskian sense) than there is in Databases."

Danny Bobrow felt that an assumption was being made: that data is costly and that planning processing is used to solve a particular problem. Michael Brodie confirmed that this is a key database issue.

John McDermott agreed with David Israel's characterization of a database as being a simple knowledge base. But for him, the distinction is unimportant. The only interesting thing about both databases and knowledge bases is that they contain information, and that there is an external agent which wants some of this information. The question for him is "Is there really a huge distinction between knowledge bases and databases?" or "Are we really engaged in the same enterprise?". He also commended that problems solved by database people are generally under-constrained, while AI problems are generally more constrained.

Rusty Bobrow characterized a class of AI problems, particularly those handled in a knowledge-intensive way, which are potentially different from what comes out from a database. He said that AI is "looking for a set of items which satisfy a complex collection of constraints. The kind of problems one is optimizing for in the database query are sets of data that satisfy a fairly simple composition of relations. In the AI case even finding one example satisfying the given constraints is hard."

Peter Szolovits made the following observation: "One of the reasons in AI why we try to build a very small complex theory within a program and build them very carefully following all the constraints, is because we are ... afraid of [it] getting out of hand." If one doesn't do this it will lead to a combinatorial explosion.

Mike Stonebraker offered his partitioning of the AI and Database world: If the data in a system fits in main memory, the search problem goes away. AI works on many problems that fit this description. If the data is very large (such as in a geological database) then searching is a serious problem. This is the kind of problems Jeff Ullman and Francois Bancilhon are tackling. And, in between these two there is the notion of a knowledge based system. Example is a financial planner that keeps the New York Stock Exchange quotations on-line.

Yannis Vassiliou feels that there are three possible research strategies in dealing with the integration of AI and Database technologies: (a) enhancements of existing systems, (b) coupling of independent subsystems, (c) integration of technology to create a new class of systems. His position is that enhancement offers a short-term partial solution, coupling offers a practical and simple solution, while integration, although most elegant, may never lead to a practically acceptable solution. He adds that the design of KBMS should be "problem-driven" in the way that Michael Brodie and Frank Manola outline in their paper.

What would a large knowledge base be like? It would be a kind of database that is built in such a way as to accommodate knowledge representation schemes. He sees coupling as the "best" way to achieve this - at least for the present. In designing a coupled system, one wants to let the various components communicate along channels so that they can make use of each other most effectively.

Hector Levesque asked how the proposed system would differ from a knowledge based system from the point of view of the end-user. Michael Brodie responded that there would not be much difference at the knowledge level. "Even after changing the knowledge based system to make it work on top of a database, one would not have changed the knowledge level itself or the user interface. However the functionality of the overall system would have been changed."

Part III

Retrieval/Inference/Reasoning

10
Notes on Inference: A Somewhat Skewed Survey

David Israel[1]

ABSTRACT *It is widely agreed* **that** *any reasonable AI system has to reason. Once it is agreed* **why** *that must be so, one can go on to look at alternative conceptions of what reasoning consist of. This chapter presents an extremely partial and incomplete survey of some of the options.*

1. Introduction

Imagine you're faced with the following problem: someone — no doubt someone with lots of money — has given you a specification for a system. One component of this system is to be a medium of representation: a language for expressing what needs to be expressed in order that the system can do whatever it's supposed to do. The client is an expert about what needs to be done and hence, perhaps, about what needs to be expressed. Still, you may want to try for a certain generality — both to cover the client's changes of mind and to accommodate, in one blow, a diversity of prospective clients. (The first contingency is as sure as death and taxes; the second — *ALAS!* — is not.) Notice that I've said nothing to delimit the purposes of the client, nothing to delimit the potential uses to which the system might be put or the environments in which it might have to operate. Is there any real chance of there being a single representational formalism that would be best along the weighted sum of all the reasonable dimensions of evaluation for all foreseeable — let alone possible — uses? Surely one has only to ask the question to get the right answer.

[1] SRI International

Now I'm going to ask you to imagine something else. Imagine you once learned a whole lot of logic and you'd like, for once in your life, to make some use of that knowledge. Some of the things you learned were that there are many logical languages, each of which can be given (typically a variety of) systematic semantic accounts. You have learned, that is, that one can state, in various ways, precisely what the sentences of such languages mean, or at least under what conditions they are true. (After looking at various AI representational formalisms, this point should seem like a **MAJOR WIN.**) Moreover, these semantic accounts all follow a pattern: they proceed by an induction tied directly to the inductive definition of the class of sentences of the language. So the semantic values (e.g., truth values) of complex sentences are determined by the semantic values of the simpler sentences out of which they are composed and the semantic values of simple sentence are themselves determined by the values of the subsentential expressions, (e.g., terms and predicates), out of which they are composed. Finally, how are the semantic values of the terms and predicates determined? Well, that depends on the kind of semantic account you want to give. For an excellent introduction to the standard — indeed, so called *classical-model theoretic* account and to the relation between such an account and the theory of relational databases, see [REIT84].

To continue, you've learned that such languages, especially, those built on the language of first order quantification theory, are very powerfully expressive indeed. So, you reason as follows: within very wide bounds, whatever my clients want/need to say, I can say in (some extension, perhaps, of) some first order language. I can teach the client enough logic to be able to read and understand my formulation of his domain — remember the point about intelligible, systematic semantic accounts — and, after a few iterations (and assuming the client doesn't change his mind about his requirements too often), I will have both formulated and analyzed the job's representational requirements.

One last bit and we're done flexing our imaginations: imagine you've read [NEWE80] and/or the two chapters by Brachman & Levesque in Section I of the current volume. So you know that, by deciding to use some standard logical language as your *analytical metalanguage*, you have not committed yourself to any decisions at the level of data structures and algorithms. You realize, that is, that using a logical language in which to represent the required domain knowledge is analogous to writing up a specification for a system, not to writing an algorithm that is supposed to meet that specification. (Put yet another way: the resulting logical representation is meant for your and your client's eyes, not — at least not necessarily — for the eyes of any interpreter.) You're free to build whatever you'd like in the way of a running system, so long as you know what you're doing; that is, so long as you know what the data structures of your formalism mean and hence have some chance of designing algorithms that will conform to and make use of their meaning. (No doubt in some terribly efficient way.) You assume that, whatever "runnable" representational formalism you adopt, there will be an effectively specifiable translation procedure mapping "sentential units" of the formalism into sentences of a formal language that includes the language of first order quantification theory. So, the syntax of this latter language can be looked at as the abstract syntax of your running formalism; the latter, a concrete realization of the former.

2. Why Reason?

What's wrong with the above picture? Well, probably, lots; but here I'm going to focus on one thing that's mostly missing. What is the system supposed to do with its data structures, say with its "sentential units" — the ones that are supposed to express claims about the application domain? No matter how smart you and your client are, the two of you aren't going to be able to formulate *explicitly* all that needs to be, or can usefully be said about the domain/tasks at hand. Moreover, you can't possibly foresee all the demands that might be made upon the representational resources of the system by other components with which it interacts, including, of course, other people. Finally, you can't predict the changes in the environment with which the system might have to cope. So, you want the system to be able to **reason**; to extract and use information implicit, in one or another sense, in what is explicitly represented. Further, you should want it to reach conclusions that, though supported by what is explicitly and implicitly represented, goes beyond it. **That's what reasoning is all about.** If you knew everything there was to know, including the "laws of change" of your environment, and could explicitly represent everything there was to be said, and if the system had, practically speaking, infinite memory — why, then, the system wouldn't have to waste its time reasoning. And you wouldn't have to waste your time designing reasonable reasoning algorithms. Of course, there would still be a *BIG* organizational and search problem for *you* to reason about, but the system wouldn't be doing any real reasoning.

So far I've simply noted that what one is after is never just a representational system; what one is after is a system that both represents and reasons. Now exactly as there isn't any real chance of there being a single representational formalism that is best, all things considered, for all plausible representational purposes; so, too, there isn't any real chance of there being a single reasoning scheme best, all things considered, for all plausible reasoning jobs.

3. Digression: A Little Logic

After all these preliminary ruminations, let's fix some ideas. Remember: you know a lot of logic and want to use it, so you decide to use a first order language as your specification language. You also know you want the system to have the capacity to reason — *to extract information implicit in what is explicitly represented.* Semantic accounts of first-order logic can be looked at as attempts to capture *one* sense of a piece of information being implicit in other information. If you have a set S of sentences and a sentence C such that it is impossible for all of the sentences in S to be true and C to be false, that is, if the truth of the members of S guarantees the truth of C, it seems natural to say that the information in S contains that in C. The notion of logical consequence is an attempt to make this sense of containment precise. Roughly: C is a logical consequence of S just in case the interpretations that make (every member of) S true make C true. Interpretations, or models, can be thought of as functions assigning truth values to sentences in virtue of what they assign to the constituent expressions out of which the sentences are composed. But what they are really are set theoretic instruments for representing alternative possible realities; each model represents a way the world - or some parts or aspects of it — might be. (Hereby hangs a long tale about the conceptual foundations of model theory.....Imagine I, or somebody, has told it.) So the sentences that get assigned the truth value **TRUE** by an interpretation are just the sentences that would be true if the world were the way the interpretation represents it as being. So, a sentence C is a logical consequence of a sentence S just in case whenever the world would be such as to make all the sentences in S true, it would also be such as to make C true.

There are a host of provably sound and (strongly) complete proof procedures for first order logic. A proof procedure for first order logic is *sound with respect to validity* just in case all sentences generated by the procedure (the *theorems*) are true in all first order interpretations. Such sentences are also called *valid.* A proof procedure is *complete with respect to validity* if every valid sentence is a theorem. A sentence is *strongly complete* if every logical consequence of a set S of sentences is derivable, by the procedure, from S. (First order logic guarantees the following *compactness* property: if a sentence is a logical consequence of an infinite set S of sentences, then it is a logical consequence of some **finite** subset of S.)

Proof procedures can be thought of as generating infinite proof trees; these trees being generated by the various possible orderings of applications of the rules of inference. Thus different procedures correspond to different trees. There are many dimensions of difference among proof procedures. Some are actually refutation procedures. They can be thought of in this way: to prove a sentence valid, one negates the sentence and shows that, on every branch of the tree, there is some atomic sentence such that both it and its negation appear on that branch. This shows that the negation of the sentence in question is inconsistent, that is one can derive a contradiction from it. By the soundness and completeness of the procedure, there is no interpretation under which the negation is true; so *its* negation — the original sentence — must be valid (true under every interpretation). To prove that a set S of sentences entails a given sentence C, one negates C and tests the resulting set of sentences — consisting of S together with the negation of C — for inconsistency. If the proof succeeds, it show that there is no interpretation under which all of the sentences in S are true but C is not, thus showing that S has C has a logical consequence.

Another important dimension of difference lies in whether the procedure takes arbitrary first-order sentences as inputs. There are procedures that require that sentences be put in a normal form. There are a variety of such forms meeting the following condition: it is provable that, for any arbitrary sentence S, there is a sentence in that normal form that is equivalent to S. Different procedures assume different normal forms. One reason for opting for conversion to normal form is that rules of inference are keyed to sentences in virtue of their logical forms; the fewer of the latter, the fewer of the former. The fewer the rules, the easier to algorithmetize.

There are, of course both normal form and nonnormal form refutation procedures, normal form nonrefutation procedures, and nonnormal form nonrefutation procedures. The classical resolution/unification method is a normal form, refutation procedure.

4. Complications and Complexity

So far I've been speaking only about proof procedures that are both sound and (strongly) complete. Some comments are in order. First, first order validity is not decidable; there can be no effective, uniform procedure for deciding whether an arbitrary sentence of first order quantification theory is valid. The same holds for logical consequence. Complete, but undecidable: If a sentence is valid, we can prove that it is; but if it is not valid (and also not the negation of a valid sentence), we may not be able to demonstrate that it's not. But that ain't the half of it. Let's look at the problem of determining the relation of logical consequence for the *monadic* predicate calculus. That is, we are looking only at those cases in which all the premises and the conclusion are sentences built up out of *one-place* predicate letters, truth functional connectives and quantification. This is all you need to represent the traditional syllogisms, such as:

All Computer Sceientists are grossly underpaid.

All AI researchers are Computer Scientists.

Therefore, all AI researchers are grossly underpaid.

This class of problems is decidable, but in nondeterministic exponential time ([LEWI78]). Or take the satisfiability problem for the sentential calculus — the logic of the truth functions. This, too, is decidable, but decisions may require nondeterministic polynomial time. (The problem is NP-complete.) Stockmeyer has calculated that, if we were to test consistency by the truth-table method among 138 atomic propositions and if we suppose that each line of the table could be tested in the time it took a light ray to travel the diameter of a proton, the test would require more than twenty billion years — the current upper estimate of the age of the universe. Of course the truth-table method is oft inefficient compared to (e.g., a resolution algorithm); but the worst case stories are the same. (The "statistics" were pointed out to me by Chris Cherniak. See [CHER84].) The moral: 2 to the 138th power is a big number. Well, that's one moral. There are no doubt others too; still it should be noted that I've simply ignored all questions about the significance of these asymptotic, worst case or upper bound analyses. For real applications, what is the actual complexity distribution like; are there small but intractable problems; etc.? (These are deep and vital questions. I pass them over.)

5. Some Responses

There are various options when faced with these seemingly horrific results for what are, after all, decidable fragments of full first order logic. (I should note that one such is the Horn clause fragment, on which **PROLOG** is based.) On one dimension there are various domain-specific heuristics. These are especially useful in interactive theorem-proving situations where the name of the game is: **PROVE THE DARN THEOREM** — and perhaps find out something useful about how mathematical reasoning actually proceeds. But I'm assuming we (at least while at this conference) aren't interested in (semi-) automatic theorem-proving in this sense. We aren't in the business of proving theorems, as an activity to be engaged in for its own sake. (I realize that the distinction I want to make — a distinction in research interests — isn't a very hard and fast one.)

In any event, the bottom line is: even where there is a complete proof procedure, or even a decision procedure, we may either have to or want to opt for an incomplete implementation. This opting is precisely what most (all?) actual **PROLOG** systems do.

Once we begin focusing in on fragments or sublanguages of full first order quantification theory (especially full first order quantification theory with identity) other options come into view. One such option centers around equational theories. These are theories expressible using only identity, individual terms, and function constants. These theories contain no relation symbols and no logical constants besides the identity symbol; so sentences in such theories look just like equations in algebra textbooks. For such theories, or for the most important cases, the computable algebras, one or another variant of a term rewriting procedure is the way to go. Again: term rewriting is just what you learned to do in algebra classes — substitute equals for equals in some set of equations. Keep going until you can go no farther and check to see if one and the same expression (modulo some trivial rewriting) ends up on both sides of the identity symbol. (And what if one wants to do both general theorem-proving and equational logic? Surely one should not shrug one's shoulders and cast all equational theories in relational form, with one or another special treatment of the identity relation. That's the way it would be done in **PROLOG**-based systems. It now looks, rather, as if one should go the opposite route. See, for instance, [JIEH85].)

Another kind of case has been explored by Ron Brachman, Richard Fikes, Hector Levesque, and myself. ([ISRA83], [BFL83b], [BPL85].) In many cases, one's (client's) domain is naturally separable into types of entities, many of which types, in turn, have subtypes. Sometimes the natural story is that the subtypes of a given type are mutually exclusive; sometimes not. Sometimes the explicitly specified subtypes of a given type exhaust the type; sometimes not. Sometimes a given subtype can be a subtype of more than one type (multiple inheritance); sometimes not. Etc... For a wide range of cases, a natural way to go is to use special purpose operations to compute various of the relationships among the types and subtypes. One thereby makes essential use of the type structure — that of a tree or a lattice, perhaps — to express the information contained in a certain set of first-order sentences, perhaps of some constrained fragment. One requires that the special purpose algorithms be at least sound with respect to the interpretations induced by the translation between first order sentences and type relationships. (One may restrict the sublanguage enough to require completeness as well. For more on this, see also [STIC84].) The simplest cases, of course, are the so called **IS-A** or type-subtype hierarchies (typically trees). Thus, one may represent the information in the syllogism above by way of an **IS-A** tree — in this case, a chain — with the node for the property of being an AI researcher connected by an **IS-A** link to the node for the property of being a Computer Scientist, which is in turn connected by an **IS-A** link to the node for the property of being underpaid. The conclusion is shown to follow simply by looking up the **IS-A** hierarchy. Finally, the following sentences of the monadic predicate calculus are alleged to represent the same information:

$$(x) \ (CompScientist \ (x) \ --> \ Underpaid \ (x))$$

$$(x) \ (AIRes \ (x) \ --> \ CompScientist \ (x))$$

$$(x) \ (AIRes \ (x) \ --> \ Underpaid \ (x))$$

6. Why Reason Soundly?

All along, I've been supposing that we want our inferential procedures to be sound, say, with respect to first order validity. But do we? Well, we do if, *but also only if,* we expect and demand that all of our reasoning be logically sound. But why should we want or expect that? No reason at all, **unless** we confuse *logically sound reasoning* with *good, useful reasoning.*

In lots of cases we will want our system to stick its neck out and conclude something not **guaranteed** to be true by the truth of what it explicitly or implicitly knows. This may involve rules not guaranteed to be sound — indeed guaranteed not to be sound. In AI circles, such rules are often called *default rules;* the reasoning involved, *nonmonotonic reasoning.* Here comes **the classic example**:

Tweety is a bird.

(Typically) birds can fly.

Therefore, Tweety can fly.

Notice that it is perfectly possible for the two premises to be true and the conclusion false. Still, the inference from the two premises to the conclusion is a fairly reasonable one — *at least in the absence of any reason to think Tweety atypical.* While we're noticing things, let us also note two other important features of this little bit of reasoning. (1) The second premise does not seem to have any adequate representation by way of first order quantificational logic. Even without the explicit hedge carried by the word "typically", the sentence "Birds can fly" simply does not mean that all birds can fly and, hence, cannot be adequately represented by some such first order sentence as:

$$(x) \ (Bird \ (x) \ --> \ CanFly \ (x)).$$

In fact, if it means anything like "Most birds can fly," it is provably outside the scope of first order expressibility. (2) If we add in, as a further premise, some reason for judging Tweety atypical - at least with respect to his (her?) ability to fly — we may have to retract our conclusion. So look at the following argument:

Tweety is a bird.

(Typically) birds can fly.

Tweety is an ostrich.

Therefore, Tweety can fly.

This second feature of such bits of reasoning is responsible for the formidable sounding characterization "*nonmonotonic reasoning*". The explanation goes as follows: the relation of logical consequence is *monotonic* in the following sense; if a set S of sentences has a sentence C as a logical consequence, then every superset of S — every set that contains all the members of S as well as other sentences — also has C as a logical consequence. So the relation is monotonic in the "size" of the set of premises. Not so, it seems, with default reasoning. Let us simply assume that our original two premise bit of reasoning was *OK* — not, of course, that it was logically sound. Adding another premise undermines the original reasoning; the new three premise argument is not *OK*. (If you like, you can consider the four premise argument you get by throwing in a statement to the effect that (typically) ostriches can't fly.) Thus, *OK* default reasoning is not monotonic in the "size" of the premise set.

I should note that I see no reason at all to believe that all good (*OK*), though not deductively sound, reasoning fits this particular pattern. Here *this* pattern might be characterized, loosely, as follows: we have some extremely useful, mostly reliable, generalization connecting (e.g., types of entity with properties) — so in our case, the type: bird with the property of being able to fly. But we don't believe that the generalization has no exceptions; still, we want to come to a conclusion about a particular instance of the type — our Tweety. In other cases, the pattern will be importantly different. So, we might want to infer a general rule from some collection of particular instances that conform with the rule. For instance, we might have recorded lots of instances of lots of different kinds of birds, most — nearly all — of which could fly, and on this basis, conclude that (typically) birds can fly. This mode of reasoning is often called *induction.* In yet other cases, we will be inferring an explanation or an explanatory pattern from phenomena (e.g., a disease from its symptoms). This mode of reasoning is sometimes called *abduction.* Then there is reasoning of the kind dubbed autoepistemic by Bob Moore. As in the following: If I had a younger brother, surely I'd know it. I know no such thing; so I don't have a younger brother. This can be thought of as a special form of abduction: what is to be explained is the fact that I don't know that I have a younger brother; the best explanation is that I just don't have one. In any event, let me repeat the main point: much perfectly good reasoning is neither monotonic nor deductively sound. (One more, especially opposite example, is that of reasoning about updates in data bases.)

There are, by the way, some comments of a complexity-theoretic nature to be said about some of these nondeductive modes of reasoning as well, but they are not of the standard computational complexity variety. That work is all done within the range of the recursive (effectively computable) functions and effectively solvable problems. With some, at least, of these *nonmonotonic* modes of inference, we are beyond the range of the recursive or even the recursively enumerable. In much of this work, for instance, there is talk of a nonmonotonic rule of inference of the following sort: given an arbitrary first order theory T and an arbitrary first order sentence A, check whether $T \cup \{A\}$ — the result of adding A to T considered now as a set of sentences — is consistent; if so, add A to T. Thus, in our example, consider the theory that consists of at least the following two sentences, together with all logical consequences of any set of sentences in the theory. (This last is just a way of saying that the theory is *closed under logical consequence* — if a sentence is a logical consequence of T, then it is in T.)

Bird (tweety)

(x) (Bird (x) --> CanFly (x))

Let A be "CanFly (tweety)". Now if one can add A to T consistently that is because no sentence incompatible with A is in T. In particular, it must be that case that the negation of A: "It is not the case that CanFly (tweety)" is not in T — is not a theorem of T. So this requirement is an attempt to capture, within the framework of first order logic, the constraint mentioned above, namely that there be no reason for thinking Tweety is atypical with respect to its ability to fly.

Given Church's Theorem that there is no decision procedure whereby to tell whether an arbitrary first order sentence can be added consistently to an arbitrary first order theory, this is not an effective rule. (This is simply another corollary of first order logic's being complete but not decidable.) That is, there is no way to tell, in general, when the rule applies. We can, of course, limit ourselves to decidable fragments of first order logic or to decidable theories. Even if we don't so limit ourselves, we can actually characterize quite precisely the place of such a procedure or rule in a recursion-theoretic hierarchy, in particular, in the Kleene-Post or arithmetic hierarchy. (I won't go into any details here; suffice it to say, a precise characterization of this problem can be had.).

In a sense these fancy recursion-theoretic analyses are a little beside the point. To see this, think about the notion of default rules, informally conceived. These are of the form: if you believe that, for example, Tweety is a bird and that typically, birds can fly, and if you have no reason to believe anything to the contrary, infer that Tweety can fly. As suggested above, one *can* analyze this in terms of the application of a noneffective procedure involving a check for consistency for arbitrary first order theories. This may be an illuminating analysis; but it had best not be thought of as a specification of an algorithm that you're going to spend time programming up and that your system is going spend time — **a whole lot of time** — executing. The point here is an analog of the point made at the very beginning of the paper about logical languages as representational formalisms. We might think of the suggested analysis as a specification that — in this case — we know cannot be fully realized, but which can guide our actual system design and implementation. Thus, one might want to think about having the system jump to conclusions retractable conclusions on the basis of default assumptions. These conclusions might then have to be retracted in the face of contrary evidence (evidence that Tweety is an oddball bird); but the system does not first have to check for the consistency of the conclusion with the current theory. Indeed, perhaps it never considers the possibility of having to retract the conclusion until such time as it explicitly represents contrary evidence. Of course, you may also want to try to design the system to be sensitive to abnormalities in its situation, so that it is reliably blocked from jumping to retractable conclusions exactly when it shouldn't so jump — that is, exactly when there are reasons for judging Tweety deviant with respect to its ability to fly. This last suggests extremely hard problems of analysis and design, so I will have nothing to say about it.

7. Concluding Remarks

I have so far not addressed myself at all to the issue of databases and database systems. So, finally: a few words — from a rank outsider — about databases (actually, a few words about relational databases). The design and intelligent use of databases obviously requires reasoning. So does the design and use of clocks; but, though clocks can and do have representational capacities — that is, they can convey or carry information, clocks don't themselves reason. How is it with databases? Note: how is it with (relational) databases, not, how is it with (relational) database systems nor, how is it with knowledge-based management systems. As for databases: by my lights at any rate, databases are like clocks; they represent, but do not reason. (Knowledge based management systems, on the other hand, are like self-loading dishwashers; they'd be wonderful to have, but they don't really exist yet.)

What could I mean by these cryptic remarks? Well, I've already had something to say about this; see my position paper in Section II, and don't want to repeat myself (again.) In that chapter, I said that, with respect to expressive power, relational databases can be thought of as representable by (finite) sets of ground atomic formulae. But I also said that this contention was completely neutral with respect to the implementation of a relational system. One way to sharpen this point about neutrality is as follows: one can — and I gather people sometimes do — think of relational data bases as if they were themselves models or interpretations of first order theories. I had earlier said that models were set theoretic representatives for collections of possible facts — or, as I put it, for ways some part of the world might be. What this comes to is that relational databases are complex data structures which are surrogates for such models. Moreover, they are — under some suitable mapping — isomorphic to those models and hence, can themselves be taken to be models. Under this conception, one need not think of the database entries as sentences or formulae of any kind; models need not consist of collections of sentences. (Indeed, usually they don't.) Query evaluation over a database is then seen as literally evaluation of a sentence in the model that **is** the database. Note that to see query processing in this way is precisely **not** to see it as a form of theorem proving — at least, if by theorem proving one means some procedure operating over (sets of) sentences. (For more on this contrast, see [REIT84]; in fact, don't just see it — read it through carefully.)

In [BI84], Ron Brachman and I suggest that one way to think of data bases is as "analog" devices. Hector Levesque has made like-sounding remarks in his Computers and Thought Lecture at IJCAI85. A happy thought is that what — if anything — we meant had something to do with what I just said about conceiving of relational databases as models of first order theories. If this suggestion makes any sense, then it's clear why there should be great difficulties in systematically merging databases with techniques derived from the AI tradition — a tradition which stresses:

(a)   Symbolic representation of information via structures whose abstract syntax is that of sentences of some logical language, and correlatively,

(b)   Reasoning systems defined over such structures in virtue of the logical form of the those sentences.

Then again, maybe this model theoretic perspective on databases is badly wrong headed.

8. The Absolute End

It will no doubt have come to the reader's attention that (1) I have not described any particular inference techniques in any detail, and (2) I have not really come to any conclusion. A partial explanation for the first is simply that I did not want to bore the reader to tears; a complete explanation for the second is that I didn't want to incite him or her to murder.

Acknowledgments

This research was supported in part by a gift from the System Development Foundation.

9. References

[BFL83b]   [BI84]   [BPL85]   [CHER84]   [ISRA83]   [JIEH85] [LEWI78] [NEWE80] [REIT84] [STIC84]

11
Current Trends in Database Query Processing

Matthias Jarke[1]

ABSTRACT *Basic algorithms and major optimization strategies for evaluating queries to relational databases are illustrated by means of an example. Relationships between AI and database techniques are emphasized and areas of active research are highlighted.*

1. Introduction

Database management systems (DBMS) manage a large collection of shared data for application programmers and end-users. The user interacts with the system by submitting requests for data selection (queries) and manipulation (updates). A sequence of queries and updates which is logically a single unit of interaction with the database system is called a transaction.

Queries and updates frequently involve access to data described in terms of their properties rather than their location. The query evaluation subsystem of the DBMS is charged with the efficient processing of such accesses. Typically, query evaluation proceeds in two steps: selecting an efficient strategy, and executing it. The first step is frequently referred to as 'query optimization' although the exact optimization of query processing strategies is usually not only computationally intractable but also impeded by the lack of precise statistical information about the database.

After a short sketch of basic query processing algorithms and some well-known improvement heuristics (section 2), section 3

---

[1] New York University and Johann Wolfgang Goethe-Universitat

describes logical transformations of queries and section 4 the cost-based optimization of access plans. Section 5 summarizes some recent extensions of query optimization concepts.

2. Basic Concepts

A database system consists of the stored data (often called the database state) and of metaknowledge about them (the database schema). This survey will use a relational framework in which the database state is conceptualized as a collection of tables or relations. Columns of the tables are called attributes, rows are called tuples or relation elements. The schema consists of a description of structural properties of the tables, a set of integrity constraints, and sometimes a set of deduction rules called 'view definitions'.

As an example, consider a database describing employees, their departments and managers, and the offices they are using. A possible schema for such a database is shown, below. Structural properties define the assignment of attribute names to relations:

> EMPLOYEE   (eno, name, marstat, salary, dno)
> DEPARTMENT (dno, dname, mgr)
> OFFICE   (floor, room, eno)

Integrity constraints apply to all levels of the database. Firstly, domain dependencies define the set of admissible values for each attribute (e.g., "married" and "single" for marstat). Secondly, database theory has analyzed a large number of dependencies between groups of attributes in a relation (keys, functional dependencies, multivalued dependencies, ...). For example, a combination of attributes is called a key of a relation if its values determine a relation element uniquely. In the example database, the following key dependencies are defined:

> key   (EMPLOYEE, eno)
> key   (DEPARTMENT, dno)
> key   (OFFICE, floor, room, eno)

An example of an integrity constraint spanning more than one relation would be the 'referential' integrity constraint that all dno values appearing in EMPLOYEE must also appear in DEPARTMENT (i.e., all employees work in existing departments). Examples of view definitions (deduction rules) will be given in section 3.

A large number of query representations exist for the relational model, including relational calculus, relational algebra, tabular and graphic notations. For our query examples, we shall use the language

SQL. Consider the query: "name single employees in computer departments who make less than 40000?"

```
SELECT    e.name
FROM      EMPLOYEE e, DEPARTMENT d
WHERE     e.salary < 40000 AND e.marstat = 'single'
AND       d.dname = 'computer' AND d.dno = e.dno
```

Usually, the most expensive operation in evaluating such queries is the execution of the 'join' term (here: d.dno = e.dno) that links the two tables. There are two ways to do this. The 'merge' method proceeds as follows. First, sort both relations by ascending dno values. Next, scan both relations in parallel. For each EMPLOYEE tuple, remember the name value if it describes a single with less than 40000 salary and if there is a corresponding DEPARTMENT tuple with dname = 'computer'. Note, that the method described here contains already some improvement on a sequential relational algebra implementation since the restriction terms and the join term are evaluated in parallel. This kind of parallelism was first proposed by [PALE72] but is still not available in all DBMS.

Alternatively, 'nested loop' solutions have been implemented. For example, the above query would translate into the following program:

```
ANSWER := [ ];
FOR EACH e IN EMPLOYEE DO
    FOR EACH d IN DEPARTMENT DO
    IF  e.salary < 40000 AND e.marstat = 'single'
    AND d.dname = 'computer' AND d.dno = e.dno
    THEN ANSWER :+ [<e.name>];
```

where :+ is an insert operator and [ ] denotes the empty relation. A closer look at this solution shows a lot of leeway for optimization. First, the inner loop should only be executed if the restrictions on EMPLOYEE hold; this is the well-known heuristic 'selection before join' which is generally attributed to [SC75]. Second, it would be useful to reduce the length of the inner loop by first preparing a list of dno's for which dname = 'computer' and then have d loop only over this reduced set. This is referred to as subquery 'detachment' first introduced by [WY76] and later generalized to more general queries, and to distributed databases where it became famous under its algebra alias 'semijoin'. Much recent database theory research deals with the question what kinds of queries can be fully decomposed in this manner (tree vs. cyclic queries). The optimized program would look as follows.

```
DNOLIST := [ ];
FOR EACH d IN DEPARTMENT DO
    IF d.dname = 'computer' THEN DNOLIST :+ [<d.dno>];
ANSWER := [ ];
FOR EACH e IN EMPLOYEE DO
    IF e.salary < 40000 AND e.marstat = 'single'
    THEN FOR EACH d IN DNOLIST DO
        IF d.dno = e.dno THEN ANSWER :+ [<e.name>];
```

Usually, merge join strategies are preferable in centralized databases whereas detachment or semijoin strategies are superior in distributed databases where the main cost component is data transfer. However, exceptions to this rule may occur in the presence of permanent access paths (e.g., indexes on certain fields). Hybrid strategies can also be developed. For example, in the merge strategy one could reduce the DEPARTMENT relation to a DNOLIST before sorting but this may make little sense if an index on dno is available for the DEPART-MENT relation.

3. Query Transformation Strategies

Several of the heuristics mentioned in the previous section can be expressed as transformations on the high-level representation of the query. For example, [JK83] represent generalized detachment and 'selection first' heuristics uniformly through nested relational calculus expressions. However, there is another class of query transformations which have to be studied on a high level to be tractable, namely the simplification of queries that contain redundant operations. One might argue that users are unlikely to formulate such queries. However, they may have no choice if the query is expressed in terms of data views rather than stored relations. This situation is typical for very high-level interfaces such as deductive databases or natural language query systems.

As an example, consider the following query as a direct translation from the natural language query: "who are the single computer people in a tax bracket under 50%"?

```
SELECT    c.name
FROM      COMPEMP c, TAX50 t
WHERE     c.marstat = 'single' AND t.eno = c.eno;
```

COMPEMP and TAX50 are views i.e., derived relations whose value is not stored but derived through deduction rules, that are defined as follows:

COMPEMP = SELECT e.*
         FROM   EMPLOYEE e, DEPARTMENT d
         WHERE   d.dname = 'computer' AND d.dno = e.dno;

TAX50 =   SELECT e.*
         FROM   EMPLOYEE e
         WHERE   e.marstat = 'single' AND e.salary < 40000
           OR   e.marstat = 'married' AND e.salary < 80000;

Stonebraker [STON75] introduced a concept of view substitution to evaluate such queries (which, incidentally, is quite similar to the way PROLOG handles queries with deduction rules). Essentially, the view definition is substituted for the view name with appropriate variable renaming. The original query (after an intermediate application of the distributive laws for AND and OR) translates to:

SELECT c.name
FROM   EMPLOYEE c, DEPARTMENT d, EMPLOYEE t
WHERE   c.dno = d.dno AND d.dname = 'computer'
        AND c.marstat = 'single' AND t.marstat = 'single'
        AND t.salary < 40000 AND c.eno = t.eno
  OR   c.dno = d.dno AND d.dname = 'computer'
        AND c.marstat = 'single' AND t.marstat = 'married'
        AND t.salary < 80000 AND c.eno = t.eno

The reader may be surprised to learn that this query can be shown to be equivalent to the simple example used in section 2. The simplification process employs a specific query representation called tableaux (introduced by [ASU79a]), in conjunction with schema knowledge.

Loosely speaking, tableaux are a tabular notation for queries whose WHERE clause contains only AND (no OR or NOT); therefore, we need two tableaux for the example. Each tableau row corresponds to a tuple variable in the query; the first row serves the same purpose as the SELECT clause in the SQL query. There is a column for each attribute in the database. The symbols appearing in the tableau are: distinguished variables denoted ai (corresponding to attributes in the SELECT clause), constants (appearing as attribute values in restrictive terms), nondistinguished variables (attributes neither being equal to constants nor appearing in the SELECT clause), blanks (attributes not appearing in a relation), and tags (relation names from the FROM clause).

eno	name	marstat	salary	dno	dname	mgr	
	a2						
b1	a2	single	b2	b3			EMPLOYEE c
				b3	computer	b4	DEPARTMENT d
b1	b5	single	<40000	b6			EMPLOYEE t

eno	name	marstat	salary	dno	dname	mgr	
	a2						
b1	a2	single	b2	b3			EMPLOYEE c
				b3	computer	b4	DEPARTMENT d
b1	b5	married	<80000	b6			EMPLOYEE t

Consider the first tableau. The schema knowledge that eno is a key of EMPLOYEE, together with the fact that the c and the t rows agree in their eno's, implies that these two rows should agree in all columns. After the necessary unification process, one of them can be deleted and we get the simplified tableau:

eno	name	marstat	salary	dno	dname	mgr	
	a2						
b1	a2	single	<40000	b3			EMPLOYEE c
				b3	computer	b4	DEPARTMENT d

which corresponds to the example in section 2, except for renaming of variables. By a similar argument, the first and third rows of the second tableau should agree in all columns; however, there are different constant values in the marstat column. Therefore, this subquery is contradictory from the point of view of the database schema and will always yield an empty answer.

The above is a simple example of 'semantic query optimization', a technique generalized by [KING80a], and by [HZ80] that employs semantic integrity constraints to transform queries into semantically equivalent ones that can be evaluated more efficiently. Not always will these methods yield simpler queries; it is possible to add restrictive terms or even joins in order to exploit indexes. Search control among the large number of possible transformations becomes a major problem with these advanced methods.

4. Access Planning

Query simplification (section 3) and evaluation heuristics (section 2) still leave a large number of possible implementation strategies. The query optimizer can sequence the operations and choose the best implementation for each one. Typically, the optimization of access plans is a three-step process (the steps may be interleaved):

1. Generate a set of reasonable-looking logical access plans; generally, these will focus on the sequence of join operations, on join implementation, and on interleaving join evaluation with restrictions.

2. Refine the plans to take into account the available physical access paths and storage structures (e.g., hash tables, indexes, sort orders, etc.).

3. Apply a model of access and processing costs to select the cheapest access plan.

Several problems make this process difficult. The first two steps are problematic because of the large number of possible plans; therefore, plans are often generated in a process of incremental concurrent generation and evaluation (e.g., using dynamic programming methods of Operations Research). However, the cost of these methods frequently leads to the application of simple heuristics that may omit good plans from consideration.

For the third step, the costs of operations must be estimated; they depend largely on the size of intermediate results. Estimation models usually make a number of assumptions about the placement of records on disk pages, and about the statistical distributions of attribute values. Serious bias can result if these assumptions are unjustified. On the other hand, cost-based evaluation cannot be just omitted, as demonstrated by the following example.

Suppose, our example company wants to have a meeting of the managers of all computer departments with employees who have offices outside the fifth floor. Assume further that each of the three database relations EMPLOYEE, OFFICE, and DEPARTMENT, resides on a different site.

This query has been written in nested form to demonstrate that it can easily be evaluated inside out by query detachment/ semijoin. Unfortunately, this solution requires the transfer of all eno's of OFFICE elements outside the fifth floor to the EMPLOYEE site, although we are really only interested in the much fewer computer employees. It would therefore be more efficient by at least an order of magnitude to transfer the dno's of the computer departments down first and then return those of them to the DEPARTMENT site (if the answer is expected

```
SELECT    mgr
FROM      DEPARTMENT d
WHERE     d.dname = 'computer'
AND       d.dno IN (SELECT e.dno
                    FROM      EMPLOYEE e
                    WHERE     e.eno = (SELECT o.eno
                                      FROM      OFFICE o
                                      WHERE     o.floor <> 5))
```

there) that qualify at the lower levels; in other words, it is more efficient to reverse the hierarchy in this case. Sometimes, even a middle-out strategy may be optimal.

5. Extensions

In recent years, query optimization has moved away from the traditional single-query, relational query language framework. On the one hand, the scope of query optimization is being extended to share resources among multiple related queries submitted by the same user at different points in time, or by multiple users simultaneously. A prerequisite is the recognition of common subexpressions not only for conjunctive queries (as provided by the tableau techniques). The optimization of batch processing, and of access path selection is being considered in this context. An interesting approach is the materialization of views (view indexing and maintenance). The simultaneous optimization of queries and updates (transaction optimization) is also being studied.

On the other hand, the queries to be optimized are getting more complex. Particular needs for query optimization arise if a DBMS is interfaced with, or extended, to an AI-based system: the combination of multiple tuple-oriented data accesses of the AI system into a smaller number of set-oriented calls; the reorganization of knowledge-base rules to simulate query optimization heuristics, as proposed by [WARR81]; and the evaluation of complex operations, such as recursion. Another area where query complexity reaches beyond standard relational calculus or algebra queries, is statistical databases whose languages include data analysis capabilities in addition to data retrieval functions. Much remains to be done to integrate these tasks.

Finally, the data structures on which the system operates may be more complex than flat records, as in the relational model. Research has been conducted on query optimization in network and hierarchical databases, mostly in the context of heterogeneous distributed database systems (cf. the work of Dayal and others at CCA). Furthermore, CAM/CAM, image databases, and office applications work on complex objects, frequently requiring recursive hierarchical structures. In such systems, the concept of a database view also takes on a substantially more complicated meaning; further research is required for advanced query and transaction processing.

6. References

[ASU79a]   [HZ80]   [JK83]   [KING80a]   [PALE72]   [SC75] [STON75] [WARR81] [WY76]

12
Logic and Database Systems

Jeffrey D. Ullman[1]

ABSTRACT *Progress toward true "knowledge-base' systems will be much harder than people imagine, if history is a guide.*

1. The Cycle of Progress

There is a pattern to the way new capabilities are realized:

1. A need is perceived, and initial experiments produce systems that allow users to program their needs.

2. The 'tricks' used by programmers are understood.

3. A second generation of systems automates the programming process to an extent, allowing the user to write in a higher-level language and skip the 'tricks.'

I could cite the progression from assembly language to Fortran or Fortran to APL as examples, but let's concentrate on the history of databases, which I see as: (1) The early systems (network etc.) gave the user the ability to program navigation through data, (2) Good ways to implement queries were understood and used in the implementation of relational systems, (3) Relational systems replaced earlier systems in many applications.

I see another example of the cycle beginning in the area of logic and databases. The need for logic-oriented languages that provide more power than relational query languages has been perceived, and examples (e.g., Prolog), that provide the capability to the programmer willing to master the navigational aspects, have been built. These navigational aspects include programmer control of backtracking through rule and term ordering. I don't think people realize how backtracking,

---

[1] Stanford University

whenever its power is used to implement anything less conventional than if-then-else control, leads to a program that is a conceptual morass.

We're now beginning to see some attempts to automate navigation in what are essentially database systems with a layer of Horn-clause logic (or even more general logic) appearing between the user and the database. These efforts range from attempts to 'compile' logic by the logic-and-databases community to efforts by Mike Genesereth to automate meta-level reasoning. I have myself started a project called NAIL! (Not Another Implementation of Logic!) to investigate algorithms for making strategy decisions in this environment automatically.

2. The Time Scale of Progress

The previous cycle of progress in database systems took roughly 15 years (1965-1980). I expect the next cycle to take roughly the same amount of time and to produce roughly the same degree of improvement in our capabilities. I have no argument for this except that the best predictor of today's weather is yesterday's weather.

On the other hand, I hear all sorts of amazing predictions about what will happen over the next few years (full speech understanding, etc.). When I compare the apparent rate of progress in the future with the rate of the recent past, I have to conclude that we went through some kind of time warp last week.

3. Differences Between Advanced Database Systems and AI Systems

There has been a considerable amount of seemingly relevant work dealing with inference strategies; for example, there are large, active communities doing automated theorem proving or proving properties of programs. The fundamental difference in approach is that these communities are still in a mode where every time they prove a theorem or prove a program correct it is an interesting event.

In comparison, a database system must respond to queries day-in, day-out, answering everything that is posed in its query language. Think of what life would be like if *1%* of all QUEL programs produced no answer or the wrong answer, or took forever even though the poser could see an easy way for the system to answer the query. Thus, the next generation of database systems needs:

1.   Methods for deciding query evaluation strategies in logical systems. These methods must be efficient, because they get applied

to each query.

2. An understanding of what class of queries can be supported by what evaluation strategies. We need a query language (which in effect includes the logical rules in the 'knowledge base') such that a response to every well-formed query can be guaranteed.

I would like to predict that work on expanding the generality of theorem-proving methods will have little impact, at least in the present cycle of progress. Rather, we need to understand the capabilities, limitations, and efficiency of the most simple of inference methods and apply them in working systems.

13
Negation in Knowledge Base Management Systems

Shamin A. Naqvi[1]

ABSTRACT *A Knowledge Base is defined as a set of closed universally quantified first-order formulas; this allows a relational database to be incorporated as a component of the Knowledge Base. A Knowledge Base Management System is defined as the system that manages the Knowledge Base. Storage of negative information in knowledge bases is impractical due to the potentially huge amount that would have to be stored. The Closed World Assumption, negation from failure to prove, and the Generalised Closed World Assumption are discussed as methods of avoiding the storage of negative information explicitly. A new method of "closing off" a Knowledge Base is presented and a system architecture for Knowledge Based Management Systems is proposed. Finally, it is shown that this architecture supports previous work in handling recursive queries in Knowledge Bases; it thus builds upon previous results and provides a coherent and unifying framework for building Knowledge Base Management Systems.*

1. Preamble

In recent years there has been a flurry of research activity in connecting and merging Database Management System (DBMS) and Knowledge Based System (KBS) Technologies (see [GM78],[GMN81],[GMN84], and [BMS83] for surveys of such efforts). The name Knowledge Base Management Systems (KBMS) is being proposed for this combined technology. It now appears that each

[1] AT&T Bell Laboratories

technology can supplement the weaknesses of the other: DBMS techniques can help in the efficient management of large amounts of information albeit the information is of a simple nature, whereas KBS techniques can allow increased functionality by dealing with more complex kinds of information.

The focus of our research is on investigating properties of knowledge bases. In our view a Knowledge Base (KB) is a set of closed first-order formulas in which all variables are universally quantified. This allows relational databases to be described as sets of ground unit formulas (informally, a formula is ground if it contains no variables). Relational views may be expressed as non-unit and nonground formulas. As an example the relation instances:

Enrolled(Student,Course) = {(John,cs100),(Peter,cs200),...}
Teach(Teacher,Course) = {Bader,cs100),(Doug,cs200),...}

can be expressed as the set of formulas:

Enrolled(John,cs100)
Enrolled(Peter,cs200)

....

Teach(Bader,cs100)
Teach(Doug,cs200)

....

and the view:

Teacher-of = natural-join(Enrolled,Teach)

can be expressed as the formula:

Enrolled(Student,Course) ∧ Teach(Teacher,Course) ⇒
Teacher-of(Student,Teacher)

Answering a query, Q, is then described as showing that Q is provable from the set of formulas in KB (i.e., KB ⊢ Q). This formulation, though expressive and elegant, suffers from efficiency problems: we do not know efficient theorem-proving techniques that can compete with query evaluation methods of databases. A way to retain the elegance and power of the logic view without a big loss in efficiency is to incorporate relational database query evaluation methods into the proof techniques. For example, in answering a query, Q, start by trying to prove that Q follows logically from the nonground formulas and when there is a need for specific ground instances in the proof, form a relational expression and ask the relational database system to evaluate it. For instance, in the above example, the query "Who is a teacher of Mark?", that is, Teacher(T,Mark), can be reduced to the formula:

Enrolled(Mark,Course) $\wedge$ Teach(Teacher,Course)

which is equivalent to the relational expression

$$\pi_{\text{Teacher}} (\sigma_{\$1=\text{Mark}} (\text{Enrolled} \times \text{Teach}))$$

A problem with this approach is that when the general formulas contain recursion the derivation of the corresponding relational expression becomes more complex [AU79] show that relational calculus can not express fixpoint queries). A solution to this problem has been proposed by Henschen and this author [HN84] which solves the problem for linear recursion and gives an efficient algorithm for transforming this recursion into an extended relational calculus program. (See the chapters by Ullman, Bancilhon, and Dayal and Manola in this book for more details on the recursion problem.) We shall talk more about this problem later in the chapter.

Another problem with this approach, and indeed with DBMS and KBS technologies, is the efficient treatment of negation when the amount of negative information is large which seems to be characteristic of many real world domains. For example, in a university environment we may know that certain students take a particular course; for all the remaining students, presumably large in number, we would be required to list them as not enrolled in that course. Such amounts of information, particularly in data intensive applications, may overwhelm a system.

Preliminary steps have been taken by Reiter [REIT78b], [CLAR78] and [MINK82] towards solving this problem. Their approaches are based on the idea of "closing off" a set of formulas by specifying that the objects mentioned in the theory are the only objects of interest in the application domain. In this paper we present a method of compiling negation based on the methods of Reiter and Clark and is more practical than Minker's method.

In a related development we show that our treatment of compiling negation is consistent with the system architecture discussed above for merging DBMS and KBS technologies. Also the current paper uses the same architecture along with the data structures of [HN84] for solving the recursive query problem. The consequence of this is that a coherent, unified and systematic corpus now exists to construct powerful and efficient KBMSs which can cope with a broad range of information and process complex queries.

The rest of this chapter is organised as follows. Section 2 examines previous work in the area of negation in databases and knowledge bases. Section 3 describes our method. Section 4 discusses unsafe negative queries in relational databases, and shows an immediate application of our method. Section 5 discusses implementation issues related to data intensive knowledge bases. Section 6 presents our proposal for a KBMS architecture, and Section 7 summarises the chapter.

The presentation is deliberately impressionistic; our intention is to convey a set of ideas that we believe can form the basis for building practical and powerful systems.

2. Previous Work

2.1. Negation in Databases

The database approach to handling negation is typified by the set difference operator of Codd [CODD79]. The relational model of data represents positive information only. The assumption here is that information not explicitly present in the database is not true. A tuple represents the existence of a relationship between its elements. From a failure to find a certain tuple in a table the converse of that relationship may be assumed as true. Thus, if no tuple exists to show "supplier S1 supplies part P2" then it is assumed that "supplier S1 does not supply part P2". For every relation scheme R in the database one can conceptually construct the complement relation $\bar{R}$ representing the negative propositions about the relationships in R. The problem is that such complement relations are generally huge and storing them explicitly is to be avoided. In such cases the assumption, that non-existence of a tuple implies the converse of that relationship, becomes extremely useful. When is it possible and consistent to make this assumption? The next section shows that such an assumption is equivalent to the Closed World Assumption made in knowledge bases and the semantics and applicability of the Closed World Assumption are also discussed.

2.2. Negation in Knowledge Bases

Following Gallaire et al. [GM78], Levesque [LEVE83] and others, a KB is a finite set of closed first-order formulas in which all variables (denoted by letters from the end of the alphabet) are universally quantified. In particular, 0-ary symbols called constants (denoted by letters from the start of the alphabet) are allowed and the assumption is made that there are as many constants as entities in the application domain. Notice that functional terms (n-ary constant symbols), such as "plus(a,b,c)" and "cons(L1,L2)" are allowed. The restriction to universally quantified variables means that skolem constants and skolem functions are not allowed in the KB. (Notice that a similar restriction exists in logic programming languages such as Prolog where functional terms such as "cons(L1,L2)" are used to construct complex terms). In order to keep the presentation simple we assume that all objects in KB belong to a single type. It shall be easy to see how the results of this chapter can be extended to systems with multiple types, as in [REIT80]. We shall usually omit writing the universal quantifier explicitly.

A negative query is a negative atomic formula in which all variables are existentially quantified. Thus $\exists x \neg P(x)$, $\neg \exists x P(x)$, and $\neg P(\text{john})$ are all valid negative queries. In this paper our concern is solely with negative queries. So we use the terms "query" and "negative query" interchangeably. Sometimes we shall have occasion to refer to the negation of a negative query α; we write this as $\neg\alpha$.

A query is answered by consulting the provability relation (i.e., $\vec{c}$ is an answer tuple to the query $\alpha(\vec{x})$ iff)

$$\text{KB} \vdash \alpha(\vec{c})$$

We would like to avoid storing negative information explicitly and make do with only positive information in the KB. One approach to this problem was suggested by Clark [CLAR78] based on the Closed World Assumption (CWA), namely, that *the information given about a predicate is all and only the relevant information about that predicate.* If the KB is finite and Horn (a KB is Horn if every formula in it is Horn; a formula is Horn if, when written in disjunctive form, it has *at most one* positive atom; it is definite Horn if it has *exactly one* positive atom) then the CWA can be implemented as the inference rule (called the "negation by failure" rule)

$$\neg(\text{KB} \vdash Q) \Rightarrow \text{KB} \vdash \neg Q$$

The negation by failure rule states that given a knowledge base, KB, we can obtain a new knowledge base, $\overline{KB}$, which contains all the negative data whose positive counterparts can not be proved from KB:

$$\overline{KB} = \{ \neg P\vec{c} \mid P \text{ is some predicate in KB},$$
$$\vec{c} \text{ is a tuple of constants,}$$
$$\text{and } P\vec{c} \text{ is not provable from KB}\}$$

It has been shown by Van Emden and Kowalski [VK76] that $\text{KB} \cup \overline{KB}$ is consistent so there is no need to explicitly represent $\overline{KB}$. The two disadvantages of this approach are that only ground atomic formulas can be assumed and that the KB is restricted to be (Definite) Horn. Many simple knowledge bases are non-Horn such as the trivial KB {Lives(John,NewYork)∨Lives(John,Chicago)}. The negation as failure rule for constructing $\overline{KB}$ does not work for non-Horn knowledge bases as the following example demonstrates.

Example 2.2.1: Let KB={Pa∨Pb}. Then since Pa is <u>not</u> provable from KB, ¬Pa∈$\overline{KB}$. Similarly ¬Pb∈$\overline{KB}$. But then KB∪$\overline{KB}$ is inconsistent.□

A way of dealing with nonground formulas is to use Clark's "completion method". It was noted by Clark [CLAR78] and Kowalski [KOWA78] that Horn formulas express only the "if-halves" of definitions which should be completed by the corresponding "only-if" parts to capture the full intended meanings. For example, the formulas

Teaches(A,cs100)
Teaches(B,cs100)

state that A and B teach "cs100". Clark and Kowalski noted that these could have been written as

Equal(X,A) ⇒ Teaches(X,cs100)
Equal(X,B) ⇒ Teaches(X,cs100)

Now, if the intention was to say that "the only people teaching "cs100" are A and B then the above statements fail to do so; this intention can be realised by completing the formulas with the "only-if" parts:

Equal(X,A) ∨ Equal(X,B) ⟷ Teaches(X,cs100)

Following this observation, Clark and Kowalski proposed that parts of a Horn KB should be completed by including the full intended IFF statements. Clark and later Apt and Van Emden [AE82] showed that if ¬Q can be inferred under the negation by failure rule then there is a corresponding first-order proof of ¬Q in Clark's completed IFF-database.

Minker [MINK82] proposes an extension of the CWA, called the Generalised Closed World Assumption (GCWA), based upon the notion of minimal models. A *model* of a set of formulas is a set of ground atomic formulas that make all formulas in the set true. A model of a KB is a *minimal model* if no proper subset of it is a model. [VK76] showed that in Horn knowledge bases if this minimal model is also a model of the KB then the KB is consistent with the CWA and that Horn knowledge bases have a unique minimal model. The following theorems state the results of Reiter and Minker.

Reiter's Theorem [REIT78a]: A ground negative atomic formula $\neg P\bar{c}$ can be assumed in a Horn KB iff $P\bar{c}$ does not belong to the (unique) minimal model of KB. □

Example 2.2.2:

KB$=\{P(a),Q(b)\}$
Minimal model of KB is $\{P(a),Q(b)\}$
We may assume $\neg P(b)$, and $\neg Q(a)$, etc. □

Minker's Theorem [MINK82]: A ground negative atomic formula can be assumed in a non-Horn KB iff $P\bar{c}$ is not contained in any minimal model of KB.

Example 2.2.3:

KB$=\{P(a)\vee P(b)\}$
MM$(KB)=\{\{P(a)\},\{P(b)\}\}$
So neither $\neg P(a)$ nor $\neg P(b)$ may be assumed. □

Example 2.2.4:

KB$=\{Q(b),P(a)\vee P(b)\}$
MM$(KB)=\{\{Q(b),P(a)\},\{Q(b),P(b)\}\}$
Since $Q(a)$ is not in any minimal model we may assume $\neg Q(a)$. □

Extensions to Minker's work have recently been proposed by Yahya and Henschen [YH85], and by Naqvi [NAQV85a]. Whilst Minker's work belongs to the class of knowledge bases we are considering in this chapter, our problem is that it is not clear how Minker's result can be used in an actual KB. To quote Minker "what remains to be addressed is how the concept can be used in a practical sense" [MINK82].

3. Closed Knowledge Bases

3.1. Motivating Example

We provide a simple example which, because it deals with a non-Horn KB and a nonground query, is not amenable to solution by the methods of Reiter, and Clark.

The query "Who is not a prefect?", $\exists x\neg\text{Prefect}(w)$, has no proof in KB. Now there is a "common-sense" notion that the prefects mentioned are the only prefects. Thus Joe is the only prefect and Sam and Peter are not. We would like to add to the KB some "closure axiom",

Example 3.1.1: Let KB consist of the following formulas:

> Graduate(Peter)
> Undergraduate(Sam)
> Prefect(Joe)
> Prefect(x) $\Rightarrow$ Graduate(x) $\vee$ Undergraduate(x)

A, such that:

> KB$\cup\{A\} \vdash \neg$Prefect(Peter)
> and KB$\cup\{A\} \vdash \neg$Prefect(Sam)

Thus, it can be assumed that neither Peter nor Sam are Prefects.

3.2. Intuitive Explanation

Our method for compiling negation is based on the idea of generating an axiom, *ejusdum generis* Clark's IFF-axioms, which "closes off" the KB with respect to a negative query. We illustrate our method by recourse to the above example. We treat the KB as an incomplete description of a subpart of the world and admit the possibility of certain individuals *in the world* but not known *in the KB*. In the above example, this amounts to saying that there are prefects, say "a", "b",...etc. in the world but are NOT KNOWN IN KB. Thus, in the world:

> Prefect(x) $\Rightarrow$ x=joe $\vee$ x=a $\vee$ x=b $\vee$ ....   (A)

Let KB(prefect) be the maximal implicative closure of the set "Prefect" in KB. So the set of individuals "a","b",... etc. (different from "joe") can be written as the set {world$-$KB(prefect)}. Now, we know from the KB formulas that KB(prefect) is the union of the sets Graduate and Undergraduate (in fact KB(prefect)=KB in this example), so we may write {world$-$KB(prefect)} as {world-(Graduate$\cup$Undergraduate)}, or simply as $\neg$(Graduate(x)$\vee$Undergraduate(x)). Axiom (A) thus becomes:

> Prefect(x) $\Rightarrow$ x=joe $\vee$ $\neg$(Graduate(x) $\vee$ Undergraduate(x))
> (B)

It is important to distinguish between the KB formula:

> Prefect(x) $\Rightarrow$ Graduate(x) $\vee$ Undergraduate(x)   (C)

and axiom (B); (C) must be satisfied by all individuals in KB (i.e., it is an integrity constraint of KB). Axiom (B) is an extensional statement about the world. (Another way of saying this is that the domain closure axiom of KB [REIT80], namely, for all constants c1,,,cn in KB:

$$x = c1 \vee x = c2 \vee ....$$

is being replaced by a domain closure axiom about the world.)

It is also important to distinguish between our assumption and that of Clark's in his IFF-completed database. In the above example, Clark's assumption is that "Joe is the only Prefect", that is, he converts:

$$\text{Prefect}(x) \Rightarrow x = \text{joe}$$

to

$$\text{Prefect}(x) \Leftrightarrow x = \text{joe}$$

But, as a consequence of this he is also forced to convert:

$$\text{Prefect}(x) \Rightarrow \text{Graduate}(x) \vee \text{Undergraduate}(x)$$

to

$$\text{Prefect}(x) \Leftrightarrow x = \text{joe} \vee \text{Graduate}(x) \vee \text{Undergraduate}(x)$$

Thus, "all graduates or undergraduates or joe are Prefects". In contrast our assumption (axiom B above) in this example is that the only invidiual known as Prefect in KB is joe.

Finally, notice that our closure axiom (B) has the contrapositive

$$\text{Graduate}(x) \wedge x \neq \text{Joe} \Rightarrow \neg\text{Prefect}(x)$$
$$\text{Undergraduate}(x) \wedge x \neq \text{Joe} \Rightarrow \neg\text{Prefect}(x)$$

which defines how some object can not be a Prefect.

In general, let $\text{CLOSURE}_{\alpha}(\text{KB})$ denote $\text{KB} \cup A$ where A is an axiom which closes off KB with respect to predicate $\alpha \in \text{KB}$. The question is then to give an algorithm for generating such axioms for a given KB and predicate.

3.3. Calculating Maximal Implicative Closures

The calculation of KB(α) can be done in several ways. The method we present here is based upon a particular data structure called the Connection Graph (CG) because previous work reported in [HN84] for the recursion problem in knowledge bases is based upon such a data structure. This affords a unified treatment of these two problems for knowledge bases. An outline of our approach is as follows. We shall represent the KB as a CG. (For the sake of simplicity, in this section, we assume that the entire KB is represented as a CG. In a later section we consider reducing the number of KB formulas that need to be represented in the CG.) Next we define the terms *linked, unlinked* and *partially linked literals.* We shall base the calculation of $KB(\alpha)$ upon these definitions.

A *literal* is a positive or negative atom and a *clause* is a disjunction of literals. It is always possible to convert a set of first-order formulas to clause form [CL73]. A *substitution* σ is a set of variable/constant or variable/variable pairs $\{x_1/c_1, x_2/c_2, ...\}$ such that, for any two variable/constant pairs, no two x_i are the same. (Note that in contrast to usual practice, as in [CL73], we allow variable/variable pairs in a substitution. Such pairs of variables are referred to as alphabetic variants.) If σ is a substitution and L a literal then $L\sigma$ is a literal obtained from L by simultaneously replacing each occurrence of the variables x_i in L by the constant terms c_i; $L\sigma$ is called an instance of L. A substitution σ is said to *unify* two literals L_1 and L_2 if $L_1\sigma = L_2\sigma$. Two or more substitutions are said to be *consistent* if their composition is itself a substitution.

Example 3.3.1: The two literals P(Peter,John,y) and P(w,John,David) are unified by the substitution $\{w/Peter, y/David\}$ whereas P(Peter,John,y) and P(y,John,David) are not unifiable.

Definition: A *Connection Graph* (CG) is a quadruple (N,E,S,P) where:

1.   N is a set of nodes; each nodes represents a literal in KB.

2.   E is a set of edges such that e, connecting the literals L_1 and $\neg L_2$, belongs to E iff L_1 and L_2 are unifiable.

3.   S is a set of substitutions such that $s \in S$ iff s is a unifier for literals L_1, L_2 of some edge in E.

4.   P is a set of clause partitions such that $p \in P$ iff it contains exactly those literals that belong to a clause of KB.

Note that edges exist between unifiable literals of opposite signs, and a partition encloses all and only the literals of a clause in KB. Figure 1 shows the CG corresponding to the KB of example 3.1.1.

A CG is a data structure; researchers have defined different operations on connection graphs. For example, Sickel [SICK76] uses CGs for loop unrolling operations, [HN84] use it for detecting particular kinds of loops, and Chang and Slagle [CS79] use them to derive a set of rewrite rules. In this paper we use them to compute the sets *linked, unlinked* and *partially linked literals.*

Consider a negative query α and a knowledge base KB, and let CG be the connection graph associated with $KB \cup \{\neg\alpha\}$. We distinguish between three kinds of literals in CG.

Partially Linked Literals: Let L and M be literals in CG connected by an edge with substitution σ. Then the instances $L\sigma$ and $M\sigma$ of L and M respectively are partially linked literals.

Linked Literals: Let L be a literal in CG. Then

1. L is linked if it is the negation of the query node; or,
2. L is linked if it is an instance of a linked literal; or,
3. If $L\sigma$ is a partially linked literal where σ is a substitution along an edge attached to L, and $L\sigma = L$ up to alphabetic variance (recall that we allow variable/variable pairs in the unifying substitutions) then L is a linked literal.

Unlinked Literals: A literal is unlinked if it has no edge attached to it in CG.

Example 3.3.2: In the CG of Figure 1, the literal Prefect(w) in partition P1 corresponds to the negation of the query literal, and Prefect(Joe) in partition P3 is an instance of it. Hence both of these are linked literals. ¬Prefect(x) in partition P2 is partially linked literal, and because of the substitution {x/w} it is a linked literal. All remaining literals in Figure 1 are unlinked. The final sets look as follows:

Partially linked set = {}; Linked = {1,2,7}; unlinked = {3,4,5,6}.

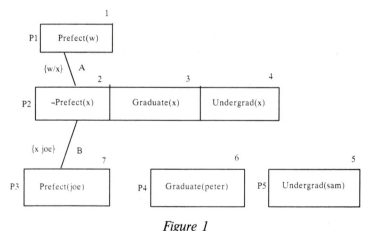

Figure 1

Example 3.3.3: Consider the CG of Figure 2. Node 1 is in the linked literal set because 1 is the negation of the query literal. {2,3,4,5,6,8,9,11,13} is the partially linked set. All of these, except node 2, are moved to the linked literal set because of the substitutions along the edges B, C, D and E. This leaves 7 and 12 unlinked.

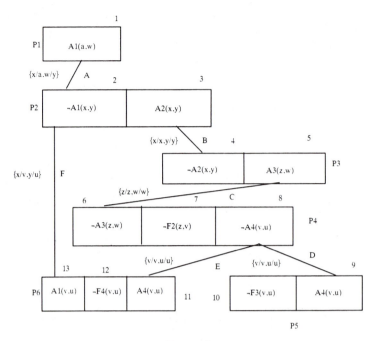

Figure 2

Example 3.3.4: Consider the CG of Figure 3. The linked literal set starts out with {1}. The partially linked literals are {2,3,4,5,6,7,8,9,10,11}. Because of the substitutions along edges B and C, nodes 2, 3, 7 and 8 are moved to the linked literal set. Note that {4,5,6,9,10,11} remain partially linked.

Intuitively, the linked literal set corresponds to the maximal implicative closure of α i.e., $KB(\alpha)$. Roughly speaking, the unlinked and partially linked sets correspond to the set {world$-KB(\alpha)$}. In fact we only need to consider the positive literals in the partially linked and unlinked sets, and only the most general instances of these positive literals at that too. Let us define this as the set UNREACHABLE$_\alpha$(KB).

Definition: Let KB be represented as a CG. Then the relation UNREACHABLE$_\alpha$(KB) consists of the general instances of all those literals in CG that are positive and belong to the unlinked or partially linked sets.

$$\text{UNREACHABLE}_\alpha(\text{KB}) = \{ \beta \mid \beta \in \text{CG}$$
$$\beta \text{ is positive}$$
$$\beta \text{ is unlinked or partially linked}$$
$$\beta \text{ is not an instance of the query literal or}$$

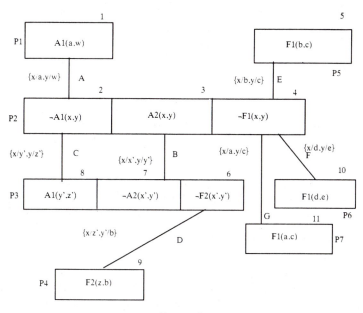

Figure 3

of any other literal in this set} □

Let UNREACHABLE-CL$_\alpha$(KB) denote the disjunction formed by the elements of UNREACHABLE$_\alpha$(KB).

Example 3.3.5: In the CG of Figure 1, the literals Graduate(x), Undergraduate(x), Graduate(Peter), and Undergraduate(Sam) are in the unlinked set. Graduate(Peter) and Undergraduate(Sam) are instances of Graduate(x) and Undergraduate(x) respectively. Thus

UNREACHABLE$_{Prefect(x)}$(KB) = {Graduate(x),Undergraduate(x)}
UNREACHABLE-CL$_{Prefect(x)}$(KB) = Graduate(x) ∨ Undergraduate(x) □

The relation UNREACHABLE$_\alpha$(KB) helps us in constructing a part of the closure axiom. The remaining part will be derived by defining a new relation INSTANCES$_\alpha$(KB) on KB. If the query is $\alpha(x)$ then INSTANCES$_\alpha$(KB) is the set of constants satisfying KB$\vdash\alpha(x)$.

INSTANCES$_\alpha$(KB) = {$\vec{\beta}$ | KB $\vdash$ $\alpha(\vec{\beta})$,
$\qquad\qquad\qquad\vec{\beta}$ is a tuple of constants}

Example 3.3.6: In the KB of example 3.1.1

INSTANCES$_{Prefect(x)}$(KB) = {Joe}

3.4. Algorithm for Generating CLOSURE$_\alpha$(KB)

The algorithm for generating an axiom to close a KB for a given negative query $\alpha(\vec{x})$ is as follows:

- Negate the query literal and add to KB. This gives $KB \cup \{\neg\alpha(\vec{x})\}$. Generate the CG for $KB \cup \{\neg\alpha(\vec{x})\}$,
- Compute the relation UNREACHABLE$_\alpha$(KB),
- Generate the clause UNREACHABLE-CL$_\alpha$(KB),
- Compute INSTANCES$_\alpha$(KB) = $\{\vec{c1},...,\vec{cn}\}$, say,
- The closure axiom is

$$\alpha(\vec{x}) \Rightarrow \vec{x} = \vec{c1} v...v\vec{x} = \vec{cn} v \neg (\text{UNREACHABLE-CL}_\alpha(\text{KB})$$

Example 3.4.1: We return to the KB of Example 3.1.1.

INSTANCES$_{\text{Prefect}}$(KB) = $\{\text{Joe}\}$
UNREACHABLE-CL$_{\text{Prefect}}$(KB) = Graduate(x) $\vee$ Undergraduate(x)
Thus, the axiom to close the KB w.r.t. the query $\neg$Prefect(x) is
Prefect(x) $\Rightarrow$ x=joev$\neg$(Graduate(x) $\vee$ Undergraduate(x))

Example 3.4.2: Here is a more complete example. The KB is

Child(Terry)
Person(David)
Martian(Goob)
Man(x) $\vee$ Woman(x) $\Rightarrow$ Person(x)
Child(x) $\Rightarrow$ Man(x) $\vee$ Woman(x)

The query, α, is $\exists x \neg$Child(x). The CG for $KB \cup \{\neg\alpha\}$ is shown in Figure 5.

INSTANCES$_{\text{Child}}$(KB) = $\{\text{Terry}\}$
UNREACHABLE$_{\text{Child}}$(KB) = $\{\text{Person}(x), \text{Martian}(x)\}$
Thus, the axiom to close the KB w.r.t. the query is
Child(x) $\Rightarrow$ x=terryv$\neg$(Person(x)vMartian(x))

4. The Negation as Failure Rule and Unsafe Negative Queries

The problem of negation in knowledge bases is that, in many applications, the amount of negative information is far in excess of the positive information. As we have discussed the usual solution to this problem is to only represent what is positively known to be true thus reducing the amount of storage needed. Queries concerning negative information are then handled under the "negation as failure" rule, namely, that failure to prove (or retrieve) a certain fact can be construed as license to assume the negation of that fact. As has already been shown the negation as failure rule can not be used in non-Horn knowledge bases. But even when the KB is Horn some queries are not answerable by the negation as failure rule as the following example shows. Let KB contain the following set of Horn formulas:

> Person (Joe)
> Graduate (Peter)
> $\forall x$ [Person (x) $\Rightarrow$ Graduate (x)]

We can ask closed queries of the form "¬Person (Peter)" which under the "negation as failure" rule returns "yes" because we fail to prove Person (Peter). However, the query "$\exists x \neg$Person (x)" under the negation as failure rule does not provide a constructive proof in which such an x can be found. (This query belongs to the class of unsafe queries defined in [ULLM83].) The recommended way to state the above query is to form the relative complement, which in this example is:

> A: $\exists x$ [Graduate (x) $\land \neg$Person (x)]

returning "Peter" as an answer. So we find that the negation as failure rule is satisfactory for a ground query. But when the query is open we must distinguish between the two forms:

> (B): $\neg\exists x P(x)$ and
> (C): $\exists x \neg P(x)$.

If it is the latter form that is required then it must be stated in relative complement form. The disadvantage of this is it requires the user to know the other entities that exist in the application domain i.e., relative complements are procedural expressions in that the user has to tell the system how to proceed in finding a solution. This is contrary to the non-procedural nature of relational calculus. For example, in the above case, we had to know about "Graduate" before we could re-state the query in relative complement form. In situations where the application domain may contain a large number of entities this information may by itself be quite prohibitive.

A side benefit of our closure axioms is that they yield the relative complement forms corresponding to queries of the form (C) above. For example, for the above KB, our method generates the closure axiom:

$$\text{D: Person}(x) \Rightarrow x = \text{Joe} \lor \neg \text{Graduate}(x)$$

whose contrapositive is:

$$\text{D': Graduate}(x) \land x \neq \text{Joe} \Rightarrow \neg \text{Person}(x)$$

Note that the antecedent of D' is equivalent to the relative complement of "$\exists x \neg \text{Person}(x)$". This topic is pursued in more detail in Naqvi [NAQV85b].

To summarize, unsafe relational calculus queries involving the negation operator present a problem to database query evaluation methods in that the negation by failure rule can not be used to solve them. The suggested method is to restate them in relative complement form. Our method can be used to generate a closure axiom that yields these relative forms automatically.

5. Data Intensive Knowledge Base

In this section we discuss issues connected with implementing the ideas discussed so far. In particular note that the complexity of calculating $\text{UNREACHABLE}_\alpha(\text{KB})$ is $O(E)$ where E is the transitive closure of edges from the clause partition enclosing α. Now if the knowledge base contains a large set of formulas then the corresponding CG will be enormous and the cost of running the UNREACHABLE algorithm may become infeasible. One manner in which the knowledge base may be large is if it contains a large number of distinct facts. Examples of such domains are genealogical databases, weather information, topological maps, financial profiles, etc, and are called data intensive domains.

Our solution to this problem involves defining a process, called *folding*, which replaces ground unit formulas by their most general instances. Thus, several instances of "parent(a,b), parent(b,c),..." can be replaced by one formula parent(x,y). The idea here is that we can hold the ground units in some separate system (a relational database for instance) and request specific facts from it if and when needed in the proof/query evaluation process. We can build the CG based only upon these general instances and the nonground and non-unit formulas of the KB. This reduces the number of nodes in the CG. But this forces us to add a modification to the definition of partially linked literal sets. The modification is: *A folded literal and the literal connected to it (by an edge), is put into the partially linked literal set only.*

Example 6.2.1: Consider the CG of Figure 3; fold the ground units F1(a,c), F1(b,c) and F1(d,e) into F1$(z1,z2)$, and the ground unit F2(z,b) into F2$(z3,z4)$. The new CG is shown in Figure 4. Recall that in example 3.3.4 (Figure 3) the set of partially linked literals was {4,5,6,9,10,11}. In Figure 4 the nodes 5, 10, and 11 have been folded into 5' and node 9 has been folded into 9'. In Figure 4 the partially linked literal set is {4,5',6,9'}. Hence the UNREACHABLE sets for these two figures will be the same after specific instances of literals have been eliminated.

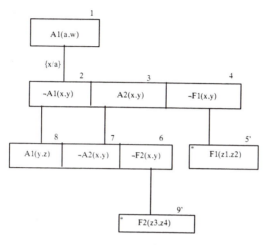

Figure 4

Note: * denotes folded literals; variable/variable pairs in substitutions are not shown.

We have thus succeeded in reducing the size of the CG for data intensive knowledge bases by folding the unit formulas into their general instances. The relational database analog is that we have represented only the schema and not the contents of the database.

5.1. Relational Databases as Components of a KB

Reiter [REIT78a,REIT78b] has presented arguments that a KB composed of a set of closed formulas can be viewed as having two components, the *extensional part*, which contains all the ground unit formulas and the *intensional part* which contains all the nonground or the non-unit formulas of KB. In such a setting it is argued that the extensional component can be realised by the relational model of data. The scheme works as follows. The intensional component (IC) contains all the nonground and non-unit formulas. Furthermore, it contains the general instances corresponding to the unit formulas in KB, called schema literals. Schema literals are the direct analogue of the relation

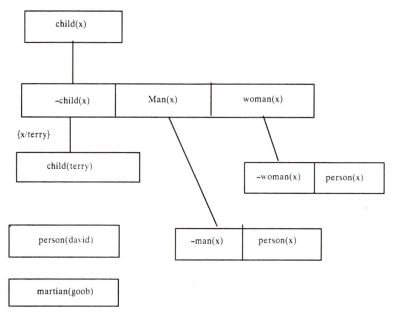

Figure 5

Note: variable/variable pairs in substitutions are now shown.

schemes of the relational model of data. Query processing in such a system proceeds by reducing a query through interactions with the formulas in IC until it can be expressed in terms of the schema literals entirely. This new form of the query is sent to another component, called the Extensional Component (EC) which translates it into a request for specific ground instances that satisfy the original request. For example, we may have the following situation [REIT78a]:

Intensional Component:
$$(\forall x,y,z) \ [\text{Enrolled}(x,y) \wedge \text{Teaches}(z,y)$$
$$\Rightarrow \text{Teacher-of}(x,z)]$$

Schema Literals:
relation:Enrolled(Student,Course)
relation:Teaches(Teacher,Course)

The query "Teacher-of(John,x)" can then be translated into the expression "Enrolled(John,x) & Teaches(z,x)" which because it is composed entirely of schema literals can be considered a primitive expression. If we assume that the extensional component is implemented as a relational database then the above primitive expression is equivalent to a join expression over the two relations Enrolled and Teaches.

In a previous paper Henschen and this author [HN84] have shown how recursive queries can be answered in knowledge bases which have an intensional component and an extensional component implemented as a relational database. The method is based upon constructing a connection graph over the formulas in the intensional component and the schema literals of the extensional component.

Our scheme for a Knowledge Base Management System is based on these ideas. We propose that the KBMS have an IC which carries out general inferencing to answer queries whereas the EC be implemented as a relational database. Readers will have noticed that the schema literals of the above approach correspond exactly to the case where we collapse the KB by folding all ground unit formulas into general instances. The CG is constructed over the formulas in the intensional component and the collapsed extensional component. Requests for ground instances are collected as shown in [HN84] and [REIT78a]. At suitable junctures these are sent off to the relational database implementing the EC. We see thus that data intensive knowledge bases do not present any practical problems to using our approach either for making assumptions in an incomplete KB or for dealing with negative information.

What is particularly appealing about this whole process is that the approach to handling recursive queries based upon the CG data structure can be used for the purposes of this paper also. So the present framework builds upon our previous work. In particular it should now be possible to build systems that can answer recursive and negative queries all based upon a common data structure and formalism.

6. System Architecture for Knowledge Based Management Systems

In recent years there has been a flurry of interest in merging KBMS and DBMS technologies. We recognise that these technologies supplement each other in certain ways, viz., DBMS is useful for efficient storage and retrieval of large amounts of simple data but its functionality is limited. On the other hand KBMS does more with the information at hand —the information is more complex— but gets into performance problems when the amount of information becomes large.

We propose the following system architecture, shown in Figure 6, for building a system that combines the strengths and supplements the weaknesses of the KBMS and DBMS areas. The Reasoning Engine contains the inferencing and search routines. It operates over a KB which has two components, the Intensional Component (IC) and the

Extensional Component (EC). IC contains the nonground or the nonatomic formulas of KB and, in our case, will be implemented as a set of Connection Graph data structures. EC contains the ground atomic formulas and may be implemented as a relational database system. What is important is that there be an interface between IC and EC which translates the requests of IC to retrieval requests which can be sent to EC. Notice that in this case EC (or the database system that implements it) is viewed as a fact management system —a view shared and proposed by Brachman and Levesque (see their chapter in the current volume).

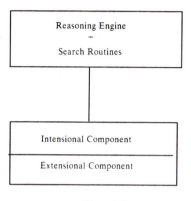

Figure 6

To reiterate, what makes this architecture appealing is that the results shown herein and in previous work combine to allow us to answer recursive and negative queries, all implemented in the same system architecture and over the same set of data structures.

7. Summary

We started this chapter by noting a need for a KB to avoid storing negative information explicitly. We showed an approach that can be used to answer negative queries in knowledge bases which store positive information only. It was also shown that for data intensive applications we can essentially work with a schema description of the domain. This sharply reduces the size of our internal data structures and plays an important part in making our proposal practical.

Finally we discussed an important and pleasing result which shows that the data structures and formalism required for the the proposal of this chapter is the same as that of previous work of Henschen and the author on answering recursive queries in knowledge based systems. This means that a coherent and unified approach exists for building powerful knowledge based systems in data intensive applications.

8. References

[AE82] [AU79] [BMS83] [CL73] [CLAR78] [CODD79] [CS79] [GM78]   [GMN81]   [GMN84]   [HN84]   [KOWA78]   [LEVE83] [MINK82] [NAQV85a] [NAQV85b] [REIT78a] [REIT78b] [REIT80] [SICK76] [ULLM83] [VK76] [YH85]

14
An Approach To Processing Queries In A Logic-Based Query Language[1]

Jeffrey D. Ullman[2]

ABSTRACT *We summarize the "capture rule" approach to planning queries in a rule-oriented database management system. Selecting from among strategies for the application of logical rules to data may be viewed as an advanced form of query optimization. Capture rules provide a framework within which a system can make such decisions. They also assist in the development of a theory of optimal strategies for logic processing. This paper surveys some of the known capture rules and suggests how they can be fit together into a system that provides "knowledge processing" with database management.*

1. Introductory Concepts

The history of database management systems can be summarized briefly as follows.[3] The first systems to provide general facilities for efficient access to massive amounts of data were "network" or "hierarchical" systems that allowed the user to write programs in a fairly low level language, such as the Codasyl Data Manipulation Language or IMS's DL/I. These languages required the user to express not only what question he wanted the system to answer, but also how that answer was to be obtained. The relational model of [CODD70] was in

---

[1] Work supported by NSF grant IST-84-12971 and a grant of IBM Corp.

[2] Stanford University

[3] See [ULLM82] for a description of the languages and systems mentioned in the following text.

a sense a great advance, because it allowed the user to specify his query without saying how the query was to be answered. Yet the relational model was not an instant success. Rather, it took roughly ten years for the query optimization problems to be solved; without solving these problems, relational database systems would be decisively less efficient than the earlier systems.

At roughly the same time as the relational model was being exploited, systems were being designed to provide a level of expression significantly greater than the relational calculus (first-order logic interpreted for relations), which is provided, in one form or another, by all the database systems just mentioned. These systems, such as Planner [SWC70], Prolog [KOWA74], and MRS [GENE83], allowed the user a more powerful query language; at the least they allow collections of Horn clauses to help define queries.

On the other hand, each of these languages requires the user to express the way in which queries are to be evaluated. Prolog uses a limited form of rule processing — top-down evaluation with backtracking. Prolog also gives significance to the order in which rules and the subgoals of rule bodies appear in the program listing, which has a powerful impact on the way the rules of an individual program are processed. The other systems mentioned give the user both the capability of, and responsibility for, choosing a query evaluation strategy, by providing a metalanguage for talking about the rules themselves. Thus, these systems are in a sense analogous to the network and hierarchical systems of two decades ago, and we need to consider how the square of Figure 1 can be completed, that is, how are we to provide efficient query processing in an advanced, rule-based data manipulation system.

Horn-clause systems	Prolog Planner, MRS	???
Database systems	Network, Hierarchical	Relational systems
	User provides navigation	System provides navigation

Figure 1: Relationships between different systems

There are a number of functions of existing database systems for which logical rules are *de facto* in use, typically through the use of the query language itself or a similar language. These include:

1.   Definition of views (e.g., [TODD76])

2.   Security (e.g., [STON75])

3.   Integrity checking (e.g., [SW74])

4.   Integration of several databases (e.g., [LITW84])

The use of logical rules for accessing a database system was proposed many years ago in such works as [GM78]. The emphasis in the "logic and databases" school was on Horn-clause logic without function symbols. Even this restricted form of logic provides the functions enumerated above and other things not provided in relational algebra, such as computation of transitive closures. The following example illustrates some of the capabilities of this form of logic. We assume the reader is familiar with Prolog notation, and we use it throughout.

Example 1: Suppose we have a database with relations

EDS(Emp,Salary,Dept)
DM(Dept,Mgr)

We might wish to secure the high salaries by allowing access only to a relation *SecureESD*, in which salaries bigger than \$100,000 are replaced by 0. The following two rules define such a relation.

SecureESD(e,s,d) :- *ESD(e,s,d)*, $s \leqslant 100{,}000$
SecureESD(e,0,d) :- *ESD(e,s,d)*, $s > 100{,}000$

Here, :- is used to mean "if", as in Prolog.

We might also wish to define a view in which employees, their salaries, and their managers (i.e., the manager(s) of the department(s) they work for) are shown. This view is formed by taking the natural join of *ESD* and *DM*, and projecting out the department; the operation can be expressed logically as:

ViewESM(e,s,m) :- *SecureESD(e,s,d)*, *DM(d,m)*

A typical query is *ViewESM(e,s,* "Jones") (i.e., print all the employees that work for Jones, and their salaries). □

1.1. The Language Model

Unlike the "logic-and-databases" approach, we shall not restrict ourselves to function-free formulas. True, much of the use of rules may be of the "database-ish" style just mentioned. However, there is an indication that the demand exists for the full computational power of a Turing machine in front of the database system. [WARR81] discusses the use of Prolog as such a front end, and indeed, most database systems allow queries to be embedded in a general-purpose language.

To provide the power of a Turing machine, one needs not only recursive Horn clauses; one needs function symbols in terms. In our examples, we shall use only the structure-forming function "cons", as in Lisp or Prolog, which we write with an infix "|". There is no loss of generality in so doing, because any function application can be simulated by "consing" a constant function name to the list of its arguments.

The reader should realize that with the addition of both recursion and function symbols to a query language, essentially all optimization problems become undecidable. We do not want to appear cavalier about this matter. In practice, we expect that one can get a lot of mileage from a few simple optimization strategies. However, we shall not even be able to decide whether any known method suffices to answer a given query, so in the final analysis we may have either to restrict the query language significantly or to inform the user occasionally that his query cannot be answered by our system.

1.2. Rule/Goal Trees

The meaning of a query in this environment is defined by a tree whose nodes correspond to the rules and the predicate symbols, which we call *goals.* A rule node in this tree is indicated by the head of the rule and the Prolog :- symbol. Its children are goal nodes corresponding to the terms in the body of the rule. The parent of a rule node is a goal node with the same predicate symbol as the head of the rule. The rule head is unified with the goal at the parent node, and the necessary substitution applies to the children of the rule node as well. Thus, the scope of any variable appearing in a rule/goal tree is a rule node and its goal children, and no more.

With each node we associate a relation. For goal nodes, the relation has components (attributes) corresponding to the variables appearing in that goal, and for a rule node, the relation is over the variables appearing in the rule head. If a goal is a database relation, we compute its relation by lookup. Other goals have their relation computed by translating the relations for each rule child and taking the union of the results. This translation involves a tuple-at-a-time calculation in which variables are translated by any substitution required by the unification between the rule head and the goal. We shall not give the details of this translation (see [ULLM85]), but the reader should be able to verify that whatever needs to be done can be done to each tuple independently.

To form the relation of a rule node, we take the natural join of the relations for its goal children.

Example 2: Consider the following rules, after [NAIS83], for merging two lists.

r_1: $M([],x,x)$:—
r_2: $M(x,[],x)$:—
r_3: $M(a \mid x, b \mid y, a \mid z)$:— $a \leqslant b, M(x, b \mid y, z)$
r_4: $M(a \mid x, b \mid y, b \mid z)$:— $a > b, M(a \mid x, y, z)$

The third argument is intended to be the merge of the two sorted lists in arguments one and two. The first two rules state that if one list is empty, the merger is the other list. Rule r_3 says that if the head of the first list preceeds the head of the second, then the merger can be formed by removing the head of the first list, merging what remains, and prepending the removed element to the result, z, r_4 makes a similar statement about the case where the second head precedes the first.

Suppose we ask the query $M(u,v,123)$ i.e., what are all the pairs of lists (u,v) whose merger is the list 123.[4] In Figure 2 is part of the rule/goal tree for this query.

Note that after two more levels of rule nodes, r_3 and r_4 will fail to unify with goals that have an empty third argument, and the tree will terminate. Suppose that we have computed the relation for $M(x, b \mid y, 23)$. It is not hard to see that the four rules together generate all pairs of lists that merge to form the list 23, that is, the relation:

---

[4] We shall use $a_1 \cdots a_n$ for a list whose i^{th} element is a_i. This shorthand leaves open whether a stands for the element a or the list of one element a, but we trust the meaning will be clear from context.

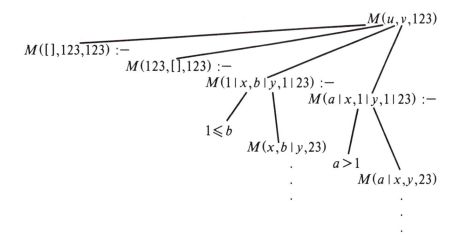

Figure 2: Part of rule/goal tree for merge example

[]	23
2	3
3	2
23	[]

However, the last of these cannot be translated into the variables of the goal $M(x,b\,|\,y,23)$, because the empty list cannot unify with $b\,|\,y$. Thus, the following relation is the one associated with this goal node:

b	x	y
2	[]	3
3	2	[]
2	3	[]

To compute the relation of the rule node $M(1\,|\,x,b\,|\,y,1\,|\,23)$:- we must join this relation with the relation associated with the goal node 1 $\leqslant b$. This sort of goal is a special case, since in principle its relation is the set of all b's $\geqslant 1$. In practice, we must represent such a relation by its defining predicate, and the join with such a relation becomes a selection. (See [ULLM85] for more details.) Since each of the b-values in the relation above exceeds 1, the selection does not change the relation. Thus, the rule node $M(1\,|\,x,b\,|\,y,23)$:- has the same relation as above.

Similarly, the goal node $M(a\,|\,x,y,23)$ contributes the relation:

a	x	y
2	3	[]
3	[]	2
2	[]	3

to the rule node $M(a\mid x,1\mid y,23) :-$.

When we consider the children of the root goal $M(u,v,123)$, and how this goal unifies with each of its four rule children, we find that the first rule contributes the (u,v)-pair $([],123)$ and the second contributes $(123,[])$. Note that r_1 and r_2 have no free variables, so there relations, technically, are each $\{\epsilon\}$ the relation with only the empty tuple. The contributions to the relation of the root node come from the unification of the root with its first two children.

The contribution of the rule node $M(1\mid x,b\mid y,1\mid 23)$ is calculated by considering each tuple in its relation, say (b,x,y). For each such tuple, the corresponding value of u is $1\mid x$, while $v=b\mid y$. Thus, this relation contributes the pairs $\{(1, 23), (12, 3), (13, 2)\}$. The remaining three possibilities are contributed by the fourth rule. $\square$

The reader may have observed that rule/goal trees are not necessarily finite. For example, if we had begun Example 2 with the goal $M(u,v,w)$, there would be no bound argument to force convergence, and the tree would in principle be infinite. In this case, the query asks for the infinite number of triples of lists such that the third is the merger of the first two.

Note that the operations used to construct relations — join, union, and tuple-at-a-time operations — are all monotone; if you add tuples to their operands, the result is not diminished. Thus, we can formally define the meaning of a query with an infinite rule/goal tree as the limit, as $n\to\infty$, of the result of considering only the top n levels of the tree.

1.3. Rule/Goal Graphs

In order to plan query-evaluation strategies we shall compress the nodes of all possible rule/goal trees into a finite number of classes. We distinguish one rule from another, and we distinguish one predicate symbol from another. Because, as we saw above, it is often significant whether or not an argument or variable is bound or free, we shall also distinguish nodes in that manner. But all other distinctions are merged, and we plan our query evaluation on a graph whose nodes represent either

1. A goal (i.e., predicate symbol) A with an *adornment* (superscript) indicating which of its arguments are bound and which are free. For example, A^{bff} represents an instance like $A(1,a \mid x,y)$, where the first argument is bound and the second and third free.

2. A rule with an adornment indicating which of its variables are bound and which are free. Conventionally, we list the bound/free information for variables in lexicographic order. For example, if a and z were bound in rule r_3 of Example 2, we would represent this situation by node r_3^{bfffb}.

Note that for technical reasons, we have switched our viewpoint from that of the rule/goal trees just described. The relation of a goal node has components corresponding to the arguments of the goal, not the variables. The change is necessary because we cannot be sure of the context in which we shall require the relation of the goal, and so we must standardize its format. It is straightforward to switch between the viewpoint of variables of rules and arguments of goals, but we should not ignore the difference.

In the basic rule/goal graph, we draw certain arcs.[5] Let A^q be a goal node. Then for each rule r with head A, there is a rule node labeled, r^p for some adornment p, that is a predecessor of A^q. The bound free information embodied in p and q must "make sense," in the following way. Adornment q makes certain arguments of A bound. Certain variables of r appear in these arguments, and all these variables are bound according to p. No other variable is bound in p.

For each rule node r^q there will be certain goal node predecessors; each atom A appearing in the body of r yields a predecessor A^q for some adornment p. Again, the adornments must make sense. In q certain variables of r are indicated to be bound. If some argument of A is formed from only those variables and/or constants, then that argument is bound according to p. Other arguments of A are not bound.

Example 3: In Figure 2 we see part of the rule/goal graph for the rules of Example 2; this part of the graph centers around the goal M^{ffb} (i.e., a query like that of Example 2 where the third argument is bound and the others free). To see why the adornments were chosen for the r_3 and r_4 nodes, note that in r_3, binding the third argument of M in the head provides bindings for variables a and z, but not for b, x, or y. Thus the proper adornment for the r_3-predecessor of M^{ffb} is r_3^{bfffb}. Similarly, in r_4, binding the third argument of M in the head binds b and z, but no other variable.

---

[5] Technically, the arcs are not fixed, and for different evaluation strategies we may prefer a different set of arcs.

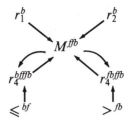

Figure 3: Part of rule/goal graph for merge example

Now consider the predecessors of node r_3^{bfffb}. Binding a and z provides a binding for the first argument of the predicate $\leqslant$, which is why we see the predecessor $\leqslant^{bf}$. It also provides a binding for the third argument of the occurrence of M in the body, which argument is z itself. However, the first and second arguments each contain free variables, so the proper adornment for the M-predecessor of r_3^{bfffb} is M^{ffb}.
□

2. Capture Rules

The general idea is to plan queries by playing a "pebbling game" on the nodes of the rule/goal graph. We "capture" a node when we know an algorithm to compute the relation corresponding to that node. This approach will be particularly effective if, as we intuitively expect, the rule/goal graph divides into many small strongly-connected components, so we can "pebble" up the acyclic graph formed from the strong components.

Each capture rule corresponds to an algorithm for computing relations; of course we only use a capture rule if the corresponding relation-computing algorithm is known to work for the node or nodes captured. A *capture rule* consists of the following parts.

1. A description of a set of nodes of the rule/goal graph that may be captured

2. A description of another set of nodes in the rule/goal graph that *support the capture*

3. Conditions on the rules corresponding to rule nodes in the captured and/or supporting sets

To apply a capture rule, we check that the conditions of (3) are met, the supporting and capturable sets meet the descriptions of (1) and (2), and that the supporting set is already captured.

Example 4: The simplest capture rules are the *basic rules* from

[ULLM85]. These rules state that:

a)   Any goal node that is a database predicate can be captured, regardless of adornment.

b)   Any rule node with an empty right side (body) can be captured with any adornment.

c)   Any node whose predecessors have all been captured can be captured.

For example, in (b), the description of the captured set is that it be a single rule node. The supporting set is empty. The condition on the rules involved is that they (really "it", since there can be only one) have an empty body.[6] □

2.1. Capture-Rule Based Systems

The motivation for thinking about capture rules is that we can plan queries thereby. A query corresponds to a goal node in the rule/goal graph that must be captured. We start by applying the simplest capture rules (e.g., the basic rules). With luck, we may capture the query node. If not, we use a more expensive capture rule, taking advantage of the nodes we already know are captured to support more captures. We proceed in this manner until we have used all capture rules available to the system, or at some point the query node is captured. In the latter case, we apply the relation-calculating methods implicit in the capture rules, and in the former case we must report that the system cannot deal with the query.

In order for the above scenario to work, there are a number of conditions on the capture rules that must be met. These are:

1.   *Efficient Test.* We must be able to determine efficiently whether or not a capture rule applies to a given set of nodes. The general notion of "efficient" is that it takes time that is only polynomial in the size of the rule/goal graph to find all applications of a given capture rule. Sometimes we are faced with a rule that can be applied in time that is the product of a polynomial in the number of nodes of the graph times an exponential in the maximum number of arguments in any goal. We call such an algorithm *semipolynomial.* Often, we are content with a semipolynomial algorithm, because the arity of predicates tends not to be large, even if the number of rules is in the thousands.[7]

---

[6] Notice that the adornments are irrelevant for the basic capture rules. It is only when we use capture rules for recursive predicates that the bound/free dichotomy is important; however, as we shall see in Section 3, it is vital in these situations.

[7] Another reason for hoping that the arity of predicates is small is that the size of

2.   *Independence.* The application of a capture rule naturally depends on what nodes have already been captured. However, we must design our capture rules so they do not depend on the rules used to capture the nodes that support a new capture, or else we could not work in passes, applying cheapest capture rules first.

3.   *Substantiation.* When we apply a capture rule, we must know that it is "substantiated," in the sense that there is an underlying way to compute the relations corresponding to the captured nodes. The algorithm used to compute these relations:

    a)   Takes as input only the bindings for the bound arguments and/or variables that the adornments of the captured nodes indicate must exist, The bindings for any one node in the set being captured must be sufficient to compute the bindings for all other members of the set,

    b)   May call only upon routines that compute relations for the nodes that support the capture; these routines are passed whatever bindings they require, and the bindings must be computed by the algorithm in question,

    c)   Must be correct, in the sense given by the rule/goal tree discussion of Section 1.

2.2. Top-Down Systems

While we have assumed in the above description of a system that we progress "bottom-up" on the rule/goal graph (i.e., proceeding from what we know we can capture to what node we wish to capture), we could also consider a "top-down" system. Such a system would start from the query node and explore ways such a node could be captured. In a top-down system, the same three conditions for good capture rules — efficiency, independence, and substantiation — would have to be met.

2.3. Some Capture Rules

In addition to the basic rules, the following kinds of rules have been considered.

1.   *Top-Down Rules.* These are rules that use a top-down substantiation (i.e., like Prolog). We shall cover some of these ideas in

---

the rule/goal graph is semipolynomial in the size of the rules. Thus, even a test that is fully polynomial in the graph size is only semipolynomial in the rule size.

detail in a separate section.

2. *Sideways Rules.* Here, bindings can be passed among sibling goals in one rule body. For example, suppose we have the rule:

$$r: A(x,y) :- B(x,z), C(z,y)$$

and we wish to capture A^{bb}. According to the basic rules, we must capture r^{bbf}, which requires us to capture B^{bf}. However, if we capture B^{bf}, we can, by definition, compute a finite set of values of z, which can be passed one at a time to a hypothetical algorithm that substantiates only the capture of C^{bb}. Similarly, we could pass the binding(s) of z from C to B and capture A^{bb} given only that C^{fb} and B^{bb} were captured. More details regarding sideways rules can be found in [ULLM85].

3. *Bottom-Up Rules.* These rules are substantiated by an algorithm that constructs all facts derivable by a set of rules from relations corresponding to some already-captured nodes. Unlike the situation where there are no function symbols, this construction is not guaranteed to converge. However, simple and easily testable syntactic conditions on the rules assure us that values not appearing in the initial relations never appear in the constructed relations. Details of the capture rule and algorithm are found in [ULLM85].

4. *Henschen-Naqvi Rules.* In [HN84] there was a suggestion for dealing with logic programs with no function symbols. While couched in general terms, the method seems most effective for "linear" rules [BANC85] (i.e., there is at most one recursive predicate in the body of any rule). In fact, the real advantage is probably limited to what Bancilhon calls the "same generation problem," finding cousins of a given individual at the same generation. This problem can be expressed by the rules:

$$SG(x,x) :-$$
$$SG(x,y) :- PAR(x,x1), PAR(y,y1), SG(x1,y1)$$

If x is instantiated, (i.e., we want to capture SG^{bf}), Henschen and Naqvi's method generates all ancestors of x, associating a generation with each.[8] Then, they work from each ancestor down the appropriate number of generations to get cousins of x.

There are a number of other ways to handle this type of rule, and depending on the subtleties of the occurrences of variables in the subgoals, and depending on the assumption of acyclicity of the underlying data, one or another algorithm for computing relations may be best. The question of capture rules to handle logical rules

---

[8] The presumption is made that the parenthood relation is acyclic.

in this general class is investigated by [NAUG85].

3. Top-Down Capture Rules

The family of top-down capture rules is very important because of the way they mimic Prolog processing. This section surveys some of the ideas in this area that have appeared in the literature.

3.1. Naish's Capture Rule

In [NAIS83] there is an idea for reordering subgoals in the rules of a Prolog program; we can view this idea as a capture rule whose substantiation is top-down evaluation of the rules involved (i.e., "backward chaining"), in the fashion of Prolog but with an appropriate order to subgoals and sideways information passing. His idea, when presented with a collection of recursive rules like the merge rules of Example 2, is to find a set of arguments of a recursive predicate, M in this case, such that each time around a cycle containing this predicate, one or more of the arguments in this set is guaranteed to be strictly smaller, and the others remain the same.

For example, one such set for the rules of Example 2 is the third argument by itself. Each recursive call, whether by rule r_3 or r_4, results in z being replaced by its own tail. A more interesting example is that the set consisting of the first and second argument also has Naish's property, since r_3 decreases the first argument and r_4 decreases the second.

To enunciate a capture rule based on this idea, we must insist that the arguments in the decreasing set are bound; top-down recursion will simply not work if these arguments are free variables. Note that this is one of the key places where distinction between bound and free adornments on nodes of the rule/goal graph must be made. In our terms, Naish's capture rule may be stated as follows. We may capture a set of nodes S provided:

1. Every predecessor of a node in S is either in S or has already been captured.

2. For each goal node G in S there is a set $A(G)$ of arguments of G with the following properties:

   a) All arguments in $A(G)$ are indicated bound by the adornment of G,

   b) In any cycle from G to itself staying within S, one or more of the arguments in $A(G)$ becomes shorter and the others are unchanged.

The substantiation for such a rule is that we can expand any goal in the set S top-down, knowing that eventually one of the arguments in the decreasing set for that goal will reach size zero. At this point, further recursion is impossible, because negative-sized values do not exist.

Example 5: Consider Figure 3, which is a part of the rule/goal graph for the rules of Example 2; these nodes center around M^{bbf} (i.e., the normal situation where we are asked to compute the merger of two lists). The set S is indicated, and it is easy to check that if we let $A(M)$ be $\{1,2\}$ (i.e., the first two arguments), then all conditions for the capture rule are satisfied. This conclusion makes sense, because if we treat the rules of Example 2 as a Prolog program, with an initial goal that instantiates the first two arguments, the program does in fact converge.

Similarly, we can capture the nodes M^{ffb}, r_3^{bffb}, and r_4^{fbffb} of Figure 2, provided we use a sideways information passing rule to bind a and b before they are passed to the predicates $\leqslant$ and $<$. That is, we must replace $\leqslant^{bf}$ and $<^{fb}$ by $\leqslant^{bb}$ and $<^{bb}$, justifying the change by the substantiation algorithm where we first recurse on M and then check that the resulting pairs of first and second arguments satisfy the inequality for each rule.

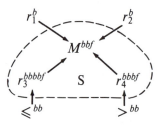

Figure 4: Another part of rule/goal graph for merge example

3.2. Top-Down Rules with Efficient Tests

Unfortunately, [NAIS83] does not give a very efficient test for applicability of his capture rule; he suggests only that we consider all cycles in the set S, whose number can be exponential in the size of S. A top-down algorithm with a fully polynomial test was discussed in [ULLM85]; it is essentially Naish's rule restricted to sets of a single argument, and with an additional condition on the form of rules to assure that the test can be made quickly.

In [SU84] a capture rule that includes Naish's was described. Moreover, a semipolynomial test for applicability of this capture rule was given, subject to some constraints on the form of rules. To show that "semipolynomial" is the best that can be done, there is a proof that when the maximum arity of relations is made a parameter of the problem, the problem is *NP*-hard.

Some conditions on the rules' form were relaxed by [APPR85], who gave a semipolynomial algorithm for an arbitrary collection of rules, subject only to the constraint that there are no function symbols in rule bodies.[9]

4. Constraints On Argument Sizes

In order to prove that a top-down capture rule such as the one appearing in Section 3 may be applied, we must be able to show that an argument size decreases going around a loop in the rule/goal graph. In the merge example, we could do so by arguing only about the syntax of the rules (i.e., an argument clearly got replaced by its tail). When there is a cascade of several predicates involved, matters are not so simple, as the following example due to E. Shapiro shows.

Example 6: The following rules define a predicate A that appends its first argument (an element) to the end of its second argument (a list), with the resulting list appearing as the third argument. We also define a predicate R whose first and second arguments are defined to be the reverse of one another.

$$r_1: A(a,[],a\,|\,[]) :-$$
$$r_2: A(a,b\,|\,x,b\,|\,y) :- A(a,x,y)$$
$$r_3: R([],[]) :-$$
$$r_4: R(a\,|\,x,y) :- R(x,z),\ A(a,z,y)$$

Suppose we want to compute the reverse of a list by instantiating the first argument of R and computing the second argument. We may use a version of the top-down capture rule that permits sideways information passing, in particular the passing of a bound value of z in r_4 from $R(x,z)$ to $A(a,z,y)$. That is, desiring to capture the node R^{bf}, we assume A^{bbf} is already captured and capture the set of nodes $S = \{R^{bf}, r_4^{bbf}\}$ with a top-down capture rule; the substantiation algorithm is exactly what Prolog would do with the four rules above.

---

[9] Technically, the rules in Example 2 for merge have function symbols on the right sides, but it is easy to rewrite these without function symbols on the right by defining a predicate $cons(a,b,c)$ with the obvious meaning.

We have no trouble justifying the capture of S, since the first argument of R is easily seen to decrease each time around the recursive loop. Further, we have no trouble capturing A^{bbf}, because the second argument of A shrinks each time around the recursion of r_2.

Suppose, however, that we wish to instantiate the second argument of R and take the reversal from the first argument. Then we must capture R^{fb}. To do so, we may assume A^{ffb} is captured; it surely may be captured since the third argument of A also shrinks going around the loop of r_2. Then we could pass information sideways from z in $A(a,z,y)$ to z in (x,z), so the recursion on R in r_4 takes us from R^{fb} to R^{fb}, rather than to R^{ff}.

However, this time, we have trouble justifying the top-down capture rule for the set $S = \{R^{fb}, r_4^{ffbf}\}$. The reason is that going around the recursive loop, y becomes z in the second argument of R, and there is no reason to believe that this recursion will converge. Fortunately, an inspection of the first two rules tells us quite clearly that the second argument of A is always shorter than the third argument; in r_1 they are of lengths 0 and 1, respectively, and r_2 gives us an easy induction that the difference between the argument lengths is preserved. $\square$

Automation of the reasoning of Example 6 is an ongoing research problem. In Ullman and Van Gelder [UG85] *unique rules* are defined; these have the property that to prove an inequality among two argument sizes, there is only one "minimal" set of other inequalities that we could attempt to prove.

Example 7: If we wish to relate the sizes of the first and second arguments of R on the left side of r_4 above, we must relate variables x and y. The only way x and y could be related is through z, and that requires

1. Relating the two arguments of the occurrence of R on the right (which we have to do anyway), and,

2. Relating the second and third arguments of A.

Thus, r_4, and the other rules in Example 6 incidentally, are unique rules. See Ullman and Van Gelder [UG85] for an exact definition of the concept. $\square$

Of course, not all unique rules allow us to prove the inequality we desire between argument sizes. However, there is an efficient test whether an inequality can be proven by the simple form of argument suggested by Example 7, given that all the rules involved are unique. Curiously, the problem reduces to one of Markov decision chains that can be solved by an algorithm of [ERIC78]. The complexity of the problem in the case that rules are not unique, but we are still restricted to proving inequalities between pairs of arguments of the same predicate symbol, is unknown.

Often the relationships among argument sizes can be expressed as a polytope (intersection of half-spaces) in the space of all vectors of length k of nonnegative integers, where k is the number of arguments of the predicate symbol. Van Gelder [VANG85] explores methods for finding polytopes that behave as fixed points of a set of rules; that is, assuming the possible argument size combinations on the right sides of rules lie in the polytope, then the possible points for the left sides also lie in the same polytope.

If we could compute such polytopes efficiently, we would have a sufficient condition for a relationship among the sizes of two or more arguments of the same predicate symbol. Like the method alluded to in Example 7, it only provides a sufficient condition; there is no known algorithm to decide in all cases whether an inequality holds.

5. Research Directions

In a sense, research on "capture rules" is trivial. Steal somebody's idea for processing rules of a special form, or of no special form, couch the idea as a capture rule, and call it a triumph for theory. However, this process ignores the key element of efficiency, which enters at two levels.

1. Comparisons between different rule-processing strategies have not been worked out satisfactorily. For example, how does one tell if the rule of Henschen and Naqvi [HN84] is the best of known alternatives for a given set of rules?

2. The efficiency of the test for applicability of the capture rule itself has to be considered. For example, it is easy to think of situations more general than those of Section 3 where a Prolog program will converge. But how quickly can these situations be recognized?

Another interesting and important open problem along the lines of (2) concerns sideways information passing. Intuitively, one can find an exponential number of different ways to pass information among subgoals on the right sides of n rules. Is it really NP-hard to determine whether a node of the rule/goal graph can be captured using sideways rules only, given a set of initially captured nodes?

Finally, the issue discussed in Section 4, proving relationships among argument sizes, needs further thought. Is it NP-hard to determine whether the inequality inference strategy of Ullman and Van Gelder [UG85] works, when the rules are nonunique? Even if rules are unique, how does one determine what inequalities one needs to prove, without violating the independence criterion for capture rules discussed in Section 2?

6. References

[APPR85] [BANC85] [CODD70] [ERIC78] [GENE83] [GM78] [HN84] [KOWA74] [LITW84] [NAIS83] [NAUG85] [STON75] [SU84] [SW74] [SWC70] [TODD76] [UG85] [ULLM82] [ULLM85] [VANG85] [WARR81]

15
Naive Evaluation of Recursively Defined Relations

François Bancilhon[1]

ABSTRACT *We address the problem of evaluating a recursively defined relation. We are given an equation of the form:*
$$R = f(R)$$
where f is a monotonic relational algebra expression and we want to evaluate the least fixpoint of that equation. We first recall that there is a simple naive evaluation of this solution and we argue that its performance is poor because it generates duplicate computations.

To solve this problem of duplication, we define a simple differential calculus on relational expressions. The goal is to see how a relational expression of the form f(R) increases when R is replaced by R+dR. The differential is thus defined as f(R+dR) - f(R). We give simple rules to compute the differential of relational expressions, using join, composition, union, intersection, projection, and selection. We also give optimized expressions for the differential when specific conditions, such as functional dependencies, hold. Finally, we show how the differential of an expression can be used to produce an "optimal" evaluation of a least fixpoint. This is done (i) by giving a logic-based definition of performance, and (ii) demonstrating a relational algebra program that computes the least fixpoint of a recursive equation and showing some optimal properties of that relational algebra program.

[1] Database Program, Microelectronics and Computer Technology Corporation, 9430 Research Blvd., Austin, Texas 78759

1. Introduction

One way to build a Knowledge Base Management System (KBMS) is to extend the functionality of a Database Management System (DBMS). Relational DBMS are particularly well suited for this purpose since they are already based on first order logic and provide some deductive capabilities. But even though relational DBMS have a deductive power through their view mechanism, this capability is limited to non-recursive, safe formulae. So, for instance, simple operators such as the transitive closure of a binary relation cannot be expressed in such a system [AU79]. Thus, the problem of recursive query evaluation must be solved, in order to extend the functionality of a relational DBMS to that of a KBMS.

This problem has recently received a lot of attention in the literature [CH80,CH82a, and CH82b]. Several approaches have been suggested, most of them fairly complex to implement. Two cases are distinguished: in the *general* case, the relation to be evaluated is subject to some selection operator (or, in terms of logic, some of its attributes are bound) and the problem is to make an intelligent use of these bindings; in the *degenerate* case we want to evaluate the entire relation.

In [CHAN81], a method is proposed to deal with a special type of rule in the degenerate case. [NH83, NAQV84, and HN84] propose a compilation-based method to deal with a special type of rule in the general case. In [ULLM85], a general framework is proposed to describe various strategies of evaluation of logical queries. [MS81a] presents a general method based on the predicate connection graph that applies only to the degenerate case.

We plan to demonstrate in this paper that, in the degenerate case, there exists a simple algorithm, the *semi-naive evaluation*, which has good performance. Naive, bottom-up evaluation of recursively defined relations has already been suggested in the literature [AU79, MS81a, and ULLM85], but its performance has never been clearly established. In this paper, we show that, with a slight improvement, it can be made fairly efficient. This is an interesting result, since it means that a very simple strategy can be used to evaluate recursive queries.

A simple way to compute a relation defined by a recursive rule of the form $r = f(r)$, where f is a relational algebra expression, consists of executing the following program:

> $r = \phi$;
> while "r changes"
> do $r := f(r)$.

It is guaranteed that if f is monotonic (and a simple sufficient condition for that is that f does not contain any difference operator), and if all the base relations referenced in f are finite then this program will produce the least fixpoint solution of the equation in a finite (but not necessarily bounded) number of steps.

We call such a program a *relational algebra program* or RAP and this particular RAP the *naive evaluation* of the fixpoint of f.

We can make the following remarks concerning this method of naive evaluation:

i.   It is simple and it works. It is simple in the sense that extending a relational database system to handle such a RAP is straightforward in implementation. Therefore there is a simple and general method for evaluating a recursively defined relation. Thus the only ground on which we should discard such a method is performance.

ii. It is not very efficient. Without specifying any further what our measure of efficiency is, let us point out one of the major drawbacks of the method: assume at step i that we have evaluated a value of the r relation and call this value $r(i)$.
Step $i+1$ will consist in evaluating $r(i+1) = f(r(i))$.
Since f is monotonic and the initial value $r(0)$ was empty, then

$$r(i) \subset f(r(i)).$$

Thus $f(ri)$ can be rewritten:

$$r(i) + dr(i),$$

where $dr(i)$ denotes the new tuples generated by step $i+1$.
Step $i+2$ of the algorithm will then evaluate

$$r(i+2) = f(r(i+1)) = f(r(i) + dr(i)).$$

In this process, we are re-evaluating $f(ri)$, which we had already done at step $i+1$. Thus naive evaluation generates a lot of duplicate computation.
Therefore, at each step, instead of computing that entire set $f(r)$, it would be nice to compute only the effect of dr since $f(r)$ is already known. What we need for this is to evaluate $f(r+dr) - f(r)$. Let us now find a way to evaluate this "differential" and apply it to the evaluation of the least fixpoint of f.

2. Differential of Relational Algebra Expressions

We define a simplified *relational algebra expression* [ULLM82] as follows:

i.   Base relations are relational algebra expressions

ii.   If f1 and f2 are relational algebra expressions then so are:
        (f1 + f2) where + denotes set union; (we have chosen this
        unusual notation to make the differential formulae more intui-
        tively appealing)
        (f1 * f2) where * denotes "join" (we only consider equi-join
        here)
        (f1 o f2) where o denotes "composition" (we define composition
        as join followed by a projection on the non-join attributes)
        (f1 ∩ f2),
        (f1 × f2).

iii.   If f is a relational algebra expression then so are:
        Π(f) where Π denotes "projection".
        σ(f) where σ denotes "selection".

Obviously the syntax defined here is not sufficient to fully
describe the expression (join attributes, projection attributes, and selection conditions are not specified), but the level of detail is sufficient to
provide for rules that evaluate the differential. Let us now assume that
we want to vary one base relation r, while leaving all the others constant. The expression f defines a function f(r). We define the
differential of f as the function:

$$df(r,dr) = f(r + dr) - f(r)$$

where r and dr are assumed disjoint and where - denotes set
difference.

Theorem 1.

Given the expression describing f, the expression describing df
can be evaluated recursively as follows:

1. $d(f1 + f2) = (df1 - f2) + (df2 - f1)$

2. $d(f1 o f2) = ((f1 o df2) + (df1 o f2) + (df1 o df2)) - (f1 o f2)$

3. $d(f1 * f2) = (df1 * f2) + (f1 * df2) + (df1 * df2)$

4. $d(f1 \cap f2) = f1 \cap df2 + df1 \cap f2 + df1 \cap df2$

5. $d(f1 \times f2) = f1 \times df2 + df1 \times f2 + df1 \times df2$

6. $d\Pi(f) = \Pi(df) - \Pi(f)$

7. $d\sigma(f) = \sigma(df)$

8. $dr0 = \phi$
     where r0 is a constant.

Proof:

1. d(f1 + f2) = ((f1 + df1) + (f2 + df2)) - (f1 + f2)
    = (df1 + df2) - (f1 + f2)
    = (df1 - f2) + (df2 - f1)

2. d(f1 o f2) = ((f1+df1) o (f2+ df2)) - f1 o f2
    = ((f1 o f2) +(f1 o df2) + (df1 o f2) + (df1 o df2))
    - f1 o f2
    =((f1 o df2) + (df1 o f2) + (df1 o df2)) - f1 o f2

3. d(f1 * f2) = ((f1 + df1) * (f2 + df2)) - (f1 * f2)
    = (f1 * f2 + f1 * df2 + df2 * f1 + df1 * df2) - (f1 * f2)
    = (f1 * df2 + df2 * f1 + df1 * df2) - (f1 * f2)
    = (f1 * df2 + df2 * f1 + df1 * df2)

4. d(f1 ∩ f2) = ((f1 + df1) ∩ (f2 + df2)) - (f1 ∩ f2)
    = (f1 ∩ f2 + f1 ∩ df2 + df1 ∩ f2 + df1 ∩ df2)
    - (f1 ∩ f2)
    = (f1 ∩ df2 + df1 ∩ f2 + df1 ∩ df2) - (f1 ∩ f2)
    = (f1 ∩ df2 + df1 ∩ f2 + df1 ∩ df2)

5. d(f1 × f2) = (df1 + f1) × (df2 × f2) - f1 × f2
    = df1 × df2 + df1 × f2 + f1 × df2 + f1
    × f2 - f1 × f2
    = df1 × df2 + df1 × f2 + f1 × df2

6. dΠ(f) = Π(f+df) - Π(f)
    = Π(f) + Π(df) - Π(f)
    = Π(df) - Π(f)

7. dσ(f) = σ(f+df) - σ(f)
    = σ(f) + σ(df) -σ(f)
    = σ(df) - σ(f)
    = σ(df)
    because f ∩ df = φ and σ(X) ⊆ X => σ(df) ∩ σ(f) = φ.

These expressions are still fairly complex. But, in many cases, taking into account the specific properties of relations, we can optimize them, as the following theorem demonstrates:

Theorem 2

1.   If f1 + df1 and f2 + df2 are disjoint, then:
      d(f1 + f2) = df1 + df2,

2.   Let X and Z be the set of non-join attributes in f1 and f2 and let
      Y be the setof join attributes:
      If f1 + df1: X → Y (by this we denote the fact that the functional
      dependency X → Y holds in (f1 + df1) or f2 + df2 : Z → Y
      then:
      d(f1 o f2) = (df1 o f2) + (f1 o df2) + (df1 o df2)

3.   If the set of attributes on which the projection is done contains a
      key of f + df then:
      dΠ(f) = Π(df).

It is clear that the expressions (1), (2), and (3) are simpler versions of
expressions (1), (2), and (7) from theorem 1.

Proof

1.   If f1 + df1 and f2 + df2 are disjoint, then so are f1 and df2
      and f2 and df1. Hence df1 - f2 = df1 and df2 - f1 = df2.

2.   We shall use the following two lemmas:

Lemma 1

If R: X → Y and S(YZ) ∩ S'(YZ) = φ
then R(XY) o S(YZ) ∩ R(XY) o S'(YZ) = φ

Proof

Assume that there exists a tuple (x,z) in R(XY) o S(YZ) ∩ R(XY) o
S'(YZ).
Then (x,z) ∈ R(XY) o S(YZ)
=> there exists y1 such, that (x,y1) ∈ R(X,Y) and (y1,z) ∈ S(Y,Z)
(x,z) ∈ R(XY) o S'(YZ)
=> there exists y2, such that (x,y2) ∈ R(X,Y) and (y2,z) ∈ S'(Y,Z).
R: X → Y => y1 = y2
Therefore, (y1,z) belongs both to S(Y,Z) and S'(Y,Z), which contrad-
icts the hypothesis.
Q.E.D.

Lemma 2

If R+R': X → Y and R(XY) ∩ R'(XY) = φ
then R(XY) o S(YZ) ∩ R'(XY) o S'(YZ) = φ

Proof

Assume that there exists a tuple (x,z) in $R(XY)$ o $S(YZ)$ $\cap$ $R'(XY)$ o $S'(YZ)$.

Then $(x,z) \in R(XY)$ o $S(YZ)$

$=>$ there exists $y1$ such that $(x,y1) \in R(X,Y)$ and $(y1,z) \in S(Y,Z)$

$(x,z) \in R'(XY)$ o $S'(YZ)$

$=>$ there exists $y2$ such that $(x,y2) \in R'(X,Y)$ and $(y2,z) \in S'(Y,Z)$

$R+R': X \rightarrow Y => y1 = y2$ therefore $(x,y1)$ belongs both to $R(Y,Z)$ and $R'(Y,Z)$, which contradicts the hypothesis.

Q.E.D.

Let us now use the lemmas to prove that:

> If $f1 + df1: X \rightarrow Y$, then
> $d(f1 \text{ o } f2) = (f1 \text{ o } df2) + (df1 \text{ o } df2) + (df1 \text{ o } f2)$

Note that the other case $(f2 + df2: Z \rightarrow Y)$ derives from this one in a straightforward way.

We know that:

$$d(f1 \text{ o } f2) = ((f1 \text{ o } df2) + (df1 \text{ o } f2) + (df1 \text{ o } df2)) - (f1 \text{ o } f2)$$

Since $X \rightarrow Y$ in $f1$ and $df2 \cap f2 = \phi$ by lemma 1 we have:

$$(f1 \text{ o } df2) \cap (f1 \text{ o } f2) = \phi$$

thus $d(f1 \text{ o } f2) = (f1 \text{ o } df2) + (((df1 \text{ o } f2) + (df1 \text{ o } df2)) - f1 \text{ o } f2)$

Since $X \rightarrow Y$ in $f1 + df1$ and $df1 \cap f1 = \phi$ then by lemma 2 we have:

$$(df1 \text{ o } df2) \cap (f1 \text{ o } f2) = \phi \text{ and } (df1 \text{ o } f2) \cap (f1 \text{ o } f2) = \phi$$

thus $d(f1 \text{ o } f2) = (f1 \text{ o } df2) + (df1 \text{ o } df2) + (df1 \text{ o } f2)$

Q.E.D.

3. If the attribute on which we do the projection contains a key, then the projection does not contain any duplicates. Therefore, assume that $\Pi(f) \cap \Pi(df)$ is non-empty. Then there exists a tuple x that belongs to both $\Pi(f)$ and $\Pi(df)$; that tuple contains a key appearing in both f and df; hence a contradiction.

Q.E.D.

3. Using Differential to Compute Least Fixpoints

Let us now return to the problem of evaluating a recursively defined relation.

Theorem 3

Consider the following series:

$$r(0) = \phi \qquad\qquad (1)$$
$$dr(0) = f(\phi) \qquad\qquad (2)$$

$$r(n) = r(n\text{-}1) + dr(n\text{-}1) \qquad (3)$$
$$dr(n) = df(r(n\text{-}1), dr(n\text{-}1)) \qquad (4)$$

The term $r(n)$ converges to the least fixpoint solution of the equation $r = f(r)$. Moreover, when all the constant relations of the expression f are finite, it converges in a finite number of steps.

Proof:

From (1), (2) and (3) we can see that:

$$r(n) = r(0) + dr(0) + dr(1) + dr(2) + \ldots + dr(n\text{-}1) \quad (5)$$

Moreover, (4) and the definition of df yields:

$$dr(n) = f(r(n\text{-}1) + dr(n\text{-}1)) - f(r(n\text{-}1))$$
$$dr(n) = f(r(n)) - f(r(n\text{-}1)) \qquad\qquad (6)$$

Thus (5) and (6) give:

$$\begin{aligned}
r(n) = \quad & r(0) + f(r(0)) \\
& + f(r(1)) - f(r(0)) \\
& + f(r(2)) - f(r(1)) \\
& \quad\ldots \\
& + f(r(n\text{-}1)) - f(r(n\text{-}2))
\end{aligned}$$

Therefore, $r(n) = f(r(n\text{-}1))$ and $r(0) = \phi$. This shows that the $r(n)$ series converges to the least fixpoint of the equation $r = f(r)$
Q.E.D.

Corollary:

The following RAP computes the least fixpoint of the equation $r = f(r)$:

```
old-r := φ;
old-dr := dr;
```

```
while dr ≠ φ do
  begin
  dr := df(old-r, old-dr);
  r := old-r + old-dr;
  old-dr := dr;
  old-r := r
  end;
```

The above RAP is clearly better than the naive one, since it does not recompute $f(r)$ entirely at each step of the iteration. We shall call this RAP the *semi-naive evaluation* of the fixpoint of f. The claim we make in this paper is that this semi-naive evaluation has "good" performance. To make such a claim we must first establish some criteria for performance.

4. Performance of RAP

Let us first establish the performance of the natural evaluation of a relational algebra expression. We shall assume that the expression is evaluated bottom up (from the base relations up).

Given a relational algebra expression f, we perform the following:

i.   We give a unique name to each sub-expression in f. If the same sub-expression appears several times, we give it the same name every time.

ii. For each sub-expression fi, we associate with it a couple of rules (the case of the + operator), or a single rule, (all other cases) as follows below. (On the left hand side we put the sub-expression, then the associated rule name and the associated rule):

f' = f1 + f2	rf'1:	f' ← f1
	rf'2:	f' ← f2
f' = f1 o f2	rf':	f' ← f1 o f2
f' = f1 ∩ f2	rf':	f' ← f1 ∩ f2
f' = f1 × f2	rf':	f' ← f1 × f2
f' = Π(f1)	rf':	f' ← Π(f1)
f' = σ(f1)	rf':	f' ← σ(f1)

Note that in this process we have given a unique name to each production rule.

Given an evaluation of the expression, we generate a trace as follows: for each tuple x produced by a rule r from tuple x' (a case of select, union and projection) or from tuples x1 and x2 (a case of join, intersection, and cartesian product) we memorize a "firing" $<r,x,x'>$ or $<r,x,x1,x2>$. Therefore, $<r,x,x'>$ means that the system has deduced x from x' by applying rule r; and $<r,x,x1,x2>$ means that the system has deduced x from x1 and x2 by applying rule r.

Note that in this model the measure of complexity of the join, the cartesian product, the intersection, and the selection is the size of the result; the measure of complexity of the union is the sum of the sizes of the arguments (each tuple present in both arguments is going to fire twice); the measure of complexity of the projection is the size of the argument. These measures are the result of the choice of a logic based model of the computation.

Now, this measure of complexity can be naturally extended to RAP: all we have to do is keep a trace of the RAP the same way we kept a trace for the evaluation of the expression.

Let us now introduce two characteristics of "good" computations:

Definition.

The execution of a RAP is .I "duplicate free" if its trace does not contain the same firing twice.

"Duplicate free" means that the same rule is never fired twice with the same data. It does not mean, however, that the same tuple is not produced twice. For instance, projection is a duplicate-free operator; however, it can generate the same tuple several times (but from different tuples, which will make it different firings).

Definition.

The execution of a RAP is *useless free* if every tuple appearing on the left of a firing, and which is not in the result set, also appears on the right of a firing.

This means that every tuple produced in the execution of the program is either in the result set or is used to produce some other tuple. In other words all tuples that are produced are "useful" as final or intermediate results.

Let us now give conditions whereby RAPs can satisfy such properties.

Definition

Let r1 and r2 be two relations. Their join is *lossless,* with the result of their join projected on the attributes of r1 is r1. Their intersection is *lossless* with respect to r1, if the result of their intersection is r1.

Thus, this definition is simply a refinement of the standard lossless join definition.

The first result is trivial:

Theorem 4

The bottom-up evaluation of a relational expression is duplicate free.

Theorem 5

Let f be a relational expression. Its evaluation is useless free if and only if:

i.   All selections that are not the identity are performed on base relations.

ii.   All joins and intersections are lossless with respect to the non-base relations they involve.

Proof

(only if)

Assume there exists a selection that does not concern a base relation. Then it has as an argument a temporary relation. Since the selection is not the identity, at least one tuple of that temporary relation will not be used later; hence the computation is not useless free. Now assume that there exists a lossy join or intersection on a temporary relation. The same phenomenon appears here: one tuple at least is lost in the join and is therefore not used. Hence the computation is not useless free. Q.E.D.

(if)

It is easy to see that union, cartesian product, lossless join, identity and projection are useless-free operations. (They essentially "use" all the tuples of their arguments). Now, if all the other operations involve only base or result relations as arguments, then the whole computation is useless free. (Base relations are not derived, therefore no "useless" tuple is produced, and result relations are always useful by definition). Q.E.D.

Theorem 6

The execution of the semi-naive evaluation is duplicate free.

Proof:

We prove this by induction: the main idea of the proof is that, if r and dr are disjoint, while computing df(r+dr) we never fire a rule that was fired while computing $f(r)$.

Step 0: The result is true for $f(r) = r0$ where $r0$ is a constant.

In this case, $dr0 = \phi$. Therefore, we do not fire any rule to compute df, and there is no duplication.

Step 1: The result is true when $f = r$.

In this case, $df = dr$ and dr being disjoint from r, there is no duplication.

Induction step: Assume it is true for f1 and f2, and let us prove it for:

1. $f = f1 + f2$
   $d(f1 + f2) = (df1 - f2) + (df2 - f1)$
Then the deductive part is simply df1 and df2 and $df1 \cap f1 = df2 \cap f2 = \phi =>$ no duplication.

2. $f = f1 \, o \, f2$
   $d(f1 \, o \, f2) = ((f1 \, o \, df2) + (df1 \, o \, f2) + (df1 \, o \, df2)) - (f1 \, o \, f2)$
Each tuple produced by the evaluation of $((f1 \, o \, df2) + (df1 \, o \, f2) + (df1 \, o \, df2))$ is produced by the join of some tuples x1 and x2; and it is not possible that $x1 \in f1$ and $x2 \in f2$, because one of x1 and x2 is in df1 or df2 and thus does not belong in f1 or f2, hence no duplication.

3. $f = f1 \cap f2$
   $d(f1 \cap f2) = f1 \cap df2 + df1 \cap f2 + df1 \cap df2$
Each tuple produced by the evaluation of df is in both df1 and df2, and therefore cannot belong to $f1 \cap f2$, hence no duplication.

4. $f = \Pi(f1)$
   $d\Pi(f1) = \Pi(df1) - \Pi(f1)$.
The deductive part is $\Pi(df1)$, and, df1 being disjoint from f1, there is no duplication,

5. $f = \sigma(f1)$
   $d\sigma(f1) = \sigma(df1)$
df1 being disjoint from f1, there is no duplication in the deduction.
Q.E.D.

Theorem 7

Let $r = f(r)$ be a fixpoint equation. If the bottom-up evaluation of df is useless free, then so is the semi-naive evaluation of the fixpoint of f.

Proof

At each step of the recursion we compute a new *dr*from and the base predicates. If the evaluation of *df*is *dr*.By it is clear that all tuples will have been useful to produce the last dr (which belongs to the result of the RAP).
Q.E.D.

Theorems 6 and 7 establish the quality of the semi-naive algorithm: it never duplicates a deduction and it never does anything useless. Provided, of course, that df is useless free (which we regard as a standard query optimization problem). To do better than the semi-naive evaluation, we would have to eliminate redundancy (i.e., the fact that the same tuple can be produced from different firings); and this seems to be a very difficult problem.

The main contribution is to have transformed the problem of evaluating a recursively defined relation into that of optimizing a relational query df.

5. Conclusion

Let us end by describing the semi-naive evaluation of a classical example: the transitive closure of a binary relation. The recursive rule defining the transitive closure of r1 is:

$$r = r \text{ o } r1 + r1$$

The differential of f is therefore:

$$df = (dr \text{ o } r1) - r$$

Therefore the semi-naive evaluation is:

```
r := φ;
dr := r1;
old_dr := r1;
while dr ≠ φ do
  begin
  dr := old_dr o r1 - r;
  r := r + old_dr;
  old_dr := dr
  end.
```

The main limitation of this work is that we only address the case of evaluating the entire relation. If we are to compute only a selection of the relation, then naive evaluation is not useless free any more. (Essentially, all the tuples that will not be selected will be useless). We

There are several possible extensions to this result. More work needs to be done on the problem of optimizing differential expressions:

1.   It would be interesting to see how the expression of the differential could be optimized under acyclicity conditions of f, since, in that case, the only thing we would have to check would be whether any tuples (and not any new tuples) were generated at each step of the recursion.

2.   Note that we have given the condition for simplification in terms of properties of f + df, but, in general, f and df are evaluated from specific sub-expression. It is therefore necessary to be able to derive properties of f and df from the properties of their sub-expressions.

Finally, the results should be extended to the case of more than one recursively defined relation.

In this paper, we have studied a particular case of the problem of recursive rule evaluation: the case of a single rule when the entire relation must be evaluated (i.e., no selection is performed on the resulting relation). We have shown that a simple strategy, the semi-naive bottom-up evaluation, is sufficient in this case. We have also proposed criteria for measuring the performance of rule-based systems, and have shown that, according to these criteria, the performance of the semi-naive evaluation is good. More precisely, we have converted the problem of optimizing an iterative relational algebra program into that of optimizing a straight line program (i.e., a standard relational query).

6. Acknowledgements

I wish to thank Mimmo Sacca for a careful proofreading of the paper and for proposing a major improvement of theorem 2.

7. References

[AU79] [CH80] [CH82a] [CH82b] [CHAN81] [HN84] [MS81a] [NAQV84] [NH83] [ULLM82] [ULLM85]

16
Knowledge Base Retrieval

W. A. Woods[1]

ABSTRACT *This chapter discusses a number of differences between traditional database retrieval and the retrieval problems that arise from the large knowledge bases of rules that occur in many expert systems applications. It outlines several principles and techniques applicable to these problems, including a basic principle of* **factoring**. *In particular, conceptually factored, taxonomic representation systems such as* **KL-ONE** *appear to be well suited to such applications. Such knowledge structures can be used to perform a kind of abstract "parsing" of a situation, using the patterns and schemata of the knowledge base as a "grammar." The way in which elements of the knowledge base are accessed in this process differs substantially from the way in which elements of a traditional database are accessed. To handle large knowledge bases of rule-like information, it will be necessary to combine insights of knowledge representation research with those of database organization and retrieval.*

1. Introduction

In traditional database retrieval, the database consists of a large collection of records with a relatively straightforward and regular structure (sets of attribute-value pairs or relational instances). The query is a structured pattern which matches and filters the data. In contrast to this, many rule-based expert systems have a large knowledge base of schemata or rule patterns whose structures are more similar to traditional database queries than they are to traditional data elements. Conversely, these patterns and schemata are sometimes invoked by

---

[1] Applied Expert Systems, Inc.

situations that are more like typical data elements in a relational data-base than typical database queries -- that is, the input to an expert system is typically a set of answers to questions or a situation described by some kind of data entry (e.g., a patient history), much like a set of relational instances.

This comparison is illustrated in Figure 1. If we align the elements of a knowledge base management system for an expert system with those of a traditional database management system (DBMS) on the basis of relative size, then we get the obvious correspondence between expert system input and the database query and between the knowledge base and the database. If however, we align them on the basis of structure and function — aligning those things that are like relational instances with things that are like relational instances and aligning generic patterns that match relational instances with similar patterns, then we get the counter intuitive result that the knowledge base of an expert system aligns with the query of the DBMS and the input of the expert system aligns with the database of the DBMS. That is, one can think of certain expert systems as like a traditional DBMS except that the database of relational instances is rather small and not worth optimizing, while the analog of the query (i.e., the knowledge base of rules) is large and the issues of importance have to do with structuring the system of rules for efficiency.

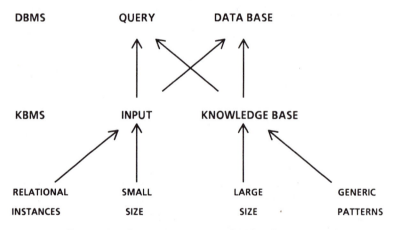

Figure 1: Comparison of a KBMS with a DBMS
The alignment is direct on the basis of size but crossed
on the basis of the pattern/instance distinction.

We can elaborate the comparison further: In a traditional DBMS, the queries are small, pattern-like, and contain variables. The database is a large set of relational instances containing no variables. An update consists of adding or changing a relational instance in the database. The result is a set of relational instances that satisfy the query. In many expert systems, the knowledge base is large, pattern-like, and contains variables. The input is comparatively small, and usually consists of relational instances with no variables. An update consists of adding or changing a pattern or a rule in the knowledge base, and a result is a structure of patterns that the input satisfies. In a traditional DBMS, the pattern-like element is used once and thrown away, while the set of relational instances is carried forward from problem to problem. In many expert systems, the input relational instances are thrown away after use (or kept only for reference) while the collection of pattern-like elements is carried forward from problem to problem and is the object to which backup, version control, security, consistency checking, multiple access, and ongoing maintenance is applied. This alignment is summarized in Figure 2.

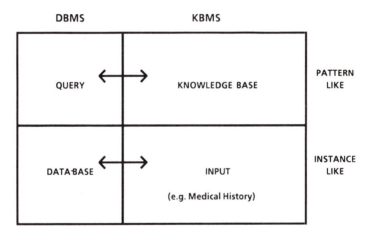

Figure 2: Functional Correspondence between a DBMS and a KBMS

Of course, the above characterization is an oversimplification. Many expert systems contain a database of relational instances as well as a pattern knowledge base, and either can be large. Thus an expert system's knowledge base may contain both facts and rules. Moreover, an expert system frequently constructs a dynamic knowledge base of intermediate results (usually consisting of facts, but possibly containing rules as well), and there are some unique issues associated with such dynamic components of a knowledge base. In this chapter, however, I want to explore the question:

"What are the retrieval problems associated with supporting a large knowledge base of rules where the knowledge base is more pattern-like and the "query" is more data-like than in traditional database systems?"

Examples of kinds of systems that would have this characteristic include: medical diagnosis systems, systems for interpreting visual scenes and physical mechanisms, situation assessment and crisis monitoring systems (e.g., reactor control, process control, network monitoring), knowledge-based language understanding systems, intelligent assistants of various kinds, and any system whose role is some analog of a mechanical creature reacting to a changing world using some body of knowledge.

Such systems use a knowledge base of rules or schemata in very different ways than the traditional filtering and report-generation operations on databases. For example, a Prolog program of 1,000,000 or more Prolog rules would need a retrieval operation embedded in an inner loop of its reasoning process that would find all of the rules that were unifiable with the current goal. A knowledge-based language understander would need to invoke a search of a knowledge base for each input utterance to find all of the schematic situations that could account for the input. Specifically, it would need to find situations in which a speaker, knowing what the system believes its user to know, and wanting what the system believes its user to want, would say something of the kind that the system has just received as input.

Among the kinds of querying operations that one would like to support for such environments are: finding rules that match a portion of the current situation, finding a collection of schemata that together provide a comprehensive account of the current situation, finding the most complete partial account of the current situation that is consistent with known schematic relationships, finding all the rules whose patterns unify with a given goal specification, finding the most specific patterns that match or unify with a given goal, and finding all the rules whose patterns are similar to a given specification (to within a specified tolerance).

2. Some Problems

Given a knowledge-based system with large numbers of situation-action rules, it becomes infeasible to find the rules that match a given situation by systematically considering each rule. One needs to have some way of reducing the computational load. One way is to index the rules according to some salient feature that will be easily detectable in the input situation and can then be used to find a much more limited set of rules to apply, much as inverted files are used to index relational instances. This has been done in many systems and certainly reduces the number of rules that need to be considered as compared with an exhaustive consideration of each rule. However, it has several limitations. There may be some values of the index key for which there are still a large number of rules to consider. For example, in the natural English question-answering system, **LUNAR** [WOOD73], the verb "be" had a large number of rules to account for different senses of the word. In an extended version of LUNAR, the number of such rules could become quite large.

Another limitation of key-word indexing is that there can be certain constructions for which there is no single easily detected feature that is strongly constraining as to possible meaning. For simple question answering systems, one can design the language to exclude such cases, but for general fluency of expression, this is not possible. In this case, there may be no useful index key that can be used to select a sufficiently constrained set of rules to try.

Also, in elliptical sentences, the constraining key may be deleted, and although one can have the rules indexed by other keys as well, the remaining ones may not sufficiently constrain the set of rules that need to be considered. A more serious version of this problem occurs if the key word has been mistyped and the system is required to perform some error correction or other helpful response.

Finally, even when the set of rules has been constrained to a relatively small set, there is frequently a good deal of sharing of common conditions among the pattern parts of different rules. For example, the rules "if A and B then C" and "if A and E then D" share the condition A. Considering each rule independently results in testing these conditions separately for each rule.

3. Factored Knowledge Structures

An approach to solving the above problems is to use a "**factored knowledge structure**". In such a structure, the common parts of different rules are merged so that the process of testing them is done only once. With such structures, one can effectively test all of the rules in a very large set, and do so efficiently, but never consider any single rule individually. At each point in a factored knowledge structure, a test is made and some information gained about the input. The result of this test determines the next test to be made. As each test is made and additional information accumulated, the set of possible rules that could be satisfied by the input, is gradually narrowed until eventually only rules that actually match the input remain. Until the end of this decision structure is reached, none of these rules is actually considered explicitly.

The most common example of factoring is the well-known "decision tree" in which a cascade of questions at nodes of a tree leads eventually to selection of a particular "leaf" of the tree without explicit comparison to each of the individual leaves. If the tree is balanced, then this leads to the selection of the desired individual leaf in $\log(n)$ tests rather than n tests, where n is the number of leaves of the tree. Another example of factoring is the mechanism in ATN grammars [WOOD70] whereby common parts of different phrase structure rules are merged, thereby avoiding redundant processing of common parts of alternative hypotheses. A simple example of the technique is illustrated by the following pair of Prolog rules:

s(X,Y) :- p(X,X1), s(X1,Y1), c(Y1,Y)

s(X,Y) :- p(X,X1), c(X1,Y).

These two rules have the same first and last subgoals, but the first rule has an additional middle subgoal. If an ordinary Prolog interpreter matches the first subgoal of the first rule, but fails on the middle subgoal, then it backtracks to the next rule and reattempts to satisfy the subgoal p(X,X1). If, however, these rules were factored together so that the common initial subgoal was shared, as illustrated in Figure 3, then upon failing to achieve s(X1,Y1), the interpreter could merely pick up at the point in the process where the two rules began to differ and attempt immediately to satisfy c(X1,Y) in the second rule.

The factoring in this case has not only elminated the duplication of the testing of p(X,X1), it has actually eliminated the bactracking associated with two alternative hypotheses. Factoring thus provides a "least commitment" or "wait and see" strategy that effectively postpones the consideration of distinct hypotheses until more information is available; in this case, whether s(X1,Y1) succeeds or not. This can greatly reduce the number of alternative hypotheses that need to be explored by backtracking or other forms of nondeterminstic search, sometimes eliminating the need to consider alternatives entirely.

Factoring is important for two distinct objectives. The efficiency of computation through elminating duplication and deferring the need to enumerate alternative hypotheses is one aspect. A second aspect deals with the ease and reliability of specifying and updating a knowledge base. When common parts of several rules are represented separately, they must be specified and updated separately. In such cases, there is always the potential for inconsistent updates. It requires effort to be sure that one has found all of the different places where a given piece of information is stored in order to insure consistency of updating. When common parts of rules are factored together, there is only one place where the common part is located and hence only one place to make changes. The term **"conceputal factoring"** [WOOD80] refers to aspects of a knowledge representation structure that support this kind of locality of specification and revision. In many cases, the

s(X,Y) :- p(X,X1), s(X1,Y1), c(Y1,Y)

s(X,Y) :- p(X,X1), c(X1,Y)

Becomes:

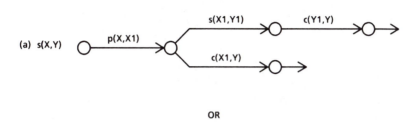

OR

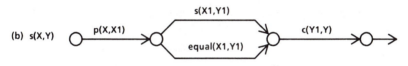

Figure 3: Factored Prolog Rules

same kinds of factoring transformations will support both conceptual and computational efficiency goals, while in other cases these two issues can make incompatible demands.

Figure 3a illustrates a factored structure in which efficiency of computation alone is the consideration. Although this structure shares the common subgoal $p(X,X1)$, it does not capture the fact that the final subgoals of the two rules are essentially the same. (Notice that they are not exactly the same, due to differences in variable names.) Figure 3b illustrates a further factoring that captures the commonality of the final subgoals as well. It also brings the variable names into a consistent form, so that (for example) if at some later point one wanted to refer to the first variable of the c predicate, independent of whether the first or the second rule had succeeded, one could refer to it consistently as $Y1$. (This move required introducing an equality predicate to handle the variable alignment.)

Factoring transformations can be performed either manually, or in some cases by means of a compiler. Thus, for example, our Prolog rules could have been transformed into a form equivalent to Figure 3a or 3b automatically by a compiler. This could achieve the computational efficiency effects of factoring without requiring the programmer to consider the issue. However, it would not have achieved the conceptual efficiency effects, since the programmer still uses a notation in which common elements are specified independently. A desirable characteristic of a knowledge representation system would be to structure the representation in such a way that the efficiency of specification and updating are supported by a conceptually factored notation, while computational efficiency is achieved by a compiler that optimizes the structure for efficiency. For example, mature Prolog compilers support the use of embedded conjunctions and disjunctions in their rules, allowing a Prolog programmer to perform the conceptual factoring equivalent to Figure 3b by writing the rule as:

s(X,Y) :- p(X,X1), (s(X1,Y1) or equal (X1,Y1)), c(Y1,Y).

Beneath the surface, the Prolog compiler must treat an expression like this in something like the way indicated in Figure 3b — that is, there is a preserved state immediately following the p(X,X1) term from which the process will pick up and attempt the equal(X1,Y1) subgoal if the s(X1,Y1) subgoal fails. Thus, figure 3b can be thought of as representing what a compiler would produce for such embedded operations.

For simple cases such as the above example, a linear or indented grouping of subexpressions, bounded by parentheses, provides a relatively clear and readable way to capture the conceptual factoring advantages discussed above. For larger and more complicated examples, repeated application of the same technique produces unreadable complexity. In this case, creating explicit named states as intermediate reference points (as in an ATN) can sometimes help to conceptually organize the subgoals. Similarly, the creation of named intermediate subgoals (the equivalent of "pushing" in an ATN) can capture commonly used constellations of subgoals.

In summary, factoring provides several things. It provides a locality for processing that supports efficiency of computation, and it provides a locality for specification and updating that supports ease of knowledge base management. It is only one step further to observe that the same locality that supports ease of updating can also supportx machine learning, since generalization and induction algorithms can find in one convenient place each of the components of a behavioral specification that might be altered to modify the behavior. Such techniques are discussed in the chapter by Mitchell. Other uses of knowledge factoring are discussed in the chapters by Bauchilon and by Ullman.

4. Generalized Transition Networks

"**Generalized transition networks**" or **GTN's** [WOOD78b] are a formalization of the notion of factoring in terms of an abstract automaton that generalizes the factoring capacities of an ATN grammar. In an ATN grammar, legal sequences of words and phrases are specified in terms of a network of states similar to that of Figure 3b. For each kind of phrase that the grammar can recognize there is an initial state to begin such a phrase and a network of transitions leading from state to state corresponding to the order in which constituent words and phrases can occur in such a phrase. There are many algorithms for using such a grammar to recognize a sentence. The simplest is to initiate a non-deteministic search process in the initial state of the top level constituent (e.g., the initial state for a sentence) which proceeds to compare transitions from that state against the input string and advances to a new state if a comparison is successful. Comparison of a phrase transition (e.g., a noun phrase) against the input is done by recursively invoking a similar process starting with the initial state of the desired phrase type. Such recursively invoked processes, if successful, will "consume" a portion of the input string corresponding to the phrase they have recognized and will return to the invoking process with an analysis of that portion of the input.

The idea of a GTN stems from the following observation: In an ATN, the set of transitions leaving a given state does double duty — both specifying the alternative possible next states that one can reach as a result of testing some condition on the input utterance, and also specifying implicitly that the test is to be made immediately to the right of the previous constituent in the input string. Thus, in following a sequence of arcs through an ATN grammar, one is both following the sequence of tests and hypothesis refinements that go on in the process of recognition and also following the left to right sequence of constituents in the input sentence. For many applications (e.g., medical diagnosis), the input is not a simple linear sequence of symbols. In such cases, an ATN-style characterization of a sequence of information gathering activities is still desirable,even though the constituents of the situation do not occur in a left-to-right sequence (e.g., the order in which the patient lists his symptoms is not usually important. A GTN provides the appropriate automaton for such applications. It keeps the general state transition structure of an ATN, but removes the implicit assumptions about the kind and location of the testing operations that result in a transition. When following a sequence of transitions through a GTN, one will still be following a sequence of hypothesis refinement operations, but there will no longer be any implicit left-to-right assumptions about the successive tests. Rather, explicit instructions at the state nodes will indicate where tests are to be performed and how successive tests relate to previous ones.

GTN's can be used to find rules in a large rule set that match a given input situation. In general, GTN's can be thought of as a class of abstract automaton that corresponds to the kind of situation to which factoring insights can be applied. A GTN is essentially an abstract, recursive, nondeterministic search machine. Anything that searches some space by moving through a space of partial hypotheses can be modeled by a GTN. Conversely, insights about formal transformations of GTN automata that improve efficiency of search can be applied to any such application. In particular, I will propose that a GTN is the class of automaton to think of as an answer to the question, "What kind of an abstract machine can execute the output of an optimizing compiler for hypothesis search problems?".

That is:

1.   If the knowledge of the behavior that a machine is to exhibit is expressed in a knowledge base of rules, and,

2.   If the knowledge base also contains some information about the control of that knowledge, and,

3.   If both of these are expressed in a "declarative" representation that does not directly determine the procedural application of the knowledge,

     then the following questions are of interest:

(a)   What is the nature of the actual process that will run when the compiler has finished operating on these declarations?; and

(b)   What is the nature of the "object code" produced by that compiler?

This object code should be thought of as a program for an abstract GTN automaton.

5. Knowledge-Based Query Understanding—an Example

As an example of the issues discussed above, consider the problem of constructing an intelligent, knowledge-based, natural language question-answering system. [WOOD78a] presents a general technique for semantic interpretation of English queries into a formal semantic representation in such systems. It can be used to access information across multiple databases possibly differing in structures and conventions. This technique has been used successfully in a number of systems including LUNAR [WOOD73]. An essential ingredient in this technique is the interpretation of English queries into an extended predicate calculus that formalizes a notion of generalized quantification in terms of operations of enumeration, filtering, and iterated action. Primitive enumerators, conditions, and actions can then be defined for a variety of different databases and database structures. This perspective provides a common high level abstraction in which to integrate not only the contents of databases with different representational paradigms, but even the results of concrete actions in the external world (e.g., by mechanical sensors and manipulators). For example, the framework can accommodate a query such as, "How many bolts are in bin 23?" in a situation in which the answer is to be determined by a robot physically counting the bolts in a physical bin of a warehouse.

A key element of the above technique is the use of **enumeration functions** to characterize the range of quantification of the generalized quantifiers. Enumeration functions have the ability to enumerate, one element at a time, the elements of a class. This is the minimal assumption necessary to obtain an operational capability. The functions make no assumptions about the nature of the organization of the data or the process that performs the enumeration. Enumeration functions provide a uniform treatment of a retrieved set, a computed set, or a set discovered as a result of a search. They also deal uniformly with single or multiple valued functions, and functions whose value's uniqueness may depend on the circumstances. (For example, "the flight from Boston to Chicago" is an appropriate description only if there is only one flight from Boston to Chicago.")

The interpretation of the meanings of questions in this framework involves the use of a large number of "pattern ⇒ action" rules similar to the "if-then" rules of many expert systems. Special indexing conventions are used, capitalizing on the feature of English that most constructions have a distinguished word called the head of the construction (e.g., the verb of a verb phrase). The heads can be used to index the rules so that rules that could apply to a given phrase can be quickly identified. This mechanism is sufficient to handle most situations with a limited subject domain with reasonable efficiency. However, it would become inadequate in a number of circumstances — such as having an encyclopedic domain of knowledge or dealing with potential ellipsis or erroneous input (in which the critical head may be missing or incorrect). A more adequate treatment would result from organizing the knowledge base of semantic interpretation rules as an appropriate GTN. (See for example [WOOD80].)

Another requirement for knowledge base retrieval comes from pragmatic considerations in language understanding. The level of interpretation performed by most current question answering systems is that of a literal interpretation -- taking the query to mean literally what it says, without taking any account of what the user might have intended without explicitly saying so. For example, the query, "List the departure time from Boston of all flights that go to Chicago" would construct a procedure that would diligently attempt to determine the departure time from Boston of every known flight whose destination is Chicago, regardless of whether that flight originates in Boston or even goes anywhere near Boston. Needless to say, people are not normally so careful in expressing their requests to say only precisely what they mean. Cohen et al [CPA81] present a variety of examples that further illustrate this point. It is now clear that providing fluent natural language communication between a person and a database will require a substantial amount of knowledge and reasoning about the user's beliefs and goals and their relation to the knowledge in the database. Supporting this kind of reasoning will require substantial attention to the structuring and organization of the necessary knowledge in the spirit of the factoring issues discussed above. (For a further discussion of these issues see the two chapters by Webber.)

Furthermore, for some applications, the determination of how a query should be answered can involve a knowledge-based reasoning component. For example, in an early question-answering system developed at Harvard [WOOD79], the framework discussed above was coupled to an ATN grammar used for parsing English queries to obtain a question-answering system that could answer questions about its own ATN grammar. Examples are: "How many arcs leave state S/NP?", "Is there a path from S/ to VP/?", or "How many nonlooping paths connect S/ to S/NP?". An interesting characteristic of this system is that although there are no pre-existing bona fide objects in the database corresponding to paths through the network, enumeration functions can nevertheless be defined to enumerate paths and can be used by the generalized quantifiers of the system to quantify over such paths. Thus it is possible to quantify over classes of entity that are implicit but not explicit in the underlying database.

A second interesting characteristic of the ATN database example is that there are a variety of different algorithms for enumerating paths through a network depending on whether only paths rooted at a given node are of interest, only paths that lead to a given destination are of interest, only nonlooping paths are of interest, etc. Many of the classes of path that one might be interested in are genuinely infinite, although the nature of the query may sometimes guarantee a finite computation even on an infinite class. The upshot of these complexities is that a knowledge base of different enumeration techniques, paired with a description of the kind of situation in which they are appropriate, is necessary in order to determine how to perform a given enumeration. A technique called **"Smart Quantifiers"** [WOOD78a] uses this knowledge base to determine an appropriate technique for performing the enumeration for each quantification. Smart quantifiers can also determine when the computation would be more efficient if the order of nesting of quantification were altered, can inform the user if the computation requested might not terminate or will be combinatorically expensive, etc.

6. Knowledge Representation Systems

From the above discussion it should now be clear that there are a variety of applications of knowledge bases of rules. In cases where the number of such rules is small, one can think of such rules as an unorganized collection of independent entities, and the processing overhead of finding an applicable rule and applying it is not excessive. However, as such knowledge bases become large, the time involved in accessing and using the rules becomes an issue and it becomes necessary to have an appropriate organization and structuring of the knowledge base. Moreover, the conceptual problems of maintaining a large knowledge base of rules are significant — (e.g., maintaining a consistent semantic interpretation of the terms used, finding and updating rules as conditions change or erroneous behavior is discovered, or finding other rules that need to be changed as a result of a change in a given rule). These issues motivate somewhat different optimization considerations than those that usually apply to conventional relational databases.   Many of the issues of both conceptual factoring and computational efficiency discussed above are applicable to this general problem.   For example, in many knowledge representation systems (referred to variously as semantic nets, conceptual taxonomies, frame systems, etc.) knowledge is conceptually factored according to a hierarchy or a generalization lattice so that specific information such as "canaries can sing" is stored at a low level in the lattice, while more general facts such as "birds can fly" and "mammals have warm blood" are stored at higher level concepts from which they are inherited by more specific ones (unless overridden by more specific exceptions).

Such problems constitute one area of knowledge representation research in the artificial intelligence community. In this section, I will introduce some terminology associated with the knowledge representation system KL-ONE [BS85], a knowledge representation system oriented around a taxonomy of structured concepts. In the next section I will discuss some of the uses of such a taxonomy for organizing a knowledge base of rules.

A **concept** node in KL-ONE is associated with a set of **roles** (a generalization of the notions of attribute, part, constituent, feature, etc.) and a set of **structural conditions** expressing relationships among them. Concepts are linked to more general concepts by explicit links. The more general concept in such a relationship is called the **superconcept** and is said to **subsume** the more specific **subconcept**. Some of a concept's roles and structural conditions are attached to it directly, while others are inherited indirectly from more general concepts.

The concepts and roles of KL-ONE are similar in structure to the classical data-structure notions of record and field or the "frame"/"schema"/"unit" and "slot" of much AI terminology. However, they differ subtly in function and interpretation since they are motivated more by an attempt to model the semantics and conceptual structure of an abstract space of concepts than by issues of data structure and retrieval operations. This difference manifests itself in a variety of details, such as the way subsumption is defined and used, the presence of associated structural conditions attached to a concept, and the representation of explicit relationships between roles at different levels of generality.

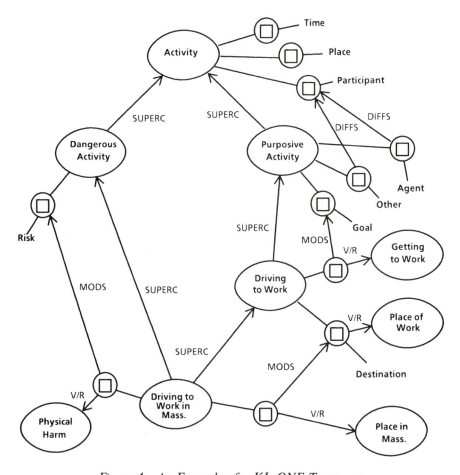

Figure 4: An Example of a KL-ONE Taxonomy

An example of a KL-ONE taxonomy is illustrated in Figure 4. In this figure, concepts are represented by ellipses, and roles are shown as circled small squares. At the top of the figure is a high-level concept of Activity. This concept has roles for Time, Place, and Participants, which are inherited by all concepts below it. Immediately below Activity is the concept for a Purposive Activity, which differentiates (DIFFS) the general role for Participants into an Agent (which is the participant that has the purpose) and Other Participants. Purposive Activity introduces a new role called Goal to represent the purpose of the activity.

Below this is a fairly specific (but still generic) concept for Driving to Work. This concept modifies the Goal of Purposive Activity by adding a value restriction (V/R) Getting to Work, indicating that whatever fills the Goal role must be an instance of Getting to Work. It also introduces a new role, called Destination, whose value restriction is a Place of Work. A structural condition (not shown) attached to the concept would specify how the Place of Work related to the Getting to Work goal (i.e., it is the Destination of the Getting to Work goal). Driving to work in Massachusetts is, in turn, a specialization of Driving to Work, whose Destination is restricted (MODS) to be a Place in Massachusetts. It is also a specialization of a Dangerous Activity whose Risk is Physical Harm.

The figure illustrates the kind of taxonomy that one would expect to have in an intelligent computer agent. It includes both very high level abstractions and quite specific concepts. Moreover, there is always room for the insertion of new levels of abstraction in between existing ones. In fact, there is a well-defined classification procedure implemented in the KL-ONE system that can automatically place a new description into such a taxonomy linked by SUPERC connections to the concepts which most specifically subsume it and those which it in turn subsumes.

There is not room here for a full discussion of KL-ONE or of the issues of knowledge representation in general. For further details, the reader is referred to [WOOD75; WOOD83; BS85] and to the survey chapter by Levesque elsewhere in this volume. We will, however, consider some of the motivations for the use of a taxonomic classification structure such as KL-ONE.

7. The Need for Taxonomic Organization

Having introduced some KL-ONE terminology and a rough idea of what a KL-ONE network looks like, let us return to the problem of recognizing what rules apply to a situation and see what such a taxonomy can do for us. In most expert system applications, a task description will often satisfy several rules simultaneously, no one of which will account for all of the task nor supplant the relevance of the others. For example, adding an object to a display is simultaneously an example of changing a display and of displaying an object. Advice (i.e., the action parts of the rules) associated with both activities must be considered. Moreover, one situation description may subsume another (more specific) description and their advice may either supplement or contradict each other. Thus, conventions are required to determine which advice takes precedence when conflicts arise.

For independent rules in a classical "production rule" system, such conflicts are only discovered when an instance of a conflicting situation occurs as input. When using a taxonomic classification structure, however, the subsumption of the conditions of one rule by another can be discovered when the rule is assimilated into the taxonomy, at which time the person entering the rule can address the question of how the two rules should interact. The advice associated with the more specific rule can then explicitly include the information to override or supplement the more general rule. It is only slightly more difficult to determine whether two existing rules could be satisfied by a common instance (when neither subsumes the other), and such tests can also be incorporated into the process that assimilates a new rule into a knowledge network.

This view of assimilating rules into a taxonomic knowledge structure not only facilitates the discovery of interactions at input time, but also promotes a compactness in the specification of the rules themselves. By relying on the fact that concepts inherit information from more general concepts, one can usually create the concept for the pattern part of a new rule by merely adding a minor restriction to an existing concept. In KL-ONE, when one wants to create a situation description that is more specific than a given one, it is only necessary to mention those attributes that are being modified or added; one does not have to copy all of the attributes of the general situation. Aside from conserving memory storage, this also facilitates updating and maintaining the consistency of the database by avoiding the creation of duplicate copies of information that may then have to be independently modified, and could accidentally be modified inconsistently. The use of such a taxonomy thus has advantages both for conceptual efficiency of knowledge base maintenance and for organizing the knowledge for run time efficiency.

The ability to assimilate new descriptions into an existing taxonomy at any level permits an evolutionary system design that achieves the same standards of rigor as a "top-down design" without requiring concepts to be defined in a predetermined order. For most applications, even if one could get the initial design carefully laid out in a rigorous top-down mode, subsequent changes (e.g., required changes in accounting policies induced by new tax laws) will require an ability to modify a system in more flexible ways. A system's taxonomy of recognizable situations should be viewed as an evolving knowledge structure that continues to be refined and developed throughout the lifetime of a system, just as it is for human beings.

8. Conclusions

This chapter has presented a number of differences between traditional database retrieval and the problems of retrieval that arise from the use of large knowledge bases of rules in expert systems applications. Several principles and techniques that are applicable to these problems were described. The basic principle of factoring, as embodied in a GTN, is applicable to a wide class of knowledge-based applications where the knowledge base is large. In such cases, an indexing structure that can be functionally modelled as a GTN can be used to classify the situation and find the relevant information to apply. In particular, conceptually factored, taxonomic representation systems such as KL-ONE appear to be well suited to such applications. These knowledge structures can be used to perform a kind of abstract parsing of the situation, using the patterns and schemata of the knowledge base as its "grammar." The way in which elements of the knowledge base are accessed in this process differs substantially from the way in which elements of a traditional database are accessed. These accesses will require techniques that are analogous to and generalizations of traditional parsing algorithms together with new memory organization techniques to avoid thrashing. They may also require parallel processing architectures and algorithms to achieve reasonable response times. A substantial challenge lies ahead of us to combine the insights of natural language understanding and knowledge representation research with those of database organization and retrieval in order to develop the techniques necessary to handle large knowledge bases of rule-like information.

9. References

[BS85] [CPA81] [WOOD70] [WOOD73] [WOOD75] [WOOD78a] [WOOD78b] [WOOD79] [WOOD80] [WOOD83]

Discussion

Jeff Ullman discussed the development of automatic planning techniques for query evaluation in Databases. Early systems required the user to state queries so that the method of obtaining the answer was explicit. Then came the Relational Model which offered a higher level of abstraction thus contribut towards more natural query languages. Much work was done on optimisation techniques. Several relational calculus languages were developed. However, these languages varied in the amount of detail they required from a user in order to answer a query. AI languages such as Planner and MRS allow the user to specify how a query is to be evaluated. Prolog, on the other hand, claims to free the user from the need to provide such detail. However, the fact that a Prolog user must consider the order of rules and terms, appears to contradict this claim. [Editors' note: This issue was also addressed by Mike Stonebraker in the discussion that followed David Warren's presentation.]

Concerning research methodology, Jeff Ullman feels that advances in the next ten years will best be achieved by starting with relational databases and enhancing them with features that upgrade the level of abstraction.

Danny Bobrow wondered whether advances could be made by enhancing Prolog technology or by another approach.

Jeff Ullman and Bill Woods discussed different views of theorem proving. Some feel that the answering of even simple database queries is theorem proving, while others restrict the use of the term "theorem proving" to the solution of hard mathematical problems.

David Israel continued the discussion on theorem proving. He stressed that there is no such thing as a universally good theorem prover; it was also noted that domain knowledge is important in speeding up the performance of a theorem prover. He wondered about the applicability of results from complexity theory to theorem proving because most of the focus is on worst case analyses. Worst cases though are often not known in advance at the design stage. Again, knowledge of the problem domain seems to be particularly important.

Concerning KBMSs, he felt that the emphasis should not be on theorem proving **per se**. Rather, theorem provers will be important as components of large systems. He concluded by noting that the main difference between KBMSs and DBMSs was that DBMSs exist.

Shamim Naqvi discussed his work on characterizing negative and incomplete knowledge in reasoning systems. He is interested in finding out when is the Closed World Assumption (CWA) applicable and when can negative information be assumed. His results, he feels, have applications both to Databases and AI. In his presentation he stressed that his work permits answers to negative queries without the need to explicitly represent negative information.

Bill Woods is concerned with efficient storage of rules and the handling of large incompatible databases, for expert system applications. For knowledge base optimisation, he proposes a technique called factoring, which merges common parts of different rules, patterns and schemata. Factoring provides efficient computations and updates, by exploiting locality. An added advantage is that locality may aid automatic learning.

Bill Woods also discussed knowledge base semantics, agreeing with Ron Brachman and Hector Levesque on the need for a Knowledge Level view. Bill Woods wants to formalise the understanding of reasoning, but feels that relying on First Order Logic leaves out some important matters, such as reasoning about beliefs and the meaning of an atomic predicate. He feels that conceptual structures from natural language processing (descriptors, predications and actions) are needed for query operators.

He stressed the need for the availability of an enumeration function in the implementation of KBMSs which retrieve one value at a time. This provides a minimal facility for retrieving sets, computing sets and doing search. It also allows the uniform implementation of single- and multiple-valued expressions, as well as reasonable handling of infinite sets. In addition, it suggests a role for user interaction, especially when costs of a query are high.

In response to a question by Francois Bancilhon, Bill Woods explained that his proposal can make use of parallel processing facilities, if they where available.

Part IV

Extending Database Management Systems

17
Database Management: A Survey

Michael L. Brodie[1]

ABSTRACT *This chapter presents and illustrates the basic concepts of database management, outlines the major research topics, and presents the key results and future directions of database management research. Database concepts and motivations are compared and contrasted with those in Artificial Intelligence.*

1. Database Concepts

During the past 15 years, databases have evolved from being simple file systems to being collections of data that concurrently serve a community of users and several distinct applications. For example, an insurance company might store in its database the data for policies, claims, investments, personnel, payroll, and planning. Although databases can vary in size from very small to very large (e.g., from hundreds to millions of records), most databases are shared by multiple users or applications.

Typically, a database is a resource for an enterprise (e.g., insurance company) in which three human roles are distinguished in relation to the database. A database administrator is responsible for designing and maintaining the database. Application programmers design and implement database transactions and application interfaces (e.g., screens). Finally, end users use prepared applications and, possibly, high level database query languages.

The design of database applications can be stated as follows: Given the information and processing requirements of an information system, construct a representation of the application that captures the

---

[1] Computer Corporation of America

static and dynamic properties needed to support the required transactions and queries. To the greatest extent possible, the static and dynamic properties common to all applications should be represented in the database. That is, a database represents the properties common to all applications, hence it is independent of any particular application. The process of capturing and representing these properties in the database is called **database design**.

The representation resulting from database design must be able to meet ever-changing requirements of existing or new applications or to be modified easily to do so. A major objective of database design is **data independence** which concerns insulating the database and the associated applications from logical and physical changes. Ideally, the database could be changed logically (e.g., add objects) or physically (e.g., change access structures) without affecting applications, and applications could be added or modified without affecting the database.

Static properties include objects, object properties (sometimes called attributes), and relationships among objects. Dynamic properties include query and altering operations on objects and relationships among operations (e.g., to form complex operations called transactions). Properties that cannot be expressed conveniently as objects or operations are expressed as semantic integrity constraints. A **semantic integrity constraint** is a logical condition expressed over objects (i.e., database states) and operations (i.e., state transitions). Examples of integrity constraints are:

Each student must have a unique student number.

For each enrollment, there must be both a student and a course.

The number of students enrolled in a course must not exceed the enrollment limit for that course.

To enroll in a course, a student must meet the prerequisites for that course.

A manager must earn more than the employees managed.

The result of database design is a schema that defines the static properties, and specifications for transactions and queries that define the dynamic properties. A **schema** consists of definitions of all application object types, including their attributes, relationships, and static constraints. Corresponding to the schema will be a data repository called a **database** which consists of instances of objects and relationships defined in the schema. A particular class of processes within an application (e.g., paying benefits within an insurance company database) may need to access only some of the static properties of a predetermined subset of the objects. Such a subset, which is called a **subschema** or **view**, is derived from the schema much as a query is defined.

Associated with the schema concept is a notion of **logical database integrity**. A database exhibits logical integrity if the values in the database are legal instances of the types in the schema and if all semantic integrity constraints are satisfied.

The purpose of a database is to answer queries and to support database transactions. A **query** can be expressed as a logical expression over the objects and relationships defined in the schema and results in identifying a logical subset of the database. A **transaction** consists of several database query and altering operations over objects in a subschema and is used to define application events or operations. Transaction are atomic since all steps of a transaction must complete successfully or the entire transaction must be aborted (i.e., no part of a transaction is committed before the whole transaction is completed). The primary criteria for the database is that it exhibit logical and physical integrity and remain secure in the face of potential errors or malicious use by multiple users or transactions.

A **data model** is a collection of mathematically well-defined concepts that help one to consider and that express the static and dynamic properties and integrity constraints for an application. (In practice, most data models have been developed intuitively. Formal definitions, if they exist, have been made after their development.) They include concepts for defining schemas, subschemas, integrity constraints, queries, and transactions. A data model includes a constrained type system (i.e., fewer types than a high level programming language) for defining objects and operations on objects. Unlike most AI knowledge representation schemes, data models provide a procedural semantics based on elementary database altering operations (i.e., insert, update, and delete) and on the concept of an update transaction. Altering and query operations are an essential part of a data model.

A data model provides a syntactic and semantic basis for tools and techniques used to support the design and use of databases. Tools associated with data models are languages for defining, manipulating, querying, and supporting the evolution of databases. Most existing database management systems provide a **Data Definition Language** (DDL) for defining schemas and subschemas, a **Data Manipulation Language** (DML) for writing database programs, and a **Query Language** (QL) for writing queries.

Many database languages combine both query and manipulation. These languages can be provided on a stand alone basis, embedded as call statements in a host language such as COBOL (these two cases are typical in commercial systems), or integrated directly into a high level programming language such as ADAPLEX [SFL83] and TAXIS [MW80].

A **database management system** (DBMS) is a system that implements the tools associated with a data model (e.g., the DDL, DML, and QL and the processors needed to implement schemas and execute transactions and queries) [DATE81, 83] [ULLM82] [SB83].

2. Data Models: Knowledge Representation in Databases

Data model concepts are closely related to knowledge representation concepts in AI. Issues of common interest include: expressive power, modelling capabilities (e.g., abstraction), languages, inference (i.e., search), truth management (i.e., integrity maintenance), and formal definition of the representations.

There is some controversy between AI and Database people about what is modelled in databases. Database people contend that databases model parts of the real world (i.e., information systems applications). Some AI people contend that databases do not provide interpretations in which individuals (e.g., objects in the real world) are identified with representations in the database that are used in any reasoning. They claim that databases store and manipulate data structures (at the symbol level) as opposed to representing knowledge (as perceived at the knowledge level) and supporting inference.

A middle ground between these extremes is that DBMSs provide some interpretation but depend largely on user intuition and that databases do represent knowledge and provide elementary inference capabilities. For further discussions about this see each chapter in Section II and the two chapters by Levesque and Brachman.

The concepts of data model and data languages came about with the relational data model at a time when the three classical data models (i.e., **hierarchic**, **network**, and **relational**) were being developed. Discussions of data model concepts can be found in [DATE81] [ULLM82] [BROD84].

The classical data models are based on common concepts (e.g., records, attributes, relationships, unique valued identifying fields) that were inherited from their ancestors, simple file systems. However, the notation and some concepts are unique to each model. Hierarchic and network data models represent objects in records that are organized, using 1:N binary relationships, as nodes in trees and networks, respectively. These data models provide primitive operations and record-at-a-time navigational facilities.

Unlike the relational languages, hierarchic and network languages are more representational (i.e., users must deal with more storage and implementation features), but they have a richer set of inherent constraints (e.g., built-in relationship types). The navigational and representational aspects of these languages are historical; non-navigational and less representational languages have been proposed for these models.

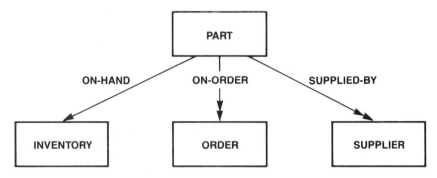

Figure 1: Network PART SCHEMA with 1:M Relationships

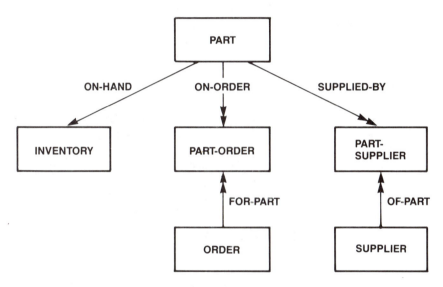

Figure 2: Network PART SCHEMA with N:M Relationships

The following example illustrates concepts common to hierarchical and network data models. Figure 1 illustrates a schema for a database concerning parts. Objects are represented by labelled boxes. Relationships are represented by labelled, directed edges. Single headed directed edges represent 1:1 relationships. Doubled headed edges represent 1:N relationships. This schema does not directly support N:M relationships between SUPPLIER and PART (i.e., a part is supplied by several suppliers and a supplier can supply several parts) and between

ORDER and PART. Representing an N:M relationship in network schemas requires the introduction of "link" record as illustrated in Figure 2. Figure 1 is a network schema with a strict hierarchical structure (i.e., each object has one "parent" or "owner"). Hence Figure 1 can be considered a hierarchical schema. Figure 2 has objects with two "owners" (e.g., PART-ORDER is owned by both PART and ORDER), hence is not a hierarchy.

Hierarchic and network queries and transactions are navigational. They follow logical connections from one record to another reading and writing information as they go. The navigational transaction in Figure 3 orders parts from a preferred supplier for those parts in the given list that are below 17 in the inventory. The transaction is written against the schema in Figure 1. Note the two nested loops in the transaction.

For each P *in* PART-LIST
do:
    Find PART *where* PART.P# = P.P#
    Get INVENTORY *via* ON-HAND *from current* PART
    If Quantity-On-Hand < 17
    Then Do
        SUPLOOP: *Get next* SUPPLIER *via* SUPPLIED-BY
            from current PART
            If SUPPLIER.S# = O.PREFERRED-S#
            Then Do:
                Insert via ON-ORDER *for current* PART
                ORDER (DATE = TODAY, PART# = P.P.#,
                SUPPLIER = P.S.#,
                QUANTITY-ON-ORDER = PART.RE-ORDER,
                DISCOUNT = SUPPLIER.DISCOUNT);
                End SUPLOOP
            End do;
            Else If SUPPLIER *is last within* SUPPLIED-BY
                Then Print ("Preferred Supplier" P.PREFERRED
                    "of PART" P.P# "missing")
                Else End SUPLOOP;
    End do;
End do;

Figure 3: Record-at-a-Time Navigational Transaction

The relational data model is based on the mathematical concept of a relation, on set theory, and on predicate calculus. A relation is a set of n-tuples. A tuple can be used directly to represent both objects and N:M, n-ary relationships. For example, Figure 4 illustrates a relation representing an enrollment entity or object.

ENROLLMENT(*STUDENT#*, *COURSE#*, TERM,GRADE)
STUDENT(*STUDENT#*, ...)
COURSE(*COURSE#*, ...)

Figure 4: ENROLLMENT: An N:M Relationship
between STUDENT and COURSE

Enrollment represents both an n-ary relation between the four attributes and an N:M relationship between STUDENT and COURSE
objects (i.e., a student can enroll in N courses and a course can have
M students enrolled).

The relational algebra and calculus provide a set oriented query
and access facility that can also be used to define schemas and constraints. Figure 5 illustrates a relational schema equivalent to the network parts schema given in Figure 1. Objects here are represented by
relations. Attributes that take part in the key are in italics. Relationships are value-based, that is, a relationship can be established by
matching values of corresponding attributes (via a join operator). For
example, a join between ORDER and PART based on equal PART#
values establishes the ON-ORDER relationship in Figure 1. Just as
with the network schema, a "link" relation must be added to represent
an N:M relationship as in Figure 6.

PART(*PART#*, COLOR, WEIGHT, RE-ORDER)
SUPPLIER(*SUPPLIER#*, PART#, ADDRESS, DISCOUNT)
ORDER (*DATE, PART#, SUPPLIER#*, QUANTITY-ON-ORDER,
   DISCOUNT)
INVENTORY(*PART#*, QUANTITY-ON-HAND)

Figure 5: Relational PART SCHEMA with 1:N Relationship

The transaction in Figure 7 is the set-oriented, relational version of the
navigational transaction in Figure 3.

PART(*PART#*, COLOR, WEIGHT, RE-ORDER)
SUPPLIER (*SUPPLIER#*, ADDRESS, DISCOUNT)
PART-SUPPLIER (*PART#, SUPPLIER#*)
ORDER (*ORDER#*, DATE)
ORDER-ITEM (*ORDER#, PART#, SUPPLIER#*,
   QUANTITY-ON-ORDER,DISCOUNT)
INVENTORY(*PART#*, QUANTITY-ON-HAND)

Figure 6: Relational PART SCHEMA with N:M Relationships

> *For each* P *in* PART-LIST, S *in* SUPPLIER, I *in* INVENTORY
> *where* P.PART# = I.PART#
> *and* I.QUALITY-ON-HAND < 17
> *and* S.PART# = P.PART
> *and* P.PREFERRED-S = S.S#:
> *Insert* ORDER (DATE = today, PART# = P.PART#,
> SUPPLIER# = S.SUPPLIER#, DISCOUNT = S.DISCOUNT,
> QUANTITY-ON-ORDER = PART.RE-ORDER);

Figure 7: Set-Oriented Relational Transaction

Whereas the navigational form explicitly uses two nested loops, the set-oriented form uses no explicit loops. The relational query processor determines an execution strategy for processing the set.

Due to an ever-growing need to capture more meaning of the information stored in a database (if only by improved data representation and organization) to provide higher level data modelling concepts, a new generation of data models evolved, called **semantic data models** [BROD84]. Some of these models were extensions of classical data models, whereas others were developed in response to other influences. Some semantic data models were defined based on mathematical theories, mostly First Order Logic, in order to make use of a well understood semantics and to rely on associated computational and analytical tools. For example, Reiter [REIT84] proposed a reformulation of the relational data model based on the proof theory of first order logic, thereby providing a direct means to extend the semantics of the model.

Most semantic data models were influenced by semantic networks. They are generally object oriented and provide at least four types of primitive relationships between objects: classification (instance-of), aggregation (part-of), generalization (is-a), and association (member-of).

Three distinguishing characteristics of data models are the means they provide for expressing integrity constraints, object relationships, and operations.

First, consider **semantic integrity constraints** which provide general means for expressing conditions not directly expressible in terms of the objects and operations of the data model. They are used to prevent updates that would violate logical database integrity. Data models differ from each other in the constraints that they can be used to represent. Constraints that can be expressed directly in one model may require complex logical expressions in other data models. For example, a generalization relationship between objects would have to be expressed by means of complex and specific logical expressions using the relational model, whereas it could defined directly using a semantic data model that supports generalization.

Second, consider the representation of **object relationships** which is an essential capability of data models. File systems do not explicitly support relationships. The hierarchic and network data models provide direct means for representing 1:1, 1:N, and restricted N:M relationships between objects. The relational data model provided direct means (the n-ary relation) for representing general N:M relationships (as in the above example). Semantic data models influenced by semantic networks attempt to model more application oriented relationships (e.g., married-to, Works-for, is-part-of, likes, etc.). Some data models provide a small fixed set of relationship types with which all application relationships must be represented (e.g., using the hierarchic data model, all relationships must be hierarchic). Other data models provide general mechanisms for representing any application relationship (e.g., a labelled edge in a semantic network). Some data models support semantic relativism since there is no distinction between objects and relationships.

Third, consider the **query and altering operations** of a data model. The altering operations define the update semantics of database objects and the query operations define the query power of the database. Different operations produce different data models, even over the same data structures, just as different inference mechanisms over the same data structures produce different knowledge representation schemes. It can be argued that the network and relational data models differ largely in their operations and not in their data structures.

Most attempts to integrate AI and Database concepts have concerned data models and knowledge representation (as outlined in the preface to this book and survey by Borgida on Conceptual Modelling and the chapter by Greenspan, Borgida and Mylopoulos).

3. Database Research Topics

Database research can be divided into two areas: database system and implementation research concerned with designing and developing DBMSs, and logical database research concerned with concepts, languages, and methodologies for using DBMSs. Clearly the logical issues determine systems and implementation requirements. Whereas the primary emphasis has been on the former area (i.e., basic database technology), logical issues are receiving more attention as database technology is being applied to new application domains (e.g., CAD/CAM, statistics, office automation, knowledge bases). The new domains require extensions of the current database paradigm. For example, whereas current DBMSs handle simple, regularly structured data, new DBMSs must handle all types of data, both structured and unstructured (e.g., text, voice, image), and with complex structure (e.g., engineering data) [BBDM84; SIGM83]. These new logical requirements will pose new challenges to extend basic database technology. To meet the challenges, the emphasis is now to shift back to basic database technology (such research is discussed in the chapters by Dayal and Smith and by Stonebraker).

Database theory is fundamental to both research areas. **Database theory** is the application of mathematical techniques to the solution of problems related to the design, implementation, and use of DBMSs. It is based primarily on the underlying mathematical foundation of the relational data model. Applications of database theory will be discussed in the next two subsections. The chapters by Naqvi, by Ullman, and by Boncilhon all address topics in database theory.

The following two subsections outline the key concepts, major research results, and future research directions for the two areas within database research.

3.1. Database Systems and Implementation Issues

Database systems and implementation issues include concurrency control, query optimization, data structures and algorithms, performance evaluation, database systems reliability, database machines, DBMS architectures, security, and distributed databases. These topics are covered in more detail in [DATE83; ULLM82].

Since a database is primarily a shared resource, it must be accessed by multiple transactions. In a banking database, for example, many transactions must access the accounts database. The objective is to provide the maximum amount of concurrent access, rather than requiring one-at-a-time access. At the same time, transactions must be prevented from interfering with the correct operation (using some definition of "correctness") of other transactions. For example, two transactions may attempt to modify the same account at the same time. **Concurrency control** mechanisms attempt to provide correct, concurrent access to a DBMS by two or more database transactions.

Currently, the primary correctness criterion is "serializability", meaning that the effect of running the transactions concurrently is the same as the effect of some serial schedule. Thus, the transactions need have no knowledge that any other transactions are running. A well-developed theory now exists for serializability, and techniques exist for verifying that individual concurrency control mechanisms are correct according to this criterion. The most effective implementation mechanism is two phase locking, in which all locks are requested before any locks are given up [ULLM82].

Current research is directed at identifying correctness criteria other than serializability that may be appropriate in some applications, and that may require less computational overhead than mechanisms that guarantee serializability. Such new correctness criteria frequently take advantage of special application semantics and system knowledge of transaction semantics, and sometimes transaction semantics require explicit knowledge of concurrent activity by individual transactions.

Query optimization concerns the efficient evaluation of queries over a database [KRB85] (see also the survey on query processing by Jarke). The processing of queries that involve relational operations such as selection, projection, and join operations are well understood. Optimization research is concerned with the more expensive database operations, which for centralized databases is the join operation, and which for distributed databases is intersite processing. Optimization is done in conjunction with storage techniques and by using information (e.g., access statistics) maintained by the DBMS. The structure of the problem is well-understood and heuristics exist for most subproblems. Database theory has provided query decomposition algorithms, query simplification mechanisms based on tableau, and semi-join theory for optimizing joins [MAIE83]. In an area called knowledge-based query optimization, semantic integrity constraints are used to reduce query evaluation costs. Current research has two main goals. The first is to develop a framework with which to integrate existing heuristics. The second is to expand the class of queries that can be optimized (e.g., to those that include transitive closure, aggregation, quantifiers, and outer joins).

Integrity maintenance attempts to ensure that after an update the database is consistent with a set of predefined integrity constraints. Integrity constraints can be expressed as queries that must always return a true value. Hence, integrity maintenance is closely associated with query processing. Although the semantic issues for integrity constraints are relatively well-understood (e.g., the declarative expression of semantic integrity constraints) and some computational results exist, a theory or body of techniques do not support their efficient maintenance.

Data structures and algorithms research was well established before database research began. The results of most research into storage and access structures are directly applicable to databases. Recent database research has addressed dynamic storage structures including hashing, B-trees, and index sequential directories. Some well known heuristics exist for physical database design, and a general theory is beginning to emerge for file structures. Recently there has been a resurgence of interest in the design and analysis of dynamic hashing based, in part, on results from computational complexity of retrievals and updates and motivated by the need to store new types of data (e.g., spatial) and to support new types of processing (e.g., spatial search, recursion).

Performance evaluation of database systems is an emerging research area. Data structures and algorithms have been studied independently and some attempts have been made to study entire systems. A framework for performance prediction has been proposed based on an analytical model that uses a queueing network. Such a framework would be used to investigate the interdependencies between various design decisions. To date, however, no theory or technique has been developed.

Database system reliability in an unreliable computing environment involves backup and recovery of database transactions. The correctness criteria is based on atomic commitment (i.e., if an entire transaction does not succeed then all its effects on the database are undone). Although many techniques exist [VERH78], a general theory has not yet evolved.

Database machine research concerns direct hardware support of database processing for dramatic improvements in processing speed over very large databases. It now appears that the original conception of database machines will not provide the performance improvements originally expected. Current research is directed at new forms of database hardware (e.g., parallel processing, in-core databases, very large cache memories - see the chapter by Cullingford, Garcia-Molina, and Lipton).

DBMS architectures concern the software components of a DBMS, the interfaces between the components, and the languages presented to users (the chapter by Manola and Brodie considers such issues in the KBMS context). Early research and development concentrated on centralized DBMSs. An early proposed architecture, called the ANSI/SPARC Framework [DATE81] identified more than 40 components and interfaces. A major contribution of the framework was the three-schema approach (i.e., external schemata for user views, a conceptual schema that integrates external schemata, and an internal schema that defines physical storage structures). The framework attempted to permit multiple data models to be used for external schemata. This led to a need for more expressive data models for the conceptual schema onto which external schemas could be mapped. The development of relational DBMSs such as INGRES [STON76] and SYSTEM R [AC76] resulted in a few well understood DBMS architectures [SB83]. These architectures reflect the structure of the query processing and concurrency control algorithms employed. As the functionality and processing algorithms become better understood, improved DBMS architecture can be developed to reflect improved modularity based on a better understanding of DBMS operations.

Database security concerns defining and ensuring only authorized access to databases. Significant research results include query modification and authorization definition. Query modification involves modifying queries before they are executed so that they access the database according to predefined access restrictions (i.e., integrity as well as security). Authorization definition involves defining and granting to users the access rights to relations. Work also has been done on secure database, particularly for statistical databases. Current research is directed at the more general problems of access control in the context of version control or configuration management [BBDM84] (see also "Context Structure/Versioning: A Survey" by Bobrow and Katz in this volume) and at problems of preventing users from inferring data they are not authorized to access from data they are authorized to access.

Distributed databases provide the appearance of a centralized database when, in fact, there are two or more distinct (e.g., geographically distant) databases. The use of distributed databases is motivated by the need to integrate data that actually reside in different locations (e.g., accounts at individual bank branches) into a single (virtual) database (e.g., the database of all accounts in all branches). Distributed databases offer several potential advantages: efficiency (e.g., increased parallelism, processing local data locally), reliability (e.g., site failure does not make the system fail), and modularity (e.g., easier to add new nodes than to modify a centralized system). Distributed database systems are either homogeneous (i.e., each site runs the same DBMS) or heterogeneous. The heterogeneous class involves the complexity of translating between multiple systems and data models in addition to distribution itself.

Currently there are no commercial distributed DBMSs (DDBMSs). Tandem's ENCOMPASS, and to some extent IBM's IMS, provide two-phase commitment protocols and atomicity of distributed transactions. However, neither provides the appearance of a centralized database.

The correctness criterion for distributed databases is the maintenance of the illusion of a centralized database. The problems of centralized DBMSs are more complex in DDBMS. Reliability is more complex since there are multiple sites plus communication networks each of which could fail. To improve reliability, multiple copies of data frequently are maintained on different sites, so that the data will be available even if sites go down. This also improves performance by increasing opportunities for parallel access and by placing data near where it will be used. However, it complicates update processing because the system must ensure that updates to data are correctly propagated to all copies of the data, and that concurrency control is maintained during this propagation. Similarly, query optimization is complicated because the optimizer may choose from among multiple copies of data, each involving differing communication delays. Moreover, since there are potentially multiple sites involved in processing a given query, it may be possible to produce an evaluation strategy that allows multiple sites to work in parallel in satisfying a query. The methods used for querying, updating, and concurrency control must take into account that some system component may fail at any given point in the process in order to retain sufficient information to recover from the failure without adversely impacting data consistency.

Problems also arise due entirely to the distributed environment (e.g., data allocation, heterogeneous databases, data replication, atomicity of distributed transactions). Again, database theory provides a basis for reasoning about access to distributed replicated data and to the correctness of concurrency control algorithms and deadlock [DATE83; ULLM82].

Generally, theories for processing distributed databases are as well-developed as the corresponding theories for centralized databases. The two-phase commitment protocol generally is accepted as the most effective implementation mechanism to ensure the reliability of distributed transactions. One of the distributed sites, which is designated as the coordinator, must ensure that all sites guarantee that the distributed transaction is be committed (i.e., completed) correctly. The coordinator sends a precommitment message to all sites asking each site to vote for or against commitment. If all sites vote for commitment, the coordinator sends a message to each site to commit the transaction. If one "no" vote is received or if any site does not respond, the transaction is aborted. Database theory has produced correctness proofs for distributed recovery algorithms. Open problems concern reaching agreement (i.e., whether all sites have successfully completed their part of a transaction) among processes in a distributed database.

Future distributed processing research is directed at relaxing the correctness criterion to more loosely coupled databases and the problems of network partition. A network partition concerns the continuous operation of the system in the face of communication and site failures that sever all communication paths between two or more subsets of the sites.

There are four main types of DDBMS. They can be characterized by their architectures which are listed below in order of increasing implementation complexity.

- Federated (loosely coupled) DDBMS operate autonomously and communicate only occasionally in order to support remote query and update operations.

- Integrated Homogeneous DDBMS provide the illusion of a centralized DBMS by tightly coupling multiple homogeneous DBMSs. Homogeneity simplifies the problem of translating data and operations between DBMSs. Three such systems are: SDD-1 [RBFG80], R* [WDHL82], and the DDM [CDFG83].

- Heterogeneous DDBMS. SIRIUS-DELTA [LBEF82] integrates heterogeneous DBMSs by means of language translation. A single logical database is presented to users via a global schema. Operations over the global schema are translated into corresponding operations on local DBMSs.

- Multidatabase DDBMS. MULTIBASE [LR82] provides a logically integrated, retrieval-only user interface to physically nonintegrated, distributed, heterogeneous DBMSs. It permits existing DBMSs to be added to the DDBMS for query and local autonomy for update. A high level data model permits complete logical integration of local schemata by means of a view mechanism based on generalization. Users can express single queries against a centralized view without knowing any details about the multiple heterogeneous databases actually in the system. Unlike SIRIUS-DELTA, incompatibilities and overlaps between databases can be resolved in MULTIBASE.

3.2. Logical Database Issues

Logical database research issues include data models and languages, and database design and administration.

Data model research has focused on logical aspects of databases and on concepts, tools, and techniques for database design [BROD84]. The primary concerns have been for the logical representation of objects. Theoretical work has been done in the areas of defining data model semantics [REIT84], treatment of null values, database design techniques based on the relational data model (normalization) [MAIE83; ULLM82], specification and verification of schemas and transactions, analysis of query languages, query processing, query optimization, view update, (universal relation) interfaces, constraint analysis, and applying logic to a variety of traditional database problems (see the Survey of Logic and Databases by Naqvi).

One of the main strengths and distinguishing characteristics of semantic data models is that they provide powerful means for expressing semantic integrity constraints. Future research in the static semantics of data models will be based on information modelling requirements to be defined for new application domains (e.g., engineering databases, knowledge bases). The most important extensions concern complex objects (i.e., objects composed of many smaller objects). Other requirements include semantics for reasoning about time, space, recursion, causal relationships, modalities, incomplete information, default information, and anomalous information. The chapter by Dayal and Smith proposes particular data model extensions for recursion, and time and space semantics.

Semantic data model research also has contributed to procedural semantics. Classical data models include elementary database altering operations (e.g., insert, update, delete) that maintain the constraints specified by the database schema. These operations obey the static semantics defined in the schema. For example, entity integrity (e.g., uniqueness) is maintained in the relational model. Recently, abstract data types have been proposed for the definition of objects, views, and view updates. The chapter by Dayal and Smith proposes adding an abstract data type facility to a data model. Current research is focusing on further integrating transactions with data models since there are no efficient computational models for abstract data types.

Database language research is an integral part of data model research. A major thrust of formal database theory and (informal) database semantics research has been to define the semantics of database languages. The results have provided well-defined languages for dealing with records (for classical data models) or objects and relationships (for semantic data models). The semantics referred to concern the meaning of queries (i.e., the precise definition of the evaluation of queries and the correctness of query evaluation algorithms).

Database theory establishes the power of relational languages (e.g., transitive closure cannot be expressed). Significant work has been done on the interfacing of programming languages with DBMSs (e.g., loose coupling via workspaces or cursors [AC76], integration with a host language [SFL83], tight coupling [SCHM77]). Other database language research has concentrated on user interfaces and database front ends. Topics in this area include natural language and graphics interfaces to databases, database environments [REIN84], and human factors [SHNE80].

Database design and administration concerns the design of database applications and the administration of DBMS and database resources. Database administration (DBA) concerns a human function, called a database administrator, and the associated methods and tools required to use a DBMS effectively.

A major DBA function is the design of database applications. Database design involves a database design and development life cycle, which includes conceptual, logical, and physical design stages. Conceptual design is done by means of objects, events, and organizational principles (e.g., generalization) to meet logical requirements. Logical design involves expressing the conceptual design by means of a classical data model of the target DBMS. Physical design involves selecting the most efficient data encodings, data structures, storage element sizes, indexes, access paths, and algorithms to meet performance requirements.

Database theory has produced dependency theory (normalization) [ULLM82; MAIE83], which addresses some aspects of logical design. Algorithms have been developed for aspects of the view integration problem (i.e., designing a global schema from several overlapping views or subschemata). In addition, (intuitive) methodologies have been developed for logical design [OST84]. Other methodologies, based on software engineering principles, have been proposed for the design of both schemata and transactions at the conceptual level [BR84; BMW84]. Data modelling tools are discussed in [REIN84].

Future research in database design will depend on advances in data modelling. Research currently is directed at design methodologies, heuristics, and algorithms, as well as at the development of environments that provide methodological and tools support for the entire database design and development life cycle [REIN84]. Expert systems have been developed to aid in physical database design (i.e., automating database designers rules). Research is needed to address distributed database design (e.g., data replication, fragmentation), design verification (e.g., by simulation or analysis), and database redesign (i.e., restructuring and reorganization).

4. Extending DBMSs to Manage Knowledge Bases

A **knowledge base management system** (KBMS) might be a system that provides highly efficient management of large, shared knowledge bases for knowledge-based systems. Motivations for KBMSs and related research issues are raised throughout this book. DBMS technology will contribute to KBMSs largely at the Symbol level but guided by developments at the Knowledge level.

There will be two levels at which to consider information in a KBMS: the knowledge level and the computational level (also called Symbol level — see chapters by Levesque and Brachman and the chapter by Levesque). The knowledge level can provide mechanisms for the development, refinement, and debugging of a knowledge representation scheme (e.g., data model and the associated knowledge base) for a particular application and for evaluating its adequacy, soundness, completeness, consistency, validity, etc. The computational level, on the other hand, can provide tools for the efficient implementation of a knowledge base, and operations for information retrieval, manipulation, and management.

DBMS technology will provide the core technology at the computational level. Key features will include traditional database management functions for large shared databases such as (semantic) data models; languages (i.e., definition, query/browsing, manipulation, transaction); semantic integrity definition and maintenance; storage/search structures; search and update optimization; concurrency; security; error recovery; and distribution of data and processes. AI technology will provide the basis for the knowledge level which will provide the means with which to represent and reason about the knowledge base represented at the Symbol level.

The required functionality of these KBMSs and the nature of integration of Knowledge Base and Database technologies is the topic of this book.

Acknowledgement

I am grateful to Umeshwar Dayal and Frank Manola whose reviews of an earlier version of this survey led to significant improvements in both content and presentation.

5. References

[AC76] [BBDM84] [BMW84] [BR84] [BROD84] [CDFG83] [DATE81] [DATE83] [KRB85] [LBEF82] [LR82] [MAIE83] [MW80] [OST84] [RBFG80] [REIN84] [REIT84] [SB83] [SCHM77] [SFL83] [SHNE80] [SIGM83] [STON76] [ULLM82] [VERH78] [WDHL82]

18
A Brief Survey of Logic and Database Systems

Shamim A. Naqvi[1]

ABSTRACT *In recent years several research efforts have concentrated on describing databases as first-order logical languages. There are two expectations of this exercise. Firstly, that it allows theoretical investigations of the properties of database systems. Secondly, that extending database query languages to first-order logic would yield powerful systems. This paper presents a brief survey of the field of logic and databases. Some discussion of advantages and disadvantages is given.*

1. Introduction

The sources for this report are [GM78, GMN81, GMN83, ULLM83]. This report presents a survey of the field of Logic and Databases which describes databases in terms of first-order logical languages. There are two expectations of this exercise. Firstly, that theoretical investigations of the power, expressiveness, flexibility, optimality and other properties of databases can be carried out. Secondly, that the coupling of the expressive power of First-Order Logic (FOL) with the capability of database systems to store and access elementary information will provide powerful systems that can be used in AI applications. In this paper the term *database* stands for the relational model of data and *logic* denotes FOL.

At the heart of the field of Logic and Databases lies the simple observation that some tuple $<t_1, t_2, ..., t_n>$ in a relation p can serve as an interpretation for the First-Order (FO) predicate term $p(t_1, t_2, ..., t_n)$.

---

[1] AT&T Bell Laboratories

Thus the data in the relations of the database serve as a model of some first-order theory. Queries to the database are to be evaluated as true or false with respect to this model.

One way in which FOL can be coupled with databases is to use logic to capture the semantics of database operations and the integrity constraints on the data, in one consistent and uniform language, at the same time providing increased functionality.

Another view of the above argument states that the relational model of data is the data structure (with the appropriate operators to manipulate this structure) that stores facts. What the database provides is a *fact management service* [BL84b] in a reliable and efficient manner. How this service is implemented and provided under the time and efficiency constraints is internal to the working of the database system. Given a database as a collection of facts, DB, we can externally view DB as representing facts in a propositional fashion. A query "q" is then true if DB implies "q" which we write as DB |— q. Now DB |— q iff (DB ⊃ q) (i.e., if "q" is a theorem of DB). The implication is that databases are FOL systems in which the class of inferences is constrained to meet certain restrictions of time and space. Choosing a suitable fragment of FOL for which efficient decision procedures can be constructed is a matter of considerable current research particularly in logic programming efforts [WARR77, CAMP84].

In this introduction, we have outlined some of the reasons behind the research in logic and database systems. In section 2 we review the work done in using the greater expressive power of FOL in database systems; it is shown that this increase in power and generality imposes certain requirements on how databases can be perceived as FO theories. This is explored in section 3. Finally, section 4 lists the salient points made in this report.

2. The Expressive Ideal

A claim of the field of Logic and Databases is that FOL provides increased expressiveness to conventional database systems in that negative, disjunctive and recursive information can be stated. We examine these in turn.

In general, a given fact about some situation implies a large number of other deduced facts. For example, knowing that John teaches course 'cs100' only (positive information) leads one to conclude that John does not teach 'cs200', 'math200', etc. for all courses known in the database (negative information). This allows one to not only answer the trivial query "Does John teach 'cs100'?" but also queries of the form "Does John teach 'cs200'?". The problems associated with negative information are: (1) Under what circumstances can negative information be deduced? (2) How should the potentially large amount of negative information be handled? (3) Under what circumstances can negative information be used in an intuitively correct manner?

In the relational model the usual assumption made is that if a tuple does not exist in an instance of a relation then it exists in the complement of that relation. Thus, the relation TEACH(teacher, course) contains all course offerings and ¬TEACH(teacher, course) lists all courses that are not taught by the corresponding teachers. Customarily the complement relation is not made explicit for reasons of efficiency. It must be emphasized that this is a semantic assumption in the relational model. The analogous assumption made in logic-based systems is called the Closed World Assumption (CWA), which asserts that if a statement Q cannot be proved then the statement ¬Q should be taken as true. Thus, if one cannot prove that "John teaches 'cs200'," then it should be concluded that "John does not teach 'cs200' ".

When is the CWA intuitively correct? It can be shown that if the FO theory is Horn then negative information is not needed and that the CWA is logically consistent [REIT77] (A FO theory is Horn if all formulas in it are Horn; a formula is Horn, if when written in disjunctive form, it has at most one positive atom). The counterpart of the CWA is the Open World Assumption (OWA), which states that the only answers that can be returned to a query are precisely those which can be logically proved from the database. In other words, failure to prove a statement cannot lead to assuming the negation of the statement. For most domains the OWA seems to be the intuitively correct assumption. If one has no statements whether or not "John teaches 'cs100'," then the implication is that one can make no statement about whether John does or does not teach that course. Now, for Horn databases, the results of [REIT77] show that query evaluation under the OWA is equivalent to query evaluation under CWA. This means that negative information is not needed and that the set of answers under the CWA and the OWA for a given query with respect to the database is the same.

In cases where the domain cannot be modelled by Horn clauses (e.g., John teaches 'cs100' or 'cs200' but we do not know which), one must use the OWA. Minker [MINK81] has investigated databases with disjunctive information and finitely many constants; he proposes an interesting extension of the CWA called the Generalized Closed World Assumption (GCWA). The central idea of the GCWA can be explained as follows. A model of a theory is a set of atomic formulas that makes all statements of the theory true. A model is said to be minimal if no proper subset of it is a model. The GCWA states that a negative ground fact, ¬P(a), can be assumed in a theory, T, iff P(a) is not in any minimal model of T. For example, let T={Pa∨Pb}. We show that the CWA can not be used. Since Pa is not provable, by CWA ¬Pa is true. Similarly ¬Pb is true. But {Pa∨Pb,¬Pa,¬Pb} is inconsistent. However, GCWA can be used. The three models of T are {Pa} and {Pb} and {Pa,Pb} of which the first two are minimal. Since both Pa and Pb exist in some minimal model therefore neither ¬Pa nor ¬Pb can be assumed. Extensions to the GCWA have been proposed by Yahya and Henschen [YH85], and Naqvi [NAQV85a].

Clark [CLAR78] and Kowalski [KOWA79] propose an interesting solution for modelling a world under both the OWA and the CWA. They maintain that the OWA amounts to specifying information by "if-half" definitions and allows gaps in our world knowledge; the CWA on the other hand corresponds to full "if-and-only-if" definitions and does not allow gaps in our world knowledge. This has the advantage that the open and closed worlds can be mixed in the same database, applied to different relations, or to different instances of the same relation.

CWA is a form of non-monotonic reasoning in that new information when added to an existing theory may invalidate some previous conclusions. For example, if we have a theory T={q⊃p} then we may assume ¬p from our failure to prove "p" under the CWA. If we now add "q" to T, then T ∪ {q} implies "p". Reiter [REIT83a] has shown that for Horn theories the completion axioms of Clark [CLAR78] serve as a heuristic for McCarthy's circumscription schema for doing non-monotonic reasoning [MCCA80].

Finally, FOL allows recursive information to be stated in databases. Recursion occurs naturally in many domains with hierarchical structures (inventories, scheduling, part hierarchies for CAD/CAM, routing and path finding). Conventional database languages are too weak to express recursion. In such cases, data is retrieved by application programs in a piecemeal fashion and then the recursion is performed outside the database. Aho and Ullman [AU79] advocated that recursive queries be allowed in databases; Chandra and Harel [CH79] show that relational calculus augmented with a least fixed point operator is equivalent in expressive power to Horn clause programs. Henschen and Naqvi [HN84] show an approach where a recursive query expressed in FOL can be translated into a sequence of database operations, and in certain subcases of recursion show more efficient translation schemes. There is considerable recent interest in the optimisation of recursive queries in databases (see papers by Dayal and Bancilhon in the current volume).

3. Databases, *Mutatis Mutandis*

Given the above situation regarding the expressiveness of query languages based on FOL it is natural to ask how databases can be perceived as First-Order Theories. There are two ways in which we can view the relational model of data through FOL. Each approach has some benefits. Various researchers have adopted one or the other of these approaches, the choice being dictated largely by the domain of discourse, intended application and personal preference.

3.1. The Deductive Approach

This approach has been studied by Reiter [REIT77,REIT80], Minker [GM78], and several other researchers. The perceived world is represented as a first-order theory with equality. More precisely, the facts in the world are represented as the set of ground unit wffs of the first-order theory. The set of proper axioms is the set of wffs representing positive and negative information. The set of theorems of the first-order theory constitutes the implicitly derivable information. Queries to the database are treated as theorems to be proved from the axioms of the underlying theory.

The proper axioms of the first-order theory can take two forms in the deductive approach. An axiom may state some derivable information, as "the parent of a parent is a grandparent," or an axiom can state a property that the underlying database must preserve (i.e., an integrity constraint). How a particular axiom is used is up to the system. Axioms that define new relations in terms of existing relations can be used for deducing new theorems. Axioms which are used as Integrity Constraints can also be used to answer queries as well as to verify the correctness of incoming update requests.

A popular variation on the above general approach is to consider all the ground atomic formulae of the theory to constitute the relational database called the Extensional Database (EDB), and the non-ground formulae as the proper axioms of the theory, called the Intensional Database (IDB) (see [GM78] and [HN84] for details). To answer queries in this case, the theorem prover attempts to prove the corresponding theorem over the IDB. When some ground atomic formulae are needed in the proof, a relational database request is formulated and sent as a query to the EDB. This approach recognizes the fact that relational technology can handle large sets of ground atomic formulae more efficiently than general theorem-provers.

Obviously the advantages of the Deductive Approach are that there is complete freedom in expressing the domain information that one desires to represent. But this generality is hurt by the semi-decidability of first-order theories. Reiter [REIT77] avoids the decidability problem by proposing a first-order theory which has no partial functions. In the absence of function signs, the halting problem is decidable. This limits the expressive power of the first-order theory as certain statements about the domain of discourse may not be expressible without function signs. In defense, Reiter points out that many interesting domains can be described by function-free theories.

It can be seen that disjunctive information can be represented naturally in the Deductive Approach. However, this leads to indefinite answers. For example, an answer to a query may be "john or peter" but it may not be possible to decide on one individual as the correct answer. It can be shown that if only Horn clauses are used in the theory then no indefinite answers can arise.

Finally, the FO theory in the Deductive Approach contains the equality axioms. Equality axioms have long posed serious efficiency problems for theorem-provers. Reiter [REIT80] shows that if the database contains the axioms $c_i \neq c_j$ for all constants c_i $\{i=1,...,n\}$ in the database then the only equality axiom required to be included in the theory is (%for% x)x=x. This reduces considerably the computational overhead on the theorem-prover, particularly, since the axioms $c_i \neq c_j$ can be indexed efficiently.

3.2. The Model-Theoretic Approach

Historically, this was the first approach studied by researchers. In this approach, preferential treatment is accorded to the elementary information (i.e., to the relations in the database). Logic is used as a query language. In other words the relational database is a model of a first-order theory and queries are treated as expressions which are true or false with respect to the database. It is possible to evaluate the truth-value of any expression in the first-order theory by performing algebraic manipulations on the database. This is in the spirit of Codd [CODD72] where expressions in relational calculus are interpreted on the database in terms of relational algebraic operations. The notion of relational completeness of query languages introduced by Codd [CODD72] is a measure of the expressive power of a query language and he has shown that the operations of set union, set difference, project, cartesian product and restrict are sufficient to decide the truth-value of expressions in predicate calculus. Languages interpretable in terms of these five operations are said to be relationally complete and the database is said to be an interpretable or computable model of the first-order theory [KONO81].

There are four different kinds of query languages based upon the use of single vs. many-sorted logics in conjunction with whether the primitive objects range over tuples or domains. The tuple relational calculus [CODD72] is based upon a one-sorted logic in which objects range over tuples. QBE [ZLOO77] is based on a one-sorted logic in which the objects range over domains. Many-sorted logics have been used by [GM78], [REIT77], [KONO81] among others. Integrity constraints are stated as the proper axioms of a FOL that the database must satisfy at all times. Any updates to the database may not take the database to a state in which these axioms are violated. Finally, queries are expressed as well-formed formulae (wffs) to be translated into algebraic operations on the relational database.

Another use of axioms in the model theoretic approach is to use them to provide answers that are perennially true. Consider the integrity assertion that all suppliers who supply widgets live in London. Now, a query asking: "Is it true that all suppliers who supply widgets live in London" can be answered directly from the integrity constraint rather than from the database. In fact, another kind of query could be introduced: "Is it always true that all suppliers who supply widgets live in London". The second query asks for an answer that must hold in all future consistent states of the database whereas the first one interrogates the current state of the database. The latter type of query is called a closed query and admits yes/no answers. Closed queries may be answerable by recourse to the integrity constraints, thus saving the interaction with the database.

The major advantage of the model-theoretic approach lies in evaluating the truth value of wffs with respect to the database. This implies that existential quantifiers and function signs can be used freely in the proper axioms of the theory and the queries to the model. As long as the wffs can be translated into equivalent relational algebraic operators, the decidability issues in deduction will not arise. The disadvantage is that disjunctive and negative information has been very hard to represent in this approach.

4. Summary

Here are the main points again:

- Negative, disjunctive and recursive information is difficult to represent in relational calculus; first-order database query languages handle such information naturally.

- Relational databases can be described as first-order theories in essentially two ways, the model-theoretic approach, and the deductive approach.

- The model-theoretic approach corresponds to the traditional manner of imposing predicate calculus on a relational database. The disadvantages of this approach are the inability to express disjunctive, incomplete and implicit information. The major advantage is the decidability of the query answering process.

- The deductive approach views the relational database as the ground units of a first-order theory (with types) and the proper axioms as the implicit information in the database. The disadvantage of the approach stems from the semi-decidability of first-order logics and the performance issues associated with deduction.

- Solutions to the problems associated with negative information are based upon the CWA and, more recently, on the circumscription schema of McCarthy.

5. References

[AU79] [BL84b] [CAMP84] [CH79] [CLAR78] [CODD72] [GM78] [GMN81] [GMN83] [HN84] [KONO81] [KOWA79] [MCCA80] [MINK81] [NAQV85a] [REIT77] [REIT80] [REIT83a] [ULLM83] [WARR77] [YH85] [ZLOO77]

19
PROBE: A Knowledge-Oriented Database Management System[1]

Umeshwar Dayal
John Miles Smith[2]

ABSTRACT *Existing database management systems will be inadequate for many of the information processing applications (e.g., business and industrial automation, CAD/CAM, and military command and control) of the future. Our objective is to develop an advanced DBMS called PROBE that will handle more of the information types and intensional knowledge relevant to the new application areas. Our approach is to enhance existing DBMSs with (a) Abstract object types as the basis for defining new objects and operations and for integrating specialized processors, (b) Dimensional (space and time) concepts, which are the common characteristic of many of the new information types, and (c) Recursive predicates and queries, which provide intensional knowledge processing (deductive question-answering) capabilities. In each case, it is necessary to augment both the logical (data model, query language) components and the physical (storage structures, access methods, query processor) components of the DBMS. We describe approaches to addressing all these issues. We demonstrate via examples the dramatic performance improvement that can result if the DBMS optimizer is made cognizant of the information types and knowledge used by the application programs.*

---

[1] This work was supported in part by the National Science Foundation under award number DCR-8360576, and is currently being supported by the Defense Advanced Research Projects Agency and by the Space and Naval Warfare Systems Command under contract number NO0039-85-C0263. The views and conclusions contained in this paper are those of the authors and do not necessarily represent the official policies of the National Science Foundation, the Defense Advanced Research Projects Agency, the Space and Naval Warfare Systems Command, or the U.S. Government.

[2] Computer Corporation of America

1. Introduction

For a long time, database management systems (DBMSs) have been regarded as a superior way of automating clerical record keeping functions for business data processing applications. It is now recognized that DBMS capabilities will be needed in many decision making and information processing applications that have different requirements and constraints from those found in traditional record keeping. These applications will be characterized by the requirements of access to a variety of information types and access to substantial, possibly evolving, shared knowledge bases. Examples of such applications occur in business automation, industrial automation, computer-aided design and manufacturing, military command and control, and cartography. Attempts to use existing DBMSs for these applications have generally failed because of lack of required functionality and performance. Our objective is to develop a new generation DBMS, called PROBE, that will meet these requirements.

Information processing systems of the future will be a combination of integrated components. There will be components for intelligent problem solving (e.g., expert systems), components for specialized user interfaces (e.g., workstations, natural language processors), components for specialized data processing (e.g., image enhancers, geometric modellers), and components for shared information management. The actual configuration and distribution of functionality across these components to meet a given set of specifications will be an engineering decision. Figure 1 shows one possible architecture for interconnecting the components [SMIT84].

Users access the system primarily by invoking functions of an intelligent application. The intelligent application may provide a user interface capability (e.g., a natural language processor or speech processor) or a problem solving capability (e.g., a diagnostic expert system). The intelligent applications utilize a shared base of information (data and knowledge), in addition to some private information.

The function of the advanced DBMS is to protect the shared information by providing integrity control, authorization, global query processing, concurrency control, and recovery, and to isolate users from the details of physical data storage and retrieval.

Under the control of the DBMS are the specialized data processors. Typically, each processor operates on data stored using a special representation. For example, an image processor may be designed for the enhancement of images stored in raster-scan format. The operations supported by these specialized processors are integrated into the data manipulation language of the DBMS. All data sent to, or generated by, the specialized processors is catalogued by the DBMS. Thus, the information management umbrella of the DBMS is extended to *all*

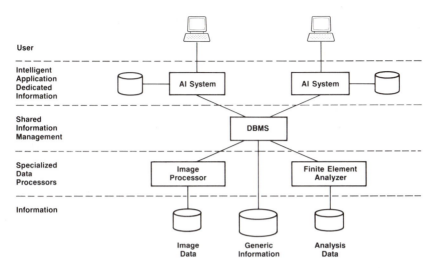

Figure 1: Architecture of an Integrated Information Processing System

kinds of information needed by the applications.

The DBMS lies at a critical point in this architecture. It must efficiently handle all accesses to shared information on secondary storage on behalf of all application transactions.

The key idea in improving performance is that the more the DBMS "understands" about a transaction, the more scope the DBMS has for optimizing that transaction. The worst situation for optimization is when the DBMS receives, during the course of a transaction, a large number of isolated information requests. Without knowing the overall context of these requests, the DBMS has no choice but to respond to them individually. All opportunities for global optimization, which is where the highest payoffs can be attained, are lost. Our approach is to make the DBMS cognizant of the information types and general knowledge used by many applications, and to correspondingly enhance the optimizer to exploit this additional knowledge.

DBMSs provide two kinds of knowledge representation capabilities: extensional (explicitly stored facts in the database) and intensional (defined as views or by queries over the stored database).

Extensional knowledge includes the stored *data* (specific facts about individual objects, for example airplane No. 123ABC consumed 200 gallons of fuel on sortie 3 on January 1); and *metadata* (schemas that describe general facts about classes of objects, for example airplanes consume fuel on missions). Extensional knowledge is represented using the *data model* of the DBMS.

In their ability to represent extensional knowledge, modern semantic data models such as DAPLEX [SHIP81, FLRR84] are comparable to semantic network-based knowledge representation languages used in artificial intelligence (AI) such as NETL [FAHL79], PSN [LEVE77], and KL-ONE [BRAC80]. A DAPLEX schema is a semantic network of entity types, functions (relationships) between types, and taxonomies (IS-A or generalization hierarchies) of entity types.

Intensional knowledge is a collection of *constraints* (e.g., an airplane can be scheduled on a mission only within its range; adjacent lines on an integrated circuit chip must be at least 5 microns apart) and *rules* for deriving new data (facts) from the stored data. In existing DBMSs, these rules are expressed as view definitions in the query language. Views can include virtual entity types, virtual functions, and virtual taxonomies. For example, consider a DAPLEX database consisting of two entity types: Employee and Department, and two functions: Department-of-Employee (which relates an Employee to his Department) and Manager-of-Department (which relates a Department to the Employee who is its manager).

A virtual function, Manager-of-Employee (which relates an Employee to the Employee who is his manager) can be defined to be the join (composition) of the two stored functions. The use of view definitions for intensional knowledge representation in DBMSs is analogous to the use of logic rules to define predicates in AI languages such as PROLOG [CM81]. For instance, a logic rule for expressing the definition of Manager-of-Employee is: if Employee(e) and Department(d) and Employee(m) and Department-of-Employee(e,d) and Manager-of-Department(d,m) then Manager-of-Employee(e,m).

Once a view has been defined, users can pose queries against it. These queries are translated by the system into queries that can be executed against the stored data. For example, the query "Find the manager of employee John Doe" is translated into "Find the manager of the department of employee John Doe." This query modification technique [STON75] has the same effect as the use of deduction for question answering in AI systems. However, in contrast to AI systems, DBMSs devote considerable attention to *efficient* processing of queries against views that are defined over large databases on secondary storage.

The key problem in knowledge representation in DBMSs is that existing query languages are too weak to capture all essential intensional knowledge. Specifically, since most existing query languages have the power of first order predicate calculus, they are incapable of expressing recursion [AU79]. For example, no language equivalent to first order predicate calculus can express the transitive closure of the Manager-of-Employee relation. As a result this knowledge has to be embedded in application programs, and is unavailable to the DBMS for optimization. On the other hand, logic-based AI languages such as PROLOG do permit recursive definitions in rules.

Recursion arises naturally in many applications that have to do with scheduling, planning, routing, and path finding. Often, recursion is inherent in the data structures occurring in the application (e.g., part hierarchies in a CAD/CAM application, feature hierarchies in a cartographic application, task precedence constraints in a planning or scheduling application). While these recursive structures can be stored extensionally in existing databases, they cannot be defined intensionally as the results of queries.

We propose to enhance the view definition and query language capabilities of an existing DBMS to include recursion, and correspondingly to extend DBMS query processing techniques to efficiently process recursive queries. These issues are discussed in Section 2.

The second limitation of DBMSs available today is their inability to process many of the information types encountered in the new applications. These DBMSs were designed specifically for business data processing applications. Hence, they can effectively store and access only formatted alphanumeric data in the form of files of records. However, many information processing applications require other types of information (e.g., maps, charts, drawings, blueprints, photographs, images, signals, geometric models, and text, in addition to formatted data). Also, the results of processing are best presented in terms of these information types (e.g., on graphic terminals) rather than as alphanumeric records. Currently, these other types of information must be extracted from a variety of separate storage systems, and manually integrated with formatted records stored in a database. Such manual processing is arduous and susceptible to errors and delays.

Extending a DBMS individually to support each information type occurring in each application would be undesirable. The DBMS would soon become complex and cumbersome, and may not be able to handle new information types that may have to be added in the future. The approach should be fundamental — to identify common characteristics of these information types — and extensible.

Our approach is based on two observations. The first observation is that most of the information types that are not satisfactorily handled by current DBMS technology share a common characteristic: dimensionality (i.e., objects of these types are oriented in space and/or time). Human beings live in a dimensional world, so it is not surprising that dimensional information is predominant in many applications. Our approach is to enhance the data model and query language of an existing DBMS with dimensional (i.e., spatial and temporal) semantics; and correspondingly to augment the DBMS's physical data structures, access methods, and query processing algorithms to include dimensional information processing. We discuss this issue in Section 3.

The second observation is that it is not feasible to implement *all* information processing within a DBMS. New types and new operations may have to be added in the future. Also, special purpose processors (e.g., image processors, map processors, signal processors, key word-based information retrieval systems) have been developed (and will continue to be developed) for some of these information types. It would be wasteful to reimplement these specialized kinds of processing within the DBMS. A better solution is to couple these specialized processors to the DBMS in such a way that (a) the operations supported by them are made available to users who can include them in transactions, and (b) the DBMS can optimize globally all processing in the system. Our approach is to make type definitions in the data model extensible. New types and new operations, and also the types and operations supported by specialized processors, can be incorporated into the DBMS as abstract object types. Correspondingly, the DBMS query optimizer also must be made extensible. The concept of abstract object types generalizes the concept of abstract data types, which has been imported into the literature on databases [BROD80, SRG83, BB84b] from the area of programming languages. What has been lacking is the efficient integration of processing of abstract data types with conventional database processing. The abstract object type concept addresses this omission. We discuss this issue in Section 4.

2. Recursion

Recursion arises naturally in many important applications (e.g., inventory control, part hierarchies for CAD/CAM, scheduling, routing and path finding). Unfortunately, the query languages of existing DBMSs are too weak to express recursion. Consequently, application programs must be written to retrieve data piecemeal from the database and then to perform the recursive computation outside the DBMS.

Performance can be improved dramatically by enhancing the query language and query processing capabilities of the DBMS to handle some forms of recursion. The following example illustrates this point.

Consider a DAPLEX database containing Task entities with functions Task-Name, Duration, Scheduled-Start, Manager, and Successors. (The Successors function relates each task t to tasks that cannot be started until t is completed.) The schema of the database is shown in Figure 2a. Notice that the database may be thought of as a directed acyclic graph in which each node is a task (labelled with the

a. *DAPLEX Schema:*

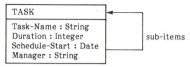

b. *Iterative Application Program to Compute Affects(t):*

```
Function Affects(t : Task) returns set of Task
begin
  initialize Affects(t) := ∅
  retrieve Successors(t) into Temp            /* DBMS query */
  while Temp ≠ ∅ do
    begin
      Affects(t) := Affects(t) ∪ Temp
      for each t1 in Temp
        retrieve Successors(t1) into Temp1    /* DBMS query */
      endfor
      Temp := Temp1
    end
end
```

c. *Definition of Affects using DAPLEX-like syntax:*

```
for t in Task
  define Affects(t) to be
  {t' in Task where t' is in Successors(t)
          or t' is in Affects (Successors(t))}
endfor
```

Figure 2: An Example of Recursion

corresponding task name) and each edge reflects the Successors function, i.e, there is an edge (t1,t2) iff t2 is in Successors(t1). Suppose a user is interested in finding the tasks that might potentially be affected if task t17 is delayed. The recursive Affects function (which is the transitive closure of the Successors function) is not definable in the first-order query languages of most existing DBMS. Hence, the above query might have to be written as an application program that successively calls the DBMS as it descends each level of the task Successors hierarchy. An iterative program that performs this computation is shown in Figure 2b. Assume that each task precedes 10 others, and that there are 7 levels of the hierarchy below t17. The cost of running this program would then be $1 + 10 + 10^{**}2 + \ldots + 10^{**}7$ random accesses to secondary storage, which (at 10 msec. each) would require approximately 34 hours.

On the other hand, making the DBMS cognizant of the recursive definition makes it possible for the DBMS to optimize the entire query by exploiting its knowledge of physical database structures and access paths. Figure 2c shows a DAPLEX-like definition of the virtual function Affects. Suppose the Task entities are stored in a topologically ordered file called Successors as follows. Each record of the file corresponds to an edge of the Successors graph (i.e., it has a Source and a Destination field, together with their level numbers and perhaps other attributes of the Source or Destination nodes). (Since the graph is directed and acyclic, we can assign a level number to each node in the obvious way: nodes with no predecessors are at level 0; the level of any other node is the length of the longest path into it.) The file is sorted by ascending level number of the Destination field. Further, suppose that there is an index on the Source field.

Then, the query to compute Affects(t17) can be evaluated as follows. Use the index to locate the first Successors record where Source = t17. Add the Destination node and its level number to the Output file. Sequentially scan the Successors file from this record onwards, adding nodes to the Output file as follows. Read a page of the Successors file. For each record (x,y) on it, if y is already in the Output file, then go to the next Successors record; else, if x is t17 or is in the Output file, then add y and y's level number to the Output file; else go to the next Successors record. Note that since Successors is ordered by the level number of its Destination field, the nodes in the Output file will also be ordered by increasing level number. Hence, for each page of Successors, to determine if any Source node x or Destination node y is in the Output file, scan the Output file in reverse (starting with the most recently added records) until the level number becomes smaller than the minimum level number on the Successors page.[3]

Assume that there are 10,000 records in the Successors file, stored 10 to a page, and that 90% of these occur after t17. Also, assume that there will be 1000 records in the Output file, stored 50 to a page, and that for each page of Successors, an average of 9 pages of the Output file have to be scanned. Then, the cost of retrieving all nodes affected by t17 is the sum of the cost of locating the first record with Source = t17 (2 page accesses, say), the cost of scanning all records after t17 in the Successors file (900 page accesses), the cost of writing the Output file (20 page accesses), and the cost of matching nodes in Successors with nodes already in the Output file (9 X 900 page accesses), i.e., a total of 9022 page accesses, which (at 10 msecs. each) take 1.5 minutes — a three orders of magnitude improvement in preformance over the simple iterative algorithm.

Incidentally, this example also illustrates a shortcoming of the approach to coupling logic-based AI languages such as PROLOG with existing DBMSs that is advocated in [REIT78c, CMT82, VCJ83, JCV84, YOKO84]. The "application program" in the example may well be a Horn clause logic program that uses the DBMS to store and retrieve facts (extensional knowledge). Figure 3 shows such a program

---

[3] This algorithm is similar to the sort-merge implementation of the relational join operation, where the inner relation is sorted on the join attribute but the outer relation is not. The only difference is that in our algorithm the inner relation can grow while the algorithm runs.

to define the Affects relation over the Task database of Figure 2.

Definition of Affects using Horn clause logic rules:

if Task(t1) and Task(t2) and Successors(t1,t2) then Affects(t1,t2)
if Task(t1) and Task(t2) and Task(t3) and Successors(t1,t2) and
Affects(t2,t3) then Affects(t1,t3)

Figure 3: Definition of Affects using Horn Clause Logic Rules

The inference engine (interpreter) associated with the logic programming language can then be used to answer queries such as "Find all t such that Affects(t17,t)" involving both extensional knowledge (stored in the database) and intensional knowledge (expressed in the Horn clause). The PROLOG interpreter or any other AI inference engine that uses standard resolution theorem proving techniques would perform poorly, because these engines work by unifying formulas and by instantiating them with one fact at a time; when the facts are stored in a database, this results in expensive tuple-at-a-time access to the database [VCJ83]. An alternative approach, described in [REIT78c, CHAN78, CMT82, JCV84, YOKO84], is to "batch" data requests from the inference engine before accessing the database. However, where the intensional knowledge being used by the inference engine includes recursion as in our example, then even this batching of data requests is inefficient. Because the query language of the target DBMS is only first order, the batching technique will, at best, produce a sequence of queries similar to those produced by the iterative program of Figure 2b. As we have seen, a DBMS capable of optimizing recursive queries directly could do much better.

Extending DBMSs with capabilities for processing recursion involves three research issues:

1. Finding special forms of recursion to put into the DBMS

2. Designing a query language that provides facilities for defining recursive queries and views, especially in such a way that the optimizable special forms can be easily recognized

3. Augmenting existing database storage structures, access paths, and query processing techniques to efficiently process these special forms of recursion

The simplest form of recursion is transitive closure. Some proposals for tacking on this operation to existing query languages (e.g., QBE [ZLOO77] , SQL [JAME82, CLEM81]) exist in the literature, but no attempt has been made to generalize it or to develop efficient query processing algorithms. At the other extreme is general recursion as found in general purpose programming languages such as LISP.

Clearly, it is infeasible to add general recursion to a DBMS query language, since it would render the query language computationally complete, and hence, undecidable. The approach taken in [MINK78, REIT78c, CHAN78, CMT82, JARK84, YOKO84] is to add the power of recursive function-free Horn clause programs to a relational query language. This is motivated by the results that a Horn clause program is equivalent to an existentially quantified first order relational query followed by one application of a least fixed point operator [CH82c] and that these queries can be evaluated by a simple iterative algorithm [AU79]. Improvements to the simple iterative algorithm using a differencing technique are described in [BAYE85], and in the chapter by Bancilhon (in this volume). [IOAN85] develops conditions for recursive Horn clause programs to be bounded and decomposable into programs that are less expensive to execute. [HN84, ULLM85], and the chapter by Ullman on query processing (in this volume) develop a number of "capture rules" that improve efficiency in special cases; these special cases are based on the propagation of information in the recursion, rather than on the special properties of the database structures and computations that occur most frequently in applications. For instance, function symbols have been largely ignored because in general they could result in non-terminating computations. However, in practical applications, the recursive functions to be computed often have algebraic properties that guarantee termination.

Our approach is evolutionary and pragmatic. First, we generalize transitive closure to a point where it captures many important applications, without sacrificing opportunities for efficient processing over large databases. For these special cases we exploit and adapt many well-known graph traversal algorithms. Later, as efficient algorithms for other, more general, forms of recursion are discovered, these forms can be incorporated.

We proceed formally as follows.

For mathematical simplicity, we shall use relational terminology in the rest of this section (i.e., we shall assume the database and the views to consist of relations, instead of entities and functions). The mapping to DAPLEX entities and functions is fairly straightforward.

A view X over a database D is defined by an equation of the form $X = f(D)$. Recursive views are defined by recursion equations. the general form of a recursion equation is $X = f(X,D)$. We seek a relation $X = LFP(f,D)$ that is the "least" fixed point of the equation. "Least" means that every other solution exceeds LFP in a partial ordering. Set inclusion is the partial ordering used in previous work; we will use a slightly stronger ordering that permits a tuple to be replaced by another tuple with the same key, but "better" data values (e.g., a shorter path).

In general, there is no guarantee that a recursion equation has a least fixed point, or that even if one exists, there is an algorithm to compute it efficiently. So we will exploit classes of functions f that exhibit good behavior.

We focus on a special class of recursion equations, called *path problems*. The simplest path problem is the transitive closure of a binary relation R. A binary relation R can be represented as a graph. Each attribute value in R corresponds to a node, and each tuple (x,y) in R corresponds to a directed edge from x to y. The *transitive closure* of R is the relation X where $(v1,v2)$ is in X iff the graph has a path from v1 to v2. Using the notation of relational algebra, the transitive closure is the LFP of the recursion equation

$$X(x,y) = R(x,y) \bigcup \text{project}(x,y)[R(x,z) \text{ equijoin } X(z,y)].$$

Transitive Closure identifies paths between node pairs $(v1,v2)$, but for most applications, we want additional information about the set of paths between v1 and v2.

Generalized transitive closure (GTC) is used to solve these more general path problems. Consider a relation R that contains two attributes to represent vertices and other attributes to represent properties (labels) of edges. For notational simplicity we assume only one edge property. Thus the tuples in R have the form (x,y,d) corresponding to a directed edge from vertex x to vertex y with property d. Then, GTC also has three attributes. For each pair of vertices v1 and v2, GTC contains a tuple $(v1,v2,d)$ that summarizes the set of all paths from v1 to v2; i.e., d is computed from the third attribute ("edge property") values of all tuples in R of the form $(v1,v2,d)$. For example, given path length, we might find the shortest of all paths connecting each pair of vertices.

GTC uses two operators to summarize information. *Concatenator* (*Con*) is applied when two paths $(x,z,d1)$ and $(z,y,d2)$ are concatenated to produce a path $(x,y,d3)$ whose label d3 is computed from the labels d1 and d2 of the two paths being concatenated. In shortest path applications, concatenator adds the path lengths.

Suppose there are several paths $(x,y,d1)$, $(x,y,d2)$,..., going from x to y. *Aggregator* (*Aggr*) replaces the set of paths with a tuple (x,y,d) whose label d is computed from the labels d1, d2, ..., of the set of paths being aggregated. To compute the shortest path, Aggregator selects the tuple with shortest length di; in load limit problems it would select the tuple with the highest value of di, and so on.

Formally, the generalized transitive closure of relation $R(x,y,d)$ is the minimal solution to the recursion equation

$$X = Aggr\{ R \bigcup \text{project}[Con(R \text{ join } X)]\}.$$

The join condition is usually equality, though some applications need more complex join conditions. For example, to connect two airline flights, in addition to matching the source and destination cities, there should be enough time left between the arrival of one flight and the departure of the other. This requires an inequality join condition. Propositional deduction can also be expressed as a path problem with an equality join condition, and hence can be optimized using the techniques described here. For deduction in predicate calculus (as performed by PROLOG), the join condition tests for unification. Again, the benefit of expressing deduction as a path problem is that it makes it possible to consider optimization. Figure 4 summarizes some well-known path problems.

An extensive theory of path problems is developed in [CARR78] and [AHU76].

Application	Property	Aggregator	Concatenator
Shortest path	length or time duration	min	+
Critical (longest) path	length or time duration	max	+
Maximal capacity path	capacity	max	min
Most reliable path	reliability (between 0 and 1)	max	×
Bill of materials	item count	+	×
List all paths	edge name	∪	concatenation
List any path	edge name	chooseany	concatenation
Propositional deduction	proposition	chooseany	concatenation

Figure 4: Examples of Path Problems
The join condition in all these problems is equality; i.e., paths are constructed recursively by matching the terminus of one path with the origin of another.

Path algebras, using operations that correspond to Concatenator and Aggregator are defined. Myriad algorithms for computing GTC under various restrictions are given. The choice of algorithm depends on the difficulty of the algebra and the complexity of the graph structure.

Topologically-ordered Recursion is a class of recursion where the tuples in LFP(f,D) can be ordered as $t1,t2,t3,...$ such that each tuple ti can be computed from tuples $t1,t2,...,t(i-1)$ and database D. The intersection of topologically ordered recursion and path problems yields the class of path problems on acyclic graphs (i.e., problems of computing GTC on acyclic graphs).

Using a topological ordering of the nodes, we can compute the GTC one node at a time. Information about paths terminating at a node v can be computed without referencing nodes beyond v. We call this simple procedure a *topologically ordered traversal*.

The algorithm for computing Affects(t17) was an implementation of topologically ordered traversal using database file structures. While Affects was an example of simple transitive closure, the same algorithm can be used to compute generalized transitive closure, as the next example illustrates.

Reconsider the Task database of Figure 2. To construct the Affects function, it was sufficient to determine whether a path exists between two tasks. For GTC problems, it is important to determine not only the existence of paths, but also to perform computations along paths. For instance, we might be interested in defining a view that tells how a delay D0 in one task T0 would affect other tasks.

The definition is fairly sophisticated. It specifies for each task the earliest time at which the task can be rescheduled. For tasks that are not affected by T0, the Delayed_Start is the same as the original Scheduled_Start. A task T that is affected by T0 will be delayed iff for some predecessor, T', of T,

$$\text{Delayed\_Start}(T') + \text{Duration}(T') > \text{Scheduled\_Start}(T).$$

The virtual function Delayed_Start might be defined using DAPLEX-like syntax as shown in Figure 5.

```
for T in Task
 define Delayed_Start(T) to be
 if T = T0 then
     Delayed_Start(T) := D0
 if T is not in Affects(T0) then
     Delayed_Start(T) := Scheduled_Start(T)
 if T isin Affects(T0) then
     Delayed_Start(T) :=
             max({Scheduled_Start(T)} ∪
                 {Delayed_Start(T') + Duration(T')
                  where T isin Successors(T')})
 endfor
```

Figure 5: Definition of Delayed_Start

For example, if T0 is task t17 and D0 is day3, then this view can be used to ask the query "Which tasks will be delayed if task t17 is delayed till day3?" Assume as before that the Successors file is stored topologically ordered by level number of the Destination field, and that there is an index on the Source field. A topologically ordered traversal strategy starts from t17 and traverses the hierarchy forward in topological order computing Delayed_Start. This strategy is implemented by an algorithm similar to that for constructing Affects. The only change is that for every node that is added to the Output file, its currently computed Delayed_Start is recorded. Thus, for each record (x,y) of the Successors file, if x and y are both in the output file, then replace Delayed_Start(y) by max {Delayed_Start(y), Delayed_Start(x) + Duration(x)} else if x is in the Output file and y is not, then add y to the output file setting Delayed_Start(y) to max {Scheduled_Start(y), Delayed_Start(x) + Duration(x)}. Nodes for which Delayed_Start > Scheduled Start can be output to another file during the above topological traversal.

We have remarked that a large number of algorithms for implementing generalized transitive closure operations exist [CARR78, AHU76, AU79]. Examples of these algorithms are: Warshall's algorithm, Schnorr's algorithm, Dijkstra's algorithm, Topologically ordered traversal, and the Iterative algorithm of [AU79]. The algorithms have various restrictions. Schnorr's algorithm applies only to GTCs with aggregator "chooseany", Dijkstra's applies only to a special subset of GTC (e.g., finding shortest paths when all edges have non-negative lengths, most reliable path, maximal capacity path). Topologically ordered traversal works only for GTCs on acyclic graphs. The iterative algorithm works only for path algebras that satisfy a monotonicity property.

Most previous work assumed that data is stored in main memory. Incorporating these algorithms into a DBMS will require three major tasks in future research. The first task will be to adapt the algorithms to work with data on secondary storage as we have done for topologically ordered traversal in our examples. The second important task, then, will be to combine the processing of recursion with the processing of conventional database operations such as selection, projection, and join.

GTC operations were defined in [MERR84] and a topologically ordered traversal algorithm for computing GTC over data in secondary storage was described. However, no attempt was made to integrate this algorithm with other DBMS query processing algorithms. Of particular importance is the use of selections to reduce the cost of processing recursion. Users will seldom want to see an entire recursive view (e.g., the entire transitive closure of a relation). The system must take advantage of these restrictions.

The examples below show some restrictions that might be imposed on path problems. They are expressed as restrictions on paths. Note that quantified restrictions (the first two predicates below) and restrictions on aggregates (the third predicate) arise naturally.

a.   Find paths that include one or all of a particular set of points. Usually, one wishes to specify the start or end point. For example, "Find all paths between Boston and Washington." These points may be used as the start of the database traversal.

b.   Find paths all of whose edges satisfy some predicate. For example, "Find all paths consisting of edges with reliability 0.8 or more." The traversal can skip edges that do not satisfy the predicate.

c.   Find paths that satisfy some monotonic predicate on the whole path. For example, "Find all paths that are less than 300 miles long." We can stop tracing a path as soon as the predicate is no longer satisfied (e.g., as soon as the length exceeds 300 miles).

When more than one selection condition is specified, there may be a choice of topologically ordered traversals. Consider the query, "Find tasks managed by Jones that are affected by t17." We could start from t17 and traverse the hierarchy downward (as we did before), testing each task for the condition Manager=Jones; or, we could use an index to locate tasks where Manager=Jones and traverse the hierarchy upward to t17. The costs of these traversals may differ significantly depending on the parameters of the database.

Some work on combining selection with the iterative algorithm is described in [AU79]. In that paper, the authors consider strategies for processing a query of the form "Selection(LFP(relational algebra expression))." They give sufficient conditions for moving the selection inside the iteration.

It is necessary to go further in two directions. First, we must give similar rules for topologically ordered traversal and other algorithms that are far more efficient (and complicated) than simple iteration. Second, the theory must be extended to expressions that include arithmetic, grouping, and other operators. That is, we must take it from transitive closure to generalized transitive closure.

Combining projection with selection and recursion is also important, since we may not need to retrieve entire paths, but only some selected nodes (or their attribute values) along selected paths. For example, "Find all tasks affected by t17," "Find all tasks that will be delayed as a result of delaying t17 to day3." As we have seen, for these cases the Output file need not record paths or even edges.

For a more complicated example that combines joins, selections, projections, and IS_A relationships with recursion, see Figure 6.

The third major task in adding recursion to a DBMS is to extend the cost model and heuristics used by the optimizer in generating efficient query evaluation plans.

The final issue is how to extend the query language and view definition syntax to include facilities for recursive definition. Some DBMSs provide a rudimentary recursive definition/query facility. For

Schema:

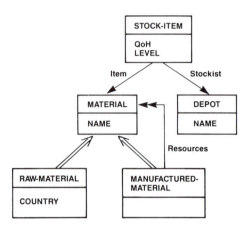

Definition of a Virtual Function called Affects from Material to Depot

```
for m in Material
   define Affects to be
   {d in Depot where (for some s in Stock-Item :
      Stockist(s)=d and Item(s)=m)
   or (for some mm in Manufactured_Material :
      m isin Affects (Resources (mm))} endfor
```

Query: If the Iran/Iraq reduces the Oil Supply, which depots will be affected?

```
for r in Raw_Material where Name(r) = Oil
            and (Country(r) = Iran or Country(r) = Iraq)
   for d in Depot where d isin Affects(r)
   retrieve Name(d)
   endfor endfor
```

Figure 6: Defense Material Supply Example

example QBE [ZLOO77] contains a recursion mechanism that can be used only on binary relations that form a tree.

Three alternative approaches to expressing GTC in a query language can be considered. One is to provide a procedural syntax in which the user writes a path traversal program [GUTT84, KHIS84]. This approach suffers from two obvious shortcomings: procedural specifications of knowledge are notoriously difficult to write and to modify; and, as the example of Figure 2b shows, the knowledge is too fragmented to be used effectively by the optimizer. Hence, it is entirely up to the user to write efficient programs, as illustrated in [KHIS84] for the shortest path problem.

The second approach is to embed PROLOG-style Horn clause logic rules in view definitions, as we did in our examples. Such definitions are declarative, and, hence, easier to write and to modify than procedures. However, it might still be difficult for an optimizer to recognize that some collection of Horn clauses is actually defining a path problem, and to extract from the Horn clauses the parameters necessary for optimization.

The third approach is to use query templates with which the user specifies merely the components of the recursion equation defining the path problem, viz., **R**, the Concatenator and Aggregator operators, and the join condition, as we did in Figure 4. This syntax may be the easiest to use and to recognize. However, it may not be readily extensible to other optimizable forms of recursion that may be discovered in the future. These tradeoffs must be examined in future research.

3. Dimensional Information

As described in Section 1, the need to process a wide variety of information types, including many forms of spatial and temporal information, is a key requirement of the new applications to be supported by PROBE. Numerous attempts have been made to store different information types in existing DBMSs [BLAS80, UM80, GS82]. While it is possible to extract formatted data from any type of information and to store the extracted data in records, conventional DBMS techniques are not satisfactory for processing dimensional information for several reasons. First, even if dimensional information is stored in a conventional DBMS, conventional data models are too weak to capture the extensional dimensional semantics. As a result, the DBMS cannot set up efficient access paths and access routines for processing the information. Second, conventional DBMS query languages are too weak to represent the intensional dimensional semantics. The result is that even routine dimensional queries may be extremely difficult to express, and if they can be expressed at all, are too convoluted for effective analysis by DBMS query optimizers. Third, conventional DBMS access paths and storage structures are often inefficient for dimensional information. The DBMS is thus unable to optimize processing of dimensional information, and orders of magnitude performance degradation can occur.

For example, assume that during the design of an aircraft, a computer mockup of the aircraft is being constructed for parts whose geometric descriptions are stored in a design database. A simplified DAPLEX schema for this database is shown in Figure 7. Each part has an idno and other symbolic attributes (weight, material, etc.). In addition, each part has spatial attributes including the location of its center, and its enclosing envelope (approximate shape), which, for simplicity, we assume to be given by a box (rectangular parallelopiped oriented parallel to the X, Y, and Z axes).

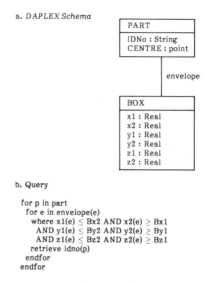

Figure 7: Simplified Design Mock-up Example

Each box is fully described by six attributes: x1, x2, y1, y2, z1, z2. Suppose we wish to determine which parts have envelopes that overlap some region, also defined by a box B (whose attribute values are Bx1, Bx2, By1, By2, Bz1, Bz2). (This is an over-simplified version of a query that is often posed during interference checking.) This query can, with a little effort, be written in DAPLEX (see Figure 7b). However, none of the conventional DBMS access methods (sequential scans, hashing, indexes, B-trees, etc.) are helpful for efficiently executing the query. If there are 100,000 parts, and the Part file occupies 10,000 pages, then a brute force sequential scan of the file will require 10,000 page accesses. On the other hand, suppose the DBMS were to maintain a spatial index structure consisting of an array, each cell of which contains a list of the parts whose envelopes overlap the cell. Then, if box B overlaps 10 cells and each cell contains 10 overlapping parts, the query requires less than 100 page accesses. [GS82] describes experimental results to substantiate the claim that existing DBMS access methods are inadequate for many information types.

Finally, conventional DBMSs do not provide general and efficient means of coupling special purpose hardware or software processors (e.g., geometric modellers, image processors) with the DBMS itself. This means that these DBMSs cannot make the best use of specially tailored processors for some of the new information types through global query optimization techniques. Again, orders of magnitude performance degradation can occur as a result of this deficiency. We return to this problem in Section 4.

To avoid these problems, there have been attempts to handle multiple information types by using a DBMS in combination with other file structures outside the control of the DBMS [FLRR84, FCKH80, HL82, LOHM83]. Typically, special ad hoc file structures are developed for the unconventional information types, while the DBMS is used to store conventional formatted data. To connect all data together, pointers are stored in DBMS records to aid in locating related data on external files. This approach has major disadvantages. The use of external files outside the control of the DBMS is really a throwback to the pre-DBMS era with all its attendant problems. The responsibility for data integrity, concurrency control, and recovery rests on all the application programs instead of on an integrated DBMS. Also, data independence is compromised: changes to the external file structures to gain performance may invalidate existing application programs. Finally, the onus of logical integration and global access planning also rests on the application programmer.

Our approach is to provide direct DBMS support for dimensional information. This involves four research issues:

1. Extending the database extensional knowledge representation to accommodate dimensional semantics,

2. Extending the query language to express dimensional queries,

3. Extending the database physical data structures to accommodate dimensional semantics, and

4. Providing general and efficient mechanisms to incorporate specialized processors.

We discuss the first three issues here and defer the fourth to Section 4.

The dimensional semantics to be built into the data model must encompass the three common representations of spatial information:

-   *solid* representation: In this technique, space is divided up into various-sized pieces. A spatial characteristic of an entity (e.g. its shape) is then represented by the set of these pieces associated with the entity. In some representations, the pieces may be of fixed size. For example, a grid might be imposed on a map to divide it into square segments. The shape of a country on the map might then be represented by the collection of segments it (wholly or partially) includes. The finer the grid is, the closer the approximation this collection becomes to the actual shape. In other representations, the pieces may be of variable size and shape. The various forms of "constructive solid geometry" [REQU80] used in CAD applications are examples of this representation.

-    *boundary* representation: In this technique, a spatial characteristic
     of an entity is represented by a line segment (or other boundary).
     For example, using this approach, the shape of a country on a
     map might be represented by a collection of line segments
     defining the outline of the country. Again, the shorter the line
     segments are, the closer the approximation this collection
     becomes to the actual shape. Curves of various sorts might also
     be used.

-    *abstract* representation: In this technique, topological relationships
     having specific spatial semantics, such as CONTAINS, IS-NEXT-
     TO, ABOVE, and BELOW, are defined in the data model and
     used to associate entities.

Temporal information may be treated as a one-dimensional case
of spatial information. The temporal semantics built into the DBMS
must include three aspects of time: intervals or duration, discrete points
(e.g., versions in a CAD/CAM application), and abstract topological
relationships (e.g., BEFORE, AFTER, DURING).

Underlying all these representations of spatial and temporal
(dimensional) information are two important concepts: *space* and *dimension.* A *space* is defined as a collection of dimensions. A dimension is
a named direction (i.e., a linearly ordered set), optionally with scale and
units. Examples of declarations using these concepts are:

X-MAP-AXIS, Y-MAP-AXIS   *DIMENSION* INTEGER *BY* MILE;
             ORDER   *DIMENSION*

           PLANAR   *SPACE* X-MAP-AXIS(0), Y-MAP-AXIS(0);
           LINEAR   *SPACE* ORDER;

Note that these concepts allow the definition of spaces having many
different characteristics, as well as an arbitrary number of dimensions.
An origin may optionally be defined, as shown in the PLANAR example.

Once the dimensions and spaces of interest to an application have
been defined, the next step is to define entity types to represent objects
that are located in these spaces. Primitive types such as POINT and
INTERVAL may be built in. Other types can then by defined in terms
of these primitive types, as illustrated in Figure 8.

The dimensional representation of entities is orthogonal to the
relationships and taxonomy of those entities that would be defined in
DAPLEX.

The concept of space provides a universal frame of reference against
which these relationships and taxonomy can be interpreted.

X-AXIS, Y-AXIS, Z-AXIS : *DIMENSION* REAL
CUBIC: *SPACE* X-AXIS (0.0), Y-AXIS (0.0), Z-AXIS (0.0)

type CUBIC-Point is Point in CUBIC
    X-COORDINATE : Point in X-AXIS
    Y-COORDINATE : Point in Y-AXIS
    Z-COORDINATE : Point in Z-AXIS

type Box is INTERVAL in CUBIC
    X-SPAN : INTERVAL in X-AXIS
    Y-SPAN : INTERVAL in Y-AXIS
    Z-SPAN : INTERVAL in Z-AXIS

type PART is entity in CUBIC
    idno : String
    center : CUBIC-Point
    envelope : Box

Figure 8: Dimensional Type Declarations

Figure 9 shows spatial analogues of the IS-A and "component" relationships. In the lefthand figure, the spatial relationship S designates a spatial version of a conventional "IS-A" relationship. This relationship indicates that the space for entity type B is the same as that for entity type A, but at a finer level of detail (such as would be seen in "zooming in" on the object). In the right-hand figure, the spatial relationship S represents a spatial "component" relationship. This relationship indicates that the space for B may be given by a transformation matrix relative to the space for A. In this case, B objects are spatially enclosed by A objects.

Using the concept of a spatial inclusion relationship and the concept of recursion from the previous section, we can model structured objects that are located in space (and time). A structured object is an object that is composed of other objects and relationships among them. For instance, a part may be composed of other parts; an integrated circuit module may be composed of other modules, connections and wires; a complex feature such as an industrial park may be composed of other features such as buildings, smokestacks, gardens, and ponds; a document may be composed of sections and front matter. In many applications, these structured objects are the units for integrity control, concurrency control, and recovery. For instance, in a computer aided design application, it may be necessary to lock an entire part assembly (i.e., a part together with its component parts) if the part is to be redesigned. Similarly, if an integrated circuit module is deleted, the deletion must be propagated atomically to all its components. Efforts to extend the relational model to handle structured objects are described

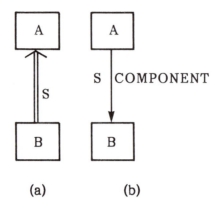

Figure 9: Spatial Links

in [HL82, LP83, BB84b]. However, no attempt has been made to capture the dimensional properties of structured objects, which are important in many applications.

X-AXIS, Y-AXIS, Z-AXIS : *DIMENSION* REAL
    CUBIC : *SPACE* X-AXIS (0.0), Y-AXIS (0.0), Z-AXIS (0.0)

```
┌─────────────────────────────┐
│ PART                        │
├─────────────────────────────┤
│ IDNo : String               │
│ SHAPE : GEOMETRY            │
│ CENTRE : CUBIC-Point        │
└─────────────────────────────┘
S│        ↑    ↑
COMPONENTS
   │    │PARENT
   │    │   IS-OF-TYPE
   ↓    ↓
┌─────────────────────────────┐
│ COMPONENT                   │
│ INSTANCE                    │
├─────────────────────────────┤
│ ORIENTATION:                │
│ MATRIX (3,3) OF REAL        │
└─────────────────────────────┘
```

```
type PART is entity in CUBIC
         idno    :   String
        SHAPE    :   GEOMETRY
   COMPONENTS    :   spatial set of COMPONENT-INSTANCE
       CENTER    :   CUBIC-Point

type COMPONENT-INSTANCE is entity in CUBIC
transformed by ORIENTATION
relative to PARENT
   ORIENTATION   :   MATRIX (3,3) of REAL
     IS_of_TYPE  :   PART
        PARENT   :   PART
```

Figure 10: Part Hierarchies as Dimensional Structured Objects

Structured objects are quite easily modelled in DAPLEX: entity-valued functions can be used to describe their structure. In fact, for structured objects that are located in space, the spatial versions of these entity-valued functions can be used to relate structured objects with their components. Properties of a structured object can be defined recursively in terms of properties of its components, or vice versa. Thus, the orientation of a component object relative to its parent can be defined by a transformation matrix, as illustrated by the Part hierarchy example of Figure 10. Alternatively, the spatial extent of a parent object may be defined by aggregating the spatial extents of its components, as illustrated by the Document example of Figure 11.

Having extended the extensional knowledge representation capabilities of DAPLEX, the query language must correspondingly be extended. We add a collection of dimensional predicates such as OVERLAPS, PRECEDES (along some specified dimension), CONTAINS. Figure 12 shows how the query of Figure 7b can be rewritten using the built-in dimensional predicate OVERLAPS.

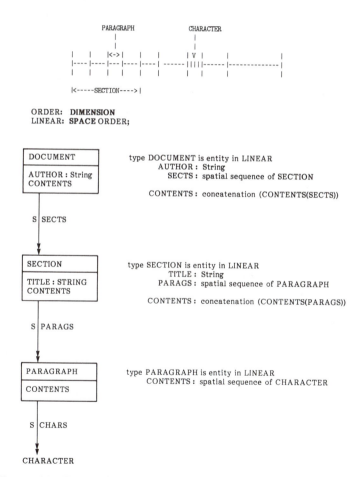

Figure 11: Documents as Dimensional Complex Objects

Given B : Box with some X-SPAN, Y-SPAN, Z-SPAN values:

```
for p in Part where OVERLAPS (envelope(p), B)
      retrieve idno(p)
endfor
```

Figure 12: Dimensional Query on Parts

For more complicated examples, we introduce the concept of a *region*, which generalizes the concept of an interval. A region is a sub-space optionally having size, shape, position or structure. The position and shape could be interactively specified via a graphics interface.

For example, consider the text data type defined in Figure 11, and the query "display occurrences of 'Kadaffi...Chad' in intelligence report and list sections spanned." The declarations and query involved are shown in Figure 13.

INTEL_REP: DOCUMENT;

T: region of INTEL_REP where FIRST(T) = "Kadaffi"
        and LAST(T) = "Chad";

```
for each T in INTEL_REP
      RETRIEVE(T);
      for each S in SECTION where OVERLAPS(contents(S), contents(T))
            RETRIEVE(TITLE(S));
      endfor
endfor
```

Figure 13: Dimensional Query on Documents

Finally, since the result of many spatial queries is better displayed graphically rather than textually, the "retrieve" command can be generalized to a "display" command that includes a specification of the display layout of the result.

In considering the augmentation of physical DBMS structures, it is useful to relate the additional components necessary for dimensional information processing to those used in conventional database processing. Conventional database structures used to implement DAPLEX are shown in Figure 14a, while the additional structures required for spatial information are shown in Figure 14b. Given an entity of a specified type, a RECORD structure gives the function values of the entity. Given a function value, an INDEX structure or HASHING is used for associative access (i.e., to find all entities of a type having that value). Given an entity, LINKS or CLUSTERING are used for sequential access to locate all related entities of the same or of different types.

Analogously, the SPATIAL NEIGHBORS structure would be used for sequential access in space, the SPATIAL INDEX structure for associative access, and the RECORD structure is used to find all spatial and non-spatial function values. Different indexing techniques are required for different applications. For example, K-D-B trees [ROBI81] are good for point entities in sparsely populated space, while cellular arrays [SRG83] and grid files [NHS84] are good for intervals in densely populated space. R-trees [GUTT84] are dynamic index structures. The text example described previously might use spatial links, while the CAD/CAM example involving the aircraft design might use a cellular array. Even when spatial links are used, physical clustering may be important as a way to optimize access to closely-related data. An example of a SPATIAL NEIGHBORS structure that provides physical clustering is the Z-ordering of [OM84].

a. Conventional Physical Database Structures

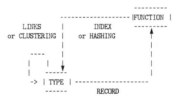

b. Spatial Physical Database Structures

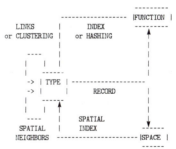

Figure 14: Conventional and Dimensional Physical Structures

Finally, the DBMS optimizer must be enhanced to take advantage of the new dimensional semantics and the new storage structures and access paths. Especially interesting optimizations are possible when recursion and dimensional knowledge are used in combination. For example, consider the part hierarchy of Figure 10 and the query "Find all parts that overlap some given region R." A topologically ordered traversal could start at the top of the part hierarchy, test these parts for overlap with R; then trace the COMPONENTS and IS_of_TYPE functions to the next level of the hierarchy, compute the transformed coordinates using ORIENTATION, test for overlap with R; and so on until the atomic parts at the leaves of the hierarchy are reached. The semantics of spatial inclusion can be used to advantage: when a part P that does not overlap with R is found, do not visit any of its descendants in the hierarchy, since none of these descendants can possibly overlap with R (because they are spatially enclosed within P). Additional performance gains can be obtained through the use of spatial indices of the type described before. However, because part geometries are described in relative coordinate systems, instead of a single global system, we have to associate one spatial index with each part in the hierarchy. At each stage of the hierarchical traversal, the spatial index associated with a part can then be used to determine which components of the part overlap R. This use of spatial (and non-spatial) monotonic predicates to improve the efficiency of hierarchical traversal was described in [RHM84]. The technique described there will be extended in future research.

4. Extensibility

The DBMS must be capable of evolving to meet the requirements of a diversity of applications. In particular, its repertoire of data types, of physical storage structures, and of access methods to implement these new data types must be extensible. Also, there might be specialized hardware or software processors for some of these data types. It would be both wasteful and inefficient to reimplement the specialized processors directly within the DBMS. On the other hand, there are clear advantages to bringing these processors under the control of the DBMS. It must be possible to couple these processors via hardware or software interfaces to the DBMS and to describe their salient features (especially the information types and operations supported) to the DBMS.

We believe that the proper approach to the general and efficient incorporation into the DBMS of both: (a) new data types defined by augmenting the DBMS's logical and physical structures, and (b) new data types defined by the use of specialized processors, is the use of abstract object types. >From the point of view of the user, an abstract object type is like an abstract data type; the type is a "black box" whose internal structure cannot be seen by the user. The only operations applicable to the type are revealed in the schema (i.e., declared in the definition of the abstract type) as extensional knowledge.

An example of such an abstract type might be the GEOMETRIC type that gives the geometric description of a part in a CAD/CAM application and was left undefined in Figure 10. This abstract type is shown in Figure 15. Since the internal structure of the new type GEOMETRY is not visible to the user, it might be implemented either as a built-in DBMS type, or by special purpose hardware designed for geometric processing, without this difference affecting the user.

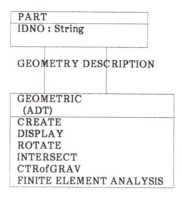

Figure 15: Geometric Abstract Data Type

The idea of abstract data types has been current in the research literature on programming languages (and to some extent on databases) for some time (see, for example, [BROD80, SRG83, BB84b]). What has been lacking is a way to properly integrate processing of such abstract types with conventional types. To take a simple example illustrating this point, suppose the GEOMETRIC data type defined above has been implemented using a special purpose geometric processor. Then suppose a query is submitted to find parts satisfying the conjunction of some non-spatial condition (e.g., made of some specified material or weighs less than some specified amount) and some spatial condition (e.g., when rotated, can fit into some specified space in a specified assembly). A query optimizer would have to choose among various strategies, including:

a.   Process the non-spatial part of the query and pass all parts satisfying the condition to the geometric processor to see if they satisfy the spatial part of the query.

b.   Process the spatial part of the query using the geometric processor and test all parts satisfying the spatial condition to see if they satisfy the non-spatial condition.

c.   Process both the spatial and non-spatial parts of the query simultaneously (the geometric processor can presumably operate in parallel with the DBMS query processor) and intersect the resulting sets of parts to determine those that satisfy both conditions.

Abstract types provide a novel twist to query optimization in the knowledge-oriented DBMS. For built-in data types, the cost of executing different operations is known and can be incorporated directly into the optimizer's cost model. However, if, in the interests of physical data independence ("information hiding"), the abstract type is treated as a black box by the DBMS query processor i.e., the details of the type's physical representation and of the algorithms used to implement its operations are hidden from the DBMS query processor, then no global optimization is possible. To enable the query optimizer to construct efficient strategies involving abstract types, it is important to specify abstract properties (e.g, commutativity, associativity, distributivity) of the types' operations, and important implementation parameters such as response time and volume of data returned. We call these data types that have two interfaces (one visible to the user and the other to the DBMS query processor) abstract object types.

The global optimizer will have to be driven by the descriptions of the abstract object types.[4] Such a description-driven query optimizer will enable the knowledge-oriented DBMS to evolve. Not only will it be easy to add new types and operations, but also new algorithms for existing types and operations. The design of a description-driven optimizer is a challenging research problem.

5. Conclusion

In Sections 1-4 we have emphasized the central role of DBMSs in shared information processing systems of the future. Using examples drawn from various applications, we have shown that it is necessary to enhance existing DBMSs if they are to successfully meet the challenging information management needs of these applications. Three important areas for enhancement have been identified: processing general knowledge expressed as (possibly recursive) view definitions and queries; handling of multiple information types (especially those with dimensional characteristics); and the integration of specialized processors for some of these information types. In each area, we have identified the principal problems in incorporating the capabilities into a DBMS. We have described promising approaches to solving these problems. Future stages of this work will construct detailed solutions, integrate them with existing DBMS technology, and develop a prototype of the enhanced knowledge-oriented DBMS.

Finally, additional research issues pertaining to general-purpose knowledge-oriented DBMSs have been identified. We discuss some of

---

[4] This query optimization problem generalizes the global query optimization problem in MULTIBASE [DAYA85] and the distributed query compilation problem in System R* [DSHL82]. In these systems, for reasons of local autonomy (information hiding), it is important to shield the optimizer from details of physical data storage, access paths, and local query processing strategies at foreign sites.

these below.

1. Operational knowledge processing issues: Many applications require *operational* knowledge (e.g., what must be done to make aircraft ready for reconnaissance missions). This type of knowledge is usually expressed in the form of situation-action rules. For example, an automated inventory control application may use the following rule: if the sum of the quantity-on-hand and quantity-on-order of an item drops below a specified threshold, then reorder the item from a supplier in good standing." A management support application may use the following rule: "if an employee's performance review is due a month from today then notify the employee's manager."

   In addition to capturing operational knowledge used by applications outside the DBMS, situation-action rules can be used in many ways inside the DBMS to improve and enhance some of its traditional functions. Examples of these functions are: integrity and access control, flexible concurrency control, version control, view update propagation, exception reporting, alerting and notification, and performance measurement.

   Unfortunately, existing DBMSs are limited in their ability to capture and process operational knowledge. Existing DBMSs are largely *passive* repositories of knowledge. Hence, even though it is always possible to store situation-action rules in database structures (e.g., in relations [SWA83]), the DBMS does not spontaneously use this knowledge. It uses the stored knowledge only when invoked by a user's query or transaction. Thus, an application that requires the use of operational knowledge must pose queries to the DBMS to evaluate the situation parts of its rules. For example, an inventory control application must periodically query the database to determine if the sum of the quantity-on-hand and quantity-on-order of any item has dropped below the threshold.

   Clearly, it would be more effective if the DBMS were *active* (i.e., if it continuously monitored the situation parts of the rules, and, whenever one was satisfied, invoked the corresponding action). Rudimentary active facilities in the form of triggers or alerters [ASTR75, SWA83] have been described for existing DBMSs. However, the only situation-action rules supported are of the form of "if relation R is updated (via an insert/delete/modify command) by user U at time T then execute query Q." General trigger capabilities have been described for the QBE system, but the hard research issues dealing with efficient implementation have not been addressed [ZLOO82].

Some AI languages such as OPS use situation-action rules as their central knowledge representation mechanism [FM77]. However, their techniques for evaluating these rules will be inefficient over large databases on secondary storage.

In [DHMR84] we describe some promising approaches to efficiently implementing active DBMSs.

2. Application design issues: How will knowledge be distributed between the application and the database? The knowledge representation facilities of the DBMS come close to matching those of the AI languages in which intelligent applications (e.g., expert systems) are written. It will be important to distinguish between shared knowledge (e.g., domain knowledge), which must be embedded in the database, and application-specific knowledge (e.g., problem solving strategies), which will typically be embedded in the application system.

3. Interface issues: We have talked about extending a textual query language such as DAPLEX. However, for many of the application areas under consideration, graphics or screen-oriented interfaces will be more appropriate. (This is especially true of applications that process dimensional information.) The interface will be used to input data, to formulate queries, and to present results. Different applications may well require different types of interfaces. For example, two-dimensional table or form oriented interfaces such as QBE [ZLOO82] and DACOS [KBB83] have been proposed for office applications. A graphics query facility has been found effective in military command and control applications [FLRR84]. A screen-oriented interface to a DBMS for CAD/CAM applications is described in [HR85].

4. Transaction Management issues: Different applications may impose different requirements on the system for concurrency control and recovery. The standard correctness criterion for concurrency control that is used in existing DBMSs is serializability [EGLT76]. It is likely that for many applications, serializability is too rigid a criterion, and that more flexible rule-based concurrency control is preferable. For instance, instead of blocking conflicting actions by two users, it might be sufficient to notify them (or a third user) of the conflict. Alternatively (in military applications

where availability is critical), it might be acceptable to perform both actions, and then subsequently take steps to compensate for any resulting inconsistencies [BGRC83]. CAD/CAM applications typically have to deal with large complex data objects and long transactions [HL82, LP83]. It is likely that for these applications, version control (management of multiple versions of a data object reflecting various stages of the design, analyze, and manufacture cycle) and extract management (management of large pieces of the database that are retrieved from the shared "public" database into a "private" workspace, manipulated, and then written back into the shared database) may be more important than strict concurrency control [HL82, LP83]. This may also be true of other applications that require lengthy processing of large data objects. For example, an image analysis expert system might extract $10^{**}14$ bits of data pertaining to an image from a geographic database, analyze the image data, and then write the results of the analysis into the database. The conventional concurrency control and recovery techniques that were developed for business data processing applications (where transactions run for a few seconds and manipulate only a handful of records) will be inadequate for the new kinds of applications envisioned for the knowledge-oriented DBMS.

We expect to address these issues in future research.

Acknowledgment

The ideas and examples presented in this paper have grown out of discussion with some of our colleagues at CCA, most notably Hai-Yann Hwang, Frank Manola, Arnon Rosenthal, Jack Orenstein, and Sandra Heiler.

6. References

[AHU76] [ASTR75] [AU79] [BAYE85] [BB84b] [BGRC83] [BLAS80] [BRAC80] [BROD80] [CARR78] [CH82c] [CHAN78] [CLEM81] [CM81] [CMT82] [DAYA85] [DHMR84] [DSHL82] [EGLT76] [FAHL79] [FLRR84] [FLRR84] [FM77] [GS82] [GUTT84] [GUTT84] [HL82] [HN84] [HR85] [IOAN85] [JAME82] [JARK84] [JCV84] [KBB83] [KHIS84] [LEVE77] [LOHM83] [LP83] [MERR84] [MINK78] [NHS84] [OM84] [REIT78c] [REQU80] [RHM84] [ROBI81] [SHIP81] [SMIT84] [SRG83] [STON75] [SWA83] [ULLM85] [UM80] [VCJ83] [YOKO84] [ZLOO77] [ZLOO82]

20
Learning Improved Integrity Constraints and Schemas From Exceptions in Data and Knowledge Bases

Alexander Borgida
Tom Mitchell
Keith E. Williamson[1]

ABSTRACT *In order to set up efficient storage structures and detect errors in the data being stored, the designers of data and knowledge base management systems must initially build schema and integrity constraints that anticipate the kind of facts that are to be stored. The purpose of this chapter is to demonstrate some ways in which a KBMS can be endowed with the ability to refine its schema on the basis of the data actually stored so far. In particular, due to the unpredictability and evolution of the natural world, as well as possible errors made by designers, a KBMS must be tolerant of occasional deviations from the norms set out during design -- in other words, it must accommodate exceptions. Two techniques are presented through which a computer system can suggest modifications and additions to the current definitions and semantic integrity constraints of a knowledge base by "learning" from the exceptions encountered. One schema refinement method is based on generalizing from example exceptions to form descriptions of classes of similar objects. The other technique refines integrity constraints by "explaining" the occurrence of exceptions in terms of a detailed theoretical world-model, and then generalizing to those cases where similar explanations hold.*

---

[1] Department of Computer Sciences, Rutgers University, New Brunswick, New Jersey 08903

1. Introduction

Knowledge bases are computer systems which maintain information about some aspect of the real world. This information is retrieved by users in order to make decisions and is updated as the world evolves. Traditionally, this knowledge about the world has been partitioned into two parts: i) a *schema* of generic, time-invariant information[2], and ii) the *facts*, which are specific, volatile and occur in large quantities.   From the user's point of view, the schema describes what concepts the knowledge base knows about (e.g., the classes and properties of a semantic data model [BORG85a] or semantic network [FIND79]) and what constraints exist on the possible relationships between objects (e.g., integrity constraints of various kinds).

Unfortunately, the schema of the knowledge base may not reflect entirely accurately the corresponding aspects of the world. This is due to the irregularity, variability and complexity of the world, the fact that it evolves over time, and that the schema design is arrived at through an inherently error-prone process of interviewing the end-users. Traditionally, all information entering the database had to be shoe-horned to fit the schema, which meant that either the schema had to be overly-general or the exceptional facts had to be omitted from the database, leading to incompleteness. However, recently developed techniques [BORG85b] permit the storage and access of information which does not conform to the constraints imposed by the schema, but which nonetheless reflects the correct state of the real world. In addition to allowing the knowledge base to reflect reality more accurately, this allows the *system itself* to determine that the schema is somehow wrong by examining the data actually stored. This chapter investigates the possibility of having automatic aids that identify cases in which the number of exceptions mounts to the point where a change in the schema is indicated, and then suggest to the database administrator possible improvements to the schema. In this sense we are describing part of a computer system which might be called a "database administrator's assistant". In particular, this chapter presents methods for proposing refinements to the integrity constraints and definitions of the KB based on an analysis of the exceptions encountered so far. This work is founded on, and extends, techniques for generalization from examples in the field of Machine Learning in Artificial Intelligence.

Our plan is to first present a particular language for describing the schema of knowledge bases — essentially a "semantic data model". In section 3, we illustrate both the need for permitting violations to constraints to persist in a particular KB and the utility of generalizing from

---

[2] The schema resembles in some ways the terminologic component of AI knowledge representation schemes such as Krypton [BFL83a].

such exceptions. We then review a mechanism which allows such exceptional information to be stored and accessed in the database. Section 4 describes some ways in which a computer system might aid in the refinement of a KB schema based on the exceptions to it encountered so far, and   Section 5 proposes a technique to accomplish this based on empirical generalization. In Section 6 we present a more powerful technique for learning from exceptions based on explanations of why the exception occurred.

2. Languages For Describing Concepts and Objects

Inspired by research on "semantic data models" in databases and semantic network schemes in AI, we have adopted a framework in which a particular state of our knowledge is described as a collection of **object descriptions**: every object is an instance of one or more **classes**, and has zero or more **attributes/properties**, which relate it to other objects, and thus describe it. Note that each object has a distinct identity independent of the values of its attributes.

The schema of such a knowledge base then specifies two things: **(1)**. The *definition of the classes* available in this KB, including their name, the attributes applicable to each of their instances, the range of possible values for every attribute, and constraints on the membership of various classes (such as subclass relationships); this essentially defines a typing mechanism for KB objects. **(2)**. Additional semantic *integrity constraints* (ICs), expressed in some logical language, which limit the possible relationships expressed in the KB.

Briefly, the schema serves several purposes:

1.   From the user's point of view, the schema describes the "domain of discourse" of the KB, and verifies the correctness of data being stored, thereby detecting data-entry errors which have been found to occur frequently in practice.

2.   From the KBMS point of view, the schema aids in achieving various forms of efficiency: (a) *storage efficiency* (e.g., by allowing concise codes to be assigned to enumerated types), (b) *faster retrieval* (e.g., fixed-length record schemes can be used for storage when attributes and their ranges are known; or the subclass hierarchy can be used to suggest vertical and horizontal splitting strategies [CDFL82]), (c) *compile-time optimizations of programs*: by using type information, one can often eliminate run-time type checking, (d) *semantic query optimization*: integrity constraints can be used to find faster access paths to the data [KING80a].

The language of class definitions used in this work will be introduced through an example, relying on the reader's ability to generalize.

According to the definition in Figure 1, the class of EMPLOYEE objects is a subclass of PERSONs (i.e., every EMPLOYEE instance is also a PERSON instance) with attributes **name, degree, jobCat, wages** and **supervisor**. Furthermore, **names** of employees are strings of no more than 25 characters, **degree** can be one of HSGD, BS, MS or PhD, **jobCat** is an integer between 1 and 7, **wage** is a decimal number in the range 0.00 to 80000.00, and the **supervisor** of an employee must also be an employee.

EMPLOYEE = = PERSON *with*
    [name : STRING(25)]
    [degree : {'HSGD, 'BS, 'MS, 'PhD}]
    [jobCat : 1.77]
    [wages : 0.00 .. 80000.00]
    [supervisor : EMPLOYEE]

Figure 1: Definition of EMPLOYEE class

Note that as usual in semantic models, classes "inherit" the attributes of their super-classes. Hence, if PERSONs have **age** and **address** attributes, then so will EMPLOYEEs. In addition, when defining a subclass one can also specify a restriction on the range of an existing attribute; for example, PERSONs may have had **age** defined to have range 0..130, but for EMPLOYEEs this may be restricted to 14..90.

The definition of a class such as EMPLOYEE specifies *necessary* properties for objects belonging to that class, but it is up to the user to explicitly assert that an object is an instance of it (i.e., there is no recognition of objects). Other classes have sufficient conditions determining membership. For example, secretaries are by definition exactly those employees who have job category 6. Such classes are described by selecting some "definitive" property specifications (in the above case, **jobCat** being 6) as tests applicable to a base class (EMPLOYEE, in the above case):

SECRETARY = = EMPLOYEE
    such that
        [jobCat: 6..6]
    with
        [wages: 0.00 .. 20000.00]
        [typingSpeed: 20..80]

Note that test-defined classes may also have additional necessary conditions attached to them.

A KB state then records information about the current state of the world by keeping track of the membership of objects in classes, and the known property values of objects. For example, the KB may contain the following information about an object emp45 at some moment:

[emp45 IN EMPLOYEE]   [emp45 IN PERSON]
[emp45 name "karl marx"]   [emp45 age 88] [emp45 jobCat 4]

This can be summarized in the form

EMPLOYEE <emp45> ([name= "karl marx"] [age=88] [jobCat=4])

leaving it to be inferred from the subclass hierarchy that emp45 is also a PERSON.

The language of class definitions allows one to capture certain constraints on the possible facts in the KB. Most obvious are the *property range constraints* limiting the possible ranges of property values. In a natural extension to the syntax of class definitions, we allow nested class definitions as a way of imposing additional such constraints. For example, the following definition ensures that fathers of persons are male:

PERSON *with*
    [gender : {'male, 'female}]
    [father : PERSON *such that* [gender : {'male}]]

Constraints which cannot be expressed in the restricted language of class definitions must be stated as *integrity constraints* in a first-order language where attribute names are considered as functions, class names are unary predicates and other primitive predicates include $=$, $\neq$, as well as the numeric and string comparators. For example, the following two constraints state that all employees must have supervisors, and that these must earn more than their subordinates:

(x) EMPLOYEE(x) $\Rightarrow$ (supervisor(x) $\neq$ null)
(x) EMPLOYEE(x) $\Rightarrow$ (wages(x) $<$ wages(supervisor(x)))

3. Exceptions in Knowledge Bases

3.1. On the occurrence of exceptions

In most practical situations the schema developed during database design does not describe perfectly the world in the sense that there will occasionally be information that needs to be stored, but that contradicts the constraints of the schema. One reason for this is the *variability* of the real world: It is often neither feasible to anticipate, nor desirable to capture all possible situations that may occur in the world. Philosophers have long been aware of the difficulties involved in defining "natural kinds" -- concepts which occur in everyday experience rather than being formally defined. Unfortunately KBs often hold information exactly about such natural domains. Two other reasons for the schema being inadequate are of potentially greater significance here: The first is that the world is not static -- it evolves, and new unanticipated situations may arise. The second is that database design is an art, not a science, often pursued by someone unfamiliar with the application domain; hence the schema may simply be wrong if the designer does not understand or express properly the situations described by users, or if users are unable to articulate their implicit knowledge.

The following examples illustrate a variety of situations where the current KB definition is plausibly inappropriate, requiring exceptional facts to be stored. In each case there are certain modifications that could reasonably be made to the schema by generalizing from a series of such exceptional occurrences.

- A few employees may be paid more than $80,000.00, thus violating the constraint on **salary**; unfortunately, the upper bound will always be debatable ($100,000?, 1,000,000?), and using such a high bound eliminates the main *raison d'être* of the constraint: to detect errors. Following a number of individual exceptions, we might recognize though that the 80,000 limit on salaries does not apply to presidents and vice-presidents in a company.

- Occasionally, an employee may be hired in a foreign country, as a sales agent for example, and his contract may stipulate a salary in some foreign currency (e.g., French Francs). Because of fluctuating exchange rates it is not possible to store the actual value in dollars, as are all other salaries. If the company's operations in France increase considerably, we would want the schema to reflect the fact that these employees are paid in different currency.

- Because of work on a new classified project, some employees may receive security clearances of various degrees. The company then desires to record this information in the database for possible future references. If this occurs with sufficient frequency, eventually we may want to add the definition of this attribute to one of the classes in the schema.

- In some special cases, a person may earn more than his/her supervisor. In fact, entire classes of exceptional situations may arise, such as employees who work overtime, or supervisors who are on leave.

- Although social security numbers are supposed to be unique, occasional employees may have duplicate numbers or may not yet have such numbers if they arrived in the USA recently. On the other hand, it is easy to see how the uniqueness of social security numbers could be (mis)stated as the formula:

(x,y) (EMPLOYEE(x) ∧ EMPLOYEE(y)) ⇒
SocSec#(x) ≠ SocSec#(y)

which is missing an antecedent to the implication, namely that x
be distinct from y.

• Although it is reasonable to describe the class of valid addresses
for a country like the USA, it seems unreasonable to describe the
addresses of *all* the countries in the world just in case someone
from that country is encountered. However, if correspondence
with some particular country becomes frequent, then a description of its addresses can be profitably added to the schema. At
issue here are the necessary attributes for an address (e.g., department or county names), as well as their legal values.

The above examples show that knowledge bases (i) need the
flexibility to accommodate at runtime special cases not sanctioned by
the schema, and (ii) under appropriate circumstances, need to be able
to adjust their schema, including integrity constraints. We present next
a synopsis of the techniques for accommodating exceptional values
presented in [BORG85b], concentrating on those features which are
relevant to the problem of learning from exceptions.

3.2. Accommodating exceptions in knowledge bases

Only two kinds of facts can be stored in the KB using the
language introduced above: the membership of objects in classes, and
the property values of objects. Such facts are entered through two primitive update operations, **modifyProperty** and **createObject**, and are
retrieved by the operator **getValue**. These operators indicate that some
fact being stored violates the definitions in the schema by **signaling a
violation**. This is a well-known technique used in programming
languages to indicate other error situations such as division by 0, arithmetic overflow, etc. Once such an error is detected, the user or program is normally supposed to take some alternative action by executing
a **handler**, which may for example ask for a correction to the data being
stored. If, however, the user insists on storing a particular fact, because
it is accurate despite the contradiction with the schema, the user will
be allowed to **resume** the update operation, which will have the effect
of storing an exceptional value. In this chapter we will treat only exceptional property values, though exceptional instances of classes can be
dealt with in an analogous manner.

The presence of exceptional values in a KB leads to a number of
problems that must be resolved. The most interesting problems arise
because a KB has multiple users, as well as pre-defined programs which
utilize its data. If these are not made aware of the presence of

exceptional facts, they are likely to produce non-sensical results (e.g., adding a salary value in French Francs to a running total of dollars, or attempting to find the **state** attribute of a French address[3]). Our solution to this problem lies in the repeated use of the violation-handling mechanism: exceptional values are marked when stored, and the act of accessing such data later on gives rise to another violation — essentially a warning or echo of the earlier problem. Again, the user/program has the choice of taking some alternate action in a handler, such as using a different value (e.g., converting the salary using the current exchange rate), or **resuming** the retrieval, in which case the actual value stored is returned. Exceptional property values are marked by creating an instance of the special class

> EXCEPTIONAL *with*
> > [prop : PropertyIdentifier]
> > [obj : AnyObject]
> > [class : ClassIdentifier]

and it is this instance which is used as a violation to signal that a property value requires careful handling.

For example, if the we tried to store an exceptionally high salary for croesus

> **modifyProperty** (croesus,wages,90000)

and we **resume**d this after the violation of the constraint on EMPLOYEE wages was signalled, then we would create some object e1, shown below,

> EXCEPTIONAL <e1> ([prop=wages] [obj=croesus]
> [class=EMPLOYEE])

and e1 would be raised as a violation when we tried to retrieve croesus' salary using **getValue**(croesus, wages). The same mechanism can also be used to store new attributes — ones not mentioned in the schema. For example, one can record the security clearance code of a particular employee by resuming the operation **modifyProperty**(croesus, securityCode, 10), and creating an appropriate instance of EXCEPTIONAL.

Violations of ICs are signalled in an identical manner to those of property range constraints. Whenever the user resumes such a violation, he may "blame" this on the value of zero or more properties, which are marked exceptional. For example, if the constraint

> notOverManager : (x) EMPLOYEE(x) $\Rightarrow$
> > (wages (s) < wages (supervisor (x)))

---

[3] France, of course, does not have states.

fails when x=croesus then any of the following facts may be exceptional: wages(croesus), supervisor(croesus), or wages(supervisor(croesus)).

Accommodating exceptions to ICs leads to a second problem: once we allow the violation of an IC to persist because it is a special case, then the constraint will henceforth be inconsistent with the database. This means that the IC will not be able to distinguish between errors in more recent updates and "false alarms" due to the old exception. For example, if after an update croesus earns more than his supervisor, then the constraint **notOverManager** will always be false as long as his and his supervisor's salary do not change. We therefore propose to modify the IC so that this "false alarm" is avoided yet the constraint continues to detect errors in future updates. In this chapter we adopt the relatively straightforward approach of considering every IC to be actually of the form:

$$constr_i : (\omega) \; SPECIALconstr_i(\omega) \vee \Phi(\omega)$$

where $constr_i$ is the label of the rule, ω is a sequence of variables, Φ is the original form of the constraint, and $SPECIALconstr_i$ is a predicate which prevents the original form from being evaluated for special cases. Initially, $SPECIALconstr_i$ is everywhere false, but as exceptions are encountered and "excused" for various argument tuples $\delta_1, \delta_2, ...,$ the definition of $SPECIALconstr_i$ becomes

$$SPECIALconstr_i(\omega) \Leftrightarrow \omega = \delta_1 \vee \omega = \delta_2 \vee \cdots$$

Thus, after encountering croesus as an exception, the constraints concerning managers' salaries would actually look as follows:

(x)(SPECIALnotOverManager(x) ∨
    (EMPLOYEE(x) ⇒ (wages(x) < wages(supervisor(x)))))

SPECIALnotOverManager(x) ⇔ (x=croesus)

In summary, we have proposed to accommodate exceptions to constraints in KBs by 1) marking exceptional information using objects in the KB so that information *about* exceptions can be maintained, 2) using an exception handling mechanism to alert the user when exceptional information is being manipulated, as well as when constraints are violated, 3) modifying integrity constraints so that they are consistent with the exceptional facts. For the interested reader, a considerably more general and complete proposal for exception handling is presented in [BORG85b]. This includes considerations about software engineering issues, implementation, accountability, and techniques for dealing with transactions. In addition, we provide a more refined theory of how to deform ICs in a minimal way, including model and proof-theoretic accounts of this phenomenon.

4. Learning from Exceptions

A user can determine that a schema is ill-designed only by using it: by making updates and retrieving information from the knowledge base described by the schema. We have argued earlier that exceptional facts provide *prima facie* evidence of problems with the definitions of classes and integrity constraints. Since such exceptions are now present in the KB itself, we can consider developing computer tools that examine these exceptions and that propose, when appropriate, possible improvements to the schema.

The first question to address is what kinds of changes to the schema should be considered. We will restrict our attention to incremental modifications of the following sort:

1. *Restricting the circumstances when an IC is checked.* Thus "All employees earn less than their supervisors" could be qualified with "unless their supervisor's status is part-time." Such qualification takes place by defining the predicates SPECIALc, occurring in all constraints, in a more general way than just by enumeration; for example, by describing a new class whose instances include all the exceptions.

2. *Adding a new attribute specification to a class definition.* For example, a securityCode property could be added to the EMPLOYEE class, or some subclass, such as COMPUTER_EMPLOYEEs.

3. *Changing an attribute specification on an existing class.* If a property range constraint, such as employee salaries being less than $80,000, is too restrictive, then it is possible to expand the range to a point where no exceptional values remain outside the range. At the same time, one can look for subclasses to which the original constraint applies without exceptions (e.g., secretaries), and add the old attribute specification to these classes.

4. *Defining a new class and placing it in the existing subclass hierarchy.* An alternative to adding the securityCode property directly to the EMPLOYEE class would be to create a subclass CLEARED_EMPLOYEE of EMPLOYEE, with property securityCode, among others. A different example: if all employees who earn over $80,000 (and hence are exceptions to the salary range constraint) have jobCat 1 or 2, then perhaps a subclass UPPER_LEVEL_MANAGEMENT of employees should be created for them.

There are many other possible changes to a schema (dropping attributes, changing their names, making ICs stronger or adding new ones, etc.) but the information present in exceptional facts seems to support mainly the changes listed above.

The following are some of the benefits of the above mentioned changes:

- The process of generalization will typically admit additional objects as exceptional, without the need for user intervention. Thus fewer exceptions will need to be excused in the future. This gain could be significant since introducing and accessing exceptional facts involves the overhead of handling violations and excuses for them, as well as modifying constraints.

- Refined ICs may be more useful for semantic query optimization, and even evaluating ICs may be faster: checking a single attribute value may be faster than searching through a sequence of disjuncts to see if any apply.

- The addition of new attributes and classes gives the user a refined vocabulary for expressing queries and updates.

- The increased vertical/horizontal splitting provided by new classes in the hierarchy might be used to improve retrieval efficiency.

The following section presents a technique for characterizing the class of currently known exceptions, and thence adjusting the schema to accommodate them. This technique locates commonalities for sets of objects based on their class memberships and property values, with the limitation that these commonalities must be expressible in the language of schema definitions. The subsequent section presents an alternative method for deriving descriptions of exception classes, based on "explaining" the occurrence of exceptions in terms of a detailed theoretical world-model.

5. Using Empirical Generalization For Schema Refinement

5.1. The utility of empirical generalization

Suppose we have an algorithm Descr which infers a class description given a set of objects {a1,a2,...}. In particular, it provides the definition of the/a most specific class which contains all these objects, given the language of class definitions from Section 2. Thus, Descr will output class definitions that consist entirely of "definitive" attribute specifications attached to some least general existing class which contains these objects as instances.

Descr can be used to accomplish some of the goals stated earlier as follows:

1. *Restricting the circumstances when an IC is checked.* If for some constraint c, the predicate SPECIALc is defined as:

$$\text{SPECIAL}c\,(x) \Leftrightarrow x = e_1 \lor x = e_2 \lor \cdots \lor x = e_n$$

as a result of a number of exceptions e_1, e_2, $\cdots$ e_n, then replace this definition by:

$$\text{SPECIAL}c\,(x) \Leftrightarrow \text{DESCR}\,(\{e_1, e_2, \cdots e_n\})\,(x)$$

so that a generalized repair to c is effected.

2. *Adding a new attribute specification to a class definition.* Suppose that some new attribute attr, which does not appear in the schema, has been introduced in several exceptional facts: attr $(a_1) = v_1$, $\cdots$, attr $(a_n) = v_n$. Then propose that the attribute specification [attr : Descr($\{v_1, ..., v_n\}$)] be added to the least class containing $a_1, ..., a_n$.

3. *Changing an attribute specification on an existing class.* If for some class C, which currently has property definition [p : E], there are many exceptional property values $p(a_1) = v_1, ..., p(a_n) = v_n$, then find the most general existing subclass(es) C' of C to which the constraint [p : E] can be restricted (i.e., such that C' does not contain any of the exceptional objects $a_1, ..., a_n$); if the constraint on p has not been refined between C and C', then augment the definition of C' with [p : E], and generalize the constraint on C to be [p : Descr (E $\bigcup$ $\{v_1, ..., v_n\}$)].

Introducing new classes is of course another way to modify the schema. In general, the decision to introduce a subclass is a heuristic one, classes being defined in order to represent collections of objects to which certain properties are restricted, and/or collections over which ICs or queries may be quantified. Specifically, in each of the cases in the above list there are several classes that may be useful if added to the database schema:

1. While modifying constraints, there is evidence for a new class Descr($\{e1, ...\}$) describing the objects to which the constraint did not apply.

2. While adding a new attribute specification, there is evidence for the existence of the class describing objects to which the attribute applied, Descr $(\{a_1, \cdots\})$ as well as the set of values for the new property, Descr $(\{v_1, \cdots\})$.

3. When an attribute specification is modified, there is evidence for a class to which the old definition applied, Descr $(C - \{a_1, \cdots\})$ as well as a more general class for the range of that property Descr $(E \bigcup \{v_1, \cdots\})$.

There is a tradeoff between adding new classes to make communication with the KB more convenient, and the confusion caused by the presence of too many marginally useful class definitions. In order to protect the DB manager from a blizzard of suggestions for class definitions, suggestions for class definitions that appear to be useful should be placed in a "suggestion box"; a second program then sifts through these to find evidence for truly useful definitions, sometimes as an amalgam of several individual suggestions. The details of this algorithm are currently under investigation.

The following scenario summarizes the proposals made so far: The DB administrator's assistant keeps track of violations and exceptions to constraints in the schema. When prompted by the DB administrator or when sufficient evidence is accumulated, it suggests one or more alternative changes to the schema to be carried out. The decision on when enough evidence has been accumulated to suggest changes is heuristic, and may be based on absolute or relative numbers of exceptions, and the "goodness" of the induced description, which measures how useful or precise the description is. The DB administrator has the final decision about which changes, if any, to implement. In fact, the administrator may choose to modify the class suggestions by removing or relaxing certain property restrictions for example (because they were the result of coincidences in the particular sample of exceptions), or by making some property constraints necessary rather than sufficient conditions for class membership.

5.2. The generalization algorithm

Descr takes as input a set of object descriptions, and produces a class description which has as instances these objects. This should be the "most specific" such class, in the sense that any other class which would have them as instances would subsume this class. This is desireable in order to maintain the ability of constraints to detect errors: a most specific class makes the SPECIAL predicate apply to the fewest cases, and hence applies the actual test of the IC to most objects. We describe first how to achieve this goal, and deal with other, possibly conflicting, goals for Descr in the following subsection.

The fundamental idea of the algorithm is to consider the objects to be described $a_1, a_2, \cdots$ one by one, and in each case deform the current class description by the least amount necessary to have it also describe the current object. The description of the set of exceptions is initialized to be the first exceptional instance. The next exceptional instance is then compared against this. Whenever part of the class description is too restrictive, that part is generalized by one of the rules below. In the technical terminology of machine learning, the algorithm

Descr makes a specific-to-general breadth-first search [MITC82] [MCM83] to induce a description for a set of objects.

1. *Introduce/Expand Range* — A range of values can be introduced or expanded to cover a new scalar data value (string, number, enumeration). For example, to describe salaries of 40,000 and 60,000 respectively, the attribute specification [wages: 40000..60000] will be necessary. In the case of strings, the generalization will be based on the length of the strings.

2. *Introduce/Generalize Class* — An existing class can be introduced or generalized (using the IsA hierarchy) in a description to cover a new data value, especially an entity object. For example, [supervisor : ACCOUNTANT] can be generalized to [supervisor : EMPLOYEE], if the next example's supervisor is not an accountant. In this generalization process, one uses the least class in the hierarchy of classes which subsumes both the old class and the new value. Note that this generalization could also be applied to scalar values if the language allowed classes of scalars, such as EMPLOYEE_AGES, to be defined.

3. *Drop Attribute Specifications* — Descriptions are pruned by dropping attribute specifications which are not uniformly applicable. For example, in generalizing a description from "EMPLOYEE *such that* ..." to "PERSON *such that* ...", one must eliminate references to attributes which are specific to EMPLOYEEs but do not occur on PERSONs. Specifications are also dropped when they are redundant or vacuous, such as in "EMPLOYEE *such that* ... [degree : {'HSGD,'BS,'MS ,'PhD}]." This form of elimination must be done only after Descr has generalized the description so that it describes *all* of the input objects.

4. *Introduce Attributes* — A reference to a particular instance of a entity class can be generalized by introducing a description of its attributes and then generalizing them. For example, [supervisor : EMPLOYEE<e14>] is generalized to also describe [supervisor : EMPLOYEE<e21>] by the attribute-specification

>   [supervisor : EMPLOYEE *such that* [age : 30..38]
>   [degree : 'BS] [jobCat : 3..4] [wages : 50k..60k]
>   [supervisor : EMPLOYEE<e43>]]

in the case they both have e43 as supervisor and 'BS degrees. This generalization is accomplished by a recursive call to the Descr procedure on the values of the respective property (**supervisor** in the above example). This can lead to a sudden growth in the size of the descriptions, or worse, it can lead to infinite recursion, as in the case when persons have spouse attributes whose values are also persons. Therefore, a limit on the depth of attribute descriptions must be imposed.

For example, suppose we want to find a description for the following 3 employees:

RESEARCHER <e41> ([age=35] [degree=PhD] [jobCat=2]
[wages=85k] [supervisor=EMPLOYEE<e56>])
RESEARCHER <e57> ([age=45] [degree=MS] [jobCat=2]
[wages=90k] [supervisor=EMPLOYEE<e56>])
EMPLOYEE <e66> ([age=50] [degree=PhD] [jobCat=1]
[wages=95k] [supervisor=EMPLOYEE<e78>])

The initial description would be [RESEARCHER<e41>]. The second researcher e57, forces this description to be generalized to:

[RESEARCHER *such that*
[age : 35 .. 45] [degree : 'MS .. 'PhD]
[jobCat : 2] [wages : 85k .. 90k]
[supervisor : EMPLOYEE<e56>]]

The third employee e66, forces this description to be generalized to:

[EMPLOYEE *such that*
[age : 35 .. 50] [degree : 'MS .. 'PhD]
[jobCat : 1 .. 2] [wages : 85k .. 95k]
[supervisor : EMPLOYEE *such that*
[age : 45 .. 60] [degree : 'MS .. 'PhD]
[jobCat : 1 .. 2] [wages : 70k .. 78k]]]

Assuming that the limit on the nesting of attribute descriptions is set to two, and that employees e56 and e78 have different supervisors, the description of their supervisors became [supervisor : EMPLOYEE]. This was then dropped as a redundant restricition since employees' supervisors are always employees.

As presented here, Descr returns a single description. However, for several reasons Descr must actually return a *set* of descriptions. First, there may be more than one maximally specific class in the schema that contains an object. For example, someone may be both an EMPLOYEE and a CUSTOMER at the same time. Second, the subclass relationship need not in general form a tree, so that two classes may have more than one most specific subsumer in the IsA partial-order. For these reasons, Descr actually maintains a set of maximally specific descriptions, as in [HAYE76] and [VERE78]. This set is initialized to be the minimal classes containing the first object to be described. Given another object, Descr generalizes each description in the set as described earlier. In "climbing" the generalization hierarchy, the set of most specific descriptions may grow if there is more than one parent. On the other hand, when one description in the set is generalized, it may now subsume one of the other descriptions and hence is no longer necessary. In this case, the set of most specific descriptions will shrink.

In order to modify the schema, it is necessary to arrive at a single class description, given the set produced by Descr. One step towards this goal is to prune the set of descriptions by taking into consideration *negative examples*: objects which should NOT be covered by the class generalized by Descr from a list of examples. Such negative examples are not immediately obvious in our case, since non-exceptional objects may well be included into generalized classes. For example, although all employees earning more than $80,000 have job category 1 or 2, there may be some persons who fit this description and still have wages below $80,000; this would not however detract from the validity of a modified constraint which states that "All employees other than those with jobCat 1 or 2 earn less than $80,000". Remembering that our goal is to retain the ability to detect errors, observe that the best candidates for negative examples are those circumstances where the current constraint did detect a violation that was NOT excused — a real data entry error. In other words, a constraint can be considered over-generalized if it no longer detects some of the errors it caught earlier. Therefore, of the set returned by Descr, only the descriptions that cover the fewest such negative examples need to be preserved. If following this there are still several descriptions left, all of them are added to the "suggestion box" mentioned earlier, which will have the responsibility of ranking various suggestions and possibly amalgamating them.

Finally, note that the current generalization algorithm can easily handle the case when the data model allows *multi-valued properties*, as in DAPLEX [SHIP81], since in that case object descriptions would simply have the form "EMPLOYEE<e78>   (...[supervisor=e12] [supervisor=e75] ...)", and multiple attribute values are treated just like attribute values of independent objects.

5.3. Estimating the Relevance of Attribute Specifications

There is an inherent conflict between the various goals for finding the generalization of a set of examples. On the one hand, we have looked so far for a *most specific* description of a set of exceptional objects, because this minimizes the set of objects for which the original integrity constraint is not checked, and hence allows continued detection of errors. In finding a most specific description, the algorithm Descr may generate spurious restrictions based on accidental commonalities in the data, unless we have a very large sample of exemplar objects. For example, a subclass of employees is likely to have few PhD's among them, and hence the restriction [degree: 'HSGD..'MS] may be suggested, although it is not necessarily relevant to characterizing this set. Also, Descr may introduce circular reasoning along the lines: "The employees who earn over $80,000 are those who satisfy the constraint [salary : 85000..120500]". The presence of such spurious attribute specifications is problematic for two reasons: it makes integrity constraints more expensive to check, and it allows fewer objects to be special, thus circumventing our goal of eliminating the need to excuse exceptional cases. These two problems can be resolved by selectively eliminating all but the most "essential" attribute specifications in a description. However, if we drop too many property restrictions or the wrong ones, the constraint expressed in the schema will become over-generalized, thereby making it less effective for detecting errors. Heursitics are therefore necessary in order to decide which attribute specifications can or cannot be dropped from a description.

A two-phase approach is advocated here: first generate candidate constraints which should be dropped from a description, then check to see if actually removing them leads to problems. In this second task, negative examples are used in the same way as when pruning less desirable descriptions among the set generated by Descr. Also, if the number of entities in the database which satisfy a description increases dramatically when some attribute specification is dropped, then the resulting description has a good chance of being overly general; this provides a second global heuristic for determining when an attribute constraint is essential. This heuristic is not currently being used, relying instead on statistical information on the distribution of values in the database, as explained below.

This leaves the problem of deciding which constraints to try to drop in a description, since it may not be feasible to try all combinations, and since there may not be enough positive and negative examples to work with. For this purpose, we introduce the notion of **relevance**: an evaluation of which attribute specifications are more relevant to the generalization at hand, so that irrelevant ones can be discarded. The following are some heuristic sources of relevance.

- Classes, and their properties, which are closer to a particular class in the superclass hierarchy are more relevant to it than ones further away. In particular, the new attributes introduced when a subclass is defined would seem to be most relevant to each other and to that subclass.

- When using Descr on values violating an IC, then the other classes and properties mentioned in the IC are likely to be relevant.

- When describing objects that are exceptional with respect to the range constraint of some attribute p, then their p property is irrelevant to this characterization. (this prevents circular descriptions.)

- The statistical distribution or frequency of certain values in the database can also be used in deciding relevance. For example, if certain values of a property p are infrequent in the database then the absence of those values in a restriction is not very significant (e.g., since 'PhD degrees are relatively rare, the constraint [degree: HSGD..MS] is less likely to be relevant). Conversely, if a value of a property occurs very frequently in the database then the absence of these property values in a set of examples is quite significant (e.g., job categories 6 or 7, representing low-ranking employees, are quite frequent, so that the restriction [jobCat: 1..2] is likely to be significant, rather than accidental). These intuitions should eventually be made more precise through the proper application of statistical techniques which establish whether there are significant differences between the distributions of property values for the general population and the set of exceptional objects.

As an example, if the description learned at the end of the last section was being used to describe employees who violated the constraint [wages: 0.00 .. 80000.00] on EMPLOYEE, then the following description would be more appropriate:

EMPLOYEE *such that*
[degree : 'MS .. 'PhD]
[jobCat : 1 .. 2]

Several attribute restrictions were dropped. The **age** attribute is less relevant than **degree** and **jobCat** since it was introduced for PERSONs and not specifically for EMPLOYEEs. The **degree** and **jobCat** restrictions were also kept because they were statistically significant. On the other hand, the **wage** attribute is irrelevant to characterizing independently employees with high wages, so it was dropped. The supervisors' **age** and **wage** attributes were dropped for similar reasons, while the supervisors' **degree** and **jobCat** were dropped since thresholds for statistical significance are increased with each level of attribute nesting (in effect, making the requirements for keeping nested attribute descriptions more stringent). Note that in order to avoid dependence on the order of examining the examples during the generalization process, the pruning of descriptions is delayed until after the algorithm Descr completes.

In order to combine the suggestions of the various sources of information about the merits of dropping some property range constraint we use a weighted sum of the individual estimates. The exact numbers for this computation, as well as the thresholds to be used for cut-offs can only be determined empirically. For this reason, most of the learning algorithm described above has been implemented as a prototype PROLOG program, and we plan to carry out experiments to determine, among others, the appropriate definition of relevance. We also continue to refine and look for new heuristics for determining relevance.

6. Explanation-Based Improvement Of Integrity Constraints

The technique for generalizing from exceptions introduced in Section 5 is relatively robust, to the extent that it always produces some generalization, although not necessarily the "best" one. Unfortunately it suffers from a number of limitations which appear to be intrinsic to the approach.

First, a considerable number of exceptions is needed in order to obtain a reliable generalization, one that is not cluttered by spurious restrictions resulting from coincidences. The semantic notion of "relevance" was introduced in the otherwise syntactic technique of the original Descr algorithm precisely in order to crop the descriptions being suggested for consideration. It is however desirable to obtain less heuristic and finer grained guides to relevance, and to require fewer exceptions to learn from.

Secondly, the previous technique only produces generalizations in the restricted language of class definitions that we have defined, and as such is incapable of achieving generalizations involving disjunction and negation. Nor does it allow terms in the description which relate multiple attributes of an object (e.g., $\text{wages}(x) < \text{commissions}(x)$).

More significantly, the Descr algorithm obtains only generalizations of homogeneous sets of exceptions. This means that if a constraint has more than one universal quantifier, $(x)(y)\Phi(x,y)$ for example, then unary predicates E1 and E2 can be learned describing sets of exceptional x and y values respectively; this however allows only those modifications to the constraint that use unary predicates E1 and E2 (e.g., $(x)(y)\ (\text{E1}(x) \land \text{E2}(y)) \lor \Phi(x,y)$), and therefore ignores many useful refinements of constraints which would be of the form $(x)(y)\ \text{E}(x,y) \lor \Phi(x,y)$ say.

In this section we illustrate the basic principles of a different approach to learning from exceptions, one which is capable of overcoming these limitations in some situations, using considerably more computation and knowledge. This technique follows the recent trend in machine learning to *explanation-based generalization*. The fundamental idea of such an approach is to use *domain specific knowledge* to explain why a certain situation has occurred, and then to extract from this explanation the salient features which generalize to other similar situations. In our context, this would mean finding an explanation of why a particular exception to a constraint was allowed to persist, and then modifying the constraint so that it does not consider sets of values for which this explanation holds.

The key to such an approach is the presence of a *theory* for generating explanations, a theory which in our case would express the semantics of the terms used in the KB description, and as we shall see, assumptions and rules of thumb commonly made in this domain. Although this kind of knowledge would not normally be available in a standard database system (data dictionaries are not expressed formally) we are in the fortunate situation of dealing with Knowledge Base Management Systems, which could reasonably be seen to possess a theory of the database. For example, a medical or design database may have associated expert-systems, which contain knowledge that might form the basis of such a theory of the domain.

In particular, we will take the stance that there exists some theory of the domain for which the KBMS is built, and that this theory in principle defines the valid states of the KB. Unfortunately, this theory may be so complex that it is not feasible to check whether the database is consistent with it. For example, for an architectural CAD database, we may have the full laws of physics to see whether a building will stand or not, but it is surely impossible to perform an analysis of a skyscraper from first principles[4]. For this reason, the ICs used in the KBMS are seen as compiled rules of judgment which can be verified efficiently and whose role is to detect errors which are expected to occur given certain assumptions about normal activities in the world. These ICs may however be overly restrictive when new, unusual circumstances occur. It is then the role of our system to generalize the IC as much as necessary in light of the fact that some previously unexpected situations have in fact arisen. We want however to avoid generalizing the constraint to the point where it is equivalent to (and as expensive to evaluate as) the original theory; the specific examples of exceptions are therefore used to guide the generalization process along this narrower path.

Figure 2 summarizes the class of problems considered here. In particular, we assume that an exception has been found to some integrity constraint Φ which is in the form of a universally quantified formula

$$(\underline{x})(A1(\underline{x}) \wedge \ ... \wedge An(\underline{x})) \Rightarrow C(\underline{x})$$

An exception is a tuple of values $\underline{a}$ such that $\Phi(\underline{a})$ is inconsistent with the current database. The task is to determine a refined constraint that

---

[4] Similar situations hold in all science-based practical disciplines such as engineering and medicine.

Given:

- A constraint of the form $(\underline{x})\ \Phi(\underline{x})$, where $\underline{x}$ is a sequence of variables.

- A theory of the domain consisting of laws and default assumptions.

- A database instance where this constraint is violated and this violation has been allowed by the user to stand as an exception.

Determine:

- A modified version of the constraint that accommodates the given exception and similar exceptions, and which is of the form $(\underline{x})($ SPECIAL$c(\underline{x}) \vee \Phi(\underline{x}))$

Figure 2: The Problem of Modifying Constraints

covers the observed exception, as well as "similar" cases. Thus, the problem of refining the constraint is reduced as before to a problem of generalizing from the example exception to find the general category of similar exception situations.

Originally, we may desire to find an explanation of why $\Phi(\underline{a})$ was false — (i.e., why the constraint had to be violated in this case). In general, an *explanation* is a proof of $\neg \Phi\ (\underline{a})$ from premises which are either general axioms from the theory of the domain or facts from the current database. If such an explanation can be found, then we will be looking to characterize those objects $\underline{x}$ for which "the same proof" can be repeated.

It seems however that our goal above is too restrictive: rather than explaining why the exceptional case *had to occur*, we can be satisfied with an explanation of why the constraint *didn't have to hold* in this case. One way to find such an explanation is to evaluate a general *justification* of the original integrity constraint Φ, in order to determine where it breaks down in the case of $\underline{a}$, and then find an explanation of this break-down, from which we can generalize once again to similar cases.

Consider, for example, an IC for a knowledge base regarding storage of physical objects, which states that boxes should not be placed on top of vases:

$$(x,y)\,(BOX(x) \wedge VASE(y)) \Rightarrow \neg ON(x,y)$$

This is a reasonable constraint because vases are generally fragile, because one should not place heavier objects on fragile objects, and because boxes tend to be heavier than vases. This rationale for the constraint is exactly the kind of information we assume appears in the justification associated with the constraint. Figure 3 illustrates the justification associated with this constraint.

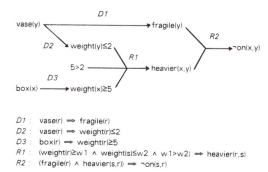

D1 :   vase(r) ⟹ fragile(r)
D2 :   vase(r) ⟹ weight(r)≤2
D3 :   box(r) ⟹ weight(r)≥5
R1 :   (weight(r)≥w1 ∧ weight(s)≤w2 ∧ w1>w2) ⟹ heavier(r,s)
R2 :   (fragile(r) ∧ heavier(s,r)) ⟹ ¬on(s,r)

Figure 3: Justification for $(x,y)[BOX(x) \wedge \text{VASE}(y)) \Rightarrow \neg\text{ON}(x,y)]$

Notice in this figure that the justification is a proof of the correctness of the constraint, based on premises that include the default rules and definitions shown in the figure. For ease of exposition, proofs are restricted here to be derivations of the consequent of Φ from its antecedents and other facts in the database, using Modus Ponens and implications derived from the theory of the domain. In the above example, assuming that vases are typically Fragile and that vases typically weigh less than two pounds, while boxes typically weigh at least 5 pounds, then it follows from the definitions of Fragile and Heavier that boxes do not belong on top of vases. Thus, the IC may be viewed as a "compiled" summary of this finer grain chain of reasoning involving the underlying domain theory.

This kind of justification can be used both to rationalize an encountered constraint exception, and to infer a more correct, refined version of the constraint. For example, consider the exception to this constraint shown in Figure 4. This exception involves a particular vase, *a*, and box, *b*, such that *ON(b,a)*. Given such an exception, there are many possible hypotheses regarding the general class of exceptions that should be accommodated in the revised IC. For instance, one might hypothesize that the constraint should be waived whenever the box is red and the vase is blue, or whenever the two objects have the same owner. The following paragraphs summarize how a justifiable generalization can be inferred from analyzing this single exception instance, and the justification of the violated IC.

The method for generalizing from the exception instance $<a,b>$ to a general exception class, SPECIAL*c*, (which is then used to revise the IC) may be summarized as follows:

1.   Consider the justification of the IC in order to determine an explanation that allows the exception instance to violate the

a = = VASE
    [Owner = Smith]
    [Color = Green]
    [Destination = Islamorada]
    [Acquisition-Date = September, 1982]

b = = BOX
    [Owner = Smith]
    [Color = Red]
    [Contents = styrofoam]
    [Volume = 3 cubic feet]
    [Density = 0.2]
    [AcquisitionDate = November 1984]

ON(b, a)

Figure 4: Exception to $(x,y)[(BOX(x) \wedge VASE(y)) \Rightarrow \neg ON(x,y)]$

constraint. In particular, step back through the intermediate assumptions in the justification of the constraint, and attempt to prove the negation of each assumption for the *specific instance* (e.g., given the assumption $R(x,y)$ from the justification, prove $\neg R(a,b)$). To complete the proof it may be necessary to rely on statements in the underlying domain theory, as well as particular features known to be true of the current exception instance in the database.

2. Once a negated assumption has been proven, isolate the features of the current exception instance **a** on which the proof is based. These features define a general class of exception instances for which this proof will carry through, and therefore constitute a justifiable exception class. Thus, define the revised IC ask $(\mathbf{x})[(A(\mathbf{x}) \wedge \neg SPECIALc (\mathbf{x})) \Rightarrow C(\mathbf{x})]$, where $SPECIALc(\mathbf{x})$ is the conjunction of features of **a** mentioned in the proof.

Consider the application of this method to the current example. The system would begin by attempting to prove the negation of the various intermediate assumptions shown in the justification of the constraint in Figure 3. In this case, the system fails to prove $ON(b,a)$ since it cannot find any reason why if a is not on b, b should be on a.[5] However, it does succeed in finding a proof that $\neg Heavier(b,a)$, which

---

[5] Note that if there was an explanation of why the exception, which is $Box(b) \wedge Vase(a) \wedge ON(b,a)$, had to occur, then there would be an explanation for $ON(b,a)$ itself.

negates the step Heavier(x,y) in the constraint justification. Figure 5 shows this proof, and the rules necessary to complete it.

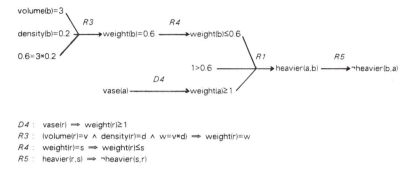

D4 :   vase(r) ⟹ weight(r)≥1
R3 :   (volume(r)=v ∧ density(r)=d ∧ w=v*d) ⟹ weight(r)=w
R4 :   weight(r)=s ⟹ weight(r)≤s
R5 :   heavier(r,s) ⟹ ¬heavier(s,r)

Figure 5: The Excuse for Box b and Vase a

Notice that the proof involves deducing the weight of box *b* from its volume and density as given in the database. Thus, the excuse for this exception is that its weight is not consistent with the default assumption that boxes weigh more than five pounds.

Once such a proof has been found to excuse the exceptional instance, the final step is to determine the most general features of this instance that are necessary for the proof/excuse to carry through. It can easily be seen from the explanation in Figure 5 that the proof depends only on the Density and Volume of box *b*, and not on other features such as its Color or Owner. Thus, the proof allows the system to resolve the problem that was so troublesome to the earlier syntactic generalization method: determining which features of the example are relevant. On this basis, one could propose the new IC

$$(x,y)[[(BOX(x) \land VASE(y)) \land$$
$$\neg((Volume(x)=3) \land (Density(x)=0.2))]$$
$$\Rightarrow \neg ON(x,y)].$$

While the revised IC described above is correct, the exception class that it describes is still not very general. A stronger generalization can be obtained by analyzing the steps of the proof to determine the weakest precondition necessary for the chain of proof steps to successfully carry through. Using a process similar to goal-regression [NILS80] the weakest precondition for the entire proof is determined by beginning with the generalized result of the proof (¬ Heavier (x,y)), then working back through the proof, computing for each inference step the weakest preconditions necessary for it to produce the desired result.[6] This

---

[6] At each step, in the regressed assertions there will be a conjunct C that was added by the right-hand-side (rhs) of the rule R that was used at that step in the proof. Unify C with the rhs of R, obtaining the most-general-unifier (mgu). Substi-

process is repeated until the corresponding assertions are computed for the starting point of the proof.

In our example, the initial assertion ¬Heavier(x,y), when regressed through the rule R5, yields Heavier(y,x). The next step yields weight(y)$\geqslant$w1 $\wedge$ weight(x)$\leqslant$w2 $\wedge$ w1>w2. Regressing this through rule D4 gives vase(y) $\wedge$ weight(x)$\leqslant$w2 $\wedge$ 1>w2. Regressing this through the rules R4 and R3 yields the assertion vase(y) $\wedge$ volume(x)=v $\wedge$ density(x)=d $\wedge$ w2=v*d $\wedge$ 1>w2, which after some simplification becomes vasey(y) $\wedge$ volume(x)*density(x)<1. If these conditions are satisfied, then the proof that ¬Heavier(x,y) will carry through. Thus, the resulting generalized IC (after simplifying to remove the redundant constraint vase(y)) is

$$(x,y)\,[[(BOX(x) \wedge VASE(y)) \wedge$$
$$\neg((Volume(x) * Density(x))$$
$$< 1)] \Rightarrow \neg ON(x,y)].$$

In summary, notice that if we trace back the proof of C(**a**) from A1(**a**),..., An(**a**), at any step of the explanation we use a propositional rule of the form $p_1 \wedge p_2 \wedge \cdots \Rightarrow q$, which is obtained by instantiating the variables of some axiom needed to establish C(**a**). Assuming that q is false in the current database, we try to find an explanation for why ¬q should be the case. If we fail, then since q is false, the corresponding step in the justification is incorrect for one of two reasons: one or more of the p's are themselves false, or the rule is invalid. The first case is covered by repeating the process: by locating one or more p_i which are false and trying to find an explanation for why ¬p_i should be the case. To cover the second case, we could look for an explanation of *notsign* ($p_1 \wedge p_2 \wedge \cdots \Rightarrow q$). However, if such an explanation existed then it would have contained an explanation of ¬q, which we had looked for already.

In our example, we found that the box *b* was not heavier than *a*, and thus discovered that the box was atypical. In other circumstances, we might have found that the vase was not fragile, because it was made of metal or onyx. The point is that it was the circumstances surrounding the given exception instance that determined which of these explanations was explored, and hence limited the generalization: only default assumptions contradicted by actual data are considered. Thus, while the theory underlying the constraints may support a great many elaborations of the constraints, only those that are needed to explain encountered exceptions will be considered. To see the significance of this point, think of all the possible elaborations that might be possible for a

---

tute the mgu into R, producing an instance of the rule. Also, substitute the mgu into the set of regressed assertions. Delete C from the regressed assertions, and add the left-hand-side conjuncts of the rule instance to the regressed assertions.

simple constraint like the one above, if one had to consider possibilities like packing on the moon, in space stations, in shelves, etc., all of which are covered by a basic theory of physics.

The above discussion indicates the potential importance of using a theory of the domain to explain exceptions to ICs in order to automatically refine the statement of the constraint. Our exploration of this line of work is in the early stages, and is related to other recent work in the AI literature on explanation-based generalization: [MITC83], [SWMB85], [WINS83]. For an overview of work in this field, see [MITC86]. Below we summarize some of the assumptions and issues associated with this approach.

- *Limitations on applicability.* Note that it will not always be possible to construct an explanation excusing the exception instance for violating the IC. In the above example, for instance, if the Volume or Density of box a were not known, then it would not be possible to prove the negation of the intermediate assertion Heavier(x,y). In this case, the weaker empirical generalization methods must be applied.

- *Degree of generalization.* Note that while this method produces *justifiable* repairs to the IC, it does not always produce the strongest possible generalization. In particular, from the analysis of the above example, one does not find that steel vases may also be excused (because they are not fragile). The generality of the exception class computed by this method depends on the particular example and the particular chain of inference steps involved in its explanation. As noted earlier, this is in fact a positive feature, since it assures that elaborations of the constraints will be tuned to the types of exceptions encountered.

- *Importance of the underlying theory.* In general, the underlying theory must be inconsistent with the actual IC if it is to explain the negation of part of its justification. And if the justification is itself derived from the theory, rather than given separately by the designer, then the theory itself is inconsistent. As we have seen in the above example, the explanation involves default assumptions that summarize what is *usually* the case, and therefore leads us into the poorly-understood field of common-sense reasoning. For example, we might know that salaries increase with education level and with experience of an employee; but what do we do in cases where *b* has more education but less experience than *c*? We must therefore be very careful, ensuring at least that any particular explanation be self-consistent (i.e., not involve inconsistent assumptions). Furthermore, the theory may be incomplete or approximate: for example, in a KB on employee salaries, the theory may state that the more somebody works the more they should earn, without giving a quantitative relation among these parameters. In such cases, the theory might not be strong enough to *prove* the exceptional instance is acceptable. However, it may be that even an imperfect theory may allow one to guide the more empirical generalization methods (such as Descr, described in an earlier section). Thus, we believe that research on combining empirical generalization methods with use of imperfect theories is an important area for further research.

7. Summary

The presence of exceptional facts which violate the constraints stated in the definition of a knowledge base provides evidence that its schema may be incorrect or inappropriate. Exceptions of certain kinds may be quite common if, for example, the KB schema was improperly designed to begin with, or if the application domain has shifted slightly since the original design. We believe that intelligent computer tools can be built to help the KB administrator *redesign* the schema, based on the exceptions encountered so far. Toward this end, we have presented two different Machine Learning techniques, and illustrated how they could be used to automatically repair errors in the KB schema.

An empirical method has been presented that can be used to determine the features common to some set of objects. These common features constitute a description of the class containing these objects, which can then be used to adjust the KB schema in various ways. We also presented a second, analytical method for repairing incorrect constraints. This technique uses a single exemplary exception to guide the search for an *explanation* of why the constraint does not hold for this case — an explanation based on an underlying domain theory including default assumptions. The explanation is then generalized to cover other potential exceptions which fit the same pattern.

Based on the preliminary work reported here, we feel there is good reason to pursue the development of Machine Learning methods for supporting KBMS's. The empirical generalization method has been implemented but not used extensively, while the explanation-based method has been worked out only for a few hand examples. We therefore plan to further implement and experiment with the methods described here in order to gain a better understanding of the capabilities of the generalization methods, and the ways in which they can be used to refine various aspects of the knowledge base schema. While substantial progress must still be made, the potential impact of this line of work on automating the management of complex KBMS is significant.

Acknowledgments:

Certain portions of this chapter have been presented under the title "Accommodating exceptions in databases, and refining the schema by learning from them", by A. Borgida and K. Williamson, in the *Proceedings of the 11th VLDB Conference*, Stockholm, 1985. By permission of the VLBD Foundation. This research has been supported by the National Science Foundation under grants No. MCS-82-10193 and DCS83-51523, and by Rutgers CAIP.

8. References

[BFL83a]   [BORG85a]   [BORG85b]   [CDFL82]   [FIND79]
[HAYE76] [KING80a] [MCM83] [MITC82] [MITC83] [MITC86]
[NILS80] [SHIP81] [SWMB85] [VERE78] [WINS83]

21
Organizing A Design Database Across Time

R. H. Katz[1]
M. Anwarrudin[2]
E. Chang[3]

ABSTRACT *A design database organizes the complex description of an artifact, arranged as a hierarchical composition of components across multiple design representations. To complicate matters, the structure must also evolve over time. We describe a way to structure a design database across time, accomplished by viewing it from the perspective of three orthogonal "planes:" one for versions, one for configurations, and one to denote equivalences across configurations.*

1. Introduction

The objective of design is to create real-world artifacts. In this paper, we are concerned with how to represent such an artifact as a machine processable description. The activity of design is complicated, and is mirrored in the complexity of design description. This arises for several reasons. First, a design can be viewed from different perspectives. For example, the description of a building as seen by a structural engineer, a plumber, or an electrician are all different, yet they interact and thus must be correlated: a wire conduit cannot be placed in the

---

[1] Computer Sciences Division Electrical Engineering and Computer Science Dept. University of California, Berkeley

[2] Visiting Industrial Fellow with the U. C. Berkeley CAD/CAM Consortium, on leave from Digital Equipment Corporation, 75 Reed Rd., Hudson, MA.

[3] Computer Sceinces Division Electrical Engineering and Computer Science Dept. University of California, Berkeley

.

same location as a water pipe, the building's structure must be able to support the pipe loads, etc.

Second, designs are constructed as hierarchies. Hierarchy is generally accepted as the most effective method for *reducing* the complexity of a design, by making it more intelligible to designers and easier to process by design tools. However, hierarchy *complicates* the design description by introducing considerable additional structure, i.e., *configurations*. The design database must now include information that describes how composite objects are built up from component objects.

The third source of complexity is that the entire description, across representations and within hierarchies, will evolve over time. Individual portions of the design are superceded by new versions. Experimental versions ("alternatives") may be created, and these must be included in the description as well. To maintain the design history, new versions do not overwrite the existing design description, and at least some portion of the history must be kept available on-line.

Thus, the design description must be organized across time, as well as across representations and hierarchy. In this paper, we will describe how to organize the design description across three orthogonal dimensions: the version, configuration, and equivalence planes. The version plane organizes the evolutionary and alternative versions of a design object across time. The configuration plane organizes the description of a particular version of an object in terms of versions of its components. The equivalence plane ties together versions of objects which are different representations of the same real world object.

The rest of the paper is organized as follows. In the next section, we define our terminology. We then follow with a detailed discussion of the three description planes: versions, configurations, and equivalences. Another mechanism for organizing a design database, based on layers and environments, is described in section 6 and is compared with our own mechanism. Finally, we give our summary and conclusions.

1.1. Definition of Terms

A design database consists of a collection of interrelated *design objects*. Each object is a logical aggregate of information about the design. Consider the design of a microprocessor. A "microprocessor datapath layout" object would describe the layout of the microprocessor's datapath. A related object might be the "microprocessor datapath transistor" object, which describes the same portion of the design in another representation, in this case transistor schematics. The real world "microprocessor datapath" object is actually represented by a collection of objects, each describing it in terms of one design representation. The equivalence of the layout and transistor objects will be represented explicitly.

We distinguish between an object, such as the "microprocessor datapath layout," and a particular instance of that object, containing a specific collection of layout primitives that together describe the datapath layout. Over its lifetime, an object is represented by many different instances. Within the context of design databases, we call these instances *versions*. The distinction is important, and must be supported explicitly. It should be possible to associate an object's versions with the object.

Design objects are constructed hierarchically. They can either be *composite* or *primitive*. Primitive objects cannot be further decomposed into components, while composite objects are composed of more primitive composite and primitive objects. For example, the "microprocessor datapath layout" object may be a composite of the "microprocessor ALU layout," "microprocessor register file layout," and the "microprocessor shifter layout." In this way, configuration information can be closely related to the hierarchical composition of objects. A *configuration* is usually defined in terms of a collection of versions of related objects. Thus, a datapath version which incorporates specific versions of its components, forms a configuration for that portion of the design.

2. The Version Plane

The version plane organizes the many versions an object has over its lifetime into a version history. Perhaps the most natural organization is to arrange them as a linear sequence based on time of creation. However, most design environments require more flexibility. Because of the experimental nature of design, an object may have more than one valid version at a time. We call these simultaneously valid descriptions *alternatives*. When one version is created by making changes to another existing version, we call the new version a *derivative* of the older.

Figure 1 shows the organization of the version plane for object V. The subscripts indicate the order of creation. Versions may also have time ranges associated with them to denote their valid lifetimes. In the figure, derivatives are aligned along the vertical axis, while alternatives are along the horizontal axis. Every object must have an initial version. The initial version of V is V[0]. Alternative versions V[1], V[2], and V[3] are derived from V[0]. Of these four versions, one would be distinguished as the "current" or preferred version, which could still be V[0] even after the other versions had been created. New derivatives can be created from previously superceded versions, as long as the new derivative is a descendant of the current version.

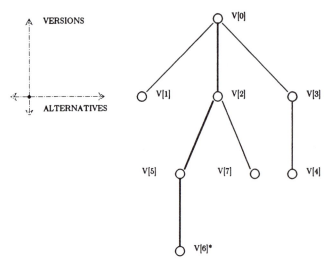

Figure 1: The Version Plane

A hierarchy is imposed on the versions of an object. The order of creation is indicated by the subscripts. Parallel versions are alternatives, while versions in series are derivatives. At any point in time, one leaf version is distinguished as "current" (marked by an asterisk). The path from the root to the current version is the "main derivation."

Once currency has moved down the tree, no new derivates in parallel with the current version can be created.[4]

To see how the version history of Figure 1 could have been derived, consider the following sequence of events. $V[0]$ is created and made the current version. $V[1]$, $V[2]$, and $V[3]$ are created as alternative derivatives of $V[0]$. $V[4]$ is then derived from $V[3]$. At this point, $V[2]$ is declared as the current version, and no further derivatives of $V[1]$, $V[3]$, or $V[4]$ can be created without changing currency. $V[5]$ is derived from $V[2]$, and in turn, $V[6]$ is derived from $V[5]$. Note that $V[2]$ remains the current version. $V[7]$ is created as a new alternative derived from $V[2]$. Now $V[6]$ is made current, disallowing further derivations from $V[2]$ or $V[7]$.

---

[4] The details of manipulating currency are not described here. The idea is that a version server would allow designers to move currency around in a manner that is consistent with the system release policy of the design team.

3. The Configuration Plane

Figure 2 shows a portion of the configuration plane rooted at object instance U[i]. Configurations are formed by combining versions of different objects to form composites. For example, V[j] is formed from the particular versions of W, X, and Y denoted by W[k], X[l], and Y[m]. Since composition information is associated with each composite object, we can think of a version of a composite object as simultaneously defining its configuration.

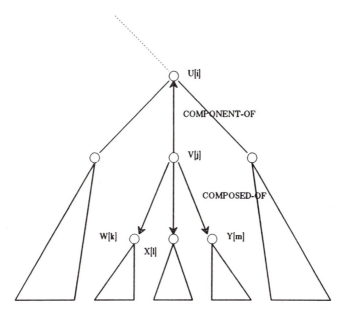

Figure 2: The Configuration Plane

Object V is composed of objects W, X, and Y, and is a component of U. The jth version of V is configured from the kth, 1th, and m^{th} versions of W, X, and Y respectively. The configuration plane, which organizes objects to form composite objects, is orthogonal to the version plane, which organizes the different instances of the same object.

The version and configuration planes are orthogonal, as Figure 3 demonstrates. The configuration plane shows how objects are constructed as a hierarchy of components, while the version plane shows how instances of individual objects have evolved over time (i.e., version histories).

At the time of its creation, the object instance V[j] is composed from instances of the objects W and X, but which instances? We defer, until Section 6, a discussion about when instances are bound to

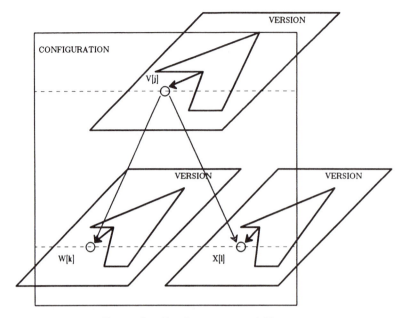

Figure 3: Configuration and Versions

> *The version and configuration planes are orthogonal. An object version is configured from components and is configured into composites. It is also a derivative of some other version in its own version plane. For example, object instance V[j] is configured from instances W[k] and X[l]. Each is also derived from some previously created object instance in its individual version plane.*

configurations.

4. The Equivalence Plane

A real world object will be described in terms of more than one representation. In our approach, each alternative representation is described by an individual object, whose instances are arranged on its version plane and who each participate in their own configuration planes. The third orthogonal in the description space is the equivalence plane, which correlates equivalent object instances across configurations in alternative representations.

Figure 4 shows how the object V is described in terms of the objects V', V", and V'", each in a different design representation and each having instances participating in a different configuration. Their instances, V'[i], V"[j], and V'"[k] are joined together through the equivalence plane.

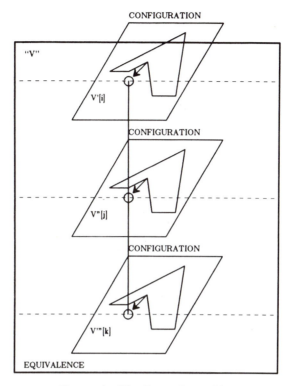

Figure 4: The Equivalence Plane

Configurations in different design representations are correlated through the equivalence plane. In this figure, three different represen-tations of the object V are grouped together by an equivalence object.

The object V, which is generic in the sense that it is associated with no particular representation, can define its own version plane whose instances can participate in configurations.

5. Layers and Environments vs. Versions and Configurations

Goldstein and Bobrow [GB81] have advocated a layered approach for object database management that is compatible with the design data-base structuring discussed here. There are two choices for how to bind object instances into configurations: statically, at the time of instance creation, or dynamically, when the configuration is acquired for pro-cessing. Layers provide a mechanism that supports dynamic configuration binding.

A *knowledge base* contains a collection of related objects. These are partitioned into *layers* by the knowledge base's administrator. Layers form the unit of version creation. The initial layer contains the original instances of the objects in the knowledge base, the second layer contains new objects added to the knowledge base and new instances of existing objects that have changed. Each object is uniquely identified, and instances that are different versions of the same object have the same identifier. A composite object is formed by including the identifiers of its components within its description. Conceptually, the binding to actual object instances takes place by searching through the design layers for the first instance that has the required identifier.

The power of the layering approach is that determination of which versions of objects are "current" is left to the designer. He can specify the order in which the layers should be searched, dynamically determining the ordering among versions. The specification of layer ordering is called an *environment*. There can be many user-defined environments for each knowledge base. The first definition of an object found in the specified order is its version within that environment. An environment can be implemented as an index structure mapping unique object identifiers into object versions, taking account of the specified order of the knowledge base's layers (e.g., see [KL84]). An environment can also contain layers from the designer's private workspace, thus making it easy to form alternative descriptions without affecting the public copy of the knowledge base.

Dynamic binding of configurations appears to be useful during the exploratory phases of design, when a new version of a portion of the system is being created. However, once a new system version has been released and placed in the public archive of the design description, the configurations must be bound to specific object instances.

6. Summary and Conclusions

An instance of a design object participates in three important structural relationships: (1) how it has been derived from other instances of the object (versions), (2) how it has been composed from more primitive object instances (configurations), and (3) how it participates as a particular view in one design representation of the real world object being designed (equivalences). This is shown in Figure 5. The interrelationships among these leads to much of the complexity of the structure of a design database.

Most configuration management systems mix the concepts of versions and configurations, and rarely support equivalences. It has been our view that structural relationships such as these should be separated

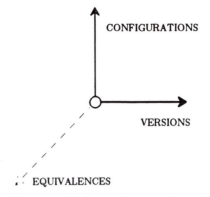

Figure 5: The Structural Relationships an Object Participates In

out for explicit support by the database system. By doing so, the design management system can take on some of the task of keeping the design description consistent. In addition, explicit support for these relationships should make it easier to develop the design tools that need to traverse the design description, for example, design library browsers and "snap together" system assemblers.

Research supported by National Science Foundation Grant ECS-8403004 and a grant from the National Semiconductor Corportation.

7. References
[GB81] [KL84]

22
Triggers and Inference In Database Systems

Michael Stonebraker[1]

ABSTRACT *There is a collection of database applications (such as real time control) which may be best accomplished using collections of triggers. The paradigm in which an initial action recursively triggers dependent actions is often called forward chaining. In addition, database support for large knowledge bases requires at least a simple inferencing capability. When a retrieve command cannot be satisfied using only stored data, a data manager must determine if a rule in the knowledge base can be used to reformulate the query. In this way, one works from the desired data toward database facts which must be ascertained using backward chaining.*

In this paper we show how forward chaining and backward chaining can both be supported by simple extensions to a relational query language. Moreover, we demonstrate extensions to a conventional lock manager which will efficiently implement the new constructs. Lastly, the extensions to support backtracking are described.

1. Introduction

In real time control applications such as power plant monitoring and control of sonar systems, a collection of sensors periodically (or continuously) present data to a database system. When certain data patterns are sighted, appropriate actions must be taken. For example, if the flow of coolant past a given sensor falls below a certain value, then

---

[1] University of California, Berkeley, CA.

an auxiliary pump should be activated. One way to implement such applications is through a collection of trigger [ESWA75] or alerters [BC79]. In business data processing applications, triggers may provide a useful mechanism for propagating updates to dependent (or replicated) data elements. (However, there are many who dispute this point of view).

In a trigger driven application an initial update to the database will cause dependent updates, which may recursively cause further updates. This forward chaining process quiesces when there are no new dependent triggers.

Conventional database management systems (DBMS) are useful for efficiently storing large quantities of rigidly formatted data. However, when DBMS's are applied in applications containing both large amounts of data and "knowledge", they usually fail to provide facilities to manage the knowledge-based portion. Applications which have a knowledge base generally require the capability to store rules of the form:

if (condition) then (result)

For example:

if a person is a manager
then he has a key to the executive lounge

Moreover, such applications require automatic inference on the rules in the knowledge base. For example, if a user asks:

Does John have a key to the executive lounge?

then the data manager must detect that the information is not stored in the database, that there is an appropriate rule to consult, and that the desired query is:

Is John a manager?

The process whereby a desired retrieval iteratively causes auxiliary retrievals until one yields an appropriate result is called backward chaining, and is the basic control tactic used in Prolog [CM81] and many other artificial intelligence (AI) languages.

When multiple rules can be applied, then backtracking is often a useful feature. Suppose there is an additional rule:

if a person is disabled
then he has a key to the executive lounge

If John is not a manager, the system should backtrack to determine whether John is disabled. Backtracking on failure is a common control tactic in AI languages, and can be applied in both forward chaining and backward chaining systems.

In this paper simple extensions to a relational query language QUEL [STON76] are proposed to support the storage of rules and both forward and backward chaining as control strategies. As such capabilities similar to those in Planner [HEWI71] can be integrated into a data base management system. Moreover, simple extensions to a lock manager to efficiently implement the language proposals are suggested. Section 2 treats forward chaining and its proposed locking implementation, while Section 3 discusses backward chaining. Then, Section 4 indicates how to extend both facilities to support backtracking, while Section 5 presents two alternative locking systems which can support the necessary locking constructs. In the next section the proposed mechanisms are contrasted with a alternate implementation tactic based on views. Lastly, Section 7 contains some concluding remarks.

Even though the context for our proposal is the data sublanguage QUEL and the INGRES database system, the ideas can be easily used in any relational DBMS with minor modifications. Although an expert system example might be a more appropriate vehicle for illustrating our constructs, in the interest of simplicity and brevity the standard EMP relation:

EMP (name, salary, age,dept, manager)

will be used instead. Other work on coupling knowledge bases and databases is described in [BJ84, CW84, JCV84, MW84, SW84, WARR81].

2. A Proposal For Triggers

2.1. Language Constructs

A QUEL command such as:

```
range of E is EMP
replace EMP (salary = E.salary)
where EMP.name = "Mike"
and E.name = "Bill"
```

will set Mike's salary equal to that of Bill. The command can be rerun at any time to reperform the replacement.

In order to turn a QUEL command into a trigger, it must logically execute indefinitely. We propose the following syntax:

```
range of E is EMP
replace ALWAYS EMP (salary = E.salary)
```

where EMP.name = "Mike"
and E.name = "Bill"

This command sets Mike's salary equal to Bill's salary, and then logically continues to execute indefinitely. Hence, whenever Bill's salary
is changed, the new value will immediately propagate to Mike's salary.
Using this feature, any QUEL operation, postpended with ALWAYS,
becomes a trigger.

2.2. Support For Triggers

Any ALWAYS command can be processed with the assistance of
a special kind of lock, called a "trigger-me" lock (T lock). The compatibility between T locks and normal read and write locks is specified in
the following table:

	R	W	T
R	ok	no	ok
W	no	no	##
T	ok	no	ok

An ALWAYS command is executed repeatedly by the user's INGRES
process until it no longer has an effect. Then, INGRES reexecutes the
command, and sets T locks on all the database objects read or written
by the command (i.e. all the objects satisfying the where clause). Then
the command is placed in a relation:

DORMANT (t-id, quel-command, user)

When a user U, submits an INGRES command which attempts to write
an object on which a T lock is held (case ## above), U's INGRES process obtains the requested lock and continues processing. In parallel
the lock manager releases all T locks held by the command in the
DORMANT relation and activates it using the stored user-id to achieve
access control. The only required DBMS facility is the ability to submit
a QUEL command from inside the lock manager.

All commands which hold a T lock on the object written by the
user command are awakened. In this way, the DBMS performs a (logically parallel) breadth-first exploration of tree of dependent commands.
Section 4 will present an alternate exploration method using a depth-
first search and backtracking.

Triggers can be canceled by running an INGRES delete command
on the DORMANT relation. At this time, all T locks held by the command must be removed. Alternatively, one could extend QUEL with a

CANCEL command as follows:

CANCEL trigger-id

In this case, the user must be informed of the trigger-id for later use in a CANCEL command.

Of course, T locks must be persistent (i.e., survive crashes of the hardware or DBMS). Moreover, very fine granularity locks (on records or even on fields of records) will be helpful in avoiding unnecessary "wake-ups" of triggers caused by updating some other object inside a lockable granule. In addition, lock escalation is desirable to prevent triggers which read many data elements from setting an enormous number of fine granularity locks. The locking system must also be carefully designed to deal correctly with "phantoms" [GRAY78]. Not only must the locking system guarantee that an update to any qualifying object will awaken the trigger, but also it must guarantee that any insertions to the database that happen to qualify will also awaken the trigger. Such insertions are called phantoms. For example, the insertion of a new employee with a name equal to "Mike" must cause the example ALWAYS command to be awakened. Section 5 presents two implementation alternatives which satisfy these goals.

The above facilities will set Mike's salary equal to Bill's whenever Bill's salary is changed, and in addition, if Mike's salary is inadvertantly changed, it is immediately reset to Bill's value. In some circumstances one might not want a direct update to Mike's salary to be undone in this fashion. Such an effect can be accomplished by a different modifier on QUEL commands (e.g., WEAKLY) and trigger-me locks which are held on objects which are read but not written. Unfortunately, the phantom problem appears difficult to solve with WEAKLY commands.

The above trigger system is based primarily on QUEL, and requires no new syntax or query processing extensions. Also, it is as efficient as the fineness of lock granularity of the locking system. Moreover, only modest changes are required to a DBMS to support ALWAYS commands and T locks. Lastly, no theorem prover or exotic data structures are required to identify which commands to trigger; the lock manager simply identifies W-T lock conflicts.

ALWAYS commands support one form of inferencing. For example, a database update can trigger a command in the DORMANT relation. This awakened command can trigger a third, and so forth. This forward chaining will stop when no new triggers are awakened by active commands. In this way, one can find all consequences of a particular update. However, the above mechanism is not able to perform backward chaining from a desired goal to a set of facts. The mechanism in the next section supports this alternate construct.

3. Backward Chaining

3.1. Language Constructs

Consider another modifier to QUEL commands, DEMAND. For example,

    range of E is EMP
    replace DEMAND EMP (hair = E.hair)
    where E.name = "Bill"
    and EMP.name = "Mike"

The normal meaning of this command is to make Mike's hair color the same as Bill's. However, DEMAND commands are not directly executed; rather, a form of "lazy evaluation" is used. When someone requests the hair color of Mike, he is made aware of the effect of the DEMAND command in a way to be described. DEMAND commands are called "lazy triggers," and require a slight modification to the relational model.

A normal relation consists of tuples, each with a collection of stored fields. In the EMP relation these are name, salary, age, dept, and manager. In addition, lazy triggers can provide data values for columns which are not stored (e.g., hair color in the EMP relation). Hence, each tuple in a relation has a collection of stored fields and a collection of fields with values provided by lazy triggers. Lazy triggers need not provide a value for a given field for each tuple in a relation. Consequently, the unstored field can vary from tuple to tuple. One view of lazy triggers is as a means of extending a relation with new fields which have values only for a subset of the tuples.

3.2. Support for DEMAND Commands

A DEMAND command is executed until the collection of objects which it will update is determined. Then execution is halted without any modification to the database, and the command is stored in a DORMANT-2 relation

    DORMANT-2 (c-id, command, user-id)

Additionally, "Missing Data" locks (M locks) are set on the collection of objects which the command would have updated. The compatibility matrix for M locks is the following: When a read lock is set on an object which has an M lock set (case !! below), an R-M conflict algorithm is run. M locks are held indefinitely and are only withdrawn when the corresponding DEMAND command is deleted.

	R	W	M
R	ok	no	!!
W	no	no	no
M	no	no	ok

QUEL processing is slightly different if DEMAND fields are present. The regular parser will reject a command which requests data which does not appear as a stored field in a relation. This rejection must be delayed, because there may be a lazy trigger to provide the desired data. An execution plan is then carried out and a retrieval command is decomposed into a collection of single relation subcommands, S, of the form:

> range of R is relation
> retrieve (R.t1, ..., R.tj)
> where Q(R)

Here, Q(R) is a qualification involving only the tuple variable R, and the target list contains a collection t1, ..., tj of fields of R. The DBMS will acquire locks during the processing of each S.

If S requests a read lock on an object which has a M lock set, the R-M conflict algorithm below must be executed. In this algorithm the DEMAND command D, holding the M lock is of the form:

> replace DEMAND X (d1 = f1, ..., dn = fn)
> where QUAL

Hence, D updates data items d1, ..., dn with values computed using the functions, f1, ..., fn whenever the qualification QUAL, is true. Also, X is the tuple variable which specifies the relation to update.

R-M Conflict Algorithm

1. Make a copy of the query S and delete from the qualification all clauses which have already been evaluated to true for the current record. Substitute into the query any data items which are stored in the current record, and call the resulting query S'. It will contain only references to non-stored data items. If D does not provide values for any data items, then terminate the algorithm, and continue query processing for S on the next DEMAND command D' which has an M lock on the current record, or on the next appropriate tuple.

2. In D replace each occurence of the tuple variable X by R. Add all range statements of D to those of S. Create S'' by replacing every reference to R.dj in S' by fj and adding the qualification QUAL

from D.

3.   Execute the modified query S'' normally and return any qualifying tuples produced as part of the result for S. Continue query processing for S on the next DEMAND command with an M lock on the current record, or on the next appropriate tuple.

For example, suppose the user requests the hair color of Mike:

retrieve (EMP.hair) where EMP.name = "Mike"

Moreover, suppose the following two lazy triggers are in effect:

range of E is EMP
range of F is EMP
D1:   replace DEMAND E (hair = F.hair)
where E.name = "Mike"
and F.name = "Bill"

range of G is EMP
D2:   replace DEMAND G (hair = "green")
where G.name = "Bill"

The request for Mike's hair color will collide with the M lock held by D1. At this time the clause "EMP.name = "Mike"" has been evaluated. Hence, the remainder of the query, S', is simply:

retrieve (EMP.hair)

The algorithm will use D1 to produce the following command:

range of F is EMP
retrieve (F.hair)
where EMP.name = "Mike"
and F.name = "Bill"

(A smarter algorithm would avoid the redundant check for Mike's name, which is guaranteed to be true at this point.) This second retrieve command is run normally and will collide with the M lock held by D2. When the collision occurs, the system will be executing the subquery:

retrieve (F.hair)
where F.name = "Bill"

and will have evaluated "F.name = "Bill" " to true. Hence, the algorithm will be run again to produce:

retrieve (hair = "green")
where F.name = "Bill"

This query will return "green", which will be iteratively returned to the top level query and added to the answer. Since there are no other qualifying records, the query processing plan will exit, producing a single answer "green" as the result of the query.

The advantage of this scheme is that little new syntax is needed. If fine granularity locking is supported, the R-M conflict algorithm will be rarely activateed unless the lazy trigger affects the request. Hence, the scheme should be very efficient. Also, there is no need for a special indexing structure for DEMAND commands to identify relevant lazy triggers.

This mechanism will implement backward chaining because a retrieve command will activate those lazy triggers which provide required data. These in turn may activate other lazy triggers which will ultimately retrieve facts from the data base. This backward chaining is similar to that accomplished by PROLOG; however, it does not support backtracking. If there are two or more rules that apply at a given point, all are executed in a random order. The next section extends the previous constructs to support backtracking.

4. Priorities and Backtracking

4.1. Introduction

Suppose a general rule with some exceptions is desired. For example, all employees over 40 have a wood desk and others have a steel desk. However, Bill who is 45 has a steel desk, Mike who is 35 has a wood desk, and Sam has the same kind of desk as Bill. Using the proposed inference system this can be expressed as five DEMAND commands:

D1: replace DEMAND EMP (desk = "wood")
     where EMP.age > 40
D2: replace DEMAND EMP (desk = "steel")
     where EMP.age < = 40
D3: replace DEMAND EMP (desk = "steel")
     where EMP.name = "Bill"
D4: replace DEMAND EMP (desk = "wood")
     where EMP.name = "Mike"
     range of E is EMP
D5: replace DEMAND EMP (desk = E.desk)
     where EMP.name = "Sam"
     and E.name = "Bill"

Two problems must be solved. First, a priority system must be devised to support evaluating the last three DEMAND commands in preference to the first and second. Second, only if a higher priority DEMAND command fails should a lower priority command be executed. For example, to determine the kind of desk that Sam has:

retrieve (EMP.desk) where EMP.name = "Sam"

command D5 and then D3 should be utilized, resulting in the answer "steel." However, if Bill is not an employee, these commands will return a null answer. In this case one should "backtrack" and try a lower priority command (D1 or D2 depending on Sam's age). In no case should all applicable DEMAND commands be used, since this will produce the answer "wood, steel" if Bill is an employee and Sam is under 40.

A similar situation exists with triggers. If two or more triggers apply, one might want to execute the one with highest priority. If that trigger fails to produce a desired answer, the DBMS should backtrack and try a lower priority trigger.

For example, suppose new employees are inserted into the EMP relation with no department specified. They are then assigned to a department using the following triggers:

T1:   replace ALWAYS EMP (dept = "shoe")
       where EMP.dept = null
       and EMP.age > 40

T2:   replace ALWAYS EMP (dept = "admin")
       where EMP.dept = null
       and EMP.manager = "Smith"

       range of E is EMP
T3:   replace ALWAYS E (dept = EMP.dept)
       where EMP.name = "Bill"
       and E.name = "Mike"
       and E.dept = null

T4:   replace ALWAYS EMP (dept = "trainee")
       where EMP.dept = null

The desired effect is to place new employees managed by Smith in the admin department, new employees over 40 not managed by Smith in the shoe department, Mike in the same department as Bill, and everyone else in the trainee department.

To achieve the desired effect, the triggering process should stop when a desired goal (in this case assigning a department to a new employee) succeeds. Moreover, all four triggers apply to a new employee over 40 named Mike who works for Smith; hence a priority system is required to activate the triggers in the order T3, T2, T1, T4.

Lastly, there may be situations where a collection of triggers have been executed, no new ones have been activated, and the goal has not been reached. In this case, the system should backtrack (i.e., undo the effect of one or more triggers) and try a lower priority alternate collection of triggers.

Consider the situation of hiring a new employee named Sam. First Fred must be moved to the toy department to make room for Sam. Moreover, George must be transferred from the toy department to the admin department to make room for Fred. If one of these changes fails (for example because George does not work in the toy department) then Sam must be placed in the trainee department and Fred restored to his original position. This situation can be expressed by the following collection of triggers:

> range of E is EMP
> T1:   replace ALWAYS EMP (dept = "toy")
>   where E.name = "Sam"
>   and E.dept = null
>   and EMP.name = "Fred"
>
> range of E is EMP
> T2:   replace ALWAYS EMP (dept = "admin")
>   where E.dept = "toy"
>   and E.name = "Fred"
>   and EMP.dept = "toy"
>   and EMP.name = "George"
>
> range of E is EMP
> T3:   replace always E (dept = "shoe")
>   where E.dept = null
>   and E.name = "Sam"
>   and EMP.name = "George"
>   and EMP.dept = "admin"
>
> T4:   replace ALWAYS EMP (dept = "admin")
>   where EMP.name = "Sam"
>   and EMP.dept = null

In this case triggers T1, T2, and T3 will be executed in order to produce the desired effect. However, if trigger T2 or T3 fails, their effects should be backed out, and trigger T4 executed instead.

The mechanisms for DEMAND and ALWAYS commands are slightly different, and we consider them separately.

4.2. Support for DEMAND

Consider an extra modifier for DEMAND commands:

replace DEMAND PRIORITY EMP (desk = "wood")
where EMP.name = "Mike"

To use priorities and backtracking, the keyword PRIORITY must be added to all potentially conflicting DEMAND commands. The effect of a PRIORITY command is similar to an ordinary DEMAND command, except it activates the following prioritization scheme.

Although priorities can be "hardwired", a flexible system is probably more useful. When a PRIORITY DEMAND command is inserted, the database system can easily ascertain which other PRIORITY DEMAND commands conflict with the new one and on what objects the conflict occurs. (This information is available from the lock manager). The user would be required to specify for each such object the priority of his command relative to conflicting commands. This could be done by making insertions into a relation:

PRIORITY-M (id-of-higher, id-of-lower, object)

The composition of PRIORITY-M for the desk example of the previous section would be:

PRIORITY-M	id-of-higher	id-of-lower	object
	5	2	Sam
	3	2	Bill
	4	1	Mike

Using this priority information, the lock manager can form an ordered list by priority of command-ids for each object. In the R-M conflict algorithm, the highest priority conflicting command must be used first.

The user must specify backtracking with the keyword PRIORITY on a retrieve command, for example:

retrieve PRIORITY (EMP.desk) where EMP.name = "Sam"

With this modifier, the R-M conflict algorithm must be altered slightly:

Whenever the algorithm says:

continue on the next command C' which holds
an M lock on the current record

substitute

continue on the next command ONLY
IF THE CURRENT COMMAND PRODUCED
AN EMPTY ANSWER

The modified R-M algorithm, the use of a RETRIEVE PRIORITY command, and the insertion of DEMAND PRIORITY lazy triggers will provide the desired priority-backtracking scheme.

4.3. Support for ALWAYS

To use priorities and backtracking, an ALWAYS command must specify the keyword PRIORITY:

> replace ALWAYS PRIORITY EMP (dept = "shoe")
> where EMP.dept = null
> and EMP.age > 40

When a user inserts such a trigger, the lock manager can ascertain conflicting triggers and the collection of conflicting objects. Registration of a trigger includes inserting information into a PRIORITY-T relation similar to the PRIORITY-M relation above. The lock manager uses the PRIORITY-T relation to order all conflicting T locks. On a W-T conflict, the highest priority trigger is awakened first.

The user must indicate that he desires a priority backtracking trigger solution. At the time he makes an update that will activate triggers, he must specify the keyword PRIORITY, for example:

> append PRIORITY to EMP (name = "Mike",
>   age = 25, salary = 2000)

Additionally, he must specify what goal should stop the priority/backtracking algorithm. A simple solution would be to have a built-in goal which is satisfied if a trigger activated no new dependent triggers but modified the database. To obtain greater generality, we propose that a user will will state both his triggering update and his goal in a transaction. The goal is a retrieve command with the keyword PRIORITY which is reached when the command has a non-empty answer. The following transaction has a goal of placing Mike in a department:

```
begin transaction
    append PRIORITY to EMP (name = "Mike", ...)

    retrieve PRIORITY (EMP.dept)
    where EMP.name = "Mike"
end transaction
```

The following three modifications to DBMS processing must be used in the presence of PRIORITY retrieves and updates:

1.   A savepoint [GRAY78] must be established for the current transaction before any trigger is activated as a result (either directly or through a chain of intermediate triggers) of a PRIORITY update.

2.   Only the highest priority trigger is activated.

3.   If an empty answer to a PRIORITY retrieve command is observed and there are no triggers still processing, then backup to the last transaction savepoint, and have the lock manager activate the next trigger in priority order.

The use of ALWAYS PRIORITY commands, the use of transactions with a PRIORITY update followed by PRIORITY retrieve, and modest changes to QUEL processing will implement a general priority-backtracking scheme. The highest priority trigger will be activated and cause a sequence of forwardly chained actions. If the goal is not achieved, the system will backtrack (by undoing changes back to a savepoint) and recursively try the next lower priority trigger, until a solution is found or until all applicable triggers are exhausted.

5. Implementation of T and M Locks

A straight-forward approach would be to place T and M locks in the same lock table holding R and W locks. In this case, one must cope with a lock table of widely varying size which must be made recoverable. Moreover, phantoms must be correctly handled. Lastly, all triggers must run inside the scope of the transaction which contained the initial update, and will thereby be backed out if the transaction is aborted.

The first objective can be satisfied by using extendable hashing for the lock table instead of conventional hashing. The second objective requires writing T and M locks into the log as part of the process of registering a new DEMAND or ALWAYS command. Moreover, the lock table must be checkpointed along with ordinary data. Database recovery code can now restore T and M locks after a crash. This presents only modest implementation difficulties.

The phantom problem poses more serious issues. Systems which perform page level locking (e.g., [RTI84, CHEN84]) have few difficulties supporting correct semantics in the presence of phantoms. However, finer granularity locking is required for efficient T and M locks. Systems which perform record level locking can allow detection of phantoms by holding locks on index intervals in the leaf nodes of secondary indexes as well as on data records [ASTR76]. Hence, a transaction which modifies a tuple will hold a write lock on the tuple and on the appropriate index interval for any modified field for which a secondary index exists. An insert will, of course, add a new record and associated index entries. Such an insert must wait if it will fall in a locked index interval. Of course, a transaction which splits a B-tree index page must wait until there are no locks held on any index records in the page.

The general mechanism can be restated as one of holding record level locks on data and index tuples. Then, a write must be delayed if it will fall adjacent to a tuple which is locked. Adjacency means "logically adjacent in Tuple Identifier order" for B-tree data records and indexes; adjacency means "in the same hash bucket" for hashed records and indexes.

The same adjacency tactic can be applied to T and M locks. T locks must be held on data and index records, and a trigger will be awakened if a write lock is set on the adjacent index record or data record. Moreover, a DEMAND command will hold M locks on data records. If a write lock is set on an adjacent data record, the DEMAND command must be reregistered to potentially cover the inserted record(s).

The only problem with the adjacency approach is that a B-tree page split will cause all triggers holding locks on the page to be awakened and all DEMAND command holding write locks to be reregistered.

The phantom problem and the logging problem appear easier to solve if an alternate strategy is employed. Consider storing the M and T locks in data and index records themselves. Systems which support variable length records can simply add as many T and M locks to each record as necessary. Such locks are automatically recoverable by current conventional techniques. The phantom problem requires the above adjacency algorithm; however, structure modifications (e.g., B-tree page splits) do not cause extra overhead. Moreover, since the extra locks are stored separately from R and W locks, extendable hashing is not a prerequisite for the lock table. Lastly, lock escalation can be handled by storing an extra record at the front of each page or relation indicating that all enclosed objects are locked. This record is automatically recoverable, and the run-time system must simply guarantee that it looks for this special record before accessing any enclosed object.

The only drawback of this second alternative is that a second implementation of a lock manager must be coded for T and M locks.

6. Comparison With A View-Oriented Scheme

We illustrate the view based scheme suggested in [ULLM85, IOAN84] by performing the hair color example from Section 3 using views. Consider the following collection of view definitions:

        range of E is EMP
        define view EMP (E.all, hair = "green")
        where E.name = "Bill"

        range of E is EMP
        range of E1 is EMP
        define view EMP (E1.all, hair = E.hair)
        where E.name = "Bill"
        and E1.name = "Mike"

The interpretation is that EMP can be both a stored relation and a collection of view definitions. Moreover, the actual value of EMP is the union of the stored relation and the view definitions.

If the following query is specified

        retrieve (EMP.hair) where EMP.name = "Mike"

it will be run on the stored relation to produce an empty answer. In addition, it will be run on both view definitions for EMP using the standard query modification procedure in [STON75]. This produces two queries:

        retrieve (E.hair) where
        E.name = "Mike"
        and E.name = "Bill"

        and

        retrieve (E.hair)
        where E.name = "Bill"
        and E1.name = "Mike"

A simple theorem prover can ascertain that the first query is false; alternately, the query can be run to produce an empty answer. The second query produces an empty answer when run on the stored relation. However, when passed again through the view mechanism, it will be modified to produce the query which will yield the desired answer.

The problem with this approach is apparent. The view machinery contains no mechanism for indexing the collection of EMP views which are logically unioned. Previous work [ROUS82] has concentrated on indexing to speed materializing the tuples in a view and not on restricting the number of view definitions which must be evaluated. Therefore, the system must try all view definitions to find the subset which yield the answer. Hence, redundant queries will be executed leading to considerable inefficiency. Alternately, some sort of a theorem prover must be built into the view mechanism to limit the number of specifications which must be evaluated. This will be a sophisticated piece of software, and theorem provers are not noted for their execution efficiency.

In the case that there are a very small number of view definitions associated with a given relation, then a view-based scheme has obvious advantages. For example, if there is only one view definition which augments a stored relation, then at most two queries must be run to satisfy any command. Moreover, if views are cascaded, then the query modification algorithm [STON75] can be run iteratively producing at the end a small number of queries to optimize and execute. Plan optimization is performed only over these ultimate queries. On the other hand, the approach in Section 3 forces query planning to be done every time a new sub-query is constructed and query optimization will be performed over a larger collection of smaller queries. Optimization at the end is sure to result in a more efficient plan.

However, the technique in Section 3 is especially effective in discarding irrelevant rules in the case that there are a large number that might apply but only a few that actually do. A view oriented scheme performs this function much less efficiently. Hence, the composition of the application will determine which mechanism will work better.

6.1. Conclusions

This paper has suggested mechanisms to support rule processing using both forward and backward chaining in a relational database system. These require only minor extensions to the query language and locking system. Moreover, modest additional changes can support backtracking on failure in either environment. The proposed facilities are advantageous because they are easy to understand, easy to implement and can be efficiently supported. Moreover, no additional data structure is required to index either DEMAND or ALWAYS commands. This can be contrasted with systems such as OPS5 [FORG81], which require such indexing.

Additionally, it appears possible to have simultaneous backward and forward chaining, if easily defined compatibility between T and M locks is established. One might suggest a solution such as the following:

> replace (...) where ...
> PARALLEL
> retrieve (...) where ...

The replace command would start a collection of forward chaining triggers, and at the same time the retrieve would activate backward chaining. The forward chaining triggers could thereby provide data required by the backward chaining inference engine.

Our approach is not without drawbacks, however. For example, it is difficult to support a field which is physically stored for some records and computed by a lazy trigger for others. If the field has an index and a query uses this index as an access path, the locking system will fail to activate the appropriate DEMAND commands. Hence, lazy triggers are restricted to non-stored fields. Also, redundant clauses are often evaluated using the R-M conflict algorithm, leading to a loss of efficiency in processing DEMAND commands.

Acknowledgement

This research was sponsored by the U.S. Air Force Office of Scientific Research Grant 83-0254 and the Naval Electronics Systems Command Contract N39-82-C-0235.

7. References

[ASTR76] [BC79] [BJ84] [CHEN84] [CM81] [CW84] [ESWA75] [FORG81] [GRAY78] [HEWI71] [IOAN84] [JCV84] [MW84] [ROUS82] [RTI84] [STON75] [STON76] [SW84] [ULLM85] [WARR81]

23
Extensible Database Systems

Michael J. Carey
David J. DeWitt[1]

ABSTRACT *The design of database systems capable of supporting non-traditional application areas such as expert systems and related AI applications, CAD/CAM and VLSI data management, scientific and statistical applications, and image/voice applications has recently emerged as an important direction of database system research. These new applications differ from conventional applications in a number of critical aspects, including data modeling requirements, processing functionality, concurrency control and recovery mechanisms, and access methods and storage structures. The goal of this project is to simplify the development of database management systems for new applications by designing and prototyping a new generation of database systems. Our research is directed towards producing a core database system that can be easily extended to meet the demands of new applications. This system will permit extensions to the data modeling, query processing, access method, storage structure, concurrency control, and recovery components of the system. We are currently considering the use of object-oriented programming and rule-based specification techniques as bases for this work.*

[1] Computer Sciences Department University of Wisconsin Madison, WI 53706

1. Introduction

Until recently, research and development efforts in the database management systems area were focused on supporting traditional business applications. The design of database systems capable of supporting non-traditional application areas including knowledge base management, image/voice applications, engineering applications for CAD/CAM and VLSI data, and scientific/statistical applications has now emerged as an important new direction for database system research. These new applications differ from more conventional applications like transaction processing and record keeping in a number of important areas:

1. **Data modeling requirements**. Each new application area requires a different set of data modeling tools. The object types and interrelationships among them used by a knowledge representation scheme (see the chapter by Levesque on Knowledge Representation) or for a VLSI circuit design are quite different from the data modeling requirements of a banking application.

2. **Processing functionality**. Each new application area has a specialized set of operations that must be supported by the database system. As an example, consider an expert database system for ship identification. Such a system would most likely contain a large database of satellite images and a rule-based system for locating ships within an image. It makes little sense to talk about doing a relational join operation between two satellite images or between a satellite image and the signatures of a set of ship types. Instead, the system will want to use a specialized image recognition algorithm to compare the satellite images with those of the relevant types of ships. As we will discuss in more detail below, we contend that it does not make sense to implement such algorithms in terms of relational database operations (or CODASYL or hierarchical data model primitives either).

3. **Concurrency control and recovery mechanisms**. Each new application area also has slightly different requirements for concurrency control and recovery mechanisms. A concurrency control mechanism is needed to coordinate access by simultaneous users so that each user is insured access to a consistent state of the database, and a recovery mechanism is needed to make sure that the database remains consistent despite hardware and software failures. However, different applications may have different notions and requirements for consistency. While locking and logging are the accepted mechanisms for conventional database applications, a versioning mechanism looks most appropriate for engineering applications. For image databases, which tend to be principally accessed in a read-only fashion, perhaps no concurrency control or recovery mechanism is needed.

4. **Access methods and storage structures**. Each new application area also has dramatically different requirements for access methods and storage structures to facilitate fast access to data stored on disk. Consider knowledge base management applications, for example. In the chapter on Knowledge Base Retrieval, Woods describes the problems associated with supporting efficient access to a large rule base. The problem he points out is that for certain types of knowledge base systems, the entries in the database (consisting of a large number of rules) look more like queries in a traditional database system, while the queries are similar to the data elements of a typical relational system. Another related example is the work of Wise and Powers [WP84], who developed an access method for indexing PROLOG clauses using superimposed code words to enhance access to large rule bases during the process of unification. Of course, different application domains have other requirements. Access and manipulation of VLSI databases is facilitated by new spatial access methods such as R-Trees [GUTT84]. Storage of satellite image data is greatly simplified if the database system supports large multidimensional arrays as a basic data type (a capability provided by no commercial database system at this time), as storing such images as tuples in a relational database system is generally either impossible or terribly inefficient.

A number of new applications for database system technology have emerged in the past few years, and it is clear that new applications will continue to emerge. Three alternative solutions to the problem of providing the database system technology needed by current and future applications seem fairly obvious. We call these solutions the "PL/I" approach, the "custom" approach, and the "coupled" approach. We comment on these three alternatives in more detail below.

1. The first approach, which we refer to as the "PL/I" approach, is to build one monolithic database system that satisfies the needs of all application areas. Like PL/I, the resulting system would undoubtably be complex to use and its performance would most likely be disappointing. Furthermore, large monolithic software systems tend to be complex to extend and difficult to maintain.

2. The second strategy, which we call the "custom" approach, would be to construct a new (custom) database system for each new application. Obviously this approach would provide excellent performance for each application area. However, since database systems are difficult and time-consuming to construct, there would be a long lead time between the recognition of the need and when the system could be brought on-line. Also, new results on algorithms and access methods appear fairly frequently in the database

literature, and such improvements would probably be difficult to incorporate once the system was up and running. Furthermore, although each application is different, the resulting systems would inevitably contain a number of similar pieces of software.

3.   The third approach, which we term the "coupled" approach, is to build interfaces for these new application areas on top of existing or slightly extended database systems [GS82, STON83, HL82]. An example of using this approach for constructing a knowledge base management system is proposed in the chapter by Vassiliou. At first glance, this approach appears promising. In Section 2, we will address why systems produced using this approach will inevitably provide unacceptable performance.

We feel that the most promising solution is a different one altogether, to design and prototype a new generation of database management systems. The goal of our research is to design a core database management system that is easily extended to meet the demands of new applications. We envision that the system will permit extensions to the data modeling, query processing, access method, storage structures, concurrency control, and recovery components of the system. While we would like to make these extensions as simple to accomplish as possible (i.e., by a database administrator), in practice what we really expect is that it will take a programmer a relatively short period of time (e.g., 2-3 months) to add the desired extensions. Initially, we will explore using an object-oriented approach as the basis for the proposed system. In Section 3, we will present an overview of the system and our initial research objectives.

The database system PROBE, as described in the chapter by Dayal and Smith, represents a cross between our approach and the "PL/I" approach. For example, while both systems permit the extension of the basic types through an abstract data type mechanism, PROBE has built-in support for versions, primitives for processing certain types of recursive queries, and multidimensional indices. While each of these features is attractive, our approach is to make such capabilities part of our basic toolkit but not to include them in every database system built using our core system.

2. Extending Existing Database Systems

Since relational database systems are now widely available, there are a number of efforts underway to utilize such systems as the basis for knowledge base, scientific, statistical, CAD/CAM, and VLSI database management systems. In this section we will explore in detail why we feel that this approach will produce systems with disappointing performance.

As a first step in understanding this claim, consider the reasons given by Date for using a database system [DATE81]:

1. Insure data independence
2. Reduce redundancy in stored data
3. Share stored data
4. Enforce standards
5. Centralize application of security restrictions
6   Balance requirements of conflicting user groups
7. Maintain data integrity

The software required to achieve these objectives varies. No software is needed to reduce redundancy in the stored data, to permit sharing of stored data, to enforce standards, to centralize application of security restrictions, or to balance conflicting requirements. To obtain data independence (which is "the immunity of application programs to changes in storage structures or access methods" [DATE81]), the database system needs schema-driven query processing routines. That is, all operations on the database must be performed according to a model of the logical and physical database design that is captured in the schema. Concurrency control and recovery software is needed to maintain data integrity during concurrent access by multiple users and during hardware and software failures.

Consider, on the other hand, the internal structure of a typical relational database management system as shown in Figure 1.

Of the software modules in Figure 1, the query processing routines, concurrency control, and recovery modules are really the only necessary ones.[2] The remaining pieces (query optimization and compilation, scans, storage structures and access methods, and buffer management) can really be considered as "glue". This is not to say that the glue is not important. Rather, it is really only there to insure that the system has reasonable performance. Furthermore, the glue varies from data model to data model. For example, a CODASYL system has little or no need for sophisticated query optimization and compilation modules.

When one attempts to build a database system for a new application using a relational database system as the basis, a number of problems arise. First, the appropriate glue for a relational database management system is frequently the wrong glue for the new application area.

---

[2] Even the user interface can be viewed as unnecessary, as it need be present only to support an ad-hoc query interface.

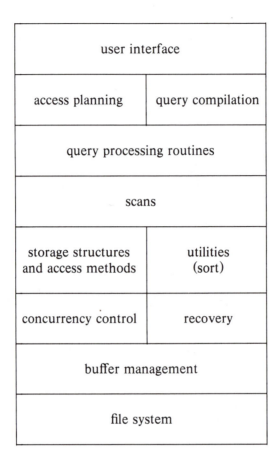

Figure 1: Architecture of a Typical Relational DBMS.

Consider, for example, the CAD/CAM application shown in Figure 2. The access methods provided by a relational system (i.e. one dimensional indices) are not adequate for a CAD/CAM environment. As a solution, Guttman recently introduced a new access method called R-trees for handling searches on spatial data [GUTT84]. As another example, specialized access methods are also needed for supporting efficient access to large rules bases in knowledge base management systems, as discussed earlier. Similar problems also arise in the area of buffer management. In [KOSH84], we showed that for operations on a statistical database, significant gains in performance can be obtained by letting the operation itself control the replacement of pages in the buffer pool rather than using a generalized buffer manager.

While one could cite a number of other examples, these examples should make it obvious that the glue for a relational system is simply

CAD/CAM Interface
Relational DBMS

Figure 2:   One Approach to CAD/CAM Database Management

not the right glue for most (and perhaps all) of the emerging application areas. Furthermore, it appears that each of these applications will have its own glue, just as relational, CODASYL, and hierarchical database systems do presently.

In [STON83, STON84], Stonebraker addresses adding abstract data types and abstract indices to INGRES [SWKH76] and implementing QUEL as a data type as a way of addressing the needs of new application areas. While the proposed additions to INGRES are certainly a step in the right direction, we do not feel that they go far enough. In particular, even with the abstract indices proposal, a good deal of the wrong glue remains (access planning and buffer management). Furthermore, it is not obvious[3] that anybody other than RTI or the University INGRES group could add a new access method such as R-trees to INGRES.

We contend, instead, that a new strategy for implementing database management systems is needed which permits glue to changed/added/deleted in order to customize the system for its intended application. In addition, we feel that although all applications-oriented database systems will have query processing routines and concurrency control and recovery mechanisms (as it is these components that really make a piece of software a database system), each of these mechanisms will also vary from system to system. For example, while one might be able to implement an expert database system by adding deduction and a rule base to a relational database system, a statistical database system must support sophisticated data analysis routines (e.g., regression analysis) as its basic query processing capabilities [KOSH84]. Furthermore, it is generally accepted that standard two-phase locking and logging (which are the algorithms most commonly used in a relational database system) are not the right concurrency control and recovery mechanisms for rule-based knowledge management systems [CDG84] or CAD/CAM database systems [LP83].

---

[3] This is based on our experiences using INGRES code as a basis for the front end of DIRECT [DEW179].

In the following section we will outline our research plan for designing and prototyping an extensible database system. This system will make it simpler (though maybe not trivial) to implement database systems for new application areas.

3. Research Objectives

As a solution to the problems outlined above, we propose to design, prototype, and evaluate a new generation of database management systems. The goal is to produce a prototype system that can be easily extended to satisfy new and future applications while still providing excellent performance. Our principal research objectives include:

1. Definition, exploration, and evaluation of alternative architectures for an extensible database system

2. Query optimization and compilation techniques that permit the addition of new operators at the data model level and the addition of new access methods

3. Concurrency control and recovery techniques

4. Query processing strategies

5. Buffer management policies

Following completion of the research phase of this project we intend to implement two prototypes. The first will be that of a conventional relational database management system. Such an effort will serve two functions. First, by seeing how long it takes to build such a system, we will be able to see how realistic our claims of "easy" were. Second, we have found from past work [CDKK85, BDT83] that benchmarking is a very effective way of illustrating performance bottlenecks in a system. By benchmarking the performance of a conventionally developed relational database system such as INGRES against that of a relational system developed using our extensible database management system, we will be able to identify performance bottlenecks in the new system and determine whether the approach provides a satisfactory level of performance.

We will also construct a second prototype system to illustrate that the system can be used successfully for new application areas. Three alternatives look appealing. An expert database system would require extending the first prototype to include new data objects for storing rules and new query processing routines for executing the rules. A prototype for a statistical database system would illustrate the flexibility of the system for supporting complex operations on the database (e.g., multivariate regression analysis) and operator driven buffer replacement strategies. A third alternative might be a database system for

CAD/CAM. Wisconsin's Mechanical Engineering department is very active in this area and could serve as a user community as well as a source of guidelines for developing the system.

3.1. A Preliminary Architecture for an Extensible Database System

We are currently examining the use of an object-oriented approach as the basis for an extensible database system. An object-oriented approach appears attractive for the following reasons:

- First, a number of researchers have shown that objects[4] are useful as data modeling tools. Examples of this application of objects can be found in [WEBE78, BS78, RS79, SK84b]. In [WEBE78] classes are used to represent entity sets and relationships between entity sets. For example, in a supplier-parts database, there would three classes: one for the suppliers entity set, one for the parts entity set, and one for the relationship between suppliers and parts. Instances of the class supplier correspond to supplier objects (i.e., actual suppliers). Associated with the supplier class is a data structure corresponding to the attributes of the entity set and procedures to add/delete suppliers, to change the address of a supplier, etc. The operators associated with the supplier-part class (e.g., no_longer_supplies, new_supplier_of) would be implemented using the operators provided by the supplier and part classes. The operators available to the user of such a system are exactly those provided by the outermost set of classes.

- Objects have also been shown to be a reasonable implementation strategy for database systems. In [BD81a, BD82] we have shown that by using one class for each modeling construct provided by the data model (e.g. the relation construct in the case of the relational data model), the high level operators associated with the data model (e.g., joins, selects, etc.) can be implemented entirely in terms of the operators associated with the basic class types. For the relational data model there is one class of type relation. With a supplier-parts database, instances of this class would be the objects corresponding to the suppliers, parts, and SP relations.

---

[4] While we have chosen to use the word **object**, others have used **abstract data type** or **module** for the basis of their work. We consider an object to be an encapsulation of a data structure and a set of externally visible operators that operate on this data structure. For our purposes we do not care whether these operations are invoked via messages (ala Smalltalk [GR83, HAGM83, KK83]) or via procedure calls (ala Mesa [MMS79]). Each object is assumed to have a unique identifier by which it can be addressed. A **class** is a generic description of a set of like objects.

Associated with each of the objects is an implementation of all the operators associated with the class. However, the operators of each object are customized to accommodate the internal schema information (i.e., storage structures and access methods) of each relation.

- Finally, objected-oriented programming ala Smalltalk 80 [GR83] provides a very flexible approach for constructing software systems. We feel that these same characteristics should be present in a database system constructed using the object-oriented methodology.

Three other groups are presently implementing object-based database management systems. Servio-Logic [CM84] has extended Smalltalk 80 into a database system. Beech [BEEC83] has defined an object-based data model and is in the process of implementing a database system to support this model. The PROBE system described in the chapter by Dayal and Smith will incorporate the notion of objects (or abstract data types) in order to provide extensibility and the ability to integrate specialized processors into the system. While all three approaches have a similar flavor to the proposed research, they differ in their goals. Neither of the first two projects addresses using an object-based mechanism as a basis for simplifying extensions to the underlying components of the supporting database system. The PROBE system does address this problem, but they seem to be a bit less concerned with the impact of objects at the lower levels of the system (e.g., concurrency control, recovery, and buffer management) and more concerned with providing functionality such as recursion and dimensional concepts. We view our research to be complementary to these other efforts.

Figure 3 presents our first idea of a design for the proposed system. We envision a 4 or 5 level architecture. At the the bottom level of the system are a collection of storage structure objects. The second level consists of access method objects. Like a conventional database system, the function of the access method objects is to facilitate access to objects at the storage structure level. Level 3 contains query processing objects. It is the function of this level to implement the query processing functionality. Finally, at level 4 we have the data model objects. If the data model objects layer is used to directly implement the conceptual schema and operations on these entities (ala [WEBE78] and [RS79] and others, as described above) then this is the final layer. If, on the other hand, the data model objects correspond to the modeling tools provided by a data model [BD81a, BD82] (e.g., the relation construct in the relational model and the set and record type constructs in the network data model), then a fifth layer of objects corresponding to the entity sets and relationships of the conceptual schema may be present. In addition to this hierarchy of objects, additional pieces of software will be present for query optimization, query compilation, buffer management, concurrency control, and recovery. Our goal is to make these pieces of software generic by implementing them entirely using the operations associated with the classes at each of the levels.

Data Model Objects
Query Processing Objects
Access Method Objects
Storage Structure Objects

Figure 3: Architecture for an Extensible DBMS.

Associated with each object[5] are a set of operators that can be applied to the object. It is these operators that appear to be the key to constructing a flexible/extensible database management system. For example, we expect that a storage structure object will provide something like the following set of operators:

- **read** — to move the object from mass storage to main memory
- **write** — to move the object from main memory to mass storage
- **obtain shared access** — a primitive used as part of the concurrency control mechanism
- **obtain exclusive access** — a primitive used as part of the concurrency control mechanism
- **write undo information** — a primitive used as part of making updates recoverable
- **write redo information** — a primitive used as part of making updates recoverable

While these operators look rather mundane, they are a key component of our system because they provide a uniform interface to manipulating objects at the storage level. Consider, for example, the read operator. In the case of fixed length records, read is simple. The object identifier

---

[5] Or more accurately, with each class type.

is first translated to a disk address, and then the proper block is read into memory. On the other hand, the read operator for a more complex storage object that spans multiple disk blocks [CDKK85, HL82] will require a much more complex read operation. We find this approach attractive as it permits access method objects to be completely ignorant of the implementation of the storage structure objects that they provide access to.

A related problem that we will examine is how to automatically provide access methods (indexes) for many applications. An index provides a way to efficiently locate objects with certain properties or attribute values. For example, a hashed index provides fast lookup for finding objects with a particular attribute value, and a B+ tree index provides fast lookup for finding objects whose attribute value lies within a range of values. We plan to provide a set of access methods for organizing collections of objects in certain standard ways — for instance, as a *mapping*, where the access method supports exact match searches, or as an *ordering*, where the access method supports both exact match and range searches. In order for a class of objects to be indexed in these ways, the implementor of a storage structure class will have to provide routines to return an attribute value given an object (for use in building the index and searching index leaf pages), to test for attribute value equality (for searching a mapping index), and to test for attribute value precedence[6] (for searching an ordering index). Note that what we are calling "attribute values" could just be simple field values for records, or they could be derived attribute values for complex objects. An example of the latter type of attribute value might be the power consumed by VLSI circuit objects — one could build an ordering index to organize a VLSI cell library according to the power demands of the cells. Our index research will initially focus on identifying the set of standard access methods desired, such as the mapping and ordering access methods described above. Other standard access method types might support such query classes as multi-dimensional exact-match, range, and partial match queries [ULLM82, ROBI81, NHS84].

The concurrency control primitives also appear interesting. For example, obtaining write access to one type of object may result in setting (or attempting to set) an exclusive lock in a lock table and then checking for deadlock. On the other hand, if a versioning scheme [CHAN82, REED83] for concurrency control is used, invoking the "obtain write access" operator may cause a new copy of the requested object to be generated.

---

[6] Such as "less than".

Details of the operators associated with the objects at the other levels in the design have not yet been developed. In the following sections we will outline some of the research problems that must be addressed.

3.2. Query Optimization and Compilation in an Extensible DBMS

One of our early research goals is to tackle the problem of query optimization and compilation. As is obvious from reading the definitive paper by Selinger et. al. [SELI79] on this topic, query optimization and access path selection for a conventional database system is a complex piece of code to implement. As evidence of this claim, our benchmarks [BDT83] illustrate that a number of commercial products have simply left this piece of code out of their system.

Since our proposed system can be extended both by adding new operators and new access methods, query optimization becomes even more complicated. Consider the case when the set of operators is fixed and we extend the system by adding a new access method.   To exploit this new access method two things need to occur. First, algorithms must be specified for those operators that can benefit from using the new access method. Second, the query optimizer must extended to understand the CPU and I/O costs associated with using these new algorithms and access methods (plus any side effects, such as changes in the ordering of the objects that the algorithm produces, that could affect subsequent costs).

We have begun the implementation of an expert system for the query compilation and optimization process. This strategy appears attractive for several reasons. First, it seems that an expert system is ideally suited to the task of evaluating alternative access plans. This task is similar to design tasks for which expert system technology has proven useful in the past, such as configuring a computer system [MCDE80] or selecting a good hardware design given a register-level description of a computer architecture [KT83]. Our approach is similar to the optimization ideas that are proposed in the chapter on PROBE by Dayal and Smith.

The second attraction of the expert system approach to query optimization is that incorporating new access methods and operators into the optimization process will require simply that a few new rules be added. For a new access method, rules will describe the cost of accessing an object (or a collection of adjacent objects) via the access method, the query patterns for which the access method is applicable, the cost of inserting and deleting objects using the access method, and the names of the routines associated with the access method's implementation. For a new operator, rules will describe the query pattern for which the operator is applicable, the ordering properties of the operator (i.e., those that determine how it can be moved around within a query during the optimization process), the names of the alternative routines that implement the operator and their associated costs, etc. The bulk of the query optimization expert system, which will include rules that describe how to identify a "good" query execution plan, how to perform algebraic transformations on a query, how to recognize candidate access methods and operator routines, how to cut off unlikely regions of the access plan search space, and how to generate the plans themselves, will remain unchanged when new access methods and operators are added.

To test the effectiveness of the expert system approach to query optimization, we intend to use it in the construction of a new relational database machine that we are implementing. Our current plan is to use the OPS5 production system language for this purpose [FORG81], as OPS5 has been the implementation language for several successful expert systems (including [MCDE80] and [KT83]).

3.3. Concurrency Control and Recovery in an Extensible DBMS

There appear to be two main flavors of transactions that any such database system must support: short and long duration transactions. Debit/credit transactions fall into the first category, while CAD/CAM and VLSI design transactions fall into the second category. Since database systems have traditionally been designed to maximize the performance of debit/credit transactions, locking and logging are the customarily used mechanisms. On the other hand, a shadow/versioning mechanism [LP83, HL82, REED83, KL84] appears to be the best alternative for long duration transactions that must survive system crashes.

Implementing both mechanisms in one database system presents a number of interesting research problems. As should be obvious from above, each class of storage-level objects will have several concurrency control operators associated with it, and different classes may use different concurrency control mechanisms. One problem to be addressed is resolving conflicts between transactions that access objects which use different concurrency control primitives. Several researchers have examined the problems associated with the use of mixed concurrency control mechanisms [BG84, BG81a], but this work seems to preclude the storage of data in shared buffer space (i.e., each transaction needs its own private workspace). We expect our work to be more heavily influenced by the work of Schwarz and Spector on type-specific locking and log-based recovery algorithms [SS83, SS84]. In addition to the fact that Spector and Schwarz have shown locking to be applicable to objects of various abstract data types, other researchers have shown that versions can be integrated with locking [BHR80, SR81, CHAN82], and IBM researchers have described lock protocols for long duration transactions based on persistent locks (i.e., locks stored on stable storage) [LP83]. Our research in the concurrency control and recovery area will involve making it easy to tailor a well defined set of concurrency control and recovery protocols to new types of objects. In particular, we plan to investigate how long duration transactions can be supported through type-specific versioning and persistent lock protocols.

A second research problem that we are beginning to explore is how to best do concurrency control on objects at the access method level. In particular, we need to understand the relationship between concurrency control at the access method level and the concurrency control primitives used at the storage structure level.

3.4. Main Memory Management of Objects

As discussed above, each class of storage structure objects has associated with it primitives to move class instances between mass storage and main memory. Buffer management, however, will be implemented at a much higher level in the system. As predicted by Stonebraker [STON81] and demonstrated by our research [CD85, KOSH84], significant performance gains can be obtained by using an operation controlled buffer management policy instead of a more general replacement mechanism such as LRU. At any instance in time, all main memory access method and storage objects will be associated with some transaction. In the case of objects that are being shared by multiple transactions, the transaction that most recently touched the object will viewed as the owner (sort of a "hot potato" algorithm). Instead of managing the objects associated with a transaction in an LRU fashion as is done by the hot-set algorithm [SS82b], when the buffer manager needs to replace a storage object it will invoke a free-space operator associated with the query processing object. This operator will return the name of the storage/access method object that it views as the most desirable to eject from main memory. The cost of losing this object might also be returned. If the cost value is sufficiently high, the buffer manager may instead try to get space from another transaction. Alternatively, it may be possible to have all of the transactions that are sharing an object provide their estimate of its replacement cost, in which case a globally inexpensive object could be selected for replacement.

4. Conclusions

In this paper we have outlined a set of research objectives for exploring the design and implementation of a new generation of database management systems. This research work should result in the implementation of a prototype database system that permits the data modeling, query processing, access method, storage structures, concurrency control, and recovery components of the system to be easily extended/adapted. This system should be capable of satisfying the database requirements of the knowledge base management systems described in other chapters of this book.

Acknowledgements

This research was partially supported by the Defense Advanced Research Projects Agency under contract N00014-85-K-0788, by the Department of Energy under contract #DE-AC02-81ER10920 and the National Science Foundation under grant MCS82-01870.

5. References

[BD81a] [BD82] [BDT83] [BEEC83] [BG81a] [BG84] [BHR80] [BDT83] [BS78] [CD85] [CDG84] [CDKK85] [CHAN82] [CM84] [DATE81] [DEWI79] [FORG81] [GR83] [GS82] [GUTT84] [HAGM83] [HL82] [KK83] [KL84] [KOSH84] [KT83] [LP83] [MCDE80] [MMS79] [NHS84] [REED83] [ROBI81] [RS79] [SELI79] [SK84b] [SR81] [SS82b] [SS83] [SS84] [STON81] [STON83] [STON84] [SWKH76] [ULLM82] [WEBE78] [WP84]

Discussion

Umeshwar Dayal spoke mostly about an on-going project at CCA. Their main interest is in very specific extensions to existing DBMS technology. They are taking the "evolutionary" approach to KBMS design, noting that there already exists a well-defined DBMS technology for various kinds of applications, and that they are seeking to develop a new system within a three- to five- year range.

Existing DBMSs will be inadequate for many of the information processing applications of the future. The goal of the PROBE research is to enhance existing DBMS technology with the following features: (a) abstract data types for defining new objects and constructs, (b) dimensional semantics (space and time) as primitive constructs, and (c) recursion, for the representation of intensional knowledge.

He stressed the importance of putting more application knowledge (e.g., space and time semantics) into the DBMS and then to optimize it using this additional knowledge and information types specific to the application. Also noted the importance of recursion, which is currently not handled by most query languages. (Gio Wiederhold suggested that there have been a few elegant implementations of recursive query languages).

The PROBE project only started a few months ago. No prototype implementation exists yet.

Alex Borgida explained that a major problem in his view is that the world rarely follows the rules that have been recorded in a database. He wants to have systems that tolerate exceptions and then learn from them. Exceptional items are marked on ENTRY to the system; when they are subsequently ACCESSED, a special handler is needed.

Alex Borgida introduced the "Database administrator's assistant" which makes suggestions for schema changes by examining and trying to characterised the accumulated exceptions through a process of empirical generalization. A key issue in developing a generalization mechanism is the language used to express the examples. On this point, Bill Woods felt that the choice of language is a separate issue from the choice of level (or levels) of generalisation.

The issue of how constraints are used in AI and Databases was raised. Rusty Bobrow noted that in highly constrained AI systems, one wishes to find the objects which satisfy particular qualifications in an efficient manner, without exhaustive (or even just repetitive) generation and testing.

Tom Mitchell felt that Databases people use constraints for determining the acceptability of input data, while AI people use constraints for defining the specification of a system under design.

Francois Bancilhon asked whether there is a difference between integrity constraints (used to test incoming data) and derivation rules (used to restore the consistency of a database after an update). For example,

grandfather = father of father

could be expressed in either way.

Alex Borgida felt that the difference was only an implementational issue, while David Israel felt that the difference was comparable to that between axioms and rules of inference.

On the subject of how constraints are used in searching, Mike Stonebraker suggested that AI systems use a large number of constraints to aid the search for objects which meet qualifying conditions, while database systems do not use constraints for searching. Alex Borgida noted that there has been theoretical work on databases concerning the use of constraints for semantic query optimisation.

Mike Stonebraker asked whether Databases people assume that there are few constraints and many data items, while AI people assume that there is a huge number of constraints, where the order of application is very significant. Rusty Bobrow felt that COMPLEXITY is the important factor, not the number of constraints. For example, very few constraints are needed to axiomatise arithmetic, yet number theory has many hard problems.

John McDermott felt that in AI there is a need to dynamically re-evaluate the method of applying the constraints and that this is independent of both the number of constraints and the amount of data. Some felt that there is a strong parallel between an AI search with several constraints on one hand and a DB query with several qualifications on the other.

Danny Hillis noted that constraints help provide solutions to AI problems, which are often under-constrained to start with. On the other hand, it was noted that some database query languages are heavily constrained so that the only questions that can be asked are those which have an efficient solution.

Danny Bobrow noted that AI systems often combine and transform two or more constraints. He then asked what rules are used in combining DB constraints and performing reasoning in query optimisation. Gio Wiederhold responded that databaase queries are often over-constrained since the user does not have a precise model of the database. This allows for some optimisation. He also noted Jonathan King's work which does reasoning on rules and considers alternative evaluation strategies (during which rules are ADDED).

Rusty Bobrow felt that at the Knowledge Level, the knowledge content is the same, whether one is considering a constraint or query optimisation information.

Michael Brodie stressed that constraints are important for database updates (as well as queries). Some felt that relatively few AI systems are concerned with updates, while others felt that this was an important AI research topic. In general, the overall feeling was that both queries and updates are important for both AI and Databases.

Bonnie Webber felt that researchers need to address the issue of maintaining consistency in a knowledge base as its knowledge is built up. Rusty Bobrow drew a parallel with the "procedural-declarative controversy" in AI. Just as one issue in that controversy was that knowledge can be used in many different procedures, the moral for KBMS is that knowledge constraints can be used in many different ways.

Randy Katz described a way to structure a design database across time. This is accomplished by viewing a database from the perspective of three orthogonal planes: one for versions, one for configurations and one to indicate equivalences across configurations.

Commenting on the general thrust of the workshop, Randy Katz noted two basic viewpoints: (a) The "database-centric" view, where the database is the center of the system and the applications a thin shell around it; according to this view, as much application-specific logic as possible is put into the database; (b) The "application-centric" view, where the application is the center, with the database being just one of many support tools. There is quite a bit of confusion as to where these two points of view overlap and what are the boundaries of each.

His view of the evolution of databases is that they support those features which were efficiently implementable at the time. The same holds for data models as well. The major issue is: "...what we can put in our data model ... because we have an efficient way of implementing it".

Randy Katz feels that there are two sets of issues concerning design databases: one concerns representation details and the other structural details. He is basically interested in the latter: "What are the structuring primitives for organizing a design database?". For him, the three most important structural relationships are the notions of version, configuration and equivalence across representations. He is also interested on the issue of maintaining correlations across different representations.

His basic approach to the problem of dealing with design databases is to extend conventional databases, with the notions of version, configuration and equivalence across representations and then to try to implement them efficiently. He contrasted this with a much more ambitious approach where the focus is on expressiveness, i.e., being able to describe large chunks of the world in a very elegant and complete way.

Rusty Bobrow felt that an unfair characterization of AI was being made. He felt that people think that the goal of much AI research is trying to come up with a single all-purpose language. He explained that there are many hybrid reasoning systems whose goal is precisely to be efficient in their more narrow domains. "I don't want to have it believed that the primary goal is expressiveness at the sacrifice of efficiency, or necessarily uniform expressiveness."

Ron Brachman raised a point about the desirability of having a system that would keep track of a history of versions. Randy Katz agreed, saying that in talking to real designers, what they need is the ability to view the history of things.

It turns out that there are a few reasons to want a history: (a) to find the first previous occurrence of a mistake, (b) which version of the item are we trying to service? (c) the versions of each component in a design are very important in determining the cost of implementing a revision.

Bill Woods raised a question about the size of the search space for a likely query to the version system. He felt that the cost of evaluating queries concerning versions would be very large indeed.

Given a very large knowledge base, **Mike Stonebraker** wants to provide efficient implementation of rule-based solutions.

He outlined four approaches that had been presented at the workshop: (a) Extending a particular AI language (e.g., Prolog) to handle large amounts of data, (b) Extending a particular DBMS to handle rules, the approach favoured by Stonebraker, (c) Trying to glue AI and Database systems together, and (d) Trying something new (John Mylopoulos' revolutionary approach).

John Mylopoulos felt that different approaches may be needed at different phases of designing a system. For example, a Prolog prototype could be used when specifying the rules, then an efficient DB might be used for production.

Mike Stonebraker allows rules to be specified and integrated into the DB manager. Commands of the form "Do this indefinitely" are implemented by using the already-present database lock manager. Efficiency is possible if the locks can be associated with individual objects (which is the case in commercial systems).

Ron Brachman noted that one command could be attached to several objects. Tom Mitchell asked about the overhead that would arise if a rule is very complicated. The response was that more locks will be placed in the DB and that more locks will be activated by an update.

Mike Stonebraker showed how a database can handle non-stored information, also by using special locks. Special processing is needed for missing data. For example, employees are on the same floor as a manager, and the manager's floor is unknown. Stonebraker felt that this processing was similar to unification, but some disagreed, and questioned the approach of taking intensional knowledge and making it purely extensional. This may require a large amount of DB storage, much DB processing, as well as much "pre-computing." Stonebraker felt that current DB systems have the same problems as well as efficient solutions.

In response to a question, Mike Stonebraker noted that it is not easy to obtain a list of triggers in the database.

Contradictions can be handled by assigning relative priorities to conflicting rules.

John Smith noted that there were two methodological approaches to the addition of new features to a DBMS. One is to separate each mechanism (e.g., concurrency, optimisation, recovery). Another (used by Mike Stonebraker) is to strongly couple two mechanism (e.g., triggering and locking). It may be harder to connect other mechanisms to the coupled ones. Stonebraker felt his method has advantages (including efficiency) as well as problems.

David DeWitt disagreed with Yannis Vassiliou in that he felt that coupling was not the preferred way to create a KBMS. He proposes to look at how database systems are put together so that people like David Warren do not have to start from scratch in designing their KBMS. His goal is to produce a "core database management system" for new applications such as engineering databases (CAD/CAM and VLSI design), scientific and statistical databases, expert database systems, and image/voice applications all of which differ from conventional transaction processing systems in a number of important ways.

He sees three ways to address these new applications: (a) the PL/I approach, leading to a super-Ingres, (b) build a system for every new application, (c) put the database in the center and glue on some application areas around the outside. He favors the third approach. He feels that tightly binding the systems does not make much sense. For a short-term solution it might be all right, but for most applications it would be wrong.

What he is proposing is a "generic architecture" for database systems.

John Mylopoulos felt that the basic idea was a very good one. He was unclear as to whether David DeWitt would be offering a tool kit with a number of boxes that can be used or replaced, or if he is providing a number of modules that can be extended at will. David DeWitt seemed to say that he is doing a little bit of both.

Part V

Extending Knowledge-Based Systems

24
Knowledge-Based Systems: A Survey

Peter Szolovits[1]

ABSTRACT *This survey examines the roots of knowledge-based systems in artificial intelligence research, tracing them to the early realization that vast amounts of knowledge are a key to expert-level performance in AI systems. It considers both rule-based and frame-based implementation methods and their use in tools to ease the task of system construction. The survey concludes with an assessment of the current state of the art and with suggestions for some research directions that will be critical to providing improved methods for building knowledge-based systems.*

1. Introduction

Knowledge-Based Systems are computer programs, usually based on technologies developed by AI research, which embody some aspects of human knowledge and expertise to perform tasks ordinarily done by human experts. As should be obvious, this is a sufficiently broad definition (as are all such definitions to be found in the literature) that almost anything can be force-fit under the term. The purpose of this survey is not to settle the question of boundaries, to identify the definitive "right" underlying technologies to be used, or to predict the future of knowledge-based systems, whether glorious or dark. Instead, I will give a brief introduction to the basic ideas of knowledge-based systems,[2] trace their evolution from AI research, mention a few

---

[1] Massachusetts Institute of Technology

[2] I prefer this term to the more commonly-used "expert systems" because it identifies the key role of knowledge in the system. The literature often confuses terms such as "knowledge-based", "expert", "rule-based", etc., which are not equivalent. The term "expert systems" is used either to emphasize that the system works in some sense like a human expert or to imply that it accomplishes its tasks as

examples of actual systems in current use as an indication of the state of the technology, and describe the foci of current research in the attempt to improve the capabilities of such systems.

2. The Importance of Knowledge

Until the mid 60's, most AI research was concerned with how to be very clever in figuring things out. The typical problems being addressed were ones like proving theorems, playing chess well, doing relatively complex integrations (symbolically), determining the structure of a statement in natural language. Certainly there is some simple knowledge necessary to deal with each of these problems (e.g., for chess, the rules of what constitutes the initial board, what are legal moves, and the goal of checkmating the opponent king). The emphasis of much of the research naturally focused on how to exploit this simplicity of knowledge by applying powerful heuristic principles (alpha-beta pruning) and newly-developed search methods (variable-deth quiescence analysis), and better static evaluation functions so the programs would play better chess and play it more efficiently.[3] The beginning of a break with this "pure" tradition in chess was the introduction of the "book," a compilation of many pre-planned opening moves that captured knowledge of how to play well in the beginning of a game, knowledge that did not automatically emerge from the application of the usual search methods. The emphasis, then, was to make programs that were like Sherlock Holmes: squeezing out of each meager fact the long chain of inferences that would net the prize.

Two large applied projects begun in the mid-60's, Macsyma [MACS83] and Dendral [FBL71], broke definitively with this early tradition, and identified the need for large volumes of special-purpose knowledge to permit programs to work effectively in "real-world" domains. For Macsyma's domain, symbolic mathematical manipulation, no small set of techniques would yield behavior that was any better than a laboratory curiosity when the goal was a system that helped real physicists and mathematicians solve real problems. Hundreds, perhaps thousands of special little techniques, some broadly applicable, some effective only for very particular little problems, had to be included to make the system useful.

---

well as a human expert no matter how it does it. Many writers also assume that expert systems must consist of rules, because many well-known systems use that method of implementation. It is useful to retain distinctions, however. In this paper I will use the more general term "knowledge-based system" throughout, and explicitly identify various methods of implementation.

[3] Much the same story can be told for the other fields I mentioned.

For Dendral's task, the identification of chemical compounds by analysis of their mass spectra, two theories working together suffice, in principle, to identify an unknown. One would generate all possible chemical structures of an unknown compound, and the other would predict the chemical fragments formed in the mass spectrometer from each possible structure. Each possible set of fragmentations of each possible structure of an unknown compound predicts a particular distribution of masses to be found in the mass spectrum. The one that best matches the empirically observed one is the answer. This is not a practical solution, however, because the problem is terribly combinatorial. The structure generator could be sufficiently constrained to make the program practical only by looking in the observed spectrum to try to identify likely building-blocks of the original compound.

In both these examples, AI researchers examined the methods used by human experts in the performance of such tasks, learned what knowledge they brought to bear, and explicitly encoded much of it into the program. Thus was born the idea of **knowledge-based systems**. In retrospect, Moses (co-leader of the Macsyma project) says the idea is obvious and virtually universal. Imagine you are a robot waking up in the morning. Can you figure out from first principles just how you should get out of bed and go to work? Well, first roll over on your side. Can you make a rolling motion? Will the side you roll onto support your weight or will your side be crushed? Can you swing your legs over the side of the bed? Will the bed tip over? How can you stand? Will the floor collapse? Clearly, this is not how it must go. We simply must know how to do already most things that most of us do most of the time. We have limited reasoning capacity, which must be devoted chiefly to figuring out and learning whatever is novel, and checking on our knowledge when it is important. *It is better to* **know** *than to be able to figure out.*

Two major approaches have been taken to encoding knowledge in computer programs: knowledge as rules (of inferences to be made and actions to be taken) and knowledge as frames (structures of knowledge). Both have been used in building knowledge-based systems, although the rule-based approach predominates at present. These two methods do not exhaust the field. Macsyma, for example, uses Lisp functions as its medium of implementation, buying efficiency and ease of initial construction at the expense of making its knowledge inaccessible in an explicit form.

3. Rule-based Systems

Most of Dendral's knowledge was encoded in production rules. There were rules describing how compounds were likely to fragment in the spectrometer, as well as rules for what features of the spectrum suggested which core structures in the unknown. Any production rule has a **premise** (also called (pre-)condition, left-hand-side (LHS), situation, if-part, ...) and a **conclusion** (also called action, consequence, RHS, then-part, ...). Generally, the rule encodes the knowledge that if the premise is true, then the conclusion is also true (or should be acted upon). An example of one of Dendral's suggestion rules is [FBL71]:[4]

IF there are two peaks at mass units X1 and X2 such that
$$X1 + X2 = M + 28,$$
X1 - 28 is a high peak,
X2 - 28 is a high peak, and
at least one of X1 or X2 is high,

THEN there is a double-bonded carbon and oxygen structure in the unknown.

The use of these rules was such a powerful method for exploiting the modularity of knowledge and assuring that all relevant knowledge would be used when appropriate (i.e., when its preconditions were met), that Feigenbaum and his colleagues suggested that rules were the appropriate encoding of all expert knowledge.[5]

The first knowledge-based system project that began with a very clear, rule-based architecture was Mycin [SHOR76]. It was intended to encode the knowledge of expert doctors specializing in infectious diseases, and to give consultations on patients with bacterial infections of the blood and (later) with meningitis. Unlike in Dendral, where the rules were run in response to the presence of data matching their premise (**data-driven**), Mycin's rules were **goal-driven**, so that the system began with a goal (Determine what treatment, if any, should be given the patient), and tried to use those rules whose conclusion included the desired goal. Thus, any rule like "If ... then the appropriate treatment is twice-daily doses of streptomycin" would be considered, and the premises of the rule would become new goals for the program to pursue. Because these new (subsidiary) goals would, in turn, cause other rules to be brought to bear, etc., the program reasons by exploring a

---

[4] The idea is that X1 and X2 are the masses of the fragments including the CO structure when the rest breaks off at the C. X1-28 and X2-28 are the peaks corresponding to the fragments without the CO.

[5] Rules also became popular via the work of Newell and Simon, whose interest was to study and simulate human problem-solving. They argue effectively that rules have many of the right characteristics for recreating the behavior of human subjects working on problems like cryptarithmetic, chess, and logic.

dynamically-constructed branching and/or tree of subgoals. Conjunctions appear because each rule's premise is typically a list of conditions, all of which must be true for the rule to be applicable. Disjunctions usually appear because more than one rule can make a conclusion matching a goal.[6] Ultimately, there would be no rules to conclude a particular premise; the program would then simply ask the user (or, in principle, a patient database) whether the premise were true. The system thus works from its goals back to questions to the user, and the technique is called **backward chaining** or **goal-directed rule invocation**. In such a scheme, a rule is not invoked just because its premise holds. It is invoked only if the conclusion it can reach is sought. Such systems can therefore fail to exploit some known data, unless they explore a chain of goals and subgoals that ultimately require those data in a premise. Redirecting the attention of such a program simply by telling it new information is, thus, not possible. The focus on goals, however, provides a natural organization of the reasoning process toward what is desired, and can produce a series of reasonably organized questions from the program as it methodically tries to achieve its goals.

Other systems, especially ones involving the interpretation of data or response to changing situations, work forward from the data. Chaining is still, possible because the conclusions of one rule, perhaps intermediate steps in reasoning, might match the premises of others. Such a system generates a tree of conclusions, branching out from the input data. This approach is called **forward chaining** or **data-directed rule invocation**.[7] Pure forward-chaining systems are innately responsive to the data they are given, but it is difficult to control the direction in which they head, because no explicit goals are provided. Nevertheless, the first commercially used knowledge-based system, DEC's XCON (developed by J. McDermott as R1 [MCDE82b]) is written in OPS5, a forward- chaining rule system. Many other commercial applications, currently in prototype form or early use, also use this approach. In these, control information ("Here is what I intend to do next") is often encoded along with data and conclusions in the data structures manipulated by the system.[8] One frequently-occurring combination of these

---

[6] Mycin and some other systems also include a pseudo-probabilistic mechanism for tracking the certainty of rules and conclusions. In this case, all possible rules are applied even if (without probabilities) some would be logically redundant, because each new conclusion can strengthen the certainty of a disjunction.

[7] **Chaining** expresses the idea that intermediate goals or conclusions are possible, thus permitting several steps of inference or interpretation between the initial data and final conclusions, or between the initial goal and the required data. This is an important concept, because rule-based systems that do not allow or use chaining make "one-shot" decisions reminiscent of simple decision tables.

[8] Aspects of both forward and backward chaining can be combined in a single system. One successful, rather natural method for doing so is to use a forward-chaining system in which both premises and conclusions of rules may include **goal**

two methods is found in diagnostic applications, wherein initially-presented data are processed by a forward-chaining system to generate an interesting set of hypotheses to explain those data, the system then attempting to confirm or refute those hypotheses by backward chaining to generate useful additional questions to ask. Other, more flexible, control structures that permit the intermixing of data and goal-directed inference, have also been built.

4. Frame-based Systems

Human knowledge appears to be "chunked" around many concepts that interrelate closely-coupled bits of knowledge. From research in the 60's on semantic networks and memory organizations, Minsky distilled his **frames** theory in a seminal paper in the early seventies [MINS75]. It suggests that knowledge should be represented as a set of frames, corresponding to objects, actions, and attributes of interest. Each frame (e.g., of a birthday party) has, in turn, a set of **slots** that represent other frames closely related to it (whose birthday it is, which guests, what activities, what's to eat, what presents, etc.). In addition, the frame has **unary predicates** encoding what frames may fill other slots (guests must be people, perhaps; things to eat must be edible, pleasant to eat, not poisonous, etc.) and **n-ary** predicates among the slots (alcohol is a good drink for an adult party, but Kool-Aid is appropriate for kids). Slots may also have **defaults**, indicating a likely or possible filler if no other information is available (cake and ice cream is a good guess for food), and **attached procedures** or **daemons** that can calculate some value autonomously when appropriate. Three types of daemons are **if-added**, which runs when a new value of a slot is asserted, and implements a type of forward-chaining inference; **if-needed**, which runs when a slot value is sought but not yet available, thus implementing backward chaining; and **if-removed**, which is supposed to clean up after a previously-asserted value is retracted.[9]

---

predicates. The backward chaining use of a rule such as "If A and B then C" is then achieved by the forward chaining rule "If (GOAL C) and A and B then C," and instead of beginning with C as the goal, the system begins with (GOAL C) as a datum. It is also necessary to have a rule like "If (GOAL C) then (GOAL A) and (GOAL B)," or perhaps some more efficient variant, to assure the backward propagation of goals [DDSS77].

[9] False information can propagate more false information; if it is corrected, the if-removed daemons are supposed to chase down its false consequences and remove them too. This mechanism never worked well in practice, and has been superseded (at least in principle) by keeping explicit dependency information, such as in a Truth Maintenance System (TMS) [DOYL79].

Other capabilities in frame systems include automatic inheritance of attributes and relationships from general categories to specific instances (e.g., because birds can fly, Bill, my pet canary, can fly) without including that specific knowledge in the database.[10] Higher-level structures such as similarity networks (what could it be if it looks like an adult birthday party but has no guest-of-honor? A wake, perhaps?) have also been proposed but not often exploited.

Knowledge-based systems based on frames often use a simple basic reasoning method called **frame instantiation**. Create an instance of a frame representing some particular entity in the world (e.g., a diagnostic hypothesis, a particular trip to be taken, a circuit to be designed) and then systematically fill in its slot by finding or instantiating other frames as fillers. One early program working this way was GUS [BKNT77], an assistant travel planner. Its initial frame to be instantiated might be a trip, which would in turn have slots for a traveler, an itinerary, etc. An itinerary would, in turn, consist of a sequence of alternating travel and stay segments. A travel segment frame would include the dates and times of travel, the type of transportation, its fare, etc. A stay segment would include the type of lodging, costs, further slots for local transportation, etc. Predicates interlinking these would insist that stays begin just after the conclusion of travel to the same locality, etc. Daemons assure the propagation of such information, and propagate necessary changes when parts of a plan are altered.

Frame matching or identification tasks have also been frequently used, especially in diagnosis systems. A disease (or, more generally, abnormality of any system) can be represented as a frame whose slots are expected abnormalities of the system. Some slots of the frame for bladder infection might include a finding of blood and white cells in the patient's urine, for example. Slots of the frame may include other disease frames as well. For example, rheumatic heart disease may have a slot for a preceding rheumatic fever episode. If every slot of the frame under consideration matches against data about the patient (and other frames that match those data) then it is possible to conclude that frame as representing the right diagnosis. Except in textbook cases, of course, there is never a perfect match, and some machinery for estimating likelihoods or degrees of match is introduced to compare the degree to which different hypothesis frames match the data. Predicates within the frame can enforce internal consistencies, and similarity networks can be used to support differential diagnosis, which is the art of selecting those questions to ask (or tests to perform) that best

---

[10] By this argument, however, penguins must also fly, because they are birds. Problems of **defeasible inheritance** or other methods of handling or excluding exceptions have been a major problem in knowledge representation.

differentiate among competing hypotheses. Internist-I [MPM82] and the Present Illness Program [PGKS76] are two, well-known, medical diagnosis programs that take this approach.

5. Tools for Building Knowledge-Based Systems

Developers of the earliest knowledge-based systems had to build not only the rules or frames that represented their application, but also the rule interpreters and frame matchers that would run their systems. Typically, these were implemented in Lisp, though a few examples of Fortran and other languages could be found. Because some of these early knowledge-based systems were at least experimentally successful, their developers wanted to make the useful technology they had developed available to other developers. Thus, for example, Emycin [VANM81] was abstracted from Mycin to permit others to build similar backward-chaining rule-based systems, using the certainty-factor model of uncertainty. Other systems, such as Conniver, FRL, KRL, OWL, KL/ONE, OPS5, etc., and even the programming language Prolog, which were originally developed to explore issues in knowledge representation and control of reasoning, were also adopted by knowledge-based system builders as components of their systems.

In the past couple of years, we have seen the birth of a large new **knowledge tools** industry, where commercial software developers are building "industrial-strength" systems to support the encoding of knowledge and various reasoning methods to provide what are essentially new programming languages to be used for knowledge-based systems development. The goal of many of these is to be universal with respect to the approaches I have identified above; they thus attempt to support both rules and frames, data and goal-directed inference, backtracking and dependency analysis, sophisticated matching methods, constraint propagation, some models of reasoning with uncertainty, and excellent facilities for knowledge (rule and/or frame) base maintenance, display, debugging, etc. Additional capabilities explored in some of them include reasoning in different hypothetical contexts, built-in facilities for tasks such as simulation, and direct, active, graphic display of internal states that are in turn manipulable through the graphics. If the optimism surrounding knowledge-based systems in government and industry comes close to being justified, then the incentives to these toolmakers will be great, and we may anticipate that much of the research in AI representation and reasoning methods will come to be incorporated in the best tools.

6. The Practical State of the Art

In addition to Macsyma and Dendral, both 50+ man-year efforts, and to dozens of university-produced knowledge-based systems, a few commercial/industrial systems have come into daily use. The first of these was probably[11] XCON [MCDE82b], a program to help configure DEC computers; it has now been in ordinary use for several years, continues to be expanded to handle new configuration tasks, and has convinced DEC to invest further in the creation of other knowledge-based systems for its own use, as well as to support AI technology in general. Other early knowledge-based systems in daily use are PUFF [AKSF83], a small system to interpret the results of pulmonary function tests; a serum protein electrophoresis interpretation program that is now built into a medical laboratory instrument; and ACE [VSZM83], developed at Bell Labs, for scheduling telephone system maintenance. Many (perhaps 50) other systems are in some state of advanced development, testing, or early use.

All of the systems actually in routine use were built as rule-based systems, and each is based on one of the early knowledge-based systems building tools. The larger projects involved at least a half-dozen man-years of development effort, and demand continued input of effort as system requirements change and performance needs to be improved.

With our current understanding of knowledge-based systems, it is easy to build a new knowledge-based system that begins to exhibit some interesting performance rather quickly. At MIT, for example, I have been teaching a course in knowledge-based application systems for the past decade, and during the last five or six years each student (a total of about 200) has built a knowledge-based system concerning a problem of his or her choice. These systems have ranged from the trivial (twenty "one-shot" rules for choosing the ideal pocket calculator) to the very serious (one of the earliest was a house-plant diagnostician that was larger than Mycin and performed remarkably well; others have included a tax advisor, college counselors, a bridge teacher, a sailing-rule master, and an office layout planner). They were all built by one or two smart but inexperienced people, using rule- and frame-oriented tools in a period of at most two months!

Interest in AI and knowledge-based systems is so high that many companies have now decided that they must "get on the bandwagon," either by establishing an internal research group to explore the possibility of building knowledge-based systems, or by hiring one of the growing number of expert-systems software houses that help to develop prototype, proof-of-concept systems. Many of these efforts are no more

---

[11] I want to hedge on the chronology, because it is difficult to tell from the literature just when a system moves from experimental prototype to daily use.

advanced, however, than some of the student projects. It is still very unusual for these projects to move from the prototype stage to production use. As is the case with the few systems that are in use, most of these systems are being developed using knowledge-based systems tools, and most are rather simple, rule-based systems. It will be interesting to see whether many of these prototype systems will indeed progress (with a much larger investment of time and effort) to useful programs.

7. Conceptual State of the Art

Current knowledge-based systems technology, as it is used in those few systems that are in routine use, represents only a very weak initial exploitation of the promise of knowledge-based systems. Indeed, it is as if the knowledge-based systems building tools are simply being exploited by clever programmers as a new programming language, more appropriate than earlier ones for building this type of system. As a consequence, conceptual difficulties and deficiencies of the tools and methods used are typically finessed, not resolved.[12] I group the conceptual problems into three categories:

1.   There is not yet a sufficient **analysis of the generic tasks** that knowledge-based systems are performing nor any study of how techniques should be matched to those tasks.

2.   **AI models** of important aspects of the world are still either very weak or nonexistent, and knowledge-based systems tools thus don't support reasoning about any particular type of concept, such as causality, time, liquids, varying levels of detail, etc.

3.   The total amount of knowledge in most systems built to date is minuscule in comparison with the size of databases used in most organizations, and there are thus far no successful means of taking advantage of large databases in knowledge-based systems.

The third of these problems is, of course, one of the main topics of this volume. Let us consider the other two issues.

---

[12] This is, of course, a perfectly reasonable tactic on the part of someone who wants to build knowledge-based systems. A Fortran programmer doesn't fix Fortran on realizing that it doesn't support list processing well; he or she simply implements a needed kludge to solve the specific problem at hand.

7.1. Analysis of Generic Tasks

The above presentation appears to break the approaches to knowledge-based systems into two camps, depending on whether rules or frames are the basic units of representation. This comparison is a popular pastime; the choice of methods seems important to implementors; and relative merits and deficiencies of the two approaches are avidly argued. Nevertheless, this is probably only an implementation issue and not a central question. Following Newell and Simon's suggestion [NEWE82], the proper analysis of knowledge-based systems should be in terms of the knowledge they use and what they do with it, not the technique whereby they manipulate it. Intuitively, we understand that a problem of diagnosis is innately different from a problem of design, for example, and it should be obvious that the organization of a knowledge-based system for one task will be rather different from that of the other. Yet there has been very little analysis of knowledge-based systems in these terms, and there is no distilled experience on what is the appropriate structure of one or another kind of system. Furthermore, looking at the actual structures of an existing system does not clearly identify what it does at the knowledge level.[13] As an example, several critics have commented on the fact that much of the diagnostic strategy of Mycin is in fact implicitly encoded in its rules [CL81]. Thus, only by a fairly careful analysis of the whole set of rules could one determine whether the patient's clinical symptoms are used primarily to focus initially on what type of infection is present, to identify the responsible organisms, or to determine the severity of the illness (or some combination thereof). Yet from the viewpoint of what Mycin needs to know and how it uses that knowledge, this is one of the critical issues.

A few particular knowledge-level methods have been identified in knowledge-based systems built to date. These distinctions are still somewhat hazy, and I simply sketch three to illustrate what I believe is an important research direction in knowledge-based systems. One important class of knowledge-based systems performs **classification**, the selection of one among a predetermined set of possibilities as the appropriate description of a situation [CHAN85]. According to Clancey's analysis [CLAN84], the typical classification task consists of three steps: abstraction or generalization of data into descriptors, an associational leap from those data descriptions to a class, and refinement and verification of the class by examination of further data. Classification is the basic method underlying a number of diagnostic programs--those for which it is feasible to enumerate *a priori* all

---

[13] See the chapter by Brachman and Levesque, addressing the problem in some detail.

possible diagnostic conclusions.

Pople identifies **differential problem formulation** as an important knowledge-level method. The basic idea is that it is easier to differentiate among a set of alternatives than to decide for each alternative whether it is the correct one or not. In his work on Caduceus [POPL82], for example, each individual, abnormal fact about the patient suggests a large competing set of possible accounts. Pople proposes a set of problem-reformulation operators that strive to combine these sets into a single coherent differential. At root, the most powerful heuristic here is Occam's razor: the simplest, adequate explanation is the best. Some form of this type of technique appears very useful in diagnostic problems when the domain is so complex that possible solutions must be constructed, not pre-enumerated.

Several programs developed in my group exploit the notion of the **patient-specific model**, a unified description of what the program understands about a particular patient at a particular time, including primitive data, interpretations of those data, diagnostic hypotheses, testing and treatment plans, expectations of what is likely to happen with the passage of time, and known problems such as data not adequately explained by the current hypotheses [GSP78, PSS81, PSS82]. The typical use of such a model is in planning the next intervention to make (in medicine, that is either further testing, some treatment, or simply waiting to see what happens) and in later evaluating the results of that intervention by comparing the new set of data with the model's expectations. Much of therapeutic reasoning, where therapies must not only be selected but continually monitored and updated, is based on such a model.

My intuition is that there will be perhaps a few dozen basic task models such as these. Building new knowledge-based systems will be on a much more systematic basis when we have learned to characterize the basic methods, how to implement good solutions for each of them, and how to recognize these models in real domains.

7.2. Improved AI Models

Knowledge-based systems are typically about the real world. Yet the tools with which they are built "know" almost nothing about that world, except, perhaps, how to match patterns in a computer memory and apply some uniform computational process. Early knowledge-based systems were typically built by encoding mostly empirical associations extracted from expert judgment. To turn to another medical example, one might encode in a system the knowledge that tarry, brown stools might well indicate a bleeding ulcer. Such a system might be able to diagnose bleeding ulcers successfully (assuming it has many other such associations available), but it certainly does not "know" in any sense:

1. Why there is such a relationship

2. Whether it always holds, or only on occasion

3. How variations in the color might correspond to variations in the location of the ulcer

4. How long it takes to develop the symptom after the ulcer

5. What an ulcer looks like in detail

6. How blood escapes into the gastrointestinal tract

7. What transformations it undergoes to make the stool tarry and brown, or, indeed

8. That it does *cause* the identified characteristic of the stool

For simple tasks, such additional detail may not be necessary. More sophisticated programs, however, need to address these more detailed questions, and many of them lead directly to representation and reasoning problems for which AI as yet has no very good general solutions. Clearly, advances in AI research, if they provide even partial answers to such problems, will have a major positive impact on our ability to build more capable, future, knowledge-based systems.

Acknowledgements

The author's research has been supported (in part) by National Institutes of Health Grant No. R24 RR01320 from the Division of Research Resources, Grant No. R01 HL33041 from the National Heart, Lung, and Blood Institute, and Grant No. R01 LM04493 from the National Library of Medicine.

8. References

[AKSF83] [BKNT77] [CHAN85] [CL81] [CLAN84] [DDSS77] [DOYL79] [FBL71] [GSP78] [MACS83] [MCDE82b] [MINS75] [MPM82] [NEWE82] [PGKS76] [POPL82] [PSS81] [PSS82] [SHOR76]

[VANM81] [VSZM83]

25
Natural Language Processing: A Survey

Bonnie Lynn Webber[1]

ABSTRACT *The first part of this survey presents some of the basic concepts and terms used in Natural Language Processing (NLP), both in Natural Language generation and in Natural Language interpretation. The second part describes recent theoretical and applied research results. It concludes with a discussion of NLP and its relation to knowledge management systems.*

1. Introduction

Natural Language Processing (NLP) involves both computer understanding and computer generation of Natural Language text. The goal is to enable Natural Languages such as English, French or Japanese to serve either as the *medium* through which users interact with computer systems (**Natural Language Interaction**) or as the *object* that a system processes into some more useful form such as in automatic text translation or summarization (**Natural Language Text Processing**).

In the analysis of Natural Language (NL), the task is to translate an utterance, often in context, into a formal specification that the system can process further. In NL *Interaction*, such further processing may involve factual data retrieval and/or reasoning, as well as generation of an appropriate response. In *Text Processing*, understanding may be followed by generation of an appropriate translation or a summary of the original text(s), or the formal specification may be stored for later,

[1] Department of Computer and Information Science, University of Pennsylvania

to serve as the basis for more accurate document retrieval. In NL *Generation*, the task is to convert some representation of what the system wants to communicate (e.g., a fact, an explanation, a description or definition) into a clear, well-structured, and hence understandable piece of NL prose.

There are many aspects of language that speakers use in conveying meaning: lexical choice, syntactic form, semantic structure, discourse context, and pragmatic use. NLP must attend to all of these. The first part of this survey presents some of the basic concepts and terms involved in NLP. The second part discusses some major recent research results, both theoretical and applied. Finally I describe how NLP fits in with the theme of this book — the development of knowledge base management systems.

2. Concepts & Terms

The aspect of NLP that has to date received the most attention is **syntactic processing** or **parsing**. Most current techniques for parsing an input string of words involve (1) A description of the allowable sentences of the language (the **grammar**), (2) An inventory of the words of the language with their inflectional, syntactic, and possibly semantic properties (the **lexicon**), and (3) A processor which operates on the grammar, the lexicon and the input string (the **parser**). This processor either (1) Simply accepts the input string, if grammatically well-formed, or rejects it (a **recognizer**), (2) Associates the string, if well-formed, with its structure (or structures, if ambiguous) according to the grammar (an **analyser**), or (3) Associates the string with some other representation — (e.g., a 'semantic' characterization (a **transducer**)). Syntactic processing is important because certain aspects of meaning can be determined only from the underlying structure and not simply the linear string of words.

Winograd [WINO82] provides an excellent description of current parsing techniques. The one that is often most familiar to members of both database and AI communities is **augmented transition networks** or ATNs. ATNs grew out of a system for parsing context-free (CF) languages, called **recursive transition networks** or RTNs. An RTN parser consists of a set of named graphs or "networks", each consisting of a set of nodes or "states" connected by a possibly ordered set of directed labelled arcs. The labels correspond to either (1) Words or classes of words that can be recognized or "consumed" on the arc, (2) The empty symbol, indicating an arc that can be taken without consuming any input, or (3) The name of a network, which indicates that the next segment of the input string must be recognizable by that network. Each network has a start state and one or more end states. If the parser can move through a network from start to end by consuming a segment of the input string, that segment is said to be recognizable by that network.

An ATN adds to the basic RTN framework the ability to set and test variables or "registers", thereby giving it the power to recognize a wider class of languages than an RTN. However, the current trend is towards parsers and grammars which have less power. In particular, researchers have begun to give almost CF descriptions of NLs, thereby allowing them to use slightly extended versions of efficient CF parsing techniques like Earley's algorithm. Such descriptions include Generalized Phrase Structure Grammar (GPSG), Immediate Dominance/Linear Precedence (ID/LP) grammar and Tree Adjoining Grammar (TAG). These are described in Winograd [WINO82] and in recent conference proceedings of the Association for Computational Linguistics (ACL).

The second aspect of NLP, **semantic analysis**, is concerned with extracting context-independent[2] features of a sentence's meaning. These include the **semantic roles** played by the various entities mentioned in the sentence - e.g., in the sentence "John unlocked the toolbox," "John" serves as the **agent** of the unlocking and "the toolbox" serves as the **object**; in "This key will unlock the toolbox," "this key" serves as the **instrument**. Context independent aspects of sentence meaning also include **quantificational information** such as cardinality, iteration, and dependency. For example, in the sentence "In every car, the mechanic checked to see that the engine was working," the checking is **iterated** over each car. In this, the identity of the engine **depends** on the identity of the car, while that of the mechanic doesn't, and the **cardinality** of engines per car is one. Thus there are as many engines as cars, but possibly only one mechanic.[3] The **representational formalism** used by the system for semantic analysis (e.g., first order predicate calculus, case grammar, conceptual frames, procedures, etc.) is usually chosen for its ability to convey those aspects of semantics that the system requires for later processing. For example, if temporal position (past/present/future) is not significant, it will not be captured in the formalism. A good discussion of techniques for semantic analysis is given in Tennant [TENN81].

---

[2] Context here refers to discourse context, the particular text or interaction being attended to. This is discussed as the third aspect of NLP.

[3] It was called to my attention that in the domain of *automobile racing*, there is one mechanic per car, and that is the way that the sentence would be understood. Thus the notion of discourse *context* needs to be distinguished from the discourse *domain*. The *domain* establishes the semantics, and while the semantics of a term or phrase may vary from domain to domain, within any one domain, there are discourse context independent aspects of sentence meaning.

Most NLs allow people to take advantage of (1) **Discourse context**, (2) Their **mutual beliefs** about the world and, (3) Their **shared spatio-temporal context** to leave things unsaid or say them with minimal effort. Thus the purpose of a third phase of NLP, **contextual** or **discourse analysis**, is to elaborate the semantic representation of what has been made explicit in the utterance with what is implicit from context. Two major linguistic devices that contextual analysis must deal with are **ellipsis** and **anaphora**.

Ellipsis involves leaving something unsaid. To handle ellipsis computationally, techniques are required for recognizing that something is indeed missing and for recovering the ellipsed material. When the utterance is a sentence fragment and not a complete sentence, it is fairly easy to recognize that something is missing — for example:

> User: What is the length of the JFK?
> System: <some number of feet>
> User: The draft?

Note that since parsers are usually designed for well-formed input, to handle sentence fragments either the system's grammar must be revised or a special error recovery routine must take over after the parser fails.

Now it may still be the case that an utterance is syntactically well-formed but still elliptic in that some needed conceptual material is missing — for example:

> User: What maintenances were performed on plane 3 in May 1971?
> System: <list of maintenances>
> User: What maintenances were performed on plane 48?

In the user's second question, the time period of interest is missing, and the question should not be answered until it is recovered. (It is clearly May 1971.)

A common technique for recovering ellipsed material is based on semantic features. For sentence fragment ellipsis, the previous discourse is searched for the most recent utterance containing a constituent with the same features as the fragment. The utterance minus that constituent is taken as the ellipsed material. For conceptual ellipsis in a syntactically well-formed sentence, the previous discourse is searched for the most recent utterance with a constituent having the required semantic features. That constituent is taken to be the ellipsed material. In each case, a new well-formed sentence is then constructed and processed as if the ellipsis had never occurred. For instance in the first example, both "length" and "draft" are properties of ships. Thus, given the fragmentary utterance "The draft?", "What is --- of the JFK?" is found as the ellipsed material. The question "What is the draft of the

JFK?" is then interpreted and answered normally. This technique works often, but does not constitute a general solution. A more powerful solution has been developed based on *recognizing a user's goals in producing an utterance*, but has only been found computationally efficient in very narrow task-oriented domains. This is discussed further under **pragmatics**.

Anaphoric expressions include definite pronouns such as "he", "she", "it", "they" and definite noun phrases such as "the mechanic", "the cars", etc. These words and phrases only refer uniquely because of the context in which they are uttered: there is clearly more than one mechanic in the world (except when your car won't start and the temperature is under 10 degrees F.), and there is no single set of individuals identifiable as "they". The problem is that all anaphoric expressions must be resolved in order to complete the semantic intepretation of a sentence.

Early computational approaches to anaphora resembled those for dealing with ellipsis: entities described in previous sentences were examined for the most recently mentioned one with appropriate semantic features. Now **recency** has been replaced by the notion of **focus** as a basis for anaphora resolution. **Immediate focus** reflects the particular thing the speaker is talking about, **global focus** involves things associated with it or in which it participates, and gives a sense of what may be talked about next. Techniques have been developed for tracking immediate focus, projecting ahead from the current utterance what may be focussed on in the next one. This is useful for resolving anaphora, in that it predicts what entities are likely to be respecified anaphorically. Several recent computational approaches to discourse phenomena are well described in [BRAD82].

A fourth phase of NLP, **pragmatics**, takes into account the speaker's **goal** in uttering a particular thought in a particular way — what the utterance is being used to do. In an interaction, this will influence what constitutes an appropriate response. For example, an utterance which has the form of a yes/no question or an assertion may have the goal of eliciting information (e.g., "Do you know how to delete a control-Z?," "I can't get the 'set file protection' command to work.") Because it is inappropriate (and possibly at times dangerous) to take a user's utterances literally or to assume that the user will take those of the system literally, computational techniques must be devised for relating the syntactic structure and semantic content of an utterance to its pragmatic function.

One important approach to this problem has been to view language understanding as **plan recognition**. The actions (either communicative or physical) that constitute a person's plan may be motivated in one of two ways: (1) *Goals in the world* that the person wants to accomplish, or (2) *Aspects of an already ongoing interaction* that need attention - for example, confusion over the speaker's foregoing utterance may lead the listener to the act of seeking clarification.

To understand a plan recognition approach to NL understanding, consider a user seeking particular information from a system. The user's utterance — a well-formed sentence or an ellipsed fragment — is taken as a request for information that the user believes he needs in order to accomplish some goal, a goal which is not as yet presumed to be known to the system. Just as a medical diagnosis system uses rules which link findings back to those diseases which commonly manifest them, the plan-recognition system uses rules which link utterances back to those domain goals which need the intended information in order to be achieved. For example, consider the utterance "The train to Windsor?" made to a system serving as train information clerk [ALLE82]. The system interprets this as a request: the user wants to know some property of that train in order to fulfill his goal. The system then tries to figure out what that goal is, in order to figure out what information the user might be requesting. There are only two possible goals considered: meeting a train and boarding one. The description "train to X" does not match that of an incoming train, so the user's goal is taken to be boarding the Windsor train. To board a train, one needs to know its departure time and track. Since the system doesn't have evidence of the user knowing either of these properties, it responds with both - "It leaves at 3:15, from track 7." Currently, it is only by limiting the domain and hence the range of possible goals the system needs to consider that such a plan-based approach to pragmatics within NLP becomes feasible.

Because pragmatics takes into account that language is being used for a purpose, it also takes into account that speakers and listeners have **expectations** about the form and content of utterances, based on **normal conventions of language use**. This has been well described by the philosopher Paul Grice [GRIC75], who noted that speakers respect a "cooperative principle" of conversation (by either upholding it or purposely flouting it), which he further specified in terms of conversational maxims of "quantity", "quality", "manner" and "relation". For example, the quantity maxims state:

Make your contribution as informative as is required (for the current purposes of the exchange). Do not make it more informative than is required.

The cooperative principle and its maxims are important to NLP because, if a system doesn't interpret its user's utterances in accord with normal conventions of use and doesn't itself conform to such behavior, the user is likely to be confused or misled by the system's responses. In particular, the cooperative principle and its maxims reveal a method of implicit communication which Grice termed **implicature**. An implicature is basically an aspect of an utterance's interpretation which makes no contribution to its truth value (i.e., semantics) but constrains its appropriateness in discourse. For example:

Q: Is there a gas station on the next block?

R: Yes.

The simple "yes" answer **implicates** to Q that, as far as R knows, the gas station is able to provide its normal services and hence fulfil Q's probable goal. Q reasons that if R knew that the gas station was closed and hence couldn't fill Q's needs, R would have said so - i.e., "Yes, but it's closed." Thus a system must be as aware of implicatures (both the user's and its own) as it is aware of what is communicated explicitly.

The growing body of research on pragmatics within NLP is described in part in [BRAD82] and in the conference proceedings of the ACL and the International Conference on Computational Linguistics (COLING).

As for fitting the pieces together, there is no single architecture for NLP. Some systems have a single processor for syntactic, semantic, contextual, and pragmatic analysis, with no distinction made as to the source of that knowledge. Some systems keep the knowledge sources separate but apply them simultaneously, extracting whatever can be derived at the moment, using whatever information is available. Other systems are modular, separating the knowledge sources and specifying when they should be applied. Efficiency, extensibility, and transportability are some of the important issues when evaluating a NLP system.

So far this discussion of basic concepts has been presented in terms of NL understanding. Complementing this is a growing body of work on NL generation. Here I want to discuss the ways in which NL generation differs from NL understanding.

Generation addresses two questions: *what to say* and *how to say it.* Under the first heading come such questions as *What does the other participant need to know?* When users ask questions, they need to know the answer or to know that their question does not make sense. They may also need to know things they haven't thought to ask. Or the system, in watching over the user's shoulder, may have recognized that the user has made a mistake or is doing something the hard way. The user should be told this, without having asked. *In what terminology should the information be conveyed?* If we tell medical personnel that a drug therapy program is trying to "check sensitivities," will they know what that means or must our explanation be given in terms of what "checking sensitivities" means? *How explicit does a text have to be?* In explaining a causal chain, is it sufficient to just give the endpoints and assume that the user will be able to make the connection, or is it necessary to explicitly describe the intermediate links?

Under the question of "how to say it" fall such questions as:

- What is to be presented explicitly?
- What linear order should it be presented in?
- What underlying structure should it reflect?
- According to whose point of view should it be presented?

A system should be able to identify what it can omit from its explicit message because the user already knows the information or because the information will be communicated implicitly through lexical, syntactic, or organizational choices. We would also like a system to make use of appropriate sentence and paragraph structures. Ideally we would like a system to describe things from the user's point of view so as to make the description easier to understand. For example, identifying and repairing syntactic programming errors is much simpler if compiler error messages reflect the user's point of view and errors he may have made, rather than the effects of those errors on the compilation process.

A second way in which NL understanding and generation differ is in the way the processes are commonly factored. NL understanding is commonly factored into syntax, semantics, discourse analysis, and pragmatics, as above. Generation, on the other hand, is commonly factored into three components:

- Content Determination
- Text Planning
- Realization as a NL Text

Content determination involves identifying information that supports general decisions about what to include in the text - for example, what to include in an explanation, what to include in a persuasive argument or justification, what to include to show the similarities and differences between two kinds of things (often with respect to the task at hand). Clearly content determination goes beyond the purely linguistic processes described for NL understanding, requiring an ability to examine the system's knowledge base and/or computational structures and determine what is available, relevant to the generation task. Note also that for anything to be generated, the knowledge to be conveyed must have been represented. Thus researchers have frequently found that they must extend the **knowledge representations** they work with to support the needs of text generation.

Texts have several levels of structure, which customarily conform to familiar patterns. **Text planning** involves embodying the intended content in an evolving multi-level pattern that is appropriate to (1) The function the text is to serve, (2) The intended audience, and (3) The amount of content to be conveyed. For example, explanations of physical processes are often presented with the overall structure of a temporally ordered chain of causes and effects, with a definite start and a definite end, even when things are essentially simultaneous [SS81]. Devices are described in terms of either their functional or their physical decompositions. Comparisons of things are done either by describing each one in turn or by interleaving their descriptions so that points of similarity and difference are revealed [MCKE85].

Finally this embodied information structure must be **realized in context** as part of a text. This requires (1) Appropriate lexical choices in how to describe and specify things, given the intended audience, the function of the descriptor or specification and the preceding discourse, and, (2) Appropriate syntactic choices, given the intended focus of the current sentence and the structure of the preceding discourse.

While syntax, semantics, discourse and pragmatics all play a role in NL generation, it seems that their operation must be much more integrated than in language understanding. However, further work in generation should make this clearer.

3. Major Research Results

In order to understand the challenge of NLP, one should be aware of our current set of tools. For example, over the years we have learned to understand enough about parsing to be able to produce efficient parsers with broad coverage [BB84a, ANLP83]. Further work on understanding the real syntactic demands of NLs should enable us to simplify (and hence speed up) these parsers even more.

Semantic analysis has been dominated by work done outside NLP on knowledge representation formalisms. This has provided us with tools for representing aspects of meaning, but does not solve the problem of what aspects of an utterance we need to represent. The only epistemology we really know how to deal with is that of the first order predicate calculus. Perhaps recent linguistic and philosophic work on "situation semantics" [BP83] will give us a better sense of events, actions and time, to improve the output of semantic analysis and to provide a better base for generation.

Discourse analysis, I believe, has seen greater progress than semantic analysis, perhaps because discourse features such as anaphora and ellipsis can be given a mechanistic, structural account, while semantic analysis requires a handle on meaning and the outside world. We have computational accounts of anaphora in terms of discourse models [WEBB82] and focussing mechanisms [GJW83, SIDN82] that not only provide a substantive basis for system implementation, but also have been adopted in linguistics. We have been able to adapt these notions to generation, to allow a system to use anaphoric terms appropriately [MCKE85]. Similar accounts are needed of the various ellipsis phenomena, but I don't think these will be long in coming.

Pragmatics is an active area of research. We have learned that we must model and make use of the user's goals in trying to understand his utterances and generate appropriate responses. However, we are still at an early stage in developing computational mechanisms for doing so. Similarly, we are constantly learning more about standard conventions of language use, but are still at an early stage in enabling systems to understand and make use of them.

Probably the most relevant research result for readers of this book is work on assembling some of the pieces together to enable factual NL access to database systems. We have transportable NL interfaces which comprise not just the interface itself and its syntactic and semantic capabilities, but also the tools for simplifying the porting of the interface to a new domain [BATE84, MOSE84, ANLP83].

4. NLP and Knowledge Base Management Systems

NLP will play a more important role for knowledge base management systems (KBMS) than it has been called upon to play for database management systems. It will play an important role in creating knowledge bases, and it will facilitate user/system interactions.

With respect to the creation of knowledge bases, one cannot deny the quantity of existing written material that should be assimilated into appropriate knowledge bases. Just think of the millions of volumes and journals currently in the National Library of Medicine and being added to every day. It is beyond our capacity to do this assimilation by hand. The state of NL text processing must advance to the point of being able to create (or at least to aid in the creation of) the large knowledge bases that useful KBMSs will demand.

With respect to interaction, I take the main responsibility of a KBMS to be the communication of information. What is special about the situation of a user confronting a KBMS? On the one hand, a KBMS will be able to represent more information than a DBMS (either implicitly or explicitly), and to capture more of the complexities of the domain represented. It will be able to combine that information to derive new and perhaps unanticipated results. As such, a KBMS must take responsibility for enabling users to understand both what it has said in answer to users' questions and why it has said it. I contend that we have no other means for fulfilling these functions of clarification and justification than NL interaction.

On the other hand, users confronting a KBMS will expect to be able to work with them in solving larger, more ill-formed problems than before. How can a user convey such a problem to a system, except through NL? Formulaic interactions such as through menus or formal languages do not provide for the kind of well-documented user/system negotiations needed to both circumscribe a problem and identify its solution or at least relevant information. Users will also have less sense of what a KBMS can do for them, and it behooves a KBMS to take more initiative in offering relevant information. Again, it is through NL that such offers will make sense.

In conclusion, NL is our best and most highly developed tool for the complex act of commmunicating knowledge. It is hard to image the use of a KBMS without it.

5. References

[ALLE82] [ANLP83] [BATE84] [BB84a] [BP85] [BRAD82] [GJW83] [GRIC75] [MCKE85] [MOSE84] [SIDN82] [SS81] [TENN81] [WEBB82] [WINO82]

26
Questions, Answers and Responses: Interacting with Knowledge-Base Systems

Bonnie Lynn Webber[1]

ABSTRACT *The purpose of this chapter is to examine the character of information-seeking interactions between a user and a knowledge base system (KBS). In doing so, I advocate that a clear distinction be made between an* **answer** *to a* **question** *and a* **response**. *The chapter characterizes questions, answers, and responses, the role they play in effective information interchanges, and what is involved in facilitating such interactions between user and KBS.*

1. Introduction

We begin with the extreme view that the main responsibility of a database system, expert system, or future **knowledge base system** (KBS) is the communication of information. From this it follows that no matter how sophisticated their archival or reasoning capabilities, without development of their communicative powers, these systems will be less than fully useful. There is evidence that information is best communicated **interactively**, person to person — evidence that comes from the advantages of individual tutoring over lectures and text books, the use of consultants rather than reference books, etc. Further, such interactions typically involve several interchanges, consisting of **requests** and **responses**. So, until we have other evidence, we[2] are working under the assumption that the same will hold true for

---

[1] Department of Computer and Information Science, University of Pennsylvania.

[2] By "we", I believe I can include our own group at Penn, groups at BBN, SRI, University of Massachusetts, Berkeley, University of Hamburg, ISI, Yale, as well as groups elsewhere.

information communication between human and machine. The goal of our research is to facilitate such interactions. This chapter is meant to describe requests and responses, the role they play in information interchange, and what is involved in facilitating such interaction between a user and a KBS.

2. Theoretical Framework

A **question** is a request by the speaker for the respondent either to *inform* him of some information or to *perform* some act. (This difference can be illustrated by the two questions "Can you speak Spanish?" and "Can you please speak Spanish?". The former is, ambiguously, either a request for information about the respondent's abilities or a request for a performance, while the latter can only be a request for a performance.) An **answer** is the information or performance directly requested. (This has been called elsewhere a "direct answer".) A **response** comprises the respondent's *complete informative and performative reaction* to the question, which can include elements of each of the following:

1.   An answer

2.   Additional information or actions that are salient to the answer

3.   Information or actions *instead of* an answer

4.   Additional information provided or actions performed that are salient to this substitute for an answer

The following question has a variety of responses, which include elements of each type:

Q: What's the combination of the printer room lock?

Response R1 below is simply a direct answer.

R1:   It's 8-9-8.

Response R2 contains both an answer and an additional salient action that will show the questioner how to apply the answer.

R2:   It's 8-9-8 <Simultaneously keying in the numbers to show how>

R3 contains both an answer and additional salient information — i.e., that the answer should not be taken as holding correct indefinitely (which might otherwise have been assumed).

R3:   It's 8-9-8, but Ira changes it every week.

R4 below does not contain an answer, but rather two kinds of information instead of an answer that is, first, rejection of the question ("I don't know, therefore I'm not the right person to have asked") and then a suggestion as to an alternative source of the requested information.

> R4:   I don't know. Why don't you ask Ira?

R5 just contains an action instead of an answer, which presumably cannot be revealed to the questioner.

> R5:   <Respondent keys in the numbers without revealing them to the questioner>

And finally, R6 just contains information instead of an answer.

> R6:   The door's open.

Note that all these responses address (to the best of R's abilities, constrained only by other possible simultaneous obligations) that which R believes to be Q's immediate goals (i.e., getting into the printer room now). They may also address an inferred long-term goal (i.e., getting into the printer room another time). I shall return to this point later.

Making this distinction between answers and responses and among the various potential components of a response allows a clean separation between (1) The information or action the *questioner* (Q) attempts to elicit and, (2) The material that the *respondent* (R) feels is necessary or useful to contribute to the interaction. They are different issues and affect different aspects of system behavior.[3]

Notice that interacting with systems *per se* does not necessarily confer the role of questioner (Q) on a user and the role of respondent (R) on the system. Expert Systems are known to need and request additional information from their users during the course of an interaction, although so far a user's ability to reply to such questions has been limited to giving a number or choosing a menu item.

In the first part of this chapter, I will characterize with examples the different kinds of information that are requested in interactions.[4] Following this, I will review work on what constitutes a cooperative answer and indicate some computational approaches to the problem. Finally, I will discuss types of responses with respect to (1) What

---

[3] I am not claiming that a question ever has to be responded to or that a response, if forthcoming, will directly follow the question — for example, a clarification sub-dialogue may intervene between question and response [LEVI83]. But while a question may be ignored, if one *explicitly refused* to answer it, the response would include information of the third type given above, and if one also *explained* one's refusal, the response would include information of the fourth type.

[4] I am not concerned with the *form* questions take. Excellent work by Allen [ALLE82] and others suggest approaches to discovering the direct information requested through an indirect question or elliptic utterance.

information they contain, (2) What motivates the inclusion of a particular information in a response, and (3) What computational work has been done towards providing them.

I hope that, after reading this chapter, the reader will conclude that a distinction between answers and responses is important for both theoretical and practical reasons: theoretically, it allows us to develop a cleaner description of the phenomena and, practically, it allows more modularity in system design.

3. Questions

He didn't have the answers, and in a way I suppose I didn't have the questions either. [LAL82, p. 394]

What is the information or performance that Q attempts to elicit through a question? Since the primary focus of this paper is answers (Section 4) and responses (Section 5), I will present only a brief catalogue of the kinds of information that someone might request, illustrated by example. While this catalogue does provide an account of all the different questions that I've looked at in naturally-occuring interactions with experts, it is probably not complete. On the other hand, it does suggest more things than we currently know how to deal with. The catalogue is organized by the *type* of information Q attempts to elicit, not in terms of the *goal* that Q hopes to satisfy through the information received (e.g., in terms of requests for *definitions* rather than of requests for *clarification*) since goals can be satisfied in several different ways. As I noted earlier, **answers** address this requested information: R may also choose to include, in **response**, information that attempts to address Q's goals in other ways. (In each of the following examples, I have given R's full response. The information they contain will be discussed in Section 5.)

Before I begin, I should comment on classifying questions automatically. This may be relatively simple if, as in standard database systems, the only questions a system can answer concern the truth of some statement or the referent of some description (see below). If a question cannot be so interpreted, it cannot be answered. Moreover, even if the system incorrectly classifies a true/false question as a request for the referent of some description, it will usually not hurt the user, who will be able to figure out from the system's answer whether or not the given statement was true — for example:

On the other hand, if a system is capable of answering many types of questions, there will often be syntactic clues as to type. For example,

Q: Do any breccias contain more than 220ppm sodium?
R: S10017 460ppm
   S10046 320ppm

Q: What's an <X>?

can only be a request for a definition. On the other hand, classifying a question may require inferring Q's goals. For example, Carberry [CARB85] describes a procedure that infers Q's task-related plans and discourse goals in order to interpret ellipsed utterances as requests for definitions, requests for the referent of a description, requests for the truth value of a statement, expressions of surprise, etc.

The examples given below come primarily from transcripts of naturally- occuring interactions — transcripts of the Philadelphia radio show "Harry Gross: Speaking about Your Money" and transcripts of employees of the IRS talking with IRS Tax Service Representatives about filing their income taxes. The few examples taken from other sources are credited to those sources. Note that in the examples taken from actual interactions, it is sometimes the seeker of expertise asking the question and sometimes the expert himself. As I noted earlier, KBSs will have to play both roles: understanding and generating questions, understanding and generating responses.

First, one can question whether or not a statement is true. Such questions are most often used to obtain information, to elicit a performance, or to verify that one has understood something correctly.

Q: Now on that 1040, do I just file my income from this job?
R: No. You have to put all of your income.

Q: I see - now the money market fund and the all saver's certificate, they're not the same are they?
R: No — oh no — a money market fund is a mutual fund, an all saver's certificate is a certificate that you get from your bank which is tax free for federal purposes up to two thousand of interest.

In both responses, "no" constitutes the answer, with additional goal-related information provided in the first response and justification provided in the second.

Secondly, one can question which individuals, sets, actions, events, etc., satisfy some (possibly partial) description.

Q: Could I just have that toll-free number?

R: It's 1-800-424-1040.

Q: Who has to file an estimated tax return?

R: Anyone who has an income that they're not paying with-holding tax on.

Both responses contain simply an answer.

Thirdly, one can question the meaning of some term. Such questions are often used to learn about new concepts, to understand what the respondent means by a term or phrase that the questioner understands in a particular way, or to obtain clarification of some utterance.

R: In your agreement of sale, make sure that you have an engineering inspection clause.

Q: Engineering inspection clause?

R: Right. You want that house inspected by an engineer just to make sure that there's nothing wrong with it that you might have missed. The clause stipulates that an engineer be permitted, at your expense, to inspect the house, and that if there is anything in that house that requires a repair (and you can set the amount, $250 or $500), the owner will be responsible for it, or else you will be permitted to get out of the deal.

This response contains both a definition of the term "engineering inspection clause" and justification of R's advice to have such a clause.

Fourthly, one can ask "Why is it the case that P?", expecting some explanation of P in terms of the events leading up to P (Example 1); the "standing conditions" that enable events to lead to P (Example 2); or the actor's motivation for doing P (Example 3).

[1]   Q: Why is this conductor warped?

    R: By mistake, J closed the switch, shorting the circuit. So some of the components got damaged.

[2]   Q: Why is this conductor warped?

    R: The earth's magnetic field is not negligible, exerting a strong force at right angles to the conductor in the horizontal plane. This puts a strong acceleration on the conductor, making it warp.

[3]   Q: Why?   *< i.e., Why did you pick up the green pyramid?>*

R: To get rid of it.

Q: Why did you do that?

R: To clean off the red cube.

Q: Why did you clean off that cube?

R: To put it on a large green cube.

Q: Why did you do that?

R: To stack up the red cube, a large red block, and a large green cube. [WINO72]

Explanation in expert systems [DAVI79, SWAR83] and database systems enriched with reasoning capabilities [KT81, WALK82] has focused, so far, on systems explaining aspects of their behavior:

- Why they requested some information from the user,

- Why they drew a particular conclusion.

Given their reasoning abilities, the only facts which systems have been able to identify as relevant to an explanation are reports of actions they have taken or are taking and, only more recently, the underlying standing conditions justifying these actions [SWAR83] and the strategic decisions organizing them [HCR84]. They can improve in their explanatory abilities with respect to

- The kinds of things that users will be able to request explanations of — (e.g., "What difference is my answer going to make?", "Why should I follow your advice?", "What if I don't follow it?"),

- The kinds of relevant facts (and theories relating facts) that the system can draw upon in forming explanations (e.g., it should be able to explain its advice either in terms of how it came to that advice or in terms of the expected benefits to the user in following it),

- Sensitivity to the contextually appropriate alternatives to what it's been asked to explain — allowing Q to explicitly indicate alternatives or, alternatively, using its beliefs about Q's expectations and interests to identify appropriate alternatives.

(As to the latter point, consider responding to the following question

Q: Why is my property tax $1400?

Q may expect it to be less, as it was only $1200 the previous year, or to be more, as the millage rate was increased for most areas. If such expectations are known to the system, it can use them in customizing its explanation to the appropriate alternatives.)

Finally, in this partial list of question types, one can ask whether two descriptions or statements are (roughly) paraphrases. Such questions are often used to verify that one has correctly understood something.

R: Okay, under those circumstances I would not object to see you go back into that for another six months.

Q: So you roll it over, in other words.

R: Right.

Q: That's what I'm looking at, Schedule A.

R: Okay. If you turn it over, there is the schedule B.

Q: Oh, it's on the back of schedule A?

R: Right.

4. Answers

Reporters...tend to love trials. It may be that we are transfixed by a process in which the person being asked a question actually has to answer it. [TRIL84]

There are two important things to understand about answers. First, while there may be many **correct** answers to a question, only a few of them may be **useful**, and it can make a significant difference to the questioner which of them is given. Secondly, even a correct and useful answer may be misleading, thereby creating as much of problem for its recipient as an incorrect or useles answer. To be **cooperative**, an answer must be **correct**, **useful** and **non-misleading**.

To discuss cooperative answers to each of the question types mentioned in the previous section would require more space than is available. Thus I will restrict the following discussion to cooperative answers to questions about the referent of some description. Since the bulk of computational work to date on question answering has been done in this area, this restriction seems justifiable. For computational work on answering requests for definitions, the reader is referred to [MCKE85], and for research on answering requests for explanations, the reader is referred to [DAVI79, WEIN80, SWAR83, HCR84].

4.1. Correct Answers

The **correct answer** to a question about the referent of some description is usually taken to be an enumeration or description of *all and only* those individual entities which satisfy the questioned description. Computing a correct answer is not a problem in standard database systems, all of which model a domain with a finite number of known individuals and relations. There the combination of correct retrieval algorithms, correct calculation procedures, and the **Closed World Assumption** [REIT78a] guarantees correct answers *with respect to the system's knowledge.*[5]

In other cases, it is more difficult: First, if a knowledge base reflects a full first-order theory, there is no way to guarantee that an answer is complete (i.e., that the system can identify all the relevant individuals). For any individual, it may be impossible to prove that it does or doesn't satisfy the questioned description. Moreover, if a knowledge base admits descriptions of some entities in terms of other ones (usually through functions), it admits the possibility of an infinite number of entities (implicitly) in the knowledge base satisfying the questioned description. In addition, the same entity might be included more than once in an answer under alternate descriptions [REIT78b, LEVE84a].

Secondly, if a knowledge base is purely intensional (that is, it models a collection of concepts whose extension is immaterial), there is no fixed set of terms denoting individuals (e.g., The Admiral Nimitz, the JFK, etc.), with other terms denoting sets of those individuals (e.g., ships, aircraft_carriers, etc.) [CORE85]. The decision as to whether a concept should be treated as an individual or as a subsuming abstraction [CORE85] can depend on the given question, or the question may allow several different correct answers. For example, the question

Q: List the foreign cars.

could be answered taking 'manufacturer' as individuator

R1:   BMW, Toyota, Saab, Fiat ....

or taking 'manufacturer' and 'model' as individuator

R2:   BMW318, BMW325, BMW533, Toyota Tercel, Toyota Celica, Toyota Camry, Saab 99, Saab 900, Fiat X1/9, ...

or taking 'manufacturer', 'model', and 'year' as individuator

R3:   '83 BMW318, '85 BMW325, '84 BMW533, '80 Toyota Tercel, '84 Toyota Celica, '84 Toyota Camry, '78 Saab 99,

Here there are several correct answers. However, consider the follow-

---

[5] The Closed World Assumption finesses the finiteness of a system's database, so that if the system doesn't know some fact, it simply takes it to be false. For example, if there is no non-stop flight from Philadelphia to Austin listed in the Official Airlines Guide, it is reasonable to answer that there isn't one.

up question

Q: Which of them have an engine over 2-liters?

To answer this correctly, "them" must refer back to a set of individuals at the level of abstraction given in answers R2 or R3, since engine size depends on model. That is, if "them" refers to the set of individuals from answer R1, the individual "BMW" can neither be included in nor excluded from the current answer because the 318 has a 1.8 liter engine, while the 325's engine is 2.5 liter. (A solution to the problem of getting complete answers to these questions over intensional data-bases is given in [CORE85]. He does not deal with the discourse prob-lem noted above.)

Thirdly, if a knowledge base represents only as much as it truth-fully knows (i.e., it contains disjunctive, existential, and negative asser-tions, as well as specific and universal assertions), it may only be able to give **indefinite answers** [REIT78b] to wh-questions. For example:

Q: What city is the capital of California?

R1:   San Francisco or Sacramento

R2:   An inland city in California

R3:   A California city other than LA

Levesque [LEVE84a] proposes an enriched interface language to respond more appropriately in such cases of more general variation in a knowledge base system's knowledge of the world.

Finally, if a knowledge base is **dynamic** (i.e., it is aware of how it can change over time), the problem with correct answers comes from modelling a dynamically changing process: the system may know what the correct answer was for time point T_i and may know that it expects to learn of a new correct value corresponding to time point T_{i+1}. When the question is asked (i.e., NOW), it may be *between points.* Thus the system does not have a correct answer for NOW. All the sys-tem can do is *respond* with information that is salient to the answer [MAYS83]. For example,

Q: Where's the Kitty Hawk?

R: At 0430 it was at <longitude/latitude>. I will have an update of that position at 1630.

(Note that, even if the system knows its answer to be correct for NOW, it may believe that information that it may later learn of may be more *useful* to the user. Thus, in addition to responding with the correct answer, the system may also offer to monitor for this more useful information. This will also be discussed in Section 5.)

4.2. Useful Answers

Consider the following interchange, adapted from [GREW83].

Q: Where is Joyce Chen's?
R1:   It's in Cambridge MA.
R2:   It's at 330 Ringe Avenue.
R3:   It's a half block from the Fresh Pond station on the Red Line, on the other side of Fresh Pond Parkway.
R4:   Over there.

All the answers correctly specify the location of Joyce Chen's but are not equally useful. Answer R1 would be useless if the user were already in Cambridge, trying to find the restaurant, whereas answer R2 would be equally useless if the questioner didn't know the streets of Cambridge and was wondering whether to get there by cab, subway, or walking. Answer R3 would be useless if the questioner were within sight of Joyce Chen's, while R4 would be useless if the questioner were trying to ascertain whether drinks were available (given that Cambridge is wet, while its immediate neighbors, Belmont and Arlington, are dry).

There has been some work done in both philosophy and AI on characterizing useful answers to questions. On the philosophy side, Grewendorf's [GREW83] solution revolves around the notion of a **pragmatically significant** answer. Grewendorf begins by noting philosophers' interest in the potentially infinite regress of wh-questions: the fact that for any answer "Y" to the question "Who (or what) is X?", one can always ask "But who (or what) is Y?". But in fact, the regress always does stop. So Grewendorf attempts to identify the conditions that must be met such that Q is satisfied with R's answer in an exchange like

Q: Who wrote the "Philosophical Investigations"?
R: Wittgenstein

According to Grewendorf, Q's satisfaction has to do with the **informativity** that the answer has for Q (i.e., with respect to what Q already knows — and the **usefulness** the answer has relative to the purposes of his question).

From the current perspective of AI, one might say that **informativeness** requires R to reason about Q's current state of knowledge (i.e., what he believes and how strongly) and the change that each possible answer would produce. **Usefulness** requires R to reason about one or more of Q's plans and how Q sees the requested information as enabling those plans. There has been some work in both these areas, the most relevant being (1) Cohen's work [COHE78] on planning speech acts needed to achieve some goal, (2) Appelt's work [APPE85] on planning utterances to achieve goals, where that planning uses a formal logic of knowledge and action to take account of the effect of actions on knowledge, and (3) Allen's work [ALLE82] on inferring plans and goals from appropriate queries and Pollack's work [POLL85], discussed further in Section 5, on inferring plans and goals from possibly inappropriate ones. While none of these specifically addresses Grewendorf's problem, I think these approaches could be effectively adapted to his idea of isolating and evaluating the subset of possible answers to a wh-question.

Early AI work on useful answers was done by Lehnert [LEHN81], in terms of assigning questions to **conceptual categories** which, in turn, constrain the range of acceptable answers. She is concerned with how people come up with useful answers, when the surface form of a question yields only a very literal understanding. She identifies 13 conceptual categories for questions, including *Causal Antecedent, Enablement, Instrumental/Procedural, Goal Orientation, Verification, and Causal Consequent, ...* Acceptable answers to a question are ones that fall into the same conceptual category as the question. Lehnert gives as examples the following:

Q:	How could John take the exam?	*enablement*
R1:	He crammed the night before.	*enablement*
*R2:	He took it with a pen.	*instrumental/procedural*
Q:	How did John die?	*causal antecedent*
R1:	He caught swine flu.	*causal antecedent*
*R2:	He was alive.	*enablement*
Q:	How did John get to Spain?	*instrumental/procedural*
R1:	He went by plane.	*instrumental/procedural*
*R2:	He wanted to see Madrid.	*causal antecedent*

Lehnert's system QUALM uses a discrimination net to assign a conceptual category to a question after it has been parsed into a conceptual dependency representation [SCHA75]. However, assignment of question and answer to the same conceptual category is necessary but not sufficient to guarantee that the answer is appropriate to the question. For example, Lehnert claims that there is an additional type of reasoning required for appropriate answers to negative *who* and *what* questions[6] — requests for the referents which don't satisfy the questioned

---

[6] What Lehnert categorizes as "concept completion" questions.

description. Given a question concerning what entities do not satisfy some predicate (e.g., "Who isn't here?", "What courses haven't you taken yet?", etc.), the respondent must infer what larger set of such entities the questioner has in mind — what set the respondent is being asked to partition. Lehnert calls this "universal set inference": it is a mechanism that examines the context of a question and determines appropriate constraining factors. An answer which doesn't *recognizably* select from the intended set, while containing correct assertions, would not be useful to Q. If Q doesn't recognize that R has selected from some set other than Q intended, R's response may mislead him as well.[7]

I believe the large difference between Lehnert's categorization of questions and the one presented here comes from the distinction I am drawing between *answers* and *responses.* Lehnert does not make this distinction: for her, there is only an answer, and that is the information or performance that satisfies Q's goals. Thus the entire burden of responding to a question falls on assigning it to a category that reflects Q's goal in asking it. Lehnert categorizes the question "Do you have a light?" as a *Request deserving a performative response* in order that it not be answered "Yes" or "Yes. I got a new lighter yesterday." In contrast, I take this question as a *request for the truth value of the statement,* for example, a request whose *answer* is 'yes' or 'no'). *Depending on that answer,* R might decide on a variety of responses, for example, an answer plus a performance addressing Q's goal.

R1:   Yes, here <holding out a matchbook>.

an answer plus relevant information that *justifies* that answer

R2:   No, I don't smoke.

or an answer plus information instead of that answer that nonetheless addresses Q's goal

R3:   No, but that guy there might.

R's response can depend upon, *inter alia,* (1) The answer found, (2) R's perception of its relationship to Q's goals, (3) R's beliefs about Q's ability to correctly understand the response, and (4) R's beliefs about Q's acceptance of that response. QUALM does not reason about these

---

[7] In a database system, a negative wh-question doesn't necessarily require special reasoning to determine the appropriate set to partition: consider a question like "Which students did not fail the prelims?" If "did not fail" is mapped into "passed" and there is normalized database relation (i.e., that doesn't contain null values) associating student name and prelim grade, then the canonical constraint on the relation ensures that only the relevant subset of students are checked in answering the question.

aspects separately, when it reasons about them at all. Thus I do not think it is as useful as the approach presented here. Responses will be discussed at length in Section 5.

(Note that the usefulness of an answer may also depend upon its presentation. So, even if R interprets Q's question "What is the phone number of each faculty member?" as only requesting phone numbers, unless R also informs Q, each time, of the faculty member whose number it is, his answer will be nearly useless [KAPL82].)

4.3. Non-misleading Answers

It is not enough for an answer to be correct and useful: even correct and useful answers may still be *misleading*. For example,

Q: Which ships have a doctor on board?

R: The JFK, the Admiral Nimitz,...

From R's answer, Q may conclude that the ships named there have a doctor on board and other ships not named there do not. That is, Q may be led to believe that there is a *non-empty set of ships which don't have a doctor on board*. However, if the named ships are the only ships (and Q doesn't know it), R's answer — while correct and useful — is nevertheless misleading: R should have answered "all of them," which would not have misled Q to believe in a doctor-less subset of ships.

The principles that guide this behavior are Grice's Maxims of Quantity:

Make your contribution as informative as is required for the current purposes of the exchange. Do not make your contribution more informative than is required for the current purposes of the exchange. [GRIC75]

and Joshi's modification to Grice's Maxim of Quality:

If you, the speaker, plan to say anything which may imply for the hearer something that you believe to be false, then provide further information to block it. [JOSH82]

What Joshi's modified Quality Maxim provides is a criterion for the level of informativeness needed to satisfy the Quantity Maxims: enough must be said so that the hearer does not draw a false conclusion.

How can R anticipate that Q might draw a false conclusion from answer A? Joshi and colleagues [JWW84a, JWW84b, JWW84c] discuss at least three different ways: First, R may believe that Q has an incorrect belief that can combine deductively with A to lead to a false conclusion; secondly, R may believe that Q would incorrectly conclude something by default from A (i.e., from what is typically the case) when R knows the default does not apply; or, thirdly, A may implicate[8] (because of its ordinary use) that something is the case, when actually it isn't. In the above example, an enumeration of those elements in a set that have property P implicates that there are also set elements with property ~P, even though the enumeration is consistent with it covering all the elements. The enumeration isn't false, but the implicature is. A computational account of implicature and its use in question answering is given in [HIRS85].

While the above example does not require the respondent to augment his response beyond a simple answer, most often adhering to these principles does require this. For example:

Q: How many ships have a doctor on board?

R: All 43 of them.

where besides the numerical answer requested by "how many," R indicates that they exhaust the set. This response behavior is therefore discussed further in the next section.

5. Responses

The previous section characterizes **cooperative** answers and some computational work aimed at providing them. But answers, of themselves, are not enough for effective communication, which seems to rely on R replying to a question with more than (or other than) an answer. This section discusses what **responses** offer Q, to enable effective communication.

One can categorize the component information included in responses in terms of what function each component is meant to serve. This will enable a separate account of the each thing that R decides to include in a response and why he includes them. The following classification is not exhaustive. Moreover, in some cases, the same component may be able to fulfill more than one function. If so, the communication is probably richer for it but, again, for both theoretical and practical reasons, it is useful to consider each category separately.

1.   The answer,

2.   Additional information (or an offer to provide information) that R believes Q may need in order to fulfill Q's plan,

3.   Information (or an offer to provide information) that R believes Q may need to satisfy his goal (at some level), where the plan

---

[8] An implicature is basically an aspect of an utterance's interpretation that makes no contribution to its truth value but constrains its appropriateness in the discourse.

that R believes Q to have will not fulfill that goal,

4. Additional information that R believes *justifies* or *explains* that response, so that Q will accept it,

5. Additional information or graphical presentation that R believes will *clarify* that response, so that Q will understand it,

6. Information intended to correct a misconception that Q reveals through his question, that interferes with R's ability to answer that question or with Q's ability to correctly interpret R's answer,

7. Information intended to correct a misconception that Q reveals through his question, that doesn't interfere with R's ability to answer that question or with Q's ability to correctly interpret that answer, but that R feels responsible for correcting,

8. Information that R believes that Q may need to keep from misconstruing R's answer (That is, Q's question reveals no misconception, but R suspects that Q may have partial or incorrect information that may lead him to draw a false conclusion from R's answer.),

9. Additional information (or an offer to provide such information) that R believes Q needs for his general knowledge,

10. Information as to R's attitude towards the answer,

11. Rejection of the question (often accompanied by support for such a seemingly uncooperative action).

In the following subsections, I discuss each briefly in turn,[9] noting what computational work has been done towards incorporating it into a Natural Language interface to DBMS or KBS. With respect to this classification, what have been called "indirect answers" [HR79] do not constitute a separate category. In an "indirect answer," the answer is meant to be inferred from the information given explicitly. However, this information will be one of the types mentioned above, for example:

Q: Would you like some more chicken?

R: I'll have some more carrots. *< conveys information relevant to Q's perceived goal of serving seconds>*

Q: Would you like some more chicken?

R: I'm full, thank you. *< conveys information that explains R's answer, so that Q will accept it>*

---

[9] Except for items 8 and 9, about which, regrettably, I have nothing significant to say, either theoretically or computationally.

For this reason, indirect answers do not constitute a separate type of response, but may be found as examples illustrating the various functions that are served by the component information in a response.

5.1.   Goal-related Information and Offers: Appropriate Plans

Many types of response behavior can be attributed to R's attempting to infer and address Q's plans and not just Q's explicit question. In cases where R believes Q's plans are appropriate to Q's goals, R may respond not only to the obstacle represented by the given question but to any remaining obstacles detected in the plan as well, to enable Q to overcome them [ALLE82]. For example:

[1]   Q: When does the Windsor train leave?
      R: 4pm, Gate 7.

[2]   Q: Does the Ottawa train leave at 4pm?
      R: No, it leaves at 5pm.

The additional information that R offers is intended to enable Q to overcome obstacles that R sees to Q's plan. For example, if the plan involves a description "the $x:D(x)$" that R does not believe Q knows the referent of, this constitutes an obstacle to Q's plan. Allen [ALLE82] has developed a system that does this obstacle detection in the course of inferring Q's plan and its goals. Allen does not claim that his system detects every obstacle in Q's plan. Moreover, it is selective in which of the detected obstacles it addresses. In particular, the system selects detected obstacles using the following preferences:

1.   Those goals about which R believes that he and Q disagree: either he believes they hold and Q does not, or vice versa,

2.   Those goals that are explicitly indicated as obstacles by the utterance (i.e., what's been requested),

3.   Those obstacles preventing the performance of the actions that are partially enabled by the explicitly indicated goals above,

4.   Those obstacles that are not "preceded" by other goals in the plan.

Obstacles of the first sort are misconceptions, which are discussed in Section 5.5.[10] Obstacles of the second sort are what Q seeks to

---

[10] Misconceptions are not a major focus of Allen's work, and neither his misconception obstacle recognition nor misconception correction mechanisms are well developed.

surmount through its (direct) answer. However, as will be seen with example [2], not every direct answer can be used to overcome the obstacle the question addresses, hence the inclusion of additional information. Obstacles of the third sort are the most obvious reason for including additional information that is believed to be needed to fulfill Q's plan. This is illustrated in Example [1]. Condition 4 is just a filter.

To understand this obstacle detection, consider example [1]. According to Allen, *the explicitly indicated obstacle* to Q's inferred plan of boarding the Windsor train is Q's lack of knowledge of its departure time. Moreover, Q's potential lack of knowledge of the train's departure location is an *additional obstacle* that could prevent his boarding that train: hence R provides *gate information* as well in response. In example [2], Q's inferred goal of boarding the Ottawa train is blocked by Q's indicated lack of knowledge of its departure time. Allen rightly comments that if the answer to Q's question were "yes", Q would thereby acquire this knowledge (eliminating this obstacle), but a "no" answer leaves Q with the obstacle intact: hence the additional information provided about the specific departure time, to eliminate that obstacle.

Similar behavior has also been recognized and implemented with moderate, limited success in simpler systems that do not have elaborate plan recognition machinery. In Kaplan's COOP system (a Natural Language database interface) [KAPL82], it appears as the "suggestive indirect responses" shown in the following examples:

[3] Q: Is John a senior?

    R1:   No, he's a junior.

    R2:   No, but Fred is.

[4] Q: What specialties in High Altitude Observatory do programmers from SYS have?

    R: I don't know, but you might be interested in any specialties that programmers from SYS have: <list of specialties>

If the answer to a user's question comes back "no" or empty, COOP checks to see if the question reflects particular misconceptions about the database (see Section 5.5). If there is no misconception — the answer was just negative or empty — COOP attempts to suggest relevant information that might be requested in a follow-up query by changing (in fact, broadening) the "focus" of the original question and answering the new question. In Example [3], the additional information in R1 is an answer to the question "John is an X:*class_level*" and R2, an answer to the question "X:*person* is a senior". In Example [4] the focus of the question is changed from "specialties in High Altitude Observatory" to "specialties", and the answer to the derived question included in the response. Kaplan acknowledges that determining the focus of a question cannot really be done purely syntactically as COOP does it, but requires recognition of the questioner's plans in order to figure out what he's interested in, and thus might request in a follow-up question. However, the behavior that COOP displays is useful and requires very little additional computational machinery.

HAM-ANS [WMJB83] is another system that is simpler than Allen's, which attempts to provide the user with additional interesting information beyond that requested. Like COOP, HAM-ANS attempts to anticipate a user's follow-up questions in its response, but does so in a different way: it will either provide additional case role fillers, as in Example [5]

[5]   Q: Has a yellow car gone by?

    R: Yes, one yellow one, on Hartungstreet.

or use more specific quantifiers, as in Example [6]

[6]   Q: Have any vehicles stopped on Biberstreet?

    R: Yes, two.

Both types of information are ones that HAM-ANS determines in the course of answering the user's question, so require no substantial additional computational burden. To summarize, since CO-OP provides an extended response in the case of negative answers, while HAM-ANS does so for positive answers, the two techniques for anticipating follow-on questions complement each other. The combination, in turn, can be complemented by a more expensive approach that takes the user's assumed interests and expectations into account.

Monitor offers are another way of addressing Q's plans and goals, as in

[7]   Q: Has flight AA57 landed yet?

    R: No, it's still circling. Do you want me to let you know when it lands?

The question in R's response constitutes an offer to monitor for and provide Q with additional information, when and if R learns of it. Mays [MAYS83, MAYS85] has identified the knowledge and reasoning capabilities needed by a system in order to offer *competent monitors* — that is, monitors for an event that might actually happen. (It would be uncooperative to offer something you couldn't deliver on.) Mays implemented these capabilities in a propositional, branching-time, modal, temporal logic and accompanying theorem prover [MAYS85].

The complementary problem of deciding which of the many possible competent monitors to offer is addressed by Cheikes [CHEI85], based on Allen's work — reasoning about the questioner's plans and potential obstacles to those plans. In cases where monitor offers are feasible, though, there are two kinds of obstacles, ones that R can do something about, through information R provides (as in example [1]) or actions taken (e.g., opening the door for someone burdened with packages), and obstacles that R has no control over. The former can be dealt with as Allen does, but the latter R must be able to reason about — whether they may somehow, sometime, become unblocked. If they do become unblocked, R must be able to reason about whether Q could carry out the plan at that point, or whether other constraints on Q's plan would make it impossible. (R might then suggest or help Q come up with a different plan to achieve Q's goal or an acceptable alternative, as discussed in the next section.)

In example [7], R may infer that Q plans to meet flight AA57. A precondition for meeting it is that it has landed. This is an obstacle to Q's plan that R has no control over: AA57 hasn't landed and R can't make it land. However, through reasoning about AA57's status in the future, R concludes that (1) The plane will eventually land, and that, (2) It does not know of any constraints to Q's plan that will prevent its execution when the plane does land. Hence R offers to inform Q when AA57 lands, so that Q can carry out the plan. Example [8], on the other hand, illustrates a competent monitor (i.e., R has correctly concluded that AA57 will eventually leave), but one that is incompatible with Q's likely plan of boarding AA57.

[8]   Q: Has flight AA57 left yet?

      R: No, it's still loading. Do you want me to let you know when it leaves?

Finally, suppose R knows that Q needs to be at his destination before a certain time, as in the following

[9]   Q: Has AA57 left yet?

      R: No, it's been delayed. There's no way now that you can get to LA by air before 3pm today. Can I do something else for you?

Here again, R can conclude that the obstacle to Q's plan of flying to LA on AA57 will eventually disappear (i.e., the flight will depart at some later time), but recognizes that constraints prevent Q from carrying out the plan at that time. Thus R merely justifies the "no" answer, acknowledges the inferred goal, and passes the initiative back to Q.

Related to these monitor offers is an example given earlier in Section 3.1, discussing correct answers:

[10] Q: Where's the Kitty Hawk?

>R: At 0430 it was at <longitude/latitude>. I will have an update of that position at 1630.

Here, R reasons that at least one obstacle to Q's plan (whatever it is) is Q's lack of up-to-date knowledge of the Kitty Hawk's position. R does not know when that plan is to be carried out, but concludes that: (1) It will have new, up-to-date knowledge of the Kitty Hawk's position in the future and, (2) That information may be relevant to Q's plan if it is executed after that point. The only difference is that instead of offering to monitor for the information, it just asserts its expectation of future knowledge and leaves Q to take the initiative — either asking for a monitor or checking on the information later himself. It is more passive behavior, but reflects the same kind of reasoning about goal-related information.

The final example is an indirect answer:

[11] Q: What time do you want to leave?

>R: I must be in San Diego before 10am.

This example comes from a dialogue between GUS [BKNT77], a very early, toy, expert system, and a user attempting to arrange a flight to San Diego. Q has already found out from R what day he wants to go. What [11] communicates *indirectly* is a rejection of the question — "I don't know what time I want to leave". Thus, knowing R's desired departure time remains an obstacle to Q's goal of arranging a flight for R.[11] What is communicated *directly*, however, is information that R believes is relevant to Q's overcoming this obstacle: since desired departure time is related to desired arrival time, constraints on the latter will propagate back to constraints on the former. Since users don't always know more than just some constraints on an answer, future KBSs should be able to deal with this type of response and interpret it as volunteered plan-related information.

5.2.   Goal-related Information and Offers: Inappropriate Plans

Unlike the examples in the previous section, it is often the case that Q has a desired goal to achieve but that the plan Q comes up with, which motivates the question, will not achieve it. Recognizing this, R may respond with information that facilitates Q's achieving this goal, as well as (directly or indirectly) answering the given plan-related

---

[11] Other obstacles remain as well, as would be clear if R responded with other information such as "I must be in San Diego before 10am. I'd like to take a UA flight, if possible."

question. This kind of behavior is illustrated in the following examples (the first two taken from [POLL85]):

[12] Q: Is there a way to tell mail that I'd like to deliver a message after some particular time and/or date?

  R: No. I can't really see any easy way to do this either (and guarantee it). If you really wanted to do that, you could submit a batch job to run after a certain time and have it send the message.

[13] Q: What's the combination of the printer room lock?

  R: The door's open.

[14] Q: Can I fly stand-by on this flight?

  R: No, all seats are taken. Do you want me to let you know when a flight with stand-by seats becomes available?

Questioners presume that experts know more about a domain than they do, and they expect the above sort of cooperative behavior. Such expectations have serious implications for knowledge-based systems, since if these systems do not satisfy expectations, they are likely to mislead their users [JWW84b].

Pollack's [POLL85] research addresses the question of inferring inappropriate plans underlying queries. She develops a model of responding to questions that does not rest on what she has called *the appropriate query assumption.* Abandoning this assumption requires the development of a model of plan inference that is significantly different from the models discussed by Allen [ALLE82], Cohen [COHE78] and others. Where their inference procedures are essentially heuristically-guided graph searches through the space of valid plans, Pollack's procedure involves R's (1) Reasoning about likely differences between R's own beliefs and Q's beliefs and, (2) Searching through the space of plans that could be produced by such differences. To facilitate this reasoning, Pollack has had to re-analyze the notion of plans, giving a careful account of the mental attitudes entailed by having a plan. Her account derives from the literature in the philosophy of action, especially [GOLD70] and [BRAT83].

One belief that is claimed to be necessary for Q to have a plan is that all the actions in the plan are related either by **generation** [GOLD70] or by **enablement**.[12] Consider example [12]. R's response

---

[12] Generation corresponds to what is roughly captured as the *by* locution in English: Q believes one can have a message delivered *by* telling mail to deliver a message. Enablement corresponds to the relationship captured in the STRIPS model of actions: finding out the combination to the printer room enables one to open the door. Generation and enablement are not the same: telling mail to deliver a mes-

can be explained by proposing that R infers that Q's plan consists of the following actions:

- Telling mail to deliver a message after some particular date and/or time

- Having mail deliver a message after some particular date and/or time

- Having a message delivered after some particular date and/or time

What R believes is that Q believes that the first action *generates* the second, and that the second *generates* the third. In R's response, the relation that holds between the mentioned action (submitting a batch job) and the inferred goal (having a message delivered after some particular date/time) is also generation, but here, it is R who believes the relation holds. While Pollack does not address the actual information that should be included in a response when the system detects an inappropriate plan underlying a query, it seems clear that an ability to infer such plans is requisite to responding appropriately.

Pollack's analysis can also be applied to handling other types of requests that reflect inappropriate plans. As discussed above, the phenomenon she addresses requires reasoning about the relationship of one action to another, and, more significantly, people's knowledge or beliefs about such relationships: the actions themselves can be treated as opaque. In order to handle an example such as [13], Pollack's analysis would have to be extended to allow reasoning about people's knowledge or beliefs about objects and their properties and the role that particular objects and their properties play in actions. Reasoning about the relationship between knowledge (primarily of objects) and action has been discussed in [ALLE82, MOOR84, APPE85]. In order to produce an appropriate monitor offer such as in [14], where Q cannot carry out his described action "flying standby on this flight," a system would have to combine an approach such as Pollack's with a system such as [MAYS85] discussed earlier, that could reason about the future.

5.3. Information intended to justify or explain R's response

The discussion here is limited to questions about the truth of a statement. The kind of information given in response to justify or explain their answers ranges from a description or enumeration of the simple facts supporting a 'yes' answer to an existential question (e.g.,

---

sage after some particular date and/or time does not alter the current world state in such a way that one can then have mail deliver the message.

"Do any X's Y?") to the general principles, concept definitions, and specific facts supporting or explaining any answer. Indirect answers are also discussed, where it is the explanation that is given directly, while the answer must be inferred. Knowing the grounds for a response as simple as 'yes' or 'no' makes that response that much more acceptable.

Facts provided as grounds justifiying a 'yes' answer to an existential yes/no question were illustrated in the HAM-ANS examples [5 and 6]. One of its applications involves answering questions about particular features of an image. When asked about the existence of objects in the image (or events in a sequence of images) that satisfy a particular description, it looks for and records all such instances. Thus it can easily enumerate or describe the instances to justify its positive response. (This is one case where the same information can fulfill more than one function.)

For yes/no questions in which the answer depends on the meaning of the concepts involved (rather than just their denotations), a response may include a justification in the form of a definition of the relevant concepts or a comparison of them, as in the following example.

[15] Q: I see — now the money market fund and the all saver's certificate, they're not the same are they?

R: No — oh no — a money market fund is a mutual fund, an all saver's certificate is a certificate that you get from your bank which is tax free for federal purposes up to two thousand of interest.

Work done by McKeown [MCKE85] on automatically generating answers to requests for the definition of a database term or for a comparison of two terms, based on an enriched database model, is directly applicable to providing this type of justification.

Where the system's answer to a yes/no question involves reasoning from general principles as well as from specific facts, that reasoning can be described as a way of justifying R's response. For example:

[16] Q: Is Bill citizen-of x

R: Yes

Q: Why?

R: I can show
            Bill citizen-of UK
       by using
            x citizen-of y if x born-in y
       and I know
            Bill born-in UK

The example comes from an interface to a PROLOG-based reasoner called "Query_the_User" [SERG83] which keeps a record of its proof tree. Because PROLOG is a Horn clause reasoning system (i.e., all its rules are of the form A1 & A2 & ... An ⇒ B, where all literals are positive), its proofs can be mapped directly onto reasonably comprehensible justifications. However, Horn clause logics have severe limitations since they cannot express disjunctive facts and conclusions and true negation. Soundproof methods for stronger logics, though, may bear little or now resemblance to any type of human reasoning, and texts produced directly from their proofs may make little or no sense.[13] The point is not that we cannot produce justifications of yes/no answers if a system uses an effective but unnatural proof procedure, but rather that addition work must be done on ways of mapping from general proof structures to comprehensible ones, whose translation into Natural Language makes sense.

There is another feature of good explanations that also does not come out from reading off a proof tree, even one as comprehensible as those for Horn clause logics — that is, an attempt to contrast the correct answer against relevant but incorrect alternatives. The alternatives to P are not used in proving P, and hence do not appear in any proof tree for P. Nevertheless, addressing them in an explanation makes the argument more convincing.

Where do relevant alternatives come from? The respondent R may have to identify relevant alternatives based on context, knowledge of Q and the kind of facts given in support of P, or Q may specify the alternatives explicitly, as in

[17] Q: So you would still file as a single person.

      R: Even though I'm married?

      Q: Right. Because you weren't married during the filing year, 1984.

Here R initially does not give any justification for the claim that Q must file as a single person. Then, in response to Q's yes/no question ("I

---

[13] To see this, consider a resolution proof of the following problem discussed by [MOOR80]:

> Suppose there's a stack of three blocks. Blocks are either green or blue. In the stack, the top block is green and the bottom one, blue. Is there a green block on a blue one?

This cannot be solved by a Horn clause reasoner, since it contains a disjunctive fact. The proof bears little resemblence to the clearest explanation one would offer in natural language:

> Yes. It doesn't matter what color B is. If it's green, then it is the green block on top of the blue block C. If it's blue, then A is the green block on top of the blue block B.

have to file as a single person even though I'm married?"), R produces a response which includes not only an answer ("right" = "yes"), but a justification that shows why the suggested alternative (file status = married) is not supported by the facts.

"Should" questions come up in the context of expert advisory systems (i.e., as opposed to expert diagnostic systems). There are many grounds for advising courses of action — goals to be advanced of the various parties involved, potential risks to the various parties, costs to be paid — and factors must both be identified and weighed. Justification is as important to include in response here as an answer. But notice that there are also two other possible answers when decisions depend on weighing factors: "yes and no," if the evidence seems to balance, and "it doesn't matter," if both courses of action lead to the same result, as in:

[18] Q: Should I take AI this semester?

  R1:   No. Although you've had the prerequisites for AI, you have many required courses left to complete.

  R2:   Yes. If you take it now, you'll be able to take more of the advanced topics in AI later.

  R3:   Yes and no. Although you've had the prerequisites for AI, you have many required courses left to complete. On the other hand, if you take it now, you'll be able to take more of the advanced topics in AI later. [MWM85]

[19] Q: Should I turn off the faucet?

  R: It doesn't matter. I've already shut off the main. [HR79]

McKeown [MWM85] has done preliminary work on justifying advice in the domain of student advising, where the advice can depend on both domain requirements (e.g., Physics 150 is required for a BSE degree) and user preferences (e.g., The user/student likes linguistics courses). She shows how the same action can be advised in favor of and advised against, depending on which requirements and preferences are taken into consideration.

The final example here illustrates indirect answers whose explicit response is justification for the answer, which Q must infer, as in

[20] Q: Will Bilandic win?

  R: The machine candidate always wins.

It is a presentation of modus ponens deduction which Sadock [SADO77] calls "Modus Brevis" in which, instead of a full modus ponens proof justifying the answer, only a portion of the argument is given. If Q takes R's explicit response as part of a proof of the answer, then Q must *simultaneously* identify both the answer and the proof R intends to convey.

In Example [20], there are two possible answers and two possible proofs, which depend on alternative beliefs about Bilandic that R may ascribe to Q. If R believes that Q believes that Bilandic is the machine candidate, then R has conveyed to Q both *that* Bilandic will win and *why*. If R believes that Q believes that Bilandic is not the machine candidate, then R has conveyed to Q both *that* someone else will win and *why*. If R doesn't know what Q believes, then *intonational cues* can convey the association R is drawing between Bilandic and the machine candidate, and R can assume that Q will use it in reconstructing both an answer and a proof. For example:

Q: Will Bilandic win?

R: The machine candidate ALWAYS wins.
     < *Unstressed subject allows Q to construe "Bilandic" and "the machine candidate" as coreferential, implying Bilandic will win* >

R: The MACHINE CANDIDATE always wins.
     < *Stressed subject and destressed 'always' prevent this construal, so the subject must refer to a new individual, implying Bilandic will not win* >

The point of this example is two-fold: to illustrate the use of explanation as an indirect answer and to illustrate the kind of reasoning Q must do to reconstruct both an answer and its proof. While I do not advocate inclusion of this sort of indirection in a system's response repetoire, it may be part of a user's repetoire, especially if allowed to respond in free text.

5.4. Information intended to clarify R's response

Two obvious types of information that can be used to clarify what one's answer is are *examples* and *pictures*. Examples can be used to pin unfamiliar concepts and abstract descriptions to things one's audience is familiar with and, as has been noted [RVA84], they allow one to explore the limits of generalizations and explanations. Pictures, on the other hand, address a different mental processor than text, and thus enable an information provider to illustrate the same information in another way.

Computational work on constructing examples and integrating them into responses to requests for on-line help has been done by Rissland and her students at the University of Massachusetts [RVA84]. Their on-line help system links a (primarily canned) textual explanation program with an *example generator* that generates examples on the fly, using a knowledge base of existing examples (organized into a taxonomy), together with procedures of modifying and instantiating them according to the user's needs and/or desires, and according to the current context. Particular calls to HELP result in the selection of a script-like structure (a *TEXPLATE*) of pointers to chunks of text and/or requests for explicit examples or constraints describing modifications to be made to an example. A TEXPLATE will also set up a context for interpreting future requests to HELP (e.g., a request for help with "queue" will be interpreted in the context of a previous request for help with "print").

[21] Q: help 'print'

R: PRINT queues one or more files for printing, either on a default system printer or on a specified device.

For example:
PRINT LOGIN.COM
will cause your file login.com to be printed on the default printer.

Q: help 'queue'

R: A print queue is a list of files to be printed on a specific device.

For example:

PRINT LOGIN.COM / QUEUE=NARROW

requests that file login.com be printed on the printer corresponding to the queue named 'narrow.'

The /QUEUE qualifier is synonymous with the /DEVICE qualifier. For instance,
PRINT LOGIN.COM / DEVICE=NARROW
will do the same thing.

An interpreter controls the flow through the TEXPLATES, including which user options to present and what to do in response to a user's request for futher explanation or additional examples. Since there is only a relatively small number of concepts for which HELP is available (albeit multiple ways to access them), a system such as this can be implemented in terms of an a priori set of scripts, one per concept. The next step is to generalize the techniques, so that the script for each individual concept need not be individually handcrafted.

Pictures can be used to clarify text: imagine trying to follow instructions for repairing an appliance without an accompanying diagram. Similarly, text can be used to clarify pictures, as subtitles and figure annotations attest. However, there has been little research on systems that can reason about how information should be presented — text or figures alone, or some combination of both.[14] Picture database systems do not do such reasoning: they accept requests for the set of pictures satisfying a given description. Nor do systems that allow users to query a given picture [WMJB83, CM82]. Neither reasons about optimal presentation of information in terms of pictures or text or both.

On the other hand, there was an ambitious experimental Command and Control system developed at BBN to allow a decision maker to make use of a highly intelligent graphics display through natural language interaction [BBCK79]. The goal of the system was to allow flexible generation of displays, to enable the user to understand some complex situation. In the prototype system, a user's utterance would be interpreted as a request for the creation or modification of a display — that is, simply as a request for a picture satisfying a given description. This system was able to engage in the following interaction in a domain consisting of spatial layouts of a large ATN grammar. (The present reader will have to imagine the displays.)

User: Show me the clause level network.

System: [displays states and arcs of the S/ network]

User: Show me S/NP.

System: [highlights S/NP with reverse video]

User: Focus in on the preverbal constituents.

System: [shifts scale and centers the display on the preverbal st

User: No. I want to be able to see S/AUX.

System: [backs off display so as to include S/AUX]

It is the user's second utterance, "Show me S/NP" that is of

---

[14] Steamer [HHW84] uses annotated diagrams to illustrate cause and effect relationships between steam room (power plant) controls and the parts of the hydraulic systems they affect, but the text and pictures are canned: The system does not reason about what to present.

interest here. The prototype was able to reason that, since S/NP is part of the S/ network, it is part of the previous display. Thus it can simply highlight it, to attract the user's attention.

Now suppose that the user's second utterance were, "Is S/NP in this network?" and that the system were able to respond with text as well as pictures. To answer this question, it would reason as above, as to whether S/NP were part of the S/ level network. Since it is, the system could answer "Yes". However, it might also reason that it could easily clarify its response by highlighting S/NP in the current display, since then the user could see its position within the network for himself. While this was not within the capabilities of the prototype system (nor was that system further developed), it does give some indication as to how one might go about incorporating pictures in a interactive system, in order to clarify the text.

5.5. Information intended to correct a misconception

Many of the troubles in interaction come from the fact that participants hold different views about the world and either do not realize it or fail to do anything about it. As a result, each may leave the interaction with very different beliefs about what was communicated.

Now in simple database systems, users may be able to recognize a disparity between the system's view of the world and their own: for example, they may be able to tell that the system's answer to their question is wrong or strange. On the other hand, users of complex database systems and KBSs will have less domain knowledge and expertise than the system and are thus less likely to be able to recognize a disparity. By not recognizing such a disparity, they may be confused by the system's response or, worse, they may misinterpret it and be misled. Therefore, a system must be able to recognize and respond to any disparities between its beliefs about the world and the user's beliefs about the world that the user reveals.

There are at least two kinds of beliefs that are easy to recognize. One is a belief that a particular description has a referent in the world of interest (i.e., that there is an individual or set which meets the description). Such a belief is revealed when a noun phrase is used in particular contexts. For example, for Q to ask the question "Which French majors failed CIS531 last term?", Q would have to believe that: (1) CIS531 was given last term, (2) there are French majors, and (3) there are French majors who took CIS531 last term. If R does not hold these beliefs as well, it would be uncooperative for R to give a direct answer, since any direct answer, including "None", implicitly confirms (incorrectly) that R holds these beliefs. The other kind of belief concerns what can serve as an argument to a particular relation. Such beliefs are revealed linguistically in terms of the subject and/or object of a verb. For example, the question "Which graduate students have taught CIS531?" shows that Q believes that graduate students can teach CIS531. Again, if R does not hold this belief, it would be uncooperative to give a direct answer, since any direct answer would implicitly confirm this belief, including the answer "None". In both examples, a direct answer is insufficient, and must be augmented in a response which addresses the disparity.

(In computational research in this area, disparities between the beliefs of user and system have been treated as **misconceptions** on the user's part. This approach is defensible in that the research has been done in the context of database question-answering, in which the user assumes the system has more information. Of course, in actual fact, the user may hold the correct belief, but the important thing is that the disparity be pointed out so that the answer, if given, can be correctly interpreted. In what follows, I shall also refer to these disparities as "misconceptions".)

Computational work on providing such responses has been done by Kaplan [KAPL82], again in the context of his Natural Language database interface called COOP. He addresses the misconception that a description of an entity or set has a referent in the system's database, when, according to the system's information, it does not. Mercer [MR84] addresses both the "extensional" misconceptions (Kaplan's term) that Kaplan considers, and certain misconceptions inferrable from the use of particular lexical items. Mays [MAYS80] addresses misconceptions that assume that a relationship can hold between two objects or classes, when according to the system's information it cannot. (The latter is very much like a "type violation" in a programming language.) Examples of interactions that this work supports are given below:

[22] Q: Which French majors failed CIS531 last term?

R1:   I do not know of any French majors.

R2:   I do not know of CIS531 being given last term.

[23] Q: Have you stopped taking CIS531?

R: No, I have not stopped, since I haven't started.

[24] Q: Which grad students have taught CIS531?

R: CIS531 is a grad course. Only faculty can teach grad courses.

The techniques that Kaplan, Mercer, and Mays developed to support such interactions rely on (1) The system's ability to determine, during retrieval, whether any relevant set is empty [KAPL82], (2) Its ability to determine the presuppositions[15] of the answer it plans to give [MR84], and, (3) Its having an enriched data model indicating whether sets are mutually exclusive and/or exhaustive [MAYS80]. Where Mercer's and Kaplan's approach differ is that Kaplan's system essentially infers what Q would have to believe about the world in order to have asked his question. If any of those beliefs conflict with the beliefs of the system, corrective information is included, in addition to, or instead of, an answer. Mercer's system, on the other hand, computes the presuppositions of its planned answer because, according to Gazdar's interpretation [GAZD79] of Grice's Maxim of Quality, a speaker should not say anything that has a non-true presupposition. The difference between the systems would be apparent if COOP did not make the "Closed World Assumption". Then COOP could not necessarily conclude there were no individuals satisfying a particular description if it couldn't find them. For example,

[25] Q: Do any professors that teach CSE101 teach CSE114?

If no such individuals could be found nor could individuals satisfying the embedded description "professors that teach CSE101," COOP would reply

R: There are no professors that teach CSE101.

On the other hand, if Mercer's system can prove that there is no professor who teaches CSE114, but cannot prove that its presupposition is false — that there is no professor who teaches CSE101 — it will respond

---

[15] In simple terms, a presupposition of a sentence S is a statement which, to make sense, must be true for either S or its negation.

R: No. Moreover I don't even know if any professor teaches CSE101.

Other computational work has been done on responding to object-related misconceptions [MCCO83, MCCO85]. These may be revealed through a user's utterance, either describing an object in terms of a class it doesn't belong to, incorrectly attributing some property to it, or ascribing an incorrect value to one of its properties. For example,

[26] Q: Do you have any liquid assets?

R: I have a $5k money market certificate.

Q: A money market certificate isn't a liquid asset. Your money is tied up for several years in a money market certificate. Do you mean a money market account?

[27] Q: What's the interest rate on this stock?

R: Stocks don't have an interest rate. They may pay a dividend periodically.

In this work on responding to object-related misconceptions, McCoy has concentrated on the role of discourse perspective — first, in deciding whether or not something reflects a misconception in the current context (which highlights certain attributes of an object while suppressing others) and, secondly, in deciding what information to include in an appropriate response (i.e., what would be an appropriate correction in the current context). As to the first point, McCoy observes that depending on the discourse perspective, two things may be judged as similar or different. Contrasting them in the former situation would reveal a misconception, as would equating them in the latter. For example,

[28] R: I'd like to see you hold that $10,000 coming due in a money market fund until mid-March and then get into a longer term money market certificate.

Q: Well, I was just wondering, what about a treasury bill instead?

R: That's not a bad idea, but it doesn't replace your money market certificate in any way — it's an exact duplicate. They're almost identical types of instruments, so one, as far as I'm concerned, is about the same as another.

[29] Q: I'm interested in buying some US Government securities. I was thinking about Money Market Certificates, since they are the same as Treasury Bills.

R: But they're not: they're two very different things. A Treasury Bill is backed by the government. You have to get it from the Federal Reserve. A money market certificate, on the other hand, is backed by the bank that issues it. So one is a government security while the other isn't.

In example [28], the discourse reveals both objects being viewed through the perspective of savings instruments, thereby highlighting such attibutes as interest rate and maturity date, which treasury bills and money market certificates share. In example [29], the discourse reveals that the objects are being viewed in terms of their issuer, thereby highlighting such attributes as issuing company and purchase place, which attributes treasury bills and money market certificates don't share. McCoy's approach through perspective is able to identify that contrasting the two in the first example reveals a misconception, as does equating them in the second example.

As to the second point — deciding what information to include in an appropriate response — McCoy presents a variety of correction strategies whose selection in a particular case depends on what the system believes may have led the user to the misconception. For example, if the system's model of the user (filtered by the current perspective) shows that a probable reason for the misconception is that the user believes the misclassified object is like its incorrectly posited superordinate (i.e., as distinct from a subclass of that incorrect superordinate), the system will attempt to include in its response

1.   A denial of the incorrect classification

2.   A statement of the correct classification

3.   A concession of similarity by mentioning their common attributes

4.   An override to the conceded information by noting features that define the object as belonging to its correct superordinate class

For example,

[30] Q: I want to buy some corporate bonds. Should I get preferred?

R: Preferred are not bonds, they are stock. A preferred stock is like a bond in that both have regular payments of a fixed amount. However, unlike bond payments, the company is under no legal obligation to pay preferred stock payments. In addition, preferred stock gives part ownership in the company.

There are clearly many other types of misconceptions that Q may hold that can interfere with R's ability to answer Q's questions or with Q's ability to interpret the answers correctly. One of the most subtle for advisory systems involves Q's belief in the relevance of some concept to his question, whereas, for R, it is irrelevant. R's lack of attention to such misconceptions can make it very difficult for Q to understand R's advice, as he is trying to integrate it into some very strange structure of beliefs. Examples of this can be found in Cassell's transcripts of doctor's taking medical histories [CASS85]. It is something that the developers of advisory systems will eventually have to deal with, if they are to be used by the lay public.

5.6. Information intended to prevent misconstrual

Section 4.3 discusses the problem of correct but nevertheless misleading answers. I note there that it is often not enough to *change* one's answer to avoid misleading the user. Rather one may have to augment it with additional information. It is this latter information that is discussed in this section.

Section 4.3 mentions three bases for R's anticipating Q's drawing a false conclusion from R's answer A: *deductive reasoning* involving A and a false belief that Q holds; *default reasoning*, where R knows the default does not hold; and *implicature*, where A may suggest, by virtue of its ordinary use, something that isn't the case here. The first case is similar to the situation discussed in the previous section, in which R adds information to correct Q's misconception. If R does not point out, or, better, correct Q's false belief, Q will draw an additional false conclusion from R's answer. The additional information R provides in response may point out the false belief or correct it as well.

The second case is illustrated by one of the examples in Section 2 (repeated here):

[31] Q: What's the combination of the printer room lock?

     R: It's 8-9-8, but Ira changes it every week.

One might call this an "inertial default" — typically, the referent of a definite descriptor stays the same. If R just answers Q's question ("It's 8-9-8"), Q may falsely conclude (by default reasoning) that the referent of the definite descriptor "the combination of the printer room lock" will stay 8-9-8. R provides the additional information ("but Ira changes it every week") to prevent this misconstrual.

The third case, misconstrual based on implicature, is illustrated by the example in Section 4.3 (repeated here):

[32] Q: Which ships have a doctor on board?

     R: All of them: the JFK, the Admiral Nimitz,...

The enumeration in the answer implicates "not all". If this is false, R should provide the additional information that the enumeration does cover all. Examples such as these are discussed in [JWW84a,

JWW84b].

Finally, I want to mention a fourth basis for R's anticipating that Q may draw a false conclusion from R's answer: R's belief that people typically believe X (i.e., as opposed to R's belief that people believe that typically X). Consider a user interacting with an employment database, checking out a job that looks interesting. He asks

[33] Q: What's the salary?

     R: There isn't any.

Because of this, the user rejects the job and moves on to consider others. The system's answer may be true, but the user's conclusion may be false: that is, the job may not pay a salary, but remuneration may come in other ways (e.g., tips, commission, stock options, etc.).

To anticipate and avoid such a false conclusion, R could reason about what people typically believe, and if that doesn't match the current situation, R could inform Q. That is, suppose R believes that people typically will not take non-paying jobs. R also believes that people typically believe that if a job doesn't pay a salary, it is a non-paying job. (Here, RB stands for "R believes" and QB, for "Q believes".)

(RB (*typically* Q not take a non-paying job))

(RB (*typically* QB (no salary ⇒ non-paying job)))

R, on the other hand, believes that all jobs either pay a salary or have tips or offer commission on sales or provide stock options or other free benefits or are non-paying. Moreover, R knows that this job offers a 20% commission on sales.

(RB ∀ x:job . x pays salary or x has tips or x offers commission ... or x is non-paying job)

(RB JOB617 not pay salary)

(RB JOB617 offers commission)

Given R's own beliefs and beliefs about users' typical beliefs, R should be able to anticipate that Q will not take this job (JOB617) because it is non-paying. However, R knows that while it doesn't pay a salary, it does pay commission. Thus R should also describe what reimbursement the job provides, to prevent any misconstrual.

     R: There is no salary, but there is a 20% commission on every squash racquet you sell.

The major assumption of this work on augmenting responses to prevent Q's misconstruing an answer is that one can limit the amount of reasoning that R is responsible for doing, to detect a possible reason for misconstrual. This is an important assumption, and work is currently underway to back it up.

5.7. Rejection of the question

Given the problems with answering and responding to questions appropriately, not much attention has been paid to enabling systems to justifiably refuse to answer a user's question. This is a problem that will have to be faced as database and knowledge-base systems become more selective as to whom they provide particular information (i.e., issues of privacy and security) and as such systems become aware of both their own and other systems' capabilities, thereby becoming able to offer competent "referrals". The interface aspects of this behavior are not the hard part: the hard part involves computing whether users should be provided with particular information or whether it will enable them to infer things that they aren't priviledged to, and giving a system awareness of its own capabilities and those of other systems so that it can determine whether it can provide the requested information or, if not, what system can. Notice that the latter is related to the same kind of reasoning involved in describing the user and the system's mutual beliefs about what services the system can provide, needed in order to understand and respond to the user's plan-related questions. (See Section 5.1.)

6. Conclusion

The purpose of this chapter is to examine the character of information-seeking interactions with KBSs. In doing so, I advocate that a clear distinction be made between an answer to a question and a response. From a theoretical viewpoint, it means that each type of information included in response to a question (including possibly its answer) can be separately motivated and analysed. From a practical viewpoint, it means that a system can reason separately about what it should include in response to a user's question or what a user has included in response to its question. The paper also reviews work in question answering, both theoretical and applied, so that the reader can sense the current state of the field with respect to providing the rich environment needed for effective interaction with KBSs. In line with the view stated in the first section, that the main responsibility of a KBS is the communication of information, supporting the range of behaviors described in this paper should be a top priority in future developments of KBS.

Acknowledgements

I would like to thank Aravind Joshi, Martha Pollack and Julia Hirschberg, who have given me valuable constructive comments on previous versions of this paper.

7. References

[ALLE82] [APPE85] [BBCK79] [BKNT77] [BRAT83] [CARB85] [CASS85] [CHEI85] [CM82] [COHE78] [CORE85] [DAVI79] [GAZD79] [GOLD70] [GREW83] [GRIC75] [HCR84] [HIRS85] [HHW84] [HR79] [JOSH82] [JWW84a] [JWW84b] [JWW84c] [KAPL82] [KT81] [LAL82] [LEHN81] [LEVE84a] [LEVI83] [MAYS80] [MAYS83] [MAYS85] [MCCO83] [MCCO85] [MCKE85] [MWM85] [MOOR80] [MOOR84] [MR84] [POLL85] [REIT78a] [REIT78b] [RVA84] [SADO77] [SCHA75] [SERG83] [SWAR83] [TRIL84] [WALK82] [WEIN80] [WINO72] [WMJB83]

27
Learning in Knowledge-Base Management Systems

Tom M. Mitchell[1]

ABSTRACT *This chapter argues that techniques from the field at Machine Learning may play a significant role in future Knowledge-Base Management Systems. We describe a specific knowledge-based consultant system which automatically augments its knowledge base by observing and generalizing from the problem solving steps contributed by its users.*

1. Introduction

It is now a good time for research aimed at incorporating Machine Learning techniques into Knowledge-Base Management Systems (KBMSs). The argument for this position is based on three assumptions: (1) The high cost of constructing large knowledge-bases manually represents one of the greatest bottlenecks to developing useful knowledge-based systems, (2) The difficulties inherent in formulating a perfect database schema for a new application make it essential to refine the initial schema during the course of its use, and (3) Recent progress in Machine Learning has led to new methods with the potential to help with both the above problems.

Machine Learning is the subfield of Artificial Intelligence concerned with developing computer methods for automatically acquiring new knowledge from experience. This field has seen a burst of activity over the past five years (see, for example, [MCM82,MCM85]). This work has led (among other things) to the development of several useful methods for generalizing from examples; that is, for inferring the

---

[1] Rutgers University

characteristic description of some class, given a set of training examples of that class. This task of generalizing from examples is central to both the problem of acquiring new facts and inference rules within an existing database schema, and to the problem of refining an initial database schema. The following paragraphs summarize one ongoing research effort that seeks to address the first of these problems. The second problem is addressed in the chapter by Borgida, Mitchell, and Williamson in this volume.

2. Automatically Extending the Knowledge Base

Our recent work on learning in knowledge-based systems [MMS85] is oriented toward developing a particular class of systems that automatically acquire new knowledge through experience. In particular, we define **Learning Apprentice Systems** as the class of interactive knowledge-based consultants that directly assimilate new knowledge by observing and analyzing the problem-solving steps contributed by their users through their normal use of the system. [MMS85] discusses issues related to the development of such Learning Apprentice Systems, focusing on the design of a particular Learning Apprentice System (called LEAP) for VLSI circuit design.

The LEAP system is currently being constructed as an augmentation to a knowledge-based VLSI design assistant called VEXED [MSS84]. VEXED provides interactive aid to the user in implementing a circuit (given its functional specifications) by suggesting and carrying out possible refinements to the design. A large part of its knowledge about circuit design is composed of a set of implementation rules, each of which suggests some legal method for implementing a given function. For example, one implementation rule states that "IF the required function is to convert a parallel signal to a serial signal, THEN one possible implementation is to use a shift register." LEAP is designed to learn additional implementation rules, so as to extend the knowledge base that provides the source of the system's capabilities.

VEXED is designed to make it easy to acquire training examples that form the basis for formulating new implementation rules in LEAP. VEXED provides a convenient editor-and-user interface that helps the user design circuits beginning with their functional specifications and leading to their implementation. It maintains an agenda of design subtasks (e.g., implementing the module which must multiply two numbers) initially containing the top-level task of implementing the entire circuit. VEXED repeatedly selects a subtask from the agenda, examines its implementation rules to determine whether it can suggest possible implementations for the corresponding circuit module, then presents any such suggestions to the user. The user may select one of the suggested implementation rules, in which case that rule is executed to refine the module. Alternatively, the user may disregard VEXED's suggestions and instead use the editor to refine the circuit module manually. It is in this later case that LEAP will add to its knowledge of circuit design, by generalizing from the implementation step contributed by the user to formulate a new rule that summarizes a previously uncatalogued implementation method. In general, each such implementation step/training example consists of (1) a description of some function to be implemented, (2) a description of the known characteristics of the input signals to the circuit module, and (3) a circuit entered by the user to implement the given function for the given input signals.

Given such a training example, the most straightforward method of acquiring a new implementation rule is to create a rule suggesting that the given circuit can be used to implement the given module function in precisely the given context (e.g., whenever the input signals are precisely the same as in the training example). Such a rule would clearly be so specific that it would add little of general use to the system's knowledge of implementation methods. A better approach would be to generalize the preconditions (left hand side) of the implementation rule, so that it characterizes the general class of input signals for which the given circuit correctly implements the specified function. LEAP computes such a generalization of the rule preconditions by analyzing the single training example in terms of its knowledge of circuit operation. In particular, LEAP first explains (verifies) for itself that the circuit does, in fact, work for the example input signals, then generalizes from this example by retaining only those features of the signals that were mentioned in this explanation. It is this set of signal features that is required for the explanation to hold in general, and which therefore characterizes the class of input signals for which the circuit will correctly implement the desired function. This explain-then-generalize method for producing justifiable generalizations from single examples is based on previous work on goal-directed, or explanation-based generalization methods [MITC83,DEJO82], and is potentially applicable to a large number of learning tasks involving knowledge-based systems.

Thus, LEAP represents an attempt to incorporate Machine Learning methods within an interactive problem-solving aid, in order to allow the system to build up its knowledge base through experience. There are, of course, many open research issues along this line of work (e.g., how can the system manage and utilize the logical interdependencies among facts in its evolving knowledge base?)

A second focus for applying Machine Learning to KBMSs lies in attempting to refine the initial database *schema*, based on failures observed during normal use. See the chapter by Borgida, Mitchell, and Williamson, for a discussion of approaches to this learning problem.

Research on both of these learning problems seems very worthwhile at this point, given its high potential impact and the fact that this is a relatively underexplored research direction.

Acknowledgments

This work was supported by the National Science Foundation under research grant DCS83-51523. Portions of this research were conducted during the fall of 1985, while the author was on leave from Rutgers University as a visiting professor in the Computer Science Department at Carnegie-Mellon University.

3. References

[DEJO82] [MCM82] [MCM85] [MITC83] [MMS85] [MSS84]

28
The Role of Databases in Knowledge-Based Systems

Mark S. Fox
John McDermott[1]

ABSTRACT *This paper explores the requirement for database techniques in the construction of Knowledge Based Systems. Three knowledge-based systems are reviewed: XCON/R1, ISIS and Callisto in order to ascertain database requirements. These requirements result in the introduction of the Organization Level, and extension to the Symbol and Knowledge Levels introduced by Newell. An implementation of these requirements is explored in the SRL knowledge representation and problem-solving system.*

1. Introduction

This chapter explores the requirements for database techniques in the construction of Knowledge-Based systems (KBS). While early work in Artificial Intelligence (AI) focused on techniques such as representation and problem-solving, scant attention was paid to the issues on which database (DB) research has focused (e.g., data sharing, query optimization, transaction processing). Our principal premise is that, although it has appeared that there was little intersection between the particular focus of each group, there is a significant overlap in needs. The maturing of AI techniques has recently led to their application outside the laboratory, thus thrusting upon them problems requiring DB solutions. On the other hand, DB needs have expanded to include more expressive data models and more powerful query languages (e.g.,

---

[1] Computer Science Department and Robotics Institute, Carnegie-Mellon University, Pittsburgh, Pennsylvania

supporting inference).

To ascertain KBS requirements for DBs, three KBSs are described. Each is analyzed from the perspective of the symbol and knowledge-level concepts developed by Newell [NEWE80]. Limitations inherent in this perspective are identified. A new level, the organization level, is proposed as a means of identifying and dealing with these limitations. Lastly, we discuss implementations of some of the requirements in the SRL knowledge engineering system. For a further discussion of DB technology referred to in this chapter, see the DB summary chapter by Brodie.

2. Database Requirement Analysis

In 1979-80, work began in both the Computer Science Department and Robotics Institute at Carnegie-Mellon University, exploring the application of AI to engineering and manufacturing problems. Over the years ,at least 15 KBSs have been created and are in various stages of development and production use. From this set we have chosen three systems exhibiting a variety of DB requirements.

2.1. R1: Computer Configuration

The configuration task that R1 performs takes, as input, a list of components ordered by a customer, and produces, as output, a set of diagrams displaying the interrelationships among those components. If the initial list of components is incomplete (i.e., it may not be possible to configure a functional system with that set of components) the configurer adds appropriate components in the course of determining what the interrelationships among the components should be. Because the various combinations of components that might be ordered is too large to enumerate, the only approach to a configuration task of this type is to construct (as opposed to select) an appropriate system configuration.

It would appear that constructive tasks require heuristic search, that is, a combinatorial search in which candidate-partial solutions are constructed and their potential evaluated. The nature of R1's knowledge of its task is such that R1 can for the most part avoid the combinatorial search (and thus avoid backtracking) by using small local searches at steps where there is ambiguity about what next action is most appropriate [MCDE82a]. In other words, local cues are ordinarily sufficient to drive R1 along a path to a solution. R1's search techniques make only one sort of informational demand on its environment: it requires information that will allow it to determine which of several competing actions within the same or within competing subtasks ought to be performed next. Viewing the task from this perspective, there are at most two roles that knowledge can play. One of the roles is as selector of the next action within some subtask. The other role is as initiator of a local search when there is ambiguity about which subtask and which action to select.

R1's problem-solving method always selects the next piece of knowledge (i.e., rule) to apply from among those pieces of knowledge associated with the currently active subtask. Ordinarily, only a few pieces of knowledge are relevant at any given time; a piece of knowledge is considered relevant whenever the pattern defining its relevance can be instantiated by elements describing the current state of the world. When more than one piece of knowledge is relevant, the problem-solving method relies on very general heuristics, such as the recency of the elements instantiating each pattern and the degree of specificity of each pattern to determine which piece of knowledge to apply. Thus R1's problem-solving can be characterized as follows: Given that it's involved in some task, it will take whatever next step (i.e., apply whatever knowledge) is relevant (and the step could be to initiate some subtask); if more than one piece of knowledge is potentially relevant, the choice of which step to take will be made on the basis of very general considerations. If there is no more knowledge relevant to the current task, R1's attention returns to the parent task. Whenever R1 does not have enough information to confidently prefer one possible step to all other candidates, it does some local problem-solving (searching) until sufficient information has been collected.

R1's rule base is written in OPS5 [FORG81] and contains over 4000 rules. It performs goal-directed forward chaining in order to synthesize a configuration. Information on Digital's standard parts is contained in the DBMS database system. It contains over 9000 part descriptions, with anywhere from 25 to 125 different attributes describing each part. A subset of R1's rule base implements an interface to the DBMS system. When parts and/or their attributes are required during the configuration process, the DB interface rules' actions query the DB and provide the retrieved information in the format required by OPS5 and R1. In order to support R1's processing, the DBMS provides query processing on a transaction basis. In the situation where more than one R1 is running, the DBMS supports transactions from more than one process.

R1/XCON
COMPUTER CONFIGURATION

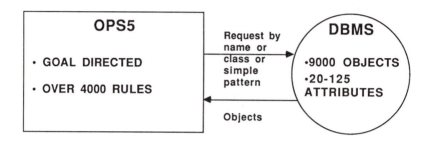

A Sample Rule

IF: The current subtask is assigning
                 devices to unibus modules
       And there is an unassigned dual port disk drive
       And the type of controller it requires is known
       And there are two such controllers neither of
                 which has any devices assigned to it
       And the number of devices which these controllers
              can support is known

THEN: Assign the disk drive to each controller
       And note that each controller supports one device

Figure 1: R1 Database Architecture

2.2. ISIS: Job-Shop Scheduling

ISIS is a knowledge-based system designed to provide intelligent support in the domain of job-shop production management and control [FS84]. Job-shop scheduling is an "uncooperative" multi-agent planning problem (i.e., each order is to be "optimized" separately) in which activities must be selected, sequenced, and assigned resources and time of execution. Resource contention is high, hence decisions are closely coupled. Search is combinatorially explosive; for example, 85 orders moving through eight operations without alternatives, with a single machine substitution for each and no machine idle time has over 10^{880} possible schedules. Many of these may be discarded, given knowledge of shop *constraints*. At the core of ISIS is an approach to automatic scheduling that provides a framework for incorporating the full range of real-world constraints that typically influence the decisions made by human schedulers. This results in an ability to generate detailed schedules for production that accurately reflect the current status of the shop floor, and distinguishes ISIS from traditional scheduling systems based on more restrictive management science models. ISIS is capable of scheduling orders incrementally as they are received by the shop, as well as reactively rescheduling orders in response to unexpected events (e.g., machine breakdowns) that might occur.

The construction of job shop schedules is a complex, constraint-directed activity influenced by such diverse factors as due-date requirements, cost restrictions, production levels, machine capabilities and substitutability, alternative production processes, order characteristics, resource requirements, and resource availability. The problem is a prime candidate for application of AI technology, as human schedulers are overburdened by its complexity, and existing computer-based approaches provide little more than a high-level predictive capability. It also raises some interesting research issues. Given the conflicting nature of the domain's constraints, the problem differs from typical constraint satisfaction problems. One cannot rely solely on propagation techniques to arrive at an acceptable solution. Rather, constraints must be selectively *relaxed*, in which case the problem-solving strategy becomes one of finding a solution that best satisfies the constraints. This implies that constraints must serve to discriminate among alternative hypotheses as well as to restrict the number of hypotheses generated. Thus, the design of ISIS has focused on:

- Constructing a knowledge representation that captures the requisite knowledge of the job shop environment and its constraints to support constraint-directed search
- Developing a search architecture capable of exploiting this constraint knowledge to effectively control the combinatorics of the underlying search space

ISIS constructs schedules by performing a hierarchical, constraint-directed search in the space of alternative schedules. The search is divided into four levels: order selection, capacity analysis, resource analysis, and resource assignment. Each level is composed of three phases: a pre-search analysis phase which constructs the problem, a search phase which solves the problem, and a post-search analysis phase which determines the acceptability of the solution. In each phase, ISIS uses constraints to bound, guide, and analyze the search.

Level 1 is responsible for selecting the next unscheduled order to be added to the existing shop schedule. Its selection is made according to a prioritization algorithm that considers order type and requested due dates. The selected order is passed to level 2 for scheduling.

Level 2 performs a dynamic programming analysis of the plant based on current capacity constraints. It determines the earliest start time and latest finish time for each operation of the selected order, as bounded by the order's start and due date. The times generated at this level are codified as operation-time-bound constraints that serve to influence the search at the next level.

Level 3 selects a particular routing for the order, and assigns reservation time bounds to the resources required to produce it. Presearch analysis begins with an examination of the order's constraints, resulting in the determination of the scheduling direction (either forward from the start date or backward from the due date), the creation of any missing constraints (e.g., due dates, work-in-process), and the selection of the set of search operators that will generate the search space. A beam search is then performed, using the selected set of search operators. The search space to be explored is composed of states that represent partial schedules. The application of operators to states results in the creation of new states that further specify the partial schedules under development. Depending on the results of presearch analysis, the search proceeds either forward or backward through the set of allowable routings for the order. An operator that generates states representing alternative operations initiates the search, in which case it generates alternative initial (or final) operations.

Once a state specifying an operation has been generated, other operators extend the search by creating new states that bind a machine and/or execution time to the operation. Various alternatives exist for each type of operator. For example, two operators have been tested for choosing the execution time of an operation. The "eager reserver" operator chooses the earliest possible reservation for the operation's required resources, and the "wait and see" operator tentatively reserves as much time as is available, leaving the final decision to level 4. This enables the adjustment of reservations in order to reduce work-in-process time. Alternative resources (e.g., tools, materials, etc.) are generated by other operators. Each state in the search space is rated by the set of constraints found (resolved) to be relevant to the state and its ancestors. This set is determined by collecting the constraints attached to each object (e.g., machine, tool, order, etc.) specified by the state and applying resolution mechanisms. Each constraint assigns a utility between -1 and 1 to a state; -1 signifies that the state is not admissible, 0 signifies indifference, 1 maximal support. The rating of a state with multiple constraints is the mean of the utilities assigned by the constituent constraints, each weighted by the the importance of the assigning constraint.

Once a set of candidate schedules has been generated, a rule-based post- search analysis examines the candidates to determine if one is acceptable (a function of the ratings assigned to the schedules during the search). If no acceptable schedules are found, diagnosis is performed. First, the schedules are examined to determine a type of scheduling error and the appropriate repair. Intra-level repair may result in the re-instantiation of the level's search. Pre-analysis is performed again to alter the set of operators and constraints for rescheduling the order. Inter-level repair is initiated if diagnosis determines that the poor solutions were caused by constraint-satisfaction decisions made at another level. Inter-level diagnosis can be performed by analyzing the interaction relations linking constraints. A poor constraint decision at a higher level can be determined by the utilities of constraints affected by it at a lower level. That is, a poorly satisfied constraint at a level 3 may be linked to a well-satisfied constraint at level 2. Only by going back to level 2 and choosing another value for the constraint at that level, which is less optimal, can the level 3 constraint's utility be increased; (e.g., to add more shifts at level 2, which is a costly decision, will increase throughput and reduce work in process time at level 3).

Level 3 outputs reservation time-bounds for each resource required for the operations in the chosen schedule. For the resources required by the selected operations, level 4 then establishes actual reservations that minimize the work-in-process time.

In addition to incrementally scheduling orders for production as they are received by the shop, the ISIS search architecture can be exploited in a reactive manner. Whenever unexpected events (e.g., machine breakdowns) cause disruptions in the existing shop schedule, ISIS needs only to reschedule the affected orders. This results in a minimal amount of change, and provides continuity in the shop schedules generated over time.

The application to which ISIS has been applied is the production of steam turbine blades. The plant has over 30,000 part numbers, 200 machines, and over 800 orders active at any time. In addition, the knowledge base contains information about operations for producing each part number (about 10 operations per part), tooling, resources, and constraints. A separate schema in SRL, a knowledge-representation language, is required for each piece of information.

The ISIS knowledge base must support parallel access by plant staff other than the schedulers. These include managers, tooling personnel, resource personnel, and marketing and sales. These accesses are made via separate terminals on the same or distributed computers. Accesses are both read and write and are addressed by schema name (i.e., unique record key). Hence a DBMS that supports multi-read/multi-write access is required, if more than one process is to be supported. The need for an extensive query language is somewhat reduced because of similar facilities provided in SRL directly.

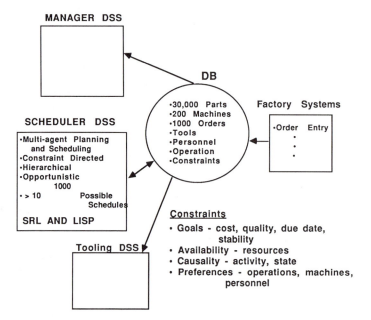

ISIS
JOB-SHOP SCHEDULING

MANAGER DSS

DB

SCHEDULER DSS

•30,000 Parts
•200 Machines
•1000 Orders
•Tools
•Personnel
•Operation
•Constraints

Factory Systems

•Order Entry

•Multi-agent Planning
  and Scheduling
•Constraint Directed
•Hierarchical
•Opportunistic
          1000
• > 10   Possible
               Schedules

SRL AND LISP

Tooling DSS

Constraints
• Goals - cost, quality, due date,
          stability
• Availability - resources
• Causality - activity, state
• Preferences - operations, machines,
              personnel

Figure 2: ISIS Process Architecture

2.3. Callisto: Project Management

A major portion of the product-development cycle is consumed in the performance and management of activities. For example, in high-technology industries such as the computer industry, thousands of activities are required to be performed in the design and prototype build of a new product. Poor performance or poor management of an activity can result in critical delays. If product development time is to be reduced, then better management and technical support should be provided for each of the activities.

The Callisto project [FSG84] [SMR86] examines the extension and application of artificial intelligence techniques to the domain of large project management. Managing large projects entails many tasks, including:

Activity

Plan generation, scheduling, monitoring and control of activities. This involves selecting activities, assigning resources to accomplish these activities, chronicling or recording the status of activities as they are performed, diagnosing deviations from the plan and repairing the plans.

Product

Maintaining a current description of the product (which is usually the outcome of a project), and determining the effects of changes to its definition (e.g., engineering change orders).

Resource

Acquisition, storage, and assignment of the many resources required to support a project.

A close observation of project tasks shows that errors and inefficiencies increase as the size of the project grows. The successful performance of project tasks is hindered by:

Complexity

Due to the number and degree of interactions among activities (e.g., resources, decisions, etc.).

Uncertainty

Of direction, due to the unknown state of other activities and the environment.

Change

In activities to be performed and products to be produced, requiring project flexibility and adaptability.

While CPM and PERT techniques provide critical path and scheduling capabilities, the bulk of the tasks are performed manually.

Callisto provides decision support and decision-making facilities in each of the above tasks. The ability to extend the capabilities found in classical approaches is due to Callisto's project model. Starting with the the SRL knowledge-representation language, a set of conceptual primitives including time, causality, object descriptions, possession, organizational authority and responsibility is used to define the concept of activities, product, and the project organization. The language is further extended by the inclusion of a constraint language that represents the constraints among activities. The modeling language provides Callisto with the ability to model both products and activities in enough detail that inferential processing may be performed.

Callisto's decision-support and decision-making capabilities include:

- Interactive generation of plans

- Interactive-change order management for products

- Multi-level scheduling of activities

500. Chronicling of activity status

- Rule-based analysis and maintenance of activities
- Automatic generation of graphic displays of project models, and
- Communication of project information among project members

These functions are constructed from a combination of five problem-solving architectures:

Object programming

Each project concept is described in terms of its information contents, as well as procedures for a variety of operations (e.g., creation, deletion, display). Thus, manipulation of these objects is achieved by sending specific messages to these objects.

Robject-based

Robjects, or responsibility objects, are program modules capable of communicating with other modules, reasoning to generate a procedure for solving their problems, and having mechanisms for generating, filtering, and archiving messages. They form an organization structure within Callisto for handling a task given by the user.

Event/Agenda-Based

Callisto robjects interpret a user's process, represented as a network of activities and states, by setting up and maintaining an agenda of goals and monitored events. The agenda facilitates or inhibits the execution of certain actions, depending on the goals. This processing facility is used in the scheduling and chronicling activities.

Rule-Based

SRL-OPS, a production-system language built on top of SRL, is used to implement managerial heuristics for project management. SRL-OPS can monitor and act on arbitrary conditions in project environment. The rule-based programming is used to evaluate activity structures and for the specification of status reports.

Logic Programming

HSRL, a Horn clause theorem prover, is used as a question answering mechanism for perusal and reporting. HSRL represents assertions and theorems within SRL.

Current research focuses on a distributed Callisto system. Each member of a project has a "mini-Callisto" to aid in managing his or her task. Each mini-Callisto is able to communicate with other mini-Callistos to collectively manage the entire project. The project management tasks supported by the mini-Callisto network are:

- **Communication** of which phase the project is in, requests for participation, and commitment to a phase

- **Definition** of activity networks for others. These networks define, at different levels of abstraction, the activities to be performed by each project member

- **Distribution** of activity network to others

- Record of **Negotiation** of the activities to be performed

- **Monitoring** of employee performance by receiving status of milestones, and perusing activities

- **Alteration** and extensions to previously defined activity networks

The knowledge base for distributed Callisto does not reside in a central location. Instead, portions of it are distributed among the project members. Communication is performed via message sending. Parallel access to a single knowledge is not provided. Access is mediated by the owning process.

3. Analysis

This section identifies issues of common interest to the database and artificial intelligence communities, using the paradigm put forth by Newell [NEWE80]. The key idea is that an intelligent system can be viewed at a variety of levels; two of the levels identified by Newell are the symbol level and the knowledge level:

- **Symbol Level**: the concern at this level is with what processing is required to bring relevant knowledge to bear in solving a problem in real time and real space. Thus the issues at this level are focused around knowledge structures and mechanisms for accessing and maintaining these structures.

- **Knowledge Level**: the concern at this level is with what knowledge is required to solve a problem, rather than with how that knowledge can be effectively used. Thus, here, the issues are focused around the content of the knowledge base, rather than its structure.[2]

We share the views of Brachman and Levesque [BL84b] that, at the knowledge level, a DB is a limited form of knowledge base; its limits are determined by the functionality it can provide an agent. But if we examine the role DBs actually play in the world, it is clear that this

---

[2] The knowledge and symbol levels are addressed throughout this book. In particular, see chapters in Section II and the two chapters by Brachman and Levesque.

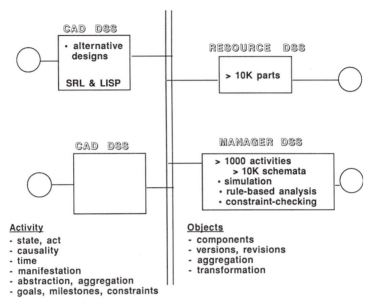

Figure 3: Callisto Distributed Architecture

knowledge-level view is incomplete. Intelligent problem-solving tends to be a group effort, involving more than one agent. A variety of issues in group problem-solving situations not considered at the knowledge level can only be resolved at a higher level, the organization level.

- **Organization Level**: the concern at this level is with how agents, each with limited knowledge, can cooperate to solve problems.

Most DB research has focused on providing capability at the organizational level and the symbol level. At the symbol level, the primary DB concern has been with time and space efficiencies. At the organization level, research has focused on the support of access to a single DB by multiple agents (i.e., processes). Most artificial intelligence research has focused on providing capability at the knowledge level and the symbol level. At the symbol level, the primary AI concern has been with flexibility and power. During the past several years, there has been a growing interest within the artificial intelligence community in issues at the organizational level and with issues of efficiency at the symbol level. Within this section, we first point to some of the areas of DB research at the symbol level that AI researchers should attend to and then discuss the intersection of interests between the two communities at the organization level. The next section discusses ways that various results of database research could be realized in the knowledge- representation language, SRL.

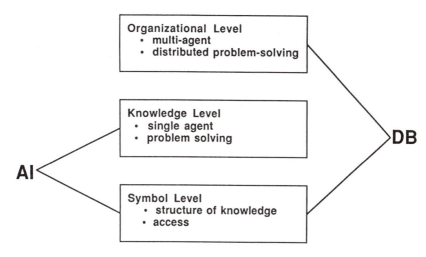

Figure 4: AI and DB Levels

3.1. Issues at the Symbol Level

Traditionally, efficiency has not been a criterion by which to measure the effectiveness of a system at the knowledge level. In fact, the knowledge level ignores the issue of how knowledge is to be structured, by relegating it to the symbol level. Nevertheless, efficiency, particularly time efficiency, is a major problem in knowledge-based systems. There are two parts to the efficiency issue: efficiency of search and efficiency of data management.

3.1.1. Efficiency of Search

Consider the case of a frame or semantic network-based, knowledge representation language, such as SRL [FWA84] or KL-ONE [BRAC77]. These representations implement a form of default reasoning by means of inheritance. The time to access a unit of information is dependent upon the amount of search to be performed in the network. Linear speed-ups in computer power do not match the possibly exponential growth in the search space of some knowledge networks.

Similarly, rule-based systems, in which the condition portion of rules is to be matched against data in working memory, may perform a great deal of search before a match is found. Systems such as R1, which has over 4000 rules and typically deals at any given time with 500 objects, each of which may have up to 125 attributes [BM84], have begun to push the limits of conventional architectures. To date, symbol level solutions have been investigated. The RETE algorithm [FORG82] is one technique for compiling the patterns (i.e., conditions) of rules into a network in order to reduce the time to test whether a rule's condition is true. But this technique has serious shortcomings, when the number of objects that need to be attended to at any given time (i.e., the number of objects in working memory) is large.

3.1.2. Efficiency of Data Management

The issue of how to manage large volumes of data has been largely ignored by AI. The approach traditionally taken is to increase the address space and store all data in virtual memory, letting the operating system worry about the rest.[3] With the application of AI to problems such as factory management, the need to store and access large volumes of data outside of virtual memory is critical. A portion of DB research has been concerned with managing the efficiency of access over a variety of storage devices.

The RETE algorithm, for example, assumes that the entire knowledge base fits in memory.[4] The issue of how to match patterns against large amounts of knowledge stored on a variety of storage devices is an issue that needs to be addressed. The problem can be broken into two parts: static and dynamic pattern matching. To the extent that a pattern is static, it is predefined and available at "compile" time for matching optimization. However, to the extent that the pattern is dynamic, it is not defined until run time and is not available for compilation. DB research in indexing methods may play a significant role in solving this problem.

Inheritance and the more general, relation-based, search also raise data management issues. The cost of such searches increases dramatically when much of the knowledge is not contained in main memory but in a DB. If such operations are to be supported, then we must reduce the time for swapping data, so that it appears invisible. Better

---

[3] Currently available Lisp machines take this approach, and do not offer DB support.

[4] The effect of the RETE algorithm, which works in main memory, is similar to materialized views in DBs supported in secondary memory.

DB fetching must also be sought. DB systems available today do not appear to provide a solution; access times to records are quite high, relative to memory access times. Solutions that include parallelism, multiple levels of caching, and intelligent pre-fetch need to be investigated.

3.2. Issues at the Organization Level

Some AI researchers have already had to address issues at the organization level. For example, Ptrans [MCDE83], ISIS, and Callisto share information with other agents (or processes), and Hearsay-II's [EHLR80] knowledge sources share knowledge via a blackboard. Consequently, issues of security and synchronization arise as well as issues of incompleteness and inconsistency. At the knowledge level, one views a knowledge base as being "owned" by a single process. The problems of security and synchronization are removed by restricting access via messages. It is then up to the process to decide what information is to be seen, when, and by whom. But distributed problem-solving systems require a variety of methods of sharing knowledge (e.g., blackboards) and thus require that the problems of security and synchronization be faced. At the symbol level, the problems of incompleteness and inconsistency are taken as a given. At the knowledge level, the problems require providing the system with the knowledge of how to qualify its judgements. But distributed problem-solving systems are collections of agents, the sum of whose knowledge may be more complete than that of any individual agent. Moreover, the nature of the inconsistencies in the sum of the knowledge may allow judgements of relative reliability. Thus, at the organization level, the task of developing a system requires providing the system with the knowledge of how to extend its own knowledge by interacting appropriately with other agents.

3.2.1. Security and Synchronization

Blackboard mechanisms such as are found in Hearsay-II provide a means by which a group of agents may jointly peruse and modify a common pool of information. Obviously, issues of synchronization occur. In addition, depending upon the role of an agent, limitations may be placed upon what information may be seen and/or modified. DB security and synchronizatiyon techniques such as transaction models and optimistic concurrency[5] control can be readily applied to

---

[5] See the Database Survey chapter by Brodie.

shared knowledge structures such as blackboards or production- system working memories. While it is at the organization level that the issue arises, it is at the symbol level that the solution will have to be implemented.

The problem of security appears in distributed systems that lack global data structures. If each agent possesses its own knowledge base, and information flows only via message passing, how is an agent to determine whether to honor requests for information from other agents? The problem of synchronization also appears when agents cooperate to solve problems. How must an agent manage the synchronization of knowledge and actions of multiple agents when working on a problem cooperatively?

3.2.2. Incompleteness and Inconsistency

In a situation when multiple agents are problem-solving in parallel, each agent may generate new knowledge. To maintain full access to the generated knowledge, each agent may have to broadcast all it knows, or make its knowledge available in a global knowledge base. The former may quickly result in saturation of the broadcast medium, while the latter may saturate the storage device and become an access bottleneck. Alternatively, an agent may not want all of the knowledge irt generates to be made available to the entire organization. In any of these cases, it is clear that one agent's model of the "world" may rapidly become incomplete. Techniques are required to decide:

- What knowledge to store locally
- What knowledge to communicate
- To whom to communicate this knowledge
- How to restrict access by other agents
- Where to look for knowledge if you don't have it

In the case where knowledge is shared among multiple agents and stored locally, an agent may extend or alter the knowledge in a manner that makes it inconsistent with another agent's understanding of the same knowledge. For example, an agent may share a description of a person with other agents, but during its problem-solving it may alter its description (e.g., guessing of the person's age) so that it is inconsistent. At some time during problem-solving, another agent may request that person's description from other agents and receive differing descriptions. How is this inconsistency to be resolved? It is not enough to maintain separate belief models; this only maintains a separation.

4. SRL

This section presents one knowledge-representation and problem-solving system, SRL,[6] and examines how it implements solutions to some of the above problems.

4.1. Language Overview

SRL is a frame-based language with the "schema" as its primitive. A schema is a symbolic representation of a single concept. Its definition is the summation of its slots and values. Slots are used to represent attributive, structural, and relational information about a concept. A schema is composed of a schema name (printed in bold font), a set of slots (printed in small caps) and the slot's values (Lisp printing conventions are observed). Values can be any Lisp expression and reference schemata, when they are strings. When printed, a schema is always enclosed by double braces with the schema name appearing at the top. The **h1-spec** schema (Figure 5) contains six slots, each of which contains a value.

{{ **h1-spec**
       IS-A: "engineering activity"
       SUB-ACTIVITY-OF: "develop-board-h1"
       INITIAL-ACTIVITY-OF: "develop-board-h1"
       ENABLED-BY: "TRUE"
       CAUSE: "h1-spec-complete"
       DESCRIPTION: "Develop specifications for the cpu board" }}

Figure 5: **h1-spec** *Schema*

Many ideas found in other representation systems have been incorporated into SRL including meta-information, demons, restrictions on legal slot value, and a context facility.

Meta-information may be associated with schemata, their slots, and values in the slots. It is represented by another schema, called a meta-schema, that is attached to the schema, slot, or value. Representing meta-information as schemata provides a uniform approach to representation. The user is provided with access functions for retrieving meta-schemata. Once retrieved, they are manipulated just as any other schema. The meta-information is printed in italics beneath the schema,

---

[6] Development of SRL began in 1977. Its contents evolved during its application to industrial problems in the Intelligent Systems Laboratory. Since 1985, many of the concepts investigated in SRL have been implemented in Knowledge Craft, a knowledge-engineering system available from Carnegie Group Inc. Pittsburgh, PA.

slot, or value to which it is attached.

{{ **hl-spec**
>   *Creator:* "mark fox"
>   *To-Create:* schemac
>
>   IS-A: "engineering activity"
>   SUB-ACTIVITY-OF: "develop-board-hl"
>   *range:* (type "instance" "activity")
>   INITIAL-ACTIVITY-OF: "develop-board-hl"
>   ENABLED-BY: "TRUE"
>   CAUSE: "hl-spec-complete"
>   DESCRIPTION: "Develop specifications for the cpu board" }}

Figure 6: **hl-spec** *Schema*

Any slot may have *facets* associated with it. Four facets are defined in SRL: DEMON, DOMAIN, RANGE, and CARDINALITY. The DEMON facet allows lisp procedures to be associated with a slot. The execution of demons is keyed to particular SRL access functions, such as filling or retrieving the value of a slot. RANGE and DOMAIN facets are used to restrict the values that may fill a slot and the schemata in which a slot may be placed, respectively. The CARDINALITY is used to restrict the number of values that a slot may contain. Values for each facet may be inherited from slots in other schemata.

As in other representation languages, a standard set of relations is provided to the user for forming taxonomic and part hierarchies. Slots and values may be inherited automatically between schemata along these relations. One of the novel representational ideas introduced by SRL is *user-defined inheritance relations* [FOX79]. In most other knowledge representation systems, several relations for inheriting slots and values are defined as part of the representation (e.g., AKO, is-a, virtual-copy). In contrast, SRL offers a facility by which users can define their own inheritance relations, allowing only slots and values of the user's choice to be inherited. In addition, slot structures can be elaborated between schemata, and slots and their values mapped arbitrarily between schemata, as need demands. Inheritance relations are represented by additional slots in a schema. A *dependency mechanism* is integrated into the inheritance facility that notes, as meta-information, the source of inherited slots and values. Here again, the user can define the dependency relations that are put into place.

Another novel feature provided by SRL is a means of *controlling the search* performed by the inheritance process. Any query of the model may optionally use a *path* to restrict which relations may be traversed while searching for a suitable value to inherit. Paths may also be used to specify the *transitivity* properties of relations. For example, a

PART-OF hierarchy for describing a car might represent the **battery** as PART-OF the **electrical system**, and the **electrical system** is PART-OF the **car**. The implicit notion that the **battery** is PART-OF the **car** (i.e., that PART-OF is transitive with itself) is represented using paths.

Contexts in SRL act as virtual copies of DBs in which schemata are stored. In the copy, schemata can be created, modified, and destroyed without altering the original context. Contexts are structured as trees in which each context may inherit the schemata present in its parent context. Hence, only schemata that are used in a context need be explicitly represented there. This avoids copying schemata that will never be used in the context. The context provides for version management and alternate worlds reasoning with SRL models.

Error handling is also schema-based. An instance of the **error** schema is created to describe each error encountered by the system. **error-spec** schemata may be defined that specify how to recover from each kind of error.

In order to support large applications, a simple DB system is integrated into SRL. The DB system provides two key access (i.e., context and schema name) to varying length records, each containing a single schema. Concurrent access is supported only for a single writer and multiple readers. Schemata are stored in a DB until they are accessed, at which time they are brought into Lisp. A *cache* of the most recently accessed schemata is kept in Lisp for quick access. When the cache becomes too large, schemata are swapped back to the DB, using recency algorithm.

4.2. Extensions to the Language

SRL serves as the core of a knowledge-engineering environment called Islisp [ISL84]. It offers a number of inference tools that operate on schemata: HSRL, PSRL, OSRL, ESRL, and KBS. HSRL [AW83] takes HCPRVR, [CHES80] a *logic program interpreter*, and alters it to use SRL models as its axioms. The system combines the modus ponens inference of logic programming systems with the representation power of SRL. In addition, the inheritance mechanism provides default reasoning, not available in logic programming environments. Similarly, PSRL is a *production rule interpreter* that operates on SRL models [RYCH84]. Production rules and their parts are represented by schemata. A subset of PSRL provides the form and execution pattern of OPS5 rules [FORG81]. OSRL provides a schema-based object programming. ESRL provides an event mechanism that enables the user to schedule events to occur either in a simulated or normal operating mode. KBS, a knowledge-based simulation system [RF82] uses ESRL to perform discrete simulations of systems modeled in SRL. Simulation objects are represented as schemata. An object's associated events and behaviors are represented as slots and values in the schema. An object's event behavior may be inherited along relations which link it to other schemata.

In addition to inference tools, system-building tools are provided. RETINAS [GREE83] is a schema-based *window system*. Schemata for windows, displays, and canvases are instantiated to build an interface. Default specifications for windows, etc., may be inherited from the prototype schemata. KBCI [ISL84] is a schema-based *command system*. Again, the **command** schema is instantiated to create commands. A command interface is defined by a collection of command schemata organized in a SUB-COMMAND-OF hierarchy. CPAK [ISL84] is a 2D graphics package based on the CORE definition. A business graphics facility is provided on top of CPAK.

4.3. Analysis

The SRL system has served as both a production-inference engine and a testbed for ideas to solve the problems raised in sections 2 and 3. Hence, we have had to worry about solving problems of efficiency while investigating solutions to the more difficult problems of incompleteness and inconsistency. In the following, we reexamine the problems raised earlier. Our "solutions" to these problems raise at least as many questions as they answer.

4.3.1. Efficiency of Data Management

Early on in the development of SRL, it became apparent that efficient access to large volumes of data would have to be provided to multiple agents. Applications such as job-shop scheduling (i.e., ISIS) and project management (i.e., Callisto) require very large DBs to be maintained, of which only a small portion is ever used by any agent at any given time. We searched for a DB system available under UNIX which had the following attributes:

- Very fast, two key retrieval (schema name and context) of varying length records

- Supporting multiple readers and writers

The search failed, so a DB system was created in-house which provided b-tree access to varying length records while supporting multiple readers and a single writer. A re-design of SRL's internal structure was performed to better integrate the DB system with the knowledge representation. A layered approach was taken:

1. **Implementation Layer**: This is the core layer at which the structures of schemata are defined in terms of of nodes, links, and metalinks. It is at this layer that indexing of static patterns is performed and maintained.

2. **Context Layer**. The definition of contexts and binding of schema/context pairs to schema structures is performed here.

3. **Database Layer**. Access to the DB is performed at this layer whenever a schema is not contained in virtual memory. Schemata are cached in main memory on demand, and are swapped out according to frequency of usage.

4. **Context Inheritance**. Inheritance of schemata between contexts is performed at this layer.

5. **Schema Inheritance**. Inheritance of slots and values is performed at this level.

6. **Distributed Knowledge Bases**. Retrieval from other separate knowledge bases is performed at this level.

The DB system has provided a significant extension to SRL's knowledge base. Large volumes of data can be maintained reliably without wasting virtual memory. Nevertheless, the cost of a DB retrieval is significantly more than a simple virtual-memory access. Better methods for storing and retrieving large numbers of schemata are still required. DB machines may hold promise in this area.

4.3.2. Efficiency of Search

A version of SRL was constructed in which rule conditions were compiled into a RETE-like network. The network was indexed directly into schemata at the implementation layer. No indexing of schemata in the DB was performed. In the case of dynamic patterns, brute force search was performed and was slow. The problem of how to index patterns has not been fully resolved in a general sense. With inheritance being a basic capability of a representation, indexing techniques have to be aware of changes not only within a schema but in schemata from which it may inherit slots and values. This is achievable in representations where inheritance is performed along classification relations (e.g., is-a, ako, virtual-copy) and slots and values are propagated to descendants upon creation. But for more complex inheritance, such as is found in SRL, the problem is much more difficult; slots and values are propagated on demand, and inheritance is user- definable and context-sensitive. Either more dynamic pattern-matching techniques are required, or restrictions will have to be placed on the functionality of the rule-base.

This still does not address the problem of whether to index schemata both in memory and in the DB, or only those in memory. An argument for the latter is that memory contains only those schemata which have been changed and require patterns to be checked. The problem here comes with the introduction of new rules: should the rule be indexed only in memory, or across the entire DB? The latter is a truly expensive operation for large DBs. We suspect that a solution to this problem lies in parallel hardware specialized for knowledge-base applications.

4.3.3. Security and Synchronization

The Callisto project provided us with a context in which to investigate the issues of security and synchronization. We were concerned with the construction of a distributed project-management system where each project member had his own version of Callisto to manage his own activities and those of the people for whom he was responsible (if any). Communication was required, concerning activities to be performed and their status among these Callisto systems.

The DB system provided for single writer and multiple reader access with a semaphore for synchronization. In the case of multiple agents, each with its own non-shareable DB, each agent could send messages to each other requesting information. The basic information access functions of SRL were extended to include the name of the agent from which to retrieve the information. This resulted in a message being sent to the appropriate agent. The agent receiving the message then determined if the sender should have access to the information and sent the appropriate reply. While this mechanism was sufficient for security purposes — an agent managed access to its own information — it was insufficient with respect to synchronization.

The problem of synchronization arose at the application level. The process of developing project activity networks is iterative, requiring many agents to review, critique, and modify them. Keeping track of the current stage of the process and activity network versions is a significant task. Much of the work we have performed in the area is nascent, and is focusing on the development of protocols, multi-agent review, critiquing, negotiation, and modification.[7] This issue is truly an organization-level problem requiring further development of the concepts of communication, cooperation, and negotiation.

---

[7] To appear as the thesis of Arvind Sathi.

4.3.4. Incompleteness and Inconsistency

The problem of incomplete and inconsistent knowledge arose also in the distributed version of Callisto. If, during an agent's problem-solving, a schema was referenced that was not contained in virtual memory nor in its DB, an attempt was made to communicate with other agents to determine the whereabouts of the schema in question. Three approaches were taken to guide the sending of messages:

1. A schema can be referred to only via another schema (i.e., the value of a slot). Since each schema contains meta-information describing the agent with whom it originated, the origin of the referring schema was used as the initial agent to communicate with.

2. Each organization contains a profile describing what *type* of schemata various agents in the organization contain. An agent looking for a schema can determine the corresponding agent by checking type description — but only if they possess the type information to begin with.

3. Lastly, each agent possesses a list of "acquaintances". As a last ditch effort, it could send a message to each of them.

These three approaches provide a reasonably powerful means of finding a schema, but does not guarantee its retrieval. Much work remains at the organization level to solve this problem satisfactorily.

The concept of *agent responsibility* was proposed as a means of aiding in inconsistency reduction. For each schema, an agent was assigned the responsibility of maintaining that schema's consistency. All problems concerning a schema's inconsistency would be resolved by the agent responsible. To support the agent's analysis, a record of transformations and communications of schemata was kept at the meta-level. If an inconsistency arose, it would be possible to trace the problem back to the source. Giving an agent the responsibility for resolving inconsistencies is only half a solution; how the inconsistencies are resolved is the other half, and that half requires further research.

5. Conclusion

The integration of Artificial Intelligence and Database technologies is a problem whose "time has come". As AI systems are extended to more complex problems requiring large volumes of information and knowledge, the need for DB support becomes apparent. The three examples described in this chapter demonstrate both the ease and the difficulty of this integration; R1, ISIS and Callisto all interface either loosely, via transactions, or tightly, via direct integration with the knowledge representation system. Though each demonstrates a successful integration of the technologies, issues of theoretical and practical importance arise.

First, a tighter integration of knowledge and data representations is required in order to allow pattern matching and search to be performed more efficiently. Without a solution to these problems, a natural complexity barrier may arise which will restrict the size and complexity of intelligent systems.

Secondly, problems arise in the design of distributed systems. In particular, issues of incompleteness and inconsistency bring into question the efficacy of current representational theories. In particular, the theory of the knowledge and symbol levels needs to be extended to include a third level, the organization level, whose focus is on multi-agent, distributed problem-solving. A sound theory for the organization will ultimately lead to solutions in distributed problem-solving.

6. References

[AW83] [BL84b] [BM84] [BRAC77] [CHES80] [EHLR80] [FORG81] [FORG82] [FOX79] [FS84] [FSG85] [FWA84] [GREE83] [ISL84] [MCDE82a] [MCDE83] [NEWE80] [RF82] [RYCH84] [SRM86]

29
An Integration of Knowledge and Data Representation

Gio Wiederhold
Robert L. Blum
Michael Walker[1]

ABSTRACT *A variety of types of linkages from knowledge bases to databases have been proposed, and a few have been implemented [MW84]. In this research note, we summarize a technique which was employed in a specific context: knowledge extraction from a copy of an existing clinical database. The knowledge base is also used to drive the extracting process. RX builds causal models in its domain to generate input for statistical hypothesis verification. We distinguish two information types: knowledge and data, and recognize four types of knowledge: categorical, definitional, causal (represented in frames), and operational, represented by rules. Based on our experience, we speculate about the generalization of the approach.*

1. Introduction

We will first review the current system organization of RX. Information stored and manipulated by RX consists of both data and knowledge. RX is a project using knowledge-based techniques in order to abstract further knowledge out of a database. The knowledge base is initially primed by acquiring knowledge from a medical expert. In subsequent operation, the knowledge base is updated by using information extracted from the database. The inference paradigm for RX is largely

---

[1] Department of Computer Science, Stanford University

based on the use of statistical techniques [BLUM82]. We will summarize here the essence of the knowledge representation.

In RX, four types of represented knowledge can be distinguished. Shallow knowledge is represented by rules, and three types of deep knowledge are represented based on the concept of frame. We will refer to these as

- Categorical knowledge
- Definitional knowledge
- Causal knowledge

The distinctions among these types are in structure, not in representation technique. In addition, there is undigested knowledge hidden in the attached database.

2. Frame Representation

Because the medical knowledge is complex and uncertain, we find that the frames have many slots and complex interconnections. An example of a populated frame describing a state the patient may have is shown in Figure 1. The information for this and subsequent figures in this paper is produced by commands to RX, as shown on the first line.

To manage the frames, they are structured hierarchically into a few categories. Within each category, the list of expected slots differs to some extent. For medical database the two prime categories are:

- States: Observations and conclusions describing the patient
- Actions: Treatments performed with the intent to change one patients state to another.

These frames, and a third category for statistical methods, to be touched on later, are descendants of single root frame.

Each frame beyond the root is categorized into a hierarchy, so each non-leaf frame must have two slots:

Generalization: Its immediate ancestor in the hierarchy

Specialization: Its immediate descendants in the hierarchy

The lowest level descendants may refer to the actual database. The subset of medicine that we are dealing with is, of course, bounded by the scope of the database being dealt with.

PL NEPHROTIC-SYNDROME

    GENL: RENAL-DISORDERS
    SPEC: (PROTEINURIA HEAVY-PROTEINURIA)
    DEFINITION: (OR (DURING --) (AND --))
    TYPE: INTERVAL
    EFFECTS: (URINE-PROTEIN-RANGE ALBUMIN
           24-HR-URINE-PROTEIN)
    MINIMUM-DURATION: 30
    MINIMUM-POINTS: 2
    INTERVALFN: MEAN-DURING-INTERVAL
    VALUE-TYPE: BINARY
    INTRA-EPISODE-GAP: 100
    INTER-EPISODE-GAP: 180
    RECORDS: INVERTED
    AFFECTED-BY: ((PREDNISONE) (
        GLOMERULONEPHRITIS) (SLE))
    PARTITION: (0 .5 1 --)
    UNITS: "gms proteinuria/24 hrs"
    PROXIES: (ALBUMIN 24-HR-URINE-PROTEIN
          URINE-PROTEIN-RANGE)
    ONSET-DELAY: 7
    MINIMUM-INTERVAL: 30
    CARRY-OVER: 30

Figure 1: A Frame from the State Branch of the Hierarchy

3. Categorical Knowledge

We have indicated that frames are hierarchically organized. This serves the first type of knowledge structuring to be considered. Figure 2 shows an example of the categorization at a high level in the hierarchy. The categorization of the knowledge has two important functions.

First of all, it follows an organization found in traditional teaching materials. By following the standard hierarchy for the subset of medicine being considered, we can be reasonably sure of having adequate coverage over the area. The hierarchical categorization of knowledge in textbooks is intended to have exactly that effect: it decomposes a larger problem into a complete set of subproblems, and so on and so on.

An important aspect of the hierarchical categorization is that it supports inheritance. Inheritance is essential to our knowledge representation, because, as we descend down the hierarchy, less information is specific to the lower level nodes and, in fact, less may be known about them. Any time a slot is empty, its values will be inherited from the superior nodes. This creates the effect of a complete knowledge representation, as is necessary for effective processing,

Respiratory Diseases:
genl:
  All Categories of Disease
spec:
  Pneumonia,
  Asthma,
  Emphysema.

Pneumonia   Asthma   Emphysema
  genl: genl: genl:
  Respiratory D.   Respiratory D.   Respiratory D.
    spec: spec: spec:
  Pneumococcal Pn.,   Allergic Asthma,   CO2 retention.
  Klebsiella Pn..   Intrinsic Asthma.

Figure 2: Frame Slots for Categorization

without having entered all of the relevant medical knowledge redundantly. This strong inheritance puts the responsibility on the frame-
definer to assure, that where a successor frame differs semantically, the
corresponding slots are properly completed. For instance, if the frame
for the class "person" has an "average-age" slot with value 35 and a specialization frame called "teenager", the "teenager" frame should have an
explicit overriding "average-age" slot value such as 16. In current
research work we are developing more complex inheritance rules, but
this choice will continue to be included, since it provides an approach
for representing non-monotonic knowledge.

In our collection of medical knowledge, the lower frames in our
area of specialization (Systemic Lupus) have most slots set individually,
while in the more peripheral areas most slot values are inherited, so
that the system there only possesses general knowledge. A snapshot of
the hierarchical arrangement is provided in Figure 3. The first part is
generated by the command **CLASS** to display the classification, and
shows the ancestors of the current node; the other part is output generated by **SPEC** to display the specialization, showing the descendants
of the current node.

4. Definitional Knowledge

Definitional knowledge provides deduction going up to higher-
level nodes of the hierarchy. Many of the final leaf nodes in our hierarchy refer to the database, and are, in essence, schema entries for database attributes. It is important when discussing medical situations to be
able to discuss them at a suitable level of abstraction. In essence, the

```
CLASS GLOMERULONEPHRITIS
      GLOMERULONEPHRITIS
      RENAL-DISORDERS
      DIAGNOSTIC-CATEGORIES
      STATES
 SPEC AUTOIMMUNE-DISORDERS
      AUTOIMMUNE-DISORDERS
           SLE
                LUPUS-NEPHRITIS
                CARDIAC-LUPUS
                CNS-LUPUS
                LUPUS-SEROSITIS
           RA
           ARTERITIS
```

Figure 3: Displaying Ancestors and Descendants

concept of a diagnosis is an abstraction from which we can draw many inferences. The diagnosis is based on the evaluation of the constellation of observed symptoms, not all of which need to be present. In simple, pathognomonic diseases, where the symptom characterizes a single disease, the inference is trivial. In our domain, rheumatic diseases, it is often complex and ambiguous. The definition of a node is, of course, not limited to nodes in its own subtree, but can be based on any nodes that can contribute information. An example of a definition for pneumonia is given in Figure 4. Note that pneumonia itself does not appear as a field in our database or as a domain value. RX is not a diagnostic tool, so we do not need to provide complex deductive mechanisms nor the mechanisms to determine the right combination of multiple diagnoses in these definitions. For deriving the statistical inference engine it is quite valid that multiple abstractions are labelled with overlapping source data and confirmed by alternative partial combinations of these source data.

Pneumonia
      definition: Temperature > 102 degrees F.
         and WBC > 10,000 cells per mm^3
         and Chest X-RAY = Lobar Infiltrate

Figure 4: Definition Slot in a Frame

It is important for RX to provide a picture of the patient state over time. We have seen in Figure 1 that there are a number of time parameters associated with a state to ensure that we have a correct picture. These time parameters include an **Onset-Time**: the state is assumed to be true before the first definite observation of its symptoms. A **Minimum-Interval-Time** is required to distinguish the state from a spurious event, and the **Carry-Over-Time** specifies an extension during which time the effects of the state are still significant to the patient.

Since the database contains many null values, we do not restrict all definitions to the state hierarchy. We are, for instance, willing to deduce that a certain disease continues if the medication, initiated when the disease was first found and appropriate to that disease, continues to be given. In fact, such a medication may mask the symptoms, so that we would be not be able to obtain the appropriate basic data in the state hierarchy alone. The medication would, of course, be found in the action subtree of the knowledge base.

We may also note, in the frames proxies, alternate findings that can support a higher-level definition.

In general, the ability to have definitions of data abstractions with alternative means of computations and candidate proxies for data is a powerful means for dealing with missing values that invariably occur in any database of realistic size.

5. Database

It is now appropriate to discuss the underlying database. Data are obtained from the databases of the American Rheumatism Association Medical Information System, which employs the Time-Oriented-Database system (TOD [WIED75]). The major relation contains data of visits made by patients having chronic diseases, so that the key is composed of patient-identifier and visit-identifier. Up to 500 attributes may be stored in a visit record, many fewer are actually collected. The database is used for statistical analysis as well as for clincal service.

The analytical database and the copy used for knowledge extraction are stored in transposed form [WIED83]. Transposition rearranges the collected data into attribute-major order, so that the physical database records store columns of the conceptual relational tables, rather than rows corresponding to tuples of the relational model. Attribute-major storage order is justified by the observation that, for analytical queries over the database, we typically request a limited number of attributes, but evaluate these attributes over a large number of patients and their visits.

In the clinical, TOD, database transpostion creates records that have a logical length equal to the number of patient visits in the database. In practice, many entries, approximately 85%, will be null, and an efficient storage representation of null and repeated values is used to compress these potentially very long records. The compression in the clinical database is invisible to the user, and the structure appears as if it were a relational table with patient-number and visit-date as key [WIED83, Chapter 4.2 and 14.2].

In the RX system, a transposed structure is used as well, now using INTERLISP. Analysis processes in RX generalize the time-history of each patient so that here only visits and attributes are transposed. For each patient we find a list of attributes, with null values omitted. From each attribute node a sublist extends, containing the data values for this patient, of length up to the number of visits made by the patient. With each value, the number of the visit is indicated. This list-oriented storage structure is not as effectively searched for statistical operations as is the corresponding data in the clinical TOD database, since cross-indexing is replaced by search.

Transposed by PATIENT
        by FRAME (States, Actions)
        by VISIT

Data attribute strings:

(Patient1
   (Aspirin ((1 30)(2 20)(3 20)(4 20)(5 20) ...))
   (Cholesterol ((1 215)(2 229)(4 230)(...))

   . . .
   (Prednisone ((1 50)(2 27)(4 25))

   . . .
   (Visit-date (1Jun80 15Jun80 12Jul80 ...)
   . . .

(Patient78
   (Aspirin ((6 10)(...))
   (Cholesterol ((1 ...))

   . . .

Figure 5: Sketch of Transposed Data Storage

Interlisp originally provided no facilities to keep such long data strings on external storage. Since the virtual addressing capability of the DEC-20 being used is limited to 256 pages of about 2500 characters each, we adopted an extension, HASHFILES, written at Stanford by William van Melle, which is now being integrated into INTERLISP systems. A single hashfile can hold 500 pages externally, and 30 distinct hashfiles were needed to store the 35 Megabytes of data in LISP format. Here the patient-number and attribute-name are the key. Figure 5 sketches the RX storage structure conceptually.

6. Causal Knowledge

The essential knowledge in RX and probably in similar systems is not captured by categorization or definition; it consists of the linkages and dependencies among arbitrary nodes from the hierarchies.

DC CHOLESTEROL

CHOLESTEROL
always is increased by PREDNISONE
regularly is increased by HEPATITIS
regularly is increased by KETOACIDOSIS
usually is increased by NEPHROTIC-SYNDROME

*note: The interpretation of the frequencies
is not linear over the range of terms.*

DF

Cell	Adverb	Probability	
1	never*	.001	* *well — hardly ever*
2	very-rarely	.005	
3	rarely	.01	
4	infrequently	.04	
5	occasionally	.16	
6	commonly	.32	
7	regularly	.64	
8	usually	.95	
9	almost-always	.99	
10	always1	.00	

Figure 6: Displaying the Causes of Cholesterol

The essence of the RX knowledge base is to maintain a deep understanding of causal effects. Applicable medical knowledge requires an expert to know how one state effects another state and, even more importantly, how one candidate treatment action affects the various parameters of the patient state. Figure 6 lists the results of a backward search to determine all the **Effects** slots that store references to the state node **Cholesterol**.

Since we are dealing in generalizations and abstractions we cannot represent their relationships as a binary condition.   It was mentioned earlier that the relationships in a medical knowledge base, or in general a knowledge base that deals in a high level of abstractions, are characterized by uncertainty. The power of generalization is that one entry can cover many instances, but, of necessity, detail is elided.

Hence, in RX, a linkage between two nodes is not represented by a single value parameter (for instance the MYCIN certainty factor), but rather by multiple essential parameters as well as further parameters that are optional. The causal relationship is represented as a set of features:

Causal linkage

intensity:	strength of effect
frequency:	frequency of occurrence in the population
direction:	positive or negative

and, optionally

setting:	applicable subset of the patient population
functional form:	equation, including covariates
distribution:	set of 10 decile values
validity:	belief: known mechanism . . . vague guess
evidence:	citation to the medical literature or to an RX experiment

Effect Pneumonia:	temperature
intensity:	.5log (severity-pneumonia)
frequency:	common
direction:	+
setting:	studied in middle-aged patients with pneumococcal pneumonia
functional form:	.5log (severity-pneumonia) + 98
validity:	widely confirmed
evidence:	[citations to the literature]

Figure 7: The relationship "**Pneumonia increases temperature**"

The parameters represent the state of our knowledge. Not shown are the interpreting functions on this knowledge. This omission is typical. The researcher has to understand the engine that operates on the knowledge in most inferential systems. It is a more serious lack here, because the linkages are much more complex and hence less obvious to the users.

The actual cause and effects are related to each other through potentially long chains. For instance, a drug being given can affect the state through a large number of mechanisms. To illustrate the complexity, Figure 8 shows the linkages through the network found when asking how a disease state, in this case **SLE**, affects the cholesterol level. The cholesterol level is one of the many clinical measurements that can be made on a patient.

The number of possible paths was pruned by computing the expected intensity from node to node, and by not displaying paths below a product threshold level. We still found quite a number of possible paths, including linkages that go back and forth from action to state and from state to state. Sometimes actions also cause follow-up actions. The sum of all these effects, some of which may be positive and some of which may be negative, with different intensities and frequencies and time delays, determine the ultimate effect on the observable state variable.

DP SLE CHOLESTEROL
      default aggregate intensity product > 0.1
    SLE {30 pct activity} increases
        NEPHROTIC-SYNDROME {1 gms proteinuria/24 hrs}
            increases CHOLESTEROL {24 mgms/dl}
    SLE {30 pct activity} is treated by
        PREDNISONE {182%} of baseline} increases
            CHOLESTEROL {14 mgms/dl}
    SLE {30 pct activity} increases
        NEPHROTIC-SYNDROME {1 gms proteinuria/24 hrs}
          is treated by PREDNISONE {143% of baseline}
            increases CHOLESTEROL {8 mgms/dl}
    SLE {30 pct activity} increases
        IMMUNOSUPPRESSION {18 pct activity} increases
          HEPATITIS {5 lu/ml of SGOT} increases
            CHOLESTEROL {6 mgms/dl}

Figure 8: Causal Paths through the Knowledge Base

RX uses this knowledge for building statistical models. If a new linkage is hypothesized, then all the existing paths must be found and controlled for in the statistical evaluation. In this particular example, a direct relationship between prednisone and cholesterol had been hypothesized earlier, and the analysis of the database showed this, within statistical limits of belief, to be a fact. This entry, leading to the linkage in Figure 8, was then automatically inserted into the knowledge base.

7. Statistical knowledge

Statistical knowledge is of only minor concern to our current exposition. We note, however, that this knowledge is categorized in a similar way as the state and action knowledge, but that here no deep knowledge is employed (i.e., there are no linkages outside of the categorization, and all the statistical operations are being driven by knowledge stored in a rule base). For completeness, a section of a log showing examples of some of those rules is shown in Figure 9. Note that the actual rules are LISP code.

8. Extrapolation

To evaluate this system as a knowledge-representation paradigm, we have to ask: How useful and how general is the structure developed to serve the RX project?

The RX knowledge and database is possibly one of the largest combinations of knowledge and data currently in existence. They are currently approximately 500 fully populated frames, 300 leaf nodes leading to database attributes. In the database is information for 1783 patients with a total of 20,000 visits. The system has been sufficiently powerful to independently rediscover and add new evidence for medical hypotheses. These results are being published in the medical literature.

This experiment demonstrates usefulness of the representation in the particular domain being covered, a medical domain characterized by complexity and uncertainty of diagnosis and treatment modalities. We are confident that it is applicable to other medical arenas as well. Beyond that we have to deal in extrapolations.

Likely application fields which lend themselves to similar analysis techniques are found in economic modeling, institutional planning, market planning, and in personnel management for large enterprises. These applications have similar characteristics:

1.   A large volume of base data is available.

2.   The relationships are complex and cannot, within our current knowledge, be completely described.

3.   Important decisions are made, based on abstract notions and characterizations.

Whether all the prerequisites exist in these fields for a successful implementation is not certain. The existence of a high-quality database, corrected through immediate feedback in daily clinical use, has been an essential factor to assure validity. The existence of well-developed statistical techniques to give reliable inferencing from many primitive facts to a high level of abstraction is another important facet of our work.

Would you like to see decision criteria for
    selecting statistical methods?
**YES
MULTIPLE-REGRESSION
RULES:
    If the independent variables are
        causally ordered,
    then do a hierarchical regression.
    otherwise do a standard regression.
PREREQUISITES:
    Multiple regression is appropriate
        when the number of independent variables
        is greater than 1
    All variables must be at least of
        measurement level = binary.
    All variables must be normally distributed.
Statistical method: MULTIPLE-REGRESSION
 The # of values recorded for the
    dependent variable for each patient must
    be > 1 + the # of independent variables.
 Next, the same minimum # of values is required for
    the independent variable of primary interest.
 To estimate the effect of the independent variable
    for a single patient, the coefficient of
    variation must be > threshold = 10 percent
 Finally, to do an individual estimation,
    the total number of events must
    be > 1 + # of independent variables.
Would you like to see the machine readable
    eligibility criteria?
**YES
Eligibility criteria:
[AND (IGEQ (#VALUES (QUOTE CHOLESTEROL) PAT)
            (ADD1 (FLENGTH VARS)))
    (IGEQ (#VALUES (QUOTE PREDNISONE) PAT)
            (ADD1 (FLENGTH VARS)))
    (GREATERP (COEF-VAR (QUOTE PREDNISONE) PAT)
            .1)
    (IGEQ (FLENGTH (ENTRIES (QUOTE PRED-CHOL)
                    NIL PAT))
            (ADD1 (FLENGTH VARS]

Figure 9: Rules to Represent Shallow Statistical Knowledge

We are sure that, as databases spread further, these prerequisites will be fulfilled at least in some instances in these or other fields.

Beyond that, the structure used satisfies some of the requirements we place on knowledge and database management [MW85]. The knowledge structure and the database are logically smoothly integrated, and can be handled operationally within a single system and computational paradigm. Important aspects such as inheritance and dependencies are well formalized, and can be manipulated consistently by the inferencing mechanisms.

At the same time, knowledge and data are well distinguished in our structure, so that the proper inferential mechanism is used for these two different types of information. The inferential and generalization power of the knowledge is strong, stronger than the power of a single database fact. Note that data can lead to new knowledge, but that knowledge can never generate data. In this context the term *data* refers to raw observations, and not to secondary elements as derived data.

Furthermore, the update mechanism differs. Even though the update concerns are minimized in our current operation, it is possible to mechanically recopy a new version of the database. Since there are multiple, identically-structured databases available within TOD for this clinical domain, storing data from different clinics in the US and Canada, it is possible to attach a copy of data from a different locale. For the process of linking new database values into the knowledge base, none of the frames of the knowledge base need to be disturbed.

The system that we have built has been constructed for the specific objective of implementing RX. It is hence not now a general tool to be distributed or exported. On the other hand, before we can have confidence to invest in general tools, it might be useful to have several handcrafted applications to illustrate appropriate principles of knowledge-base management. This, then, is the intent of this presentation.

Acknowledgement

This research receives support from the National Library of Medicine, grant number 1R18 LM4334, from the National Science Foundation as grant IST-8317858, and from the Defense Advanced Research Projects Agency, contract N39-84-C-211 for Management of Knowledge and Database. Computing facilities were supplied by SUMEX-AIM, which is supported by the National Institutes of Health under grant number RR-00785. RX research was initiated under support from the National Center for Health Services Research, grant numbers R03

HS3650 and R18 HS04389. We have profited from cooperation with the activities of the Medical Information Science group and the Knowledge System Laboratory (formerly the Heuristic Programming Project) at Stanford. John Mylopoulos provided helpful comments.

9. References

[BLUM82] [MW84] [WIED75] [WIED83]

Discussion

Bonnie Webber discussed natural language understanding systems from the point of view of such a system responding to a user. She pointed out that there is some agreement on what structures are useful for natural language processing and knowledge representation. The discussion then focused on the use of term definitions, taxonomic information and temporal reasoning in the generation of natural language responses.

Rusty Bobrow noted that taxonomic hierarchies can also be used for the semantic interpretation of sentences and the resolution of ambiguities. The same comment applies for the temporal knowledge.

Mike Brodie asked how powerful a knowledge representation scheme is needed for natural language processing. Rusty Bobrow and Bonnie Webber responded that a first pass semantic interpretation can be done with the use of a taxonomic hierarchy with possible mutual exclusions and predicate argument restrictions. A general purpose theorem prover is not necessary for handling such features. KL-ONE and NIKL, both developed at BB&N would be adequate for the task.

Bonnie Webber asked about the extend to which current DBMSs handle temporal constraints. Gio Wiederhold responded that such constraints can only be enforced through the transactions that operate on a database.

Jeff Ullman wondered about the computational feasibility of any system that uses powerful forms of logic such as those investigated for natural language processing and knowledge representation purposes. He noted that a theorem prover for propositional dynamic logic, for example, requires in the worst case double exponential time (on the length of the formula to be proven). There was considerable discussion and a variety of answers on this issue. Rusty Bobrow pointed out that practical systems don't have to solve hard problems ever. Ron Brachman added that if you are working on small problems NP-completeness (or worst) is hardly an issue. David Israel asserted that worst case complexity results are not very useful because we simply don't know enough about the actual distribution of worst cases. "...There are actual full fledged first order theorem provers that return an answer before the death of the Universe", he said. Danny Bobrow added that there is considerable interest in *reflective systems* which can be aware, at some level, of the state of their processing. For such systems, simple cases are done simply without reflecting. Hard cases, on the other hand, may require interaction with the user, consideration of resource requirements, etc.

Hector Levesque countered that it's very hard to come up with general criteria for assessing the progress made by a theorem prover and this is a fundamental bottleneck for work on reflective systems.

Mike Stonebraker noted the general agreement among discussants that "there are many hard problems yet to be solved" and the fact that the same was said five years ago. "...I wonder how much progress you have made in the last five years on building natural language understanding systems. What's the gradient of progress? What's the research payoff for investment in this area?" Bonnie Webber responded that these issue were not even under investigation five years ago. Jerry Kaplan's work on helpful responses by a system is new. So is work on plan recognition techniques for handling ellipses and on our understanding of anaphora. Rusty Bobrow added that there has also been progress on the practical front with parsers that can handle a significant fraction of English syntax and are computationally feasible.

John Smith returned to Mike Stonebraker's question. "...you make it clear that there is progress, but it's really a question of what remains to be done...I like to use the analogy of a monkey climbing a tree and is actually not making too much progree towards getting to the moon." Rusty Bobrow answered that one has to be clear about research goals. "If you talk about the general computational representation of human use of language, that's shooting for the moon. If you want to talk about useable interfaces at various levels of complexity, I think that we are already at one level."

Shamim Naqvi asked whether people like to use natural language front ends to databases or find them tedious because of the amount of typing involved. Rusty Bobrow remarked that natural language queries might be expanded into formal queries of much greater length, on the other hand he acknowledged that people do like to use telegraphic English in many situations.

Tom Mitchell introduced EXCUSES, a language feature used to explain why exceptions can be accommodated. Excuses can also help determine general repairs to a constraint.

Bonnie Webber noted that the method provides A repair, not necessarily THE correct repair.

Frank Manola asked how one differentiates good excuses from bad ones, and who judges the excuses. Tom Mitchell explained that if the user insists upon an update for which a reasonable explanation cannot be found, then the update may be allowed, but the system probably would not produce a general rule.

Tom Mitchell gave an example from "naive physics" (placing physical objects on top of each other). David Israel observed that in these situations, theorem-proving is straightforward. Mike Stonebraker observed that there is a huge number of defaults to be specified for such problems.

Tom Mitchell explained that the underlying theory would guide the production of generalisations, and claimed that this theory will very likely be incomplete. This led Rusty Bobrow to suggest that the constraints should simply be checked in advance, instead of waiting for exceptions to arise. The response is that the real world has just TOO MANY exceptions and special cases; furthermore, an incomplete theory can result in unexplained phenomena. Thus Mitchell's method may be viewed as an "example-guided incremental compilation of knowledge."

Rusty Bobrow then drew a parallel with construction codes. Some are PRESCRIPTIVE (stating what must be done), while others are PERFORMANCE-BASED (stating the results, not how they must be obtained). He felt that Tom Mitchell is starting with a prescriptive code and explaining how to relax it into a performance-based one.

Mark Fox presented a report on some of the projects he and John McDermott have been working on. He spoke about the OPS5 and SRL representation systems in some detail and some of their experiences with these systems.

The OPS5 system is a generic rule base that is able to go to a database and make a request either by name or by giving some of the attribute names. The main point stressed by Mark Fox is that within the framework of his project, he has a database system interfaced with a knowledge representation system.

The question these systems raise is: "What has all this led to? What role do databases play in knowledge based systems?" They proposed a "symbol level" where the concern is about the storing and access of knowledge and a "knowledge level" where the concern is about inferences and what can be done with this knowledge.

Their research focusses mainly on the symbol level. In this they have been mainly looking at the efficiency of search since they are dealing with very large search spaces. Also, they have been looking at possible database machines that could be used to support these systems.

Mike Stonebraker asked if their ideas about query optimization could be used in a more dynamic situation. Mark Fox replied that they have a totally dynamic system, with incremental planning and a lot of effort spent on making the system react to changes.

Yannis Vassiliou asked how are the databases actually coupled to their rule systems. Fox explained that it is different for each system. In SRL, for example, there is no concept of a separate database: the system is tightly integrated.

Bruce Buchanan brought up the point that the organizational level as they define it differs from what Simon originally meant when he coined the term. John McDermott answered that their definition allows them to bring in the System Engineering level suggested by Levesque and Brachman. Newell's knowledge level focusses on the agent that has certain kinds of capabilities; it proposes an agent-centered view. The organizational level, according to Mark Fox and John McDermott, provides means for the organization of a collection of agents on the same level.

Gio Wiederhold presented a project (called Rx), focusing on the development of a knowledge based system that uses a large database to extract knowledge from. This knowledge is either used for decision making or to extend the system's knowledge base. An interesting characteristic of his system is that it extracts knowledge from data, in contrast to conventional knowledge extraction from human experts. An underlying premise of this project is that a database may contain much more experience than any single expert. Since it demonstrates the linkage of a knowledge base and a large database, the project is also very relevant to the workshop.

The end product of this project is an advice-giving system, so Rx has been designed so that the representation of both the initial knowledge and the derived knowledge are identical.

Gio Wiederhold identifies three types of knowledge that are fully integrated in the Rx knowledge base: (a) categorical knowledge, which organizes hierarchically the concepts that are relevant to the application, (b) definitional knowledge, which employs a frame structure to represent the attributes of concepts, and (c) causal knowledge, represented by cross-links in the hierarchy.

The importance of using hierarchies is that one gets some confidence of the completeness of the knowledge base over its intended domain. This is especially important in using and drawing causal information, where one needs to assume a basically closed world.

Bruce Buchanan asked if the database was growing or static. The answer given was that it is growing by re-loading, not incrementally like the clinical database which is the source of information for the knowledge base.

Tom Mitchell asked about inferring new relationships. Gio Wiederhold explained that, at the moment, new nodes could not be created, only the links between nodes could be changed. There is research currently looking into the addition of new nodes to the knowledge base.

There was some discussion of the data vs. knowledge issue: Gio Wiederhold felt that knowledge can be generated out of data, but not vice-versa. Frank Manola asked about the derivation of scientific constants. Gio Wiederhold responded "One person's data may be another persons knowledge." Mike Stonebraker did not really see the significance of Gio Wiederhold's distinction.

In summary Gio Wiederhold stated that his project represented a first attempt to automate the extraction of statistical knowledge, and the construction of statistical models.

Part VI

Knowledge-Based System Design Issues

30
Context Structures/Versioning: A Survey

D. G. Bobrow[1]
R. H. Katz[2]

ABSTRACT *Complex system descriptions, for example, a design database or an expert system's knowledge base, will evolve over time. As these descriptions evolve, new versions of their components are created and organized into new configurations. We introduce the terminology, give examples of how versions arise, and review some proposed mechanisms for organizing complex descriptions across time. Some issues are the granularity of changes stored, simultaneity of access to different versions, and tradeoffs between storage requirements and ability to back up.*

1. Introduction

It is not surprising that complex knowledge bases evolve over time. New versions of system objects are created and are incorporated into new configurations. In large-scale knowledge bases, to support versions other than the most current one, additional mechanisms must be added both in the database and in the query language. Such alternative views are important if the knowledge base is being used to support an exploratory activity in which different users want one or more views of the knowledge base at different times, and where comparison of views is a relevant operation.

---

[1] Xerox PARC.
[2] University of California at Berkeley

Two examples of applications where versioning is important are discussed in this book. In the manufacturing application of Fox and McDermott, one needs to have views of the knowledge base that correspond to alternative plans for manufacturing. The VLSI design system discussed by Katz et al uses versioning to control the process by which parts of designs can evolve independently and be incorporated into larger designs. Our examples will come from this domain.

In this survey, we review some of the proposed methods for organizing the versions and configurations of a complex data or knowledge base. But first, we must introduce some terminology. An *object* is a logical aggregate of information.[3] In the case of a design database, an object is a logical component of the system being designed, for example, a program module or layout cell of a VLSI design. At any point in time, there is a collection of information that describes its implementation. These are its *versions*.

Complex systems are most often constructed hierarchically, with composite objects built up from more primitive component objects. We distinguish between primitive objects that have no subparts, and composite objects that do. In its simplest form, making a new version of any part of a composite object forces creation of a new verion of the composite object. It is also useful to define a *configuration* as an object that refers to a collection of versions of related objects. Figure 1 shows the distinction between configurations and versions for a simple design database represented by design files.

Different versions of the composite object denote different configurations of its components. In addition to composition, objects may have parameters (e.g., the number of bits per wire, or resistance per nanoacre). Different versions of objects may differ only with respect to the value of one or more parameters. In such cases, the issue arises as to whether to store the modification as a new version of the object, or to store changes at the granularity of the associated information (the value of *parameter3* for *obj2* is *val1* in this configuration).

If one only made improvements to objects, then it would be appropriate to think only of sequential versions. However, it is often useful to think about two versions of an object as being *alternatives*, that is, to allow a user access to more than one version at the same time. For example, one design might optimize space at the cost of speed, and another the opposite. Alternative descriptions are carried forward in parallel, allowing the object to evolve along different lines. This is particularly important in exploratory environments such as

---

[3] An object is often defined as a bundle of data together with its associated procedures (methods).

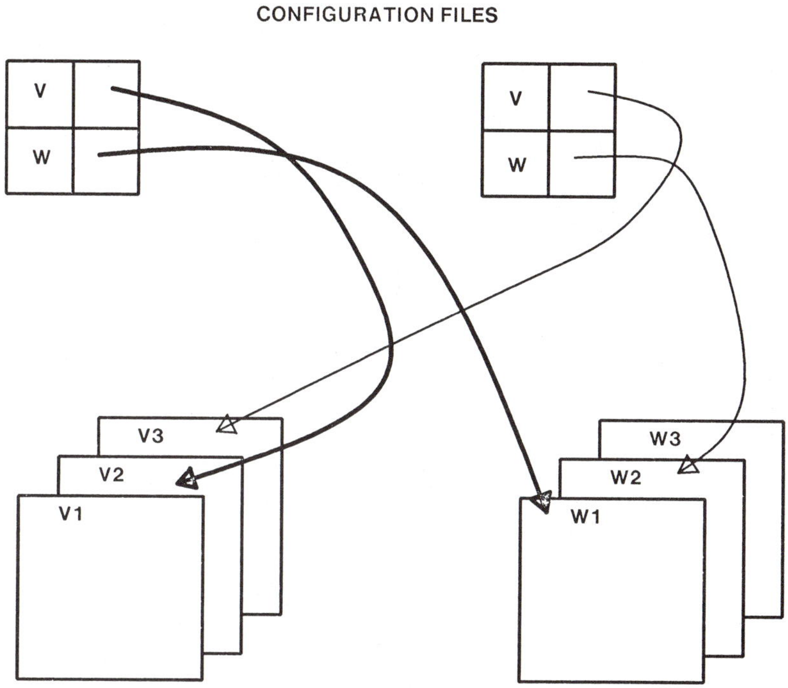

CONFIGURATION FILES

Figure 1: Configuration Files and Design Versions

A system is configured from two objects, V and W, versions of which are represented by individual design files. V version 2 and W version 1 make up the leftmost configuration, while V version 3 and W version 2 make up the rightmost one. This illustrates how a configuration file can tie together versions of individual design files to form versions of a design. In this figure, the granularity indicated is that of complete objects, and one has access to only one version of the configuration at a time.

design and expert system applications. An important variation on this theme is to allow a user of such a system to move backward in time as well as forward, undoing changes that have been made.

2. Design Life Cycle

To illustrate how versions and alternatives arise, and the operations for their creation and manipulation, consider the following system life cycle scenario (see Figure 2). It is presented for illustrative purposes only, and is not the only possible way to organize the evolution of a system.

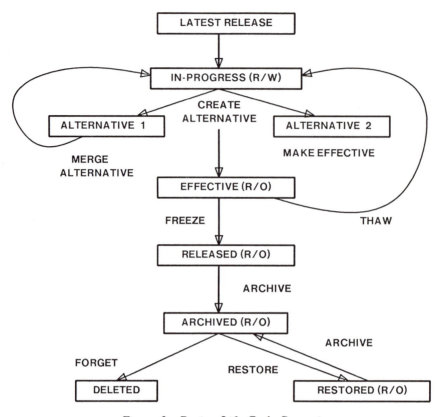

Figure 2: Design Life Cycle Scenario

*One model for a design life cycle is shown. A previous release is made
in-progress and can receive new updates. Various alternatives can be
created in parallel, and one is selected to become effective. If the
effective version is approved by the administrator, it can move on to
become a new release. Old releases are eventually moved to archive,
and eventually discarded.*

Each design object has its own *administrator*, who is responsible
for its contents. Other designers can make their own private copies,
which may be updated. We call these *alternatives*. Only the file's
administrator can incorporate the changes into the object.

A new *in-progress* version is *created* from its latest released version. Only its administrator can update the in-progress version. Other
designers can *create* alternative versions of the object. Changes to alternatives are not reflected in the in-progress version until explicitly
merged into the latter by the administrator.

Effective versions are read-only and represent a pre-release version of an object, suitable for testing before actual release. The administrator merges alternatives into the in-progress version before *making it effective*. Once effective, a file can be updated only if it is first *thawed* back into an in-progress version. Otherwise, it can be *frozen* into a *released* version.

Releases can be *archived* and later *restored*. Ancient versions are removed from the archive by being *forgotten*. Once forgotten, a version can never be reaccessed. Usually, direct access is required for the latest release, all effective versions created since the last release, and the current in-progress version. Thus, it is convenient to have several versions of each design file available on-line.

Effective versions are *checkpoints*. For example, design data must pass a battery of verification checks for self-consistency before it can be released. An effective version is a firewall, providing a capability for restoring an object to a previous consistent version known to have passed these tests.

Alternative versions, in the sense we have used them here, are different from other versions. A designer often attempts several solutions to a design problem. For example, he may design two circuits that perform the same function, one consuming less area and another less power. The design system should aid him in carrying forward multiple alternative designs in parallel. An alternative can be combined with the current in-progress version to form a new in-progress version. Because alternative designs are tentative, changes do not affect the current working copy of a design file until it is explicitly incorporated into the in-progress version.

3. Environments and Layers

[BS83] contains a description of how to implement a version and alternative mechanism that could support the design life cycle described above. The mechanism is based on the ideas originally explored in the PIE system [BG80, GB80a, GB80b]. A *knowledge base* contains a heterogeneous collection of objects. Versions and alternatives are implemented by dividing the the knowledge base into *layers*. These layers explicitly represent changes between states of the knowledge base. Rather than a change to just a single configuration, the layer should represents a coherent set of changes to a number of objects. The initial layer contains the original versions of the objects in the knowledge base, the second layer contains new objects added to the knowledge base and new versions of existing objects that have changed in creating the next version of the knowledge base, etc. Each object is uniquely identified, making it possible to reference different versions of the same object across layers.

As we have described things thus far, the user can choose a *state* of the knowledge base on which to work. A state is a selection of a single version of each object. In PIE, it is possible to switch easily between different states of the knowledge base. A state is defined by an *environment*, which specifies an ordered set of layers. The version of the object used in any environment is the one found in the most dominant layer of the set. An environment can be implemented as an index structure mapping unique object-identifiers into object versions, taking account of the specified order of the knowledge base's layers.

Layers and environments provide a flexible mechanism for organizing design versions. A user can work alternatively between different design versions. By adding a layer created in another environment, a user can incorporate in one design any changes made along another design path. An environment can also contain layers from the designer's private workspace, thus making it easy to form alternative descriptions without affecting the official copy of the knowledge base.

For more efficient usage of storage, a design file's administrator can *summarize* a design file, replacing the file with the most recent versions of all objects in the file. Since this could disrupt the view of designers who have created alternatives of the file, they have the option of making copies of all the layers they refer to in their environments. Before summarization takes place, presumably at a consistent point in a design file's evolution, its administrator snapshots the file into an archive.

In the Loops and PIE implementations, it is made easy for an individual user to compare several alternatives. PIE provided a special program which would highlight for a user the differences between two alternative versions of a structure, and allow choice of either value or construction of some compromise value. This kind of capability is most useful in support of collaborations between two equal partners, such as coauthors of a paper, where no single system administrator exists.

4. A Database Implementation of a Version Mechanism

[KL84] describes an efficient database-oriented implementation of a version mechanism for record-based files. Each record has a system-generated identifier. This is used as a key into a B-tree index of *version histories*. These are descriptors that indicate which record images are valid at different points in the history of the file. The advantage of the B-tree organization is that it is well-suited for managing collections of version histories larger than the physical main memory size.

Furthermore, the structure is organized to provide low-overhead access to the most recent version of the file, while still retaining the ability to reconstruct previous versions of the file with reasonable efficiency. For large files that do not change very much between versions (a common situation for design data), the storage overhead of the index structure is quickly amortized versus the alternative of storing separate instantiations of the complete files.

5. Summary

A variety of terms related to version management have been introduced: *objects, versions, configurations,* and *alternatives.* A possible system-life cycle was introduced to demonstrate how versions can arise. *Layers* as reification of changes, and *environments* as a mechanism for viewing multiple states of a system provide a flexible way of working with versions across time. We also mentioned one structure, a B-tree of version histories, that can be used to efficiently implement a version mechanism for very large configurations. In addition to hardware design, they can clearly be useful in the development and maintenance of large software systems. Versioning seems to us a crucial feature of future large scale-knowledge bases.

6. References

[BG80] [BS83] [GB80a] [GB80b] [KL84]

31
Conceptual Modeling of Information Systems

Alexander Borgida[1]

ABSTRACT *It is claimed that Information Systems can be developed more easily, and can be used in a more natural way, by concentrating on the semantics of the application domain. This brief review paper presents a list of general features which characterize languages that can be used for this purpose (called "conceptual modeling languages"), and distinguish them from more traditional approaches to developing database-intensive application programs. The paper considers both programming languages and languages for specifying requirements, and includes discussion of the modeling of entities, activities, and of open issues.*

1. Goals

CMLs are languages used to develop database-intensive information systems (IS), such as those for reservations and registrations, accounting and data processing, etc. They represent an evolution from traditional data processing *cum* DBMS languages towards languages for representing knowledge, and CMLs have been variously used at the requirements, design or implementation level for ISs.

An IS usually stores, retrieves, and manipulates information about some portion of the real world, and in an important sense can be viewed as a *model of that world*, or more accurately, of the *user's conceptualization of the world*. This is a fundamental tenet of the research on conceptual modeling, and suggests that IS development is like model

---

[1] Department of Computer Science, Rutgers University, New Brunswick, New Jersey 08903

building, and that using an IS is like asking questions of the model. As in physics or engineering, some models may be more perspicuous, more accurate, or easier to build than others. The goal of CMLs is:

- To make it easier to *design* and *maintain* the IS, by choosing a *vocabulary* that is more appropriate for the problem domain, and by *structuring* the IS description as well as the description process,

- To make it easier to *use* the IS, by helping the user find and interpret the stored data in order to obtain information.

As a result, CMLs claim to allow more *natural* and *direct* modeling of the world than has been the case traditionally, and conceptual models are claimed to capture the *semantics* of a situation more accurately and conveniently.

According to a rather naive philosophy, the world is comprehended in terms of conceptual *objects* or *entities*, which have associated descriptions, and are *related* to each other in meaningful ways. Furthermore, *activities* occur over time, with resulting changes in inter-relations. Both the entity and the activity descriptions are subject to *constraints* which define the concepts and distinguish "reality" from other possible worlds. Facilities are therefore needed to express all these as part of an IS model.

2. CMLs For Programming

An IS is usually built out of a database that conforms to some **data model** — general rules for specifying the structure of the data and operations on it — and application programs that manipulate this data. There are two kinds of problems with previous techniques used to build ISs:

1. Traditional data models are based on the notion of "record" (with numeric or string fields), plus sometimes "links". These primitives, however, are more appropriate for modeling the way in which the data is stored and accessed in the computer, than the concepts underlying them and their relationships.

2. General purpose languages like COBOL or PL/I provide few features which would facilitate the more restricted goal of modeling activities for IS design, and the data type structure of the host programming language is usually not integrated with that of the DBMS, often forcing extensive translation between various representations.

Programming languages for conceptual modeling ([ABRI74], [ADAP83], [ACO85], [HB80], [MBW80]) attempt to alleviate some of these problems, and we list below as aphorisms a number of features that distinguish them.[2]

First, concerning the modeling of *static* aspects:

- *Objects in the model correspond to entities in the world.* The designer is expected to set up a natural one-to-one correspondence between the entities in the enterprise and objects in the model. For example, information about a person is not spread out among several records.

- *An object is not the same thing as a name for it.* An object can exist without having a "key" (unique external identifier), and yet be distinct from other objects.

- *State relationships between objects, not their identifiers.* An important consequence of the preceding principle is that relations are asserted between objects, not their names or descriptions. The above three principles free the designer from the tyranny of external identifiers, which are often problematic and lead to inconsistencies (e.g., dangling references).

- *Express most relationships as properties of objects.* Binary relationships are seen to be most common, and *properties/attributes*, which are functions applicable to objects, are provided as a way of expressing these. Attributes make it easier to locate related objects because one can follow chains of properties without having to explicitly introduce intermediate objects: to find the **address** of a book's publisher it is sufficient to say **"address(publisher(b))"** rather than **"find x,y such that PUBLISHED_BY(b,x) and HAS_ADDRESS(x,y)"**.

- *Objects are grouped into classes.* One role of classes is to act as a "typing" mechanism for objects: a class description constrains the attributes applicable to its instances and their values.

- *Classes are organized into subclass hierarchies.* When there are many classes, the resulting hierarchy *organizes* the class descriptions and ensures that subclass instances belong to superclasses. Also, the notion of "inheritance" eliminates unnecessary duplication, since one need not repeat for each subclass definition what has been said for the superclass.

- *Classes are also objects.* Classes, therefore, are instances of "metaclasses" and may have their own attributes. This provides a natural repository for summary information (e.g., for various subclasses of books, the budgets allocated for purchasing books in that class), and meta-data (e.g., who can be the borrower of a book).

---

[2] Some of these observations have appeared earlier in [MS81b].

- *Attributes can have multiple values.* In several CMLs, attributes are allowed to have, as values, sets or sequences of entities. By adopting special notational conventions, these languages make it much easier to express iterative procedures. For example, the expression name(publisher(y)) would yield the name of the (sole) publisher of book y if publisher is defined to be single-valued, while name(authors(y)) would yield the *set of names* of the authors of book y.

- *Descriptions contain redundancy and computed information.* CMLs allow one to define classes whose instances are defined intensionally/procedurally, and properties whose values are computed, rather than explicitly stored. Redundancy accommodates differing viewpoints of users, and makes it more likely that the design of the IS is complete.

- *Use special syntax to state additional constraints.* A plethora of syntactic annotations allows one to constrain the cardinality of relationships, totality of functions, modifiability of relationships, etc. Additional constraints must be stated in a logical language.

Figures 1 and 2 below illustrate many of the above concepts.

type *Books* **is entity**
      call# : INTEGER;
      title: STRING(1..120);
      publisher: Publishers;
      writtenBy: **set of** *Authors;*
    end entity;

unique *call#* **within** *Books;*

subtype *Short_term_loan_books* **is** *Books*
    entity
      forCourse: Courses;
      requestedBy: Instructors;
    end entity;

type *Loans* **is entity**
      item: Books
      loanedTo: Borrowers
      dueDate: Dates
    end;

Figure 1: Some entity class descriptions in Adaplex [ADAP83]

Overdue_books **restriction of** *Books* **with**
     some *x* **inp** *Loans* **with**
       (this = item **of** *x)*
         & *Before(dueDate* **of** *x, $today)*

overdueFine := **derived** *overdueRate* ×
    difference($Today,dueDate **of get** *Loans* **with** *item = this*]

Figure 2: Derived class and attribute in Galileo [ACO85]

Readers familiar with Artificial Intelligence may consider many of the above features "old hat" — they appear in semantic networks and frame-languages — and AI research on KR has, in fact, been a principal source of ideas for CMLs. The following distinctions must, however, be kept in mind: i) Class descriptions are used to check the correctness of the data stored in the computer, and as type information for implementation efficiency, but NOT to recognize and classify objects, ii) Class descriptions are NOT used for "deduction", including "common sense/default" reasoning, although there has been at least one attempt to use integrity constraints for query optimization [KING80a], iii) Current CMLs are particularly inept at coping with incomplete knowledge (disjunction, negative information, etc.). Many of these differences arise because efficiency in storing, retrieving, and protecting large amounts of data is still of paramount importance to users.

Some CMLs [CODD79] [WE83] [CHEN76] have been designed with the purpose of capturing additional semantics, and facilitating user access to data. Others, like traditional data models, provide primitive update operators for adding and removing instances of classes and modifying property values. When augmented by control structures, these languages can be used to build transactions which model activities in the real world (e.g., lending a book). Distinctive features of CMLs in this regard include:

- *Primitive operations on a class can be encapsulated.* So, for example, a new librarian can never be created except by the completed HireLibrarian transaction.

- *Events with long durations can also be modeled.* Using transition networks of potential activities, borrowed from Office Automation, it is possible to model such long-term activities as participation in a clinical trial, attending a university, etc. (See Figure 3)

The major research issue for these programming languages, at the moment, is efficient implementation. At least one effort [CDFL82] has produced a high-quality, distributed DBMS for the Daplex data language, but much work remains to be done for transaction optimization, both for short and long duration transactions. In addition, there is

Figure 3: Sketch of a long-term event (script) in Taxis [BARR82]

considerable research on programming environments and tools connected to these languages.

From the purely language point of view, an important issue here, as elsewhere, is the discovery of a few orthogonal principles whose combination leads to powerful constructs. For a more detailed discussion of some of the above issues, the user may wish to consult [BORG85a].

3. CMLs For Information System Specification

A number of researchers have presented CMLs as tools for stating the specification [CHEN76], [BMS84] and even the requirements [GMB82] of ISs, with the goal that the IS will then be implemented using any available techniques, including more traditional ones.

These languages share most of the features listed earlier. However, they lack programming language facilities (loop and other control structures) and, instead, concentrate on the specification of constraints and activities. Some languages (e.g., RML - see Chapter 32) attempt to integrate in a uniform framework such as that of objects, classes, and properties, the specification of activities and assertions, and concentrate on facilities for organizing and abbreviating descriptions.

An important aspect of these works is the support of "abstraction principles" which allow large, complex models to be built according to good software engineering practices. An abstraction principle selects certain details of a description as being important or relevant at this moment, leaving the others for later stages, in a process which iteratively refines the description. *Classification, aggregation, generalization,* and *normalization* are a few of these principles discussed in the literature [SS77] [BMW84].

More generally, there is considerable concern with the process of gathering the requirements or specification, and various methodologies for doing so have been proposed [BMS84]. For example, an RML model should be built only after a global sketch of the situation has been made using a diagramatic technique such as SADT^{TM} — this sketch provides a "road map" which can be fleshed out with detailed descriptions and constraints to obtain a full model.

It is believed that such software engineering concerns will be essential in developing large KBMSs, and these form a novel contribution of research on Conceptual Modeling to work on Knowledge Representation.

4. Some Open Issues

Practically any aspect of human knowledge is of potential interest to research on conceptual modeling and CMLs. Among the significant representation issues we mention:

- *Time* — the convenient yet accurate modeling of the pervasive temporal aspect of the world.

- *Multiple viewpoints/users* — the integration of overlapping conceptual models.

- *Modeling users and communication with them* — considering user interaction as acts of communication that use the CM as a knowledge base, including the modeling of users, their beliefs and goals.

- *Acquisition* — techniques for aiding the construction and modification of models by generalizing from "examples" or discovering new correlations.

- *Exceptions* — the ability to resolve contradictions during the design of the IS, and the ability to accommodate in a shared information base unanticipated situations, including contradictions to the schema.

- *Incomplete information* — finding ways of representing and reasoning effectively with various forms of incomplete knowledge.

In addition, there are, of course, many systems issues related to the use of CMLs as specification languages, including the development of editors, consistency checkers, and efficient query processors. For example, the latter might provide answers to questions like: "Is situation X permissible according to the specification?" and could be based on specialized theorem provers, since many specifications can be viewed as collections of logical axioms.

5. Summary

CMLs hold out the hope that the development and use of ISs will become considerably easier. From the point of view of users, we have claimed that an IS is useful to the extent that 1) The "model" it stores is accurate, and 2) The information is accessible to the user.

A CML helps to preserve correctness by capturing more accurately the semantics of the world. This is done either through the constraints that are built into the language primitives (e.g., attribute values, integrity of reference, subclasses), or by allowing the designer to state semantic constraints not normally available in usual DBMS.

CMLs make it easier to access the information by:

- Modeling *naturally* the entities and activities in the world

- Using the notion of attribute — computed or stored — to access *directly* from one object all relevant related objects; this is in contrast with having to navigate storage access-paths or computed joins

- Supporting the concise manipulation of groups of entities through set-oriented operators, multi-valued attributes, and appropriate conventions

- Providing uniform access to the generic as well as the specific information usually found in the database

From the point of view of IS developers, CMLs advocate an approach which emphasizes the modelling of the real-world enterprise, as opposed to consideration of implementation issues. This approach is supported by providing a vocabulary specifically tailored for this purpose. Furthermore, the designer is aided in the task of gathering, structuring, and maintaining the IS description by the abstraction hierarchies supported by CMLs, as well as the associated automated tools.

Acknowledgments

This chapter is an abbreviated version of the paper "Features of Languages for the Development of Information Systems at the Conceptual Level", appearing in IEEE SOFTWARE, 2(1). c IEEE.; its preparation has been funded in part by the National Science Foundation under grant MCS-82-10193.

6. References

[ABRI74] [ACO85] [ADAP83] [BARR82] [BMS84] [BMW84] [BORG85a] [CDFL82] [CHEN76] [CODD79] [GMB82] [KING80a] [MBW80] [MS81] [SS77] [WE83]

32
A Requirements Modeling Language and Its Logic

Sol J. Greenspan[1]
Alexander Borgida[2]
John Mylopoulos[3]

ABSTRACT *This chapter describes aspects of a Requirements Modeling Language (RML) which can be used in the initial phases of software development. RML is based on the idea that a requirements specification should embody a conceptual world model, and that the language for expressing it should provide facilities for organizing and abstracting details, yet at the same time have qualities such as precision, consistency, and unambiguity.*

    RML has a number of novel features including assertion classes, the treatment of time, and various abbreviation techniques, all integrated into one uniform object-oriented framework based on ideas that derive from Knowledge Representation research. The precise semantics of these and other features are provided in this chapter by relating RML to a logic involving time. This demonstrates that a language can offer highly structured and convenient mechanisms for requirements specifications while having solid, mathematical underpinnings.

[1] Schlumberger-Doll Research, Old Quarry Road, Ridgefield, Conn. 06877-4108, USA

[2] Dept. of Computer Science, Rutgers University, New Brunswick, NJ 08903, USA

[3] Dept. of Computer Science, University of Toronto, Toronto, Ontario M5S 1A4, CANADA

1. Introduction

The importance of *requirements specifications* as an initial step of software development has long been apparent in Software Engineering ([IEEE77]) and its relevance to Databases, and more generally, to Information System (IS) design is clearly stated in [LGSJ80], where it was called "Corporate Requirements Analysis". The general purpose of this activity is to acquire an understanding of the goals of an enterprise and the way it functions, in order that the eventual computer system (hardware and software) be able to support its current and projected information-handling activities.

As such, the apparent subject matter of the requirements specification is *the enterprise* itself, which could potentially include one or more (existing or planned) computer subsystems. Many of the requirements specification languages mentioned in the literature (e.g., [TH77], [SWL83]) restrict their attention mainly to the characteristics of the data to be stored, and the operations on it which are to be supported by the *projected system*. This means that such important information as definitions of terms, goals, as well as performance requirements, cannot be stated uniformly in the requirements specification. However, important design and development activities such as view integration in databases rely on exactly such information. For this reason, a fundamental tenet of the present work is that the requirements must capture our understanding of the environment within which the proposed system will function. Furthermore, we believe that this information is most appropriately presented in the form of a *model of the real world*, or more precisely our knowledge of the world. Consequently, the constructs of the language have their intellectual roots in AI research on the representation of knowledge (see Levesque, this volume), specifically on ideas used by semantic networks and frame-based representation languages as well as object-centered languages such as Simula and Smalltalk.[4] Two earlier papers ([GMB82], [BGM85]) elaborated on this theme and presented a *framework* for requirements modeling. The purpose of this chapter is to present an actual language developed within this framework, together with its formal definition, and illustrate its effectiveness. A more complete discussion of relevant issues and details of RML can be found in [GREE84].

The actual features of the RML language have been shaped by a number of principles and assumptions. To begin with, a good modeling language should allow the definition of objects in the domain of discourse, the description of changes (events) in the world, and the statement of constraints and assumptions. For this reason, RML allows

---

[4] A more detailed discussion of these relationships can be found in [GREE84 and BGM85].

the description of information in three general categories: *entity, activity,* and *assertion.* By allowing the same information to be viewed from these three qualitatively different viewpoints, RML encourages *redundancy* in the specification, and hence can improve the chances of obtaining a correct and complete specification, as argued in [MCLE78] and [ROSS77].

Second, *uniformity* is an important characteristic of a language which is easy to learn and use. For this reason, RML adopts an *object-centered* view, where all information is recorded in terms of objects, inter-related by properties and grouped into classes. Each object is intended to represent some single coherent concept in the world; each relationship between objects corresponds to the real-world relationship between the respective real-world objects; and changes to model objects are supposed to model changes in the corresponding real-world object.[5]

Third, in order to manage large, complex descriptions, RML supports a structured organization based on widely used abstraction principles [SS77], [MS81b]: *aggregation, classification,* and *generalization.* Again, it applies these uniformly to all three kinds of information. Structuring activities in the same manner as data provides several advantages, as noted in [BG81b]; the other type of description unit, assertions, provide (i) The expressive power of logic, and (ii) Means of structuring complex constraints using the same abstraction principles as for entities and events, since assertions are objects themselves.

A fourth principle is to make it easier to state frequently occurring expressions and constraints. A good example of this is declaring the *type* of a relationship between two objects as an abbreviation for a frequently occurring restriction. RML offers versions of many popular devices present in languages such as SADT[6] [ROSS77] and PSL [TH77], as well as other abbreviatory techniques.

Finally, in order to facilitate the eventual implementation of the IS, RML was designed in a sense as a "sibling" of the TAXIS programming language [MBW80]. As such, RML shares with TAXIS several of the above basic principles, including the use of classes/objects/properties as fundamental building blocks, and the emphasis on the uniform support of the abstraction principles for both data and transactions. Requirements modeling and Information System design can thus be approached within the same framework.

After a brief discussion of the differences between requirements modeling and semantic (data) modeling in databases, Section 2 is

---

[5] Smalltalk is an example of a programming language based on such ideas, although it has a second fundamental principle, that of message passing.

[6] SADT is a trademark of Softech Inc.

devoted to a description of the central features of RML. Section 3 presents a possible treatment of time in requirements modeling both as an illustration of the descriptive capabilities of RML, and as a topic of independent importance for requirements. Section 4 argues for the need to present a more precise specification of RML, and proceeds to do so using a logic with temporal aspects, while the appendix outlines reasons for choosing the particular formal logic used in this chapter, as well as its exact definition.

1.1. Requirements modeling vs. Semantic (Data) Modeling

Readers may be familiar with a number of earlier efforts to capture additional semantics of the application domain for databases, collectively known as "semantic data models" (see [BROD84] for a review). Although there are clear similarities between the goals and techniques used in the requirements and semantic modeling, it is important to be aware of some significant differences.

To begin with, there is a distinction between a model capturing the semantics of the world and one modeling a proposed Information System. For example, in "world modeling" the statement "an employee may optionally have a supervisor" means that a person may or may not have a supervisor, while in "system modeling", it is normally taken to mean that the *data* may or may not be present; hence a "non-optional" property of a real object (e.g., location) may be "optional" in the system. Similarly, while people distinguish between a variety of colours, the *requirements* on the IS might be that it treat as "RED" all colours from pink to burgundy.

More significantly, a requirements model may contain models of concepts which will *not* be implemented in a computerized system. These include precise definitions of terms which need to be understood in order to implement appropriate software (e.g., "ohm", "quarterly"), as well as descriptions of concepts which relate to, but are not part of, the proposed software system (e.g., other systems, humans).

A second difference arises in the modeling of the dynamic aspects of the world. In particular, a requirements model in RML does not depict the world at a particular moment of time; instead, the model is assumed to span a time interval covering the existence of the real-world portion which is of interest, and the designer is supposed to express constraints which must have been obeyed during this interval. Metaphorically, the designer is taking a post-apocalyptic view of the world, and describes semantic conditions which characterized it. An RML model therefore is not expected to change with time as would a database, and hence RML is not a *data model* per se, since it lacks access or update operations.

Third, in RML *assertions* are first class citizens alongside entities and activities. As described in detail later, assertions are objects appearing in classes, and can therefore be organized and described using the same mechanisms as entities. This is an obvious distinction from other conceptual models and requirements specification languages where assertions only play the role of "glue".

Finally, as a statement of requirements, an RML model can be incomplete in several quite acceptable ways, including an incomplete description of how an activity is performed (contrast this with transaction definitions in IS).

2. Introduction to RML

A fundamental principle of RML is that everything that is to be described is an *object*, so that a world model consists of a collection of object descriptions. RML distinguishes *entity*, *activity*, and *assertion* objects in order to help model different kinds of things in the world.

In this framework, interesting things can be said about any object only by describing how it relates to other objects. RML represents directly binary relationships which are functions through the notion of *property* or *attribute*, leaving other relationships to be expressed through assertions.[7] Objects can also be related to each other through the *instanceOf* relationship, which acts as a typing mechanism. Depending on the kinds of instances they have, objects can be classified as *tokens* — not intended to have instances, *classes* — having tokens as instances, *meta classes* — having classes as instances, *meta meta-classes*, etc. The significant point is that classes, meta classes, etc. have associated descriptions which express commonalities about their instances. To a great extent, an RML model is a collection of class (and meta class) definitions, which describe their instances.

In addition to being able to relate objects, we also need the ability to express constraints on the possible relationships between objects if we are to provide accurate models of the real world, distinguishing it from other possible worlds. Assertions will of course be suitable for this task, but we shall present a number of other ways of expressing special kinds of constraints throughout the chapter. Their goal is to make it easier to state commonly occurring situations, and to make descriptions shorter and more intelligible.

---

[7] Properties are restricted to being single-valued (i.e., functions) in order to allow convenient application of comparators and arithmetic functions to property values.

2.1. Modeling entities in RML

Entities are used to model   objects such as persons, places, and things. The chief characteristics of such objects is that they can be meaningfully said to *exist or not at any moment of time*, and that they have an *identity* independent of their potential descriptions or relationships. Information about entities, and about all other kinds of objects, is largely presented through class definitions expressing facts about their instances. At any moment of time a class has some set of instances, which are generally intended to model objects existing in the world at that time.[8] The specification of entity classes resembles in many ways the descriptions current in semantic data models.

Consider for example the case when we wish to model the fact that every person has a name, a gender, which is male or female, an address and a nearest relative. We accomplish this by defining a class of objects, Persons, each of whose instances has properties with suitable identifiers and restricted ranges of values. The particular syntax for expressing this is illustrated in the following example:

> **entity class** *Persons* **with**
> **necessary part**
> *name : Names*
> *gender : {'Male,' Female}*
> **association**
> *address: Addresses*
> *nearestRelative: Persons*

In addition to giving the name or identifier of each property, *(name, gender, address, nearestRelative)*, the specification of a property in a class definition introduces one or more constraints on the values of this property as a function applied to instances of this class. Two mechanisms are illustrated in the above example:

- A *range* of property values allowed is specified as the class name following the colon. It indicates that the value of this property, if it exists, is an instance of that class, and hence can be qualified by the attributes defined for that class; some classes though define sets of values such as integers, strings or enumerations as in Pascal.

- A property can also be specified to belong to one or more *property categories*, which appear in bold face as prefixes to lists of

---

[8] This does not preclude the definition of a class such as PersonsWhoEverExisted, whose instances at any point may be objects that do not actually occur in the world at that time.

properties. Each property category acts as a qualifier describing in more detail some aspect of the functionality of the property.

In the above example, the range of *address* is specified to be the class Addresses, and the **association** property category specifies that a person's address may change over time (unlike his/her *name*, which is a **part**). The property category **necessary** states that every every object in the class must have a value for that property. We adopt the convention that if a property does not have a value for a particular object (e.g., the spouse of an unmarried person), it will be said to have the special value **null**, so that properties can be thought of as total, not just partial, functions.

A property category expresses some constraint on the value of a property for each instance *Inst* of the particlar class *CL* whose definition is being considered. Figure 1 is a catalogue of some predefined property categories available in RML — a list based, in part, on experience with previous specification languages (e.g., [IEEE77]). The additional property categories of Figure 2 apply specifically to entity classes.

Property categories provide a concise way of stating certain constraints which form part of the semantics of the relationships expressed by a property. They are thus a potent form of abbreviation, one whose utility is being first explored here, and for this reason we choose to allow the language user to add to the above catalogue by defining new property categories and their meaning. This is however not expected to be the normal *modus operandi.*

We illustrate many of the features introduced above by presenting next the definition of the class Patients as it might appear in the model of a company running nursing homes. We wish to state that a patient is related in significant ways to his/her medical record, nursing home and room in which he is housed, and the current payment due. A patient is also cared for by a physician, and has a certain diagnosis. A person becomes a patient by being admitted — a special class of activities described later — and stops being a patient by being discharged or dying. In addition, a patient may be affected by being assessed (e.g., his location may change). Whenever a new patient appears, he has no charges pending, and his medical records should be at the same home where the patient is. These conditions are captured formally by the RML class definition in Figure 3.

The example in Figure 3 also introduces a second technique for stating constraints, namely *property binding*, which resembles parameter binding for procedures in programming languages. It is used to further specify the relationship of an object and its properties, by restricting

---

[9] By convention, "this" refers to the instances of the class being described.

part   such properties express relationships which ordinarily do not change with time (e.g., one's name, parents) in the sense that at most one non-null object may be related to *Inst* by that **part** property. Note that parts may be null at some times.

necessary
the property value can not be null as long as *Inst* is in *CL* (e.g., a person's gender or age).

initially
the property value cannot be null at the time *Inst* becomes an instance of *CL* (e.g., a person has a mother at the time of birth).

finallythe property value cannot be null at the time *Inst* stops being an instance of *CL*. As we shall see, when the value of a property is an assertion object, the property category **finally** can be used to state that the condition holds true at the time when *Inst* stops being an instance of *CL*. Similar interpretations about when conditions hold can be given to property categories **initially** and **necessary**.

association
the property value is an entity object, though the property value may change over time; this is a default category, and many properties (e.g., a person's friends) are associations.

unique
no other instance of *CL* has the same property value as *Inst* (e.g., an employee's Social Security number).

Figure 1: Property categories applicable to objects in general

some of the attributes of property values. For example, the specification

register : AdmitPatients (person = **this**, *toHome* = *location)*

states that if *c* is the value of the *register* property of some patient b, then *person* **of** *c* is equal to *b*, and *toHome* **of** *c* equals *location* **of** *b* (i.e., a patient is registered if there has been an act of admitting patients, where the person being admitted was that particular patient, and the home to which he was admitted was the location of the patient.) Note that unlike the case of procedure invocations, it is up to the designer to specify which properties of an activity are "bound" (constrained) when that activity is related to some other object.

producer

> the property value is an event, one of whose effects is to make *Inst* appear as a new instance of *CL* (e.g., a person becomes a patient by being admitted to a hospital).

consumer

> the property value is an event one of whose effects is to make *Inst* stop being an instance of *CL* (e.g., a patient being discharged from the hospital).

modifier

> the property value is an event that affects the relationships in which *Inst* participates, but not its membership in *CL*.

Figure 2: Property categories for entities only

entity class *Patients* **IsA** *Persons* **with**
    necessary unique part
        record : Medical Records
    association
        location : Nursing Homes
        room : Rooms
        physician : Doctors
        diagnosis : Diseases
        paymentDue : $Values
    producer
        register : AdmitPatients (person = **this**[9], *toHome* = *location)*
    modifier
        assessment : Assess (patient = **this***)*
    consumer
        release : Discharge (patient =**this***)*
        decease : Certify (certifyee =**this***, status* = *dead)*
    initially
        rightPlace? : (place or record = *location)*
        startClean? : (paymentDue = *0)*

Figure 3: Definition of the entity class Patients

    Classes can also be related to each other by the IsA relation if the instances of the subclass are always to be instances of the superclass; for example, Patients form a subclass of Persons. The IsA relation is a partial order, and one advantage of stating this explicitly is that properties can be *inherited* down the hierarchy. Thus, every property definition of Persons is also a property definition of Patients (a patient also has a name, etc.), and hence need not be restated. Subclasses may have though additional constraints on these attributes, and may have other attributes applicable to them. The advantages of specialization hierarchies for entity and activity classes have been discussed in detail elsewhere [BG81b, BMW84]; specialization of assertion classes will be considered in Sections 2.3 and 3.

In RML classes are also objects, and hence are instances of other classes, called *meta classes*. These may have associated property definitions describing their own instances. For example, EMPLOYEE_CLASS might have as instances Nurses, Doctors, Administrators, etc. and each of these objects might have an *averageSalary* or *minimumPermittedSalary* — properties that are not applicable to individual employees.

2.2. Activity objects in RML

Classes of activities/events are intended to capture information about events in the world and usually have as instances at any moment of time events which are taking place then. Activity tokens have a single occurrence, over a continuous interval of time.

Events are related by properties to other events (e.g., component activities which must occur as part of this occurrence of an even)t. Events are also related to entities participating in them, and to assertions constraining them.

The additional property categories of Figure 4 are applicable specifically to activities:

The activity class *AdmitPatients* is exemplified in Figure 5. This activity has one input property, a person, and one output property, a patient.
The activity also depends on the presence of a doctor who supervises the admission, and the home where the person is being admitted. The initial conditions assure that there is room, and that the person being admitted is not already a patient (in which case the activity would be one of patient transfer, not admission). The final condition assures that the patient is the same as the person, and that his location is the home specified. Finally, we specify a number of parts which make up this activity. Note that these subactivities are not ordered in any way — it is up to the designer to state any constraints on their temporal ordering as explicit assertions. Finally, as with entity classes, events can be organized in a specialization hierarchy, with identical rules for proper specialization.

input
> the property value is an entity that participates in the event being defined and is of interest at the start time of the event; it is removed by this event from its property value class.

outputthe property value is an entity that participates in the event being defined, and is of interest at the end time of the event; it is added by this event into its property value class.

control
> the property value is an entity that affects the event being defined but whose properties and relationships are not altered by this event; note that input, output and control are all parts and hence are time invariant (except for **null** value).

actcond
> the property value is an assertion which becomes true at a point in time if and only if an instance of the event being defined begins at that point in time.

stopcond
> the property value is an assertion which becomes true at a point in time if and only if an instance of the event being defined ends at that point in time.

Figure 4: Property categories for activities

2.3. Assertions in RML

We have argued in the introduction that constraints are indispensable if we are to provide sufficiently detailed specifications. Some commonly used constraints of a restricted form have been built into the RML notation and principles through such facilities as ranges for properties, property categories, binding assertions, and rules about the IsA relation.

To deal with more general constraints, RML also provides a many-sorted First Order Logic with identity. In this language we must explicitly recognize that an RML description provides a "longitudinal" view of the world through time, so one of the sorts is that of *time points* which are assumed to be linearly ordered in an infinite sequence.[10] RML assertions may involve the following functions and predicates

---

[10] Note that these time points are abstract mathematical concepts, not calendar times; the latter are expressible in RML, as illustrated in Section 3.

activity class *AdmitPatients* **with**
   input
        person : Persons
   control
        toHome : NursingHomes
        doc : Doctors
   output
        pat : Patients
   initially
        already-in? : **not** *(person* **in** *Patients)*
   finally
        admitted? : (person = pat) **and** *(location* **of** *pat = toHome)*
   part
        getBasicInfo : Interview (whom = person)
        place : AssignRoom (toWhom = person)
        getConsult: ScheduleVisit (visitor = doc, patient = pat)
        assess : TakeVitalSigns (patient = pat)

Figure 5: Definition of AdmitPatients activity class

involving time:

- Time comparators $=$, $<$ and $\leqslant$
- Functions **start** and **stop** specifying the start and end time of an event token
- 3-place predicate **in**(x,y,s) indicating whether x is an instance of y at time s, this is written in infix notation as $(x$ **in** y **at** $s)$
- 3-place function **pv**(x,y,s) and returning the value of property y of object x at time s; the infix notation for this is $(y$ **of** x **at** $s)$.

In addition, RML assertions subsume the usual notations for the logic of arithmetic and strings, and may involve the special symbols "null" and "this". As mentioned earlier, "this" refers to prototypical instances of the class being defined, and will be viewed as a variable ranging over this class.

    Assertions must be associated with instances of a class or meta class through properties. For example, an essential part of the meaning of admitting a person is that the *location* argument of the activity agree at the end with the *location* property of the patient. This can be captured through the property "rightPlace" for AdmitPatients:

   necessary
        rightPlace: location **of** *(pat* **of this at** *stop(***this***))* **at** *stop(***this***)*
          $=$ **atHome of this at** *stop(***this***)*

In order to simplify the form of the assertions, we adopt several conventions. First, whenever the expression "**at** ..." is omitted, it is assumed to be by default "**at now** ", where **now** is a special reserved variable, which the semantics of the language interprets in a distinct way. In particular, property categories may be used to qualify the values of **now** for which an assertion will be checked. Thus, the above constraint could have been stated as

finally *rightPlace: (location* **of** *pat* **of this** $=$ *atHome* **of this***)*

since the **finally** property category considers the assertion only when **now** is the stopping time of the activity.

As a second abbreviation, the expression **of this** can be omitted in expressions appearing in the definition of a class. The previous constraint then simplifies to

finally *rightPlace: (location* **of** *pat* $=$ *atHome)*

In order to represent more general relationships than functions we will need assertions which play the role of predicates. Since uniformity is one of our guiding principles in designing RML, we have chosen to also model assertions as objects organized into classes. In this case, an assertion class is to be interpreted as a predicate declaration. In analogy with entity and event classes, instances of an assertion class will have zero or more attributes, which in this case include the free variables (arguments) of the predicate, and these variables will be typed by the usual method of property definitions. If, for example, P is an assertion class with argument properties $x1$ and $x2$ say, then at time t each instance of P is assumed to correspond to a *true* proposition, where the values of $x1$ and $x2$ correspond to constants which make the formula $P(x1,x2,t)$ true. Therefore, instances of assertion classes represent propositions which are true at that moment, in the same way as instances of entity classes represent existing entities, and instances of event classes correspond to occurring activities. Therefore in RML, in order to require that some condition be true, one must state that the property relating this condition to some object have non-null value. In other words, truth of conditions is replaced by the presence of objects in assertion classes, where logical formulas written by designers are assumed to implicitly define distinct assertion classes.

For example, the assertion IsTreatedWith, describing what treatments a patient receives, might be modeled by the class:

assertion class *IsTreatedWith* **with**
    arguments
        p : Patients
        t : Treatments

and at any moment of time *s*, this class is presumed to contain tokens which have as pairs of attributes a patient p who is receiving treatment t at time s. In other words, there is a token c in class IsTreatedWith at time s, with properties p **of** c at $s = d$ and t **of** c at $s = e$ if and only if IsTreatedWith(d,e,s) is considered to hold.

As with entities and events, in cases where the requirements become very large, there will be a need to organize the assertions themselves. For example, it may be desirable to relate one assertion with others, as was done for events and entities. Properties with assertion values can be used for this purpose, with the continued understanding that if at any moment an attribute value is not null, the corresponding assertion is true. For example, the description of IsTreatedWith can be expanded to

> **assertion class**   *IsTreatedWith* **with**
>   **arguments**
>   *p: Patients;*
>   *t: Treatments;*
>   **necessary**
>   *c1: Available(treatment =t, atPlace =* *location* **of** *p)*
>   *c2: Recommended (treatment =t, disease = diagnosis* **of** *p)*

Once again, property categories are used to impose certain interpretations on the properties. Thus the c1 attribute value cannot be null, so that for any instance of IsTreatedWith there must be an instance of Available with the appropriate properties. This is equivalent to saying that IsTreatedWith(x,y) logically implies Available$(y,\text{location}(x))$.

Some property categories specific to assertions are listed in Figure 6.

argument
> the property represents a free variable of the predicate corresponding to the class; hence for each token of this class, the values of the arguments represent one particular set of variable bindings

asserter
> an activity which makes this assertion true

denier- an activity which makes this assertion false

Figure 6: Property categories for assertions

As with other classes, assertions can now be organized into IsA hierarchies. The organization of assertions provides an index whereby the specifier can check if closely related assertions have been used before and thus specify new assertions incrementally. If some assertion is to be modified, one can also obtain an indication of what other assertions one might have to reconsider in light of this change. To be consistent with the rules relating the instances of sub and super classes for other kinds of objects, if P is an assertion subclass of Q, all instances of P must be instances of Q, and P must be more "restrictive" than Q in some sense. The natural conclusion is that P **IsA** Q only if P implies Q logically. However, we do not intend the converse to hold; namely P $\Rightarrow$ Q will not necessarily result in P **IsA** Q.

Specialization — the process of defining subclasses by describing new properties for them and restricting values for the inherited properties — proceeds with assertion classes in the same manner as with activity classes. Thus, we could define the subclass ReceivesChemotherapy of IsTreatedWith as in:

> **assertion class** *ReceivesChemotherapy* **IsA** *IsTreatedWith* **with**
> > **arguments**
> > > *p : CancerPatients*
> > > *t : CancerDrugs*
> > **necessary**
> > > *c3 : IsTreatedWith(p = p , t = 'psychotherapy)*

Thus, receiving chemotherapy is restricted to the subclass of cancer patients, and has the additional condition of requiring concurrent psychotherapy.

The above examples suggest that assertion classes serve the role of *relationships* in the Entity-Relationship model. They are useful for other reasons too, as illustrated in the following section.

3. Modeling time: an example of using RML

Although RML incorporates the notion of passage of time in a fundamental way, the language does not commit the user to any particular kind of calendar or metric on time. In order to demonstrate the capabilities of RML, we present in this section portions of a model for standard calendar time which would be useful for many applications.

To begin with, we present some philosophical observations which have guided our treatment of time in RML as well as the modeling of calendar time. First, the requirements definition is usually assumed to express WHAT is to be constructed, not HOW this is to be achieved. Therefore the requirements statement should allow the maximum possible latitude in implementations. This implies that all temporal relationships should be *explicitly* stated as constraints. Thus any temporal view which forces all activities to occur serially is unacceptable. For the same reason we must be able to represent incomplete information, or be vague to any degree desired.

Second, it seems clear that given any description of some ordinary human activity, we have at least in theory the ability to provide a description at an even finer level of detail.   From the temporal view, this means that every time period can be subdivided into finer intervals.

Of course, the time model should be able to express the everyday time concepts such as clock and calendar time, but it should also allow the definition of any time unit, not just one based on notions such as "second".

Our solution is to overlay on top of the linear time line introduced earlier a temporal scheme based on time *intervals*, along the lines of that proposed in [ALLE83] , and to note that we already have time intervals associated with activity occurrences: the beginning and end of an activity token demarcate an interval. This generalizes a proposal by Bubenko [BUBE80] for expressing ordinary time units like hours, etc. as events.

Let us introduce now some of the predicates used in describing temporal relations based on time intervals, such as "before","during", etc. These time comparators will be considered as assertion classes with two arguments, of type AnyEvent. We start by defining the most general class, TemporallyRelated as:

assertion class *TemporallyRelated* **with**
    arguments
        first : AnyEvent
        second : AnyEvent

We then define additional terms according to the hierarchy partially specified in Figure 7.

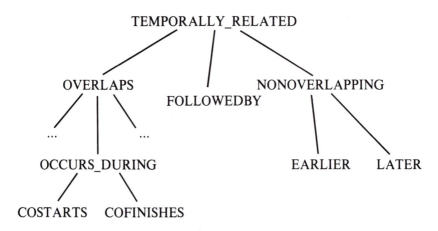

Figure 7: Hierarchy of some temporal relation terms

The hierarchy of names provides a rough guide to the intended meaning of these terms; for example, the term EARLIER is intended to relate an event which finishes *before* the other one starts, as indicated by its position under the class NONOVERLAPPING. The meaning of these constraints can be clarified by adding appropriate assertions about start and stop times. Thus OVERLAPS and OCCURS_DURING are defined in Figure 8.

assertion class *Overlaps* **IsA** *TemporallyRelated* **with**
  necessary
    atOneEnd : $(x = first$ **of this at** $ft)$
                 and $(y = second$ **of this at** $st)$
                 and $(x \neq$ **null**$)$ **and** $(y \neq$ **null**$)$
              $\Rightarrow$
              $(stop(x) > start(y)$ **or** $stop(y) > start(x))$[11]
assertion class *OccursDuring* **IsA** *Overlaps* **with**
  necessary
    atBothEnds : $(x = first$ **of this at** $ft)$
                   and $(y = second$ **of this at** $st)$
                   and $(x \neq$ **null**$)$ **and** $(y \neq$ **null**$)$
                $\Rightarrow$
                $(start(y) < start(x)$ **and** $stop(x) < stop(y))$

Figure 8: Two assertion classes for temporal relations

The above specification process incidentally illustrates the utility of hierarchies of assertion classes for defining groups of related terms: the organization of the notoriously ambiguous English time terms allows their similarities and differences to be viewed, and their meaning to be made precise for the purposes of this specification.

Once the preceding classes have been defined they can be used in assertions to specify the relationships of various activities. For example, to state that activity token a1 must precede activity a2, use a property

necessary precedence : EARLIER (first = a1, second = a2)

For convenience, hereafter adopt the convention of writing predicates with binding assertions like EARLIER(first=a1,second=a2) as EARLIER[a1,a2].

To reiterate two significant points: The above definitions of temporal terms appear now as an integral part of the requirements

---

[11] This circumlocution is required in general because the two events may not occur at the same time and hence there may not be a time when both the properties of first and second are non-null.

specification; and assertion classes can be used to structure and organize related definitions. This organizational ability is useful in light of the well known problems of gathering and modifying large amounts of details during requirements.

One way to model common time intervals, such as hours, days, etc., in RML is using event classes. To begin with, distinguish the notion of time intervals of uniform length ("one hour from now"), from specific such intervals used to measure the passage of time ("at 5 o'clock"). The distinction is necessary because time intervals like the hour in "one hour from now" are dense in the sense that at any moment of time a new time interval of that kind begins; on the other hand clock/calendar time events have unique occurrences (there is only one calendar day going on right now).

Considering the concept of ClockHour, several things need to be said: hours form chains, there is only one going on at any moment of time, how an hour relates to its minutes, the name of the hour, etc. Some of these things are properties of individual hours, and can be stated in the definition of the class ClockHour. Others, like the fact that there is always an hour occurring, are aggregate properties of the entire collection of hours, not of any particular hour. Such constraints should be stated as properties of the class ClockHour itself. Furthermore, it turns out that all time measures, including minutes, seconds, weeks, etc. have such properties.

For these reasons it is best to define a meta event-class *Standard-TimeUnits*, whose instances will include classes ClockHour, Clock-Minute, CalendarDay, etc. The definition in Figure 9 specifies a number of constraints, including: at any moment of time there is at least one event of each such kind going on (captured by the assertion property "*eternal*"); in fact, except for the end points, there is only one such event occuring at any time *("up-to-two", "unique-except-at-ends")*.[12] Each hour is specified to have an associated clock name from 1 to 24, and is related to its starting minute, successor hour, and the calendar day during which it occurs. An hour must have 60 minutes in it, and assertions about the first minute and next hour are needed, ensuring proper sequencing. (See Figure 10.) Similar assertions will be needed for ClockMinutes, CalendarDays, etc. Having defined this, to specify that the admission of patients can only begin between nine and ten o'clock in the morning, we could attach the assertion

initially *when :* (**E**xists *h) (h* **in** *ClockHours)* **and** *(clockReading* **of** *h* = *9)*

---

[12] For technical reasons discussed in [MCDE81], we should also include a "comprehension axiom" which ensures that time periods don't "shrink" infinitesimally small. We omit this here for the sake of brevity.

activity meta class *StandardTimesUnits* **with**
    necessary
        eternal : Exists t (t **in this***)*
        up-to-two: (x **in this***)* **and** *(y* **in this***)* **and** *(z* **in this***)* $\Rightarrow$
            $z = x \lor z = y$
        unique-except-at ends: (x **in this***)* **and** *(y* **in this***)* $\Rightarrow$
            $x = y \lor start(x) = stop(y) \lor start(y) = stop(x)$

Figure 9: The StandardTimeUnits meta-class

activity class *ClockHours* **in** *StandardTimeUnits* **with**
    parts
        next : ClockHours
        firstMinute : ClockMinutes (clockReading = 1)
    necessary part
        clockReading : 1..24
        onDay: CalendarDays
    initially
        sixtyMinutes:$(Exist m_1, \ldots , m_{60}, t_1, \ldots , t_{60}$
            (m_i **in** *ClockMinutes* **at** t_i*)* **and** *FOLLOWEDBY* [m_i, m_{i+1}]
            and *COSTARTS* [m_1, **this**] **and** *COFINISHES* [m_{60}, **this**]
        startingMinute : COSTARTS[*firstMinute,* **this**]
    finally
        hourChain : FOLLOWEDBY[**this**, *next*]
        nextHour'sClock : (clockreading **of** *next) = 1+mod(clockreading, 24)*
        duringDay : OCCURS_DURING[**this**, *onDay*]

Figure 10: The definition of clock hour

to the definition of AdmitPatients.

4. A definition of the semantics of RML

    Several reasons compel us to present a more formal account of the meaning of RML. To begin with, since RML has quite a number of novel features, especially relating to the manner in which constraints, hitherto expressed in English, can be precisely stated, it is important to define them precisely for the benefit of users. The process of formalization itself has forced us to consider in detail the exact meaning of the constructs, and has lead to the discovery of ambiguities and asymmetries. (See the chapter by Levesque and Brachman for a strong statement on this.)

Second, given a requirements specification, there is a range of questions that one often wishes to have answered, including:

- Is the specification consistent or self-contradictory?

- Can a particular situation arise in the (model of the) world, according to the current specifications? (e.g., "Can a patient be in several nursing homes at the same time?")

A formal semantics provides a domain where the definition of such terms as "consequence" and "consistency" can be given, and sets a standard against which to judge the correctness of any computer tools that purport to assist the user in answering the above questions.

Finally, the users and readers of the language can use the formal specification as the final arbiter in cases where there is disagreement concerning the exact meaning of some specification.

We have chosen to express the semantics of RML by providing a method to translate an arbitrary RML specification into a set of formulae in a Predicate Calculus. This provides us with proof-theory as a computational definition of notions like "consistency" and "answer to a question".[13]

Time plays an important role in our logical calculus, and it is incorporated by adding time arguments to most predicates and functions. We have eschewed more complex temporal logics (e.g., [SERN80]), and non-linear time lines because of the relative simplicity of our approach, its expressive power, and our notion of the model as a history of the world. For further discussions of these issues, see the Appendix.

4.1. The logical language with time

The following logic extends the language of RML assertions outlined in section 2.3 through the addition of new predicates and functions. The following are its basic predicates and functions.

IN(k,K,s)

> predicate asserting that token k is an instance of class K (or class k is in meta class K) at time s

PROPDEF(K,p)

> time-independent function which gives the class or meta class to which must belong the value of attribute p for instances of K;

---

[13] We wish to emphasize that at the moment this is just a theoretical possibility.

(the *definitional property* function)

PROPVAL(k,p,s)

> function which gives the value of the attribute p of element k at time s; (the *factual property* function)

START(e)

> function providing the start time of event token e

STOP(e)

> function providing the end time of event token e

IS-A(K1,K2)

> time-independent predicate asserting that class (meta class) K1 is a subclass of class (meta class) K2

OCCURS(k,K,s1,s2)

> non-primitive predicate used to specify the maximal time interval(s) s1 to s2 when k is an instance of K; definable in terms of START and STOP for events, and more generally using the predicate IN

=, ≠ predicates to determine if two objects are identical or not;

$<_T, >_T, =_T$

> predicates to compare time points

$ a special constant used to denote the null value (meaning "no value")

The symbols relating to the calculus of numbers and strings will also be used in formulas.

All free variables occurring in assertions, other than **this** and **now**, are assumed to be universally quantified, and whenever a symbol could be either a constant or a variable, it will be a variable unless expressly stated that it is a constant.

In order to avoid problems with non-sensical assertions, the logical language is made *many-sorted*[14], so that one can specify, for example, that the third argument of IN is of sort time, and hence variables or constants of sort token or property cannot be used there. In the discussion to follow we will omit the sort information, since it can be easily inferred from the context.

---

[14] See the appendix for precise definitions.

4.2. The basic axioms of RML

First, some obvious axioms describing the notion of time. These may involve two special time constants: $-\infty$ and $+\infty$, marking the ends of time ("creation" and "judgment days"), and used to represent events that last forever. The following axioms present the desired properties of time.

$$(s1 \leqslant s2) \wedge (s2 \leqslant s3) \;\Rightarrow\; (s1 \leqslant s3) \qquad \{\leqslant \text{ is transitive}\}$$

$$(s1 \leqslant s2) \wedge (s2 \leqslant s1) \;\Rightarrow\; (s1 = s2) \qquad \{< \text{ is anti-symmetric}\}$$

$$(s1 \leqslant s2) \vee (s2 \leqslant s1) \qquad \{< \text{ is a total order}\}$$

$$(s1 < s2) \Leftrightarrow (s1 \leqslant s2) \wedge (s1 = s2) \qquad \{\text{definition of } < \}$$

$$s1 < s2 \;\Leftrightarrow\; (\exists\, s)\; s1 < s \wedge s < s2 \qquad \{\text{time is dense}\}$$

$$(-\infty \leqslant s) \wedge (s \leqslant +\infty)$$

The central axioms of RML describe the way in which definitional and factual properties relate to instances and subclasses of classes.

Null-value axioms. {base predicates on $ are false, and functions on $ produce $}

$$\tilde{}\; \text{IN}(\$,K,s) \wedge \tilde{}\; \text{IN}(k,\$,s)$$

$$\text{PROPVAL}(\$,p,s) = \$ \wedge \text{PROPDEF}(\$,p) = \$ \wedge \text{START}(\$) = \$$$
$$\wedge \; \text{STOP}(\$) = \$$$

Property-value constraint. {Property values must belong to the range specified by the definitional property}

$$\text{IN}(d,C,s) \wedge \text{PROPVAL}(d,p,s) = y \wedge y \neq \$ \;\Rightarrow$$
$$(\exists\, D)\;\; \text{PROPDEF}(C,p) = D \wedge \text{IN}(y,D,s)$$

Extensional IS-A constraint. {Each instance of a subclass is in its superclass}

$$\text{IN}(d,D,s) \wedge \text{IS-A}(D,C) \;\Rightarrow\; \text{IN}(d,C,s)$$

Intensional IS-A constraint. {Inherited attributes have more specialized ranges}

$$\text{PROPDEF}(C,p) = E \wedge E \neq \$ \wedge \text{IS-A}(D,C) \;\Rightarrow$$
$$(\exists\, F)\;\; \text{PROPDEF}(D,p) = F \wedge \text{IS-A}(F,E)$$

Definition of **OCCURS** (): {maximal periods during which an object is in a class}

OCCURS(e,E,s1,s2) $\Rightarrow$ s1<s2

(OCCURS(e,E,s1,s2) $\wedge$ OCCURS(e,E,s3,s4)) $\Rightarrow$ s2<s3 $\vee$ s4<s1

OCCURS(e,E,s1,s2) $\wedge$ s1<s $\wedge$ s<s2 $\Rightarrow$ IN(e,E,s)

IN(e,E,s) $\Rightarrow$ ($\exists$ s1,s2) OCCURS(e,E,s1,s2) $\wedge$ s1$\leqslant$s $\wedge$ s$\leqslant$s2

4.3. Axioms for general class definitions

The definition of a class introduces new symbols - predicates, functions, and constants - into the language, as well as a number of axioms. In this subsection we consider those aspects of the semantics of a class/metaclass definition which are independent of the kind of class being defined (entity/activity/assertion).

Consider the definition of an arbitrary class, which has the general syntax:

<class B> **in** <meta class M> **IsA** <class C> **with**

   . . .

   <property-category π

      . . .

      <property p> : <range D> (<binding assertion ψ>)

     . . .

As a result of this definition, add B to the list of class constants, p to the list of property constants (if not already there) and add the following axioms:[15]

IS-A(B,C)   {B is a subclass of C}

IN(B,M,s)   {B is an instance of M}

PROPDEF(B,p) = D {values of p belong to D}

Property categories other than **arguments** will be represented by *predicates on properties*, and their meaning will be defined by axiom schemata. The property category states constraints about property values and the times when these constraints must hold. For example, the property category **necessary**, indicating that the property is not allowed to have null value, would be defined by:

---

[15] Here the only variables will be the ones dealing with time states.

NECESSARY (p) $\equiv$ [PROPDEF(x,p)=y $\wedge$ y $\neq$ \$] $\Rightarrow$
[IN(z,x,now) $\Rightarrow$ PROPVAL(z,p,now) $\neq$ \$]

while **initially** could be defined as:

INITIALLY (p) $\equiv$ [PROPDEF(x,p)=y $\wedge$ y $\neq$ \$] $\Rightarrow$
[OCCURS(z,x,now,t) $\Rightarrow$ PROPVAL(z,p,now) $\neq$ \$]

The other property categories are similarly defined, and a designer who wishes to introduce a new property category must define a corresponding schema.

A binding constraint ψ is a sequence of equality assertions of the form $e_1=e_2$, where e_i are property value expressions. They behave as all other assertions except that e_1 refers to a property of the *p-value* for some object, while e_2 refers to the object itself. For this purpose define a recursive program ADDOF$_x$, where X is a class, which expands this abbreviation:

ADDOF$_x$ $(p,e)\equiv$

e   if e is a constant;

e **of** p if e is a property name applicable to tokens in X;

q **of** ADDOF$_x$(p,f)   if e $\equiv$ "q **of** f"

error otherwise

Then replace a binding assertion of the form

$$p : D \ (e_{1,1}=e_{1,2}, \ e_{2,1}=e_{2,2}, \ \cdots)$$

by the property definition   p : D and by a new assertion property

$$p' : (ADDOF_D(p,e_{1,1})=e_{1,2})\wedge(ADDOF_D(p,e_{2,1})=e_{2,2})\wedge \cdots$$

whose semantics are expressed in section 4.7.

4.4. Axioms for entity classes

We begin with the axioms defining some of the constants and permanent objects which can be used to build descriptions in RML, including ANY-ENTITY, ANY-ENTITY-CLASS. If D is an entity class and M is an entity metaclass then:

IN(d,D,s) $\Rightarrow$ IN(d, ANY-ENTITY, s)

IN(D,M,s) $\Rightarrow$ IN(D, ANY-ENTITY-CLASS, s)

IS-A(NUMBERS, ANY-ENTITY) $\wedge$ IS-A(STRING, ANY-ENTITY)

We will also need axioms asserting the existence of all the numbers as instances of NUMBERS, all strings as instances of STRINGS, and defining the usual arithmetic and string operations and predicates.

The following two additional axioms will ensure that numbers and strings are distinct from all other entities.

$$IN(n, NUMBER, s) \land IN(n, K, s) \Rightarrow$$
$$\text{IS-A}(k, NUMBERS) \lor \text{IS-A}(NUMBERS, K)$$

$$IN(z, STRINGS, s) \land IN(z, K, s) \Rightarrow$$
$$\text{IS-A}(K, STRINGS) \lor \text{IS-A}(STRINGS, K)$$

In a class definition such as the one illustrated in Section 2, designers may introduce new entity class constants "in-line" by using Pascal-like enumeration or range expressions for domains D. If D is an enumerated set specifier of the form $'k1,'k2,...,'kn$, create constant symbols k1, ... kn, unless they exist already, and the axioms:

$$IN(k1, D, s) \land ... \land IN(kn, D, s)$$
$$IN(x, D, s) \Rightarrow x=k1 \lor ... \lor x=kn$$
$$\text{IS-A}(D, NUMBERS) \text{ in case k1 , ... are integers}$$
$$((\forall k) IN(k, D, s) \Rightarrow IN(k, K, s)) \Rightarrow \text{IS-A}(D, K)$$
$$((\forall k) IN(k, K, s) \Rightarrow IN(k, D, s)) \Rightarrow \text{IS-A}(K, D)$$

If the definition of D was of the form i1..i2, the first three axioms are replaced by:

$$\text{IS-A}(D, NUMBERS)$$
$$IN(n, D, s) \Leftrightarrow i1 \leqslant n \leqslant i2$$

4.5. Axioms for events

The following axioms deal with the semantics of event occurrences.

Events progress in time: $START(e) \leqslant STOP(e)$

Event tokens occur only once:

$$IN(e,A,s) \Rightarrow START(e) \leqslant s \land s \leqslant STOP(e)$$

$$(\forall_o)(\exists A)(\forall s)(START(e) \leqslant s \land s \leqslant STOP(e)) \Rightarrow IN(e,A,\mathbf{s})$$

To model events with multiple occurrences (e.g., going to school with interruptions), event classes have their own occurrence defined by the occurrence of their instances:

$$OCCURS(E, RepetitiveEventClass, s1, s2) \Leftrightarrow$$
$$\exists\ e, s, s1, s2\ OCCURS(e, E, s1, s2)$$

4.6. Axioms for assertion classes

Every time we encounter the definition of an assertion class A, with n properties p1,..., pn in the **arguments** category, we define a new $(n+1)$-ary predicate **A**, the last place of sort time. The presence of a token with argument values a1,...,an is supposed to model the assertion of **A**(a1,...,an) at that time, therefore argument values have to be unchanging and unique for each assertion token.

> IN(y,A,s) $\Leftrightarrow$ ($\exists$ s1,..., sn) PROPVAL(y, p1, s1)=a1 $\wedge$ ... $\wedge$
> PROPVAL(y, pn, sn)=an $\wedge$ a1$\neq$\$ $\wedge$ ... $\wedge$ an $\neq$ \$ $\wedge$
> A(a1,..., an, s)

> (IN(y, A, t1) $\wedge$ PROPVAL(y,p_i, t1)=v1 $\wedge$ v1$\neq$\$) $\wedge$
> (IN(y, A, t2) $\wedge$ PROPVAL(y, p_i , t2)=v2 $\wedge$ v2 $\neq$ \$)
> $\Rightarrow$ v1=v2

> y $\neq$ z $\wedge$ IN(y, A, s) $\wedge$ IN(z, A, s)
> $\Rightarrow$ ~(PROPVAL(y, p1, s)=PROPVAL(z, p1, s) $\wedge$ ...
> $\wedge$ PROPVAL(y, pn, s)=PROPVAL(z, pn, s))

4.7. The semantics of assertion formulas

Suppose that the property definition of p for some class C specifies an RML assertion ξ instead of a domain class D. First, expand some abbreviations: Restore the omitted portion "**of this**" in all property value expressions according to the procedure ADDOF$_C$ (**this**,...) introduced in Section 4.2. Also, add the special reserved variable **now** as the time argument of all predicate or function expressions which involve time but do not have an explicit time specified. Furthermore, add universal quantifiers for all free variables occurring in the expression, except **now** and **this**.

If at this point the assertion ξ does not have **this** as a free variable, then add a new assertion class constant A$_\xi$ (as with in-line entity class definitions), and replace the property definition "p : ξ" for class C by

$$p : A \; \xi$$

Then specify that A^ξ has an instance token if and only if ξ is true

$$\xi(\textbf{now}) \Leftrightarrow (\exists y) \; IN(y, A^\xi, \textbf{now})$$

and require that p have this value whenever it exists:

$$(\forall x, t) IN(x, C, t) \Rightarrow (\exists y) \; IN(y, A^\xi, t) \Rightarrow PROPVAL(x, p, t) = y$$

If ξ contains occurrences of the special free variable **this**, A^ξ must be defined with one argument property v:ANY, and change the last two axioms above to

$$(\forall w, t) \xi < w/\textbf{this}, \, t/\textbf{now} > \; \Leftrightarrow$$
$$[(\exists x) \; (IN(x, A^\xi, t) \wedge PROPVAL(x, v, t) = w)]$$

$$(\forall x, t) IN(x, C, t) \Rightarrow$$
$$[[(\exists y) \; IN(y, A^\xi, t) \wedge PROPVAL(y, v, t) = x] \Rightarrow$$
$$PROPVAL(x, p, t) = y]]$$

5. Conclusions

RML is a language which was crafted with the intention of providing users with a tool for stating requirements in the form of knowledge bases about some enterprise/world. RML shares this goal, as well as an orientation towards expressing the requirements in terms of objects organized in classes and related by properties, with several other research efforts, including [ROUS79], [BUBE80] and [BGW82]. RML is also related, though more distantly, to the work on requirements specification within the Entity-Relationship paradigm as presented in [DJNY83] for example. RML differs from the above languages and approaches in one or more of the following:

- A temporal view of the world is a fundamental part of any world model expressed in RML. Abbreviation facilities are however provided in order to allow temporal expressions to be eliminated when they are particularly simple.

- The dynamic aspects of the world are modeled by activities, which are treated uniformly with other parts of an RML model as objects in classes.

- RML demonstrates the utility of property categories as a way of expressing *concisely* commonly occurring semantic constraints on the relationships expressed by properties.

- More complex conditions constraining the possible situations allowed by the model can be expressed in a language with power equivalent to First Order Logic. More significantly, such assertions are integrated into the object-centered framework of the language. Among others, this allows assertions to be *organized* into taxonomies of classes, and by requiring assertions to be properties of objects, allows the application of property categories to them.

- Abbreviatory devices such as property binding and the elimination of predictable occurrences of special variables **this** and **now** make the statement of many constraints considerably shorter.

In summary, we believe that RML facilitates the task of stating precise and consistent specifications by providing organizational/abstraction principles, which structure large specifications and make them easier to construct and modify, as well as useful abbreviatory devices. Furthermore, by matching the features of RML with those of the TAXIS programing language, we hope to further facilitate the implementation of useful information systems.

We have presented a formal definition of the concepts in RML by giving a translation procedure from RML to a logic with temporal indices, and in this sense any RML specification is equivalent to some logical theory. However, RML makes it easier to gather, express and maintain such a set of axioms, especially when it gets large and complex. The availability of a translation from RML to logic also acts as a specification for such important concepts as "a consistent specification" and "a consequence of this specification". Although we have not done so, we believe it would be straightforward to translate RML into a system such as STROBE [SMIT83]) so that the requirements models could be created and manipulated with the help of automated tools. An important component of any implementation would of course be a consistency checker (e.g., a theorem prover).

Concerning the axiomatization of RML, observe that much of what needs to be said about entities, events, and assertion objects can be stated once for all objects, with few additional axioms characterizing the three object types. This supports our contention that RML treats these concepts in a relatively uniform manner.

In conclusion, we intend our work to be attacking part of the problem described by [GHW82], where in these authors' experience, existing specification tools were found to be rigorously formal, or else usefully structured, but not both. At the same time, we view this work as a step towards the establishment of a multi-level framework [Jarke, this volume] for the construction and efficient implementation of knowledge bases, a function that we consider crucial to the development of KBMSs.

Acknowledgements

This chapter is a revised version of an article which is to appear in the journal *Information Systems*, and appears with the kind permission of its publisher, Pergamon Press. The research reported here was supported in part by the NSERC of Canada, and the NSF of USA under grant MCS-82-10193.

6. Appendix

6.1. Some issues in the selection of a formal semantics for RML

The semantics of RML is to be described by presenting a method for translating an arbitrary RML specification into a set of assertions in a Predicate Calculus.

It appeared advantageous to use some logic as the language in which the meaning of RML is expressed because (i) Assertions in some form are already part of RML, (ii) Logics come ready-made with notions such as "consistency" and "deduction", which are relevant for a requirements language, (iii) There has been considerable work on automatic deduction, especially with First Order Languages, work which can be incorporated into computer tools that assist users in developing proper requirements.

The choice of a logical language was motivated by additional considerations. First, RML is a *specification* language, whose intended use is to place *constraints* on the potential systems implementations, with minimal possible interference with the task of the implementor; in RML one has the ability to be as precise as desired, but also to be vague. This is in contrast with languages such as programming languages, which, relatively speaking, are geared to uniformly precise specifications.

A second important characteristic of requirements languages is that they are almost always used to model or describe dynamic, as opposed to static, enterprises. This makes the notions of events and changes, together with some idea of time, of central importance to the language.

Accepting time or change as a basic fact, one is still left with a number of questions about the nature of objects and events that may occur. Is time viewed as a sequence of static snapshots so that one can always ask about "the next state"? Tied to this is usually the existence of an assumption (a general "frame axiom") that there are no changes in the domain of interest unless some *specified* event has caused them. In a requirements specification language, it would seem appropriate that the designer be required to expend extra effort in order to state such a condition as a constraint, since it limits the possible implementations. For this reason, we have chosen not to use one of the traditional programming logics, or temporal logics for programming systems ([BMP81], [DCF82]).

We have chosen to avoid more complex systems such as temporal or tense logics (e.g., [RU71], [SERN80]), or intensional logics (e.g. [MONT73]), because they do not provide any additional expressive power, only expressive convenience. Since we have ourselves built into RML several techniques for facilitating the expression of requirements, these logics are inappropriate because of their complexity, including the absence of significant automatic theorem proving capabilities in these domains. However, there is nothing to prevent us from offering the abbreviations proposed in temporal logics (e.g., a default **now** time, abbreviations for "P until Q", etc.) to *users of RML*.

The traditional way of extending a First Order language to deal with change is through the *situational calculus* ([MCCA68]), where an extra argument is added to all time-dependent functions and predicates, while events are specified through predicates on the situations they "connect". Within this general framework, several alternatives arise as to the nature of the "situations".

The weakest assumption, one adopted in programming logics and papers like [DCF82] and [MCCA68], is that there is no constraint on the ordering of situations. This, however, is obtained by modeling events as "state changes" (sets of pairs of states). This does not allow one to talk about what may happen *while* an event is occurring, and makes it difficult to talk about durations of event occurrences, among others.

It is also possible to consider time as a partial order of time points, as done in [MCDE81], [MCCA81], and tense logics, with several possible futures such that each is a total order. This is advantageous for planning actions, revising beliefs or representing the meaning of English sentences referring to future possibility, but seems superfluous baggage for our purposes, since the specification can be taken to be a "God's eye-view" of the situation, and we are not concerned with providing a formal system in which one can reason on how to achieve certain goals.

We are thus led to a metaphysically linear view of time. In the present work, we have chosen the conservative approach of using *time points* as indices, because it is relatively well understood; we are however investigating the alternative of using time intervals as primitives, as suggested in [ALLE83], since this approach avoids some thorny problems about what happens at the time points where one event starts immediately when another one stops.

6.2. On the exact nature of the formal language used

The logical language which we use for expressing the semantics of RML is a *many sorted first order language*, which has

- A non-empty set of sorts S, which in our case are not assumed to be mutually disjoint,

- A potentially infinite collection of variable symbols, each belonging to some of the sorts,

- For each n, a collection of n-ary predicate symbols, each associated with one or more *sort signatures*, which are n-ary vectors of elements in S; intuitively, each signature specifies the sort of the corresponding arguments for the predicate,

- For each n, a collection of n-ary function symbols, each associated with one or more sort signatures, which are $(n+1)$-vectors of S, and specify the sort of the arguments of the function as well as the sort of the function value,

- The standard formation rules using logical symbols $\wedge, \vee, \tilde{}, \Rightarrow, \Leftrightarrow, \forall$ and $\exists$.

Traditionally, the sorts are supposed to be distinct (i.e., an object is of one sort only), and predicates/functions have a single sort signature. We have chosen our modified definition since it considerably simplifies our task of description and because the construction in [ENDE72], which shows the equivalence of ordinary many sorted logic to standard logic, can be trivially modified to allow for the variations used here.

We extend this language with the special binary predicate $=$, and its complement $\neq$, to introduce the notion of identity. In order to deal with time, we assume a special sort T whose elements are linearly ordered by the predicates $\leqslant_T$ (before) and $=_T$ (equality for time). For convenience, strict precedence $<_T$ for time is defined in the obvious way (Hereafter, we will omit the subscript since the sort of the equality can always be determined from the context).

The remaining objects in the world are divided into four sorts: D, E, A and P, corresponding to entities, activities, assertions and properties (attributes). The first three each have subsorts: **Token, Class** and **Meta class**, so in fact there are 10 basic sorts all together. It will also be convenient to have sort **Element** representing **Token** U **Class**.

The remainder of the formalization is presented in Section 4, but with the sort information left implicit, since it is easily deducible from the context.

7. References

[ALLE83] [BGW82] [BMP81] [BG81b] [BGM85] [BMW84] [BROD84] [BUBE80] [DCF82] [DJNY83] [ENDE72] [GHW82] [GMB82] [GREE84] [IEEE77] [JARK86] [LGSJ80] [MBW80] [MCCA68] [MCCA81] [MCDE81] [MCLE78] [MONT73] [MS81b] [ROSS77] [ROUS79] [RU71] [SERN80] [SMIT83] [SS77] [SWL83] [TH77]

33
Languages and The Engineering of Large Knowledge Bases

Alexander Borgida[1]

ABSTRACT *This position paper expresses the author's opinion that the development of large Knowledge Bases is subject to the problems traditionally encountered in Software Engineering, and that these problems can be addressed by developing new knowledge representation languages and environments that pay equal attention to a number of issues: expressive power, efficiency of implementation, ease of organization and modification, supporting tools and environments. These points are illustrated by briefly considering the problem of exceptional facts in a knowledge base.*

In a fundamental way, Knowledge Bases (KBs) and the programs that use them are *software systems*. When KBs reach the stage of routine industrial use, I believe that the entire range of software engineering issues from interviewing users to testing and maintenance will be relevant to their development. However, KBs appear to form yet another restricted subclass of software systems, like office systems, information management systems, or graphics systems; they have some distinctive commonalities that can be exploited to find better ways of building KBs than could have been done with general purpose techniques (e.g., Mylopoulos proposes in his chapter a new software development paradigm for Information Systems.) As with other areas of Computer Science, significant improvements will come with the discovery of appropriate *languages* in which to describe and communicate with the KB, and with *software systems supporting* the KB development and maintenance process.

---

[1] Department of Computer Science Rutgers University

In the past, Artificial Intelligence interest in KB languages has been largely centered on *expressive adequacy and ease* — being able to make the necessary distinctions and to do so conveniently, and more recently on *computational tractability* — being able to reason effectively with the knowledge. On the other hand, until recently, database research has been directed mainly towards efficient and safe access to large, shared, collections of facts.[2] Software Engineering (or, shall we say, Knowledge Engineering) adds to the above concerns such issues as *organizing* the KB conceptually in an effective manner, and supporting *modification* of the KB — likely the most effort-intensive activity in large KBs from the point of view of the people involved. I claim, therefore, that part of the challenge of designing appropriate Knowledge-Base Management Systems lies in the development of languages that meet the varied criteria imposed by the above concerns.

To illustrate the range of issues that arise, consider the problem of exceptional occurrences in KBs.[3] To express facts about the world, we make statements involving terms that must first be defined. Unfortunately, the real world is populated mostly by "*natural kinds*": concepts that lack clear definitions and for which we have at best only guidelines or prototypes. The first problem here, therefore, is one of **representation**: What are appropriate language features to deal with definitions of concepts that are "soft"? (See also the chapters by Israel and Levesque on Inference and Knowledge Representation.) In fact, one of the distinguishing features of the human world is its general unpredictability: except for synthetic, man-made, situations it is impossible to anticipate all possibilities, including what actions need to be taken. To support human problem solving, we must therefore provide ways to live with the unexpected. One possible solution which I have explored is based on the notion of exception-handling present in many programming languages.

Once we accept the need for such features, we must consider how they can be **effectively implemented**. The traditions of knowledge representation in LISP and record-based databases represent two extremes in the spectrum of dealing with special, exceptional circumstances. The LISP KB allows a distinct data structure for every fact, thereby accommodating exceptions perfectly: essentially every fact is exceptional! Also, arbitrary LISP code can be executed as part of an exception handler in systems like INTERLISP. The price we pay for this is two-fold: (i) Inefficiency of storage and access: large KBs of LISP

---

[2] Notable exceptions to this trend are apparent in this collection, and include work on deductive databases and Knowledge-Base Management Systems such as Probe.

[3] For more details, see [BORG85b]

structures are much slower to deal with than large databases, (ii) The expense of processing data: since every object can be exceptional in any aspect, programs manipulating them must always check for possible exceptions. Traditional database management systems, on the other hand, enforce uniformity through the notion of *schema*: at the time the database is designed, a fixed pattern of facts and constraints is imposed on all the data to be stored. The result is a gain in efficiency at the cost of flexibility: facts that do not fit the schema cannot be stored. We therefore seek a scheme that combines the flexibility of AI knowledge bases with the efficiency of large databases. Or, put another way, to combine the benefits of strong typing and compilation, with the flexibility of run-time type checking and run-time specification of alternative actions.

Finally, from the Software Engineering point of view, exceptions turn out to be an important form of **abstraction**: when first developing a KB, it seems natural to ignore the rare, special cases, which should then be considered in a second pass, following the major design steps; I call this abstraction "normalization" or "special case deferment". The language features for dealing with exceptional cases should then be designed to syntactically support normalization, for example, by making exceptional cases appear like annotations or footnotes.

In addition, a number of useful **computer tools** can be developed to deal with exceptions. If we mark exceptional cases explicitly, we can consider having tools that search the KB to find inconsistencies that may have crept in — a likely occurrence, if experience with standard databases is any indication. Furthermore, heuristic tools could be used to suggest improvements to the KB design, if exceptions become too numerous and patterns begin to emerge.

In summary, if we re to deal with exceptional values in KBs, we must address issues of expressive adequacy, efficiency of implementation, software/knowledge engineering aspects such as abstraction, and computer tools that manipulate and utilize exceptional values.

The above discussion of exceptions illustrates my view of a general paradigm of developing knowledge-base languages and environments, a view which I believe will be essential if Knowledge-Base Management Systems are to become useful, practical tools.

Acknowledgement

This research has been supported in part by the National Science Foundation, under grant MCS-82-10193, and by Rutgers CAIP.

34
Control of Search and Knowledge Acquisition in Large-Scale KBMS

Matthias Jarke[1]

ABSTRACT *Large-scale Knowledge-Base Management Systems (KBMS) will require strong control for reducing the cost of search/ query processing, and for preserving consistency within the KBMS and with the system to be modeled. In DBMS, control knowledge comes as data types, integrity constraints, and procedures embedded in the database schema. As a starting point for extending these concepts to KBMS, the paper studies the use of a database controller in a setting of expert systems - database coupling. The controller is a knowledge-based system that implements intelligent uses of integrity constraints outside the DBMS.*

Further requirements of integrity managers for KBMS are derived from the analysis of a current KBMS development effort in the domain of information systems analysis and design. It is demonstrated that consistency of the KBMS knowledge bases is feasible or even desirable only if "knowledge" is related to its origins and underlying assumptions or justifications. Knowledge sharing and negotiation among conflicting assumptions and goals emerge as crucial problems.

1. Introduction

Databases feature a two-level architecture. They contain a (usually large) set of uninterpreted data stored in records, files, and indexes, and a (typically much smaller) database schema that represents

---

[1] New York University and Johann Wolfgang Goethe-Universitat

metadata. This separation — which distinguishes databases from most AI knowledge representation schemes — has efficiency reasons. It would be very costly to provide full semantic information (or even pointers to such information, as, e.g., in semantic nets) with each data item, since many data items of the same type exist. Furthermore, polynomial time search procedures [IMME82] can be used, rather than potentially more expensive inference mechanisms.

The database schema serves two purposes. Deduction rules or view definitions typically associated with ANSI/SPARCs external schema help users interpret data and derive new information from the stored data. Data structures and integrity constraints of the conceptual schema provide control over database operations.

Much research in database implementation has been based on a 'small schema assumption': few metadata manage a large amount of base data. In Knowledge-Base Management Systems (KBMS), this assumption is no longer justified. We define a KBMS loosely as a hybrid of database and semantics capabilities; for instance, a relational DBMS together with the integrity rules, inference rules, and semantic relations used by the database designer to define the 'meaning' of the data. In KBMS, the amount of base data will remain large, but there will be an tremendous growth of metadata (often called 'general knowledge'). This growth will accelerate even more, if multiple users update the knowledge bases.

In previous work, we have (implicitly) assumed that it will be the number of deduction rules where most growth can be expected. Deduction rules are conveniently expressed in languages such as PROLOG. Consequently, we built a coupling mechanism [VCJ85; JV84] that associates a logic-based expert system managing the deduction rules, with a relational database management system for ground facts. The mechanism for optimization — located in the expert system [JCV84] or in a separate database controller [JARK84] — requires copying parts of the conceptual database schema into the optimizer.

Thus, the coupling architecture still assumes that the number of relation type definitions and integrity constraints is small enough, not only to allow copying, but also to require no more than a rather naive use of PROLOG's inference mechanism. This situation is not untypical; as [MB85] points out, efficient integrity management is one of the less understood areas of database research.

This paper is a preliminary study of the consequences of relaxing the small schema assumption for integrity constraints. It also proposes some concepts for solving the problems arising from this relaxation. Our main observation is that the transition from DBMS to (multiuser) KBMS reveals the subjective and volatile nature of knowledge in knowledge bases. The concept of integrity will have to be enhanced to capture notions of knowledge sharing and negotiation among different points of view.

As a theoretical foundation, section 2 briefly reviews a number of approaches for defining the logical semantics of integrity constraints. Section 3 presents recent techniques for efficiently utilizing integrity constraints in DBMS, and demonstrates their application in a database controller concept for expert system-database coupling. Section 4 analyses the additional control requirements in KBMS, using examples from multiperson-decision support systems and systems analysis and design tools. Section 5 summarizes these requirements and outlines solution strategies that seem workable in the 1990 scope.

2. The Logic Of Integrity Constraints

The traditional two-level architecture of databases has been formalized as a model-theoretic representation. In this section, we sketch this formalism and then trace how alternative methodologies have been developed by logic and database researchers. In essence, database researchers have usually worked on the schema level alone, developing design methods, query optimization techniques, etc., for specific types of integrity constraints. In contrast, researchers in logic focused on a proof-theoretic perspective that basically collapsed the two-level hierarchy into a single level of representation, the relational theory [REIT84]. For large schemas, as in KBMS, we propose an alternative generalization. Instead of collapsing the two-level, model-theoretic approach, we suggest its extension to a multi-level hierarchy. The three options (two-level model theory, single-level proof theory, and multi-level model theory) are summarized in Figure 1. Not shown is the object- or actor-oriented approach [HEWI85a, KRAS83] which represents a more "democratic" mode of communication.

2.1. Model-theoretic Formalization

According to the model-theoretic view [NG78], the DBMS divides its knowledge about the world in two parts: rules (the database intension) and facts (the database extension). Some of the rules are chosen as integrity constraints, the rest as deduction rules. Deduction rules describe how new facts can be derived from stored facts; integrity rules describe what facts can or must be stored. (Note that integrity rules are automatically also deduction rules; however, since they enforce the existence of their extension, their use for derivation is redundant. It does not really matter whether they are included in the deduction rules or not.) Each extension must satisfy the integrity

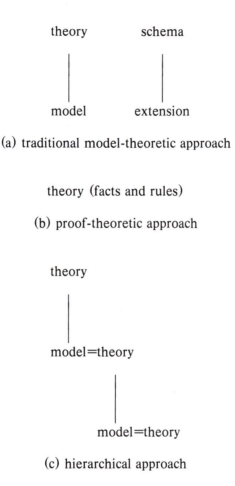

(a) traditional model-theoretic approach

theory (facts and rules)

(b) proof-theoretic approach

(c) hierarchical approach

Figure 1: Methods for Integrity Management in DBMS and KBMS

constraints in the following sense.

The database intension is understood as a theory of the world, and the database extension as an interpretation of that theory. An interpretation I is called a model of formula w iff w is true in I; a database extension D is a model of the set IC of integrity constraints iff D is a model of each w in IC. The integrity constraints are satisfied iff each database state is a model of them [NY78].

The model-theoretic view has the advantage of efficiency. Rather than testing the consistency of a new fact with the whole database, we can concentrate on the much smaller set of integrity constraints to check whether a database update violates our perception of the world. Of course, consistency (i.e., the absence of contradictions) must still be checked for the integrity constraints themselves; however, their number is assumed to be relatively small, and they are assumed to be relatively stable over time.

2.2. Proof-theoretic Formalization

In this approach, rules and facts are combined into a one-level relational theory. The set of answerable queries is the set of theorems provable from the theory, using standard first-order inference. In order to make this approach feasible, a number of completion axioms [REIT84] have to be added to the basic theory.

Since there is only a one-level theory, there can be no notion of integrity with respect to a higher-level theory. (Integrity with respect to the real world is an empirical question outside the scope of any system.) Therefore, the basic proof-theoretic approach tests for consistency and redundancy rather than integrity. If a new axiom (fact or rule) is added to the theory (=database), it is checked whether this fact is implied by existing axioms or contradicts them [BK82].

Another approach is followed in [REIT84]. The set IC of constraints is satisfied iff for each w in IC, w is *provable* from the theory (which, in this case, does not contain IC). We can use provability instead of truth in this approach, since, due to Reiter's careful choice of completion axioms, there is only one interpretation of the theory that is also a model.

This uniform solution is very elegant, and allows extensions of the theory to cover issues such as incomplete information and enhanced database semantics. [REIT84] himself points out that he is not concerned with efficiency issues. Indeed, as [BR84] show, the proposed generalizations may be computationally very expensive.

2.3. Hierarchical Knowledge-Base Management

To summarize the previous discussion, the proof-theoretic approach has more generality, but model-theoretic implementations seem more efficient in many cases. However, if the schema becomes very large, we may need metarules that decide when and how to use integrity constraints. Moreover, when some of the rules change frequently (e.g., in a design environment where the user experiments with constraints) it may be costly to check (or even undesirable to have) full consistency of all integrity constraints.

In such a case, we propose to extend the two-level hierarchy of DBMS to multiple levels of abstraction. In this architecture, each level must be a model of its immediate superior and becomes part of the theory for the levels below. Justification for the idea comes from three sources: experience in AI [SACE73; STEF81], a three-level hierarchy implemented in a database controller discussed in section 3, and the information design KBMS described in section 4. In all of these systems, there are several distinguishable levels of stability in the knowledge base that are well supported by the architecture shown in Figure 1(c).

3. Managing Integrity Constraints For DBMS

In this section, the role of integrity constraints in making DBMS behave correctly and efficiently is studied. The context is a KBMS architecture that couples deduction-based systems with DBMS through an independent entity we call a *database controller* (Figure 2). (Note that this system, although independently developed, could be seen as a highly simplified implementation of the architectures proposed in [SMIT84], and in the chapter by Manola and Brodie.) The controller knows at least the structures and integrity constraints of the DBMS schema [JCV84]. Its possible roles and functions in query processing, update execution, and rule management are now discussed and related to the key ideas database research has come up with for optimizing such operations.

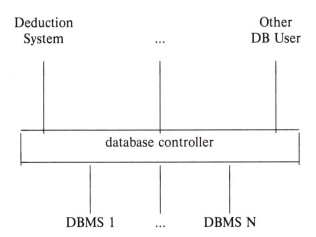

Figure 2: Coupled KBMS Architecture Using a Database Controller

3.1. Database design control

Integrity constraints in DBMS express stable knowledge about the real world. It is therefore not surprising that their most prominent use has been in database design [ULLM82]. The various forms of normalization essentially try to express integrity constraints through data structures that support a minimal subset of standard constraints.

Ideally, one would like to have a normal form in which the only constraints are domain dependencies, key dependencies, and referential integrity constraints among relations [FAGI81]. It would then be easy to enforce constraints during database updates and to utilize them for query optimization [JCV84]. Unfortunately, no normalization procedure fully achieves such a form. In other words, there will always remain a set of integrity constraints that must be expressed as more general predicates.

The same limitation applies to the so-called semantic data models [HM81] that associate procedures and integrity constraints directly with database objects. These models are based on programming language concepts of abstract data types [BROD80]. They give the programmer/designer much control over the definition of database objects, but may, at the same time, deprive the system of some scope for optimization. Moreover, the set of integrity constraints enforced automatically with most semantic data models is quite limited. Nevertheless, this approach has been followed in much recent 'expert database systems' research [SK84a]. Its main disadvantage for more general KBMS seems to be its 'objectivity'. The approach allows the designer to describe the world, but does not surface the designer's assumptions and goals (which might later be questioned if the same or another user works on the knowledge base).

3.2. Query Processing Control

The query processing subsystem of a DBMS (or an external optimizer) may employ integrity constraints to reduce the evaluation costs of queries. Methods for 'semantic query optimization' were developed almost simultaneously in database [ASU79a] and artifical intelligence [KING81] contexts. The underlying principle of both approaches is the same. Given a query predicate, P, we can add any relevant integrity constraints to it without changing the query outcome, since all integrity constraints are true by definition:

$$P \text{ AND } IC1 \text{ AND } IC2 \text{ AND } ... \text{ AND } ICn \Leftrightarrow P$$

Again, the difference between AI and DB approaches is one of generality versus efficiency. Database research focused on specific types of constraints together with special-purpose representations (e.g., tableaux [ASU79a] or query graphs [DST80]), whereas AI research discussed general first-order predicates [CFM84], together with general-purpose heuristics. We argue that both approaches should be combined in a flexible semantic query-optimization architecture, using database theory for a kernel of algorithms. The principle is shown in Figure 3. A collection of special-purpose algorithms based on database theory concepts and possibly AI heuristics ('query optimization experts') is controlled by metalevel rules that decide when and how to apply the special-purpose methods. The concept of 'capture rules' in [ULLM85] seems to follow a similar philosophy.

The implementation is based on the concept of expert systems - database coupling [VCJ85; JV84] rather than full integration. The optimizer is seen as a first step of a query-processing controller. As in a business, the controller is responsible for observing the strengths and weaknesses of the manager(s), for providing expert helpers in areas where a manager is weak, and for improving the inflow of transactions. It is easily seen from Figure 3, that decoupling the controller from its input and output systems allows the use of multiple user interfaces, as well as access to multiple (possibly heterogeneous) databases. Thus, an architecture that uses AI systems, databases, and an independent controller in between may be a feasible KBMS architecture, close to the requirements of [SMIT84]. Current work extends the system to the simultaneous optimization of multiple related queries [JARK85]. The enhanced controller will collect a batch of queries from one or more users, reorganize them by common subqueries, submit the reorganized (and usually smaller) batch to the database system(s), and monitor the further processing of the retrieved answers.

3.3. Fact Update Control

A fact update inserts, deletes, or replaces facts in a database extension, mapping a current database state into a new one. Integrity constraints determine the feasibility of a mapping. A constraint checker tests the validity of the new state (for static constraints) or of the change itself (for dynamic constraints). An early implementation introduced the principle of query modification for this purpose [STON75]. Query modification rejects invalid operations but does not automatically identify the culprit — violating data as well as violated integrity constraints [SV84].

Optimization algorithms for integrity checking reduce the number of tests and the costs of conducting them. The latter is closely related to query optimization issues, since constraint verification frequently

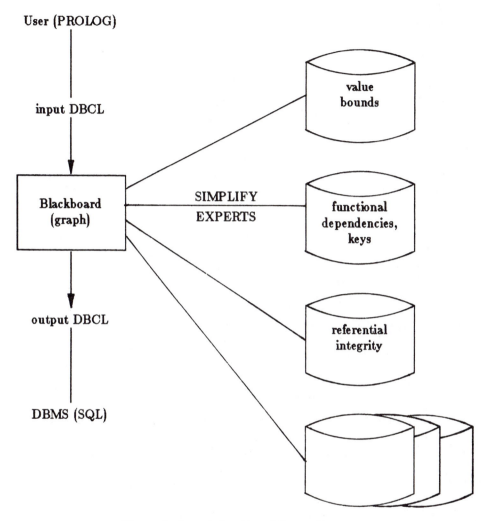

Figure 3: Knowledge-Based Query Optimizer

involves answering a database query. Constraint classification methods identify cases where such queries can be avoided, and the feasibility of an attempted update can be evaluated from metadata and operation specification alone. For example, testing key uniqueness requires a (simple) query in insert operations but none in delete operations.

Constraint simplification techniques exploit the fact that the database state, prior to an update, satisfies the integrity constraints

[NICO82]. This permits dropping a large subset of unaffected integrity constraints from consideration altogether; it also allows substantial simplification of the remaining assertions [BB82; SV84]. Moreover, many such tests can be performed prior to executing the update (i.e., based on the initial database state) and assertion simplification or compilation can be done at constraint definition time [HMN83; MORG84; SV84] (which — in DBMS, not in KBMS — is assumed to be the time of database design).

On the other hand, integrity checking can be delayed until the end of a transaction [WSK83] or even until data depending on the correctness of the update are used [LAFU82]. The latter approach is similar to tentative constraint posting in AI planning [STEF81]. While [LAFU82] demonstrates some performance advantages of this method, delayed integrity checking may increase the complexity of the tests and put long, expensive transactions at risk of being aborted after a large amount of work has been wasted. [SV84] propose a method for automatically generating checkpoints within such long transactions, to reduce this problem.

The optimization methods for integrity checking sketched above fit easily into the database controller structure. In fact, they even use the same knowledge bases. Thus, an extension of the semantic query optimizer to handle update integrity checking seems feasible. However, in contrast to the query processing case, update requests must not be batched with others (queries or updates), since concurrency control should remain in the DBMS domain.

Moreover, the previously discussed mechanisms only provide support for base data changes. If the context is extended to studying the controller's role in a KBMS coupling expert systems and databases (Figure 2), additional, subtle problems arise. On the one hand, updates to deduced facts correspond to view updates. They can be handled either by attempting to translate them back to base data updates [FC85]; or they could just be added as differential files to the deduction rule base, to be used as exceptions to the deduction rules. On the other hand, some views defined by deduction rules might be materialized, and these 'view indexes' [ROUS82; STZ84] must be maintained. Nevertheless, there seems to be no major obstacle to incorporating these aspects into the controller architecture, provided it offers adequate buffer management.

3.4. Rule Update Control

Beyond the notion of redundant integrity constraints [ULLM82], database research has contributed little to the question of how to change deduction or integrity rules. The main contributions in this area originate from AI, particularly from work in logic programming. To date, the most comprehensive study of metadata assimilation problems was done in the Japanese Fifth Generation Project [KKMF84] based on work by [KOWA81; BK82].

There are two major requirements for rule changes. First, any change should preserve satisfaction and internal consistency of the integrity constraints. Second, to reduce search costs, redundancy should be avoided unless specifically desired by the user. These requirements lead to the following algorithms.

Integrity constraints. Adding an integrity constraint leads to an exception, if it is not satisfied by the current database of facts and deduction rules. (Note that this includes the case of inconsistent integrity constraints; however, checking inconsistency first may save time.) If the new constraint is implied by existing constraints or implies that existing constraints are redundant, remove the redundant constraint. Deleting an integrity constraint is always possible, but may require recomputation of materialized views.

Deduction rules. Adding, deleting, or changing a deduction rule leads to an exception, if the new database state does not satisfy the integrity constraints. If insertion or change make any deduction rules (including the new ones) redundant, these can be removed.

Using the amalgamation of language and metalanguage proposed in [BK82], it is relatively easy to specify a proof-theoretic method for a straightforward implementation of these algorithms [KOWA81; KKMF84]. What is missing from the existing proposals, is a set of optimization strategies similar to the ones we found for the cases of query processing and fact updating.

For example, the implementation reported in [KKMF84] does not employ any assertion simplification unless manually defined by the user through an 'inconsistent' predicate in which possible violations are explicitly listed by update operation and condition. From the discussion in the previous subsection, we should expect that this could be automatically generated by the system. Here, substantial additional research is required. On the positive side, we notice that the metalevel evaluation strategy followed in the interaction of deduction system and database controller [VCJ85] carries over to the case of rule update. However, to enforce integrity at the deduction rule level, tighter integration of the database controller with the deduction system is required.

4. Integrity Requirements Of KBMS: Two Examples

The previous section discussed the feasibility of a database controller architecture for improving integrity rule management and utilization in KBMS configured by coupling deduction rule bases and fact databases. However, it is clear that these requirements, namely semantic query optimization and integrity maintenance in fact and rule updates, are insufficient for complex KBMS. In this section, two current KBMS projects serve as case studies to investigate further requirements.

4.1. Corporate Memory KBMS

A European car manufacturer has had some problems in its product design process. Two major departments, marketing and engineering, participate in a design. Each department imposes certain constraints on the process. Compromise decisions are reached and altered over several years. This process tends to work very well until close to the end, when many previous decisions and constraints are forgotten under time pressure, since there is no time for further interdepartmental consultation. In some cases, this has resulted in losses in the range of several millions.

In this context, we are developing a multiperson decision support system called MEDIATOR [JJS86] which supports a human mediator or group leader in conflict situations. As part of the data management component of this system, a simple logic-based KBMS is being designed for a network of personal computers. It is intended to provide managers of both departments with memory aids and consistency-checking mechanisms for previously accepted constraints and decisions. In building this system, two issues not covered by the previously discussed mechanisms were noticed.

First, while the need for data dictionaries at the data level is well established, there is a need for a data dictionary at the metadata level as well. This data dictionary should be used to map departmental terminologies. Since terminologies may differ significantly, there is otherwise no guarantee that relationships between constraints and decisions will be detected. Artificial intelligence for learning concepts and terminology simultaneously may be applicable [HH80; WINS79].

A second requirement, well known in expert systems, is a good explanation of the reasons for inconsistencies. This allows the user a choice to reconsider a proposed decision, or to remove an old one, with all its consequences. It has been shown in [JARK84] that integrity constraints can be a valuable help in generating such explanations, even in the simple case of query evaluation failure.

4.2. Information Systems Design KBMS

An information systems design can be understood as a hetero-geneous knowledge base consisting of knowledge representations for requirements documentation, database and transaction designs [BMW82], programs, etc. Traditionally, only the lower level representa-tions have been computerized, but recently there has been a trend to store 'runnable' specifications [BDFS82] or general requirements docu-mentation (see the chapter by Borgida et al.) as well.

In such a language environment, information systems design can be perceived as *a process of interactive, knowledge-base construction.* Hence, a workbench environment that helps designers develop a sys-tems design from requirements analysis through database and program implementation requires a fairly powerful KBMS. We are working on the initial design of such a KBMS; see also the chapter by Borgida et al. A sketch of the proposed architecture is provided in Figure 4. It cou-ples existing formal and semi-formal representations for data flow diagrams (SADT), conceptual modelling (see the chapter by Borgida et al.), rapid prototyping (PROLOG) and formal design (TAXIS [BMW82]) of database-centered information systems, and database pro-gramming (DBPL [SCHM84]).

Coupling among the layers is achieved in such a way that each layer of knowledge presents a set of integrity constraints for the next lower level. This matches the multilevel integrity hierarchy proposed in section 2.3. An attempt to implement a similar hierarchical KBMS for general systems analysis and design can be found in the frame-based system, PLEXSYS [KK84]. In addition, each layer also employs further domain-specific knowledge bases, as proposed in [JS84]. Part of the difficulties in mapping between layers is due to the fact that they address different goals: faithful representation of the real world versus efficient implementation. (Incidentally, but not co-incidentally, this corresponds nicely to the distinction between semantic and computa-tional theories of the world made in [MB85], or between knowledge and symbol level in the chapter by Levesque and Brachman.)

One consequence of this observation is that intermediate levels are needed; another is that automatic translation among the levels may be impossible, despite the introduction of specific additional knowledge bases. Another reason for the latter difficulty may be the presence of multiple participants in the design (see the left-hand side of Figure 4), with possibly different goals and assumptions. Negotiations [DS83; HEWI85a] may be needed to resolve inconsistencies based on indivi-dual differences.

The design process, and therefore the relationship among the lev-els, can be viewed as a process of successively imposing constraints (=

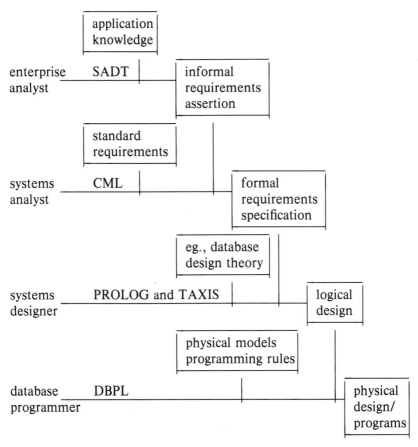

Figure 4: KBMS Architecture for Information Systems Design

adding knowledge) on the knowledge base. At first sight, these look like integrity constraints that could be easily accomodated by database techniques. However, these constraints may not follow the top-down layer structure and will usually come from different persons; moreover, each person may change his or her basic assumptions over time. The KBMS must therefore keep track of the design choices as well as of the assumptions underlying them. The need for keeping a record of versions and alternative configurations has also been recognized in CAD/CAM contexts (see the chapter by Katz et al.); the need for maintaining assumptions or beliefs has been studied in the context of so-called 'truth maintenance systems' [DOYL79]. These data are mostly needed to trace the consequences of local changes in the knowledge base, without requiring full consistency [MD80].

Surfacing the underlying assumptions is not an easy task. In [DJ85], a method is described that associates justifications with each design decision (i.e., design object), similar to [DOYL79]. However, there is also a learning mechanism that interactively generalizes the justifications in order to produce more general 'rules' used by the designer. These can subsequently be used to generate automatic justifications for new design objects, or even generate new design objects required by the rules, using an analogy-based reasoning mechanism [WINS79].

Finally, once decisions at lower levels have been made and implemented, their 'sunk costs' create new bottom-up constraints that reduce the flexibility of future choices (but also save future work). The KBMS needs tools that reflect design dependencies in order to accomodate modern methods, such as prototyping, which proceed concurrently at all levels, as well as ongoing systems maintenance.

5. Conclusion

The results of this paper can be summarized as follows. Expert systems - database coupling as proposed in [VCJ85; JV84] is a promising method for managing KBMS with large amounts of data and deduction rules but relatively small schema sizes and numbers of integrity constraints. If this 'small schema assumption' is not satisfied, a first improvement is a database controller architecture where a separate controller takes over major parts of the integrity management function for both the deduction rule base and the database. It was shown that functions like semantic query optimization, efficient integrity control during fact updates, and control of rule updates can all be accomodated in this architecture. It is expected that other AI methods for search control (such as Genesereth's procedural hints) can also be integrated.

However, several major KBMS requirements are not covered by these database-oriented methods. The following principles result from our discussion of two case studies. First, KBMS will be organized in abstraction levels corresponding (among other reasons) to levels of human or computerized decision making. Second, KBMS must be able to evolve in the presence of incomplete and subjective knowledge, making explicit the assumptions under which they operate. Levesque's 'K' operator ("the knowledge base knows that...") is a valuable tool but should be interpreted as: "the designer of the knowledge base used to believe that...".

The third and perhaps most important difference between DBMS and KBMS becomes obvious in the presence of multiple (writing) users. In the DBMS context, serializability [BG81a] guarantees execution of transactions equivalent to any serial sequence; other inconsistencies are prevented by the integrity constraints. In KBMS -- whether their users cooperate on a common problem or are in a bargaining situation -- there is a need for direct negotiation among conflicting viewpoints which is not offered by the existing or proposed transaction concepts. Fox and McDermott's chapter introduces an 'organization level' of knowledge management to address some of these problems. Another partial solution can be found in [DS83]. The chapter by Katz et al. proposes a database structure for a problem very similar to the information systems design KBMS that can be seen as complementary to the more process-oriented issues addressed here. Finally, if the KBMS is distributed, there is also a need for knowledge sharing and translation which in turn may lead to the detection of new inconsistencies and negotiations [HEWI85a].

6. References

[ASU79a] [BB82] [BDFS82] [BG81a] [BK82] [BMW82] [BR84] [BROD80] [CFM84] [DJ85] [DOYL79] [DS83] [DST80] [FAGI81] [FC85] [HEWI85a] [HH80] [HM81] [HMN83] [IMME82] [JARK84] [JARK85] [JCV84] [JJS86] [JS84] [JV84] [KING81] [KK84] [KKMF84] [KOWA81] [KRAS83] [LAFU82] [MB85] [MD80] [MORG84] [MB85] [NICO82] [NG78] [NY78] [REIT84] [ROUS82] [SACE73] [SCHM84] [SK84a] [SMIT84] [STEF81] [STON75] [STZ84] [SV84] [ULLM82] [ULLM85] [VCJ85] [WINS79] [WSK83]

Discussion

John Mylopoulos sees knowledge representation languages as playing a key role in the features, performance and the complexity of implementation of a KBMS in the same way a data model plays a key role on how easy or difficult it is to design, implement and use a DBMS.

There have been a number of features that have proven useful in Knowledge Representation and should be considered by the designers of a KBMS. For example, (a) default reasoning, as a way of dealing with ignorance and common-sense knowledge, (b) a "realization" association to represent the relationship between a concept and its implementation(s) (e.g., a stack and its linked-list implementation), (c) reflection as a means of representing knowledge about an agent's reasoning process, (d) justification as a way of keeping track of how (and why) a given assertion came to be in the knowledge base.

One should probably pick a subset of these (and other) features when trying to design a knowledge representation language, keeping in mind some of the considerations that Hector Levesque and Ron Brachman mentioned earlier.

John Mylopoulos then went on discuss his research involving the application of knowledge representation techniques to Databases and Software Engineering. In particular, he discussed a requirements modelling language under development: "...the traditional Software Engineering paradigm views requirements modelling as an activity whose aim is to provide a very abstract description of a system that is yet to be built, rather than a model of a world...We view requirements modelling primarily as a world modelling activity, and base the features of our language on knowledge representation techniques..." The language, called RML, uses a simple object-oriented framework which supports aggregation, generalization and classification, and includes an assertion sublanguage which allows for statements about the world. These assertions are themselves treated as objects.

Some of the weaknesses of the language are its size, its non-extensibility and its inability to deal with exceptions. Research on these and other issues is continuing.

Alex Borgida spoke about languages for expressing knowledge. He subscribes to the revolutionary approach to KBMS development.

He feels that knowledge representation language concerns have parallels with Programming Language research. The equivalents of compiler research is research into efficient forms of reasoning (e.g., suitable subsets of logic for which we know how to compute effectively). Also, he feels that Hector Levesque's Systems Engineering level might be better termed a Knowledge Engineering level to match software engineering. There is interesting research to be done on these aspects of knowledge representation languages, as there was on similar aspects in programming languages. As an example of some work already done in this direction, he offered the use of taxonomies, so prevalent in the AI area.

David Israel raised the question of the semantics of Alex Borgida's ideas for knowledge representation languages. Alex Borgida explained that the proposals he was making are not new semantic concepts. For example, Logic says nothing about how one organizes a set of formulas. David Israel felt that there are "other dimensions of expressive power, semantic dimensions...".

The idea of **Matthias Jarke's** work is to couple several small database systems, to permit them to communicate with each other. The focus of his work has been the coupling of relational databases and Prolog rule bases.

Much of the presentation followed the themes discussed in the session on Exception Handling and Constraints, such as how constraints are used and how optimisation is done. His system uses constraints for designing a database, checking fact updates and checking rule updates.

Optimisation can be done by compilation, assuming that rules do not change much over time and that constraints are satisfied before a set of operations is performed. By focussing on a few types of standard integrity constraints he can do some semantic query optimisation.

In response to a question by Frank Manola, Matthias Jarke said that his system does need to have knowledge of what the optimiser for the intermediate database language (e.g., SQL) is doing.

David Warren views logic programming as a means to integrate AI and database technology. He would like to build medium-size KBMSs (larger that current knowledge bases but smaller than current databases). His methodology favours an engineering approach, building down from current Prolog systems. An enhanced Prolog could provide secondary storage, better indexing, data persistence and recovery.

Mike Stonebraker noted that the order of clauses is significant in Prolog, which is not the case in relational databases. This is a problem that will be compounded in the context of a database with frequent updates.

David Warren gave examples of a query-answering system, written in Prolog. The database includes all the countries in the world and is kept in virtual memory. All rules in the database are indexed and pre-optimised through compilation. Queries, expressed in English, are translated to logic and optimized with respect to the database. Francois

Bancilhon noted that query optimization is only done for nonrecursive queries.

Gio Wiederhold asked how much reorganization would be required if there is a change in the database. David Warren responded that the database would have to be recompiled. It also seems that the different kinds of expected queries have to be given by the user in advance, to allow "compilation."

David Warren stated that speed-ups in inferencing will result from (a) the use of special processors, and (b) the exploitation of parallelism. He would also like to see an extended Prolog that would use secondary storage, more flexible and dynamic indexing, data persistence and recovery.

Turning to the fastest existing implementations, he presented the following list:

Implementation	Machine	LIPS
Edinburgh, Quintus	DEC2060	43000
Waterloo	IBM3033	27000
Quintus	VAX780	23000
Quintus	Sun-2	20000
Uppsala	LMI Lambda	8000
PopLog	VAX780	2000
M-Prolog	VAX780	2000
C-Prolog	VAX780	1500
MicroProlog	Z-80	240
Prolog-II	Apple-II	8
ESL Prolog	IBM PC	?

He expects that there will be hardware that allows speeds between 1 and 10 MegaLIPS by 1990. Some of the speedup will come from the development of Prolog processors that can process up to 500,000 LIPS. Further speedups have to come from the use of parallelism.

There was some discussion whether parallelism can speed up full unification. Dave DeWitt asked whether an extremely high-LIPS (logical inferences per second) machine could be fully exploited. If the data transfer rate from secondary storage cannot keep up with the processor, there will be a bottleneck. David Warren replied that in one part of their system, much more time is spent applying rules than retrieving facts.

Jeff Ullman asked whether the number of USEFUL LIPS can be greatly increased by straightforward introduction of parallelism. He was concerned with (a) all processors making the same inferences and (b) all processors making different inferences, which would not all be used unless things were run serially. David Warren responded that these problems can be avoided by guarding against duplication of processing and by exploiting "or" parallelism in search.

John Mylopoulos asked whether Prolog should be viewed as an alternative to a Lisp dialect or a knowledge representation language such as Krypton. David Warren replied that Prolog in its present form is a programming language that happens to have the functionality of pure Lisp and the basic functionality of a relational DBMS in terms of querying and query processing.

Part VII

Advanced Hardware for
Knowledge-Based Systems

35
New Computer Architectures: A Survey

W. Daniel Hillis[1]

ABSTRACT *Artificial intelligence and database computations have historically taxed the computational resources of available computers. There is every reason to believe that the integration of these two disciplines will be, if anything, even more demanding in this respect. It therefore makes sense to ask what kinds of computer architectures we might expect in the near future that will be able to deliver significantly greater raw computing power for this type of problem. This paper will summarize some of the most important design choices for the "new wave" of high- performance computers. It is an attempt to identify a design space in which most of the proposed supercomputer designs can be sensibly placed by listing common, key decisions that must be made in any design. To the first approximation these choices are independent, so that in principle there could be a different computer architecture for every combination of alternatives.*

The paper will only review general-purpose computer designs that are not linked to a particular algorithm or application. It will not discuss special-purpose hardware-assist devices such as database machines (RAP, CASM), systolic arrays for computing relational joins, content addressable memories, or specialized AI machines linked to a specific model of intelligence (Boltzman Machine, production machines). Instead, we will discuss the major design alternatives for building general- purpose computers with many orders of magnitude potential performance increase. By necessity these are all parallel computers involving multiple processing units. This is because there are fundamental physical limitations, such as the finite speed of light, which will limit the speed of conventional word-at-a-time computers to within,

---

[1] Thinking Machines Corporation

say, an order of magnitude the speed of existing machines. Parallel computers, on the other hand, have the potential of being hundreds of thousands of times faster, even in the near future.

Given a parallel machine with many processing units, how are they organized to work together on a problem? There are essentially four major issues, listed below, roughly in order of importance.

1. Fixed versus General Communication

In all parallel machines, some portion of the computation involves communication among the individual processing elements. In some machines such communication is allowed in only a few specific patterns defined by the hardware. For example, the processors may be arranged into a two-dimensional grid with each processor connected to its north, south, east, and west neighbor. A single operation on such a machine could send a number from each processor to its northern neighbor. Proposed connection patterns for such fixed-topology machines include rings, n-dimensional cubes, and binary trees. The alternative to a fixed topology is a general communications network that permits any processor to communicate with any other. An extreme example of an architecture with such a general communications scheme is Schwartz's hypothetical "para-computer", in which every processor can simultaneously access a common shared memory. In a para-computer, any two processors can communicate by referencing the same memory location. Depending on how such a general communications network is implemented, some pairs of processors may be able to communicate more quickly than others, but every pair can communicate. Even in general communications schemes, the supercomputer has an underlying, unchanging physical pattern of wires and cables, although it is invisible to the programmer.

The primary advantage of fixed-topology machines is simplicity. For problems where the hardwired pattern is well matched to the application, the fixed-topology machines can be faster. Examples of such matches are the use of a two-dimensional grid pattern for image processing, and a shuffle-exchange pattern for Fast Fourier Transforms. The general communications machines have the potential of being faster and easier to program for a wide range of problems, particularly problems that have less structured patterns of communication. Another potential advantage is that the connection pattern can change dynamically to optimize for particular data sets, or to bypass faulty components.

2. Coarse-Grained versus Fine-Grained

In any parallel computer with multiple processing elements, there is a trade-off between the number and the size of the processors. The conservative approach is to use as few as possible of the largest available processors. The conventional single processor von Neumann machine is the extreme case of this. The opposite approach is to achieve as much parallelism as possible by using a very large number of very small machines. We can characterize machines with tens or hundreds of relatively large processors (such as the Livermore S1 Multiprocessor) as "coarse-grained" and machines with tens of thousands to millions of small processors (such as the Goodyear MPP) as "fine-grained." There are also many intermediate possibilities.

The fine-grained processors have the potential of being faster because of the larger degree of parallelism. But more parallelism does not necessarily mean greater speed. Because the individual processors in the small-grained design are necessarily less powerful, many small processors can be slower than one large one. For almost any application there are at least some portions of the code that run most efficiently on a single processor. For this reason, fine-grained architectures are almost always designed to be used in conjunction with a conventional single-processor host computer.

Perhaps the most important issue here is one of programming style. Since essentially all serial machines would fall under the category of large-grained, the technology for programming these processors is better understood. For example, it is plausible to expect a Fortran compiler to optimize code to keep 16 processing units busy, but not 16 thousand. On the other hand, if the algorithm is written with parallel processing in mind from the start, it may be that it divides naturally into extremely large numbers of processors, a number that would be available only on small-grained machines. For example, in a vision application it may be most natural to specify a local algorithm to be performed on each point in the image, so a 1000 x 1000 image would most naturally fit onto a million processor machine.

3. SIMD versus MIMD

A MIMD (Multiple Instruction Multiple Data) machine is a collection of connected autonomous computers, each capable of executing its own program. Usually a MIMD machine will also include mechanisms for synchronizing operations between processors, when desired. In an SIMD (Single Instruction Multiple Data) machine, all processors are controlled from a single instruction stream which is broadcast to all the processing elements simultaneously. Typically, each processor has the option of executing an instruction or ignoring it, depending on the processor's internal state. Thus, while every processing element does not necessarily execute the same sequence of instructions, each processor is presented with the same sequence. Processors not executing must "wait out", while the active processors execute. There are also intermediate possibilities in the SIMD/MIMD spectrum, SIMD processors with limited autonomy or MIMD processors with multiple processing elements per instruction stream.

Although SIMD machines have only one instruction stream, they differ from MIMD machines by no more than a multiplicative constant in speed. A SIMD machine can simulate a MIMD machine in linear time by executing an interpreter which interprets each processor's data as instructions. Similarly, a MIMD machine can simulate a SIMD. Such a simulation of a MIMD machine with a SIMD machine (or vice versa) may or may not be a desirable thing to do, but the possibility at least reduces the question from one of philosophy to one of engineering: since both types of machines can do the same thing, which can do it faster or with less hardware?

The correct choice may depend on the application. For well-structured problems with regular patterns of control, SIMD machines have the edge, because more of the hardware is devoted to operations on the data. This is because the SIMD machine, with only one instruction stream, can share most of its control hardware among all processors. In applications where the control flow required of each processing element is complex and data-dependent, MIMD architecture may have an advantage. The shared instruction stream can follow only one branch of the code at a time, so each possible branch must be executed in sequence, while the uninterested processor "waits out". The result is that processors in a SIMD machine may sit idle much of the time.

The other issue in choosing between a SIMD and a MIMD architecture is one of programmability. Here there are arguments on both sides. The SIMD machine eliminates problems of synchronization. On the other hand, it does so by taking away the possibility of operating asynchronously. Since either type of machine can efficiently emulate the other, it may be desirable to choose one style for programming and the other for hardware.

4. Numeric versus Symbolic Processors

What is the difference between a "number cruncher" and a super-computer designed for symbolic processing? There are many architectures that operate extremely well for one type of operation and poorly for the other, and a few that perform reasonably well in both cases. So there is a real distinction. Since all the data operated upon by computer are internally represented as numbers, it is not exactly a distinction between numbers and symbols, but between different types of numbers and different mixes of operations upon them. Number crunchers are optimized primarily for arithmetic operations on large (usually floating point) numbers. In a typical symbolic application, multiplies and divides are rare, and floating point numbers rarer. Symbolic processors are optimized for memory reference, control flow, and secondarily for logical/arithmetic operations on small, variable-length, fixed-point numbers. In a typical symbolic application, a large percentage of the machine's time is spent in the overhead of subroutine calls, set up for non-local exits, context switching, etc. There is also a difference between symbolic and numeric computation in the complexity of data structures. In symbolic applications, data structures tend to be complex, linked, pointer patterns, scattered through memory. In numeric applications, the most common data structure is a linearly allocated array or vector. This regularity allows the efficient use of vector operations provided by machines like the Cray I.

Another difference, at least for the present, is the relative amount of time spent in program development versus program execution. Most machine utilization for symbolic processing in the United States today is for program development, rather than for program execution. The reverse is probably true for numeric applications. Part of the reason is that most symbolic applications are still in the research or testing stages, but another part is that the symbolic programs, such as Artificial Intelligence programs, are complicated, and difficult to debug. This means that hardware support of debugging and exception-detection features, such as runtime type checking, are more important for symbolic applications. This will probably remain true in the foreseeable future.

In summary, the general-purpose, high-speed computers of the future will almost certainly be parallel architectures with many processing units. How these units will communicate, how big they will be, how they will be controlled, and how many there will be are all questions that are yet to be determined. And, indeed, they will probably be determined in different ways for different machines. In any case, we can look forward to many orders of magnitude increase in raw computing power.

36
The Role Of Massive Memory In Knowledge-Base Management Systems

Richard Cullingford
Hector Garcia-Molina
Richard Lipton[1]

ABSTRACT *The Knowledge-Base Management Systems of the future will certainly require high performance hardware to cope with the substantial processing and data storage requirements. Many researchers have associated this "high performance hardware" with highly parallel computers (i.e., machines with large numbers of processing elements). In this paper we argue that this may not be the only choice. A computer with a single, high-performance processor and with massive amount of physical main memory, say on the order of tens of billions of bytes, may be especially well suited for some KBMS functions, and may vastly outperform parallel machines (with more limited memory). In this paper we outline the applications of such a machine, discussing its strengths and limitations.*

1. Introduction

A new project has recently been started up at Princeton University, in order to investigate the uses and power of large amounts of physical memory. Our central thesis is that the availability of massive amounts of physical memory, on the order of tens of billions of bytes, will change in fundamental ways how certain classes of problems are

[1] Department of Electrical Engineering and Computer Science Princeton University Princeton, N.J. 08544

solved. We also believe that this memory can be efficiently exploited by a single, high-performance processor. The programs developed for this SISD machine will trade the available space for running time, and may lead to orders of magnitude performance improvements. Even supercomputers with huge numbers of parallel-processing elements (but without massive memory) may be outperformed by a massive memory machine on memory intensive applications.

In this paper we will give a brief overview of our project, concentrating on the role that massive memory may play in a knowledge- base management system. In the next section, we present the case for a massive memory machine in a general framework. In section 3 we discuss possible database applications, and in section 4 we study how various artificial intelligence systems could take advantage of a massive memory database.

2. The Case For Massive Memory

The most immediate reason for our interest in massive memory is memory pricing trends. Memory prices are dropping very fast, currently faster than processor prices, and a massive memory will soon be economically feasible. Even at today's prices, the cost of the integrated circuits necessary to build a one gigabyte memory is below one million dollars. A complete computer may cost several times this amount, but this is still not out of proportion with the investment necessary to equip state-of-the-art installations for research or production work. Furthermore, if the price trends hold [WITH83], by the end of the decade the same million dollars will purchase about 20 gigabytes.

There are, incidentally, a number of challenging hardware problems that must be solved in order to connect the massive memory to a single processor, as we suggest. Although we do not discuss these problems in this paper, we believe that solutions exist. They range from ingenious packaging of devices to novel architectures. One candidate architecture is discussed in [GLV84].

Large memories can improve performance in a direct way, especially in programs that manipulate large data structures and have poor data locality. Examples of these programs arise in VLSI design tools, artificial reasoning, numerical analysis of sparse structures, and database applications. When these programs run on conventional machines, they cause excessive paging (called thrashing). The solution is, of course, to have sufficient physical memory to hold a significant portion of the data.

For example, D. W. Clark [CLAR79] has analyzed in detail the data reference patterns of LISP programs, including a chemical structure generator and a parser for a speech understanding system. He reports that, in order to obtain a miss ratio[2] of 0.001, between 40 and 80 percent of the data space of the programs must be resident in memory. And even this miss ratio can slow down programs significantly. For instance, if we assume, as Clark does, that a reference to secondary memory takes 5000 times longer than a reference to primary memory, then the 0.001 miss ratio implies slowing down the program by a factor of 6.

In addition to the data reference time improvements, there is an even more compelling reason to go to massive memory. In many cases, problems can be solved in entirely new ways, taking advantage of the available memory. Specific examples will be given in the following two sections, when we discuss database and knowledge base systems. However, there are two central themes that arise in trading the available memory for running time:

1. *Data Structures.* Often, the chief bottleneck in a computation is the repeated retrieval of information from a large "table". As is well known, with the proper data structures it is often possible to do this retrieval very rapidly. For example, if the table changes slowly, then it is possible, via hashing, to do the lookups in constant time, independent of the size of the table. Thus, our strategy is to store the entire table in memory so that it can be accessed in this way. It is interesting to note that when enough memory is available for such data structures, the programs outperform any parallel computer, since no number of parallel processors can do lookups faster than constant time.

2. *Learning or Caching.* Often, in a program, it is necessary to re-evaluate the same functions. For example, this is very common in recursive computations. With enough memory, tremendous performance improvements are made possible by remembering values and subsequently looking them up, rather than recomputing them. Such a strategy of learning or caching clearly requires adequate memory to store computed values. It is again interesting to note that such a strategy can dominate any number of parallel processors: if the parallel processors must compute each value over and over, because they do not have adequate memory to store them, then they may run arbitrarily slower than the learning strategy.

In the above paragraphs, we have illustrated the power of memory by comparing to parallel processing. Before moving on, we should

---

[2] The miss ratio is computed as the number of data references that caused a page fault, divided by the total number of data references.

clarify a few points regarding parallel processing. First, we are not arguing that memory is "better" than parallel processors. Both resources are very powerful. However, we believe that in some problems one or the other is more valuable. Our goal is to identify the applications where memory is more useful (i.e., the applications where most operations involve searching and manipulating large amounts of data, as opposed to performing many computations on relatively small amounts of data).

We should also clarify that we *do not* dislike multiple processors. If we could have unlimited memories and at the same time huge numbers of fast processors, we would, of course, take them all. However, given our limited resources, we are investigating the approach of investing a disproportionate amount in memories. Other researchers are opting for huge numbers of parallel processors, but, of course, assuming a fixed system cost, their system will have much less memory than ours. On memory-intensive applications, such systems may be outperformed by a massive memory system, since it may hold a significant portion of the necessary data in main memory and it can build efficient auxiliary search structures.

Given that we want to invest heavily in memory, one could argue whether the remaining resources should be invested in a single processor or in a small number of possibly lower- performance processors. We are not ruling out any of these choices, but, for our project, we are initially concentrating on having a single, high-performance processor attached to the massive memory. (This processor could act as a back-end for other processors.) This has two main advantages. First, this extreme approach makes it easier to evaluate the power of massive memory, since all of the performance gains will come from it.

Second, and perhaps more importantly, having a SISD machine greatly simplifies the system.   From the point of view of a programmer, the machine is conventional, and learning to use it will be trivial. Problems of concurrent access to memory are eliminated.

Furthermore, the availability of massive memory on a single processor will make it possible to write *data-driven* or *interpretive* programs. For these, one writes a very simple control or monitor program which uniformly retrieves data objects that are "instructions." Programs written in this fashion are simple to understand and easy to expand. Current AI rule-based [SHOR76] and production-system techniques [WH78] are examples of a data-driven programming style. These approaches have not been popular heretofore, because they tend to be slow with respect to a monolithic approach. However, a large part of the cost lies in simply accessing the required objects more or less randomly. This cost is high in a standard virtual memory system, but would not be in a massive memory machine.

3. Database Applications

Let us now consider how massive memory can be effectively utilized in a database system. Specifically, let us assume that the entire database can reside in main memory. Let us also concentrate on a type of database system that can best exploit memory: a transaction processing system. In such a system, almost all database requests, or transactions, are short, pre-compiled, and pre-loaded. Transaction processing systems are common in commercial applications such as airline reservation and inventory control. At the same time, we believe that this type of system may be common in knowledge-base management systems (KBMS). Here the database contains production or inference rules, and it must be queried repeatedly for the next rule to apply. In commercial systems, the number of CPU instructions that must be executed per transaction is small, typically between 1,000 and 10,000, not counting instructions needed for communication protocols and other system overhead. Similarly, in a KBMS, we would expect the number of instructions necessary for retrieving a rule to be in this range.

Clearly, having the database in fast memory will eliminate disk read and write delays, and will improve the performance of the system. But the impact of massive memory may be more far reaching than this. It may completely alter the structure of the system, eliminate much of the overhead, and lead to even greater performance improvements [DEWI84, GRAY83, HAGM84].

For instance, disk data structures like B-trees and indexed sequential files can be replaced with simpler, more efficient structures like hashing and binary trees. Updates to these structures will also be much simpler (e.g., there will be no need for overflow files). Since the data will be in memory, buffer management is no longer needed. As a matter of fact, concurrency control may be unnecessary: Since transactions are short, and encounter no disk delays, it is simpler and more efficient to process them sequentially. (This, of course, guarantees serializability.)

Thus, in this system, most of the work performed will be useful. If transactions take between 1,000 and 10,000 instructions, then a 10 MIPS processor will have a rate of 1,000 to 10,000 transactions per second, much higher that what is currently available on any system.

There are, however, certain questions that must be answered. For instance, is it reasonable to assume that the entire database can reside in main memory? Are the computational needs of KBMS transactions actually this small, or, in other words, would it not be preferable to have multiple processors accessing the database for additional computational power? If the database is memory-resident, how is transaction atomicity guaranteed in the face of failures? How can a 20 or more gigabyte be loaded into memory in a reasonable amount of time after a power failure wiped out the memory-resident database? In the rest of this section we briefly address these questions.

Obviously, databases come in all sizes, so a memory-resident database system will not be for all applications. However, let us make a few observations. First, in high throughput applications like the ones we are addressing, "the database" may contain large portions of archive or seldomly-accessed data, and this need not reside in memory. For example, in a credit card application, data giving the customer's name, address, current charges, and current credit limit constitute part of the high throughput database. The customer's credit history and data on his original application, on the other hand, are not part of this database, and can be handled in a conventional fashion.

Second, as we discussed in section 2, we expect a 20 gigabyte machine to be feasible by the end of the decade, and there are today several important data or knowledge bases in this range [GRAY79]. (Note that today a 20 gigabyte database requires 50 disk drives with 400 megabytes each, costing about half a million dollars.) Some KBMS applications with this type of requirement will be given in the next section.

Third, one could argue that, as memory sizes grow, data or knowledge-base sizes will grow just as rapidly, and hence memories would never catch up. This may be true in some applications (e.g., databases for satellite images), but many others have bounded or slow-growing requirements. For instance, in the lexicon learning system to be discussed in section 4, it is clear that the size of the English language is fairly stable. In a banking application, the number of accounts is related to the number of customers in a community, and this number is not doubling every two or three years as memory densities are.

Another set of questions regards the interface of the massive memory data or knowledge base to the rest of the system. There are many options here, but we currently favor attaching the massive memory to a single, high-performance processor. It would be responsible for all data searching and manipulating within the database. If there are additional, non-database computations that must be performed (e.g., communications protocols for remote teller machines, or complex inferencing), they can be executed elsewhere. That is, the massive memory and its processor become a back-end data server to the rest of the system. The reason for our choice is simplicity. We believe that a single processor can effectively process the transactions we are interested in (i.e., those with few computational requirements but significant data needs). On the other hand, if multiple processors access the database, we re-introduce the problems of concurrency control.

As we have argued, massive memory can simplify and improve the performance of a transaction-processing system, but, unfortunately, there may be one important "catch": crash recovery [HAGM84]. One complication is simply the number of components. A massive memory machine, as well as other types of supercomputers, has a large number of components, and this increases the probability of failure. However, in the case of massive memory, the components are highly regular (i.e., RAM chips) and techniques for improving reliability are well understood. Specifically, error detection and correction codes can be used, with chip overheads between 10 and 40 percent, depending on the degree of protection desired [SS82a].

A second, more serious, complication is that main memory, unlike disk, is volatile. As is well known, to tolerate a CPU crash or a media failure, we need at least two copies of the database (one can be a backup plus a log), and one of the copies must be non-volatile. In our case, the second copy must be the non-volatile one. The critical point then, is to update this second copy efficiently, *without sacrificing the performance gains brought about by the massive memory.*

There are a number of potential solutions. One simple one is to have two massive memories, two copies of the database, and a motor-generator unit for backup power. Memory writes would be performed on both memories, and hence, without any overhead, both copies would be up to date. If one of the memories fails, the second one would be available. The drawback to this solution is its cost. Doubling the memory will almost double the cost of the system. Furthermore, the backup power unit may also be expensive.

A second, more reasonable, solution is to store the second database copy on disk. This copy can be kept in the form of a database dump plus a update log. Conventional logging techniques can be used to ensure that changes to the database are recorded on disk before the actual database is modified. Although the logging techniques can be optimized for a massive memory database system [DEWI84, HAGM84], there are still potential problems: (1) Transactions must wait until their log record(s) is flushed out to disk before committing, and (2) Substantial overhead is involved in logging. Specifically, transactions cannot modify the database directly. They must instead copy the portions they will modify to buffers and, after the log entry is flushed, they must copy the modified buffers back to the database. This overhead can be significant, especially in a transaction that only has to execute 1,000 to 10,000 actual instructions on the database.

Because of these problems, we have been investigating a slightly different approach. The idea is to the update logging with a dedicated hardware device we call HALO. Its salient features are:

(a) It avoids disk delays by initially storing the log on fast, non-volatile memory. As time permits, the log is then written out to disk.

(b) Log entries are made at the word level, as opposed to the record level. This makes it possible to update the main database copy directly, without recourse to buffers.

(c) The logging is transparent to the transaction. When a transaction starts, HALO is informed and makes a begin transaction entry. All subsequent memory writes cause a log record to be created with the address involved and the old and new data values. When the transaction terminates, HALO is again informed, and an end transaction entry is made.

(d) If a crash occurs, HALO simply undoes the changes made by the currently executing transaction.

(e) If the main memory database is lost, the backup copy is loaded and the updates since the backup are played back.

We believe that such a device can remove most of the crash recovery burden from the transactions, and actually make it possible to achieve the high transaction rates we are after. The details of HALO are given in [GLH83].

Another related problem is that of managing the backup database copy. There are two steps involved in restoring a lost database. The first is to load the backup database into main memory. For this, it is clearly desirable to have multiple I/O paths, so that data can be read off various disk drives and loaded into memory in parallel. This technique is known as *striping* [SG84]. Incidentally, striping can also be useful in writing the transaction update log to disk.

The second step involves bringing the newly loaded backup database up to date. This can be achieved by re-executing the database updates that occurred after the last dump. These updates have been stored in the transaction log. In order to reduce the time it takes to play back these updates, the database should be dumped frequently. Note that transaction processing need not be brought to a halt for each dump. A so called *fuzzy dump* [ROSE78] can be taken as transactions are processed. Even though the backup database will be inconsistent, it can easily be made consistent by playing back the updates that occurred during the dump (which were saved in the transaction log).

4. Artificial Intelligence Applications

AI systems are notorious for their appetite for huge amounts of memory. Mostly, this is because of the large number of symbolic forms (usually heap-allocated) that one needs to do a reasonable job of representing the knowledge content (rules, facts, plans, and the like) of an application domain. The problem with storing such knowledge bases under a standard virtual memory regime is that access to the records/objects encoding the unit forms of the knowledge representation is likely to be essentially random. Although it is true that memory reference patterns are likely to be quite localized in such objects once they are found, the virtual memory system will typically be taking "hits" all over the address space as the AI program asks for objects. Thus, massive real memory can be expected to improve the access time for finding the objects tremendously, and thus the overall performance of the application program. We illustrate this argument with two research examples of current interest in AI and cognitive science.

4.1. Circumlocuting an On-Line Dictionary

On-line dictionaries of natural languages are extremely useful tools in a number of research areas of computer science, linguistics, and cognitive psychology. In artificial intelligence (AI), for example, associations between words and symbolic structures representing their meanings (word senses) are the basic data items used by programs which attempt to "understand" and "generate" natural language. Computational linguists are interested in the kinds of grammatical constructions the words of the language can enter into. As a third example, psycholinguists study the clustering of concepts (semantic fields) around words acquired by speakers of a language, by examining the usage of synonyms and near-synonyms of the words. These kinds of information, and more, are in principle obtainable from modern dictionaries such as the *Longman Dictionary of Contemporary English* [LONG81].

The use of such information, however, is hampered by the sheer magnitude of the data contained in a reasonably complete dictionary. In the Longman's dictionary cited above, for example, there are roughly 120,000 entries, each accompanied by several sentences describing usage, structural (e.g., syntactic) information, and pronunciation and other data. Even when the textual data is available in digital form, the amount of storage required for it (in the order of hundreds of millions of characters and up) overwhelms the primary memory capacity of all but a very few current supercomputer systems.

Why are we concerned with main-memory considerations in tasks involving on-line dictionaries? The answer lies in the essentially random-access, intricately interlocking nature of the patterns of word usage in a sentence. Note that the *sentence* is the main unit of comprehension in tasks such as machine understanding or determination of semantic fields. To a first approximation, the probability of access to a given word in a dictionary is independent of the lexical form of the words seen in a sentence so far. (The next word can be roughly predicted, however, by the *conceptual* content of the words already seen.) Thus, the time to *access* the information associated with a given word will be determined by the speed of the mass-storage subsystem rather than by main memory, in currently available computer memory hierarchies. The basic argument, then, for a massive memory in a project involving computations on tens or hundreds of thousands of words is that these computations are not feasible unless a large part of the dictionary resides in primary memory.

To make this argument concrete, we will describe a dictionary-using problem of intense current interest to practicioners of both AI and psycholinguistics. Then we will sketch how a processor with a massive memory might be used to help solve it.

The basic aim is to make available to the machine a database of word senses, pairings of lexical items and meaning structures, for a significant fraction of English. Our approach to the problem is based on the simple observation that words are usually defined, both in dictionaries and in everyday use, by *circumlocution.* In a dictionary, for example, a word (sense) will be defined in terms of sentences made up of other words. Many standard dictionaries, unfortunately, tend to be circular: a sizable fraction of the words are defined in terms of other words whose definitions end up involving the originals. The important feature of a dictionary like the Longman's, which is intended to support the learning of English as a second language, is that all the words are defined in terms of a *core vocabulary* and no others. Thus, if we can provide definitions of the core lexicon (which has about 2000 entries in the Longman's), and a conceptual analyzer of sufficient power, we can envision the acquisition of the remaining dictionary items by *associating each item with the conceptual structure built by the analyzer for the defining sentence(s).*

Consider, for example, the following definition of one sense of the word "complain," as given in the Longman's: "to express feelings of annoyance, pain, unhappiness, dissatisfaction, grief, etc. The words in the definition belong to the core vocabulary, and can be combined (by an analysis process described in [CULL85]) into a symbolic meaning structure such as:

Example 1:
(mtrans actor (person)
    to (cp part (person))
    from (cp part (person))
    mobj
        (cause con1 (episode)
           con2
           (s-change actor (person)
               attr (anger val (-3)))))
equivalences
(((actor)(from part)(mobj con2 actor)))

This representation, a data structure of the programming language Lisp, is based upon the semantic representational formalism called *conceptual dependency* [SCHA75, CULL85]. (Several other choices for the representation scheme are available.) The meaning structure expresses what it means to "complain" in terms of the following paraphrase: "there was a mental transfer *(mtrans)* of information between the mind of one person and that of a second such that the occurrence of a certain real-world episode lead to a negative change in the first person's current state of anger." Or, to put it another way, "someone told someone else that something happened which resulted in the first party's becoming angry."

To make the analysis procedure possible, several things have had to be done to the basic defining sentence. First, we have had to *expand ellipses*. Definitional sentences typically leave the reader to infer the nature of characteristic actors and objects in events. That is, the defining sentence is really an ellipsed form of a sentence such as "Walter told Geraldine that he (Walter) was annoyed by Ronald's remarks on TV." The fact that it is *people* that express and hear complaints has to be made explicit. Secondly, there is a process of *generalization* that must be mechanized, which would specify (perhaps by examination of a series of examples) that *episodes* are things to get annoyed about, or that "complain" refers to feelings of "annoyance, pain, grief" (i.e., *negative mental state-changes*).

The theory and technology of knowledge representation and conceptual analysis has begun to reach a level of development where automation of a dictionary-acquiring task along the lines sketched above is possible. What is needed is a machine capable of storing the lexical/structural/symbolic information associated with the core vocabulary in primary memory, so that access to the core items is very fast as sentences are read. We can envision either a straight dictionary-definition construction scheme in which the words of the main dictionary are read out one after the other in alphabetical order, or, more intriguingly, in terms of *semantic field* pointers. In the latter case, the dictionary would be built by defining a "key" word as sketched above, then defining "nearby" words as specified by synonyms, near-synonyms and antonyms, perhaps in a thesaurus such as Longman's.

What would be the memory requirements for such schemes? We estimate that the 2000 word core vocabulary actually contains 4-5 times as many word senses, for which symbolic structures such as (1) would have to be specified. (This is much too conservative for words such as "of" or "take", for which literally dozens of semantic readings exist. We are sketching out an order of magnitude argument here, however.) Analysis instructions would also have to be provided for the syntactic/semantic constituents the core words demand. Examination of a current conceptual analyzer [CULL85] suggests that the dictionary definitions that would need to be provided for the core words (which are extremely complicated) would amount to 500 lines of Lisp code per word sense. This is conservatively estimated as needing 40,000 characters worth of symbol and pointer storage per sense, or 400 Megabytes for the core dictionary. Compilation of the dictionary definitions and other symbolic computing techniques could bring this total down, but clearly a large memory supercomputer is required.

4.2. Belief Revision

Models of the process of commonsense reasoning must take into account two features of such reasoning. First, of course, we must handle the deduction of conclusions that follow logically from prior beliefs as well as those that are merely plausible projections from those beliefs. Secondly, commonsense reasoning often leads someone to abandon prior beliefs, for example, on discovering evidence that conflicts with those prior beliefs.

We are currently investigating the processes of belief revision by constructing an Artificial Reasoner (AR). The work is based on two recent research streams in cognitive science. First, it is based upon a body of ideas in AI about the reasoning process that goes under the rubrics of "non-monotonic" or "default" reasoning (e.g., MD80, MCAL80). Theories of this sort are concerned with the actual inference-making machinery of the reasoning process.

Second, this work is based on research on the consistency, coherence, or satisfactoriness of a reasoned set of beliefs, in particular as developed under the name "Reasoned Change in View." ([HARM85], in press, discusses this theory.) The combination of ideas of these kinds in a working AR is expected to suggest additional principles of human reasoning that differ in important respects from current systems.

To test our ideas about reasoning, we plan to apply the AR to a number of different practical domains, such as the simulation of a person learning how to get around in a new place. In any such domain, the size of the knowledge base (e.g., of contingent reasoning rules, facts currently "believed", etc.) quickly outgrows the available main memory, and the research bogs down. Like the lexicon learning project just described, access to the needed rules for keeping the reasoner going is essentially random in nature. Moreover, the "working set" of beliefs under revision is expected to be very large. Thus, a massive memory supercomputer is required for the "production runs" of an artificial reasoner.

Consider a scenario in which a reasoner already possessing a "coherent" set of beliefs about some real-world situation is given some new information which bears on those beliefs. In the cases of interest, inputs can be "contingent" in various interesting ways. They may be noisy and partially mistaken. Two inputs might contradict one another. The relevant reasoning will have to reach conclusions that are merely plausible projections from the data without being logical consequences of it. Furthermore, the domain evolves. New roads are built, repair work closes a bridge, troops are moved. All of these facets of belief revision are of direct concern to the AR.

For example, the AR might be given (possibly unreliable) information about the street map of Princeton. It must then extend its beliefs in various plausible ways, correcting errors to the best of its ability, and try to answer questions about how to get from one place to another. Clearly, the AR could go wrong in various ways. The data it gets may be inaccurate because its informant has confused left and right, has forgotten something, or has gotten the name of a street wrong. The AR may reach false conclusions from true premises merely via plausible reasoning. For instance, suppose the AR starts with the following information: (1) Princeton Street is parallel to and one block west of Harrison Street, (2) Aiken Avenue intersects Princeton Street. Then the AR may (incorrectly, as it happens) project an intersection between Aiken and Harrison.

Suppose the AR believes this: Going south on Princeton, starting at Nassau, the next street is Aiken, then Patton. Going east on Patton, the next street after Princeton is Harrison. Going north on Harrison, the next street after Patton is Aiken, and then Nassau. Going west on Nassau, the next street after Harrison is Princeton.
It is then asked how to get to Aiken Avenue from the intersection of Patton and Harrison. It concludes that the thing to do is to go north on

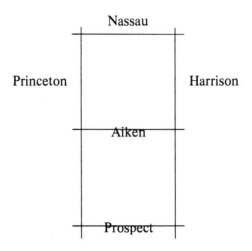

Figure 1

Harrison and the next road will be Aiken. But suppose the AR is now told that, going north on Harrison from Patton, the next street is Nassau. Then the AR must decide whether it was mistaken or this new information was mistaken. It does this by trying to leave as little as possible unexplained. If the AR supposes the informant is right, then it can suppose that the informant's opinion is the result of contact with the way things are. But then the AR may have no explanation of its own previous error. If the AR supposes the informant is mistaken, it can explain its own opinion (as deriving from contact with the way things are) but it may have no explanation of the informant's mistake. If a different informant agrees with the AR's previous opinion, then it leaves less unexplained (other things being equal) to suppose the first informant is wrong than to suppose the AR and the new informant are both wrong. If the AR remembers that it previously projected an intersection between Harrison and Aiken from the intersection at Princeton and Aiken, it may now infer that this projection is probably incorrect. It will then abandon its belief that Aiken intersects Harrison and will believe instead that Aiken does not go that far.

It will be relevant what the informant's reasons are for saying that the next intersection after Patton going North on Harrison is Nassau. If the informant has just gone and checked, that counts for more than if the informant's opinion is based on a more fallible projection from other considerations. However, the informant might be wrong even if he or she just checked (since a street sign might have been misread, a road might have been overlooked, etc.). The AR may or may not have

views about the informant's reasons (and what views it has are themselves fallible). Of course, the AR will often have to wait for more
data before it can decide what to believe.

The AR must allow not only for incorrect information about the
world but also for changes in the world. Repair work may make it
impossible any longer to get from Patton to Nassau on Harrison. Learning about the repair work will lead the AR to change its views about
how to get from one place to another, but after a time it must be ready
to try to find out whether the repair work has been completed and the
old route restored.

One thing we want to explore is the extent to which it is feasible
for the AR to keep track of its reasons for its current beliefs. People
have trouble with this, and it may be expensive in computer time and
memory to keep track of all reasons.

Problem-solving research of this kind in artificial intelligence is
typically conducted on machines of the supermini (e.g., DEC VAX-
11/780), "small mainframe" (e.g., DEC-20), or engineering workstation
(e.g., Symbolics Lisp Machine) class, using a symbolic computing
language such as Lisp or Prolog. Typical "rates of execution" for reasoning programs range from a few inferences per second to a few dozen
per second, depending on the machine type and timesharing load.
Total time for a solution run ranges from fractions of hours to several
hours.

An important reason for the low speeds of current reasoning systems is the limitation on the number of data items accessible to the
program because of main memory size. In an OPS83-type production
system [FORG84], for example, the functioning of the reasoner often
begins to bog down after a few thousand rules have been loaded. The
memory capacity required for the matching part of the productions and
the working memory is a significant fraction of the available main
memory, and the reasoner often slows to a crawl when the paging subsystem begins to run. Thus, it appears once again that a dedicated,
high-performance conventional computer with a massive memory may
make reasoning on knowledge bases having tens of thousands of items
practical.

Acknowledgements

This research was supported by the Defense Advanced Research
Projects Agency of the Department of Defense and by the Office of
Naval Research under Contracts Nos. N00014-85-C-0456 and N00014-
85-K-0465, and by the National Science Foundation under Cooperative
Agreement No. DCR-8420948. The views and conclusions contained

in this document are those of the authors and should not be interpreted as necessarily representing the official policies, either expressed or implied, of the Defense Advanced Research Projects Agency or the U.S. Government.

5. References

[CLAR79] [CULL85] [DEWI84] [FORG84] [GLH83] [GLV84] [GRAY79] [GRAY83] [HAGM84] [HARM85] [LONG81] [MCAL80] [MD80] [ROSE78] [SCHA75] [SG84] [SHOR76] [SS82a] [WH78] [WITH83]

37
Parallel Computers for AI Databases

W. Daniel Hillis[1]

ABSTRACT *A large modern computer contains about one square meter of silicon. This square meter contains roughly a billion transistors, each capable of switching up to a billion times per second, so with optimal utilization of components we could expect as many as 10^{18} interesting events per square meter per second. The human brain, for comparison, has about ten billion neurons. Coincidentally, they are also arranged in a sheet about one square meter in area. Each neuron can switch roughly a thousand times a second. A neuron connects to many other neurons, say 10^5. If we assume that each of these synapses is a switching component, then the number of interesting events per second could be as high as $10^{10} * 10^5 * 10^3 = 10^{18}$, or about the same as the computer.*

We do not really know enough about the mechanisms of the brain to make such a comparison, but since we would like to construct a thinking machine, the brain will have to serve as our only example. The result of the comparison is surprising and encouraging, especially when we consider the technical possibility of building computers with many square meters of semiconductor. Unfortunately, it is also misleading. Computers, as we build them today, are extremely inefficient in their use of components, and they become even less efficient as they become larger. The actual number of events per second per silicon square meter in a large computer today is less than a tenth of one percent of the number given above.

The reasons for the inefficiency are partly technical, but mostly historical. The basic forms of our architecture were developed under very different technologies, where different assumptions applied. Also, the problems that they were intended to solve have little similarity to

[1] Thinking Machines Corporation

the processes that underlie intelligence. The machine described here, the Connection Machine, is a step in the direction of fixing these problems. It is an architecture that better fits the technology and, hopefully, better fits the requirements of a machine that thinks.

One of the primary reasons why classical computers use their hardware resources inefficiently is that most of the silicon area is devoted to memory, and only a tiny fraction of the memory is being accessed at any given time. The bandwidth between memory and processor is typically the limiting factor on the performance of a machine. This single small path between the large memory and the large processor is what Backus [BACK78] called the "von Neumann bottleneck." The bigger we build our computers, the worse it gets.

Von Neumann and his colleagues were not stupid. In the days when wires were faster than switches and memory much cheaper than gates, it made a lot of sense to leave most of the memory and wires sitting around doing nothing as long as the expensive vacuum tubes were kept busy. The von Neumann architecture made sense. But today both memory and gates are made of the same sand, and it is the transmission of the signals over wires that is costly.

Signal transmission takes most of the time, burns most of the power, accounts for most of the failures, and costs most of the dollars. To see why this is the case, compare a gate to a wire. A typical gate takes up 10^{-5} cubic centimeters, dissipates 10^{-14} watts, switches in about 10^{-9} seconds, and has a mean time between failures of 10^{10} hours, and costs about 10^{-3} dollars. By contrast, a wire from one chip to another consists of the following: a bonded filament from die to package, a lead from package to a board, a solder joint, a trace on a printed circuit board, another solder joint, a connector (usually plated with gold), another soldered joint, a long piece of controlled impedance transmission line with a shield or ground wire, followed by joint, connector, joint, trace, joint, lead, and bond, in reverse. The transistors driving the wire typically take up about 100 times the chip area of a gate, and dissipate 100 times the power.

Propagation over the wire even at the speed of light takes a nanosecond a foot, and in typical wires it is twice that. The delay in the driver is generally many times the delay of a gate. Each part of the wire must be manufactured separately, so the total cost of driving, bonding, soldering, connectors, cable, termination, and assembly is a large fraction of a dollar. Wires also break, make and pick up electrical noise, and take up room.

Obviously, it is preferable to use gates rather than wires. They are avoided whenever possible. This was not true in von Neumann's day.

The other thing that has changed, besides our implementation technology, is the nature of the computational problems. In artificial intelligence and in symbolic computation in general, many algorithms involve relatively simple operations applied to a great deal of data. Sorting, data base retrieval, pattern matching, consistency maintenance, and vision processing are all in this category. The problems considered by von Neumann and his colleagues in calculating the memory requirements for a digital computer bear a much closer similarity to the calculations we do today on a programmable calculator [BACK78] than they do to the problems of artificial intelligence. This leads them, after an analysis of their applications, to the following assumption: "It is reasonable at this time to build a machine that can conveniently handle problems several orders of magnitude more complex than are now handled by existing machines, electronic or electro-mechanical. We consequently plan on a fully automatic electronic storage facility of about 4,000 numbers of 40 binary digits each. We believe that this exceeds the capacities required for problems that one deals with at present by a factor of about 10." [BGV46].

By contrast, the capacities required for the problems we deal with at present are on the order of 10^6 to 10^7 words. In many applications a large fraction of these words must be accessed in each cycle of the algorithm. There is every reason to believe that as programs become smarter, as they begin to incorporate more knowledge, they will operate on even more data. The problems are clearly different. Von Neumann did consider the possibility of using his machine for sorting, but came to the following conclusion: "In using an electronic machine of the type under consideration for sorting problems, one is using it in a way least favorable for its specific characteristics... ." In using the Connection Machine for problems of this type, one is using it in a way that is most favorable for its specific characteristics.

In essence, a Connection Machine is a very large number of very tiny processor memory cells connected by a programmable communications network. Each cell is sufficiently small that it is incapable of performing meaningful computation on its own. Instead, multiple cells are hooked together into data-dependent patterns called active data structures which both represent and process the data. The activities of these active data structures are directed from outside the Connection Machine by a conventional host computer. This host computer stores data structures on the Connection Machine in much the same way that a conventional machine would store them in a memory. Unlike a conventional memory, though, the Connection Machine has no von Neumann bottleneck. The memory cells themselves do the processing. More precisely, the computation takes place through the coordinated interaction of the cells in the data structure. Because thousands or even millions of processing cells work on the problem simultaneously, the computation proceeds much more rapidly than would be possible on a conventional machine.

Often the structure of a problem will suggest a natural method of solution. If very different problems repeatedly suggest a similar method of solution, you begin to have faith in the method. If your analytic and computational tools do not fit the method, you change the tools. This is the motivation for the development of Connection Machine architecture. It is a tool to match a method.

In the case of the Connection Machine, the problems to be solved originally came from artificial intelligence, specifically from models of common sense reasoning, learning, language understanding, and vision. In each of these areas there are natural methods of performing calculations with networks of simple processing/memory units operating concurrently.[2] Unfortunately, the conventional digital computer does not fit particularly well with this kind of model. A conventional computer has only a single processing unit, so the potentially concurrent operations must be performed serially, stacked up in time. Since each case involves processing sets with hundreds of thousands to millions of elements, the natural solutions become impractical. The tool does not match the method.

One response could be, and has been, to look for other methods better suited to the capabilities of the conventional computer. This has often been successful. For example, it is sometimes possible to eliminate the need for a lengthy search by using a hash table. In artificial intelligence it may be possible to avoid reasoning about large numbers of facts by building "Expert Systems" where a specific body of knowledge can be carefully arranged by a human so that just the right fact will be available at just the right time. Of course, it is not always possible to prestructure the knowledge in this way and, even when it is possible, the result is often inflexible. Hash tables depend on knowing in advance what keys will be available when you need to access a stored item. An expert system will break down when an unanticipated situation arises. Also, the intellectual effort involved in the solution seems to be directed at overcoming obstacles in the implementation, rather than obstacles inherent in the original problem.

The other approach to dealing with the mismatch is to change the tool, which is the point of the Connection Machine. The form of the Connection Machine is deliberately chosen to provide a natural solution to these problems which are handled so poorly by a conventional

---

[2] See, for example, the works of Fahlman and Feldman [FAHL79, FB81] on reasoning, Hinton and Hopfield [HS84, HOPF82] on learning, Quillian and Waltz [QR68, WP85] on parsing, Poggio [PTK85] on vision, and Minsky [MINS79] on the structure of the mind.

computer. In this sense, the Connection Machine is intended to augment the conventional computer, rather than to replace it. There are still many computations that fit well into the time-sequential, step-by-step method. It is the problems that do not fit that need our attention. In this paper, we consider a simple example problem that has a natural solution suggesting a Connection Machine-like architecture.

We will use as an example the problem of finding the shortest length path between two vertices in a large graph. The problem is appropriate because, besides being simple and useful, its solution is similar in character to the many "spreading activation" computations in artificial intelligence. The problem is this:

> Given a graph with vertices V and edges E is is a subset of $V \times V$, with an arbitrary pair of vertices a,b in V, find the length k of shortest sequence of connected vertices $a, v_1, v_2, \cdots$ such that all the edges $(a, v_1), (v_1, v_2), \cdots (v_{k-1}, b)$ in E are in the graph.

For concreteness, consider a graph with 10^4 vertices and an average of 10^2 randomly connected edges per vertex. (For examples of where such graphs might arise see Quillian, Collins and Loftus, Waltz). In such a graph, almost any randomly chosen pair of vertices will be connected by a path of not more than three edges.

The simplest algorithm for finding the shortest path from vertex A to vertex B begins by labeling every vertex with its distance from A. This is accomplished by labeling vertex A with 0, labeling all vertices connected to A with 1, labeling all unlabeled vertices connected to those vertices with 2 and so on. The process terminates as soon as vertex B is labeled. The label of B is then the length of the shortest connecting path. Any path with monotonically decreasing labels originating from B, will lead to A in this number of steps. A common optimization of this algorithm is to propagate the labels from A and B simultaneously until they meet but, for the sake of clarity, we will stick to its simplest form.

Ideally, we would be able to describe the algorithm to the computer something like this:

Algorithm I: "Finding the length of shortest path from A to B"

Label all vertices with +infinity.
Label vertex A with 0
Label every vertex, except A, with 1 plus the minimum
   of its neighbor's labels.
   Repeat this step until the label of vertex B is finite.
Terminate. The label of B is the answer.

Through the remainder of this paper we will use this path-length algorithm as an example for motivating the structure of the Connection Machine.

Assuming that each step written above takes unit time, Algorithm I will terminate in time proportional to the length of the connecting path. For the 10^4 vertex random graph mentioned above, Step 3 will be repeated two or three times, so about six steps will be required to find the path length. Unfortunately, the steps given above do not correspond well with the kinds of steps that can be executed on a von Neumann machine. Figure 1, for example, shows an almost direct translation of the algorithm into Lisp.

```
(SETQ +INFINITY 99999.)                    ;a very big number

(DEFUN PATH-LENGTH (A B GRAPH)
  (LOOP FOR VERTEX IN GRAPH          ;initialize all labels
   DO (SETF (LABEL VERTEX) +INFINITY))
  (SETF (LABEL A) 0)                 ;label a with 0
  (LOOP UNTIL (< (LABEL B) +INFINITY);repeat until b finite
   DO (LOOP FOR VERTEX IN GRAPH ;compute new labels
      DO (IF (NOT (EQ VERTEX A))
         (SETF (NEW-LABEL VERTEX)
          (+ 1 (LOOP FOR NEIGHBOR IN (NEIGHBORS VERTEX)
            MINIMIZE (LABEL NEIGHBOR))))))
      DO (LOOP FOR VERTEX IN GRAPH ;update simultaneously
      DO (IF (NOT (EQ VERTEX A))
         (SETF (LABEL VERTEX) (NEW-LABEL VERTEX)))))
  (LABEL B))                         ;return answer
```

Figure 1: Serial implementations of findpath
obscure the simplicity of the algorithm

Note that this a very inefficient program. The program runs in time proportional to the number of vertices, times the length of the path, times the average degree of each vertex. For example, the graph mentioned above would require several million executions of the inner loop. Finding a path in a test graph required about an hour of cpu time on a VAX-750.

Besides being slow, the program implements the dissimilar operations with similar constructs, resulting in a more obscure rendition of the original algorithm. Compare the way "repeat" is used in Algorithm I with the way the "loop" statement is used in the program. In the algorithm, repeat is used only to specify multiple operations that need to take place in time-sequential order, which is where the sequencing is critical to the algorithm. In the program, everything must take place in sequence. The loop is used not only to do things that are rightfully sequential, but also to operate all of the elements of a set and to find the minimum of a set of numbers. Also, because the updates are implemented sequentially, a second set of labels is used to get the same results as a simultaneous update. (In this simple example, the algorithm would give the right answer in either case without simultaneously updating the case, but this is not generally true.)

A good programmer could, of course, change the algorithm to one that would run faster. For example, it is not necessary to propagate labels from every labeled vertex, but only from those that have just changed. Not updating the label simultaneously would be another optimization. We have become so accustomed to making such modifications that we tend to make them without even noticing. Most programmers given the task of implementing Algorithm I probably would include several such optimizations almost automatically. Of course, many "optimizations" would help for some graphs and hurt for others. For instance, in a fully connected graph, the extra overhead of checking if a vertex had just changed would slow things down. Also, with optimizations, it becomes more difficult to understand what is going on. For example, would the sequential update optimization interfere with the optimization of only propagating changes? Optimization trades speed for clarity and flexibility.

Instead of optimizing the algorithm to match the operation of the von Neumann machine, we could make a machine to match the algorithm. In what follows, we design a machine to implement Algorithm I directly. It will turn out to be a Connection Machine.

We will begin by making a list of requirements necessary for a machine to implement the path-length algorithm. The first requirement is for concurrency. As Algorithm I is described, there are steps when all the vertices change to a computed value simultaneously. To implement the algorithm directly, there must be a processing element associated with each vertex. Since the graph can have an arbitrarily large number of vertices, the machine needs an arbitrarily large number of processing elements. Unfortunately, while it is fine to demand infinite resources, any physical machine will be only finite. What compromise should we be willing to make?

It would suffice to have a machine with enough processors to deal with most of the problems that arise. How big a machine this is depends on the problems. It will be a tradeoff between cost and functionality.

We are already accustomed to making this kind of tradeoff for the amount of memory on a computer. Any real memory is finite, but it is practical to make the memory large enough that our models of the machine can safely ignore the limitations. We should be willing to accept similar limitations on the number of processors. Of course, as with memory, there will always be applications where we have to face the fact of finiteness. In a von Neumann machine we generally assume that the memory is large enough to hold the data to be operated on plus a reasonable amount of working storage, say in proportion to the size of the problem. For the shortest path problem we will make similar assumptions about the availability of processors. This will be the first design requirement for the machine:

> Requirement I: There are enough processing elements to be allocated as needed, in proportion to the size of the problem.

A corollary of this requirement is that each processing element must be as small and as simple as possible so that we can afford to have as many of them as we want. This has a consequence:

> Requirement Ia: Each processing element has very little memory.

This will turn out to be an important design constraint. It will limit what we can expect to do within a single processing element. It would not be reasonable to assume both that "there are plenty of processors" and that "there is plenty of memory per processor." If the machine is to be built, it must use roughly the same number of components as conventional machines. Modern production technology gives us one "infinity" by allowing inexpensive replication of components. It is not fair to ask for two.

In the path-length algorithm, the pattern of interelement communication depends on the structure of the graph. The machine must work for arbitrary graphs, so every processing element must have the potential of communicating with every other processing element. The pattern of connections must be part of the changeable state of the machine. (In other problems we will actually want to change the connections dynamically during the course of the computation, but this is not necessary for the path-length calculation.)

From the standpoint of the software, the connections must be programmable, but the processors may have a fixed physical wiring scheme. Here again there is an analogy with memory. In a conventional computer, the storage elements for memory locations 4 and 5 are located in close physical proximity, whereas the location 1000 may be physically on the other side of the machine but, to the software, they are all equally easy to access. If the machine has virtual memory, location 1000 may be out on a disk and may require much more time to access. From the software, this is invisible. It is no more difficult to move an item from location 4 to 1000 than it is from 4 to 5. We would like a machine that hides the physical connectivity of the processors as thoroughly as the von Neumann computer hides the physical locality of its memory. This is an important part of molding the structure of our machine to the structure of the problem. It forms the second requirement for the machine.

Requirement II: The processing elements are connected by software.

This ability to configure the topology of the machine to match the topology of the problem will turn out to be one of the most important features of the Connection Machine. (That is why it is called a Connection Machine.) It is also the feature that presents the greatest technical difficulties. To visualize how such a communications network might work, imagine that each processing element is connected to its own message router and that the message routers are arranged like the crosspoints of a grid, each physically connected to its four immediate neighbors. Assume that one processing element needs to communicate with another one that is, say, 2 up and 3 to the right. It passes a message to its router which contains the information to be transmitted plus a label specifying that it is to be sent 2 up and 3 over. On the basis of that label, the router sends the message to its neighbor on the right, modifying the label to say "2 up and 2 over." That processor then forwards the message again, and so on, until the label reads "0 up and 0 over". At that point, the router receiving the message delivers it to the connected processing element.

In practice, a grid is not really a very good way to connect the routers, because routers can be separated by as many as 2 (square root n) intermediaries. It is desirable to use much more complicated physical connection schemes, with lots of short-cuts, so that the maximum distance between any two cells is very small. We also need to carefully select the routing algorithms to avoid "traffic jams" when many messages are traveling through the network at once. The important thing here is that processing elements communicate by sending messages through routers. Only the routers need to worry about the physical connection topology. As long as two processing elements know each other's address, they can communicate as if they were physically connected. We say there is a virtual connection between them. The virtual connection presents a consistent interface between processors. Since the implementation details are invisible, the software can remain the same, while technology changes, wires break, and hardware designers think of new tricks.

In the path-length algorithm, a vertex must communicate with all of its neighbors in one step. The fanout of the communication is equal to the number of neighbors of the vertex. Since a vertice may have an arbitrary number of connected edges, the fanout of a processing element must be unlimited. Similarly, a vertex may receive communication from an arbitrarily large number of edges simultaneously. This points out a corollary to the requirement for arbitrary programmable communication for a machine to match the shortest path algorithm.

Requirement IIa: A processing element must be able to send and receive from an arbitrary number of others elements.

Does this mean that each processing element must be large enough to handle many messages at once? Will it need arbitrary amounts of storage to remember all of its connections? Providing large amounts of storage would contradict the requirement (Ia) that the processing elements are small. Fortunately, there is a better method, involving the construction of fanout trees.

The term "fanout tree" comes from electrical engineering. The fanout problem comes up electrically because it is impossible to measure a signal without disturbing it. This sounds like a mere principle of physics, but every engineer knows its macroscopic consequences. In standard digital electronics, for instance, no one gate can directly drive more than about ten others. If it is necessary to drive more than this, then it can be accomplished by a tree of buffers. One gate drives ten buffers, each of which drives ten more, and so on, until the desired fanout is achieved. This is called a fanout tree.

There is a software equivalent to this in languages like Lisp, where large data structures are built out of small, fixed-sized components. The Lisp "cons cell" has room for only two pointers. Sequences of arbitrary many elements are represented by stringing together multiple cons cells. Lisp programmers use linear lists more often than trees, because they are better suited for sequential access. Balanced trees are used when the time to access an arbitrary element is important.

The use of trees to represent a network with fanout is illustrated in the figure below. Notice that each node is connected to no more than three others. (Lisp gets away with two because the connections are not bidirectional, so it does not store the backpointers.) Since a balanced tree with N leaves requires 2N-1 nodes, the number of 3-connected processing elements required to represent any graph is equal to twice the number of edges minus the number of vertices. The tree structure "wastes" memory by storing the internal structure of the tree, just as the Lisp list "wastes" a factor of two in storage by storing the links from one node to the next. Because each vertex of the graph is represented by a tree of processing elements rather than by a single processing element, there is storage and processing power at each vertex in proportion to the the number of connected edges. This solves the problem of how to handle multiple messages arriving at once. Each processing element only needs to handle a maximum of three messages. It also keeps the elements small, since each needs only the addresses that correspond to three virtual connections. There is a cost in time. A vertex must communicate data through its internal tree before the data can be communicated out to the connected vertices.

This internal communication requires Log_2V message transmission steps, where V is the degree of the vertex.

Figure 2 shows an implementation of Algorithm I in Connection Machine Lisp, a parallel Lisp designed for expressing programs for the Connection Machine. Each line of the program corresponds directly to one of the steps in Algorithm I. Each line also corresponds to a single command sent from the host to the Connection Machine.

The Connection Machine control unit interprets these commands as instructions to the appropriate individual processor/memory cells. For some expressions, for example, the final, (LABEL B), the command sent to the Connection Machine specifies a value to be returned to the host. For others, for example, the initial (SETF (LABEL ! GRAPH) + INFINITY), the command sent specifies an operation to be performed by some set of cells in the Connection Machine.

In this case, all cells that represent vertices are to set their labels to +INFINITY. The operation is performed by all such cells simultaneously. Commands generated by other portions of the program, such as the REDUCE operation, specify operations on the Connection Machine that involve communication between cells. By this method of sending high level commands, called macro-instructions, the host is able to direct the behavior of active data structures within the Connection Machine.

```
(DEFUN PATH-LENGTH (A B GRAPH)
  (SETF (LABEL ! GRAPH) +INFINITY);initialize all labels
  (SETF (LABEL A) 0)                    ;set label of A to 0
  (LOOP UNTIL (< (LABEL B) +INFINITY);update labels
    DO (SETF (LABEL (EXCEPT ! GRAPH A))
      (+ 1 (REDUCE 'MAX)) (LABEL (NEIGHBORS ! GRAPH))
  (LABEL B))                            ;return answer
```

Figure 2: The Connection Machine Lisp
implementation of findpath

In this section, we contrast the Connection Machine architecture with some other approaches to building very high performance computers. The most important distinguishing feature of the Connection Machine is the combination of fine granularity and general communication. The Connection Machine has a very large number of very small processors. This provides a high degree of parallelism and helps solve resource allocation problems. Also, the communications network allows the connectivity of these processors to be reconfigured to match a problem. This ability to "wire up" thousands of programmable processing units is really the heart of the Connection Machine concept.

Below, we summarize some of the approaches taken by other architectures.

There are a large number of ongoing efforts to push the performance of conventional serial machines. These involve the use of faster switching devices (Josephson Junction, gallium), the use of larger and more powerful instruction sets (S1), the use of smaller and simpler instruction sets (RISC), improvements in packaging (Cray) [RUSS78], and tailoring the machines to specific applications (LispM, Japan-Lispm, Scheme [SS78]). Even if the most exotic of these projects are completely successful, they will not come close to meeting our performance requirements. When performing simple computations on large amounts of data, von Neumann computers are limited by the bandwidth between memory and processor. This is a fundamental flaw in the von Neumann design. It cannot be eliminated by clever engineering.

Other researchers have proposed connecting dozens or even hundreds of conventional computers by shared memory or a high bandwidth communications network [SCHW80, SFS77, HALS79, RIEG79, HEWI80, WIDD80]. Several of these architectures are good candidates for machines with orders of magnitude in increased performance. Compared to the Connection Machine, these architectures have a relatively small number of relatively large machines. These machines have a much lower ratio of processing power to memory size, so they are fundamentally slower than the Connection Machine on memory-intensive operations.

Much closer to the Connection Machine in the degree of potential parallelism are the tesselated or recursive structures of many small machines. The most common topologies are the two-dimensional grid or torus, [SLOT78, SUTH65, BATC80] and various kinds of trees [SF82, SHAW82, BROW80]. These machines have fixed interconnection topologies. Their programs are written to take advantage of the topology. When the structure of the problem matches the structure of the machine, these architectures can exhibit the same degree of concurrency as the Connection Machine. Unlike the Connection Machine, their topologies cannot be reconfigured to match a particular problem. This is particularly important in a problem like the logic simulation, or semantic network inference, where the topology is highly irregular.

There have been several special-purpose architectures proposed for speeding up database search operations (RAP, CASSM, DBC, DIRECT, CAFS). Like the Connection Machine, these database processors are designed to perform data-intensive operations under control of a more conventional host computer. Although these machines are designed to process a restricted class of queries on larger databases, they have many implementation issues in common with the Connection

Machine. The study of these architectures has produced a significant body of theory on the computational complexity of parallel database operation [HD82].

Historically, the Connection Machine architecture was developed to implement the marker-propagation programs (NETL) proposed by Fahlman for retrieving data from semantic networks [FAHL79]. The Connection Machine is well suited for executing marker-type algorithms, but it is considerably more flexible than Fahlman's special-purpose marker propa- gator. The Connection Machine has a computer at each node, which can manipulate address pointers and send arbitrary messages. It has the capability to build structures dynamically. These features are important for applications other than marker-passing.

A systolic array [KL80] is a tesselated structure of synchronous cells that perform fixed sequences of computations with fixed patterns of communication. In the Connection Machine, by contrast, both the computations and the communications patterns are programmable. In the Connection Machine, uniformity is not critical. Some cells may be defective or missing. Another structure, similar to the systolic array, is the cellular automata [WOLF84, TOFF77, HOLL81]. In an abstract sense, the Connection Machine is a universal cellular automation, with an additional mechanism added for non-local communication. This additional mechanism makes a large difference in performance and in ease of programming.

The Connection Machine may be used as a content-addressable or associative memory, but it is also able to perform non-local computations through the communications network. The elements in content-addressable memories are comparable in size to connection memory cells, but they are not generally programmable. When used as a content- addressable memory, the Connection Machine processors allow more complex matching procedures.

In summary, the Connection Machine is a small-grained processor with general purpose communication. A 64,000 processor prototype is currently under construction at Thinking Machines Corporation in Cambridge, Massachusetts.

1. References

[BACK78] [BATC80] [BGV46] [BROW80] [FAHL79] [FB81] [HALS79] [HD82] [HEWI80] [HOLL81] [HOPF82] [HS84] [KL80] [MINS79] [PTK85] [QR68] [RIEG79] [RUSS78] [SCHW80] [SF82] [SFS77] [SHAW82] [SLOT78] [SS78] [SUTH65] [TOFF77] [WIDD80] [WOLF84] [WP85]

Discussion

Hector Garcia-Molina presented his Massive Memory Machine (MMM) Project. The kind of machine he is interested in is one with 10 to 100 gigabytes of main memory. The access times are expected to be similar to current machines. Also, he plans to use the traditional von Neumann model. The goal is to build machines that avoid the disk bottlenecks, so prevalent in data base applications. The project has two aims: (a) To show that a massive memory machine is a good idea and to identify potential applications; (b) To actually build a prototype massive memory machine. He noted that for some applications it is clearly an advantage to increase memory size rather than CPU speed. Once a certain threshold is reached and an entire database with supporting software is in main memory, the problem of implementing efficiently a database can be treated in completely different ways with new data structures and optimization techniques. Potential application areas include compilers, VLSI design and Prolog machines. He is particularly interested in DBMSs with very high performance transaction requirements.

As a starting point towards the construction of a prototype, the project will be using a VAX785 with 256 megabytes of main memory.

Questions were raised as to the feasibilty of the idea. Mike Stonebraker asserted that virtually all production database systems are CPU-bound, a problem that wasn't addressed at all by the proposed architecture. Gio Wiederhold noted, however, that some of the demand on the CPU comes from index compression, multiple address translations and other things that would be affected by the new architecture.

Peter Szolovits remarked that operations such as writing zero in all memory addresses would take for ever without special purpose hardware. One could get some idea how such a system would behave by just instrumenting a current system and subtracting the cost for I/O, interrupts, etc. The intuition is that there would be some kind of speed-up, but not a very dramatic one. What evidence to the contrary is there? Hector Garcia-Molina responded to these concerns by noting that the project should be viewed as a scientific experiment intended to find answers to these questions.

Danny Hillis talked about parallelism in general and about his prototype Connection Machine. The basic problem with traditional von Neumann machines, is that all of the processor is working for you all the time, whereas only one or two memory locations are touched per instruction. To avoid this "bottleneck", one has to build machines with many processing components. Danny Hillis sees four major directions to this idea: (a) multicomputer configurations, where existing computers are hooked up, (b) machines with many (micro-)processors, (c) machines with a fixed topology, where processors are arranged in a grid, tree or the like, (d) connection machines where a shared memory structure that can be tied to a large number of small processors in arbitrary patterns. He favours the latter direction.

The prototype under construction has 6400 processors, 32 megabytes of memory. He hopes to expand this to 500 megabytes. The application that motivated this hardware design was a VLSI simulation problem. For his machine, he is using a version of Lisp that supports parallelism by allowing parallel operations on lists.

David Warren is looking into high-performance logic programming systems through the use of parallelism. He thinks that two orders of magnitude speedup is possible. Improvements on sequential performance of Prolog programs is just as important, however. A basic requirement on parallel machines is that they will run at least as fast as a sequential machine on any program (and will hopefully run faster on most).

Prolog is especially well-suitable to parallel implementation due to its basic technique of depth-first search with backtracking. The execution of Prolog programs can essentially be viewed as involving "parallelism across time". There is a project under way at Argonne to build a Prolog compiler for a multiple high-speed processor machine. machine. The parallelism exploited by the Argonne project is "or-parallelism". The idea is to try to make a multiprocessor machine behave like a single processor one. Choice points during the execution of a program are preserved and whenever one choice fails, another one is tried. There are problems that need to be resolved in having many processors look simultaneously look at different instantiations of the same variables. In the parallel version of Prolog there are two versions of the "cut" operator: the asymmetric cut and the symmetric cut. The asymmetric cut is the same as in regular Prolog. The symmetric cut allows for a race. If this cut is reached, other processes trying to establish the same goal with this rule are aborted.

Part VIII

Epilogue

38
Concluding Remarks from the Artificial Intelligence Perspective

Daniel G. Bobrow[1]

ABSTRACT *This summary reviews some recurrent themes of the conference. We have a few suggestions about how funding might help us now. Finally, we want to pass along a suggestion that might improve the next conference.*

The first theme was the inappropriateness of all-or-none views.

Systems come in pieces. What we often want are just some of those pieces. We have to get them by using large systems that already exist, ignoring some capabilities; the hope is that we can eventually get a tool-kit such as suggested by Dave DeWitt. Even with the tool-kit idea, we have seen that people have very different assumptions about what pieces should be implemented, and what the division into parts should be, and what the important pieces are.

Tasks also come in pieces. Different kinds of tasks that can be combined in a system in different ways. Some inference can be done on either side of the knowledge system/ database boundary. As Bill Woods noted this morning, we should compare the nature of the data dealt with in AI (many generalizations and patterns, relatively few facts of any given type) to the data that to be found in knowledge bases (few generaliztions and patterns, and many specific facts). In determining features necessary in a KB/DB system, we must refer to the task we have in mind. Randy Katz pointed out special features in the design world; not all systems will stress, for example, the versioning mechanism so severely.

Groups come in pieces. As Peter Szolovits pointed out, this is true of both the AI community and the database community. Those from one community tend to think that the other is monolithic and

[1] Xerox PARC

homogeneous in its opinions. This conference was enlightning to me because I had the impression I was going to talk to "the" database community.   I was surprised to see how different some of Mike Stonebraker's beliefs are from those, for example, of Jeff Ullman. These different approaches are very important. What "database people" share, and what I learned a lot about, was the vocabulary that they use to talk to each other, and to try to talk to us AI folk.

Another theme was "We can't have it all". However, the two communities differ on what is important to keep and what is not important. Here is an incomplete list of priorities. Rather than rank-ordering them, I sorted them into three categories — those things we won't give up, and those we want, and those we will gladly give up if we need too. Of course, the "we" is the other parameter in this chart.

	AI	DB
we won't give up	partial descriptions specialized inference techniques controlled search inferences	concurrent access security persistence frequent updates large data
we want	large data	inferences
we will be glad to give up	security frequent updates	specialized inference rules controlled search

AI people start with, and won't give up partial descriptions; they don't think that many ground level (fully-instantiated) descriptions are enough.   Inference and search are the bread and butter of AI. Knowledge-based control of the search is at the heart of many problems.

What AI folk would like to add to their systems is something the DB people know a lot about — that efficient engineering to handle large amounts of data. We find that a hard problem; and that's why we are here talking about it.

Database people won't give up security, concurrent access, and persistence, which define the core of the problems they have been working on. In their systems, they expect frequent updates of large amounts of data. What they would like to add is "the smarts" — the ability to make inferences during database storage and retrieval.

The third category, what we will be glad to give up, defines where we are willing to make compromises. In our AI research, it not is not terribly important to enforce security; we believe we are dealing with a homogeneous group of friendly users. Updates don't appear to be worth optimizing because, in our limited experience, our databases are usually relatively static, and rarely accessed by more than a single person at a time.

Database people don't really want specialized inference systems; with a uniform system using a few key words, they can add some inference only slightly augmenting current mechnisms. Specialized inference, say using links in the database, or inheritance, might interfere too much with current operations and optimizations. On the other hand, some in the DB community are willing to make other tradeoffs, — for example, people dealing with geographic databases would like links if that would be a way of processing certain difficult queries.

The indication that DB people are willing to give up controlled search does not imply that they want uncontrolled search; it means that they want the database to control the search, rather than a program that must reach through the interface to the data-handling facilities. The data manager is supposed to know how the data are stored and can be retrieved efficiently. It also means that the higher level doesn't have to know.

Ronald Brachman: Where does Lisp go? Is that something that we won't give up?

Danny Bobrow: I am ready to give up Lisp several times per year. (laughter) However, it is the language in which I express my algorithms, and it does provide a significant programming environment. I need both. I can imagine some brave soul putting Lisp together with a database. I can also imagine using other languages; Prolog, for example, has a database in it.

Ronald Brachman: On the AI side, I think, we would gladly give up, and that may be surprising for the DB side, First Order Logic in a particular syntax. First Order Logic *per se* is a nonissue. But what we won't give up is the notion of semantics, and the notion of precision, and the notion of knowing what we are doing. We also won't give up the notion of knowledge, although it is easy to dismiss. There has been a long history in philosophy concerning knowledge or belief. When we talk about the knowledge level, we want to draw on that particular notion and some of these ideas.

Peter Szolovits: I think we should be careful. As far as I know, there has been no large-scale expert system with semantics that we won't give up. There are a lot people out there who would like it; but since I can't build a medical diagnosis system that has semantics right now, I have no alternative but to build one that doesn't.

Danny Bobrow: Note here an example of a difference in the AI community.

David DeWitt: What about extensional vs. intensional knowledge?

Danny Bobrow: We would not want to give up intensional knowledge. We could add this to the figure, but this is just a beginning; it provides a way of organizing criteria about combining systems. In dialogues between communities, these often-unstated criteria can lead to confusion. Metaphorically, each community stands on one leg and tries to stretch out the other leg as far as they can; but they won't give up their grounding. That is appropriate for the set of tasks they have worked on so far.

Here are some suggestions about how the funders here might help this newly emerging joint community. One is to help with the availability of systems. Take an Ingres system, for example, running on the Sun hardware. Distribute copies of it to different sites, and put some on the ARPA net. Let people have free access to gain understanding about what happens if systems are joined together.

Gio Wiederhold: You want a modifiable Ingres?

Danny Bobrow: Yes, I would try a modifiable Ingres. I would also be happy to have Ingres as a black box that I could try to use in an application.

Another useful thing that could be funded is a task that involves both groups of people. We all need to maintain code; we need versions, large files etc. There are lots of reasons why a code maintenance system could use a database and some intelligence about what is in the code. It is not necessarily the best possible research project, but it is one in which both groups have vested interests. It can expand in several directions. Larger systems require more storage of data; more intelligent systems allow more sophisticated code.

What could be improved about this conference? I didn't get initialized well enough. I read all the preprints and surveys I was given. I still would have liked an hour introduction to what is in Ingres and what it buys me. What do other systems do for me that Ingres doesn't do?

Similarly, I think it would have been useful to hear an extended description of one AI system. For example, what is in SRL+, a commercially available product. What is good about it, what are the things that people keep asking us for? This might have helped us avoid inventing things again. Mark Fox's talk was extremely illuminating, because he presented real problems with real solutions; it was delightfully concrete.

>From this base, the conference could have been directed toward planning how to solve some of the open problems of real systems.

Ronald Brachman: We tried. There were the two kinds of systems that Mike Brodie suggested that all of us think about in advance of coming here, but somehow we lost it on the first day.

Michael Brodie: Let me raise another point. You said earlier that the groups disagree within themselves. At the Pingree conference, there was an initial day of surveys and summaries. There turned out to be more fighting within each community in trying to get that across.

Danny Bobrow: I was not suggesting a survey; rather, a specific system description. One can't argue with Mark Fox or John McDermott about what ISIS does. It is hard to argue with Michael Stonebraker about what makes Ingres tick. These are examples of current systems solving real problems that could have been illuminating to those of us who have too little knowledge of the "other world."

On the whole, I thought the conference worked well, with a good balance of discusssion time and presentations. I really enjoyed hearing about new ideas and approaches to database systems, and it started me thinking in new directions in my own work. For me, it was a very valuable conference.

I want to conclude by thanking Michael Brodie, and all the people who worked so hard to make this conference so productive and enjoyable.

39
Concluding Remarks from the Database Perspective

John M. Smith[1]

ABSTRACT *The remarks summarize the conference results from a database perspective. Emphasis is placed on emerging general system concepts for knowledge base management systems.*

John Smith: Let me start by saying that the conference was extremely valuable. The most important idea to me was that there is a particle theory of AI, the idea that one could sprinkle "cognitions" on a system and make it more intelligent. It seems to me that AI and DB will never get together unless there is a comparable simplicity about the DB field. The key task for me today was to come up with a comparable theory of DBs. I have not gotten it down to a single particle, but I have isolated two particles. These are "transactions", which have the property that a system with transactions sprinkled on it suddenly can be used by many people without interference. The second particle is called "relations." These actually are not so well understood as transactions. They have the property that if you sprinkle relations on a systems, it all of a sudden makes a quantum leap in terms of performance and the size of the problems it can solve.

To summarize this workshop, the knowledge base area is the intersection of DB and AI. I wanted to identify system concepts for KBMS systems. These system concepts should have the following properties.

First, they should apply to a class of problems, so they should be general concepts. I don't mean universal, but with a certain degree of generality. Second, they should have substantial research challenge. This is not fundamental research, but a systems-oriented style of

---

[1] Computer Corporation of America

research. They also should have a potential for practical use within the next 5 years. They don't have to guarantee it, but this seems to me an operational horizon for new systems. Fourth, they should provide a substantial technology advance.

When I came to the workshop it was pretty unclear what structure a KBMS has, or even what it is. I would like to tell you the different system concepts that I observed that seem to meet these four requirements.

The first is an Intelligent DBMS, basically adding cognitions to a DBMS. I mean a relatively specific thing. A data management facility that makes application programs smarter in the sense that it is easier to write intelligent application programs. It processes the data in a more powerful and general way; it does not try to interpret the data as knowledge for inferences and so forth. This is a distinct, useful, and realizable system concept.

The second system concept is an AI-DB language system. A lot of AI technology is embedded in AI languages, and the goal is to add transactions and relations to AI languages. What you end up with is a tool for expressing knowledge-oriented problems where you have built-in certain facilities for handling large-scale problems and for sharing.

The third range of system concept I have termed "vertical KBMSs." Those are systems that apply to a specific area. They combine AI and DB technology in a specific application area.

The fourth thing is the most speculative (but I still think it is a system concept), what I call "pure KBS." It is trying to introduce a system that operates at the knowledge level. You can fill knowledge into the system in a simple way, you can tell it certain things, and you can ask it certain things. In that sense a pure KBS is really different from an intelligent DBMS. It is uniform; there is no distinction between data and algorithms; there is only knowledge and inference. I think after what I have heard in this conference that we could have within 5 years a medium scale, fairly general knowledge representation/inference engine.

Peter Szolovits: You have to have some bounds on that, because that is equivalent to the dreams of 25 years ago.

John Smith: I agree, but I am only talking about system concepts. It is the idea of a knowledge-representation scheme and inference engine whose semantics are defined. It may be restricted in some sense. The performance may not be satisfactory, but the tool itself could be there.

I would just like to cover these four areas and make a few comments on each of them.

First of all, intelligent database management systems. The objective is to make it much easier to write intelligent application programs. The further we can move into the intelligent direction the better. There are several people who presented ideas which high-level facilities could add to a DBMS. Those are recursion, taxonomies, daemons, dimensions in space and time, and others. The real question concerns what is implementable with reasonable effort and complexity. Some insight might be gained from work in the natural language area, because the people in this area are at the forefront of semantics.

The second subject is AI-DB language systems. Let us start at Lisp. If you add logic rules to Lisp, you have a language like Prolog. If you add situation-action rules to Lisp, you end up with a system like OPS (with daemons, it looks somewhat similar to PLANNER). The point is that AI languages have a rich taxonomic structure. To add database facilities onto this spectrum, what should we do? The current approach is to add relations and transactions to Prolog. The temptation is to take the "most advanced" AI language and the "most advanced" database system and integrate those. I am not sure what the most advanced AI language is, but there are a lot of DB languages and features beyond the relational model, and it is not at all clear what the most suitable system would be. I wonder if that is really the most sensible thing to do. Maybe the big win is to observe that the root of the AI language hierarchy is Lisp, and to add DB features to Lisp. If we had such a thing, it would have a profound effect on all languages that are based on Lisp. When one decides to do it this way, maybe one should also try to build this into hardware, a DB-Lisp machine. If you have an all-over system concept, it gives you a much sounder basis to build an advanced useable machine.

The third area I mentioned above is vertical KBMS. I don't have a great deal to say about it, but I was very impressed by what is going on. I tried to use a spectrum here from AI-oriented domains to DB-oriented domains. In this order we heard about natural languages, vision, medical applications, SE applications (John Mylopoulos), and CAD/CAM support systems. In each of these areas there are some integrations of AI and DB techniques. These areas develop techniques appropriate for their problems, but they can also be seen as a rich source for more generalized ideas and systems.

The last area is the area of pure KBSs, systems for general knowledge representation and inference. I would expect that these systems would have, at the lowest level, some kind of knowledge-representation scheme, an inference engine that works on top of that, and, as a front-end, some kind of system that allows sharing and operations like "tell" and "ask." There would be no distinction between data and algorithms; there is just knowledge. The concept is based on a clear, semantic, conceptual model to emphasis the right combination of power and performance. There will certainly be some more struggle about procedural or declarative knowledge representation; I don't have any idea what will do better. Some ideas might be borrowed from logic and the natural language research. I think that within 5 years we might have a pure, knowledge-based system.

40
Large-Scale Knowledge-Based Systems: Concluding Remarks and Technological Challenges

Michael Brodie[1]

ABSTRACT *Following observations on the status of research into Large-Scale Knowledge-Based Systems, this chapter outlines the motivations, goals, and technological challenges for LSKS technology.*

1. Concluding Remarks

The chapters in this book describe current and future needs and potential benefits for a technology that integrates features of Knowledge-Based Systems (KBS) and Database Systems (DBS). Many chapters pose significant technological problems that arise in achieving integrated KBS/DBS technology; some chapters present solutions to specific integration problems. Clearly, we are currently at a very early stage of this integration.

Terms such as **Knowledge Base Management System (KBMS)** and **Large-Scale Knowledge Systems (LSKS)** are used throughout the book to denote the integrated technology. Some chapters propose lists of potential KBMS features that are of particular interest to the authors. However, there is little consensus about what a KBMS might be. The only agreement is that future KBSs will require large-scale (possibly shared) knowledge bases and that future DBMS's will require some knowledge-based capabilities.

---

[1] Computer Corporation of America

Current attempts at KBS/DBS integration described in the book include: semantics for coupling a knowledge representation language with a DBMS; architectural issues that arise when integrating a KBS with a DBS; logic-based languages for databases; DBMS extensions including recursion and time-space semantics; and providing a B-tree secondary storage mechanism for a large-scale KBS. These constitute small evolutionary steps toward the integration envisaged by most authors, in particular by John Mylopoulos (in the first chapter) and John Smith (in the Epilogue).

Most chapters take the approach that it is too early to understand generic KBMS technology. The authors consider problems and requirements of specific applications for both research results and intuition on useful KBMS features. Database researchers look for *cognitons*[2] to improve DBS (e.g., for more powerful database languages, query optimization, inference in databases, and database design, dealing with constraints) whereas AI researchers look for database technology to improve KBSs (e.g., KBS access to databases, efficient storage and retrieval for large-scale knowledge bases, and databases for AI processing such as Natural Language). Some AI and Database researchers are actually working on the same problems (cf., optimization and control of inference in AI with semantic query optimization in databases) without being aware of each other's work.

KBS/DBS integration requires a deep understanding of both DBS and KBS. Such an understanding can be obtained through joint research. Indeed, the purpose of this book is to improve communication between the KBS and DBS research communities about the integration of KBS and DBS technologies.

2. Technological Challenges

Following the Islamorada workshop, Artificial Intelligence and Database Researchers worked together to propose directions for a research program in LSKS technology. The AI researchers were Danny Bobrow, Ronald Brachman, John McDermott, and John Mylopoulos. The Database researchers were Michael L. Brodie, John Mylopoulos,[3] John Miles Smith, Michael Stonebraker, and Jeff Ullman.

The group jointly developed the following motivations, goals, and technological challenges for a LSKS research program.

---

[2] Ideas from AI.

[3] John Mylopoulos does both AI and Database research.

Future information systems will be knowledge-based and, potentially, large-scale. These systems will require capabilities such as:

- Distributed information acquisition and usage
- Knowledge-based information processing
- Large-scale information storage and retrieval

Such a system will be called a Large-Scale Knowledge-Based System (LSKS).

LSKS technology will be essential for the success of existing and proposed research programs (e.g., the Strategic Computing Initiative — SCI) which relies heavily on both KBS and DBS technologies. Current KBS technology does not provide access to or efficient management of large, shared-knowledge bases required by currently envisioned knowledge-based applications. Current DBS technology does not accommodate knowledge bases, and lacks the inference capabilities required to provide knowledge-based applications. The lack of effective integration of the two technologies leaves a significant technological gap.

A research program is required to advance KBS and DBS technologies and to develop a new integrated technology that is responsive to all LSKS needs, and to fill the technological gap.

A LSKS research program should have three key goals:

- To identify LSKS requirements and technical roadblocks
- To develop a general LSKS technology that is applicable to a variety of application areas
- To create an industry/academic community that will continue to develop LSKS technology

A LSKS research program should contribute significantly to removing technological roadblocks in the development of LSKS technology and hence in the development of these 1990s systems. It should provide a framework for identifying and providing the technology base for the functional and performance requirements of these systems.

The contribution of LSKS technology will be to reduce the cost and to increase the effectiveness of future information systems. It is estimated that in the 1990s hundreds of LSKSs will be required for different commercial and governmental applications. In addition, the availability of LSKS technology will reduce by an order of magnitude the development cost of these systems.

A LSKS research program should address the following technological challenges:

Storage Capacity

Future KBSs will require knowledge bases of 10^{10} objects or knowledge chunks (e.g., rules, frames, facts). The SCI program proposes applications with 10^6 objects. Several KBSs currently in development in both research and industry will result in knowledge bases of 10^8 knowledge chunks. Current KBS technology supports knowledge bases of only 10^3 objects. Proposed extensions (e.g., within SCI) do not address the storage of large knowledge bases. To fill this technological gap, a LSKS research program should produce LSKSs with knowledge bases of 10^{10} objects.

Knowledge Processing

As storage capacity increases from 10^3 to 10^{10} objects, challenges to knowledge processing requirements arise. These requirements do not arise for databases, and are less critical for in-core knowledge bases. A major knowledge-processing requirement concerns knowledge-base maintenance which includes support for knowledge acquisition, knowledge verification, maintenance of relationships between knowledge chunks in the face of update, and index maintenance. These goals require means by which knowledge can be stored, accessed, and manipulated just as DBMSs access data. In particular, LSKSs must be able to access knowledge bases via the reasoning mechanisms appropriate for the chosen knowledge-representation scheme, whether the knowledge base resides in-core or in secondary storage.

Knowledge Capacity

Knowledge capacity refers to knowledge processing performance over large-scale knowledge bases. It is a performance-storage measure for knowledge-based systems. Knowledge capacity can be measured by the processing rate (e.g., in LIPS[4] per MIP of hardware) and the storage capacity (in numbers of objects) and requires the knowledge processing capabilities mentioned above.

Current KBS technology supports a knowledge capacity of 10^2 LIPS per MIP over 10^3 object knowledge bases. Current DBS technology supports 10-30 elementary LIPS[5] per MIP over 10^{12} object

---

[4] LIPS, although frequently used to measure inference rates, is an imprecise term, hence it is used here only as a relative measure.

[5] A query or transaction in current DBS corresponds to elementary logical; inferences over a database. Deriving database views is an example of such inferences.

databases. Currently, there is no full inference capability over large knowledge bases.

A LSKS research program should fill the technological gap between the two disjoint extremes of current KBS and DBS technology (as illustrated in Figure 1) by providing at least the same knowledge processing speeds over knowledge bases of 10^{10} objects as is currently achieved over in-core knowledge bases of 10^3 objects. It may be possible, within five years, to produce LSKSs that have knowledge capacities of 10^2 LIPS per MIP over 10^{10} object knowledge bases.

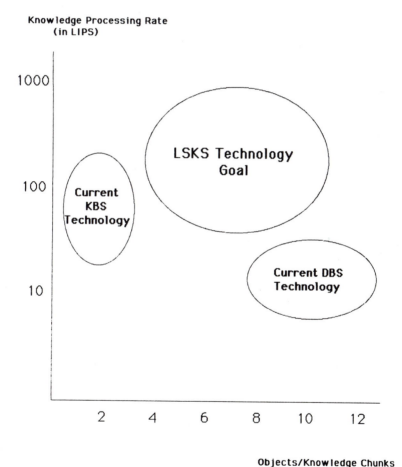

Figure 1: Knowledge Capacity

Expressive Power

As the knowledge capacity of LSKSs increases, *knowledge level* issues such as knowledge representation must be considered in detail, not only to insure uniformity and appropriateness of language semantics but also to provide a sound basis for efficient language and system implementation.

A LSKS research program should produce knowledge representation languages that address the following open problems in knowledge representation research. A major contribution of LSKS technology will be to add reasoning capabilities to DBS languages. In addition, LSKS languages should have, at a minimum, the power of first order logic with the following extensions. First, higher order operators will be provided to permit knowledge to be accessed as objects. This capability is required to achieve LSKS knowledge capacity (i.e., analysis) goals. Second, to support meta-knowledge, LSKS languages will permit explicit denotations of knowledge-base objects. Third, special purpose logics (e.g., for time and space) will be provided for the target application domains. Finally, LSKS languages will provide powerful means with which to structure knowledge.

Software Development

Software development challenges concern the effectiveness and efficiency of humans in building and maintaining LSKSs. The desired results of the technological challenges described above will contribute to this challenge. Specifically, software development in the LSKS environment will involve two major activities:

1. Knowledge Base Structuring: Knowledge engineers design the knowledge base according to the structure of specific applications.

2. Knowledge Base Maintenance: Application specialists fill out the knowledge base and modify its contents over time.

LSKS technology should provide techniques and tools to aid both activities.

The technological challenge for a LSKS research program is to provide tools and techniques that ensure that software development costs are at least as low for the vastly larger LSKSs are they currently are for small in-core KBSs and DBSs that are not knowledge-based.

LSKS technology will provide additional (as yet unmeasured) leverage for software development based on the application of both KBS technology (e.g., explanation) and knowledge bases themselves for software development and for automatic application generation. An improvement of one order of magnitude might be achieved in the next five years due to LSKS technology.

Contributors' Addresses

Advisory Committee
Danny Bobrow
Xerox Corporation
Palo Alto Research Center
3333 Coyote Hill Road
Palo Alto, CA 94304
415-494-4367
Bobrow@PARC

Ronald Brachman
Bell Laboratories
600 Mountain Avenue
Murry Hill, NJ 07974
415-496-4631
decvax!allegra!rjb

Michael Brodie
Computer Corporation of America
4 Cambridge Center
Cambridge, MA 02142
617-492-8860
brodie@cca

John McDermott
Department of Computer Science
Carnegie-Mellon University
Pittsburgh, PA 15213
412-268-2599
McDermott@CMUA

John Mylopoulos
Department of Computer Science
University of Toronto
Toronto, Ontario
CANADA M5S 1A4
416-978-5180
jm%utai%toronto.csnet%csnet-relay

John M. Smith
Computer Corporation of America
4 Cambridge Center
Cambridge, MA 02142
617-492-8860
jsmith@cca

Michael Stonebraker
549 Evans Hall
Department of Electrical Engineering
and Computer Science
University of California, Berkeley
Berkeley, CA 94720
415-642-5799
mike@berkeley

Research Agency Representatives

Ted M. Albert
Data Administrator
United States Geological Survey
806 National Center
Reston, VA 22092
703-860-6086

Bernard Chern
Design, Manufacturing, and
Computer Engineering Division
National Science Foundation
Room 1108
1800 G. Street, NW
Washington, DC 20550
202-357-7508
Chern@USC-ISI

Stephen Guptill
Chief, Branch of Analysis
United States Geological Survey
521 National Center
Reston, VA 22092
703-860-6345

J. Allen Sears
Information Processing
Techniques Office
Defense Advanced Research
Projects Agency
1400 Wilson Blvd.
Arlington, VA 22209
202-694-5921
Sears@USC-ISIA

Research Participants

François Bancilhon
Microelectronics and
Computer Technology Corp.
9430 Research Boulevard
Austin, TX 78759-6509
512-343-0860
Bancilhon@MCC

Robert J. Bobrow (Rusty)
Bolt, Beranek & Newman, Inc.
Department of Artificial Intelligence
10 Moulton Street
Cambridge, MA 02138
617-497-3601
Rusty@BBNG

Alex Borgida
Department of Computer Science
Rutgers University
Hill Center, Busch Campus
New Brunswick, NJ 08903
201-932-4744
borgida@red.rutgers.edu

Bruce Buchanan
Heuristic Programming Project
701 Welch Road
Stanford University
Standord, CA 94305
415-497-0935
Buchanan@Sumex-AIM

Umeshwar Dayal
Computer Corporation of America
4 Cambridge Center
Cambridge, MA 02142
617-492-8860
dayal@cca

David DeWitt
Computer Sciences Dept.
University of Wisconsin-Madison
1210 West Dayton Street
Madison, WI 53706
608-263-5489
dewitt@wisconsin.arpa

Mark Fox
Robotics Institute
Carnegie-Mellon University
Pittsburgh, PA 15213
412-268-3832
Mark.Fox@cmu-ri-isl1

Hector Garcia-Molina
Dept. of Electrical Engineering
and Computer Science
Princeton University
Princeton, NJ 08544
609-452-4633
hector%princeton@csnet-relay

Mike Genesereth
Department of Computer Science
Stanford University
Stanford, CA 94305
415-497-0324
GENESERETH@SU-SCORE

Danny Hillis
Thinking Machines Corporation
245 First Street
Cambridge, MA 02142
617-876-1111
DANNY@THINK.COM

David Israel
SRI International - EK268
333 Ravenswood Avenue
Menlo Park, CA 94025
415-859-4254
Israel@SRI-WARBUCKS

Matthias Jarke
711 Merrill Hall
New York University
90 Trinity Place
New York, NY 10006
212-285-6079
B20,M-JARKE@NYU20
effective Oct. '85 on leave at:
Johann Wolfgang Goethe-
Universitaet Frankfurt
Fachbereich Informatik
Dantestrasse 9
D-6000 Frankfurt am Main
West Germany

Randy Katz
Computer Science Division
Electrical Engineering and
Computer Science Department
Evans Hall
University of California, Berkeley
Berkeley, CA 94720
415-642-8778
randy@berkeley

Hector Levesque
Department of Computer Science
University of Toronto
Toronto, Ontario M5S 1A7
Canada
416-978-3618
hector%toronto.csnet@csnet-relay

Frank Manola
Computer Corporation of America
4 Cambridge Center
Cambridge, MA 02142
617-492-8860
manola@cca

Tom Mitchell
Department of Computer Science
Rutgers University
Hill Center, Busch Campus
New Brunswick, NJ 08903
201-932-3259
MITCHELL@RUTGERS

Shamim Naqvi
Bell Laboratories
600 Mountain Avenue
Murray Hill, NJ 07974
201-522-5101
decvax!allegra!san

Peter Szolovits
Laboratory for Computer Science
545 Technology Square
Cambridge, MA 02139
617-253-3476
PSZ@MIT-MC

Jeffrey D. Ullman
Dept. of Computer Science
Stanford University
Stanford, CA 94305
415-497-1512
ullman@su-score

Yannis Vassiliou
Graduate School of Business
Administration
New York University
90 Trinity Place
New York, NY 10006
212-598-7536
spirakis.acf1@nyu

David H. D. Warren
Dept. of Computer Science
The University of Manchester
Manchester M13 9PL
England

Bonnie Lynn Webber
Dept. of Computer
and Information Science
The Moore School
University of Pennsylvania
Philadelphia, PA 19104
215-898-7745
bonnie%upenn.csnet

Gio Wiederhold
Computer Science Department
Jacks Hall 436
Stanford University
Stanford, CA 94305
415-497-0685
wiederhold@SUMEX-AIM

Bill Woods
Applied Expert Systems
5 Cambridge Center
Cambridge, MA 02142
617-492-7322
wwoods@bbn

Student Assistants

Ellis Chang
Computer Science Division
Electrical Engineering and
Computer Science Department
Evans Hall
University of California, Berkeley
Berkeley, CA 94720
415-642-8778
chang%ucbernie@UCB-VAX

Goetz Graefe
Computer Sciences Dept.
University of Wisconsin-Madison
1210 West Dayton Street
Madison, WI 53706
608-244-6073
graefe@WISC-DB

Brian Nixon
Department of Computer Science
University of Toronto
Toronto, Ontario
CANADA M5S 1A4
416-978-4299
nixon%Toronto@CSNet-Relay

Martin Stanley
Department of Computer Science
University of Toronto
Toronto, Ontario
CANADA M5S 1A7
mts%Toronto@CSNet-Relay

References

[ABRI74]
Abrial, J.R., "Data semantics," in *Data management systems*, J.W.Klimbie and K.L.Koffeman, eds., North Holland, Amsterdam, 1974, pp. 1-59.

[AC76]
Astrahan, M. M., D. D. Chamberlin, et al., "System R: Relational Approach to Database Management," *ACM Trans. Database Systems*, 1, 1976.

[ACO85]
Albano, A., L.Cardelli, and R.Orsini, "Galileo: A strongly typed, interactive conceptual language", *ACM Trans. on Database Systems*, Vol.10, No.2, June 1985, pp.230-260.

[ADAP83]
"ADAPLEX: Rationale and Reference Manual," Technical Report CCA-83-03, Computer Corporation of America, May 1983.

[AE82]
Apt, K., M. van Emden, Contributions to the Theory of Logic Programming, *J. of the ACM 29, 3*, 1982.

[AHU76]
Aho, A., J. E. Hopcroft, and J. D. Ullman, *The Design and Analysis of Computer Algorithms*, Addison-Wesley: Reading, Massachusetts, 1976.

[AKSF83]
Aikins, J. S., Kunz, J. C., Shortliffe, E. H., and Fallat, R. J., "PUFF: An Expert System for Interpretation of Pulmonary Function Data", *Computers and Biomedical Research*, Vol. 16, pp. 199-208, 1983. Reprinted in [CS84].

[ALLE82]
Allen, J., "Recognizing Intentions from Natural Language Utterances", In M. Brady (editor), *Computational Models of Discourse*, MIT Press, Cambridge MA, 1982.

[ALLE83]
Allen, J., "Maintaining knowledge about temporal intervals", *Communications of the ACM,* Vol. 26, No. 11, November 1983, pp. 832-843.

[ANLP83]
Bea Oshika, Program Chair (editor), *Proc. of the Conference on Applied Natural Language Processing,* Association for Computational Linguistics, Santa Monica Ca, 1983.

[APPE85]
Appelt, D., *Planning English Sentences,* Cambridge University Press, Cambridge England, 1985.

[APPR85]
Afrati, F., C. H. Papadimitriou, G. Papageorgiou, and A. Roussou, "On testing convergence of the Sagiv-Ullman capture rule", unpublished memorandum, Dept. of CS, Stanford Univ., Private communication, Feb., 1985.

[ASTR76]
Astrahan, M. et. al., "System R; A Relational Approach to Data", *ACM-TODS,* June 1976.

[ASU79a]
Aho AV, Sagiv Y, Ullman JD, "Equivalences among relational expressions", *SIAM Journal of Computing,* 8:2, 218-246, 1979.

[ASU79b]
Aho, A.V., Sagiv, Y. and J.D. Ullmann, "Efficient optimization of a class of relational expressions", *ACM Transactions on Database Systems,* Vol. 4, No. 4, December 1979, pp.435-454.

[AU79]
Aho, A., J. Ullman, "Universality of Data Retrieval Languages", *Sixth ACM Symposium on Principles of Programming Languages,* 1979.

[AW83]
Allen, B.P., and J.M. Wright, "Integrating Logic Programs and Schemata", *Proceedings of the 8th International Joint Conference on Artificial Intelligence,* Karlsruhe, West Germany, 1983.

[BACK78]
Backus, J., "Can Programming Be Liberated From the von Neumann Style?" *Communications of the ACM,* (8): 613-641, 1978.

[BALZ80]
Balzer, R., et al., "HEARSAY-III: A Domain-Independent Framework for Expert Systems," *Proc. AAAI Conference,* August 1980.

[BANC85]

Bancilhon, F., "On recursive rule evaluation in a knowledge base system", *Proc. Islamorada Workshop on Large Scale Knowledge Base and Reasoning Systems*, M. L. Brodie, ed., CCA, Cambridge, Mass, 1985.

[BARR82]

Barron,J. "Dialogue and process design for Interactive Information Systems using Taxis", *Proc. SIGOA Conf. on Office Information Systems,* June 1982, Philadelphia, PA, pp.12-20.

[BATC80]

Batcher, K.E., "Design of a Massively Parallel Processor," *IEEE Transactions on Computers*, C-29 (9), 1980.

[BATE84]

Bates, M., "Accessing a Database with a Transportable Natural Language Interface", In IEEE Computer Society (editor), *Proc. First Conf. on Artificial Intelligence Applications*, IEEE, December, 1984, pages 9-12.

[BAYE85] Bayer,

"Query Evaluation and Recursion in Deductive Database Systems," *Proceedings of the Islamorada Workshop on Knowledge Base Management Systems*, February 1985 (to be published in [BROD86]).

[BB82]

Bernstein PA, Blaustein BT, "Fast methods for testing quantified relational calculus assertions", *Proceedings ACM-SIGMOD Conference*, Orlando, Fl, 39-50, 1982.

[BB84a]

Bates, L. and Bobrow, R., "Natural Language Interfaces: What's Here, What's Coming, Who Needs It", In W. Reitman (editor), *Artificial Intelligence Applications for Business*, pages 179-194. Ablex, Norwood NJ, 1984.

[BB84b]

Batory, D. S., A. P. Buchmann, "Molecular Objects, Abstract Data Types and Data Models — A Framework", *Tenth International Conference on Very Large Data Bases*, August 1984.

[BBC80]

Bernstein, P., B. Blaustein, and E. Clarke, "Fast Maintenance of Integrity Assertions Using Redundant Aggregate Data," *Proc. Sixth VLDB,* October 1980.

[BBCK79]

Brachman, R., Bobrow, R., Cohen, P., Klovstad, J., Webber, B. and Woods, W., "Research in Natural Language Understanding - Annual Report: 1 Sept 78 - 31 Aug 79", Technical Report 4274, Bolt Beranek and Newman Inc., August, 1979.

[BBDM84]

Brodie, M. L., B. Blaustein, U. Dayal, F. Manola, and A. Rosenthal, "CAD/CAM Database Management" in *IEEE Database Engineering Newsletter*, R. Katz (ed.), Special Issue on Engineering Data Management, July 1984.

[BC79]/

Buneman, P. and Clemons, E., "Efficiently Monitoring Relational Databases", *ACM-TODS*, June 1979.

[BCGK83]

Blaustein, B. T., R. M. Chilenskas, H. Garcia-Molina, C. W. Kaufman, and D. R. Ries, "Maintaining Replicated Databases Even in the Presence of Network Partitions," *Proc. Third Symposium on Reliability in Distributed Software and Database Systems,* Clearwater Beach, FL., IEEE, October 1983.

[BD81a]

Baroody, A.J. and D.J. DeWitt, "An Object-Oriented Approach to Database System Implementation", *ACM Transactions on Database Systems*, Vol. 6, No. 4, December, 1981.

[BD81b]

Barr, A. and Davidson, J., "Representation of Knowledge" in *Handbook of Artificial Intellingence*, Barr, A. and Feigenbaum E., (eds), William Kaufman, Los Altos, CA, 1981.

[BD82]

Baroody, A.J. and D.J. DeWitt, "The Impact of Run-Time Schema Interpretation in a Network Data Model DBMS", *IEEE Transactions on Software Engineering*, March 1982.

[BDFS82]

Balzer R, Dyer D, Fehling M, Saunders S, "Specification-based computing environments", *Proceedings 8th VLDB Conference*, Mexico City, 273-279, 1982.

[BDT83]

Bitton, D., DeWitt, D. and C. Turbyfill, "Benchmarking Database Systems - A Systematic Approach", *Proceedings of the 1983 Very Large Database Conference*, Florence, Italy, (October 1983), pp. 8-19.

[BEEC83]

Beech, D., "Introducing the integrated data model", Hewlett-Packard Computer Science Laboratory Technical Note CSL-15, January, 1983.

[BF83]

Brachman, R. J., Fikes, R. E., and Levesque, H. J., "Krypton: Integrating Terminology and Assertion," *Proc. AAAI-83*, Washington, DC, August, 1983, 31--35.

[BFL83a]

Brachman, R.J., R.E. Fikes and H.J. Levesque.,- "Krypton: A Functional Approach to Knowledge Representation", *IEEE COMPUTER, Special Issue on Knowledge Representation*, Vol. 16, No. 10, October 1983, pp. 67-73.

[BFL83b]

Brachman, R.J., R.E. Fikes, and H. Levesque, "KRYPTON: Integrating Terminology and Assertion," in *Proc. National Conference on Artificial Intelligence*, AAAI83, Washington, D.C, August, 1983, pp. 31-35.

[BG80]

Bobrow, D. G., I. P. Goldstein, "Representing Design Alternatives", *Proc. AISB Conference*, Amsterdam, 1980.

[BG81a]

Bernstein, P., and N. Goodman, "Concurrency Control in Distributed Database Systems", *ACM Computing Surveys*, 13(2), June 1981.

[BG81b]

Borgida, A. and S. Greenspan, "Data and activities: exploiting hierarchies of classes", *Proc. Pingree Workshop on Data abstraction, Databases and Conceptual Modeling,* ACM SIGMOD Record Vol.11, No.2, February 1981.

[BG84]

Boral, H. and I. Gold, "Towards a Self-Adapting Centralized Concurrency Control Algorithm", *Proceedings of the 1984 SIGMOD Conference*, Boston, Ma., 1984.

[BGK85]

Bobrow, D. G., I. P. Goldstein, R. H. Katz, "Context Structures/Versioning: A Survey", *Islamorada Workshop on Knowledge and Data Bases*, Islamorada, FL, February 1985.

[BGM85]

Borgida, A., S.Greenspan, J.Mylopoulos, "Knowledge representation as the basis for requirements specifications", *IEEE COMPUTER, Special issue on Requirements Engineering*, Vol.18, No.4, April 1985, pp. 82-90.

[BGRC83]

Blaustein, B. T., H. Garcia-Molina, D. R. Ries, R. M. Chilenskas, and C. W. Kaufman, "Maintaining Replicated Databases Even in the Presence of Network Partitions", *IEEE EASCON Conference*, September 1983.

[BGV46]

Burks, Arthur W., Herman H. Goldstine, and John von Neumann, "Preliminary Discussion of the Logical Design of an Electronic Computing Instrument," in Report on the Mathematical and Logical Aspects of an Electronic Computing Instrument, Pt. I, Vol. 1, The Institute for Advanced Study, ECP list of reports 1946-1957, no. 1, 1946.

[BGW82]

Balzer, R., N. Goldman, and D. Wile, "Operational specification as the basis for rapid prototyping", *Proc. ACM Software Engineering Symp. on Rapid Prototyping*, Columbia, MD., in *ACM Software Eng. Notes*, Vol.7, No.5, December 1982.

[BH80]

Ball, E. and P. Hayes, "Representation of Task-Specific Knowledge in a Gracefully Interacting User Interface," *Proc. AAAI Conference*, August 1980.

[BHR80]

Bayer, R., Heller, H., and A. Reiser, "Parallelism and Recovery in Database Systems", *ACM Transactions on Database Systems*, Vol. 5, No. 2, June 1980.

[BI84]

Brachman, R, and D. Israel, "Some Remarks on the Semantics of Representation Languages," in in Brodie, Mylopoulos, Schmidt (eds.), *Conceptual Modelling: Perspectives from Artificial Intelligence, Databases, and Programming Languages*, Springer-Verlag, New York, 1984, pp. 119-142.

[BJ84]

Brodie, M., and Jarke, M., "On Integrating Logic Programming and Data Bases", *Proc. 1st International Conference on Expert Data Base Systems*, Kiowah, S.C., Oct 1984.

[BK82]
Bowen KA, Kowalski RA, "Amalgamating language and metalanguage in logic programming", in Clark KL, Taernlund S-A (eds.), *Logic Programming*, London: Academic Press, 153-172, 1982.

[BKNT77]
Bobrow, D.G., Kaplan, R.M., Norman, D.A., Thompson, H. and Winograd, T., "GUS, A Frame-Driven Dialog System", *Artificial Intelligence*, Vol. 8, pp. 155-173, 1977.

[BL84a]
Brachman, R. J., and Levesque, H. J., "The Tractability of Subsumption in Frame-Based Description Languages," *Proc. AAAI-84*, Austin, TX, August, 1984, pp. 34-37.

[BL84b]
Brachman R.J. and H.J. Levesque, "What Makes a Knowledge Base Knowledgeable? A View of Databases from the Knowledge Level", *Proceedings of the First International Workshop on Expert Database Systems*, Kiawah Island, SC, USA, October, 1984.

[BLAS80]
Blaser, A. (ed.), *Database Techniques for Pictorial Applications*, Springer-Verlag: New York, New York, 1980.

[BLP84]
Brachman, R. J., H. J. Levesque, and P. F. Patel-Schneider, "What Makes a Knowledge Base Knowledgeable? A View of Databases from the Knowledge Level," in L. Kerschberg (ed.), *Expert Database Systems*, Proc. First Intl. Workshop on Expert Database Systems, Kiawah Island, S.C., October 1984.

[BLUM82]
Robert L. Blum, "Discovery and Representation of Causal Relationships from a Large Time-Oriented Clinical Database: The **RX** Project", *Lecture Notes in Medical Informatics No. 19*, Lindberg and Reichertz (eds.), Springer-Verlag, New York, 1982, 242 pp.

[BM84]
Bachant, J. and J. McDermott, "R1 revisited: four years in the trenches". *The AI Magazine*, Vol. 5, No. 3, 1984.

[BM86]
Brodie, M. L., and Mylopoulos, J. "Knowledge Bases and Databases: Semantic vs Computational Theories of Information", *New Directions for Database Systems*, Gad Ariav and Jim Clifford (Eds.), Ablex Publishing Co., New York, to appear 1986. Also Computer Corporation of America Report CCA-TR-85-01.

[BMN84]

Gallaire, H., J. Nicolas, J. Minker, *Advances in Database Theory*, Vol. 2, Plenum Press, New York 1984.

[BMP81]

Ben-Ari, M., Manna, Z. and Pnueli, A. "The temporal logic of branching time.", In *8th ACM POPL Symposium*, January, 1981. pp. 164-176.

[BMS83]

Brodie, M., J. Mylopoulos, J. Schmidt, *Conceptual Modelling: Perspectives from Artificial Intelligence, Databases and Programming Languages*, Springer-Verlag, 1983.

[BMS84]

Brodie, M.L., J.Mylopoulos and J.W.Schmidt, Eds. *On Conceptual Modelling: Perspectives from Artificial Intelligence, Databases and Programming Languages*, Springer Verlag, New York, 1984.

[BMW82]

Borgida A, Mylopoulos J, Wong HKT, "Methodological and computer aids for interactive information systems development", in Schneider HJ, Wasserman AI (eds.), *Automated Tools for Information Systems Development*, Amsterdam: North-Holland, pp. 109-124, 1982.

[BMW84]

Borgida, A., J. Mylopoulos, and H. K. T. Wong, "Generalization/Specialization as a Basis for Software Specification," in [BMS84], pp. 87-114.

[BMW86]

Borgida, A., Mitchell, T., and Williamson, K., "Learning Improved Integrity Constraints and Schemas from Exceptions in Databases and Knowledge Bases", in this volume.

[BORG85a]

Borgida, A., "Features of languages for the development of Information Systems at the Conceptual level", *IEEE SOFTWARE*, Vol.2, No.1, pp.63-73, January 1985.

[BORG85b]

Borgida, A., "Language features for flexible handling of exceptions in Information Systems", *ACM Trans. on Database Systems*, Vol. 10, No. 4, December 1985.

[BP83]

Barwise, J. and Perry, J., *Situations and Attitudes*, MIT Press, Cambridge MA, 1983.

[BPL85]
Brachman, R, V. Pigman, and H. Levesque, "An Essential Hybrid Reasoning System: Knowledge and Symbol Level Accounts of Krypton," in *Proc. Ninth International Joint Conference on Artificial Intelligence*, Los Angeles, CA, August, 1985, Vol I, pp. 532-539.

[BR84]
Brodie, M. L., and D. Ridjanovic, "On the Design and Specification of Database Transactions," in [BMS84].

[BRAC77]
Brachman R.J., "A Structural Paradigm for Representing Knowledge," (Ph.D. Thesis), Harvard University, May 1977.

[BRAC80]
Brachman, R. J., "An Introduction to KL-ONE", in R. J. Brachman, et al. (eds.), *Research in Natural Language Understanding*, Annual Report, Bolt, Beranek and Newman, Inc., Cambridge, Massachusetts, 1980.

[BRAD82]
Brady, M., *Computational Models of Discourse*, MIT Press, Cambridge MA, 1982.

[BRAT83]
Bratman, M., "Taking Plans Seriously", *Social Theory and Practice*, 9:271-287, 1983.

[BROD80]
Brodie, M. L., "The Application of Data Types to Database Semantic Integrity", *Information Systems,* Vol 5, No. 4, 1980.

[BROD84]
Brodie, M. L., "On the Development of Data Models," in [BMS84], 1984.

[BROD85]
Brodie, M. *Summary of Panel Discussion on Knowledge Base Management Systems*, Kiawah Workshop on Expert Database Systems, October 1984.

[BROW80]
Browning, S.A., "A Tree Machine," *Lambda Magazine*, 1 (2): 31-36, 1980.

[BS78]
Brodie, M. and H. Schmidt, "What is the use of abstract data types in databases?", *Proceedings of the 1978 VLDB Conference, pp. 140-141, 1978.*

[BS83]

Bobrow, D. G., M. Stefik, "The LOOPS Manual", Xerox Palo Alto Research Center, (1983).

[BS85]

Brachman, R.J. and Schmolze, J., "An Overview of the KL-One Knowledge Representation System," *Cognitive Science 9*, 1985, pp. 171-216.

[BSR80]

Bernstein, P., D. W. Shipman, and J. B. Rothnie, Jr., "Concurrency Control in a System for Distributed Databases (SDD-1)," *ACM Transactions on Database Systems,* Vol. 5, No. 1, March 1980.

[BUBE80]

Bubenko, J., "Information modeling in the context of system development."
Proceedings of IFIP 80, Tokyo, 1980. pp. 395-411.

[CAMP84]

Campbell, J., *Implementations of Prolog*, (ed. J. Campbell), Ellis Horwood Series in Artificial Intelligence, 1984.

[CARB85]

Carberry, S., "A Pragmatics-based Approach to Understanding Intersentential Ellipses", *Proc. of the 23rd Annual Meeting*, pages 188-197. Association for Computational Linguistics, University of Chicago, Chicago IL, July, 1985.

[CARR78]

Carre, *Graphs and Networks*, 1978.

[CASS85]

Cassell, E.J., *Talking with Patients, Volume I: The Theory of Doctor Patient Communication*, MIT Press, Cambridge MA, 1985.

[CD85]

Chou, H.T. and D.J. DeWitt, "An Evaluation of Buffer Management Strategies for Relational Database Systems", *Proceedings of the 1985 VLDB Conference*, Stockholm, Sweden, August, 1985.

[CDFG83]

Chan, A., U. Dayal, S. Fox, N. Goodman, D. Ries, and D. Skeen, "Overview of an Ada Compatible Distributed Database Manager," *Proc. ACM SIGMOD Conf. 83*, San Jose, CA, May 1983.

[CDFL82]

Chan, A., S. Danberg, S. Fox, W.K. Lin, A. Nori and D. Ries, "Storage and access structures to support a semantic data model", *Proc. 1982 VLDB Conference*, Mexico, September 1982.

[CDG84]
Carey, M., DeWitt,D., and G. Graefe, "Concurrency Control and Recovery for PROLOG - A Proposal", in *Expert Database Systems*, Benjamin/Cummings Publishing Co, to appear.

[CDKK85]
Chou, H.T., DeWitt, D.J., Katz, R., and A. Klug, Design and Implementation of the Wisconsin Storage System, *Software Practice and Experience*, August, 1985.

[CFLR81]
Chan, A., S. Fox, K. Lin, and D. Ries, "The Design of an Ada Compatible Local Database Manager," Technical Report CCA-81-09, Computer Corporation of America, Cambridge, Mass., 1981.

[CFM84]
Chakravarthy US, Fishman D, Minker J, "Semantic query optimization in expert systems and database systems", in [KERS84], 1984.

[CH79]
Chandra, A.K., D. Harel, "Computable Queries for Relational Databases", in *Proc. 11th. Sym. on Theory of Computing*, 1979.

[CH80]
Chandra, A. and Harel, D., "Computable Queries for Relational Data Bases", *JCSS 21, 156-178*, 1980.

[CH82a]
Chandra, A. and Harel, D. , "Horn Clauses and the Fixpoint Query Hierarchy", *Proceedings First PODS*, 1982.

[CH82b]
Chandra, A. and Harel, D., "Structure and Complexity of Relational Queries", *JCSS 25, 99-128*, 1982.

[CH82c]
Chandra, A., D. Harel, "Horn Clause Queries and Generalization", *ACM SIGACT-SIGMOD Symposium on Principles of Database Systems*, 1982.

[CHAN78]
Chang, C. L., "DEDUCE 2: Further Investigations of Deduction in Relational Data Bases", in H. Gallaire, J. Minker (eds.), *Logic and Data Bases*, Plenum Press: New York, New York, 1978.

[CHAN81]
Chang, C., "On the Evaluation of Queries Containing Derived Relations in Relational Database", in *Advances in Data Base Theory* Vol.1. H.Gallaire, J. Minker and J.M. Nicolas (eds.), Plenum Press, New York, pp 235-260, 1981.

[CHAN82]
Chan, A., et al, "The Implementation of an Integrated Concurrency Control and Recovery Scheme", *Proceedings of the 1982 SIGMOD Conference*, Orlando, Florida, 1982.

[CHAN85]
Chandrasekaran, B., "Generic Tasks in Expert System Design and Their Role in Explanation of Problem Solving", *Proceedings of the Workshop on AI and Distributed Problem Solving*, May, 1985.

[CHEI85]
Cheikes, B., "Monitor Offers on a Dynamic Database: The search for relevance", Technical Report CIS-85-43, Dept. of Computer and Information Science, University of Pennsylvania, October, 1985.

[CHEN76]
Chen, P.P.S., "The Entity-Relationship model: towards a unified view of data.," *ACM Trans. on Database Systems*, Vol. 1, No. 1, March 1976, pp. 9-36.

[CHEN84]
Cheng, J. et. al., "IBM Database 2 Performance: Design, Implementation and Tuning", *IBM Systems Journal*, February 1984.

[CHER84]   0
Cherniak, C., "Computational Complexity and the Universal Acceptance of Logic," in *The Journal of Philosophy*, Vol. LXXXI, No. 20, December, 1984.

[CHES80]
Chester, D., "HCPRVR: an Interpreter for Logic Programs," *Proceedings of the National Conference on Artificial Intelligence*, 1980.

[CL73]
Chang, C., R. Lee, *Symbolic Logic and Mechanical Theorem Proving*, Academic Press, 1973.

[CL81]
Clancey, W.J. and Letsinger, R., "NEOMYCIN: Reconfiguring a Rule-Based Expert System", *Proceedings of the Seventh International Joint Conference on Artificial Intelligence*, Vol. 2, 1981, pp. 829-836. Reprinted in [CS84].

[CLAN84]
Clancey, W. J., "Classification Problem Solving", *Proceedings of the National Conference on Artificial Intelligence (AAAI-84)*, pp. 49-55, August, 1984.

[CLAR78]
Clark, K., "Negation as Failure", in [GM78], 1978.

[CLAR79]
D. W. Clark, "Measurements of Dynamic List Structure Use in Lisp," *IEEE Transactions on Software Engineering*, Vol. SE-5, Num. 1, January 1979, pp. 51-59.

[CLEM81]
Clemons, E., "Design of an External Schema Facility to Define and Process Recursive Structures," *Proceedings of the ACM Transactions on Database Sytems*, Vol.6, No.2, June 1981, pp. 81-92.

[CM81]
Clocksin, W. and Mellish, C., *Programming in Prolog*, Springer-Verlag, Berlin, Germany, 1981.

[CM82]
Conklin, J. and McDonald, D., "Salience: the key to the selection problem in natural language generation", *Proceedings of the 20th Annual Meeting*, pages 129-135. Assoc. for Computational Linguistics, University of Toronto, June, 1982.

[CM84]
Copeland, G. and D. Maier, "Making Smalltalk a Database System", *Proceedings of the 1984 SIGMOD Conference*, Boston, Ma., 1984.

[CMS83]
Cammarata, C., D. McArther, and R. Steeb, "Strategies of Cooperation in Distributed Problem Solving," *Proc. IJCAI83*, Karlsruhe, August 1983.

[CMT82]
Chakravarthy, U. S., J. Minker, and D. Tran, "Interfacing Predicate Logic Languages and Relational Databases", *First International Logic Programming Conference*, France, September 1982.

[CODD70]
Codd, E. F., "A relational model for large shared data banks", *Comm. ACM*, Vol. 13, No. 6, pp. 377-387, June 1970.

[CODD72]
Codd, E.F., "Relational Completeness of Database Sublanguages", *Data Base Systems* (Ed. R. Rustin), Prentice Hall, 1972.

[CODD79]
Codd, E.F., "Extending the database relational model to capture more meaning," *ACM Trans. on Database Systems*, Vol. 4, No. 4, December 1979, pp. 395-434.

[COHE78]
   Cohen, P., "On Knowing What to Say: Planning Speech Acts", Technical Report 118, Dept. of Computer Science, Univ. of Toronto, January, 1978.

[CORE85]
   Corella, F., "Semantic Retrieval and Levels of Abstraction", In L. Kerschberg (editor), *Expert Database Systems*, Benjamin Cummings, New York, 1985.

[CP84]
   Ceri, S., Pelagatti, G.: *Distributed Databases. Principles and Systems*, McGraw-Hill, 1984.

[CPA81]
   Cohen, P.R., Perrault, C.R. and Allen, J., "Beyond Question Answering." In W. Lehnart & M. Ringle (Eds.), *Strategies for Natural Language Processing*, Lawrence Erlbaum Associates, Hillsdale, NJ., 1981.

[CS79]
   Chang, C., J. Slagle, Using Rewriting Rules for Connection Graphs to Prove Theorems, *Artificial Intelligence 12, 2*, 1979.

[CS84]
   Clancey, W. J. and Shortliffe, E. H., *Readings in Medical Artificial Intelligence: The First Decade*, Addison Wesley, 1984.

[CULL85]
   R. E. Cullingford, *Natural Language Processing: A Knowledge Engineering Approach*, Totawa: Allanheld & Rowman, 1985. (In press)

[CW84]/
   Chang, C. and Walker, A., "PROSQL: A Prolog Programming Interface with SQL/DS", *Proc. 1st International Conference on Expert Data Bases*, Kiowah, S.C., Oct 1984.

[DATE81]
   Date, C.J., *An Introduction to Databases Systems,* 3rd ed., Addison-Wesley, Reading, MA, 1981.

[DATE83]
   Date, C. J., *An Introduction to Databases Systems,* Volume II, Addison-Wesley, Reading, MA, 1983.

[DAVI79]
   Davis, R., "Interactive Transfer of Expertise", *Artificial Intelligence*, 12(2):121-157, 1979.

[DAVI84]
Davis, R., "Diagnostic Reasoning Based on Structure and Behavior", *Artificial Intelligence*, Vol. 24, 1984, pp. 347-410.

[DAYA83]
Dayal, U., "Processing Queries over Generalization Hierarchies in a Multidatabase System," *Proc. Ninth International Conference on Very Large Data Bases*, October 1983.

[DAYA85]
Dayal, U., "Query Processing in a Multidatabase System", in W. Kim, D. Reiner, D. Batory (eds.), *Query Processing in Database Systems*, Springer-Verlag: New York, New York, 1985.

[DCF82]
deCastilho, J.M.V., M.A. Casanova, and A.L. Furtado. "A temporal framework for database specifications.", In *Proceedings 8th VLDB Conference*, Mexico, September 1982. pp. 280-291.

[DDSS77]
deKleer, J., Doyle, J., Steele, G., and Sussman, G. J., "AMORD: Explicit Control of Reasoning", *Proceedings of the ACM Symposium on Artificial Intelligence and Programming Languages*, 1977, pp. 116-125.

[DEJO82]
DeJong, G., "Automatic Schema Acquisition in a Natural Language Environment", in *Proceedings of the Second National Conference on Artificial Intelligence*, pages 410-413, Pittsburgh, PA, August, 1982.

[DEWI79]
DeWitt, D.J., "DIRECT - A Multiprocessor Organization for Supporting Relational Database Management Systems", *IEEE Transactions on Computers*, June 1979, pp. 395-406.

[DEWI84]
D. J. DeWitt et al, "Implementation Techniques for Main Memory Database Systems," *Proc. SIGMOD 84*, Boston, June 1984, pp. 1-8.

[DF84]
Deering, M., and J. Faletti, "Database Support for Storage of AI Reasoning Knowledge," in L. Kerschberg (ed.), *Expert Database Systems*, Proc. First Intl. Workshop on Expert Database Systems, Kiawah Island, S.C., October 1984.

[DHMR84]
Dayal, U., H. Y. Hwang, F. Manola, A. Rosenthal, and J. M. Smith, "Knowledge-Oriented Database Management, Phase I, Final Technical Report", CCA-84-02, Computer Corporation of America, Cambridge, Mass., August 1984.

[DJ85]
Dhar V, Jarke M, "Learning from prototypes", *Proceedings Sixth International Conference on Information Systems*, Indianapolis, In, 1985.

[DJNY83]
Davis, C.G., S.Jajodia, P.A.Ng, R.Yeh (eds). *Entity-Relationship approach to Software Engineering*, North Holland, 1983.

[DK75]
Davis, R., and J. King, "An Overview of Production Systems," Memo AIM-271, Stanford Artificial Intelligence Laboratory, 1975.

[DOYL79]
Doyle, J., "A Truth Maintenance System", *Artificial Intelligence*, Vol. 12, 1979, pp. 231-272.

[DS83]
Davis R, Smith, RG, "Negotiation as a metaphor for distributed problem solving", *Artificial Intelligence*, 20, 63-109, 1983.

[DSHL82]
Daniels, D., P. Seliger, L. Haas, B. Lindsay, C. Mohan, A. Walker, and P. L. Wilus, "An Introduction to Distributed Query Compilation in R*", in *Distributed Databases,* H. J. Schneider (ed.), 1982, pp. 291-309.

[DST80]
Downey PJ, Sethi R, Tarjan RE, "Variations on the common subexpression problem", *Journal of the ACM*, 27, 4, 758-771, 1980.

[EGLT76]
Eswaren, K. P., J. N. Gray, R. Lorie, and I. L. Traiger, "The Notions of Consistency and Predicate Locks in a Database System", *Communication ACM*, 19, 11, November 1976.

[EHLR80]
Erman L.D., F. Hayes-Roth, V.R. Lesser, and D.R. Reddy, "The Hearsay-II Speech-Understanding System: Integrating Knowledge to Resolve Uncertainty", *Computing Surveys*, Vol. 12, No. 2, June 1980, pp. 213-253.

[ENDE72]
Enderton, H.B. "A mathematical introduction to logic" Academic Press, 1972.

[ERIC78]
Erickson, R. D., "Optimality of stationary halting policies and finite termination of successive approximations", TR — 33, Dept. of OR, Stanford Univ.

[ESWA75]/
Eswaren, K., "A General Purpose Trigger Subsystem and Its Inclusion in a Relational Data Base System", RJ 1833, IBM Research, San Jose, Ca., July 1975.

[FAGI81]
Fagin R, "A normal form for relational databases that is based on domains and keys", *ACM Transactions on Database Systems*, 6:3, 387-415, 1981.

[FAHL77]
Fahlman, S. E., *NETL: A System for Representing and Using Real World Knowledge,* MIT Press, 1979.

[FAHL79]
Fahlman, S.E., *NETL: A System for Representing and Using Real-World Knowledge*, MIT Press, 1979.

[FB81]
Feldman, J.A. and D.H. Ballard, "Computing with Connections," TR7, Department of Computer Science, University of Rochester, 1981.

[FBL71]
Feigenbaum, E.A., Buchanan, B.G. and Lederberg, J., "On Generality and Problem Solving: A Case Study Using the DENDRAL Program", in *Machine Intelligence 6*, Meltzer, B. and Michie, D. (eds.), American Elsevier, New York, 1971, pp. 165-190.

[FC85]
Furtado A, Casanova M, "Updating relational views", in Kim W, Reiner D, Batory DS (eds.), *Query Processing in Database Systems*, New York: Springer-Verlag, 206-217, 1985.

[FCKH80]
Friedell, M., R. Carling, D. Kramlich, and C. F. Herot, "The Management of Very Large Two-Dimensional Raster Graphics Environments", *Workshop on Picture Data Description and Management*, August 1980.

[FIND79]
Findler, N.V., "Associative Networks: Representation and Use of Knowledge by Computer", Academic Press, New York, 1979.

[FLRR84]
Fox, S., T. Landers, D. R. Ries, and R. Rosenberg, *DAPLEX User's Manual*, Computer Corporation of America, Cambridge, Massachusetts, 1984.

[FM77]
Forgy, C. L., and J. McDermott, "OPS — A Domain-Independent Production System Language", *Fifth International Joint Conference on Artificial Intelligence*, Cambridge, Massachusetts, 1977.

[FORG79]
Forgy, C. L., "On the Efficient Implementation of Production Systems," Ph. D. Dissertation, Carnegie-Mellon University, 1979.

[FORG81]
Forgy, C., "OPS5 User's Manual", Technical Report No. CMU-CS-81-135, Carnegie-Mellon University, 1981.

[FORG82]
Forgy, C.L., "Rete: a fast algorithm for the many pattern/many object pattern match problem", *Artificial Intelligence*, Vol 19, No 1, 1982.

[FORG84]
C. L. Forgy, "The OPS83 Report," Department of Computer Science, Carnegie-Mellon University, May 1984.

[FOX79]
Fox M.S., "On Inheritance in Knowledge Representation", *Proceedings of the Sixth International Joint Conference on Artificial Intelligence*, pp. 282-284, Tokyo Japan, 1979.

[FS84]
Fox M., and S. Smith, "ISIS: A Knowledge-Based System for Factory Scheduling", *International Journal of Expert Systems*, Vol. 1, No. 1, 1984.

[FSG84]
Fox M., A. Sathi, and M. Greenberg, "The Application of Knowledge Representation Techniques to Project Management", *Proceedings of the IEEE Workshop on Principles of Knowledge-Based Systems*, Colorado, 1984.

[FSG85]
Sathi A., Fox M., and M. Greenberg, "Representation of Activity Knowledge for Project Management", *IEEE Transaction on Pattern Analysis and Machine Intelligence*, Vol. PAM-7, No.5, September 1985, pp. 531-552.

[FWA84]

Fox M.S., J.M. Wright, and D. Adam, "Experiences with SRL: An Analysis of a Frame-based Knowledge Representation", *Proceedings of the First International Workshop on Expert Database Systems*, Kiawah Island, SC, 1984.

[GARC83]

Garcia-Molina, H., "Using Semantic Knowledge for Transaction Processing in a Distributed Database," *ACM Transactions on Database Systems*, Vol. 8, No. 2, June 1983.

[GAZD79]

Gazdar, G., "A Solution to the Projection Problem", in Oh, C.-K. and Dinneen, D. (editors), *Syntax and Semantics*, pages 57-90. Academic Press, New York, 1979.

[GB80a]

Goldstein, I. P., D. G. Bobrow, "A Layered Approach to Software Design", in D. Barstow, H. Shrobe, G. Sandwall (editors) *Interactive Programming Environments* IP [GB80b]   Goldstein, I. P., D. G. Bobrow, "Descriptions for a Programming Environment", *Proc. 1st Ann. Conf. Am. Assoc. Art. Int.*, (August 1980).

[GB81]

Goldstein, I. P., D. G. Bobrow, "Layered Networks as a Tool for Software Development", *Proceedings 7th International Joint Conference on AI*, August 1981.

[GBM82]

Greenspan, S., A.Borgida, and J.Mylopoulos. "Capturing more world knowledge in the requirements specification", Proc. 6th International Conference on Software Engineering, Tokyo, 1982.

[GBW83]

Geschke, M. J., R. A. Bullock, and L. E. Widmaier, "TAC*II — An Expert Knowledge Based System for Tactical Decision Making," Master's Thesis, Naval Postgraduate School, Monterey, CA, June 1983.

[GENE83]

Genesereth, M. R., "MRS: a metalevel representation system", HPP — 83 — 28, Dept. of CS, Stanford Univ., 1983.

[GHW82]

Guttag, J., J.Horning, and J.Wing. "Some Notes on Putting Formal Specifications to Productive Use", Xerox PARC Report CSL-82-3, June 1982.

[GJW83]
Grosz, B., Joshi, A.K. and Weinstein, S., "Providing a Unified Account of Definite Noun Phrases in Discourse", *Proc. 21st Annual Meeting*, pages 44-50. Assoc. for Computational Ling., Cambridge MA, June, 1983.

[GKLS81]
Goodman. N., R. Katz, T. Landers, J. M. Smith, and L. Yedwab, "Database Integration and Incompatible Data Handling in MULTIBASE — A System for Integrating Heterogeneous Distributed Databases," Technical Report CCA-81-06, Computer Corporation of America, Cambridge, Mass., May 1981.

[GLH83]
H. Garcia-Molina, R. Lipton, and P. Honeyman, "A Massive Memory Database System," Technical Report 314, Department of Electrical Engineering and Computer Science, Princeton University, May 1983.

[GLV84]
H. Garcia-Molina, R. Lipton, and J. Valdes, "A Massive Memory Machine," *IEEE Transactions on Computers*, Vol. C-33, Num. 5, May 1984, pp. 391-399.

[GM78]
Gallaire, H. and Minker, J. (eds.), *Logic and Data Bases.* New York, Plenum Press, 1978.

[GMB82]
Greenspan, S., J.Mylopoulos, A.Borgida, "Capturing more world knowledge in the requirements specification", *Proc. 6th International Conference on Software Engineering*, Tokyo, 1982.

[GMN81]
Gallaire, H., J. Nicolas, J. Minker, *Advances in Database Theory*, Vol. 1, Plenum Press, New York 1981.

[GMN84]
Gallaire, H.,J. Minker, J. Nicolas, *Advances in Database Theory*, Plenum Press, Vol. 2, 1984.

[GOLD70]
Goldman, A., *A Theory of Human Action*, Prentice-Hall Inc., Englewood Cliffs NJ, 1970.

[GR83]
Goldberg, A. and D. Robson, *Smalltalk-80: The Language and its Implementation*, Addison-Wesley, 1983.

[GRAY78]/
Gray, J., "Notes on Data Base Operating Systems", RJ 2254, IBM Research, San Jose, Ca., August 1978.

[GRAY79]
Gray, J., "Notes On Database Operating Systems", in *Operating Systems: An Advanced Course*, R. Bayer, R. M. Graham and G. Seegmuller (eds.), pp. 393-481, Springer-Verlag, 1979.

[GRAY81]
Gray J, "The transaction concept -- virtues and limitations", *Proceedings 7th Very Large Data Base Conference*, Cannes, 144-154, 1981.

[GRAY83]
J. Gray, "What Difficulties Are Left in Implementing Database Systems", Invited Talk at *SIGMOD Conference*, San Jose, CA., May 1983.

[GREE83]
Greenberg M., "RETINAS User's Manual", Internal report, Robotics Institute, Carnegie-Mellon University, Pittsburgh PA, 1983.

[GREE84]
Greenspan, S. "Requirements modeling: A knowledge representation approach to software requirements definition", Ph.D. Thesis, Dept. of Computer Science, University of Toronto, 1984; also CSRG Report No. 155.

[GREW83]
Grewendorf, G., "What Answers can be Given?", in F. Kiefer (editor), *Questions and Answers*, pages 45-84. D. Reidel Publishing Company, 1983.

[GRIC75]
Grice, H. P., "Logic and Conversation", in P. Cole and J.L. Morgan (editors), *Syntax and Semantics*, Academic Press, New York, 1975.

[GS82]
Guttman, A. and M. Stonebraker, "Using a Relational Database Management System for Computer Aided Design Data", *IEEE Database Engineering*, Vol. 5, No. 2, June, 1982.

[GSP76]
Gorry, G. A., Silverman, H., and Pauker, S. G., "Capturing Clinical Expertise: A Computer Program that Considers Clinical Responses to Digitalis", *American Journal of Medicine*, Vol. 64, March, 1978, pp. 452-460.

[GSP78]

Gorry, G. A., Silverman, H., and Pauker, S. G., "Capturing Clinical Expertise: A Computer Program that Considers Clinical Responses to Digitalis", *American Journal of Medicine*, Vol. 64, pp. 452-460, March, 1978.

[GUTT84]

Guttman, A., "R-Trees: A Dynamic Index Structure for Spatial Searching", *Proceedings of the 1984 SIGMOD Conference*, Boston, Ma., 1984.

[HAGM83]

Hagmann, R., "Preferred classes: a proposal for faster Smalltalk-80 execution", in *Smalltalk-80: Bits of History, Words of Advice*, G. Krasner, Editor, Addison-Wesley, 1983, pp. 323-330.

[HAGM84]

R. Hagmann, "A Crash Recovery Scheme for a Memory Resident Database System," Unpublished manuscript, July 1984.

[HALS79]

Halstead, R.H., "Reference Tree Networks: Virtual Machine and Implementation," MIT/LCS/TR-222, Massachusetts Institute of Technology, Laboratory for Computer Science, Cambridge, MA, 1979.

[HARM85]

G. H. Harman, *Reasoned Revision of Belief.*

[HAYE76]

Hayes-Roth, F. "Patterns of Induction and Associated Knowledge Acquisition Algorithms", In Chen, C. (editor), *Pattern Recognition and Artificial Intelligence.* Academic Press, New York, 1976.

[HAYE85]

Hayes, P., "Some problems and non-problems in representation theory" in *Readings in Knowledge representation*, Brachman, R., and Levesque, H., (eds), Morgan Kaufman, Los Altos, 1985.

[HB80]

Hammer, M. and B.Berkowitz, "DIAL: A programming language for data intensive applications," *Proc. ACM-SIGMOD Conference*, May 1980, pp. 75-92.

[HCR84]

Hasling, D., Clancey, W. and Rennels, G., "Strategic Explanations for a Diagnostic Consultation System", *Intl J. of Man-Machine Studies*, 20:3-20, January, 1984.

[HD82]

Hawthorn, Paula B. and David J. DeWitt, "Performance Analysis of Alternative Database Machine Architectures," *IEEE Transactions on Software Engineering*, SE-8 (1): 61-74, 1982.

[HEND75]

Hendrix, G. "Expanding the Utility of Semantic Networks Through Partitioning", Proceedings IJCAI-75, Tbilisi, USSR, 1975.

[HEWI71]

Hewitt, C., "Planner: A Language for Proving Theorems in Robots", *Proc. 1971 Internation Joint Conference on Artificial Intelligence*, 1971.

[HEWI72]

Hewitt, C., *Description and Theoretical Analysis (Using Schemata) of PLANNER: A Language for Proving Theorems and Manipulating Models in a Robot*, Ph.D. thesis, Dept. of Mathematics, MIT, Cambridge, MA, 1972.

[HEWI80]

Hewitt, C.E., "The Apiary Network Architecture for Knowledgeable Systems," *Proceedings of Lisp Conference*, Stanford, 107-118, 1980.

[HEWI85a]

Hewitt C, "Implications of open systems", in Jarke M (ed.), *Managers, Micros, and Mainframes: Integrating Systems for End Users, London: John Wiley & Sons, 1985.*

[HEWI85b]

Hewitt, C., "The Challenge of Open Systems", presented at the Artificial Intelligence Conference, Capri, Italy, 1985.

[HH80]

Haas N, Hendrix GG, "An approach to acquiring and applying knowledge", Technical Note 227, SRI International, Menlo Park, Ca, 1980.

[HHW84]

Hollan, J., Hutchines, E. and Weitzman, L., "STEAMER: An Interactive Inspectable Simulation-based Training System", *AI Magazine*, 5(2):15-28, Summer, 1984.

[HILL85]

Hillis, W. Daniel, *The Connection Machine*, The MIT Press, 1985.

[HIRS85]

Hirschberg, J., "Scalar Implicature", PhD thesis, University of Pennsylvania, December, 1985.

[HL82]
Haskin, R. and R. Lorie, "On Extending the Functions of a Relational Database System", *Proceedings of the 1982 ACM SIGMOD Conference*, Orlando, FL, 1984, pp. 207-212.

[HM75]
Hammer, M. M., and D. J. McLeod, "Semantic Integrity in a Relational Data Base System," *Proc. International Conference on Very Large Data Bases*, September 1975.

[HM81]
Hammer, M. and D.McLeod, "Database description with SDM: a semantic data model," *ACM Trans. on Database Systems*, Vol. 6, No. 3, Sept. 1981.

[HMN83]
Henschen LJ, McCune WW, Naqvi SA, "Compiling constraint-checking programs from first-order formulas", in Gallaire H, Minker J, Nicolas J-M (eds.), *Advances in Database Theory 2*, New York: Plenum Press, 145-169, 1983.

[HN84]
Henschen, L. J. and S. A. Naqvi, "On compiling queries in recursive first-order databases", *J. ACM, Vol. 31, No. 1, pp. 47-85, January, 1984.*

[HOLL81]
Holland, John H., "Genetic Algorithms and Adaptation," Technical Report No. 34, University of Michigan, 1981.

[HOPF82]
Hopfield, J.J., "Neural Networks and Physical Systems with Emergent Collective Computational Abilities," *Proceedings of the National Academy of Sciences USA*, (79): 2554-2558, 1982.

[HR79]
Hobbs, J. and Robinson, J., "Why Ask?", *Discourse Processes*, 2, 1979.

[HR85]
Heiler, S. I., and Rosenthal, A., "G-WHIZ: A Visual Interface for the Functional Model with Recursion", submitted to *11th International Conference on Very Large Data Bases*, 1985.

[HS84]
Hinton, G.E. and T.J. Sejnowski, "Learning semantic features," *Proceedings of the Sixth Annual Conferences of the Cognitive Science Society*, Boulder, CO, 1984.

[HWL83]
Hayes-Roth, F., D. A. Waterman, and D. B. Lenat, *Building Expert Systems*, Addison-Wesley, Reading, Mass., 1983.

[HZ80]
Hammer, M. and S. Zdonik, "Knowledge-based query processing", *Proc. 6th VLDB Conference*, Montreal, 1980, pp.137-147.

[IEEE77]
IEEE Trans. on Software Engineering, Vol. SE-3, No. 1, January 1977.

[IMME82]
Immerman N, "Relational queries computable in polynomial time", *Proceedings 14th ACM Symposium on Theory of Computing*, San Francisco, Ca, 147-152, 1982.

[IOAN84]
Ioannides, Y., et al., "Enhancing INGRES with Deductive Power", *Proceedings of the 1st International Workshop on Expert Database Systems, Kiowah SC, October 1984.*

[IOAN85]
Ioannides, Y., "A Time Bound on the Materialization of some Recursively Defined Views", *Proceedings of the Eleventh Conference on Very Large Data Bases*, 1985.

[ISL84]
ISL, "Intelligent Systems Laboratory Software Systems Manual", Internal report, Robotics Institute, Carnegie-Mellon University, Pittsburgh PA, 1984.

[ISRA83]
Israel, D., "Interpreting Network Formalisms," in N.J. Cercone (ed.), *Computational Linguistics*, International Series in Modern Applied Mathematics and Computer Science, Vol. 5, 1983, Pergamon Press, Toronto, pp. 1-13.

[JAME82]
James, G., and W. Stoeller, "Operations on Tree-Structured Tables", X3H2-26-15 Standards Committee Working Paper, 1982, pp. 81-92.

[JARK84]
Jarke M, "External semantic query simplification: a graph-theoretic approach and its implementation in PROLOG", in [KERS84], 1984.

[JARK85]

Jarke M, "Common subexpression analysis in multiple query optimization", in Kim W, Reiner D, Batory DS (eds.), *Query Processing in Database Systems*, New York: Springer-Verlag, 191-205, 1985.

[JARK86]

Jarke M., "Control of Search and Knowledge Acquisition", in this volume, 1986.

[JCV84]

Jarke M, Clifford J, Vassiliou Y, "An Optimizing PROLOG Front-end to a Relational Query System", *Proceedings ACM-SIGMOD Conference*, Boston, Ma, 296-306, 1984.

[JIEH85]

Jieh Hsiang, "Refutational Theorem Proving using Term-Rewriting Systems," in *Artificial Intelligence*, Vol. 25, March, 1985, pp. 225-300.

[JJS86]

Jarke M, Jelassi MT, Shakun MF, "MEDIATOR: Towards a negotiation support system", to appear in Shakun MF (ed.), *Evolutionary Systems Design: Policy Making under Complexity*, San Francisco: Holden Day, 1986.

[JK83]

Jarke, M. and J. Koch, "Range nesting: a fast method to evaluate quantified queries", *Proc. ACM SIGMOD Conference*, San Jose, 1983, pp.196-206.

[JK84]

Jarke, M., Koch, J., "Query optimization in database systems", *ACM Computing Surveys*, 16:2, 1984, pp. 111-152.

[JOSH82]

Joshi, A.K., "Mutual Beliefs in Question Answering Systems", in N. Smith (editor), *Mutual Belief*, Academic Press, New York, 1982.

[JS84]Jarke M, Shalev J, "A database architecture for supporting business transactions", *Journal of MIS*, 1:1, 1984.

[JV83]

Jarke, M., and Y. Vassiliou, "Coupling Expert Systems with Database Management Systems," NYU Symposium on Artificial Intelligence Application for Business, May 1983.

[JV84]

Jarke M, Vassiliou Y, "Coupling expert systems with database management systems", in Reitman WR (ed.), *Artificial Intelligence Applications for Business*, Norwood, NJ: Ablex Publ., pp. 65-85, 1984.

[JWW84a]

Joshi, A., Webber, B. and Weischedel, R., "Preventing False Inferences", *Proceedings of COLING-84*, Stanford CA, July, 1984.

[JWW84b]

Joshi, A., Webber, B. and Weischedel, R., "Living Up to Expectations: Computing Expert Responses", *Proceedings of AAAI-84*, Austin TX, August, 1984.

[JWW84c]

Joshi, A., Webber, B. and Weischedel, R., "Default Reasoning in Interaction", *Proceedings of 1984 Workshop on Non-Monotonic Reasoning*, AAAI, Menlo Park CA, October, 1984.

[KAPL82]

Kaplan, J., "Cooperative Responses from a Portable Natural Language Database Query System", M. Brady (editor), *Computational Models of Discourse*, MIT Press, Cambridge MA, 1982.

[KBB83]

Kaufman, C. W., J. Barnett, and B. T. Blaustein, "The DACOS Forms-Based Query System", *Journal of Telecommunication Networks*, 1983 (pp. 463-482).

[KELL86]

Keller, A.M., "Choosing a View Update Translator by Dialog at View Definition Time, *IEEE Computer*, Jan.1986.

[KERS84]

Kerschberg L, ed., *Expert Database Systems*, New York: Springer-Verlag, to appear, 1984.

[KHIS84]

Kung, R., E. Hanson, Y. Ioannidis, T. Sellis, L. Shapiro, and M. Stonebraker, "Heuristic Search in Database Systems", *Proc. First Int'l Workshop on Expert Database Systems,* October 1984, pp. 96-107.

[KING80a]

King, J., "Intelligent Retrieval Planning", *Proc. 1st Natl. Conf. on AI*, pp.243-245, August 1980.

[KING80b]

King, J. "Modelling Concepts for Reasoning about Access to Knowledge, *Proc.of the ACM Workshop on Data Abstraction, Data Bases, and Conceptual Modelling,* Pingree Park CO, June 23--26, 1980, ACM-SIGPLAN Notices, Vol. 16, No. 1, January 1981.

[KING81]

King JJ, "QUIST: A system for semantic query optimization in relational data bases", *Proceedings 7th VLDB Conference,* Cannes, France, pp. 510-517, 1981.

[KK83]

Kaehler, T. and T. Krasner, "LOOM — Large objected oriented memory for Smalltalk-80 systems", in *Smalltalk-80: Bits of History, Words of Advice,* G. Krasner, Editor, Addison-Wesley, 1983, pp. 323-330.

[KK84]

Kotteman JE, Konsynski BR, "Dynamic metasystems for information systems development", *Proceedings Fifth International Conference on Information Systems,* Tucson, Az, 187-204, 1984.

[KKMF84]

Kitakami H, Kunifuji S, Miyachi T, Furukawa K, *Proceedings International Symposium on Logic Programming,* Atlantic City, NJ, 131-142, 1984.

[KL80]

Kung, H.T. and C.E. Leiserson, "Systolic Arrays," in *Introduction to VLSI Systems,* C.A. Mead and L.A. Conway, Addison-Wesley, sec. 8.3, 1980.

[KL84]

Katz, R. H., T. J. Lehman, "Database Support for Versions and Alternatives of Large Design Files", *IEEE Transactions on Software Engineering,* Vol. SE-10, No. 2, March 1984.

[KONO81]

Konolige, K., "A Metalanguage Representation of Relational Databases for Deductive Question-Answering Systems", in *Conf. on Very Large Databases,* Montreal, 1981.

[KOSH84]

Koshafian, Setrag, *A Building Blocks Approach to Statistical Databases,* Ph.D. Thesis, Computer Sciences Department, University of Wisconsin, June, 1984.

[KOWA74]

Kowalski, R., "Predicate logic as a programming language", *Proc. 1974 IFIP Congress,* pp. 569-574, North Holland, 1974.

[KOWA75]
Kowalski, R., "A Proof Procedure Using Connection Graphs," *J. ACM*, 22 (4), October, 1975, pp. 572-595.

[KOWA78]
Kowalski, R., Logic for Data Description, In [GM78], 1978.

[KOWA79]
Kowalski, R., *Logic for Problem Solving*, Elsevier, 1979.

[KOWA81]
Kowalski RA, *Logic as a database language*, Imperial College, London, 1981.

[KP81]
Koenig, S. and Paige, R., "A transformational Framework for the Automatic Control of Derived Data", *Proceedings Seventh VLDB*, Cannes, France, September 1981.

[KRAM86]
Kramer, B. "Representing Control Knowledge", PhD thesis, Department of Computer Science, University of Toronto, (forthcoming).

[KRAS83]
Krasner G, ed., *Smalltalk-80*, Reading, Mass: Addison-Wesley, 1983.

[KRB85]
Kim, W., D. Reiner, and D. Batory (eds.), *Query Processing in Database Systems,* Springer-Verlag, New York, NY, February 1985.

[KRD85]
Kim, W., Reiner, D. and Batory, D. (eds.), *Query Processing in Database Systems*, Springer-Verlag, 1985.

[KT81]
Kellogg, C. and Travis, L., "Reasoning with Data in a Deductively Augmented Data Management System", H. Gallaire (editor), *Advances in Data Bases*, pages 261-295. Plenum Press, 1981.

[KT83]
Kowalski, T., and D. Thomas, "The VLSI Design Automation Assistant: Prototype System", *Proceedings of the 20th ACM-IEEE Design Automation Conference*, June 1983.

[KUIP85]
Kuipers, B., "Qualitative Simulation in Medical Physiology: A Progress Report", MIT/LCS/TM-280, MIT Laboratory for Computer Science, Cambridge, MA, June 1985.

[LAFU82]
Lafue GME, "Semantic integrity dependencies and delayed integrity checking", *Proceedings 8th VLDB Conference*, Mexico City, 292-299, 1982.

[LAL82]
Lang, K., Auld, R. and Lang, T., "The Goals and Methods of Computer Users", *Int. J. Man-Machine Studies*, 17:375-399, 1982.

[LBEF82]
Litwin, W., J. Baudenant, C. Esculier, A. Ferrier, A. M. Glorieux, J. La Chimia, K. Kabbai, C. Moulinoux, P. Rolin, and C. Stranget, "SIRIUS Systems for Distributed Database Management," in *Distributed Databases*, H. J. Schneider (ed.), North Holland, 1982.

[LEHN81]
Lehnert, W., "A Computational Theory of Human Question Answering", A. Joshi, B. Webber and I. Sag (editors), *Elements of Discourse Understanding*, chapter 6, pages 145-176. Cambridge University Press, 1981.

[LEVE77]
Levesque, H., "A Procedural Approach to Semantic Networks", TR-105, Dept. of Computer Science, University of Toronto, 1977.

[LEVE81]
Levesque, H. J., "The Interaction with Incomplete Knowledge Bases: A Formal Treatment," *Proc. IJCAI-81*, Vancouver, 1981, pp. 240-245.

[LEVE83]
Levesque, H., The Logic of Incomplete Knowledge Bases, In [BMS83].

[LEVE84a]
Levesque, H., "Foundations of a Functional Approach to Representation", *Artificial Intelligence*, 23(2):155-212, July, 1984.

[LEVE84b]
Levesque, H. J., "The Logic of Incomplete Knowledge Bases," in [BMS84], pp. 165-186, 1984.

[LEVE84c]
Levesque, H., "A fundamental tradeoff in Knowledge Representation and reasoning", *Proc. of the CSCSI/SCEIO Conf.*, London, Ontario, 1984.

[LEVE84d]
Levesque, H., "A logic of explicit and implicit belief", in *Proc. of the AAAI-84 Conference*, Austin, Texas, 1984.

[LEVI83]
Levinson, S., *Pragmatics*, Cambridge University Press, Cambridge England, 1983.

[LEWI78]
Lewis, H., "Complexity of Solvable Cases of the Decision Problem for the Predicate Calculus," in *Proc. 19th IEEE Symposium on Foundations of Computer Science*, 1978, pp. 35-47.

[LGSJ78]
V.Lum, S.Ghosh, M.Scholnick, D.Jefferson, S.Su, J.Fry, T.Teorey, B.Yao, "1978 New Orleans Data Base Design Workshop Report", IBM Report RJ2554(33154)7/13/79.

[LIPS79]
Lipski, W., On Semantic Issues Connected with Incomplete Information Databases, *ACM Trans. on Database Systems 4,3*, Sept. 1979.

[LITW84]
Litwin, W., "MALPHA, A Multidatabase manipulation language", *Proc. IEEEDEC*, April, 1984.

[LOHM83]
Lohman, G. M., et al., "Remotely Sensed Geophysical Databases: Experience and Implications for Generalized DBMS", *ACM SIGMOD International conference on Management of Data*, 1983.

[LONG81]
P. Proctor (ed.), *Longman Dictionary of Contemporary English*, Bath, UK: Longman Group, Ltd. 1981

[LONG83]
Long, W. J., "Reasoning About State from Causation and Time in a Medical Domain", *AAAI*, 1983.

[LORI81]
Lorie, R. A. , "Issues in Database for Design Applications," IBM Research Report RJ3176, IBM Research Lab., San Jose, CA, July 1981.

[LP83]
Lorie, R. and W. Plouffe, "Complex Objects and Their Use in Design Transactions", *Proceedings of the Engineering Design Applications of the 1983 ACM-IEEE Database Week*, San Jose, CA, May 1983.

[LR82]
Landers, T., and R. L. Rosenberg, "An Overview of MULTI-BASE," in *Proc. 2nd International Symposium on Distributed Data-bases,* H. J. Schneider (ed.), Berlin, W. Germany, September 1982.

[LZ74a]
Liskov, B., and Zilles, S., "Programming with Abstract Data Types," *SIGPLAN Notices,* Vol. 9, No. 4, 1974.

[LZ74b]
Liskov, B. and Zilles, S., "Specification Techniques for Data Abstraction", Transactions on Software Engineering, Vol. 1, No. 1, March 1975, 7-19.

[MACS83]
"Macsyma Reference Manual -- Version 10", MIT Laboratory for Computer Science Report, Cambridge, Mass., January, 1983.

[MAIE83]
Maier, D., *The Theory of Relational Databases,* Computer Science Press, Potomac, MD, 1983.

[MAYS80]
Mays, E., "Failures in natural language systems: application to data base query systems", fIProc. First National Conference on Artificial Intelligence (AAAI), Stanford CA, August, 1980.

[MAYS83]
Mays, E., "A Modal Temporal Logic for Reasoning about Change", *Proc. 1983 Assoc. for Computational Linguistics Conference,* Cambridge MA, June, 1983.

[MAYS85]
Mays, E., "A Temporal Logic for Reasoning about Changing Data Bases in the Context of Natural Language Question-Answering", In L. Kerschberg (editor), *Expert Database Systems,* New York: Benjamin Cummings, 1985.

[MB85]
Mylopoulos J, Brodie ML, "AI and databases: semantic vs. computational theories of information", in Ariav G, Clifford J (eds.), *New Directions for Database Systems,* Norwood, NJ: Ablex Publ, 1985.

[MBW80]
J. Mylopoulos, P. Bernstein and H.K.T. Wong, "A language facility for designing interactive database-intensive systems", *ACM Trans. on Database Systems,* Vol. 5, No. 2, June 1980, pp. 185-207.

[MCAL80]
D. McAllester, "An Outlook on Truth Maintenance," MIT AITR-551, August 1980.

[MCCA68]
McCarthy, J. "Programs with common sense." In *Semantic information processing*, M.Minsky (editor), The MIT Press, 1968.

[MCCA80]
McCarthy, J., "Circumscription, A Form of Non-Monotonic Reasoning", *Artificial Intelligence 13,* 1980.

[MCCA81]
McCawley, J. *Everything linguists ever wanted to know about logic, but were afraid to ask.,* University of Chicago Press, 1981.

[MCCO83]
McCoy, K., "Correcting Misconceptions: What to Say", *CHI'83 Conference Human Factors in Computing Systems,* Cambridge MA, December, 1983.

[MCCO85]
McCoy, K., "Correcting Object-related Misconceptions", Technical Report MS-CIS-85-57, University of Pennsylvania, Dept. of Computer and Information Science, 1985. Ph.D. Thesis.

[MCDE80]
McDermott, J., "R1: An Expert in the Computer Systems Domain", *Proceedings of the First Annual National Conference on Artificial Intelligence,* Stanford, CA, 1980.

[MCDE81]
McDermott, D. "A temporal logic for reasoning about processes and plans." Technical Report 196, Dept. of Computer Science, Yale University, March, 1981.

[MCDE82a]
McDermott, J. "R1: A Rule-based Configurer of Computer Systems", *Artificial Intelligence,* Vol. 19, No. 1, 1984.

[MCDE82b]
McDermott, J., "R1's Formative Years", *Artificial Intelligence Magazine,* Vol. 2, No. 2, 1982, pp. 21-29.

[MCDE83]
McDermott, J. "Extracting Knowledge from Expert Systems", Proceedings of IJCAI-83, Karlsruhe, West Germany, 1983.

[MCKE85]
McKeown, K., *Text Generation: Using Discourse Strategies and Focus Constraints to Generate Natural Language Text,* Cambridge University Press, Cambridge, England, 1985.

[MCLE78]
McLeod, D. "A semantic database model and its associated structured user interface", PhD Thesis, MIT, 1978.

[MCM82]
Michalski, R.S., Carbonell, J.G. and Mitchell, T.M (eds.), *Machine Learning: An Artificial Intelligence Approach*, Tioga Press, 1982.

[MCM83]
Michalski, R., Carbonell, J. and Mitchell, T., *Machine Learning: An Artificial Intelligence Approach.*, Tioga Publishing Company, 1983.

[MCM85]
Mitchell, T., Carbonell, J., and Michalski, R. (eds.), *Machine Learning: A Guide to Current Research*, Kluwer Academic Press, 1986.

[MD80]
D. V. McDermott and J. Doyle, "Non-Monotonic Logic I," *Artificial Intelligence*, Vol. 13, 1980

[MERR84]
Merrett, T. H., *Relational Information Systems*, Reston Publishing: Reston, Virginia, 1984.

[MINK78]
Minker, J., "An Experimental Relational Database System Based on Logic", in H. Gallaire, J. Minker (eds.), *Logic and Databases*, Plenum Press: New York, New York, 1978.

[MINK81]
Minker, J., "On Indefinite Databases and the Closed World Assumption", Univ. of Maryland Technical Report No. 1076, 1981.

[MINK82]
Minker, J., On Indefinite Databases and the Closed World Assumption, 6th Conf. on Automated Deduction, New York, in *Lecture Notes in Computer Science*, no. 138, (ed. D. Loveland), Springer-Verlag, 1982.

[MINS75]
Minsky, Marvin, "A Framework for Representing Knowledge", in *The Psychology of Computer Vision*, Winston, Patrick H. (ed.), McGraw-Hill, New York, 1975.

[MINS79]
Minsky, M., "K-Lines: A Theory of Memory," Massachusetts Institute of Technology Artificial, Intelligence Laboratory Memo 516. Reprinted in *Cognitive Science*, (1980) 117-133, 1979.

[MITC82]
Mitchell, T., "Generalization as Search", *Artificial Intelligence 18(2)*, pp.203-226, March 1982.

[MITC83]
Mitchell, T., "Learning and Problem Solving", *Proc. of IJCAI 83*, pp.1139-1151, Karlsrhue, Germany, August 1983.

[MITC86]
Mitchell, T., Keller, R., and S. Kedar-Cabelli, "Explanation-Based Generalization: A Unifying View" *Machine Learning*, Vol. 1, No. 1, Kluwar Academic Press, January 1986.

[ML84]
Mylopoulos, J. and Levesque, H., "An Overview of Knowledge Representation", in *On Conceptual Modelling: Perspectives From Artificial Intelligence, Databases and Programming Languages*, Brodie, M., Mylopoulos, J., and Schmidt, J. (eds.), Springer-Verlag, 1984.

[MMS79]
Mitchell, J.G., Maybury, W., and R. Sweet, "Mesa Language Manual", Xerox Research Center, Palo Alto, CA, 1979.

[MMS85]
Mitchell, T., Mahadevan, S. and Steinberg, L., "LEAP - A Learning Apprentice for VLSI Design", in *Proceedings of the Ninth International Joint Conference on Artificial Intelligence*, August 1985.

[MONT73]
Montague, R. "The proper treatment of quantification in ordinary English." In J.Hintikka, J.Moravics and P.Suppes (editors), *Approaches to natural languages*, Reidel, 1973. pp. 221-242.

[MOOR80]
Moore, R., "Reasoning about Knowledge and Action", Technical Report 191, SRI International, 1980.

[MOOR84]
Moore, R.C., "A Formal Theory of Knowledge and Action", in R.C. Moore and J. Hobbs (editor), *Formal Theories of the Commonsense World*, Ablex Publishing, Norwood NJ, 1984.

[MORG84]
Morgenstern M., "Constraint equations: declarative expression of constraints with automatic enforcement", *Proceedings 10th VLDB Conference*, Singapore, pp. 291-300, 1984.

[MOSE84]

Moser, M., "Domain Dependent Semantic Acquisition", IEEE Computer Society (editor), *Proc. First Conf. on Artificial Intelligence Applications*, pp. 13-18. IEEE, December, 1984.

[MPM82]

Miller, R. A., Pople, H. E., Myers, J. D., "INTERNIST-1, An Experimental Computer-Based Diagnostic Consultant for General Internal Medicine", *New England Journal of Medicine*, Vol. 307, August 19, 1982, pp. 468-476.

[MR84]

Mercer, R. and Rosenberg, R., "Generating Corrective Answers by Computing Presuppositions of Answers, not of Questions", *Proceedings of the 1984 Conference*, pp. 16-19. Canadian Society for Computational Studies of Intelligence, University of Western Ontario, London, Ontario, May, 1984.

[MS81a]

McKay, D. and Shapiro, S., "Using Active Connection Graphs for Reasoning with Recursive Rules", *Proceedings 7th IJCAI*, pp 368-374, 1981.

[MS81b]

McLeod, D. and J.M.Smith. "Abstraction in Databases", *Proc. of Workshop on Data Abstraction, Databases and Conceptual Modelling*, M.L. Brodie and S. Zilles (eds.), ACM SIGMOD Record Vol.11, No.2, January 1981.

[MSS84]

Mitchell, T.M., Steinberg, L.I., and Shulman, J.S., "A Knowledge-Based Approach to Design", In *Proceedings of the IEEE Workshop of Principles of Knowledge-Based Systems*, pages 27-34. IEEE, December, 1984.

[MW80]

Mylopoulos, J., and H. Wong, "Some Features of the TAXIS Data Model," *Proc. 6th International Conference on Very Large Databases*, Montreal, Que., Canada, October 1980.

[MW84]/

Missicoff, M. and Wiederhold, G., "Toward a Unified Approach for Expert and Data Base Systems", *Proc. 1st International Conference on Expert Data Base Systems*, Kiowah, S.C., Oct. 1984.

[MWM85]

McKeown, K., Wish, M. and Matthews, K., "Tailoring Explanations for the User", *Proceedings of the 1985 Conference*, Int'l Joint Conference on Artificial Intelligence, Los Angeles CA, August, 1985.

[MYLO80]

Mylopoulos, J. "A Perspective for Research on Conceptual Modelling", Proceedings Pingree Park Workshop on Data Abstraction, Databases and Conceptual Modelling, Pingree Park, Colorado, 1980.

[NAIS83]

Naish, L., "Automatic generation of control for logic programs", TR 83/6, Dept. of CS, Univ. of Melbourne, 1983.

[NAQV84]

Naqvi, S., "Interfacing Prolog and Relational Databases: The Problem of Recursive Queries", *Proceedings 1st International Workshop on Expert Database Systems*, Kiawha, October 1984.

[NAQV85a]

Naqvi, S., Some Extensions to the Closed World Assumption, submitted for publication.

[NAQV85b]

Naqvi, S., Negative Queries in Horn Databases, submitted for publication.

[NAUG85]

Naughton, J., Work in progress, Dept. of CS, Stanford Univ., 1985.

[NEWE80]

Newell, A., "The Knowledge Level," Presidential Address, American Association for Artificial Intelligence, AAAI80, Stanford University, Stanford, CA (19 August 1980), in *AI Magazine*, Vol., No. 2 (Summer 1981), pp. 1-20.

[NEWE82]

Newell, A., "The Knowledge Level", *Artificial Intelligence*, Vol. 18, No. 1, 1982, pp. 87-127.

[NG78]

Nicolas J-M, Gallaire H, "Data base: theory vs. interpretation", in [GALL78], 1978.

[NH83]

Naqvi, S. and Henschen, L., "Synthesizing Least Fixed Point Queries into Non-recursive Iterative Programs", *Proceedings IJCAI 83*, Karlsruhe, 1983.

[NHS84]

Nievergelt, J., Hinterberger, H., and K.C. Sevcik, "The Grid File: An Adaptable, Symmetric Multikey File Structure", *ACM Transactions on Database Systems*, Vol. 9, No. 3, (March 1984), pp. 38-71.

[NICO82]
Nicolas J-M, "Logic for improving integrity checking in relational databases", *Acta Informatica*, 18, 227-253, 1982.

[NILS80]
Nilsson, N., *Principles of Artificial Intelligence*. Tioga Publishing Company, 1980.

[NY78]
Nicolas J-M, Yazdanian K, "Integrity checking in relational databases", in [GALL78], 1978.

[OGLL84]
Overbeek, R.A., J. Gabriel, T. Lindholm and E.L. Lusk, "Prolog on Multiprocessors", Internal Report, Argonne National Laboratory, Argonne, Illinois 60439, 1984.

[OM84]
Orenstein, J. A., and T. H. Merrett, "A Class of Data Structures for Associative Searching", *ACM SIGACT-SIGMOD Symposium on Principles of Database Systems*, 1984.

[OST84]
Olle, T. W., H. G. Sol, and C. J. Tully (eds.), *Information Systems Design Methodologies: A Feature Analysis*, North Holland, Amsterdam, September 1984.

[PALE72]
Palermo, F.P., "A data base search problem", *Proceedings 4th Computer and Information Science Symposium*, Miami Beach, 1972, pp.67-101.

[PGKS76]
Pauker, S. G., Gorry, G. A., Kassirer, J. P., Schwartz, W. B., "Toward the Simulation of Clinical Cognition. Taking a Present Illness by Computer", *The American Journal of Medicine*, Vol. 60, June, 1976, pp. 981-996.

[PILO83]
Pilote, M. "A Framework for the Design of Linguistic User Interfaces", PhD thesis, Department of Computer Science, University of Toronto, 1983.

[POLL85]
Pollack, M., "Information Sought and Information Provided", *Proceedings of CHI'85*, pages 155-160. Assoc. for Computing Machinery (ACM), San Francisco CA, April, 1985.

[POPL82]

Pople, H. E., Jr., "Heuristic Methods for Imposing Structure on Ill-Structured Problems: The Structuring of Medical Diagnostics", in *Artificial Intelligence in Medicine*, Szolovits, P. (ed.), Westview Press, Boulder, Colorado, 1982, pp. 119-190.

[PSS81]

Patil, R. S., Szolovits, P., and Schwartz, W. B., "Causal Understanding of Patient Illness in Medical Diagnosis", *Proceedings of the Seventh International Joint Conference on Artificial Intelligence*, Vol. 2, 1981, pp. 893-899. Reprinted in [CS84].

[PSS82]

Patil, R. S., Szolovits, P., and Schwartz, W. B., "Information Acquisition in Diagnosis", *Proceedings of the National Conference on Artificial Intelligence*, 1982, pp. 345-348.

[PTK85]

Poggio, T., V. Torre, and C. Koch, "Computational vision and regularization theory," *Nature*, Vol. 317: 314-313, 1985.

[QR68]

Quillian, M. Ross, "Semantic memory," in *Semantic Information Processing*, M. Minsky (ed.), MIT Press, 227-270, 1968.

[RBFG80]

Rothnie, J. B., P. A. Bernstein, S. Fox, N. Goodman, M. Hammer, T. A. Landers, C. Reeve, D. W. Shipman, and E. Wong, "Introduction to a System for Distributed Databases (SDD-1), *ACM Trans. Database Systems.* 5, 1, March 1980.

[RBS84]

Rychener, M. D., R. Banares-Alcantara, and E. Subrahmanian, "A Rule-Based Blackboard Kernel System: Some Principles in Design," *Proc. IEEE Workshop on Principles of Knowledge-Based Systems*, December 1984.

[REED83]

Reed, D., "Implementing Atomic Actions on Decentralized Data", *ACM Transactions on Computer Systems*, V 1, N 1, (March 1983).

[REIN84]

IEEE Database Engineering Newsletter, D. Reiner (ed.), Special Issue on Database Design Techniques, Tools, and Environments December 1984.

[REIT77]

Reiter, R., "An Approach to Deductive Question-Answering", BBN tech. report no. 3649.

[REIT78a]
Reiter, R., Deductive Q-A on Relational Databases, In [GM78].

[REIT78b]
Reiter, R., On Closed World Databases, In [GM78].

[REIT78c]
Reiter, R., "Reductive Question-Answering on Relational Data Bases", in H. Gallaire, J. Minker (eds.), *Logic and Data Bases*, Plenum Press: New York, New York, 1978.

[REIT80]
Reiter, R., Equality and Domain Closure in First-Order Databases, *J. of the ACM 27,2*, 1980.

[REIT83a]
Reiter, R., "Circumscription Implies Predicate Completion (Sometimes)", *Proc. of AAAI Conf.*, Pittsburgh 1982.

[REIT83b]
Reiter, R., Towards a Logical Reconstruction of Relational Database Theory, In [BMS83].

[REIT84]
Reiter, R., "Towards a Logical Reconstruction of Relational Database Theory," in [BMS84], 1984.

[REQU80]
Requicha, A. G., "Representations for Rigid Solids: Theory, Methods, and Systems", *ACM Computing Surveys*, 12, 4, December 1980.

[RF82]
Reddy Y.V. and M.S. Fox, "KBS: An Artificial Intelligence Approach to Flexible Simulation", CMU-RI-TR-82-1, Robotics Institute, Carnegie-Mellon University, Pittsburgh PA, 1982.

[RH83]
Reimer, U., and U. Hahn, "A Formal Approach to the Semantics of a Frame Data Model," *Proc. IJCAI-83,* Karlsruhe, 1983.

[RHM84]
Rosenthal, A., S. Heiler, and F. Manola, "An Example of Knowledge-Based Query Processing in a CAD/CAM DBMS," *Proceedings 10th International Conference on Very Large Data Bases*, March 1984.

[RICH81]
Rich, C., "Inspection Methods in Programming", Ph.D. thesis, MIT, MIT-TR-604, 1981.

[RICH82]

Rich, C., "Knowledge Representation Languages and Predicate Calculus: How to Have Your Cake and Eat it too", Proceedings AAAI-82, Pittsburgh, 1982.

[RIEG79]

Rieger, C., "ZMOB: A Mob of 256 Cooperative Z80A-Based Microcomputers," Computer Science Tech. Rep. Series TR-825, University of Maryland, College Park, MD, 1979.

[RVA84]

Rissland, E., Valcarce, E. and Ashley, K., "Explaining and Arguing with Examples", *Proceedings of the Natl. Conf. on Art. Intelligence*, pages 288-294. AAAI-84, University of Texas at Austin, August, 1984.

[ROBI81]

Robinson, J. T., "The K-D-B Tree: A Search Structure for Large Multidimensional Dynamic Indices", *Proceedings of the 1981 SIGMOD Conference*, Ann Arbor, MI., 1981.

[ROSE78]

D. Rosenkrantz, "Dynamic Database Dumping," *Proceedings 1978 SIGMOD Conference*, May 1978.

[ROSS77]

Ross, D. T., "Structured Analysis(SA): A Language for Communicating Ideas," *IEEE Trans. on Software Engineering*, Vol. Se-3, No. 1, Jan. 1977.

[ROUS79]

Roussopoulos, N., "CSDL: a conceptual schema definition language for the design of data base applications", *IEEE Trans. on Software Engineering*, Vol. SE-5, No. 5, Sept. 1979.

[ROUS82]

Roussopoulos N, "View Indexing in Relational Databases", *ACM Transactions on Database Systems*, 7:2, 258-290, 1982.

[RS79]

Rowe, L. and K. Schoens, "Data Abstraction, Views, and Updates in RIGEL", *Proceedings of the 1979 SIGMOD Conference*, Boston, MA., 1979.

[RTI84]

Relational Technology, Inc., *INGRES Version 3.0 Reference Manual*, December 1984.

[RU71]

Rescher, N. and A. Urquhart. *Temporal Logic*, Springer Verlag, 1971.

[RUSS78]
Russell, R.M., "The Cray-1 Computer System," *Communications of the ACM*, 21 (1): 63-72, 1978.

[RYCH84]
Rychener M., "PSRL User's Manual", Technical Report, Robotics Institute, Carnegie-Mellon University, 1984.

[SABM73]
Shortliffe, E., Axline, S.G., Buchanan, B.G., Merigan, T.C. and Cohen, S.N., "An Artificial Intelligence Program to Advise Physicians Regarding Antimicrobial Therapy", *Computers and Biomed.Res.*, Vol. 6, No. 6, Dec.1973, pp.544--560.

[SACE73]
Sacerdoti ED, "Planning in a hierarchy of abstraction spaces", *Proceedings 3rd IJCAI*, 412-422, 1973.

[SADO77]
Sadock, J., "Modus Brevis: The Truncated Argument", *Proceedings of the 1977 Meeting*, pages 545-554. Chicago Linguistics Society, Chicago IL, 1977.

[SB83]
Schmidt, J. W., and M. L. Brodie, *Relational Database Systems: Analysis and Comparison*, Springer-Verlag, New York, NY, 1983.

[SC75]
Smith, J.M., and P.Y.T. Chang, "Optimizing the performance of a relational algebra database interface", *Communications of the ACM*, 18,10, October 1975, pp.568-579.

[SCHA75]
Schank, R., *Conceptual Information Processing*, North-Holland, Amsterdam, 1975.

[SCHM77]
Schmidt, J.W., "Some High Level Constructs for Data of Type Relation", *ACM Transactions on Database Systems, 2,3*, September, 1977.

[SCHM84]
Schmidt J.W., "Database programming: language constructs and execution models", in Ammann, U. (ed.), *Programmiersprachen und Programmentwicklung*, Heidelberg: Springer-Verlag, 1-26, 1984.

[SCHW80]
Schwartz, J.T., "Ultracomputers," *ACM Transactions on Programming Languages and Systems*, 2 (4): 484-521.

[SELI79]
Selinger, P.G., et. al., "Access Path Selection in a Relational DBMS", *Proceedings of the 1979 SIGMOD Conference*, June 1979.

[SERG83]
Sergot, M., "A Query-the-User Facility for Logic Programming", P. Degano and E. Sandewall (editor), *Integrated Interactive Computing Systems*, pages 27-41. North-Holland, 1983.

[SERN80]
A.Sernadas, "Temporal aspects of logical procedure definition", *Information Systems*, Vol.5, No.3, 1980, pp. 167-187.

[SF82]
Sequin, C.H. and R.M. Fujimoto, "X-Trees and Y-Components," Report UCB/CSD 82/107, Computer Science Division (EECS), University of California, Berkeley, CA.

[SFL83]
Smith, J. M., S. A. Fox, and T. Landers, "ADAPLEX Rationale and Reference Manual," Technical Report CCA-83-08, Computer Corporation of America, Cambridge, MA, May 1983.

[SFS77]
Swan, R.J., S.H. Fuller, and D.P. Siewiorek, "CM* — A Modular, Multi-Microprocessor," *Proc. AFIPS Conf.*, (46): 637-643.

[SG84]
K. Salem and H. Garcia-Molina, "Disk Striping," Technical Report 332, Department of Electrical Engineering and Computer Science, Princeton University, December 1984.

[SHAW82]
Shaw, David Elliot, "The NON-VON Supercomputer," Department of Computer Science, Columbia University.

[SHIB85]
Shibahara, T. "Explicit and Active Use of Causal Knowledge: A Knowledge-Based Arrythmia Recognition System", PhD thesis, Department of Computer Science, University of Toronto, 1985.

[SHIP81]
Shipman, D., "The Functional Data Model and the Data Language DAPLEX," *ACM Transactions on Database Systems*, Vol. 6, No. 1, March 1981.

[SHNE80]
Shneiderman, B., *Software Psychology,* Winthrop, Cambridge, MA, 1980.

[SHOR76]
Shortliffe, E. H., "MYCIN: Computer-based Medical Consultations", American Elsevier, New York, 1976.

[SICK76]
Sickel, S., A Search Technique for Clause Interconnectivity Graphs, *IEEE Trans. on Computers C-25,8*, Aug. 1976.

[SIDN82]
Sidner, C. L., "Focusing in the Comprehension of Definite Anaphora", in M. Brady (editor), *Computational Models of Discourse*, MIT Press, Cambridge MA, 1982.

[SIGM83]
Engineering Design Applications: Proc. ACM SIGMOD, San Jose, CA, May 1983.

[SK84a]
Shepherd A, Kerschberg L, "Constraint management in expert database systems", in [KERS84], 1984.

[SK84b]
Shepherd, A. and L. Kerschberg, PRISM: A Knowledge Based System for Semantic Integrity Specification and Enforcement in Database Systems", *Proceedings of the 1984 SIGMOD Conference*, Boston, Ma., 1984.

[SLOT78]
Slotnick, D.L., et al., "The ILLIAC IV Computer," *IEEE Transactions on Computers*, C-17 (8): 746-757.

[SMIT82]
Smith B.C., "Reflection and Semantics in a Procedural Language", PhD thesis, Laboratory of Computer Science, MIT, 1982; also MIT/LCS/TR-272.

[SMIT83]
R. G. Smith, "Strobe: Support for structured object knowledge representation", *Proc. 8th Intern. Joint Conf. on Artificial Intelligence*, Karlruhe, W.Germany, August 1983.

[SMIT84]
Smith JM, "Expert database systems: a database perspective", in [KERS84], pp. K:1-22, 1984.

[SR81]
Stearns, R., and D. Rosenkrantz, "Distributed Database Concurrency Controls Using Before-Values", *Proceedings of the 1981 SIGMOD Conference*, Ann Arbor, MI., 1981.

[SRG83]

Stonebraker, J., B. Rubenstein, A. Guttman, "Application of Abstract Data Types and Abstract Indices to CAD Databases", *ACM SIGMOD Database Week — Engineering Design Applications,* 1983.

[SRM86]

Sathi, A., Roth, S., and T.E. Morton, (1986), "Callisto: An Intelligent Project Management System", *AI Magazine*, to appear.

[SS77]

Smith, J.M., and D.C.P.Smith, "Database abstractions: aggregation and generalization", *ACM Trans. on Database Systems*, Vol.2, No.2, June 1977, pp.105-133.

[SS78]

Steele, Guy L. Jr., and Gerald Jay Sussman, "The Revised Report on SCHEME: A Dialect of Lisp," AI Memo 452, Massachusetts Institute of Technology.

[SS81]

Stevens, A. and Steinberg, C., "A Typology of Explanations and its Application to Intelligent Computer Aided Instruction", Technical Report 4626, Bolt Beranek and Newman Inc., March, 1981.

[SS82a]

D. P. Siewiorek and R. S. Swarz, *The Theory and Practice of Reliable System Design*, Digital Press, 1982.

[SS82b]

Sacco, G. M. and M. Schkolnick, "A Mechanism for Managing the Buffer Pool in a Relational Database System Using the Hot Set Model", *Proceedings of the 1982 Very Large Database Conference*, Mexico City, Mexico, (September 1982), pp. 257-262.

[SS83]

Schwarz, P.M., and A.Z. Spector, "Recovery of Shared Abstract Types", Technical Report No. CMU-CS-83-151, Carnegie-Mellon University, October 1983.

[SS84]

Schwarz, P.M., and A.Z. Spector, "Synchronizing Shared Abstract Types", *ACM Transactions on Computer Systems*, Vol. 2, No. 3, August 1984.

[STEF81]

Stefik M, "Planning with constraints (MOLGEN)", *Artificial Intelligence*, 16, 111-170, 1981.

[STIC82]
Stickel, M. E., "A Nonclausal Connection-Graph Resolution Theorem-Proving Program," *Proc. AAAI-82*, Pittsburgh, PA, 1982, pp. 229-233.

[STIC84]
Stickel, M., "Automated Deduction by Theory Resolution," SRI Technical Note No. 340, Menlo Park, CA, 1984. (A version of this paper is to appear, under the same title, in *J. Automated Reasoning*, 1985.)

[STON75]
Stonebraker, M., "Implementation of Integrity Constraints and Views by Query Modification", *Proc. 1975 ACM-SIGMOD Conference*, San Jose, Ca., May 1975.

[STON76]
Stonebraker, M., et al., "The Design and Implementation of INGRES," *ACM Trans. Database Systems,* 1, 3, September 1976.

[STON81]
Stonebraker, M. R., "Operating System Support for Database Management", *Communications of the ACM*, V 24, N 7, (July 1981), pp. 412-418.

[STON83]
Stonebraker, M., et. al., "Application of Abstract Data Types and Abstract Indices to CAD Databases", *Proceedings of the Engineering Design Applications of the 1983 ACM-IEEE Database Week*, San Jose, CA, 1983.

[STON84]
Stonebraker, M., et. al., "QUEL as a Data Type", *Proceedings of the 1984 SIGMOD Conference*, Boston, Ma., 1984.

[STZ84]
Shmueli O, Tsur S, Zfirah H, "Rule support in PROLOG", in [KERS84], 1984.

[SU84]
Sagiv, Y. and J. D. Ullman, "Complexity of a top-down capture rule", STAN − CS − 84 − 1009, Dept. of CS, Stanford Univ., July, 1984.

[SUTH65]
Sutherland, I.E., "SKETCHPAD: A Man Machine Graphical Communications System," Massachusetts Institute of Technology, Lincoln Laboratory Tech. Rep. 296.

[SV84]
> Simon E, Valduriez P, "Design and implementation of an extendible integrity subsystem", *Proceedings ACM-SIGMOD Conference*, Boston, Mass, 9-17, 1984.

[SW48]
> Shannon, C. and Weaver, W., *The Mathematical Theory of Computation*, the Univ. of Illinois Press, 1962, reprinted from the Bell System Technical Journal, 1948.

[SW74]
> Stonebraker, M. and E. Wong, "Access control in a relational database management system by query modification", *Proc. ACM National Conf.*, pp. 180-187, 1974.

[SW84]/
> Sciore, E. and Warren, D.S., "Toward an Integrated Database-Prolog System", *Proc. 1st International Conference on Expert Data Bases*, Kiowah, S.C., Oct 1984.

[SWA83]
> Stonebraker, J., J. Woodfill, E. Anderson, "Implementation of Rules in Relational Data Base Systems", Memorandum UCB/ERL, 83/10, University of California, Berkeley, California, 1983.

[SWAR83]
> Swartout, W., "XPLAIN: A System for Creating and Explaining Expert Consulting Programs", *Artificial Intelligence*, 21:285-325, 1983.

[SWC70]
> Sussman, G. J., T. Winograd, and E. Charniak, "Micro-planner reference manual", MIT — AI 203a, AI Lab., MIT, Cambridge, Mass., 1970.

[SWKH76]
> Stonebraker, M., Wong, G., Kreps, P., and G. Held, "The Design and Implementation of INGRES", *ACM Transactions on Database Systems*, V 1, N 3, (September 1976), pp. 189-222.

[SWL83]
> N.C.Shu, H.K.T.Wong and V.Y.Lum, "Forms approach to requirements specification for database design", *Proc. SIGMOD 83 Conference*, San Jose, Ca., May 1983.

[SWMB85]
> Smith, R.G., H.A. Winston, T.A. Mitchell and B.G. Buchanan, "Representation and use of explicit justification for knowledge base refinemnent", *Proc. 9th IJCAI*, Los Angeles, CA. August 1985.

[SY82]

Sacco, G.M. and Yao, S.B., "Query optimization in distributed database systems", *Advances in Computers*, Vol. 21, Academic Press, 1982, pp. 225-273.

[TARS55]

Tarski, A., "A Lattice-Theoretical Fixpoint Theorem and its Applications", *Pacific Journal of Mathematics*, 5, 2, June 1955 (pp. 285-309).

[TENN81]

Tennant, H., *Natural Language Processing*, Petrocelli, 1981.

[TH77]

Teichroew, D., and E. A. Hershey, III "PSL/PSA: A Computer-Aided Technique for Structured Documentation and Analysis of Information Processing Systems," *IEEE Trans. on Software Engineering*, Vol. SE-3, No. 1, Jan. 1977.

[TODD76]

Todd, S. J. P., "The Peterlee relational test vehicle---a system overview", *IBM Systems J.*, Vol. 15, No. 4, pp. 285-308, 1976.

[TOFF77]

Toffoli, Tommaso, "Cellular Automata Mechanics," Tech. Rep. 208, Logic of Computers Group, CCS Department, The University of Michigan.

[TRIL84]

Trillin, C., *Killings*, Ticknor and Fields, New York City, 1984.

[TW84]

Tick, E., and D.H.D. Warren, "Towards a pipelined Prolog processor", *New Generation Computing*, Vol 2, no 4, pp. 323-345, 1984.

[UG85]

Ullman, J. D. and A. Van Gelder, "Testing applicability of top-down capture rules", STAN $-$ CS $-$ 85 $-$ 1046, Dept. of CS, Stanford Univ., 1985.

[ULLM82]

Ullman, J. D., *Principles of Database Systems*, Computer Science Press, Rockville, Md., 1982.

[ULLM83]

Ullman, J.D., *Principles of Database Systems*, Computer Science Press 1983.

[ULLM85]

Ullman, J., "Implementation of Logical Query Languages for Databases", *ACM Transactions on Database Systems*, Vol. 10., No. 3, pp. 289-321, 1985

[UM80]

Uno, S., and H. Matsuka, "A Relational Database for Design Aids System", *Workshop on Picture Data Description and Management,* August 1980.

[VANG85]

Van Gelder, A., "Deriving relations among argument sizes in logic programs", unpublished manuscript, Dept. of CS, Stanford Univ., 1985.

[VANM81]

van Melle, W., "System Aids in Constructing Consultation Programs", UMI Research Press, Ann Arbor, MI, 1981.

[VASS80]

Vassiliou, Y., A Formal Treatment of Imperfect Information in Database Management, Ph.D. thesis, Dept. of Computer Science, Univ. of Toronto, 1980.

[VCJ83]

Vassiliou, Y., J. Clifford, and M. Jarke, "How Does An Expert System Get Its Data?", *Ninth International Conference on Very Large Data Bases,* 1983.

[VCJ85]

Vassiliou, Y., Clifford, J., and Jarke, M., "Access to Specific Declarative Knowledge by Expert Systems," *Decision Support Systems,* Vol. 1, No. 2, 1985.

[VERE78]

Vere, S. A., "Inductive learning of relational productions", In Waterman, D. A. and Hayes-Roth, F. (editors), *Pattern-Directed Inference Systems.* Academic Press, New York, 1978.

[VERH78]

Verhofstad, J. S. M., "Recovery Techniques for Database Systems," *ACM Computing Surveys,* 10, 2, June 1978.

[VK76]

Van Emden, M., R. Kowalski, The Semantics of Predicate Logic as a Programming Language, *J. of the ACM 23,4,* 1976.

[VSZM83]

Vesonder, G. T., Stolfo, S. J., Zielinski, J. E., Miller, F. D., and Copp, D. H., "ACE: An Expert System for Telephone Cable Maintenance", *Proceedings of the Eighth Joint Conference on Artificial Intelligence, Vol. 1, 1983, pp. 116-121.*

[WALK82]

Walker, A., "Automatic Generation of Explanations of Results from Knowledge Bases", Technical Report RJ3481, IBM San Jose Research Laboratory, May, 1982.

[WARR77]

Warren, D., "Implementing Prolog -Compiling Predicate Logic Programs", University of Edinburgh, DAI report nos. 39 and 40, 1977.

[WARR81]

Warren, D.H.D., "Efficient Processing of Interactive Relational Database Queries Expressed in Logic", *Proc. of the Seventh International Conference on Very Large Data Bases*, Cannes, France, pp. 272-281, 1981.

[WBW85]

Gio Wiederhold, Robert L. Blum, and Michael Walker, "An Integration of Knowledge and Data Representation", in this volume.

[WDHL82]

Williams, R., D. Daniels, L. Haas, G. Lapis, B. Lindsay, P. Ng, R. Obermarck, P. Selinger, A. Walker, P. Wilms, and R. Yost, "R*: An Overview of the Architecture," *Proc. 2nd International Conference on Databases: Improving Usability and Responsiveness*, Jerusalem, Israel, 1982.

[WE83]

Wiederhold, G. and R. Elmasri "A formal high-level query language for the Entity-Relationship Model", *ER Approach to Information Modeling and Analysis*, P.P.Chen ed., North Holland, 1983

[WEBB82]

Webber, B. L., "So What Can We Talk about Now", in M. Brady (editor), *Computational Models of Discourse*, MIT Press, Cambridge MA, 1982.

[WEBE78]

Weber, H. "A Software Engineering View of Database Systems, *Proceedings of the 1978 VLDB Conference*, pp. 36-51, 1978.

[WEIN80]

Weiner, J., "BLAH, A System which explains its Reasoning", *Artificial Intelligence*, 15:19-48, 1980.

[WESS81]

Wesson, R., et al., "Network Structures for Distributed Situation Assessment," *IEEE Transactions on Systems, Man, and Cybernetics*, Vol. SMC-11, No. 1, January 1981.

[WH78]
D. Waterman and F. Hayes-Roth (Editors), *Pattern Directed Inference Systems*, Academic Press, New York, 1978.

[WIDD80]
Widdoes, L.C., "The S-1 Project: Developing High Performance Digital Computers," *Spring COMPCON 1980*, 282-291, 1980.

[WIED75]
Gio Wiederhold, James F. Fries, and Stephen Weyl, "Structured Organization of Clinical Databases"; *Proceedings of the National Computer Conference*, 1975, AFIPS Vol.44, pp. 479-485.

[WIED83]
Gio Wiederhold, *Database Design*, McGraw-Hill Book Company, New York, Second edition, January 1983, 768 pp.

[WIED84]
Wiederhold, G., "Knowledge and Database Management", *IEEE Software*, Vol. 1, No. 1, January 1984, pp.63--73.

[WIED85]
Gio Wiederhold, "Knowledge versus Data", position paper, in this volume.

[WINO72]
Winograd, T., *Understanding Natural Language*, Addison-Wesley, New York, 1972.

[WINO82]
Winograd, T., *Language as a Cognitive Process*, Addison-Wesley, 1982.

[WINS79]
Winston PH, "Learning and reasoning by analogy", *Communications of the ACM*, 23, 12, 689-703, 1979.

[WINS83]
Winston, P., "Learning by Augmenting Rules and Accumulating Censors", *Machine Learning: An Artificial Intelligence Approach*, Volume II, Michalski, Carbonell, and Mitchell eds., Kaufman-Morgan Publishers, 1986.).

[WITH83]
F. G. Withington, "Winners and Losers in the Fifth Generation," *Datamation*, December 1983, pp.193-209. (These forecasts also appear in "Future Information Processing Technology, 1983," Institute for Computer Sciences and Technology of the ***LINE MISSING IN ORIGINAL FILE***.

[WM77]

Wong, H.K.T., and Mylopoulos, J., "Two Views of Data Semantics: Data Models in Artificial Intelligence and Database Management," *INFOR*, 15, 3, 1977.

[WMJB83]

Wahlster, W., Marburger, H., Jameson, A. and Busemann, S.,
"Over-Answering Yes-No Questions: Extended responses in a NL
interface to a vision system", *Proceedings of the 8th IJCAI*, pages
643-646. IJCAI, Karlsruhe, West Germany, August, 1983.

[WOLF84]

Wolfram, Stephen, "Cellular Automata as Models of Complexity,"
Nature, 311 (4): 419-424, 1984.

[WOOD70]

Woods, W.A., "Transition Network Grammars for Natural
Language Analysis," *Communications of the ACM, Vol. 13, No. 10*,
October 1970, pp. 591-606.

[WOOD73]

Woods, W.A., "Progress in Natural Language Understanding: An
Application to Lunar Geology," *AFIPS Conference Proceedings,
Vol. 42.*, 1973, pp. 441-450.

[WOOD75]

Woods, W.A., "What's In a Link: Foundations for Semantic Net-
works," in D. Bobrow and A. Collins (Eds.), *Representation and
Understanding: Studies in Cognitive Science*, Academic Press, New
York, 1975, pp. 35-82.

[WOOD78a]

Woods, W.A., "Semantics and Quantification in Natural Language
Question Answering", *Advances in Computers, Vol. 17*, Academic
Press, New York, 1978, pp. 1-87.

[WOOD78b]

Woods, W.A., "Generalizations of ATN Grammars," in Woods,
W.A. & Brachman, R.J., (Eds.) *Research in Natural Language
Understanding*, BBN Report No. 3963, Bolt Beranek and Newman,
Inc., Cambridge, Mass., 1978.

[WOOD79]

Woods, W.A., *Semantics for a Question-Answering System*, Garland
Publishing, Inc., New York, 1979.

[WOOD80]

Woods, W.A., "Cascaded ATN Grammars", *American Journal of
Computational Linguistics, Vol. 6, No. 1*, January-March 1980, pp.
1-12.

[WOOD83]

Woods, W.A., "What's Important about Knowledge Representation?" *IEEE Computer, Vol. 16, No. 10*, October 1983, pp. 22-27.

[WP82]

Warren, D.H.D., and F.C.N. Pereira, "An efficient easily adaptable system for interpreting natural language queries", *American Journal of Computational Linguistics*, Vol 8, No 3-4, pp. 110-122, 1982.

[WP84]

Wise, M. J. and D. M. Powers, "Indexing PROLOG Clauses via Superimposed Code Words and Field Encoded Words", *Proceedings of the 1984 Symposium on Logic Programming*, Feb. 6-9, 1984.

[WP85]

Waltz, David and Jordan B. Pollack, "Massively Parallel Parsing: A Strongly Interactive Model of Natural Language Interpretation," *Cognitive Science*, 9 (1): 51-74, 1985.

[WSK83]

Weber W, Stucky W, Karszt J, "Integrity checking in database systems", *Information Systems*, 8:2, 125-136, 1983.

[WY76]

Wong, E., and K. Youssefi, "Decomposition - a strategy of query processing", *ACM Transactions on Database Systems*, Vol. 1, No. 3, September 1976, 223-241.

[YH85]

Yahya, A., L. Henschen, "Deduction in Non-Horn Databases", *Journal of Automated Reasoning, 1,* No. 2, 1985.

[YOKO84]

Yokota, H., et al., "An Enhanced Inference Mechanism for Generating Relational Algebra Queries", *ACM SIGACT-SIGMOD Symposium on Principles of Database Systems*, 1984.

[ZLOO77]

Zloof, M. M., "Query-by-Example: A Data Base Language", *IBM Systems Journal*, 16, 4, 1977 (pp. 324-343).

[ZLOO82]

Zloof, M. M., "Office-by-Example: A Business Language that Unifies Data and Word Processing and Electronic Mail", *IBM Systems Journal*, 21, 3, 1982.

Index